Parliamentary Reform
1640 - 1832

PARLIAMENTARY REFORM
1640-1832

JOHN CANNON
Reader in History, University of Bristol

CAMBRIDGE
At the University Press
1973

Published by the Syndics of the Cambridge University Press
Bentley House, 200 Euston Road, London NW1 2DB
American Branch: 32 East 57th Street, New York, N.Y.10022

© Cambridge University Press 1972

Library of Congress Catalogue Card Number: 72-83588

ISBNS
0 521 08697 3 hard covers
0 521 09736 3 paperback

Printed in Great Britain
at the University Printing House, Cambridge
(Brooke Crutchley, University Printer)

Preface

I should first like to express my appreciation of the kindness of my colleagues in the Department of History at the University of Bristol, and particularly of David Large, for his willingness to help on all occasions. I am also greatly indebted to the staff of the University Library for their patience and understanding.

Dr W. A. Speck of the University of Newcastle has helped me by placing at my disposal his unrivalled knowledge of the electoral history of the early eighteenth century.

Like all university teachers, I have benefited greatly by discussions with students, past and present. I should particularly like to mention Nigel Boardman, Sue Hearder, Linda Colley and Ian Colwill.

Lastly, my debt to fellow historians working in this field is great and obvious. I have tried to acknowledge it wherever possible. If I have inadvertently ironed out the subtleties of their arguments, I can offer only the plea of good faith.

J. A. C.

BRISTOL

Contents

Abbreviations

Albemarle	George Thomas, Earl of Albemarle, *Memoirs of the Marquis of Rockingham and his contemporaries*, 2 vols., 1852
Althorp	D. le Marchant, *Memoir of John Charles, Viscount Althorp, Third Earl Spencer*, 1876
Arbuthnot	*The journal of Mrs Arbuthnot 1820–32*, ed. F. Bamford and the Duke of Wellington, 2 vols., 1950
Broughton	Lord Broughton, *Recollections of a long life*, 4 vols., 1909
Buckingham	*Memoirs of the court and cabinets of George III*, 4 vols., 1855; *Memoirs of the court of George IV*, 2 vols., 1859; *Memoirs of the court and cabinets of William IV and Victoria*, 2 vols., 1861, by the Duke of Buckingham and Chandos
Bulwer	H. L. Bulwer, *The life of Henry John Temple, Viscount Palmerston*, 3 vols., 1870
Burke Corr.	*The correspondence of Edmund Burke*, ed. T. W. Copeland, 10 vols., 1958 onwards
Burton	*Diary of Thomas Burton*, ed. J. T. Rutt, 4 vols., 1828
Cal.S.P.Dom.	*Calendar of State Papers, Domestic series*
Cartwright	*The life and correspondence of Major Cartwright*, ed. F. D. Cartwright, 2 vols., 1826
CJ	*Journals of the House of Commons*
CJI	*Journals of the House of Commons of Ireland*
Cobbett's Parl. Debs.	*Cobbett's Parliamentary Debates*, 1803–12, 22 vols.
Creevey	*The Creevey papers*, ed. Sir H. Maxwell, 2 vols., 1904
Croker	*The correspondence and diaries of John Wilson Croker*, ed. L. J. Jennings, 3 vols., 1884
Despatches	*Despatches, correspondence and memoranda of the Duke of Wellington*, ed. the Duke of Wellington, 1867–80
Early Correspondence	*The early correspondence of Lord John Russell 1805–40*, ed. R. Russell, 2 vols., 1913
Ellenborough	Lord Ellenborough, *A political diary*, 1828–30, ed. Lord Colchester, 2 vols., 1881
Fortescue	*The correspondence of King George the Third*, ed. Sir J. Fortescue, 6 vols., 1927
Gent. Mag.	*The Gentleman's Magazine and Historical Chronicle* by Sylvanus Urban

Greville	C. C. F. Greville, *A journal of the reigns of King George IV, King William IV & Queen Victoria*, ed. H. Reeve, 1874–87
Grey and William IV	*The correspondence of the late Earl Grey with H.M. King William IV*, ed. Henry, Earl Grey, 2 vols., 1867
HMC	Reports of the Royal Commission on historical manuscripts
LJ	*Journals of the House of Lords*
Parker	C. S. Parker, *Sir Robert Peel*, 3 vols., 1891
Parl. Debs.	*The Parliamentary Debates from 1812 onwards*, printed by T. C. Hansard
Parl. Hist.	*The Parliamentary History of England from the earliest period to 1803*, 36 vols., 1816
Parl. Reg.	*The Parliamentary Register, or History of the proceedings of the House of Commons of Ireland*
P.P.	Parliamentary Papers
Pitt. Corr.	*Correspondence of William Pitt, Earl of Chatham*, ed. W. S. Taylor and J. S. Pringle, 4 vols., 1838
Princess Lieven	*Correspondence of Princess Lieven and Earl Grey*, ed. G. le Strange, 3 vols., 1890
Porritt	Edward and Annie Porritt, *The unreformed House of Commons*, 2 vols., 1903
Russell	*Memoirs and correspondence of Charles James Fox*, ed. Lord John Russell, 4 vols., 1853
State Trials	*A complete collection of state trials*, compiled by T. B. Howell, 1809
Three diaries	*Three early nineteenth century diaries*, ed. A. Aspinall, 1952
Trevelyan	G. M. Trevelyan, *Lord Grey of the Reform Bill*, 1920
Wharncliffe	C. Grosvenor and Lord Stuart of Wortley, *The first Lady Wharncliffe and her family (1779–1856)*, 2 vols., 1927
Wyvill	*Political papers chiefly respecting the attempt…to effect a Reformation of the Parliament of Great Britain*, 6 vols., 1794–1802

OF INNOVATIONS

'He that will not apply new remedies must expect new evils;
for Time is the greatest Innovator.'

Bacon

Introduction

'A state without the means of some change', wrote Edmund Burke in his *Reflections on the revolution in France*, 'is without the means of its conservation.' The grandeur compels respect, even if Burke contrives to beg the essential question. For change, as Bacon reminds us, can no more be defied than death. What is at issue is whether change comes about by peaceful or by violent means. The answer depends, to a great extent, on whether the channels of opinion and protest in society are open or closed. The condition of the representative system and the question of parliamentary reform is thus at the very heart of modern British history.

In the years before the 1914 war it looked as though historians were about to launch a collective onslaught on the problem of reform and change in the old regime. The decade saw the publication of three works of great distinction – Edward and Annie Porritt's *The unreformed House of Commons* (1903), G. S. Veitch's *The genesis of parliamentary reform* (1913), and J. R. M. Butler's *The passing of the Great Reform Bill* (1914). During the war these works were powerfully augmented by Charles Seymour's *Electoral reform in England and Wales* (1915) – the first scholarly study of the consequences of the Reform Act – and by P. A. Brown's *The French revolution in English history* (1918). But this initiative was not followed up. Porritt's promised work on the campaign for parliamentary reform was never produced, and the studies of Sir Lewis Namier, which dominated the thirties and forties, emphasized stability rather than change. Indeed, one might suggest that Namier, by the very brilliance of his success, helped to arrest a promising line of development. His method of structural analysis was – as Sir Herbert Butterfield pointed out – ill-adapted to registering change, producing an X-ray rather than a moving picture. The tendency, too, to widen Namier's conclusions to embrace the whole eighteenth century – indeed, even to overflow into the previous and subsequent centuries – encouraged the concept of the eighteenth century as a vast monolithic bloc. In fact, the period which I have in chapter two called 'Pudding time' was of comparatively short duration, and a student of the eighteenth century must surely be struck by the way in which the character of the period changes, subtly but inexorably, decade by decade.

During the last twenty years the investigation of the forces promoting change has been resumed in such works as Sir Herbert Butterfield's *George III, Lord North and the people* (1949), G. Rudé, *Wilkes and liberty* (1962), E. C. Black, *The Association* (1963), J. Norris, *Shelburne and Reform* (1963), and in the writings of Professor I. R. Christie. At the same time, work on the politics of Anne's reign – notably by Professor J. H. Plumb, Dr Holmes and Dr Speck – has tended to reveal the differences between that period and the era of the Pelhams and to emphasize the vigour and vitality of Augustan political life. There have also been admirable contributions to our understanding of the political problems of the early nineteenth century, particularly M. Roberts, *The Whig party 1807–1812* (1939), A. Mitchell, *The Whigs in opposition, 1815–30* (1967), and F. O'Gorman, *The Whig party and the French revolution* (1967). Two other thought-provoking books studying different aspects of the period are E. P. Thompson, *The making of the English working class* (1965) and H. J. Perkin, *The origins of modern English society, 1780–1880* (1969).

But although the political background is fast being reinterpreted, and much work of a specialist character has been done on parliamentary reform, no one has so far attempted to draw the threads together.

Of the temerity of such an undertaking I am acutely aware. 'The tasks of the more general historian', one recent editor has remarked, 'have become so complex that he has little hope of accomplishing anything except the provision of easy targets for criticism by his more specialized colleagues.'[1] Organizing a volume on parliamentary reform is so much an exercise in leaving things out that one wonders at times what has been left in. 'Parliamentary reform' is, for instance, so wide a term that a fairly austere definition is necessary if the subject is to have any cohesion. I have therefore limited my enquiry to the two most important aspects of reform – namely changes in the franchise and changes in the distribution of seats. I have discussed other proposals, such as the duration of Parliaments, qualification of members and the ballot – only in relation to these main themes. In limiting myself in this way I have had to ignore or neglect many interesting and significant aspects of political and constitutional development. I can only plead that to pursue, over a period of two hundred years, every suggestion for electoral change would result in a monstrous and shapeless volume, in my judgement of no use to anybody. I have however tried to indicate where some further discussion of these themes is to be found.

Similar considerations apply to the overall balance of the book, which has been determined by what has already been published. Mr Thompson's book has, for example, treated the extra-parliamentary side of radical reform so fully that it has enabled me to concentrate more on the parliamentary side. I have devoted a chapter to the problems of Scottish and Irish reform in the 1780s because little work has been done on them in this period: I dismissed them fairly lightly in the 1830s because Professor Gash dealt with them in some detail.[2] In the 1830–2 crisis I have given

---

[1] J. P. Cooper in *The new Cambridge modern history*, IV, 7.
[2] *Politics in the age of Peel*, ch. 2.

little attention to Francis Place and his friends, partly because their activities have been very fully documented, and partly because I agree with D. J. Rowe, the historian of London radicalism, that they were more the chorus to the drama than the leading actors.[1]

The decision to begin the enquiry in the mid-seventeenth century, and not, more conventionally, in the 1760s, was not mere antiquarianism. It serves to place the whole reform question in a different time scale. First, it is remarkable how little the arguments employed, both for and against reform, changed between the army debates of 1647 and the debates of Wilkes' day and after. Where Rainborough talked at Putney of the rights of the 'poorest he alive', Wilkes talked of 'the meanest mechanic'; Colonel Rich, with his fears of a legal proscription, had his counterpart nearly two hundred years later in the Duke of Wellington, who was convinced that reform must lead to a 'revolution by due course of law'. Secondly, an investigation of the Commonwealth reforms dispels the suggestion that is sometimes heard – that the unreformed system was in some way appropriate to the eighteenth century but was rendered inadequate by industrial development and population growth: it establishes that, in some respects, the representation was inadequate before 1640. Thirdly, it underlines the enormously conservative nature of the eighteenth-century political settlement.

It is perhaps scarcely necessary to point out that in isolating one theme for treatment one runs the risk of distorting the overall picture. I have not, for example, tried to give a total assessment of the 1688 revolution, which would be quite outside my brief. But in observing that an opportunity for reform was missed, I do not mean to imply – in contrast to some commentators – that the Glorious Revolution was other than important, necessary, and salutary.

My own interest has been to trace the relationship between ideas and actions – to see why arguments which are pressed ineffectually at one moment become politically viable the next. If I have, as some will certainly think, given undue attention to the parliamentary scene, it is not through too uncritical a belief in the rationality of man but because the key problem was how and why an unreformed Parliament could be brought to reform itself. At an early stage in preparing the book, I was struck by two observations. In 1811 Major John Cartwright wrote to Christopher Wyvill discussing the tactical problem. Each man had devoted a lifetime to the cause of reform. 'How is a despotism to be *reformed*? This is the point we have to consider. We are to remember that the despotism being legislative, it must be the very *agent of its own reformation*...What say the examples of our ancestors? It was a great national effort, headed by the barons, that first subdued the mind of the despot, John, and extorted,

[1] *London radicalism 1830–43: a selection from the papers of Francis Place*, p. xxvii.

from his *fear*, Magna Charta. . . And just so it is fear alone, that, from the *borough-faction* can ever extort a PARLIAMENTARY REFORM.'[1] These sentiments I found echoed in James Fitzjames Stephen's book, *Liberty, equality and fraternity*, published in 1873 as a counterblast to the pious liberalism of John Stuart Mill. 'Look at our own time and country,' demanded Stephen, 'and mention any single great change. . . not carried by force, that is to say, ultimately by the fear of a revolution.'[2] These observations have stayed in my mind during the writing of this volume, and in the concluding chapter I have looked back on the achievement of reform to decide whether Stephen would have been justified in claiming it as an illustration of his contention.

[1] *The life and correspondence of Major Cartwright*, ed. F. D. Cartwright, II, 7–8.
[2] *Liberty, equality and fraternity*, ed. R. J. White, 70.

1

Anarchie or blest reformation

The mitre is downe, And so is the crowne,
And with them the coronet too;
Come clownes and come boyes, Come hober-de-hoyes,
Come females of each degree;
Stretch your throats, bring in your votes,
And make good the anarchie.
And 'Thus it shall goe', says Alice;
'Nay, thus it shall goe', says Amy;
'Nay, thus it shall goe', says Taffie, 'I trow',
'Nay, thus it shall goe', says Jamy.[1]

Reformers in the eighteenth century were apt to meet the charge of
innovation by insisting that they sought merely to restore the representative system to its original principles and pristine purity. Much misplaced
ingenuity was devoted to expositions of what those principles were and
how they had been subverted. T. H. B. Oldfield, one of the more sensible
of the reformers, claimed that the representative system was 'as ancient
as the establishment of civil society in the world', and his *Representative
history of Great Britain,* as well as chapters on 'Representation in the time
of the Saxons and Danes', included learned asides on Cassivellaunus and
Vortigern.[2] In sober fact it would be hard to say at what period, if ever,
the representation, with any semblance of adequacy, reflected either the
distribution of population or of wealth in the kingdom. The borough
representation, in particular, was from its earliest days somewhat haphazard: even in the thirteenth century insignificant villages were sometimes
summoned and important towns neglected.[3]

The basis of the later representative system was that of the reign of
Edward I, during which the practice of summoning two knights from
each shire became standard, and the general pattern of the borough
representation was established. In county representation few changes

[1] From *The Anarchie, or the blest reformation since 1640,* a royalist ballad of October 1648,
printed in the Percy Society collection, ed. T. Wright. It was subtitled, 'Being a new
song, wherein the people express their thankes and pray for the reformers'.
[2] The attitude of reformers towards the past is discussed in H. Butterfield, *George III,
Lord North and the people, 1779–80,* 344–52, and in J. E. C. Hill's essay on 'The
Norman Yoke' in his *Puritanism and revolution.*
[3] M. McKisack, *The parliamentary representation of the English boroughs during the
Middle Ages,* 19–20.

were subsequently made. The most important was an act of 1430 which, complaining of the great number of persons 'of small substance or of no value' who cast votes, restricted the franchise henceforward to freeholders worth forty shillings per annum.[1] Of the 202 boroughs sending members to Parliament on the eve of reform in 1830, 125 were enfranchised during the reign of Edward I. The subsequent additions did little to bring the representation up to date. Henry VI summoned Wootton Bassett, Westbury, Hindon, Heytesbury and Gatton, none of which can have been of significance, even in the fifteenth century, and all, except Westbury, doomed to extinction under schedule A in 1832. The 51 boroughs enfranchised in Tudor times contained a high proportion of obscure hamlets and decayed ports: more than half of the new creations were totally extinguished in 1832, and a further 6 lost one member. Nor were the restorations much more fortunate. Of 19 boroughs to which representation was restored by the Tudors, 4 finished in schedule A and 4 more in schedule B.[2] The Tudor additions, if anything, made the representation less satisfactory, joining man-made oddities to those, such as Old Sarum and Dunwich, produced by the vicissitudes of time.

It is clear from documentary evidence as well that many of the Tudor creations and restorations were of little importance in their own day. Professor Neale has demonstrated that Newton, Lancs., which first sent members in 1559, was an insignificant borough.[3] John Leland's *Itinerary* furnishes more evidence. Aldborough, when he visited it in the 1530s, was 'now a small village', and its twin town, Boroughbridge, 'but a bare thing'; the most remarkable feature of Bossiney, enfranchised in 1553, was 'the ruins of a great number of houses'; Camelford was 'that poor village', and St Germans 'but a poor fisher town'. In 1571, in a Commons debate, the existence of 'decayed towns' and 'old ruins' was taken for granted.[4] Nevertheless, the pressure for seats was such that creations and restorations went on, often in the face of royal disapproval.[5] Thomas Wylson, Elizabeth's Secretary of State, resisting with success the proposal to enfranchise Newark in 1579, declared that there were already over-many burgesses, and that there would be 'a device hereafter to lessen the number for divers decayed towns'.[6]

[1] 8 Henry VI c. 7.
[2] Schedule A included Tregony, Orford, Hedon and Yarmouth; the schedule B boroughs which lost one member were Woodstock, Droitwich, Petersfield and Thirsk. East Retford had already been reformed. The other towns were Wigan, Lancaster, Liverpool, Preston, Andover, Newport I.o.W., Beverley, Ripon, Lichfield and St Albans.
[3] *The Elizabethan House of Commons*, 189.
[4] *The journal of all the Parliaments during the reign of Queen Elizabeth*, collected by Sir Simonds D'Ewes (1682), 168–9.
[5] The reasons for this pressure are discussed in J. E. Neale, ch. vii, and by A. L. Rowse, *Tudor Cornwall*, 91–4.
[6] Quoted Neale, 146.

It was not to be expected that the absurdities of the representative system would escape the tidy and logical mind of James I. In his proclamation for a new Parliament in 1604, sheriffs were instructed not to send writs to any boroughs that were 'so utterly ruined' that they could not furnish sufficient residents either to elect or to serve.[1] The sheriffs ignored the message: none of the old boroughs was struck off, and two that had once been represented, Evesham and Harwich, were restored. Towards the end of his reign the King refused to approve a bill giving two members each to county Durham, Durham City and Barnard's Castle, maintaining that some decayed towns, such as Old Sarum, would have to be extinguished before new ones could be brought in, and on his behalf Sir Robert Heath, the Solicitor-General, resisted proposals to restore the franchise to Amersham, Marlow and Wendover, three Buckinghamshire boroughs whose rights had lapsed.[2]

The growing antagonism between monarch and Parliament made it unlikely that any 'device' from the crown for a comprehensive reform would be acceptable. Substantial additions to the representation were made however in the period 1604–41 by the grant of two burgesses each to the Universities of Oxford and Cambridge, the enfranchisement of three new boroughs, and the restoration of a further sixteen, mostly by resolution of the House of Commons.[3] These changes did little to remedy the defective representation. 'In the nature of the case', wrote Lady de Villiers, 'the restored boroughs tended to be towns that had seen better days.'[4] Northallerton, in Camden's description, was 'nothing else but a long, broad street', and Ilchester he dismissed as 'at this day of small account'.

Another way in which the House of Commons could influence the representation was through its right to determine disputed elections, established as a result of Goodwin's case in 1604. The opposition to the court during the 1620s almost invariably supported attempts to extend the franchise: in each of fifteen disputes between 1620 and 1629 involving a borough franchise, the decision was for a broad interpretation.[5] That

---

[1] G. W. Prothero, *Select statutes*, 281; Camden Society, *The Egerton papers*, ed. J. P. Collier, 384–8.

[2] *Cal.S.P.Dom.*, 1623–5, 266; T. H. B. Oldfield, *Representative history of Great Britain*, III, 86–7.

[3] Tiverton, Bewdley and Tewkesbury were newly enfranchised; of the sixteen others, seven ended up in schedule A – Weobley, Ilchester, Milborne Port, Amersham, Wendover, Okehampton and Seaford: two more – Ashburton and Northallerton – were in schedule B. The rest were Cockermouth, Malton, Pontefract, Hertford, Marlow, Honiton and Bury St Edmunds.

[4] 'Parliamentary boroughs restored by the House of Commons, 1621–41', *English Historical Review*, 67 (1952).

[5] The fifteen were Oxford, Rochester, Sandwich, Chippenham, Pontefract, Cirencester, Dover, Newcastle-under-Lyme, Colchester, Bridport, Boston, Warwick, Lewes,

this was a deliberate policy can hardly be doubted. In February 1621 the House resolved, apparently as a general principle, that the election of burgesses belonged 'not to Mayor and Aldermen alone, but to the commons and inhabitants'.[1] In May 1624 it repeated that where there was neither custom nor charter, the election should be in the inhabitant house-holders, and on 8 May 1628 the Committee on Elections issued a strong statement that the franchise in all boroughs belonged to the commoners, 'and that nothing could take it from them, but a Prescription, and a constant Usage beyond all memory'.[2] The same principle was adopted in a bill to regulate elections brought forward in 1621, which declared that borough elections should be made 'by the greater number of freemen inhabitants; in such places where there are not twenty four freemen, by the Inhabitants, excluding only such as receive alms of the parish; and if not twenty four inhabitants, then by the greater number'. In the counties, where the decline in the value of money had produced a great increase in the number of voters, the qualification was to be raised to eighty shillings, but as a counterweight copyholders of ten pounds a year were to be enfranchised.[3]

The Commons persisted with their attitude during the early days of the Long Parliament. Seven boroughs had their parliamentary representation restored, and in the disputed elections for Wallingford and New Windsor the House found decisively for the broader franchise.[4] In two other disputed elections, questions of general principle emerged. On 19 November 1640, on the case of Marlow, a discussion arose on the right of the poor to vote: a majority of the speakers whose views were recorded supported the suggestion, and Sir Simonds D'Ewes maintained that 'the poorest man ought to have a voice, that it was the birthright of the subjects of England'. In the debate on the borough of Tewkesbury, a week later, the issue was the definition of the word 'commonalty': though John Pym argued that it referred to the freemen only, others insisted that it 'comprehended the whole inhabitants'. Even in the case of Salisbury, where the House found for the narrow franchise – according to D'Ewes out of sympathy for the members returned – it was alleged by some speakers that it was 'the general law of England that all free men should have voices'.[5]

Gatton and Exeter. The matter is also discussed by J. H. Plumb, 'The growth of the electorate in England from 1600 to 1715', *Past & Present*, no. 45 (1969), 100, who reaches similar conclusions.
[1] *Commons debates, 1621*, ed. W. Notestein, F. H. Relf & H. Simpson, V. 13.
[2] *CJ*, I, 792, 893.
[3] Notestein, ed. *Commons debates, 1621*, IV, 421–2.
[4] The restored boroughs were Ashburton, Honiton, Cockermouth, Malton, Northallerton, Okehampton and Seaford. For the disputed elections, see *CJ*, II, 47 and *The journal of Sir Simonds D'Ewes*, ed. W. Notestein, 120–1, 361.
[5] *Journal of Sir Simonds D'Ewes*, 42–3, 69–70, 542–3, 430–2.

The motives behind this liberal policy seem to have been a mixture of high principle, antiquarianism and political calculation. In the euphoric phase before a revolution or civil war, it is not unnatural to find some members of the propertied classes bidding for the support of their social inferiors: the assistance may be of value, while the potential dangers of the proceeding are masked by more immediate animosities. Sir Simonds D'Ewes, who spoke strongly for the broader franchise, based his arguments primarily on his understanding of 23 Henry VI c. 14, which he interpreted as giving every citizen the right to elect: he was not, however, unaware of the tactical considerations, remarking that if the franchise were restricted to the select number, 'we shall have such sent as great men will command'.[1]

The implication of this attitude towards the franchise is that the parliamentary opposition assumed that the general populace was informed on political and religious matters and would normally support them in an anti-court policy. It is also clear that the defects of the representative system were recognized long before fighting broke out in 1642. The exigencies of war were to release, if only temporarily, those forces for whom franchise reform and redistribution were not mere debating or antiquarian matters, but cardinal political principles, which had to be implemented if they were to play any permanent part in the government of the country. The somewhat vague advocates of the rights of the poor had soon to ask themselves how far they were prepared to go in that direction.

*   *   *   *

In March 1646, when the last sizeable royalist force surrendered at Stowe-on-the-Wold, Sir Jacob Astley told his captors: 'you may go to play, unless you will fall out among yourselves'. His jibe became true quicker perhaps than he could have hoped. With the need to construct a peacetime settlement, and the problem of what part, if any, the King was to play in it, the dissensions of the victors began to reveal themselves. In July 1646 Richard Overton published his *Remonstrance of many thousand citizens*, in which he argued for a free press, religious toleration, annual parliaments and the abolition of the monarchy. 'Ye have', the members of the Long Parliament were told, 'long time acted more like the *House of Peers* than the *House of Commons*...it is evident, a change of our bondage is the uttermost is intended us.'[2] The question of parliamentary reform was raised more specifically in a pamphlet composed in

[1] *Journal of Sir Simonds D'Ewes*, 137, 431. See also the evidence produced by R. L. Bushman, 'English franchise reform in the seventeenth century,' *Journal of British Studies*, vol. 3, no. 1 (1963).
[2] Printed in D. M. Wolfe, *Leveller manifestoes of the Puritan revolution*, 112–30.

October 1646 by John Lilburne, during one of his spells of imprisonment in the Tower. Most of *London's liberty in chains discovered* is concerned with civic issues and is an appeal for a more democratic city government. But towards the end of the pamphlet, almost parenthetically, Lilburne branches out into wider themes, beginning with an attack upon the royal prerogative, which allows the King to enfranchise 'what paltery townes he pleaseth'. To be bound by laws in the making of which one has no voice is 'meer vassalage'. The distribution of parliamentary seats is completely defective: Yorkshire, twice as big and three times as populous as Cornwall, has far fewer members, while Durham, 'my poor country', has none at all. Were he still living there, declared Lilburne, he would not pay one sixpence in taxes until representation were granted – thus anticipating by some one hundred and eighty years the proposal to withhold taxes to gain reform. 'And therefore', he concludes,

> me-thinks it were a great deale of more justice and equity to fixe upon the certain number of the men, that the House of Commons should consist of at 500, or 600, or more, or lesse, as by common consent should be thought most fit; and equally to proportion out to every county, to chuse a proportionable number, suitable to the rates, that each county by their bookes of rates are assessed, to pay towards the defraying of the publique charge of the kingdom.

Lilburne's influence may be seen in the *Representation of the army*, issued on 14 June 1647, and probably the work of Henry Ireton, Cromwell's son-in-law.[1] By this time relations between the army and Parliament had deteriorated almost to breaking point: in response to attempts to engineer its disbandment, the army had commenced a menacing march on London. It was, Parliament was sharply reminded, no 'mere mercenary army', which had abandoned the rights of citizens, but men who had taken up arms in defence of 'our own and the People's just rights and liberties'. The Long Parliament should set a term to its own existence and afterwards proceed by triennial elections. After denouncing the 'multitude of burgesses for decayed or inconsiderable towns (whose interest in the kingdom would in many not exceed or in others not equal ordinary villages)', the *Representation* called for a remodelling of constituencies 'in proportion to the respective rates they bear in the common charges and burdens of the kingdom'.[2] These suggestions were repeated in more specific terms in the *Heads of the proposals* on 1 August, in which it was argued that the seats taken from the decayed boroughs

---

[1] R. W. Ramsey, *Henry Ireton*, ch. vii.

[2] The paragraphs on redistribution are not included in the text as printed by J. Rushworth, *Historical collections*, VI, 564–70, but are given by A. S. P. Woodhouse, *Puritanism and liberty*, 403–9, based on the Cambridge edition.

should be allotted to the 'great counties that have now less than their due proportion'.[1]

The reply of the radicals, issued three months later as the *Agreement of the people*, declared as a first principle for a redistribution, 'according to the number of the inhabitants' – a significant change of emphasis from property and taxation.[2] This document became the basis for the debates of the army council at Putney on 28 and 29 October and 1 November. It is an indication of how the centre of power had shifted that the most systematic discussion of the principles of government ever held in England should take place, not in Parliament, but in the army. Cromwell's cautious attitude revealed itself from the outset:[3]

> Truly this paper does contain in it very great alterations of the very government of the kingdom, alterations from that government that it hath been under, I believe I may almost say, since it was a nation ...Therefore, although the pretensions in it, and the expressions in it are very plausible, and if we could leap out of one condition into another that had so specious things in it as this hath, I suppose there would not be much dispute – though perhaps some of these things may very well be disputed. How do we know if, whilst we are disputing these things, another company of men shall (not) gather together, and put out a paper perhaps as plausible as this...And not only another, and another, but many of this kind...Would it not be confusion? Would it not be utter confusion? Would it not make England like the Switzerland country, one canton of the Swiss against another, and one county against another?

It was an argument with which reformers were to become wearisomely familiar in the years ahead. But the extent to which the existing system of representation was regarded as inadequate may be seen from the fact that the need for a substantial redistribution of seats was admitted on all sides. Ireton assured Rainborough – his most determined adversary in many other matters – that on this subject at least there was no reason for them to differ – 'I will agree with you, not only to dispute for it, but to fight for it and contend for it.'[4]

The dispute over the franchise cut deep however, and revealed a disagreement between moderates and radicals that was to dog reform move-

[1] Rushworth, VII, 731–6. The proposal for triennial parliaments was changed to biennial. There is of course a great deal on all these documents not concerned with parliamentary reform, on which I do not comment.
[2] S. R. Gardiner, *Constitutional documents of the Puritan revolution, 1625–1660*, 3rd ed., 333–5.
[3] Woodhouse, 7. This is a better text of the Putney debates than the Camden Society volume edited by C. H. Firth. Cromwell's remarks read like a prose version of the ballad quoted above p. 1.   [4] Woodhouse, 77.

ments for generations to come. Manhood suffrage, in the view of Ireton
and Cromwell, would necessarily lead to the overthrow of property and
the utter destruction of civil society.[1]

It has been suggested that the proposals of the Levelling party fell far
short of manhood suffrage.[2] There is no doubt that in the course of the
discussions Cromwell presumed that, under no circumstances, would
those in receipt of alms, or servants, be admitted to the franchise, and the
point was not disputed.[3] Furthermore, the *Agreement of the people*, presented to Parliament in January 1649, expressly reserved the franchise to
persons ordinarily contributing towards poor relief, excluding those who
were 'servants to, or receiving wages from, any particular person'. Yet
the examples are not decisive. One commentator has denied the contention
that 'servants' in seventeenth-century usage meant wage-earners,[4] while
the *Agreement* of 1649 was a compromise proposal and can scarcely be
regarded as containing the pure milk of Leveller doctrine. Two more
recent contributors to the debate are agreed in attacking the 'new
orthodoxy' of Professor Macpherson, and stress the variety of views
among the Levellers themselves.[5]

In the face of so formidable a barrage of scholarship, the wisest course
is to revert to the original texts. It is hard, in my view, to read the Putney
debates and still believe that the Levellers intended a substantial proportion of the male community to be without the right to vote. Ireton, at one
stage, assumed that the proposal of the radicals was that 'every man that
is an inhabitant is to be equally considered': Rainborough, far from
denying that this was a fair interpretation of their views, retorted that
'the poorest man in England is not at all bound in a strict sense to that
government that he hath not had a voice to put himself under'. A little
later, Cromwell demanded to be told where it would all end if 'men that
have no interest but the interest of breathing' were to have the vote. Here,
surely, was the moment for the Levellers to intervene and complain that
he was grossly distorting their attitude? But, on the contrary, Maximilian
Petty affirmed that 'every Englishman that is an inhabitant of England
should choose and have a voice in the representatives', and John Wildman
continued to assert that, since government should be based upon the free

[1] For the argument repeated two hundred years later, see Macaulay's speech of 3 May
1842 on the People's Charter: 'I believe that universal suffrage would be fatal to all
purposes for which government exists…and that it is utterly incompatible with the very
existence of civilisation.'
[2] C. B. Macpherson, *The political theory of possessive individualism*, ch. iii.
[3] Woodhouse, 82–3.
[4] P. Laslett, *Historical Journal*, vol. 7, no. 1, p. 152.
[5] J. C. Davis, 'The Levellers and Democracy', *Past & Present*, no. 40 (1968); D. E.
Brewster & R. Howell, 'Reconsidering the Levellers: the evidence of *The Moderate*',
Past & Present, no. 46 (1970).

consent of the governed, 'there is never a person in England [but ought to have a voice in elections]'. The whole discussion confirms the impression that the Leveller spokesmen were skilful and adroit debaters and renders it difficult to credit Professor Macpherson's contention that what they really advocated was the exclusion from the franchise of well over half the adult males.[1]

The essence of the moderate argument was that only those with a stake in the country could be trusted to exercise the franchise – 'all those', in the words of Ireton, 'who have any permanent interest in the kingdom'. Inescapably bound up in its prosperity they would be obliged to put the nation's interests first. The counter-argument, that men had a natural right to be represented, seemed to Ireton and Cromwell dangerously vague – what other natural rights might they discover for themselves? 'If you do, paramount to all constitutions, hold up this law of nature', demanded Ireton, 'I would fain have any man show me their bounds, where you will end, and why you should not take away all property?' Rainborough replied that property would be protected by the Law of God – '*thou shalt not steal*'. To this, Colonel Rich objected that, under manhood suffrage, property could be attacked by perfectly legal means: 'it may happen, that the majority may by law, not in a confusion, destroy property; there may be a law enacted, that there shall be an equality of goods and estate'. On this point, the security of property, the debate rocked backwards and forwards, with little room for compromise. 'All the main thing that I speak for is because I would have an eye to property', admitted Ireton – to be met with Rainborough's rejoinder: 'I would fain know what the soldier hath fought for all this while? He hath fought to enslave himself, to give power to men of riches, men of estates, to make him a perpetual slave.'[2]

These differences were not reconciled. That time-honoured mode of prevarication – to refer the matter to a committee – was adopted, but the radicals on the committee succeeded in carrying a resolution in favour of manhood suffrage, excluding only beggars and servants, and the whole

[1] Woodhouse, 52, 53, 59, 61, 66. I find Professor Macpherson's attempt to set aside these remarks unconvincing. Though I take his point that Cromwell and Ireton may have misunderstood or misrepresented the Leveller position, I do not understand why, in very candid exchanges, their misrepresentation was not challenged. It is not enough to say, as Professor Macpherson does, that the Levellers 'did not trouble to contradict it'. Controversialists are rarely so obliging.
[2] Woodhouse, 58, 59, 63, 57, 71. Rainborough's final remark calls to mind the attack by Jean-Paul Marat on the moderate French constitution of 1791, with its distinction between 'active' and 'passive' citizens: 'what shall we have gained by destroying the aristocracy of birth if it is to be replaced by the aristocracy of wealth? It would have been better to have kept the privileged orders, if we are now to groan under the yoke of these *nouveaux riches*.' Cromwell's instinctive distrust of rational reform was erected into an intellectual system by Edmund Burke.

controversy flared up again at the general council, where Cromwell once more denounced the Levellers' proposals as leading to anarchy. The result was yet another committee. Nothing emerged from it, and the resumption of fighting in the spring and summer of 1648 brought constitutional disputations to an end for the time being.

In November 1648, with Cromwell's approval, John Lilburne began work on a revised draft of the *Agreement of the people*.[1] The franchise proposals, spelled out in more detail, were an attempt at compromise, substantially enlarging the existing electorate, yet falling short of manhood suffrage: the vote was to be restricted to citizens ordinarily paying towards poor relief, except those who were 'servants to, or receiving wages from, any particular persons', or in receipt of alms. The proposals for the redistribution of seats were the most detailed and elaborate yet produced. The old system was almost completely overthrown. 170 of the existing parliamentary boroughs were to lose their representation: only 28 leading towns or cities were to retain individual representation, with one or two members. The remaining seats, up to a total of 300, were allotted to the counties, in approximate proportion to their tax burden. Yorkshire with 13 seats, Kent, Devon and Lincoln with 11, Essex and Suffolk with 10, were the new giants: Cornwall, with 44 seats under the old distribution, was to be reduced to 6, Wiltshire was to fall from 30 to 7, and Dorset from 20 to 6.

One can do no more than speculate on what basis Lilburne's proposals were made. He could have made use of the general assessment of March 1648, but this had the disadvantage, for his purpose, that very few towns were separately treated.[2] The Irish assessment of 1641 has also been suggested,[3] but the correlation is not particularly evident. A more positive correlation seems to be with the ship money assessment of 1636.[4] This had the reputation of being a very accurate survey – in the view of its critics, so that administrative injustice should not be added to political provocation.[5]

By the time the new proposals came to be considered by the council of officers at Whitehall in December 1648, Pride's Purge had taken place, and the army was in a stronger position to impose its views on Parliament. Though most of the discussion at council took place on the religious question, the army leaders made certain changes in the constitutional

---

[1] D. M. Wolfe, 291–303. See also J. W. Gough, 'The Agreements of the People, 1647–9', *History*, N.S., xv, 334–41, and V. F. Snow, 'Parliamentary Reapportionment Proposals in the Puritan Revolution', *English Historical Review*, 74 (1959), 409–42.
[2] *Acts and ordinances of the Interregnum, 1642–60*, ed. C. H. Firth & R. S. Rait, I, 1107–11.   [3] Snow, 426–7.
[4] Printed as an appendix to M. D. Gordon, 'The collection of ship money in the reign of Charles I', *Trans. Royal Hist. Soc.*, 3rd series, IV, 141–62. I have shown the degree of correlation in appendix one.
[5] *Diary of Thomas Burton*, ed. J. T. Rutt, II, 214 ff.

proposals before submitting them to the Rump Parliament in January 1649. The total number of members of Parliament was to be increased from 300 to 400, and the number of boroughs separately represented to be raised to 46. The first or second Parliament, under the revised constitution, was given the responsibility of allocating the remaining seats to counties still under-represented.

The detailed changes made by the army leaders seem to have been a genuine attempt to make the redistribution more equitable rather than a merely conservative reappraisal. Lilburne's original proposals had already dealt tenderly with Oxford and Cambridge, which were to retain their university representation at one seat each, and were allocated a borough seat each in addition. The revised proposals cleared up certain anomalies and oversights. The Cinque Ports, which had been left out, were given 3 seats between them, and separate representation was given to Bury St Edmunds, King's Lynn, Yarmouth, Nottingham and Lincoln, somewhat haphazardly omitted from Lilburne's lists. The decision to strengthen the borough representation brought in more towns of respectable size such as Winchester, Derby, Chichester, Barnstaple, Durham and Hull, even if special pleading enabled Dorchester to wriggle back into the representation for no very obvious reason, other than being a county town.[1] In one respect the army officers showed themselves more radical than Lilburne in proposing to award seats to Leeds and Manchester, which had never previously had members. London, severely under-represented in the original scheme, was left under-represented, and Middlesex savagely reduced – clearly as part of a general policy. The representation of Wales was substantially increased – from 18 seats out of 300 to 35 seats out of 400 – in defiance of the tax burden.[2]

Prodded into activity, the Rump Parliament now commenced its own investigations, setting up on 15 May 1649 a committee to make recommendations.[3] Ireton was himself a member of the working party, though his departure for Ireland two months later means that he can have taken little share in its deliberations. Progress was slow. Bound up with the question of reform was the continuation of the Rump Parliament itself, and the members showed little desire to bring it to an end. After six months they appear to have decided to accept the proposals of the *Agreement* in principle, though they had made no decision about the franchise or the borough representation. On this occasion we can with greater confidence say on what the proposed distribution was based. John

[1] Dorchester had a charmed life. It escaped again in 1832, being included in schedule B in the first bill, but reprieved in the third.
[2] For London, see below p. 16. The generous treatment for Wales is discussed by V. F. Snow.
[3] *CJ*, VI, 210.

Moyle, member for East Looe, wrote to Robert Bennett on 13 November 1649:[1]

> Since I writ this, the committee, that was appointed by the House to bring in a model for a new representative have made report to the House what progress they made in that business. The number they think fit to be reduced to 400, and the rule by which they went on for <u>the numbers of each shire in the nation is the Army's monthly rate,</u> <u>that is one representative for every £200,</u> so Cornwall, being £2000 per mensem, is to have 10 representatives, Devon 20, London & Middlesex with the liberties 25, and so the rest of the shires according to the abovesaid proportion. But the matter being of so great concernment, as it indeed is, the business was again referred to the same committee.

When the committee reported again in January 1650, things were little further forward. The difficult question of the franchise was left for more mature consideration. With the exception of London, cut to seven members, no town was given separate treatment: instead the House was asked whether it wished some 'particular distribution' for other places. In short, the scheme bore all the hall-marks of procrastination. After desultory discussions during the summer, the next two years were allowed to elapse with nothing decided.

In March 1653, under the shadow of imminent dismissal, the Rump returned once more to the subject. The earlier proposals were taken out, dusted, and debated in considerable detail. This time the full rigour of rational reform was modified in favour of the traditional system. The committee's recommendation that the county franchise should be based once more on the forty-shilling freehold was rejected,[2] and a resolution carried by 21 votes to 17 that the right to vote should be in persons possessing property, real or personal, of £200.[3] For the first time Scotland and Ireland were to be included, with 33 and 37 members respectively. Although according to Ludlow the intention was to frame the representation 'in as near a proportion as was possible to the sums charged...for the service of the state,'[4] once the House began to discuss the proposals county by county, it restored many of the old parliamentary boroughs, some of which had little claim to consideration – Bedford, Buckingham, Penryn, East and West Looe, Honiton, Poole, Queenborough, Woodstock, Newcastle-under-Lyme, Andover, Reigate, Chichester and

---

[1] I am indebted to Miss Linda Colley for drawing my attention to this reference in *HMC Hodgkin*, 47.
[2] *CJ*, VII, 273.
[3] This was the franchise adopted under the Instrument of Government and is discussed subsequently.
[4] *Memoirs*, ed. C. H. Firth, I, 334.

Arundel.[1] The bill was still not completed when, on 20 April 1653, Cromwell terminated the Parliament's existence.[2]

* * * *

The next constitutional experiment, Barebones or the Little Parliament of 1653, has so often been described in ludicrous terms that its importance could easily escape unacknowledged. In the first place, though an interim measure, it was the first complete reconstruction of the representative system to be implemented: all the previous plans had remained mere paper proposals. Secondly, Scotland and Ireland were included in a united Parliament. Thirdly, although its members were nominated and not elected, the distribution was avowedly based upon the tax burden.[3] With the exception of London, which was granted four seats, representation was limited to the counties: Yorkshire was allocated 8 members, Devon 7, Norfolk, Suffolk, Essex, Kent and Lincoln 5 each, down to Monmouth and Rutland with 1 each. The four Northern counties – Northumberland, Cumberland, Westmorland and Durham – were treated as a group and awarded four members. Wales and Ireland had 6 each, and Scotland 5, out of a grand total of 136 representatives.

The failure of Barebones Parliament made a new constitutional settlement necessary. This was the *Instrument of Government*, promulgated in December 1653 – the first and only written constitution for Britain and the most ambitious reform of the electoral system undertaken before 1832. Its authorship has been attributed to Lambert, but, as Professor Roots has remarked, 'the ghost of Ireton broods over the whole Instrument',[4] and it must be seen against the background of the discussions of the previous seven years. Executive responsibility was lodged in the Lord Protector, assisted by a Council of State. The legislature, to be elected triennially, was to number 460 persons, 30 each from Scotland and Ireland, and 25 from Wales: there was to be no second chamber.[5] Its franchise provisions repeated the formula of the abortive Rump Parliament bill,

[1] *CJ*, VII, 265–6, 268, 270. The text refers to Newcastle-upon-Tyne, but since the representation of Staffordshire is amended, I take it that Newcastle-under-Lyme was intended. Andover was denied a seat on 16 March, but given it when the matter was reopened on 23 March. Proposals to award representation to Plympton and Kingston-on-Thames were defeated.
[2] Blair Worden, 'The Bill for a New Representative: the dissolution of the Long Parliament, April 1653', *English Historical Review*, 86 (1971), defends the Rump from the familiar charge of seeking to perpetuate its own authority.
[3] A. Woolrych, 'The calling of Barebones Parliament', *English Historical Review*, 80 (1965). [4] I. Roots, *The great rebellion, 1642–1660*, 182.
[5] The working of the Scottish provisions is discussed by P. J. Pinckney, 'The Scottish Representation in the Cromwellian Parliament of 1656', *Scottish Historical Review*, XLVI (1967), 95–114. He concludes that there was more genuine representation than is often allowed.

real & personal

giving the county vote to owners of estates worth £200. No alteration was made in the franchise of those boroughs that remained and it is clear that the old and variegated rights of voting were retained.[1] The *Instrument* followed the previous proposals in sweeping away a large number of the existing parliamentary boroughs, which were reduced to 104, the total of seats falling to 131.[2] But although this was scarcely more than half the boroughs that had been represented in the Long Parliament, it was more than double the number that the *Agreement of the people* of January 1649 had proposed to enfranchise. In this respect, as in many others, the *Instrument of Government* adopted an intermediate position. In particular, a tenderness can be detected towards the old parliamentary boroughs, some of which were retained in defiance of strict logic, and almost all of which were given precedence over previously unrepresented competitors.[3] The county representation was increased from 78 seats under the Long Parliament to 238.

Opinion has differed as to the motives behind the redistribution. Gardiner saw it as an attempt to strengthen the middle classes at the expense of the country gentlemen, who controlled many of the borough seats: Trevor-Roper, turning the Gardiner thesis on its head, argued that it represented a move by the country gentlemen to fortify their own position by augmenting the representation of the counties, where they were solidly entrenched.[4] To reject both interpretations may seem perverse, yet each exaggerates the effect of mere distributive reform. Since the great majority of seats, county and borough, were already in the hands of the country gentlemen it is difficult to see how any redistribution could, in itself, have changed the position.[5] Franchise reform was another matter, and it is significant that the agreement between Ireton and Rainborough broke down at this point.

[1] E. Jenks, *The constitutional experiments of the Commonwealth, 1649–1660*, p. 86, wrote that the anomalies of the borough franchise had been 'swept altogether away' by the *Instrument*. But the disputed returns for Yarmouth in 1654 and King's Lynn in 1656 establish that the old borough franchises were still in operation. On another occasion the House resolved that the old franchises were not to be disturbed. *CJ*, VII, 369, 441–2, 392.
[2] The Isle of Ely and Isle of Wight, each accorded two seats, are treated as counties: the Universities, with one seat apiece, are treated separately. I do not know why Jenks, p. 87, includes Whitby among towns given representation under the *Instrument* for the first time.   [3] See appendix two.
[4] S. R. Gardiner, *History of the commonwealth and protectorate, 1649–56*, III, 171ff.; H. Trevor-Roper, 'Oliver Cromwell and his Parliaments', in *Essays presented to Sir Lewis Namier*, ed. R. Pares & A. J. P. Taylor. G. D. Heath III, 'Making the Instrument of Government', *Journal of British Studies*, vol. 6, no. 2 (1967) follows Gardiner.
[5] This seems to be borne out by the conclusions reached by A. Everitt, *The community of Kent and the great rebellion, 1640–1660*, 295. Comparing the *Instrument* returns with those of previous Parliaments, he remarks 'Precisely the same kind of gentry were elected'.

Another historian has warned us that it would be a mistake to see the changes as an attempt at 'pure' reform.[1] In one sense the advice is beside the point, since hardly any political reform can be 'pure', if by this is meant that it can be devised on abstract mathematical principles with no party or social group gaining any advantage from it. But even if we had not Ludlow's assurance that the *Instrument* changes were modelled on the Rump Parliament proposals, their kinship with the reforms mooted since 1647 would be plain to see, and the basic principle had been that the distribution of seats should relate to the tax burden.[2] The recasting of the representation has all the hall-marks of a genuine attempt at utilitarian reform, and those anomalies which were perpetuated, such as the continued representation of Dunwich and Queenborough, serve only to underline the logic of the rest of the scheme. Once the principle had been accepted that representation should relate to the tax burden, the main provisions – for the abolition of decayed boroughs and the augmentation of county representation – followed automatically, though how far strict logic was to be pressed was still a matter for political judgement. The disparity between the burden of taxation shouldered by the counties and by the towns was so great that the inclusion of too many boroughs would wreck the underlying principle. Whereas comparatively modest counties, such as Warwickshire, Bedfordshire and Hertfordshire, were assessed for ship money at £4000 p.a., and the larger ones, such as Kent, Lincoln and Somerset at £8000 p.a., only seven towns were assessed at £500 or more. The contributions from some of the old parliamentary boroughs were minute. Dunwich was assessed at £4 p.a., Wilton and Appleby at £5, Clithero and Newton at £7, Aldeburgh at £8, Queenborough, Shoreham, Castle Rising, Camelford and St Mawes at £10, and a dozen others at £20 or less. Rutland, by far the smallest of the counties, was assessed at £800, greater than forty of the smaller parliamentary boroughs put together. Yorkshire and Devon combined paid more than all the parliamentary boroughs of 1640, if London is excluded.

Nor was it an easy task to find large towns, previously unrepresented, as substitutes for the decayed boroughs. Manchester, Leeds, Halifax and Durham were brought in, but of the forty towns paying the greatest ship money assessment, only two – Cranbrook and Leeds – were without representation in 1640. All the towns individually assessed for ship money and unrepresented in the Long Parliament – 39 in all – paid a total of £2400 – i.e. only a little more than was paid by the county of Huntingdon.

The *Instrument of Government* allocations included of course anomalies, some of which were clearly the result of special pleading. London and

[1] J. R. Pole, *Political representation in England and the origins of the American Republic*, 6.
[2] *Memoirs*, I, 386–7.

Middlesex were particularly under-represented. Whereas Yorkshire, assessed for ship money at £12,000, was given 22 seats, London, assessed at £14,000, was given 6; Middlesex, paying £5000, was also given 6, while Sussex, paying the same, received 14 seats. This was a deliberate act of policy, as the debates on the *Instrument* in December 1654 make clear. To the objection that London, paying one-sixteenth of the total assessment, was entitled to better treatment, it was replied that 'London's interest was too big already' – implying that London merchants found seats for nearby counties and boroughs. This in itself would cast doubt on Gardiner's contention that the electoral changes had been made for the advantage of the middle-class element.[1]

In other cases the special pleading can be plausibly conjectured. The borough of Newark had a reasonable claim to representation. There had been an attempt to secure enfranchisement during the reign of James I, and with a ship money assessment of £120 it was one of the most substantial unrepresented towns – certainly entitled, on rational grounds, to preference over East and West Looe, which kept their representation under the *Instrument*. But Newark had been a royalist stronghold in the first civil war, and had carried out a stubborn and protracted resistance well into 1646. Its claim to representation was ignored during the Commonwealth, but after the Restoration it was brought in, 'on account of its loyalty to King Charles I' – being, in fact, the last addition to the unreformed representative system. One may suspect that Windsor, the largest old parliamentary borough not to be continued under the *Instrument*, also suffered for its royalist associations.

If Newark was unlucky, Queenborough in Kent was the reverse. With a ship money contribution of only £10 its chances of surviving reform must have seemed feeble. The first and second *Agreements of the people* swept it aside. But when the Rump Parliament in March 1653 came round to discussing the question further, one of the members for the borough, Sir Michael Livesey, was still present, and acted as teller in his own cause: on the casting vote of the Speaker, the borough was reprieved.[2] Included in the representation by the *Instrument of Government*, its parliamentary existence was again challenged in December 1654, when certain members argued that its seat ought to be transferred to a more important town or to the county. On this occasion the new member, Augustone Garland, turned aside the subject with a quip, and a further respite was granted.[3] Dunwich, an even more curious survival, also escaped abolition, the proposal to transfer its seat to Aldeburgh being

---

[1] Burton, vol. I, p. cx.
[2] *CJ*, VII, 268.
[3] Burton, vol. I, p. cxi; *CJ*, VII, 396. Though the House subsequently changed its mind, *CJ*, VII, 411, it was itself dismissed and Queenborough suffered no harm.

defeated by 72 votes to 59. Other boroughs were less fortunate. Woodstock, granted one member under the *Instrument*, had its representation transferred to Banbury.

The Cromwellian distribution, for whatever reasons undertaken, anticipated in the most striking fashion the ultimate remodelling in 1832. Of the 56 boroughs in schedule A, deprived of both seats in 1832, 53 had been abolished under the *Instrument of Government*: of the rest, East and West Looe had been given a joint seat, while Queenborough and Dunwich had, as we have seen, been the subject of discussion. In the schedule B group of boroughs, which lost one seat, 24 of the 30 had disappeared in the Cromwellian reform. Only Launceston, Dartmouth, Lyme Regis, Reigate, Rye and Arundel survived in 1654 but lost one seat in 1832. A further four boroughs, dropped in 1654, had been reformed previous to 1832 – Shoreham, Cricklade, Grampound and East Retford. Putting the same argument in a different way, of the 102 parliamentary boroughs that remained in the representation in 1654, only 9 failed to survive the 1832 reform intact. Manchester, Leeds and Halifax, enfranchised for the first time by the Cromwellian reform, were among those boroughs added in 1832.

The similarity between the Commonwealth reform and the 1832 Act exists, of course, only negatively – in the boroughs disfranchised. The great industrial towns to which the representation was extended in 1832 were things of the future. But the parallel reinforces the argument that the Cromwellian reform was utilitarian in character: the redistributed seats went to the counties, not out of political machiavellianism, but because there was no alternative in the rural society of Stuart England.

The army officers who framed the *Instrument* could permit themselves radical gestures on redistribution since their provisions for the county franchise seem to have been of a conservative nature. Article xviii of the new constitution substituted for the forty-shilling freehold a franchise in persons possessing estate, real or personal, to the value of £200. Though the new definition allowed property other than land to be represented, giving the vote to merchants, the qualification was fixed so high that it must have curtailed dramatically the county electorate. Such a conjecture would accord with repeated admissions by the supporters of the Protectorate that the regime was highly unpopular with the lower orders. The fact that the franchise was borrowed from the Rump Parliament proposals also suggests that it was intended to be limited.

Discussion of the £200 franchise is dogged by lack of evidence and by the eccentricity of some later comments. Professor Trevor-Roper remarked of the *Instrument* that it 'preserved the old property qualifications and thus the same social level of representation' – which appears to miss the point completely[1] – and while Mr Snow observes that the new franchise was broader than the old one, he offers no evidence for the assertion. The only close study of its operation is concerned with the Cheshire election of 1656.[2] But despite a wealth of detail, it is far from conclusive, partly because the election did not go to the poll. Mr Pinckney draws attention to the large number of persons, apparently supporters of John Bradshaw, who were not allowed to vote, and concludes that they were 'a middle or even lower middle class group' who had profited from the revolution. It is not immediately clear why a group recently enfranchised by Cromwell should be supporting one of the most persistent critics of his regime. An alternative explanation is that they were the old forty-shilling freeholders, excluded under Cromwell's new franchise, and registering their resentment. In their subsequent petition, they were specifically referred to as 'freeholders and such as had voices at that election'. If they were indeed the newly-excluded freeholders, it would explain why the sheriff refused a poll and why he intended to hold the election in a small hall.[3] When the Parliament assembled and the Cromwellians lost control of the situation, there is no doubt that the republican opposition favoured an extended franchise. They carried first a proposal to restore the vote to the forty-shilling freeholders, and then to substitute the old franchise for the new one provided by the *Instrument*. It is clear that these resolutions passed in defiance of the regime.[4]

[1] In *Essays presented to Sir Lewis Namier*. I do not quite understand what Professor Trevor-Roper means. There was no property qualification for members of Parliament to be either preserved or changed, while the franchise was unquestionably altered.
[2] P. J. Pinckney, 'The Cheshire election of 1656', *Bulletin of the John Rylands Library*, 49 (1966–7).
[3] At the Herefordshire election of 1656, freeholders not worth £200 were also refused a vote. *HMC Portland*, III, 208. At the Wiltshire election of 1654 the under-sheriff, acting on behalf of the Cromwellian party, is reported to have taken an opposite line, and allowed persons of less than £200 to vote. Ludlow, *Memoirs*, I, 387–90 and appendix five.
[4] *CJ*, VII, 391–2, 410–11. Richard Cromwell was teller for the minority on the first vote. On 1 January 1655 the opposition failed narrowly to enfranchise copyholders as well. Two pamphlets in the Thomason collection add further light. *A memento for the people about their election of members for the approaching Parliament* (1654), though supporting the regime, gives inadvertent support to the view that the county franchise at £200 must have been restrictive. It remarks that 'the encouragement & respect to trades being of great consequence to the Commonwealth, it was not thought fit to restrain the choice in cities and boroughs to those only who were worth £200... Neither is that restriction of electors for counties any straightening of the election, but an enlargement thereof, full of reason;... now, by the Lord Protector, every man, though a copyholder, or a man of personal estate, if he be worth £200 is made a chooser, as well as freeholders.' But it is clear that the forty-shilling freeholders did not retain their franchise. Prynne said more bluntly that the new *Instrument* had 'disabled many thousands of their votes in elections': *A summary collection of the principal fundamental rights, liberties, proprieties of all English freemen*, 6 Nov. 1656. When the regime's own apologists did not understand what was intended, the confusion of sheriffs and historians seems more excusable.

One final piece of evidence may be cited which seems to confirm that the consequence of the £200 franchise must have been a sharp reduction of the electorate. In 1679 Shaftesbury proposed the same franchise as part of his bill to regulate elections. The argument behind the proposals was spelled out in a supporting pamphlet. Deploring that the fall in the value of money meant that the forty-shilling freeholders were now men of 'mean and abject fortune...under the temptation of being corrupted by the inveiglements of a little money or a pot of ale', Shaftesbury proposed that the county electorate be reduced to one-quarter its existing size, so that the 'ungovernable multitude' would be replaced by the 'optimacy'. Other provisions made it clear that the intention was to reserve power to men of 'wealth and substance'.[1]

Few reforms, however disinterested, are implemented without some benefit to their authors. Though the *Instrument*'s generous treatment of the old parliamentary boroughs meant that the traditionally dominant counties – Cornwall, Somerset, Wiltshire, Sussex and Hampshire – were better off than they would have been under the *Agreement of the people* proposals, the overall effect was to strengthen the Eastern counties as against the Western ones. Whereas in 1640 the 'hard-core' royalist counties of the North and West mustered 206 seats against 119 belonging to the 'hard-core' parliamentarian, under the *Instrument* the ratio had changed to 125:135 – that is the parliamentary counties, which had previously been in a clear minority, were in 1654 placed in a slight majority.[2]

* * * *

The franchise and redistributive reforms of the *Instrument of Government* survived Cromwell's lifetime, despite efforts by his first Parliament to question them. Though by the *Humble Petition and Advice* of 1657 a second chamber was added, the other provisions remained unaltered.

The movement back to traditional forms of government was powerfully reinforced after the death of Cromwell when the Council decided that Richard Cromwell's first Parliament should be summoned according to

[1] Shaftesbury had, of course, been a member of Cromwell's Council of State. The pamphlet entitled 'Some observations concerning the regulating of elections for Parliament' is in J. Somers, *A collection of scarce and valuable tracts*, 1st. coll., 1, 63. The bill is commented on by J. R. Jones, *The first Whigs*, 53–4.
[2] Definitions of this kind are necessarily crude and conceal all kinds of local variation, but my 'hard-core' royalist counties are Cheshire, Cornwall, Devon, Dorset, Gloucestershire, Herefordshire, Lancashire, Oxfordshire, Shropshire, Somerset, Wiltshire and Worcestershire: the 'hard-core' parliamentarian are Bedfordshire, Cambridgeshire, Essex, Hertfordshire, Huntingdonshire, Lincolnshire, Middlesex, Norfolk, Northamptonshire, Rutland, Suffolk, Surrey and Sussex. W. C. Abbott, *The writings and speeches of Oliver Cromwell*, III, 385 appears to deny that the redistribution brought the parliamentarians any advantage.

the ancient usage. Ludlow suggested that the intention was to harness as much support as possible to the new regime: a contemporary pamphlet, *England's confusion*, hinted that the government hoped more easily to control the old parliamentary boroughs.[1] Accordingly, in January 1659, the members for Grampound, St Mawes, Hedon, Gatton and all the other restored boroughs took their seats once more in the House of Commons, and the election committees resumed their customary investigations into disputed returns for Horsham, Petersfield, Malton, Tiverton, Poole and Haslemere.

Even at this late stage, however, it was not certain that the old representative system would be retained in its entirety. When the inhabitants of co. Durham petitioned on 31 March 1659 for representation, which they had enjoyed under the *Instrument*, the House was sympathetic: a committee to bring in a bill was appointed, and several members spoke strongly in favour of a general reform.[2] Though the decision in May 1659 to summon back the survivors of the Rump Parliament implied that all the intervening constitutional provisions had been abandoned, the case for a more equitable distribution of seats remained. On 9 August the clerk of the Parliament was ordered to search for the bill for a new representative which the House had been considering six years earlier, and in October another committee was appointed to make recommendations. On 4 February 1660 the Rump resolved that it should be recruited, to a total of 400 members, according to the 1653 distributive arrangements, and four days later that the forty-shilling franchise should continue to operate.[3] The redistribution was never put into effect. While the House deliberated, Monck and his troops arrived from Scotland. The following month a bill to dissolve the Long Parliament was passed, and a new Parliament, under the old franchise and the old distribution, summoned for 25 April. The time for experiments was over.

*   *   *   *

How can one explain the emergence in the 1640s of these liberal and democratic ideas? A complete answer would demand a survey of the political, economic and intellectual developments in Europe from the Renaissance onwards. But the most immediate impulse came from the Reformation. First, the nature of Protestantism made it a fertile seedbed for dissidence in both church and state: individual judgement was a

---

[1] *Memoirs*, II, 48–9; *Somers Tracts*, 3rd coll., II. The elections are discussed in G. Davies, 'The Election of Richard Cromwell's Parliament, 1658–9', *English Historical Review*, 63 (1948). There had been strong rumours in the spring of 1658 that Oliver Cromwell intended to summon a traditional Parliament: see James Wainwright to Richard Bradshaw, 19 February 1658, *HMC 6th Report*, 442.

[2] *CJ*, VII, 622; Burton, vol. IV, 309–12.

[3] *CJ*, VII, 752, 790, 791, 834, 837; *HMC Leyborne-Popham*, 129–30, 144.

solvent of all authority, and could not be confined to religious matters. Seventeenth-century thinkers like Hobbes and Bossuet, who argued that religious disunity must lead to political discord, could produce much evidence to support their views. Secondly, the creation in the course of the sixteenth century of large numbers of subjects at permanent variance with their rulers stimulated the demand for guarantees of toleration and rights of legitimate opposition. Though medieval thinkers, such as John of Salisbury, had of course recognized the right of tyrannicide, it was regarded as an exceptional and extraordinary weapon to restore a natural order that had been perverted. Post-Reformation writers developed theories that implied a permanent share in government by subjects. 'Political liberty as a fact in the modern world', it has been written, 'is the result of the struggle of religious organisms to live.'[1]

The great issues in the political thought of the sixteenth and seventeenth centuries were, therefore, allegiance and sovereignty. From the Reformation sprang conflicting and opposed currents. While in many countries the immediate result was to strengthen the power of the crown through the control exercised over national churches, it also unleashed forces of protest that challenged monarchical authority. The clash produced a century full of turbulence and disorder, as estates struggled with princes throughout western Europe.

It is therefore less a contradiction than a corollary that the 'age of absolutism' should witness the enunciation of theories of social contract and limited sovereignty. Subjects were led to develop their own doctrines of resistance lest they be ground to dust beneath princely power. In France, the most distinguished statement of royal authority, Bodin's *Six livres*, was followed within three years by *Vindiciae contra tyrannos*, in which the rights of subjects were upheld. In Scotland, Buchanan's *De jure regni*, published in 1579, received its counter-blast nineteen years later in James I's *True law of free monarchies*, which declared kings to be the 'breathing images of God upon earth' and free from human restraint.

To these general factors may be added others more particular to England. Social and economic change was strengthening the middling ranks of society and rendering an absolutist and patriarchal government increasingly inappropriate. By the end of Elizabeth's reign the House of Commons, in a new mood of assertiveness, was probing the royal prerogatives.[2] Though republicanism was still a remote and unlikely contingency, the example of the Dutch showed a people defying their lawful

[1] J. N. Figgis, *Studies of political thought from Gerson to Grotius, 1414–1625*, quoted by D. B. Robertson, *The religious foundations of Leveller Democracy*, 121.

[2] Or, more properly, a revival of former assertiveness if Professor Roskell's contention of the vitality of medieval Parliaments is accepted. 'Perspectives in English Parliamentary History', in *Historical studies of the English Parliament*, II (1399–1603), ed. E. B. Fryde & E. Miller.

ruler with success and reaping, into the bargain, a rich commercial reward. To the aspirations of powerful groups of his subjects Charles I tendered an uncomprehending negation. The liberties of the subject, he declared defiantly from the scaffold, in no way consisted in having a share in government: 'a subject and a sovereign are clean different things'. It was a view fast becoming outmoded, first in England, later in the rest of Europe.

The various proposals for reform of Parliament in the Commonwealth and Protectorate period were in part derived from the general discussion of sovereignty but more immediately arose from the exigencies of the political situation. First, the needs of war gave influence, however briefly, to groups who could never hope to participate permanently in government unless sweeping changes were effected. Secondly, the claim of Parliament to represent the people prompted enquiry whether the people's wishes could be expressed through the existing system. When in January 1649 the House of Commons tried to justify the King's trial, it declared that 'the people are, under God, the original of all just power', and that the Commons, 'being chosen by, and representing the people, have the supreme power in this nation'.[1] But who were the people, and in what sense did the House represent them?

From the intricate network of causation two themes may be identified which reappeared throughout the long history of the struggle for reform. The first, the link between religious nonconformity and reform, has already been mentioned. From Overton and Lilburne in the 1640s, through Priestley and Price in the 1780s, to the enactment of Catholic Emancipation in 1829, the connection runs. A second, but less obvious link, was between civic affairs and reform of Parliament. In the conditions of pre-industrial England, with travel difficult and hazardous, most people lived out their lives in their local communities: local affairs were certainly more immediate, and perhaps more important to them, than national politics. In many towns, power was in the hands of self-appointed cliques. It is no coincidence that one of the earliest statements of the case for parliamentary reform should arise from Lilburne's discontent with the government of London, nor that the Reform Act of 1832 should be followed, within three years, by municipal reform.

The importance of the Commonwealth period in formulating and developing those arguments which were to dominate discussion of reform until 1832 does not need elaborating. It produced in Harrington's *Oceana* a major contribution to political thought, which expounded the relationship between property and political power, and advocated an agrarian law, manhood suffrage and the ballot. Yet it was a false dawn. Indeed, the identification of reform with civil disturbance postponed for generations

[1] *CJ*, VI, III.

any overhaul of the representative system. The upper classes were sobered by the glimpse of anarchy: in Cromwell's reception of the Levelling proposals of 1647, in his emphasis on order, continuity and stability, we can perceive the case for the Restoration. Radical schemes, such as manhood suffrage, law reform and the abolition of tithes, came to be discussed not because economic change had reached the point when political change had to follow, but because the privileged classes, in their schism, had called in the lower orders of society to do the fighting. As in France in 1793 concessions had to be made, however temporarily, to the 'passive' citizens. Through their membership of the victorious parliamentary army the lower ranks possessed a power that they could not, in any normal period, sustain, and as soon as the army was disbanded their chance was gone. Sexby's retort to Ireton's conservatism in the Putney debates conveys all the bitterness of men who felt themselves duped: 'had you thought fit to let us know...you would have had fewer under your command'.

2

Pudding time

When George in pudding time came o'er,
And moderate men looked big, Sir;
My principles I chang'd once more,
And so became a Whig, Sir.   *The Vicar of Bray*

The hundred years that followed the Restoration of Charles II were the
most conservative in modern British history. For generations the spectre
of Oliver was seen behind reform. 'Remember', warned Lord Chancellor
Clarendon in 1662, 'how near Monarchy hath been dissolved, and the
Law subverted, under pretence of reforming and supporting government,
law and justice...There is an enemy amongst us...towards whom we
cannot be too vigilant...the Republicans and Commonwealth's Men.'[1]
Forty years on the message had scarcely changed. It was their duty, the
Rev. Charles Leslie informed his readers, never to forget the Revolution
of Forty-One, 'wherein three flourishing kingdoms were set all in a flame,
which yet that ocean of blood could not quench; the laws and constitution
were totally subverted under the pretence of preserving them inviolate'.[2]
'The word *Commonwealth*', wrote a pamphleteer in 1702, 'frights men
like a Goblin.'[3]

   Yet throughout the whole period scarcely any writer on the subject of
government failed to deplore the inadequacy of the representative system.
Sir William Petty, in his *Political Arithmetic*, deployed the utilitarian
argument that reform of the representation would help to promote the
prosperity of the nation by enabling government to function more smoothly.
Clarendon and Burnet were agreed in commending Cromwell's redistribution of seats; Locke found it ridiculous that 'the bare name of
a town' could send up as many members as a county – 'this strangers
stand amazed at, and everyone must confess needs a remedy'; Jonathan
Swift included the representation among his Publick Absurdities; Defoe
expressed scorn for a system which allowed villages to 'send up gentlemen to represent beggars'. David Hume, in his essay on a perfect commonwealth in 1742, sketched out a plan for a more equal representation,

---

[1] *Parl. Hist.*, IV, 252–3.
[2] 'The New Association', part II, *A collection of tracts on several political subjects*.
Dr Henry Sacheverell took up the same theme in his celebrated sermon, 'In perils
amongst False Brethren'.
[3] 'The claims of the people of England', *State tracts of William III*, III, 7.

[24]

coupling it with a drastic reduction in the number of county voters. Even that most cautious of jurisprudents, Sir William Blackstone, admitted that it was a 'misfortune' that so many deserted villages were still represented. Nothing was done. Sir Thomas Littleton, speaking in a debate of 1675, allowed that Oliver's settlement was 'more proper', but added – as though aghast at his own candour – 'hopes you will not remedy such an inconvenience by so gross an injustice'.[1]

The revolution of 1688 disturbed the existing order as little as possible. Indeed, that was the feature which commended it in the following century to such unadventurous politicians as Henry Pelham, Lord North and the Marquis of Rockingham. It was, as the Whigs never wearied of proclaiming, a *preserving* revolution. The nation was saved from the perils of popery and absolutism: what more could be desired? The feebleness of Jacobite resistance, save in Ireland, made it unnecessary for the revolutionaries to appeal for support to the mass of the people – thus avoiding the distressing consequences of the 1640s. The success of the Glorious Revolution helped to perpetuate the representative system for another 150 years. Critics were reminded that they could count themselves fortunate that they did not, like Prussians, French or Spaniards, live under the sway of despots. 'No wooden shoes' was a great comfort. Though 'nations not so blest as thee must, in their turns, to tyrants fall', Britons never, never, never would be slaves.

Bolingbroke, in his *Dissertation on Parties*, lamented the opportunity missed in 1688. 'The revolution was, in many instances, and it ought to have been so in all, one of those renewals of our constitution that we have often mentioned...the communities, to whom the right of electing was trusted, as well as the qualifications of the electors and the elected, might have been settled in proportion to the present state of things.'[2] That such a reform was not attempted was no oversight. Lady Mordaunt rejoiced in 1689 that there was in the Convention 'an occasion not only of mending the government but of melting it down and making all new',[3] but she could hardly have been more at variance with the framers of the revolutionary settlement, concerned above all that things should not get out of hand. Thomas Wharton, author of *Lilliburlero* and one of the most devoted supporters of the revolution, expressed the view of the majority of mem-

[1] Sir W. Petty, *Political arithmetic*, ch. v; Clarendon, *History of the rebellion*, ed. W. D. Macray, v, 299; G. Burnet, *History of his own time*, 1833 ed., v, 281–2; J. Locke, *An essay concerning...civil government*, ch. xiii, paras. 157 and 8; J. Swift, *Of publick absurdities in England*; D. Defoe, *The freeholders plea against stock-jobbing election of Parliament men*; D. Hume, *The idea of a perfect commonwealth*; W. Blackstone, *Commentaries*, Book 1, ch. two; A. Grey, *Debates*, iv, 2.
[2] Letter XVIII.
[3] Quoted by P Laslett, 'The English Revolution', *Cambridge Historical Journal*, vol. xii, no. 1, 40.

bers of Parliament when he declared that the government should be settled 'as near the ancient government as can be', and Sir John Maynard, the lawyer, warned the Convention against listening to coffee-house reformers: 'take care of overloading your horse, not to undertake too many things'.[1]

Those few pamphlets that urged radical reform were afforded little attention. *Now is the time – a scheme for a commonwealth* advocated a conciliar government on the Venetian pattern, not unlike the scheme implemented in Sweden thirty years later on the death of Charles XII, and warned against 'barely changing our *master*'. *Some remarks upon government*, a more cogent and persuasive tract, argued that very considerable alterations were needed, and called for secret ballot, redistribution of seats and franchise reform: the Convention, elected as it was, could not be regarded 'truly and fairly' as representing the people. This last argument, hinted at in the Convention by Sir Robert Sawyer and others, received short shrift: 'I say, we represent the valuable part, and those that deserve a share in the government', countered Sir George Treby. Behind the constitutional wrangling lay the old issue of property. The doctrine that James had 'abdicated' and that the people must elect his successor seemed to many Tories fraught with subversive possibilities: 'if we were in the state of nature', Heneage Finch, the member for Oxford University, reminded his colleagues, 'we should have little title to any of our estates'. The lesson of the Putney debates had not gone unheeded.[2]

The experience of Edmund Ludlow in the 1688 revolution underlines its conservative nature. A prominent Commonwealthman and regicide, he had taken refuge in Switzerland after 1660. In 1689, thinking that his time had now come, he returned to his native land. Instead of receiving preferment as he had anticipated, the House of Commons addressed the King for his arrest as one of the murderers of Charles I. He departed hastily for Switzerland which he never left again.[3]

The reluctance of the governing class to disturb an old fabric may be judged from the case of the borough of Stockbridge during the Convention Parliament. Stockbridge was an unimportant Hampshire town, with fewer than 100 voters, enfranchised during the reign of Elizabeth. In November 1689, after a disputed election in which both candidates were disqualified for bribery, the House of Commons sent the bailiff and three other inhabitants to gaol, and it was moved to disfranchise the borough and award the two seats to the county. This was in itself the most conservative measure of reform possible since it could only add to the influence

---

[1] Grey, *Debates*, IX, 29, 32.
[2] *Somers Tracts*, 2nd coll., vol. III, 420; *State tracts of William III*, I, 149; Grey, *Debates*, IX, 13, 18, 21–3.
[3] *CJ*, x, 280, 282; Grey, *Debates*, IX, 398.

of the landed gentry. But the debate revealed little enthusiasm for change. Sir William Williams, knight of the shire for Carnarvon, warned that 'you break the ice by this, and give a handle to throw boroughs into counties, and another Parliament may throw counties into boroughs'. Two other members took the same line. John Hawles, nervous perhaps for his tenure of Old Sarum, recalled the experiences of the Commonwealth, while Sir John Trevor begged the House not to remove 'old landmarks'. The matter was allowed to drop. Two more attempts to reform the borough after further acts of bribery foundered during the next five years in the same way, and one hundred years later the House was still considering proposals for the disfranchisement of Stockbridge and deciding that they were premature.[1]

The other occasion which might have furnished the opportunity for a comprehensive reform of the electoral machinery was the Act of Union with Scotland in 1707, which brought into being the Parliament of Great Britain. It was not taken. 'Your universal or general union', wrote one commentator, 'which must carry along with it the destruction of the constitution of both kingdoms and the resurrection of another in their room is no more to be expected than the annihilation of this world.'[2] The negotiators contented themselves with adding 45 Scottish members to the English House of Commons and 16 representative peers to the House of Lords. The Union itself however was a tacit admission at last that some of the Commonwealth experiments were worthy of imitation, and the Protectorate arrangements were followed in the grouping of the 66 Scottish burghs into districts of four or five.[3] To some opponents of the Union the groupings were a source of grievance: was it right, demanded James Hodges, that so many Scottish burghs should lose their separate representation, 'while England does not disfranchise one, though it may not contain a dozen freeholds'.[4]

In other respects too the new arrangements offered little comfort to reformers. The Scottish representative system, which was perpetuated, was even more defective than that of England and Wales. In the burghs

[1] *Parl. Hist.*, v, 433–5; *CJ*, VIII, X, XI, XLVIII, *sub* Stockbridge. Another notoriously corrupt borough, Hindon, was threatened with extinction 1702–3 but escaped by courtesy of the House of Lords. A pamphlet of 1702, *The representative of London and Westminster in Parliament examined and considered*, *Somers Tracts*, 1st coll., 2nd vol. refers to a bill 'in agitation' in 1701 to extend the right of voting in boroughs of less than 100 voters to the neighbouring freeholders. The bill made no progress. See also E. Hamilton, *The Mordaunts, an eighteenth-century family*, 52.
[2] 'An essay upon the Union of the Kingdoms of England and Scotland', *Somers Tracts*, 4th coll., vol. III, 113.
[3] Edinburgh alone was given separate representation. According to Clarendon, one of Charles II's reasons for not perpetuating the Union in 1660 was that he 'would not build according to Cromwell's models'. *Life of Clarendon*, 1857 ed., I, 362.
[4] Quoted Porritt, II, 24–5.

control was exercised by narrow self-electing oligarchies, while the forty-shilling freehold in the counties was so tightly interpreted under Scottish law that the electorate was diminutive. In the largest of the Scottish constituencies, Aberdeenshire, a mere 178 persons were entitled to vote – fewer than in the village of Hindon. In the smaller counties, the dearth of voters was extraordinary – 7 in Orkney and Shetland, 12 in Buteshire, and 18 in Cromartyshire. The total electorate of the Scottish counties in 1788, after a good deal of vote-splitting had taken place, was only 2662 – about half that of the city of Bristol.[1]

There is some evidence which suggests that certain Scots may have tried to secure franchise concessions. At the first general election subsequent to the Act of Union, in 1708, there were thirteen petitions to the House of Commons from the 45 Scottish constituencies – far more than in proportion from the English. Several of the county elections involved disputes about the franchise. In Perthshire it was alleged that one candidate had brought to the poll 'a great number of gentlemen who never pretended a right to vote in that county, and who, by the Laws of Scotland, have no right to elect'. Similar allegations were made for Fifeshire, Roxburghshire, Ross-shire, Elginshire and Clackmannanshire. In Bruntisland, one of the component burghs of the Dysart group, it looks as though some townsfolk hoped to break open the old oligarchy. It was complained of the commissioner from that burgh that he had no legal authority, 'only a pretended insufficient one from a few of the Commonalty, electing him by way of poll, which is contrary to the manner of elections, settled by the Act of Parliament'. The protesters gained one victory. A petition from Aberdeenshire declared that the eldest sons of Scottish peers had been elected for many places and that if this were permitted 'electors and free-holders in future time will never be able to withstand so powerful an interest, but rather, by continual discouragements, the majority of them must become subservient to the nobility'. The House upheld the complaint. In no other respect does the attempt to liberalize the Scottish system seem to have met with success.[2]

The ultimate effect of the Union was to support the *status quo* by adding substantially to the security of the Hanoverian regime. The military threat posed by a semi-independent Scotland disappeared in the course of time, and Scottish regiments won battle honours in the creation of empire. The electoral arrangements promoted governmental stability in a most direct way. The smallness of the Scottish electorate and the penury of the

---

[1] C. E. Adam, *The view of the political state of Scotland in the last century*. This is shown by D. G. Henry, *Scottish Historical Review*, 46, to have been the work of Laurence Hill. The total burgh electorate has been estimated at about 1250. A. V. Dicey & R. S. Rait, *Thoughts on the union between England and Scotland*, 290, n. 1.

[2] *CJ*, XVI, 15, 21, 23, 27; *Parl. Hist.*, VI, 757–8.

Scottish representatives made government influence paramount, and many ministers in the course of the century had occasion to bless the Scottish bloc vote. As early as 1708 one English observer remarked that the Scottish members seemed 'very importunate to have their deserts rewarded', and towards the end of the century a disgruntled reformer declared, with pardonable exasperation, that 'an equal number of elbow chairs, placed once for all on the ministerial benches, would be less expensive to government, and just about as manageable'.[1]

* * * *

With the enfranchisement of Newark in 1673 and of Durham in 1675, the English representation took the form it was to keep, with only slight modifications, until the Reform Act of 1832. The forty counties returned two knights of the shire each, on the forty-shilling freehold franchise; 196 boroughs returned two members apiece; 5 boroughs returned one member each, and two others, London and the double borough of Weymouth and Melcombe Regis, returned four members. The Universities of Oxford and Cambridge returned two burgesses each, making a grand total of 489 members sitting for the English constituencies. In addition, Wales returned 24 members to Parliament, equally divided between the 12 counties and the 12 boroughs or groups of boroughs. Until the Act of Union with Scotland, therefore, the total membership of the House of Commons was 513: the addition of the 45 Scottish members in 1707 brought it up to 558, at which number it remained until the Act of Union with Ireland in 1800.

In the boroughs there was no uniformity of franchise, though they fall into four main groups.[2] The largest was the group of freeman boroughs, which accounted for nearly half the English borough representation; next came the inhabitant householder boroughs, under which may be included the scot and lot boroughs and the freeholder boroughs; the third group of burgage boroughs, where the right to vote had from time immemorial been attached to certain properties, was the most picturesque and anachronistic: this group included Old Sarum with its green fields, Richmond with its pigeon lofts, and Droitwich with its dried-up salt pans; in the fourth group, the corporation boroughs, the franchise was restricted to the members of a self-perpetuating oligarchy. Within these general definitions, variety was infinite, and generations of attorneys grew fat on the niceties of electoral law – whether certain borough charities could be interpreted

[1] Dicey & Rait, 262, n. 1; J. T. Callender, *The political progress of Britain* (1792), quoted by E. Porritt, *The unreformed House of Commons*, II, 5.
[2] The most careful and illuminating description is given by J. Brooke in his introductory survey to *The House of Commons, 1754–90*, I, 10–56. I have not followed Mr Brooke's classification into six groups, since the scot and lot and freeholder boroughs can be treated as variants of the inhabitant householder group.

Freeman
householder: scot-lot; freeman
burgage
corporation

as alms in such a way as to disqualify the recipients, whether residence was or was not necessary, whether the right to vote for a burgage attached to the owner or the tenant, together with innumerable disputes about the rightful election of mayors and corporations. After every general election, members of Parliament spent days in committee dealing with disputed returns, sometimes from fifty or sixty constituencies, while aged inhabitants were paraded before them to offer their quavering testimony on the ancient practices of their particular borough.

The size of the electorates varied enormously. In some of the larger constituencies, such as Westminster, Bristol and the counties, there were several thousand voters, even in the seventeenth century: at the other extreme stood Gatton, a scot and lot borough, where the number of electors had dwindled to two, Dunwich where the greater part of the town had long since fallen into the North Sea, and corporation boroughs like Buckingham, where a mere thirteen burgesses exercised the exclusive right to vote. In character they varied from a great county constituency like Yorkshire, where a disputed election could be a genuine test of public opinion, to Leominster, described by one candidate as 'like a farm, where the good wife beating the bottom of the pail, all the hogs run to the wash'; from Bath, where the members of the corporation chose men of rank and distinction, to nearby Malmesbury, where the burgesses are reported to have said that 'it was no odds to them who they voted for, it was as master pleased'.[1]

The total electorate changed considerably with the increase of population, particularly in the counties. In 1708 some 9000 persons seem to have voted in the Yorkshire contest; by 1741 it had risen to more than 15,000, and by 1807 to 23,000. The total electorate of England and Wales in 1754 was about 282,000, of which 177,000 were in the counties and 105,000 in the boroughs.[2] In relation to a population of about six and a half million,[3] this meant that roughly one in ten of the male population had the right to vote, or perhaps one in six of the adult male population. A more precise estimate would neither be possible nor particularly illuminating, since for most of the eighteenth century election contests were rare. There was no contest for Shropshire between 1722 and 1831, for Dorset between 1727 and 1806, nor for Worcestershire between 1741 and 1806. The freeholders of Wiltshire had only one opportunity to cast a vote between 1713 and 1818. At the general election of 1747 only three English counties went to a poll, and in 1780 only two. In the boroughs contests were rather more frequent, but still generations of electors might have no chance of voting. The borough of St Germans, for many years under the control of the

---

[1] *CJ*, XX, 493; LXII, 33.
[2] *The House of Commons, 1754–90*, ed. L. B. Namier & J. Brooke, I. 514–20.
[3] *Abstract of British historical statistics*, ed. B. R. Mitchell & P. Deane, 5.

Eliot family, seems never to have had a contest between the Restoration of Charles II and its abolition in 1832. Thirsk and Castle Rising seem not to have gone to a poll between 1673 and 1832. Under such circumstances, the right to vote might mean anything or nothing.

The variety of franchises in the boroughs made for some strange juxtapositions and anomalies. In Bristol some 5000 people were entitled to vote in 1754 – approximately one in three of the adult male population: in its neighbour, Bath, only the thirty members of the corporation – perhaps one in a hundred – could vote. Exeter, a freeman borough, had some 1500 voters: Plymouth, more than twice its size, had about 200; Southampton, a scot and lot borough, had 500 electors, while Portsmouth, four times its size, had only 100 electors. In some places the franchise came close to manhood suffrage and the electors must have included a large number of the lower orders – at Appleby, for instance, where there were 250 voters in a township of about 1000 persons, or at Sudbury, Honiton, Wootton Bassett, Lancaster or Ilchester. At the other end of the scale was Bury St Edmunds, where the corporation of 37 monopolized the franchise in a town of nearly 8000. The first census, in 1801, revealed that of the seven largest towns in England, four – Manchester, Birmingham, Leeds and Sheffield – were not represented at all.

But whatever defects the representative system possessed in practice were palliated in theory by the <u>doctrine of virtual representation</u>, which averred that although the poor were represented in Parliament by the rich their interests were not neglected.[1] Soame Jenyns, writing in 1765, treated it as a constitutional commonplace: 'I am well aware that I shall hear Locke, Sidney, Selden and many other great names quoted to prove that every Englishman, whether he has a right to vote for a representative or not, is still represented in the British Parliament.'[2] Burke used the doctrine as an argument against parliamentary reform in 1784 maintaining that equal representation already existed because in Parliament 'you have men equally interested in the prosperity of the whole, who are involved in the general interest and the general sympathy'.[3] In 1792 he offered a more pre-

---

[1] I refrain from putting the argument in class terms since the validity of the concept of class has been questioned for the eighteenth century. Samuel Taylor Coleridge declared that 'no such divisions as classes actually exist in society. There is an indissoluble blending and interfusion of persons from top to bottom; and no man can trace a line of separation through them.' *Table Talk*, 20 March 1831. This is similar to the view expressed by H. J. Perkin, *The origins of modern English society 1780–1880*, who argues that it was a 'finely graded hierarchy of great subtlety and discrimination.' I am not quite convinced that these shades of difference are not to be found in any society. But for the purposes of my present argument, it is enough to assume that rich and poor existed in eighteenth-century England.

[2] *The objections to the taxation of our American colonies...briefly considered.*

[3] *The works of Burke*, World's Classics edition (1906), III, 359. The editor followed tradition in attributing this speech to the debate of 7 May 1782, but internal evidence

cise definition of virtual representation as 'that in which there was a communion of interests and a sympathy in feelings and desires between those who act in the name of any description of people and the people in whose name they act, though the trustees are not actually chosen by them... Such a representation I think in many cases better even than the actual.'[1]

No very elaborate refutation of so simple a theory is necessary. It would of course be foolish to deny that in a very general sense there was a common interest between rich and poor – all men suffered, though not equally, from flood, pestilence, famine and war. Nor would one wish to dispute that the harshness of the lot of the poor was often mitigated by acts of piety, kindness and understanding on the part of their social superiors. But as a general political proposition the doctrine of virtual representation was no more than a polite fiction. Indeed the assertion that there were no fundamental differences of interest between rich and poor is hard to reconcile with the determination of the upper classes to reserve political power for men of substance. One of the most extraordinary features of eighteenth-century life – the proliferation of capital offences – is a clear warning against too sentimental a view of the relations between rich and poor in the eighteenth century.[2] One may also draw attention to the increasing severity of the Game Laws in the period,[3] the effect of the enclosures, and the extreme reluctance of the upper classes to

makes it clear that it was prepared in 1784 or later. It was probably the speech Burke would have delivered on 16 June 1784 had the House not refused him a hearing.

[1] *Letter to Sir Hercules Langrishe, Bart.* Since Burke was applying the argument to Irish affairs, he was forced to concede that virtual representation ought to have 'a substratum in the actual'.

The concept of virtual representation has had a long life, particularly in relation to women's suffrage. James Mill, writing 'On Government' for the *Encyclopaedia Britannica* in 1820, remarked blandly that 'all those individuals whose interests are included in those of other individuals may be struck off from political rights without inconvenience. In this light women may be regarded.' Nearly one hundred years later, Arnold Ward, the member for West Herts., resisted women's suffrage: 'We have maintained that in the past the interests of women have on the whole been fairly justly looked after by a Parliament of Men. I do not think that that is seriously disputed by any historian of the nineteenth century.' *Parl. Debs.*, 5th series, XCII, 498.

[2] In 1819 Fowell Buxton, the member for Weymouth, asserted that there were 223 capital offences on the statute book, of which 187 had been added since the accession of Charles II, and more during the single reign of George III than in the reigns of Plantagenet, Tudor and Stuart put together. The Duke of Sussex, speaking in 1831, contrasted the number of capital commitments in France and England – in 1827 for the former 109, the latter 1529. *Parl. Debs.*, 1st series, XXXIX, 808–9; 3rd series, VI, 1174.

[3] In 1671 the killing of game was prohibited to all save owners of land worth £100 p.a., lessees worth £150 p.a., and persons of high degree. In the course of George III's reign, thirty-two new Game Laws were added to the statute book, culminating in the Ellenborough Act of 1803 whereby anyone resisting lawful arrest was to be hanged. These encroachments on what the poor regarded as their natural rights were much resented.

commit themselves to any national system of education for the poor.[1]

The doctrine of virtual representation was not, of course, without critics in its own day. Richard Woodward, in *An address to the publick on ...the poor*, published in 1775, argued that the case of the poor was 'the strongest instance that the whole body of the people are not represented, because the interest of the poor calls for a tax on the rich, and therefore is in direct opposition to the supposed interest of all the representatives, and almost all who are concerned in electing them'. Sir William Jones was more laconic in 1782 denouncing the doctrine as '*actual* folly...there is no end of absurdities deducible from so idle a play upon words'.[2]

* * * *

It was scarcely to be expected that the generation after the Restoration would witness any major overhaul of the electoral structure. Those changes that were made – the remodelling of borough charters by the later Stuarts or the passing of the Triennial Act in 1694 – were tactical moves in the power struggle between Crown and Commons rather than attempts to improve the state of the representation. The overall tendency was towards conservative oligarchy. Even writers like Swift and Bolingbroke, who recognized the need for redistributive reform, frequently coupled it with proposals for revising the forty-shilling freehold franchise to take account of the fall in the value of money. Shaftesbury's pamphlet of 1679,[3] though strongly in favour of legislation against bribery and the abolition of rotten boroughs – several 'so inconsiderable that they contain not above three or four houses' – also advocated a savage reduction in the county electorate.

Even without legislation it was possible for the House of Commons to make considerable alterations in the extent of the electorate, since it retained the sole right of determining the franchise in boroughs where the return was disputed. Though many of the petitions were decided purely on a party basis, each side upholding whichever franchise would assist its candidate, the tendency after 1688 was to find in favour of the narrow franchise – that is for corporations against the commonalty and

[1] That the English state should be some seventy years behind its continental counterparts in providing education hardly suggests vast concern for the poorer classes. I have merely sketched out the argument at this point. The concentration by historians of the eighteenth century on the narrowly political and constitutional developments of the period means that the relations of governors and governed have been little explored. Two important pioneering enterprises are J. H. Plumb, 'Political Man', in *Man versus society in eighteenth-century Britain*, ed. J. L. Clifford, and Angus Macinnes, 'The Revolution and the people', *Britain after the Glorious Revolution 1689–1714*, ed. G. Holmes.

[2] *Speech by William Jones, Esq., to the assembled inhabitants of the counties of Middlesex and Surrey...at the London Tavern*, 28 May 1782.   [3] See above p. 19.

for scot and lot payers against the inhabitants at large. Between 1660 and 1688, while the struggle was against the monarchy, these conservative instincts seem to have been kept in check. In 51 determinations between the Restoration and the Glorious Revolution, the House upheld a broad franchise on 28 occasions and a narrow one on 23. Thereafter the ratio changed considerably. From 1688 until 1727 (the general election before the Last Determinations Act came into force) the House declared 28 times in favour of a broad franchise and 78 times in favour of a narrow franchise. The result over the years was <u>substantially to reduce the size of the borough electorate.</u> It does not necessarily follow that this was a conscious policy. A House of Commons that was increasingly conservative tended, other things being equal, to find for privileged corporations and to mistrust the general populace. In the voluminous evidence presented to the election committees one may occasionally catch glimpses of underlying political prejudices. A witness at the hearing for Milborne Port in 1702, when the issue was between scot and lot payers and the inhabitants at large, remarked that the latter were 'first permitted to poll in Oliver's usurpation'. This was in itself no great commendation, and the House duly found in favour of the narrow franchise.[1] The number of voters affected by these decisions could be large. When the election committee in 1696 resolved in favour of the corporation and burgesses at Portsmouth against the inhabitants at large, the electorate was reduced from over 450 to about 100. In 1723 when another committee upheld the scot and lot payers at Shrewsbury against the inhabitants at large, the petitioner's counsel declared his intention of objecting to 1000 voters, and the sitting members' counsel counter-objected to more than 700.[2]

A further encouragement to conservatism in electoral matters was the <u>Last Determinations Act of 1696, strengthened by that of 1729, which stipulated that the previous decision on the franchise was to be 'final to all intents and purposes whatsoever,</u> any usage to the contrary notwithstanding'.[3] This rendered the position of many corporations and borough patrons unassailable and served to freeze the existing system: not until the legislation was modified in 1788 could the franchise in most boroughs be effectively challenged. A further consequence of the Last Determinations Act, together with the Septennial Act of 1716, was to enhance the value of boroughs and to render electioneering extremely expensive.[4]

---

[1] *CJ*, XIV, 75.   [2] *CJ*, XI, 411–12; XX, 191.
[3] 7 & 8 William III, c. 7; 2 George II, c. 24.
[4] Though the supporters of the Septennial Act were concerned primarily to secure the dynasty, the advantages of oligarchy were not overlooked. The Earl of Dorset complained that triennial elections 'destroy all family interest', and the Duke of Devonshire that they occasioned 'ruinous expense'. Lord Islay maintained that 'frequent elections render our government dependent upon the caprice of the multitude'. *Parl. Hist.*, VII, 292–305.

Although estimates of the average cost of a seat are bound to be approximations, there can be no doubt that the expense rose steadily. At Malmesbury Lord Wharton demanded £400 for a seat in 1698. Giles Earle and his son William Rawlinson Earle paid £650 each for their seats in the same borough in 1727, 1734 and 1741: there was a standard tariff, the thirteen burgesses receiving £100 a head for a general election, and a further £20 for any re-elections on taking office. In 1761 Lord Tylney paid £2000 for a seat there.[1] By 1784 the average price of a seat had risen to £3000, and during the early nineteenth century £5000 or £6000 was asked.[2] The alternative to the direct purchase of a seat from a patron was to hazard a contest in one of the open boroughs. There the same inflation can be observed. Whereas Thomas Webb, a candidate for Wootton Bassett in 1690, was reported to have purchased votes at 32/6d a head, sixty-four years later John Probyn and Thomas Estcourt Cresswell were charged thirty guineas apiece in the same borough. Their joint expenses, including treating, came to £6000.[3] Though there is no evidence of direct bribery in county elections, candidates were afflicted by various charges, an act of 1745 making them responsible for the payment of poll clerks and the erection of polling booths. Their greatest expense continued to be the transport and entertainment of voters, many of them brought long distances.

These considerations made electioneering even more of a rich man's pursuit. The one measure of reform that was always guaranteed a hearing in the House of Commons was a proposal to curb election expenses and eliminate bribery. As early as 1674, in a debate on the subject, a member could complain that the cost had 'grown so vast that it goes beyond all bounds'. One of many pious pieces of legislation was an act of 1696 which forbade any 'present, gift, reward or entertainment' to voters on pain of disqualification.[4] Judging from the number of subsequent efforts, it remained a complete dead letter. Nearly a hundred years later, speaking in support of a proposal by Lord Mahon, Richard Hippisley Coxe declared that 'the necessity of such a bill must strike every gentleman, for at present there was scarcely a fortune that could support the expense of a contest at an election'. Another advocate of the bill, Charles Barrow, revealed that it had cost him 1500 guineas to transport 150 voters from London to Gloucester at the election of 1780.[5]

[1] *Letters illustrative of the reign of William III*, ed. G. P. R. James, II, 148; 'An account of money', Malmesbury borough records; L. S. Sutherland, 'Henry Fox as Paymaster', *English Historical Review*, 70 (1955).
[2] Porritt, I, 358.
[3] *CJ*, X, 522; 'Copy of a statement by William Hollister, mayor of Wootton Bassett', in the Devizes Museum, the original of which is listed as no. 187 in J. A. Neale, *Charters and Records of the Neales of Berkeley*.
[4] 7 & 8 William III, c. 4.   [5] *Parl. Hist.*, IV, 658; XXIII, 102–3.

Another blow to men of modest means was the introduction of the property qualification for members of Parliament in 1711. It was a measure that had been advocated for years. Shaftesbury had argued that 'wealth and substance' was necessary to give 'a lustre and reputation to our great council and a security to the people'. As carried by the Tory ministry of 1710 it enacted that knights of the shire must possess landed property worth £600 p.a. and burgesses £300 p.a. Though sometimes thought of purely as a party measure, it is notable that the Whigs made no attempt to repeal it after their triumph in 1715: on the contrary it was strengthened in 1717 by the adoption of standing orders tightening the supervision. It failed in its main purpose of beating off the competition of the 'moneyed interest', proving little embarrassment to the wealthy and influential, who could secure the services of accommodating lawyers or the assistance of friends, but there is some evidence to suggest that it may have been a deterrent to lesser men.[1] A remarkable tribute to the ideal of landed property, it had its counterpart in local government in the act of George II's reign which required that J.P.s should possess land to the value of £100 p.a. Clause five granted exemption from its provisions to peers and the eldest sons of peers.[2]

The consequence of these accumulated factors was that the electoral system grew increasingly oligarchical. In the early eighteenth century the county constituencies were still frequently contested. In 1702 at least 18 of the 40 counties went to the poll; in 1705 no less than 26, and in 1710 a total of 23.[3] But after 1734 the decrease in the number of contests was marked. Cheshire was contested in 8 of the 10 general elections between 1701 and 1734, and never again during the unreformed parliament; Nottinghamshire was contested in 1698, 1701, 1702, 1710 and 1722, and never again; Shropshire was contested in 6 of the 8 general elections between 1701 and 1722, but the next contest, and that of a token nature, was not until the eve of reform in 1831. Gloucestershire was contested at 8 of 10 general elections between 1701 and 1734, and only one general election subsequently.[4] Whereas 65% of the counties went to the poll in 1705, at the general election of 1747 it was only 7.5%.

[1] See, for example, John Comyns, who lost his seat for Maldon in 1715 after he had refused to take the necessary oath, and John Boteler, heir to a decayed Hertfordshire property, who lost his seat for Wendover in 1735. Examples of petitioners unable to produce the requisite qualifications are Henry Andrews (Shaftesbury, 1715), James Sheppard (Honiton, 1715), Henry Gorges (Leominster, 1717), Thomas Harrison (Steyning, 1724), George Grove (Minehead, 1728), James Bertie (Westbury, 1734) and Foster Cunliffe (Liverpool, 1734). *CJ*, XVIII, 126–9; XXII, 466–8; XVIII, 69, 71, 543; XX, 368; XXI, 66; XXII, 395, 426.
[2] 5 George II c. 18. The property qualification act for members of Parliament is 9 Anne c. 5. It also exempted the eldest sons of peers.
[3] See below appendix three.
[4] In 1784, when W. H. Hartley polled only 20 votes in a token contest.

An analysis of the 203 English boroughs reveals a similar trend, though the evidence is more fragmentary.[1] But it is certain that at least 104 boroughs went to the poll in 1710, and as many as 110 in 1722. Ludlow, a freeman borough, was contested in 7 consecutive general elections between 1705 and 1727,[2] and only once, in 1826, subsequently. Calne, a corporation borough, was contested in 1679, 1685, 1700 and 1701, and in 7 of the 8 general elections between 1705 and 1734, and not again until 1830. Dunwich, another freeman borough, was contested at 5 of the 6 general elections 1708–27, and never again.

A study of the election petitions presented to the House of Commons also suggests increasing oligarchy. In the period 1660–1702, only 15 boroughs did not at any time petition; from 1705–1774 33 boroughs did not petition; in the final period, from 1780 until the Reform Act, no fewer than 70 boroughs did not petition. The inference is that opposition to the established electoral interest became steadily harder. According to a comment by Defoe in the *Review* at the time of the general election of 1705, the trend was already apparent:

> In some towns of England, it can hardly be called an election of Members; the Corporation is small, the Electors few and poor; one man comes and buys the Lordship, and let him be what he will, he is sure to be sent to Parliament…Bramber in Sussex, Castle Rising in Norfolk, Gatton and Bletchingley in Surrey, Marlow in Buckinghamshire, and a great number of like places in England are plain instance of this.

Two more analyses must suffice. One can make a reasonable assessment of the families sharing the county representation throughout the period under survey, distinguishing the years 1660–1746, including 22 Parliaments, from 1747 to 1832, including 18 Parliaments – periods of 86 and 85 years respectively. In only 3 of the 40 counties were there more families involved in the representation in the latter period.[3] In all the others, the indications are that the representation was becoming monopolized. The figures for Huntingdon were 21–9; Buckinghamshire 19–7; Norfolk 16–7; Somerset 19–10; Sussex 22–10; Cambridgeshire 17–9; Wiltshire 16–9; Warwickshire 16–8; Bedfordshire 18–10; Oxfordshire 17–10.

[1] The figure of 203 excludes the University seats, and treats Weymouth and Melcombe Regis as one borough.
[2] As well as in 1690, 1695, 1698 and 1701.
[3] These were co. Durham, Yorkshire and Surrey. The first had no representation until 1675. The figures for Yorkshire were 15–19, but the county had four seats from 1826 onwards, and 8 new families appeared in the representation in the remaining years before reform, including, for example, Henry Brougham. In Surrey, where the figures were 12–19, the increasing influence of wealthy merchants from London seems to be the explanation. This is an unsophisticated analysis and I have not taken into account distant family relationships or female descent, but I trust the degree of error at least is a constant.

Secondly, one can form some conclusion from the average length of service of county members. A long and uninterrupted tenure of a county seat is comparatively uncommon in the earlier period. The average length of service for the members of the Parliament of 1695 was 16.99 years: by 1734 it had risen to 24.18 years. Throughout the remainder of the period it rose slowly, reaching 26.75 by 1812, and 28.0 by 1818.[1] It is difficult therefore to resist the conclusion that the smaller gentry had less chance of obtaining a county seat in the later eighteenth century than at the beginning.

An additional irritant to the lesser country gentry was that their hold on the local boroughs also diminished. An analysis of six Wiltshire boroughs shows that their catchment area in the later seventeenth century was extremely narrow.[2] The twelve members who represented Cricklade between 1660 and 1702 all had property within twenty miles of the town: of the fourteen members representing Downton between 1660 and 1713, one, John Elliott, had property seven miles away, but the other 13 had estates within one mile of the borough. In all six boroughs it was unusual until the end of the seventeenth century for the member to be other than a local man. In the reign of Anne a change begins to be apparent. James Vernon, the first stranger to sit for Cricklade, was returned in 1708, and a comment in *Dyer's Letters* in 1705, though clearly exaggerated for propaganda purposes, shows that the issue was beginning to attract attention: 'We hear that 17 strangers are like to be chosen in Wiltshire, not one of them having a foot of land in that county, to the reproach of the electors, for not having a greater value for the honest, loyal, neighbouring gentry.' As the century progressed, the trend became more marked. At Westbury, where only one of the eleven members 1660–1702 had not had property within five miles of the borough, only three of the last thirty-five members before 1832 can, by any definition, be regarded as local men. Sir Watkin Williams Wynn, speaking in 1734 in support of a motion to repeal the Septennial Act, argued that annual elections would make it impossible for place-men to bribe the voters out of their natural allegiance: 'How can it otherwise be imagined that the people would chuse persons they never saw, persons they perhaps never heard of, in opposition to gentlemen who live in the neighbourhood...and gentlemen whose ancestors have, perhaps, often represented that very place in

---

[1] For the purposes of this computation, the seventeenth-century Parliaments are treated as continuous. Length of service includes service for boroughs as well as for counties. For an estimate of the effect of the increased expectation of life, see G. P. Judd IV, *Members of Parliament 1734–1832*, 21–2.

[2] John Cannon, 'The parliamentary representation of six Wiltshire boroughs', University of Bristol Ph.D. thesis, 1958, vol. two, appendix 3. It would of course be foolish to generalize from six boroughs if the argument were not supported by other evidence.

Parliament?' He concluded with an instance of one member who boasted that he had never set foot in his constituency nor spoken to one of his constituents.[1]

Improved techniques for controlling boroughs helped patrons to close them to outsiders. As early as 1747 Lord Feversham was reported to be in command of Downton by the issue of 'snatch-papers.'[2] Once the majority of properties in a burgage borough had been acquired by one family, opposition was almost fruitless. The borough of Westbury was contested at eight out of eleven general elections between 1702 and 1747, but after the fourth Earl of Abingdon gained control there were no further contests. Weobley, in Herefordshire, was fought on nine occasions between 1700 and 1754 (exclusive of by-election contests in 1708, 1730 and 1732), but the Thynne family ultimately established so commanding a hold that all opposition ceased. Better methods of control were also devised for corporation boroughs. At Wilton it became the practice of the Herbert family to fill the corporation with relatives and friends.[3] At Malmesbury the patron allowed men of modest rank to become burgesses, but commanded their loyalty by means of a bond worth £500 against each of them.[4] In freeman and scot and lot boroughs, the corporation could often establish a decisive influence by the creation of honorary freemen, the manipulation of local charities, or the control of the poor law books.[5]

A development which facilitated the growth of oligarchy was the publication of printed poll books, which became common in the course of the eighteenth century. The taking of voters' names had been resisted by the Commons in the early seventeenth century on the grounds that it might permit pressure to be brought on electors.[6] No such inhibitions existed after the Glorious Revolution. The Last Determinations Act of 1696 included a clause instructing the clerk of the crown to keep a record of all polls and make it readily available, and was followed by a remarkable

---

[1] *Parl. Hist.*, IX, 430.
[2] 'His Lordship's method of electing members is to make a small part of one of these burgage tenures by lease to his tenants and tradesmen in the neighbourhood, which leases are by his agent delivered to them on the day of election, and after voting they are delivered up to his agent again, so that these voters are never in the possession of or receive any rent of the land by virtue of which they claim their right of voting.' 'State of the borough of Downton', Newcastle (Clumber) MSS., University of Nottingham.
[3] *The House of Commons, 1754–90*, I, 421. There were contests at Wilton in 1660, 1690, 1698, 1700, 1701, 1702, 1708, 1710, and one thereafter.
[4] *CJ*, LXII, 33–4.
[5] Porritt, I, ch. 3. Further examples of Corporation oligarchy may be found in J. H. Plumb, *Sir Robert Walpole*, I, *The making of a statesman*, 50–2. Roy Carroll, 'Yorkshire parliamentary boroughs in the seventeenth century', *Northern History*, III (1968) concludes that 'by 1730 the freedom of most of the Yorkshire parliamentary boroughs was gone'.
[6] J. H. Plumb, 'The growth of the electorate in England from 1600 to 1715', *Past & Present*, no. 45 (1969), 97.

proliferation of poll books. Though most copies were commercial ventures, produced to gratify curiosity, the use to which they could be put is made clear by the number of poll books that have survived with marginal comments by canvassers and election agents.[1]

The gradual development of oligarchy goes far to explain the dissatisfaction which many country gentlemen came to feel with the state of the representation. It was an important ingredient in the persistent Tory opposition to Sir Robert Walpole and his successors, the Pelhams. Christopher Wyvill, organizer of a reform agitation in the 1780s and himself a large landowner in Yorkshire, traced the change back to the Glorious Revolution, 'for since that period...the Crown has gradually been enabled to influence or command elections in many seaports and other places, while within the same period, in still more boroughs, the aristocracy by various unwarrantable arts, especially by creating fraudulent and fictitious votes, has destroyed the right of election, and acquired the absolute power of nomination'.[2]

* * * *

In recent years some distinguished historians have drawn attention to the vigour of political life in the reign of Anne and argued that a great part of the nation was deeply interested in the party struggle. Professor J. H. Plumb has written that between 1688 and 1715 'the voice of the electorate was able to make itself heard in many places', and has suggested that it may prove that England was 'far more democratic' in that period than immediately after 1832.[3] Dr W. A. Speck has written that the political struggle 'comprehended the electorate and even to some extent the unenfranchised'.[4] Their arguments are so compelling that it is necessary to insist on the contrast between the position in Anne's reign and forty years later. Perhaps this is most easily done by commenting briefly on two pieces of evidence cited by Professor Plumb – while acknowledging that he is well aware of the change to which I have referred. He makes an illuminating analysis of a series of poll books for contested elections in

[1] 7 & 8 William III c. 7. See also John Cannon, 'Short guide to records: Poll Books', *History*, 47 (1962).
[2] C. Wyvill, *Political papers*, III, appendix, 14–15. A parallel instance of oligarchy in ecclesiastical affairs is the suppression of Convocation, which was not allowed to meet between 1717 and 1855. Though this is usually interpreted as a triumph for erastianism, it can also be seen as a move to protect the Whig episcopate from the strictures of the Lower House of Convocation, dominated by Tory parsons. The bishops still had voices in the House of Lords: the parsons were silenced.
[3] *Past & Present*, no. 45 (1969), 116. See also *The growth of political stability in England, 1675–1725* and 'Political Man', in *Man versus society in eighteenth-century Britain*, ed. J. L. Clifford.
[4] *Tory and Whig: the struggle in the constituencies, 1701–15*, 7, and 'Conflict in Society', in *Britain after the Glorious Revolution, 1689–1714*, ed. G. Holmes. The matter is also discussed in G. Holmes, *British politics in the age of Anne.*

Suffolk during Anne's reign to establish that the ordinary freeholder may have had more independence and voted less deferentially than is commonly supposed. It would be almost impossible to make a similar analysis for the mid-eighteenth century since the necessary series of contested elections does not exist. Suffolk itself was not contested between the elections of 1727 and 1784. Between 1741 and 1768, which I regard as the period of closest oligarchy, eighteen of the forty English counties were not contested at all and four others only at one by-election. It would be owlish to conduct an investigation into the general election of 1747 to discover what degree of independence the freeholders of Lancashire, Middlesex and Staffordshire revealed without remarking that in the other thirty-seven counties the electors could not vote at all.[1] Between 1701 and 1734 a run of three consecutive contested general elections can be found for nineteen counties: between 1741 and 1784 such a sequence exists for only one county, Westmorland.[2] Plumb's evidence for the boroughs includes a reference to Amersham, a pocket borough belonging to the Drake family, where a contest in 1705 showed that there could still be political contention. But the subsequent history of the borough marks the difference. The control of the Drakes was once more challenged in 1728 and 1734 before the voters finally submitted. For the last one hundred years before it was disqualified under schedule A the peace of the borough was not disturbed and *The House of Commons, 1754–90* is able, without injustice, to dismiss it in three lines of print.

Among the factors making for a vigorous political life in the Augustan period Professor Plumb includes the 'astonishing' increase in the size of the electorate in the seventeenth and early eighteenth centuries. It is clear that the effect of the Commons' decisions in favour of narrow franchises after 1688 was mitigated by the natural increase of population and by the creation of additional voters for electoral purposes. But, once again, we find a contrast between the early and later eighteenth century. It is doubtful whether, from the Hanoverian succession onwards, the increase in the electorate kept pace with the growth of population, and in the early years of the nineteenth century it certainly fell behind. In 1715 the total population of England and Wales was some $5\frac{1}{2}$ million: by 1790 it had risen to $8\frac{1}{2}$ million, and by 1831 it stood at nearly 14 million – that is, it had increased by 155%. Plumb's estimate of the English electorate at

---

[1] Even supposing the voters of Lancashire and Staffordshire proved on investigation to be startlingly independent, it was their last chance. Since Lancashire was not again contested until 1820 nor Staffordshire until after 1832, only centenarians would get a second opportunity.

[2] My own investigations of two by-elections during Lord North's administration, though far from conclusive, do not suggest much independent voting. 'The Wiltshire election of 1772: an interpretation', *Wiltshire Archaeological Magazine*, LVII; 'Gloucestershire politics, 1750–1800', *Trans. Bristol & Gloucestershire Archaeological Society*, 79.

the end of Anne's reign was approximately 250,000. *The House of Commons, 1715–54* suggests a slightly higher figure of 261,000, of whom 160,000 were county voters. The subsequent volume of *The House of Commons* puts the county vote in 1754 at about 177,000, with 105,000 in the boroughs, making a grand total of some 282,000. Although percentages may suggest a false precision, the electorate seems to have increased in that period by some 8% against a population increase of some 18%.

To assess the electorate in the years immediately preceding 1832 is far from easy, since there were several counties where there were no contests or only token ones, and the evidence for many boroughs is similarly fragmentary.[1] There seems little doubt however that the increase in the county electorate was modest. In Kent, estimated at 8000 voters in 1754, 8848 polled in 1802; Yorkshire was estimated at 20,000 in 1754, and polled 23,000 in 1807; Dorset, estimated at 3000 in 1754, polled 3658 in a very fiercely contested by-election at the height of the reform crisis in 1831;[2] in Gloucestershire, where the poll was open ten days during the celebrated contest of 1811, the total vote was 36 fewer than in 1776. In some of the most rural counties it seems probable that an actual decline took place. In Worcestershire there was a seven days poll in 1831 and a long-established county interest was overthrown: the total poll was only 3140, whereas 3424 had voted in 1715, and probably 4000 at the contest of 1741. From the figures I have compiled, I would put the increase in the county electorate between 1754 and 1831 at not much higher than 6%.[3] During the same period, the English borough electorate seems to have increased by some 50%.[4] My estimate for the total English electorate in the years immediately before 1832 is some 344,000,[5] representing an overall increase on 1754 of something like 20%. Since during the same period the total population more than doubled, we may say with reasonable confidence that there was a sharp decline in the proportion of people who had even a formal share in the political life of the nation.[6]

[1] See appendix four.

[2] The poll lasted fifteen days and the county was said to be 'entirely polled out'. *Parl. Debs.*, 3rd series, IX, 1122.

[3] I need hardly say that these figures must be treated with caution, but in relation to the rise of population the general inference seems valid.

[4] By far the greater part of this increase was concentrated in thirteen large towns. The increase at Preston, where the franchise was widened by a decision of 1768, I put at 6300. The others were Liverpool 2400, Leicester 2300, Nottingham 2400, London 1600, Northampton 1400, Bristol 1300, Norwich 1200, Coventry 1000, Hull 1000, Southwark 1000, Dover 900 and Oxford 800. There could of course be no increase in corporation boroughs like Bath and Salisbury, and in several of the burgage boroughs the electorate declined.

[5] Boroughs 156,000; counties 188,000. The size of the electorate before 1832 is further discussed on p. 259 below and the evidence presented in appendix four.

[6] By 'formal' I mean that many of them would in practice have no chance of casting a vote during their lifetimes.

These conclusions in the field of electoral development correspond closely to what is known of economic change in the period. The most recent assessment of landed income suggests that it may, at most, have doubled between 1690 and 1790, and that the income of the landed gentry probably rose less than that of the great landlords.[1] With the cost of electioneering rising out of proportion, the gentry would be the first to feel the burden. H. J. Habakkuk has produced evidence that in the later seventeenth and early eighteenth centuries the greater landlords consolidated their estates at the expense of the lesser gentry.[2] The same period witnessed the proliferation of the great country houses – Chatsworth, Castle Howard, Houghton, Wentworth Woodhouse.[3] The establishment of the electoral supremacy of the territorial magnates was the political counterpart to these economic changes. The inability of the lesser gentry to compete for political office weakened their chances of commanding an income large enough to permit electioneering ventures and forced them to abandon the field to Shaftesbury's men of 'wealth and substance'.

* * * *

We have already noted how the prestige of the 1688 settlement helped to inhibit further change. The author of a reforming pamphlet, *Some remarks upon government*, prophesied that the eventual settlement would be unadventurous:[4]

> There is a notion generally received by the nobility and gentry of England that a mixt monarchy (just such a one as ours is, and no other) must needs be the best of governments, and that amongst all others none could boast of those advantages as that of England. This fancy is so riveted in the minds of the people (spread abroad and preached up, only to keep the people in peace, and from endeavouring an alteration, which could not be affected without the inconvenience of the sword) that I do believe all things will settle again on their old basis, and the government be rebuilt with all its irregularities.

His gloom was justified. As the constitutional settlement was crowned in turn by the heady commercial and colonial successes of the eighteenth century, complacency hardened into a national sclerosis. Few doubted that an ideal formula had been discovered. Even a work such as George Lyttelton's *Persian letters*, intended as a satire and which indeed pokes tepid fun at some conventions, is imbued with respect for the constitution, and the moral he is at pains to draw is the good fortune of the British in

---

[1] G. E. Mingay, *English landed society in the eighteenth century*, 20–5.
[2] 'English landownership, 1680–1740', *Economic History Review*, 1st series, x.
[3] Sir J. Summerson, 'The classical country house in eighteenth century England', *Journal Royal Society of Arts*, July 1959.
[4] *State tracts of William III*, I, 149.

not living under an Oriental (or by inference European) despotism. But in view of the paeans of praise from continental commentators, it is hardly surprising that the British should be so convinced of the excellence of their own institutions. Princes and philosophers combined to assure them how fortunate they were. One of the earliest visitors after the Glorious Revolution, Muralt, observed that 'si tout ce que j'entens dire de ce gouvernement est vrai, les Anglois peuvent se vanter d'avoir un grand avantage sur d'autres nations'.[1] By the 1720s the convention was so well established that Voltaire felt constrained to apologize in the preface to his *Lettres sur les Anglais* for 'not expatiating further upon their constitution ...which most of them revere almost to idolatry'. The young Frederick the Great thought the English constitution 'a model of wisdom', while Mercier, Diderot and Condorcet pined for the protection of English law. Even in the nineteenth century testimonials continued to pour in. Madame de Stael, writing a mere sixteen years before the Reform Act, paid tribute in a passage more remarkable for its fervour than its exactness: 'it is a beautiful sight, this constitution, vacillating a little as it sets out from its port, like a vessel launched at sea, yet unfurling its sails, it gives full play to everything great and generous in the human soul'.[2]

No one could suppose that these encomiums were intended to endorse every detail of the governmental arrangements, but their collective impact was to drive reformers on to the defensive, to make them appear as men who stubbornly and wilfully refused to count their blessings. Such was certainly the view of the constables of the unrepresented town of Manchester when they wrote in 1782 to the Rev. Christopher Wyvill to dissociate themselves from his reform campaign: 'it is by no means proper ...to raise disputes and dissension in the kingdom about altering and amending our excellent constitution, under which the inhabitants of Great Britain and her colonies have, for this last century, enjoyed more real liberty and property than any nation upon earth'.[3] Rarely can the good have been more evidently the enemy of the best.

In the face of this kind of pressure the advocates of reform were pushed out on to the fringes of politics. Sydney might help to devise an advanced constitution for Pennsylvania, but England was another matter.[4] Faint echoes from the Cromwellian past can be heard in the Rye House plot of 1683: Richard Rumbold, owner of the house, had been a guard on the

---

[1] *Lettres sur les Anglois*, ed. Charles Gould, 105. Published 1728 but written after a visit in 1694.
[2] *Considérations sur la révolution françoise*, 1816.
[3] Wyvill, II. 95–6.
[4] A. C. Ewald, *Life and times of Algernon Sydney*, II, 197; G. P. Gooch and H. J. Laski, *English democratic ideas in the seventeenth century*, 2nd ed., 283–4. There was to be manhood suffrage, secret ballot and equal electoral areas. The constitution finally adopted is described by C. M. Andrews, *The colonial period of American History*, III, ch. vii.

scaffold of Charles I, while West, the lawyer, was reported to have said that, as far as kings were concerned, there was 'nothing like lopping'. Their ambitions seem to have included sweeping constitutional changes. To such desperate remedies were Commonwealthmen driven.[1]

After the Glorious Revolution, the case for reform was deployed mainly by bookish radicals with antiquarian tastes. Viscount Molesworth published in 1711 a translation of François Hotman's *Franco-Gallia*, first printed in 1573, showing how French liberties had been eroded. 'A True Whig', Molesworth wrote in his preface, was 'not afraid of the name of a Commonwealthsman because so many foolish people, who know not what it means, run it down'. Thomas Hollis of Corscombe, Dorset, devoted much of his large fortune to disseminating tracts on liberty from ancient authors. Caroline Robbins, in a book of great interest, has traced the activities of these worthy men with loving care, and concludes that they 'preserved a great tradition'.[2] It would be pleasant to believe that they did more than persuade each other. The scale of their operations was small, their impact on important politicians slight, and their influence on the public at large negligible. Political achievement is built on something more direct than treatises on sixteenth-century France, warnings from seventeenth-century Denmark and morals drawn from Venice and the Roman Republic. Each generation needs to be convinced by arguments related to its own needs and drawn from its own experience. If economic and political conditions are ripe for change, it will not be halted for want of theoretical justification or historical precedent: when the unusual circumstances of the 1640s afforded opportunities for change and experiment, theory developed apace. One can hardly suppose that without the works of Molesworth and Hollis, Moyle and Trenchard, Middleton and Montagu, radicals of the 1770s would have been at a loss to know how to support their claims.

In the reign of George II, the opposition continued to show interest in place bills and shorter Parliaments, and there were abortive attempts to curtail election expenses. Just before the 1734 election Walpole's opponents sponsored a whole series of reform measures, including a place bill, a bill against bribery and corruption, and a suggestion for raising the property qualification, while a motion for the repeal of the Septennial Act collected 184 votes in the Commons against 247. A flurry of activity at the time of Walpole's downfall produced nothing more than another place act, whereby commissioners of the navy and victualling office were excluded from Parliament. In the later 1740s some of the Tories hoped to do a deal with Frederick, Prince of Wales, in which borough reform was

[1] *Cal.S.P.Dom.*, 1683, 40; T. B. Howell, *State trials*, IX, 358–519.
[2] *The eighteenth-century commonwealthman.*

at least mooted, but all vanished with his unexpected death in 1751.[1] The intention of these proposals was to curb the power of the executive rather than secure the better representation of public opinion: of any organized and sustained campaign for franchise reform or redistribution of seats, there is no trace. The regime of Walpole gave way to that of the Pelhams. The parliamentary session of 1751 was so placid that, said Henry Fox, a bird might build its nest in the Speaker's wig and never be disturbed.[2] The heroic days had gone and pudding time was come.

[1] See *Camden Miscellany*, XXIII, 181–2, ed. A. N. Newman; A. S. Foord, *His Majesty's opposition, 1714–1830*, 183–5; *Parl. Hist.*, IX, 366–482; *Gent. Mag.* (1741), 263–4, 269, 276, 378.
[2] Lord Ilchester, *Henry Fox, first Lord Holland*, I, 179.

3

A parcell of low shopkeepers

'What times do we not live in, when a parcell of low shopkeepers
pretend to direct the whole legislature.'[1]

When George III succeeded his grandfather in October 1760 there were
few indications that the ice was breaking. The accession of a King who
gloried in the name of Briton seemed to augur an era of harmony and
contentment, political controversy was muted, and the country basked in
victory over the national enemy. Yet ten years later, a vigorous, organized
reform movement was in existence, seeking support throughout the land.

England in 1760 was a wealthier, more sophisticated and better informed
country than at the succession of the House of Hanover. Forty-five years
of domestic tranquillity, scarcely interrupted by the Jacobite risings, had
wrought great changes. There had been a substantial growth of population.[2] Imports had almost doubled and exports more than doubled.[3]
Though little industrialization had as yet taken place, there had been
a marked increase in the size of many towns. A movement away from the
old centres of London had pushed the suburbs out into Middlesex and
Surrey. Liverpool and Birmingham, with populations of about 10,000 at
the accession of George I, had grown to some 25,000 and 35,000 respectively: Manchester had increased even faster. Bristol had doubled in the
period, and Nottingham almost doubled.[4] There had been a remarkable

[1] This was George III's observation to Bute after receiving a petition against the Cider
Bill from the City of London on 30 March 1763. *Letters from George III to Lord Bute,
1756–66*, ed. R. Sedgwick, 207–8.
[2] Rickman's estimate for England and Wales, quoted by B. R. Mitchell, *Abstract of
British historical statistics*, was: 1710/11 – 5,240,000; 1720/1 – 5,565,000; 1760/1 –
6,736,000.
[3] T. S. Ashton, *Economic fluctuations in England, 1700–1800*, tables 4 and 5:

	£s
IMPORTS (England and Wales):	1715 – 5.6 million
	1760 – 9.8 million
EXPORTS (England and Wales):	1715 – 6.9 million
	1760 – 14.7 million

By 1770 imports had risen to more than £12,000,000.
[4] J. A. Picton, *Memorials of Liverpool*, 159, 165, 198; C. Gill & A. Briggs, *History of
Birmingham*, I, 120; J. Latimer, *Annals of Bristol in the eighteenth century*, 194, 292;
M. D. George, *England in transition*, 101; J. D. Chambers, 'Population change in
a provincial town: Nottingham 1700–1800', in *Studies in the industrial revolution*,
ed. L. S. Pressnell, 122.

improvement in the speed, if not the comfort, of road transport, due mainly to the work of turnpike trusts. The public coach from Bristol to London, which took three days in the reign of Charles II, was making the journey in two days during the 1700s. From 1763 onwards travellers could do it in one day – albeit a long and gruelling one – and in 1775 a specially designed coach was scheduled to do it in sixteen hours.[1] 'There never was a more astonishing revolution accomplished in the internal system of any country', wrote an observer in 1767, 'than there has been within the compass of a few years in that of England.'[2]

The rise in the number and importance of the middling classes of society – clerks, merchants, teachers, doctors, attorneys, shopkeepers – manifested itself in a great increase in the publication of journals, books and newspapers. The reign of George II saw the establishment in 1731 of the *Gentleman's Magazine*, which rapidly became a national institution; its rival, the *London Magazine*, launched in 1732, lasted until 1797; the *Monthly Review*, started in 1749, and the *Annual Register*, in 1758, both saw out the century. The demand for political information was enough to persuade Edward Cave, founder of the *Gentleman's Magazine*, to brave the occasional wrath of the House of Commons in order to include reports of parliamentary debates. The 1740s saw the establishment in many provincial towns of circulating libraries. But most dramatic of all was the rise in the number of newspapers. In 1715 there was still only one daily newspaper published in London, the *Daily Courant*, founded in 1702: by 1760 there were four.[3] Provincial newspapers made their first appearance during the reign of Anne, with the *Norwich Post*, the *Bristol Post-boy* and the *Exeter Post-man*. In 1715 there were about a dozen: by 1760 the number had risen to 35, and, we are told, 'few towns of any importance lacked one'.[4] Advertising duty, clapped on by harassed ministers to exploit the new phenomenon, rose from just over a thousand pounds in 1715 to more than £8000 by 1756.[5] A writer in the *Annual Register* for 1761 commented on the increase in sophistication:[6]

It is scarce half a century ago since the inhabitants of the different counties were regarded as a species, almost as different from those of

[1] J. Latimer.

[2] Henry Sacheverell Homer, *An enquiry into the means of preserving and improving the public roads of this kingdom.*

[3] *Daily Advertiser*; *The Gazeteer and London Daily Advertiser*; *Public Advertiser*; *Public Ledger.*

[4] G. A. Cranfield, *The development of the provincial newspaper, 1700–1760*, 19–22.

[5] A. Aspinall, 'Statistical accounts of the London newspapers in the eighteenth century', *English Historical Review*, 63 (1948). The duty was raised from a shilling to two shillings for each advertisement in 1757, and the income for 1760 was £15,806. By 1770, it was £25,148.

[6] 'On the country manners of the present age', 205–8. See also J. H. Plumb, 'Political Man', in *Man versus society in eighteenth-century Britain*, 9–10.

the metropolis, as the natives of the Cape of Good Hope. Their manners, as well as dialect, were entirely provincial; and their dress no more resembling the habit of the town, than the Turkish or Chinese. But time, which has inclosed commons and ploughed up heaths, has likewise cultivated the minds and improved the behaviour of the ladies and gentlemen of the country. We are no longer encountered with hearty slaps on the back, or pressed to make a breakfast on cold meat and strong beer...The several great cities, and we might add many poor country towns, seem to be universally inspired with an ambition of becoming the little *Londons* of the part of the kingdom wherein they are situated.[1]

* * * *

To these developments the electoral system made no acknowledgement. Outwardly it remained exactly as it had been, each anomaly and oddity preserved. In practice it was more narrow and oligarchical than ever. The year 1761 can, in many respects, be regarded as the peak of aristocratic power, before it was challenged by liberal and popular movements. The number of contests at the general election was the smallest between 1702 and 1832 - and almost certainly the smallest since 1660.[2] Whereas in 1715 nearly half the boroughs and counties went to the poll, in 1761 only 4 counties out of 40 were contested, and 42 boroughs[3]

[1] This assumption of the growing importance in the community of the middle classes does not, at first sight, correspond with the extremely interesting evidence printed by H. J. Perkin, *Origins of modern English society*, 20-1. Professor Perkin relates Gregory King's estimates for 1688 to those of Patrick Colquhoun in 1803. These analyses divided society into the aristocracy, middle ranks and lower orders and attempted to estimate the numbers and wealth in each group. Though the 'middle ranks' increased in both numbers and wealth, their progress was little faster than the rest of the community, their share of the national income rising from 59.0% to 59.4%. But the definition of the 'middle ranks' included farmers, merchants, manufacturers and professional men. When the changes are studied in detail it becomes apparent that the great increase was in the wealth of the *urban* middle class. The number of families of farmers and freeholders actually *decreased* between 1688 and 1803 from 330,000 to 320,000, though their collective wealth more than doubled. But the families grouped as 'industry and commerce' rose from 50,000 to 230,000, and their wealth from £4,200,000 to £66,385,000. It would of course be unwise to rely too much on figures which may be inaccurate and certainly need interpretation, but the general inference of a vast increase in urban wealth can hardly be gainsaid. Many of the merchants, shipowners, manufacturers, engineers and warehousemen would, necessarily, live in the great unrepresented towns and the midlands and north, and others in towns where they had no share in either parliamentary or municipal politics.
[2] See Table of Contests, printed below as appendix four. The absence of provincial newspapers before 1702 makes it almost impossible to compile a list of contests for any earlier date, but there can be little doubt that many more boroughs were open between 1660 and 1702 than in the mid-eighteenth century.
[3] *The House of Commons, 1754-90*, eds. L. B. Namier & J. Brooke, appendix 1 gives forty-one contests in English boroughs, but it is clear from B. Bonsall, *Sir James Lowther & Cumberland and Westmorland elections, 1754-75*, 52, that Carlisle went to the poll in addition.

out of 203. Almost two-thirds of the English boroughs were under patronage.[1]

At almost precisely the same moment, the aristocracy seems also to have been at its most exclusive. After a rapid increase in the number of peers during the reigns of James I and Charles I, there was a slow increase thence until 1714, when the total number of temporal peers was 171. The creations of George I and II scarcely kept pace with extinctions, and in 1759 the number was only 172 – which, in terms of population, represents a slight proportional decrease. In the first two decades of George III's reign there was a further slow increase, followed by a great inflation of titles under William Pitt and his successors, until by 1837 the peerage was double what it had been in 1760. Nor did the number of baronetcies afford much hope to those who could not reasonably aspire to peerages. Baronetage creations reached a peak just after the Restoration, and in 1700 there were still 674 baronetcies in existence. Thereafter the number fell steadily to 607 in 1720, 534 in 1740, and 466 in 1760. If therefore the regime is correctly described as an aristocratic oligarchy, that oligarchy was in 1760 at its most narrow, and it is scarcely surprising that persons excluded should begin to complain.[2]

Resentment of the control exercised by small groups of magnates is a commonplace of county politics in the middle and later eighteenth century. In 1760 it was argued that the representation of Cornwall, 'the only honour the county can confer', ought to be taken in rotation, and that 'gentlemen should give way to one another where there are equal pretensions'.[3] The freeholders of Westmorland and Cumberland resisted for

[1] The survey of patronage in 1761 made by Sir Lewis Namier, *The Structure of Politics at the accession of George III* (2nd ed.), 144–8, though interpreted by him to explode 'the legend of a close Whig oligarchy', nevertheless reveals a substantial measure of oligarchical control. Of 405 English borough seats, 235 were, according to his assessment, under patronage. I would add to the list at least another 20 seats. I cannot accept the reasoning (p. 143) which excludes Chester, where the Grosvenor family held one seat without a break between 1715 and 1874, nominated to the second seat for much of the period, and spent £4000 p.a. on 'the maintenance of the Chester interest'. (*The House of Commons, 1754–90*, I, 221; G. E. Mingay, *English landed society in the eighteenth century*, 151) I would also include Bewdley (Winnington), Carlisle (Lowther), Chippenham (Bayntun), East Retford (Newcastle), Great Yarmouth (Walpole & Townshend), King's Lynn (Walpole), Lewes (Newcastle), Milborne Port (Walter), Northampton (Halifax & Northampton), Stafford 2 (Chetwynd), Stamford (Exeter), Winchelsea (Government), Winchester (Penton), Warwick (Warwick), Wootton Bassett (Bolingbroke).
[2] It might be argued that the granting of honours being a royal prerogative, reluctance to increase the peerage should be seen as royal policy rather than aristocratic exclusiveness. But though some peerages were personal acts of the ruler, the majority were matters of state, granted on the advice of aristocratic ministers not anxious to dilute their own order. In both Russia and Sweden, triumphant nobilities in 1730 and 1718 took steps to curtail the royal prerogative in this matter, and the Peerage Bill of 1719 shows the English aristocracy pursuing a similar policy.
[3] *The House of Commons, 1754–90*, I, 222.

decades the efforts of Sir James Lowther to acquire total command of the two counties.[1] At the general election of 1768 a Warwickshire freeholder, attempting to rouse an opposition, complained that it was more than sixty years since the county had been contested: 'two or three noblemen, and a few gentlemen have, during that time, thought it sufficient in themselves...to nominate and chuse two representatives for you'.[2] In the 1772 Wiltshire by-election, each side tried to assume the mantle of independents struggling against a clique: Ambrose Goddard's supporters drew attention to the 'amazing combination of Dukes, Earls and Lords' supporting his opponent, while Henry Herbert retorted that Goddard was the tool of a 'junto – a set of people who have too long pretended to dictate arbitrarily to their county'.[3] The freeholders of Somerset in 1784 declared publicly that they would never give their votes for the son of a peer.[4]

Nor could the lesser gentry, slighted in the counties, take much comfort from their local boroughs, where in the seventeenth century their ancestors had often picked up seats. Increasingly they were shut out, in the close boroughs by the nominee of the patron, in the open boroughs by affluent strangers. In the early years of the century they vented their irritation on courtiers, merchants, lawyers and brewers. From 1761 onwards they found a new object of hatred in the returned 'Nabobs' – 'gorged with the spoils of the East' and reckless of their ill-gotten wealth. But the Nabobs were themselves victims of the changing electoral conditions: so many boroughs were closed to them that they concentrated their activities on a few open boroughs, which soon acquired great notoriety. The case of General Richard Smith illustrates the point. Born in Marlborough in 1734 he amassed in fifteen years in India a large fortune and cherished ambitions of serving his native borough in Parliament. To a friend, he wrote in 1767:[5] 'If Marlborough, from the prevalence of the Bruce interest should be found impracticable (which I by no means suppose) there are two or three other boroughs in Wiltshire where a timely and proper application may possibly meet with success...For my own part, I conceive that my opponents will not readily enter the lists against me.' Forty years earlier such an attack on Marlborough would have been far from hopeless – the borough had been frequently contested up to 1734. But in the meantime the Bruce family of Tottenham Park had acquired a complete domination, which was not challenged until the eve of reform in 1826. Smith was forced to recognize that he could not hope to succeed there, and on his return to England embarked on a tour of the

---

[1] B. Bonsall. [2] *St James Chronicle*, 22/4 March 1768.
[3] *Salisbury Journal*, 3 and 17 August 1772.
[4] *Felix Farley's Bristol Journal*, 24 January 1784.
[5] R. Smith to Robert Orme, 14 March 1767, Orme MSS.

most squalid boroughs, which earned him six months imprisonment, and brought one of them to the brink of reformation.

There were thus in the 1760s two groups which might provide the nucleus for a reform movement – the middling classes, seeking participation for the first time, and the country gentlemen, pining for their old seventeenth-century pre-eminence. Though an alliance forged between them might prove a powerful political force, it could only be temporary, since the same reforms were unlikely to satisfy both.

A family that came close to representing the interests of both groups was the Beckfords. Three of them were returned to Parliament in 1754. William, the eldest brother, had represented Shaftesbury and transferred to London; Richard, next in age, won a seat in a hard-fought contest at Bristol, the second largest city of the kingdom, and the third largest urban constituency; the third brother, Julines, came in for the city of Salisbury. Their great wealth came from their Jamaica plantations and they were at home among the merchants of Bristol and London. They were also country gentlemen, taking an active part in Wiltshire and Dorset, where their estates lay: Julines Beckford was sheriff of Dorset in 1749–50, Richard was an Alderman of London, and William was twice Lord Mayor. Dislike of the great magnates seems to have been a cardinal point with them, providing the link between their Toryism and their radicalism

Two of Richard Beckford's interventions in the 1754 Parliament reveal this mixture of urban radicalism and rural conservatism. On the Bristol night watch bill of 1755 he drew a contrast between the government of London, where the citizens chose the common councilmen, and that of Bristol, where the magistrates exercised the arbitrary power of 'choosing one another, and of filling up all vacancies by a majority among themselves, without so much as asking the consent of their fellow citizens'. But in the debate on the Oxfordshire election, which turned on whether copyholders should be allowed to vote, he spoke in traditional Tory terms. Rising prices had, he observed, diminished the value of the forty-shilling freehold, with a consequent increase in the number of county voters, 'the inconvenience (of which) is now felt by every gentleman who stands candidate at a county election'. The admission of 'little copyholders' into the electorate would 'throw a great weight into the other House...the eyes of the vulgar are always dazzled with high titles and a shining equipage'.[1]

[1] *Parl. Hist.*, xv, 481–2, 455. Since I wrote the above, Marie Peters has published in the *English Historical Review*, 86 (1971), an article, 'The "Monitor" on the constitution, 1755–65: new light on the ideological origins of English radicalism'. *The Monitor* was a weekly paper founded by Richard Beckford and reflecting his views. The article does not, I think, conflict with my interpretation, though it makes the point that suspicion of the executive had been at times both a Whig and a Tory tradition, and is best described as a 'country' attitude.

Richard <u>Beckford</u> died after less than two years in Parliament, but the crusade against the aristocracy was continued by <u>William</u>. In 1753 he had attacked the Clandestine Marriage Bill on the grounds that it would 'tend to throw all the wealth of the kingdom into the hands of our nobility'.[1] In the course of the Seven Years War, in common with many of the Tories, he developed a great admiration for William Pitt, with whom he was later closely associated. At the general election of 1761 he told the London voters that the constitution was defective in allowing 'little, pitiful boroughs' equal representation with great cities, 'contrary to the maxim that power should follow property'. Six months later, in a patriot speech on the address, he declared that 'it was not the mob, nor two hundred great lords (who received more from government than they paid to it) that made us so firm: the middling rank of men it was in which our strength consisted'.[2] A series of newspaper letters in the next few years <u>kept the subject of electoral reform before the public eye.</u> *Carliolensis* in 1764 called for the abolition of rotten boroughs, and was echoed in the spring of 1766 by *Hanseaticus*: 'I must believe that the wisest man in the Convention-Parliament of 1689 could never have foreseen...either that so many English boroughs would have been monopolized, or that such monopolies would have been confirmed by such sanctions as no man is at liberty to dispute.'[3] Meanwhile, Pitt added his own weight to the argument in the course of refuting the suggestion that the Americans enjoyed virtual representation: how could they be represented through a borough which perhaps its own members never saw? This, he added, was 'the rotten part of the constitution': it could not continue a century, and if it did not drop, it should be amputated.[4] For the first time for decades a politician of the front rank had committed himself, however tentatively, to the cause of parliamentary reform.

With the approach of a general election there was a marked quickening of interest. In May 1767 John Almon, publisher to the Beckford–Temple–Pitt group, produced the first number of a monthly magazine, the *Political Register*. 'The people of England', he declared in his preface, 'are of all the nations in the world the most addicted to politics.' The early numbers were of an unsensational character, save for some scabrous frontispiece

---

[1] *Parl. Hist.*, xv, 80–1. There is much of interest on Beckford's career in L. S. Sutherland, 'The city of London and the opposition to government, 1768–74' (Creighton Lecture 1959).
[2] *London Evening Post*, 4/7 April 1761; H. Walpole, *Memoirs of the reign of King George the third*, ed. G. F. R. Barker, I, 72.
[3] *A collection of letters and essays in favour of public liberty, 1764–70*. A copy of this rather rare publication is in the Cambridge University Library. For other letters on this theme, see *A free burgess in fetters*, urging the repeal of the Last Determinations Act, and *The shadow of a boroughman*, ibid. I, 137; II, 105.
[4] *Parl. Hist.*, xvi, 100.

caricatures of the long-suffering Bute, and the publication for the first time of Wilkes' letter giving a burlesque account of his duel with Lord Talbot in 1762. In July 1767 however *An essay on the British Government* touched a theme that Almon was to develop later: 'we seem to be in a fair way of becoming...a nation of *great lords* and of *needy vassals*'. Later the same year, Almon published *The Honest Elector's Proposal*, a pamphlet arguing the case for <u>secret ballot</u>.[1]

Events in Parliament also contributed to a growing interest in electoral matters. On 26 January 1768 the House of Commons was informed of a corrupt bargain which the corporation of Oxford had attempted to strike with its members nearly two years before: hard-pressed by civic debts, it had offered re-election on payment of £4000. The House promptly committed the corporation to Newgate, while the town clerk fled to France dropping the corporation minute-book overboard in transit.[2] Beckford took advantage of the indignation, genuine or otherwise, to ask for leave to introduce a bill against bribery and corruption. It was supported by George Grenville, Pitt's brother-in-law, according to Horace Walpole out of a desire to 'flatter the country gentlemen, who can ill afford to combat with great lords, nabobs, commissaries, and west indians'.[3] At the same time, the introduction of the *Nullum Tempus* bill gave wide publicity to shady election manoeuvres in Cumberland, where Sir James Lowther, locked in a contest with the Duke of Portland, made use of a legal loophole to deprive his opponent of estates which had been in his family since the reign of William III. These spectacular instances of <u>corruption in boroughs and counties served as an admirable background for a reform campaign</u>. A pamphlet entitled *The Upholsterer's Letter to the Rt. Hon. William Pitt, Earl of Chatham*, published in January 1768, begged him to take the lead in a comprehensive reform which would award extra seats to the counties and enfranchise the great towns. 'A measure of this sort is doubtless become very necessary', wrote one reviewer.[4] The same month the *Political Register* began a series of articles apparently designed to ensure prominence for reform issues at the general election and working within the area sketched out by Beckford. The January issue contained 'cautions' to the voters to shun certain candidates, including merchants, placemen, lawyers, spendthrifts, and eldest sons of peers. This was tepid routine stuff, but in March Almon produced a special election issue, the main article of which, by *Regulus*, laid out a complete programme of reform

---

[1] By 'A freeman of King's Lynn'. It was noticed in the *Monthly Review*, XXXVII (1767), 474.

[2] John Cannon, 'The parliamentary representation of the city of Oxford', *Oxoniensia*, XXV (1960).

[3] *Memoirs of George III*, III, 113.

[4] *Monthly Review*, XXXVIII (1768) 158. The review in the *London Magazine* was less complimentary.

and begged the electorate to support only those candidates who would pledge themselves to it. It included as a matter of course an onslaught on the *grandees*, 'more formidable than ever', and traced the misfortunes of the constitution back to 1688:[1]

> The state reformers at the Revolution were so intent on binding down our *kings* to their good behaviour that they left the *grandees* in possession of powers inconsistent with the first principles of liberty ...It ought to have been settled at the great reformation of the state in 1688, that if at any time a law...should be found agreeable to the majority of the *lower* house and to the *sovereign*, it should be established, whether passed by the *grandees* or not.

It continued with a detailed indictment of the representative system:

> What could blind chance have determined more *unequal irregular* and *imperfect* than we see it at this day?...there are two members for each county. But, on comparing the extent and value of the counties, you will find that one county, as Yorkshire for instance, is of six times more value than another, as Rutlandshire. There are but six representatives (sic) for the immense contiguity of the metropolis, comprehending London, Westminster and Southwark...there are as many for Old Sarum, and one or two other rotten boroughs in that neighbourhood...
>
> The monied interest is not represented at all. One hundred millions and upwards of property wholly excluded from a share in the legislature excepting where the proprietors have other qualifications. The case is much the same with the *commercial* interest. A merchant or manufacturer, who exports to the value of half a million every year, is not represented as a merchant or manufacturer: he has not the privilege of a beggar in a Cornish borough. Accordingly, the great manufacturing towns of Manchester, Birmingham, Sheffield, etc., have no representation in Parliament. And in most towns the *corporation*, which bears no proportion to the inhabitants, either in number or property, are the only voters.

It went on to propose a large extension of the franchise to cover 'every substantial *housekeeper*', secret ballot, annual elections and economical reform.

With the publication of Almon's manifesto, reform was on the way to becoming, once more, a real issue in politics. Here was no abstract and learned discourse sent from one earnest scholar to another, but a comprehensive programme, presented to the general public, with suggestions,

---

[1] No. XII, 224–5.

however inadequate, how it might be achieved. In this way the fusion of Toryism and radicalism had created a foundation on which a reform movement might be built.

*   *   *   *

It would not have been possible for Almon or anyone else to rally much support for a reform programme had the political waters remained as calm as they had been in 1760. For the storms that had in the mean-time arisen, two men were primarily responsible – George III and John Wilkes.

To name the King in this connection may strike some readers as surprising, since distinguished historians have assured us that he was free from blame.[1] Certainly his action was unwitting, and there is little difficulty in recognizing that his intentions, if vague, were well-meant. Nevertheless, the elevation of Lord Bute to be Secretary of State and then First Lord of the Treasury was a blunder of the first magnitude, acting as a major political irritant. This is no place to conduct yet another enquiry into the constitutional propriety of the King's action. It is enough for our purposes to note that large numbers of his subjects saw in it a cause for alarm: the *Annual Register*, summarizing the opposition's case, admitted that while the monarch had the undoubted right to choose his own ministers, 'the spirit of the constitution required that the crown should be directed in the exercise of this public duty by public motives, and not by private liking and friendship'.[2]

The promotion of Bute brought about the break-up of the Newcastle–Pitt administration. Together they had presided over a government of almost unparalleled success, buttressed by enormous majorities in the House of Commons, where opposition had almost ceased, and boasting unprecedented naval and military victories. It has been pointed out that the ministry was not always without friction:[3] few are, and none in which Newcastle had a part. Yet less than a month before the old King's death Hardwicke had written to Pitt that he continually heard from Newcastle

---

[1] R. Sedgwick, introduction to *Letters from George III to Lord Bute, 1756–66*; J. S. Watson, *The reign of George III*, 7–8. Mr Sedgwick was largely concerned with a constitutional defence of the King's actions: Mr Watson attributes the political storms to 'personal antagonisms' among the leading contenders for power. Sir Lewis Namier, *England in the age of the American revolution*, 181 distributed the blame between George and Pitt: 'it was his (Pitt's) intractable, incalculable nature...which, at least as much as the immature, unbalanced obstinacy of George III produced the chaos of the first ten years of the new reign'.

[2] *Annual Register* (1763), 41 quoted by H. Butterfield, *George III and the Historians*, 49.

[3] J. S. Watson. It is not always clear what Mr Watson does think about the Pitt–Newcastle ministry. On p. 7 he observes that 'unity in common action' was exactly what they lacked; on p. 67 he remarks that the administration seemed in 1760 'to have every requirement for stability...these two ministers were complementary halves of a perfect whole'.

'how harmoniously you go on together'.[1] Pitt's conduct of the war had won him the adoration of the city of London and a national prestige not known perhaps since the heyday of Marlborough. The new King's first public act was a calculated insult to him. In his speech to the privy council on the morning of his grandfather's death he referred to the 'bloody and expensive war': only Pitt's urgent protests persuaded him to agree to the clumsy formula – 'expensive but just and necessary war' – before publication. It has been suggested that George showed restraint in not immediately dismissing Pitt and Newcastle, which, constitutionally, was within his power.[2] They were in fact reprieved because they were still needed to wind up the war and because it was more adroit if they could be made the authors of their own destruction. But that it was a stay of execution and not a pardon is clear from George's private correspondence with Bute. When that 'true snake in the grass' – as George described Pitt shortly before his accession – proved tiresome in November 1760, the King wrote that unless Pitt changed his conduct he would 'show him that aversion which will force him to resign'. In September 1761 the King told his friend: 'we must get rid of him in a happier minute than the present one'. The following month Pitt resigned when the cabinet refused to authorize strong measures against Spain, and was vindicated three months later when the same cabinet was obliged to declare war.

Newcastle, having less spirit than Pitt, lasted eight months longer. From the beginning of 1762 he was at odds with Bute over the war in Germany, and the King was predicting his imminent resignation without noticeable grief. 'The more I know of this fellow', he wrote to Bute in April, 'the more I wish to see him out of employment, and should what we have now before us come to maturity, I flatter myself that will soon be the case.'[3]

Thus, if the King did not actually kill the ministry, he took no steps to keep it alive. But worse was to follow. The resignations roused a hornet's nest. Though the opposition was weak in Parliament, as the divisions on the peace were to show, it made up for it in vituperation. Pitt did little to defend himself, but his allies Beckford and Temple set their friends in the press to work. By the spring of 1762, only eighteen months after the King's accession, journalists and pamphleteers were barking and braying at each other with furious zeal. Even the tough and experienced Henry Fox, called in to prop up Bute's administration, was staggered at 'such a clamour as was never before heard'.[4] 'Vigour and the day is ours', declared the King heroically, but Bute displayed no stomach for the

---

[1] *The correspondence of William Pitt*, ed. W. S. Taylor & J. S. Pringle, II, 71.
[2] J. S. Watson, 79.
[3] R. Sedgwick, 47, 50, 63, 79, 93–4.
[4] Quoted R. R. Rea, *The English press in politics, 1760–74*, 25.

fight. His testing-time revealed, as a subordinate tactfully put it, 'more than ordinary sensibility to unmerited reproach and abuse'.[1] To the King's consternation he insisted on resigning in less than a year. His hand-picked successor, George Grenville, took his authority too seriously, and within four months the King was negotiating privately through Bute for Pitt's return. The transaction fell through, and in the face of Grenville's reproaches the King fell back on a show of candour: 'it is true, Mr Grenville, but let us not look back, let us only look forward; nothing of that sort shall ever happen again'.[2] The reconciliation did not last and in the summer of 1765 Grenville was dismissed to make room for the Rockinghams.

The King's conduct may, of course, be explained and palliated. He was young, inexperienced, intolerant, and a poor judge of men. The end of the war was bound to create difficulties: peace settlements, victorious or otherwise, frequently provoke dissension. Pitt was touchy and unco-operative, a rogue elephant of the political scene; Newcastle was fussy, petty and suspicious; Grenville was tedious and prolix. Subjected to George's treatment they grew worse, and it is hard to resist the conclusion that he prompted many of the misfortunes of which he complained so bitterly. The outcome of these disagreements was to give part of the aristocracy a reason for a flirtation with radicalism, and, by splitting the upper classes, allow the forces of radicalism a longer run than they could have expected on their own strength.

If the King's contribution to political tumults was inadvertent, that of John Wilkes was most deliberate. In 1762, almost overwhelmed by debt, he confided that 'in this time of public dissension he was resolved to make his fortune'.[3] Accordingly he set up as patriot writer and picked a quarrel with Bute's paper, *The Briton*. It is hardly an exaggeration to suggest that Wilkes' connection with the movement for parliamentary reform was fortuitous. In the forty-five numbers of the *North Briton* there is no trace of any interest in the subject: the formula was a series of rather weary jokes on Scottish pride, poverty and presumption. There seems little, in fact, to distinguish the *North Briton* from its competitors: nevertheless its audacity evoked astonished admiration from many readers and outraged indignation from others. Repeatedly the ministers took opinion from the law officers of the crown whether it was actionable. But as soon as they moved against him – issuing a general warrant for the arrest of those engaged in the production of No. 45 – Wilkes' unique qualities began to reveal themselves. In particular, he knew how to dramatize his own situation. Before Chief Justice Pratt he declared that 'the liberty of all peers

---

[1] Sedgwick, 109; Edward Weston to A. Mitchell, 17 May 1763, Add. MS. 6823, f. 185.
[2] *The Grenville papers*, ed. W. J. Smith, II, 205.
[3] Edward Gibbon, *Journal*, 23 September 1762.

and gentlemen, and (what touches me most sensibly) that of all the middling and inferior class of the people which stand most in need of protection, is, in my case, this day to be finally decided upon'.[1]

After his release from the Tower of London, Wilkes settled down to exploit to the full the potentialities of the situation, and throughout the rest of 1763 a series of legal actions, going off at intervals like a string of fire-crackers, kept the public agog. On 6 December Pratt declared general warrants illegal and awarded Wilkes £1000 damages for the seizure of his papers.

During Wilkes' years of exile in France, following his duel with Samuel Martin and expulsion from the House of Commons, many on-lookers concluded that his political career was finished. But the excitement he had engendered was not totally extinguished, nor the vein of anti-authoritarian sentiment he had struck worked out. 'No, Wilkes, thou art not alone,' wrote one melodramatic young admirer, 'we are all outlawed, sentence is passed on all'.[2] In February 1765 when a bookseller was put in the pillory for reprinting the *North Briton* in volume form, a 'prodigious concourse of people' turned out to acclaim him.[3] 'It is a time of most licentious and plentiful abuse of all persons of eminence among us', wrote one observer in October 1765: 'discontent and dissatisfaction...grows more and more universally'.[4]

Two other factors that helped to stoke the fires of radicalism must be mentioned. The 1760s was a period of acute distress among the urban poor, caused chiefly by bad harvests, high prices and mass unemployment. The King's speech of November 1767 referred to the difficulties of the 'poorer sort of my people', and the year 1768 was marked by riots, strikes and demonstrations. In July 1768 no fewer than seven coal-heavers were hanged at Stepney for attempted murder. During the spring of 1769, at the time of Wilkes' re-elections for Middlesex, the Spitalfields weavers made repeated attacks upon work in looms, and later in the year troops had to be stationed in the troubled areas.

Contemporaries often connected these incidents directly with the political agitation. But the two most recent and thorough investigations agree that there was little political motivation, despite occasional shouts for Wilkes and Liberty.[5] The unrest certainly helped Wilkes to sustain an atmosphere of excitement and made it easier to rally mobs, but too great an encouragement to violence would run the risk of alienating the many shopkeepers and merchants among his supporters. Popular disorder, as

[1] *North Briton*, printed J. Williams, III, 175.
[2] 'The petition of an Englishman', printed in A. Stephens, *The memoirs of John Horne Tooke*, I, 61–2.
[3] *Gent. Mag.* (1765), quoted S. Maccoby, *English radicalism, 1762–85*, 36.
[4] *Letters of James Harris, first Earl of Malmesbury*, I, 131–2.
[5] G. Rudé, *Wilkes and liberty*; I. R. Christie, *Wilkes, Wyvill and reform*.

the Gordon riots were to show, might strengthen the conservative rather than the radical cause.

Other historians have drawn attention to the influence of American affairs. Professor E. C. Black has written that the American agitation 'probably contributed as much as any single factor to the direction of radical activity in Great Britain'.[1] The evidence is perhaps a little slight for so large a claim, though there is no doubt that the debates over taxation and representation had implications for both countries. Soame Jenyns developed the point in a characteristically light-hearted pamphlet of 1765 defending Parliament's right to tax the colonists: 'if the towns of Manchester and Birmingham, sending no representation to Parliament, are notwithstanding there represented, why are not the cities of Albany and Boston equally represented?'[2] It was a good debating point, but distinctly imprudent. It might serve to baffle American partisans but was equally likely to provoke the retort that Manchester and Birmingham should be directly represented. Hans Stanley, in a speech of February 1766, also moved from a discussion of the concept of virtual representation to a denunciation of reform proposals in Britain.[3] But to most British voters American affairs were remote indeed, and by the time, in the 1770s, that they had really penetrated British political consciousness, the first phase of the reform movement was over.

*   *   *   *

There is no evidence that Almon's manifesto had the slightest impact on the general election of 1768. There was no organization to follow it up, and it may be safely assumed that 99 out of 100 electors never heard of it. Nevertheless, the election produced the incident needed to turn a manifesto into a movement – the return of John Wilkes at the head of the poll for the county of Middlesex.

This, in itself, was an indication of the way in which society was beginning to change, if only in certain areas. Knights of the shire were traditionally men of broad acres, often with ancestors who had represented the county in previous centuries: they rode to the hustings at the head of hundreds of their friends and supporters. Wilkes was a most bizarre specimen, an adventurer of no property, unquestionably bankrupt, and an outlaw into the bargain. But Middlesex was no longer an ordinary county. In many places, particularly in the eastern areas, the growth of London had substituted merchants, shopkeepers and tradesmen for the tenant farmers and squires. The new class of voters was more independent

[1] *The Association*, 28.
[2] *The objections to the taxation of our American colonies...briefly considered.*
[3] 'Parliamentary diaries of Nathaniel Ryder', *Camden Miscellany*, no. XXIII, 261–2.

and less deferential than the old, and from it Wilkes drew the bulk of his support.[1]

Wilkes' election need not have had national significance. He had shown himself more dangerous outside the House of Commons than inside, and the government might have been well-advised to have adopted Barré's ironic suggestion – to destroy his popularity by a free pardon or by bringing him into the ministry.[2] The imprudent decision to force his expulsion, and in particular the resolution of April 1769 seating Henry Lawes Luttrell, produced a *cause célèbre*. Whatever the legal arguments, which few probably understood, it seemed to many moderate men manifestly absurd that a candidate who had been outpolled by four to one should be declared elected. The government's attitude armed Wilkes with issues more powerful than general warrants had ever been. Was the House of Commons superior to the electorate? Where did sovereignty reside? What was the nature of representation? For the first time for decades fundamental and profound questions were raised in British political life.

But before the issues arising from the Middlesex election could be exploited politically, two things were necessary – the creation of some kind of organization outside Parliament to inform and arouse the electorate, and an alliance with a sizeable parliamentary squadron capable of ensuring that the grievances were adequately presented and debated. The first service was attempted, however inefficiently, by the Society for the Supporters of the Bill of Rights, the second by the members of the Rockingham party.

The Society for the Supporters of the Bill of Rights was formed in February 1769 with the immediate and daunting task of paying Wilkes' debts.[3] Its moving spirit was the Rev. John Horne, a reluctant clergyman from Brentford, though the best known supporters were four members of Parliament – James Townsend, son of Chauncy Townsend, a merchant and contractor; John Sawbridge, a distiller, and brother of Mrs Macaulay, the radical historian; Sir Joseph Mawbey, a vinegar manufacturer from Vauxhall; and Sir Cecil Wray, a Lincolnshire country gentleman. But the first steps to broaden the issue of the Middlesex election into a demand for comprehensive parliamentary reform were taken by William Beckford, with whom Townsend and Sawbridge had close contacts. On 10 February 1769 the city of London, under his guidance, instructed its members to press, not merely for the rectification of Wilkes' grievances, but for shorter Parliaments, a place bill, measures against bribery and secret ballot. In the House of Commons, responding as one of the London

[1] G. Rudé, chs. 5 and 10; *The House of Commons, 1754–90, sub* Middlesex.
[2] *Parl. Hist.*, XVI, 540.
[3] For its foundation see J. Horne to Wilkes, letter xi, in *The controversial letters of John Wilkes and the Rev. J. Horne*, published by Almon, 1771.

members to his own initiative, he intervened repeatedly to denounce rotten boroughs and the overweening influence of the aristocracy. In April 1769 he took a leading part in the foundation of the *Middlesex Journal or Chronicle of Liberty*, a radical newspaper which appeared thrice weekly.[1]

The Rockingham party, some eighty strong, had little enthusiasm for parliamentary reform, and several leading members were strongly opposed to it. Their panacea for the nation's woes, as developed by Burke in his *Thoughts on the present discontents*, was their own return to power, coupled with measures for reducing the influence of the crown. Their restoration, after what had been something of a fiasco in 1765–6, was unlikely unless they could identify themselves with a cause that might command strong public support. The various opposition groups came together in May 1769 at a grand political dinner at the Thatched House Tavern, where Burke, Lord John Cavendish, Sir George Savile and some forty Rockinghams were joined by Beckford, Barré, Calcraft and Aubrey, representing the Chatham connection, George Grenville with his friends Thomas Whately and Alexander Wedderburn, and the radical reformers including Mawbey, Townsend, Sawbridge and Brass Crosby. The difficulty was to find some course of common action which would not disrupt the fragile unity so recently established. The toasts were many, fervent and suitably vague, and agreement seems to have been reached to launch a widespread petitioning movement on the Middlesex election issue. 'The whole meeting', exclaimed Temple ecstatically, 'appeared to be that of brothers, united in one great constitutional cause.'[2]

In fact, as soon as the alliance tried to do something, its motley nature became apparent. Some of its members were totally opposed to the idea of petitioning. 'These appeals to the people', wrote Lord George Sackville, 'are dangerous and may have false consequences...when once the mob and the middling people lose their respect for Parliament there is an end of all government and subordination.'[3] Lord Rockingham, on whom everything depended, was scarcely more enthusiastic and found the excesses of his new plebeian allies distressing: 'I *must say*', he wrote to Burke, 'that the thing which weighs most against adopting the mode of petitioning the King is, *where* the example was first set.'[4]

[1] L. S. Sutherland, 'The city of London and the opposition to government, 1768–74', 23; Sir H. Cavendish, *Debates of the House of Commons during the thirteenth Parliament of Great Britain*, 82, 281, 304; H. R. Fox Bourne, *English newspapers: chapters in the history of journalism*, I, 198.
[2] Temple to Lady Chatham, 9 May 1769, *Pitt Corr.* III, 361.
[3] *The House of Commons, 1754–90*, III, 393.
[4] 3 September 1769, *The correspondence of Edmund Burke*, vol. 2, ed. L. S. Sutherland, 64. The point at issue was whether petitions should be submitted to the King or to Parliament. Some argued that an appeal to the King against his Parliament was un-Whiggish. The example had first been set in Middlesex and London.

With a good deal of exertion however a campaign was got under way. Disappointments were numerous. From Sussex the Duke of Richmond wrote that his neighbours found the controversy remote and uninteresting; William Dowdeswell found Worcestershire equally reluctant to embark – 'it is amazing how in most places people of rank and fortune shrink from this measure'; Lord Temple reported a similar experience in Buckinghamshire, where the freeholders were 'in general totally ignorant of the question'. Thomas Pitt, proprietor of Old Sarum, went down to rouse Cornish indignation, and was told to put his own house in order first. In every county attempted, a rift opened between moderates, anxious to restrict the appeal to the single issue of the Middlesex election, and radicals, wishing to extend it to reform. Sir Anthony Abdy, one of Rockingham's supporters in Surrey, refused any further part in the petition, complaining of the 'wild and warm proceedings of Messrs Horne, Bellas, etc...the generality of whose opinions and ideas I cannot agree or subscribe to'.[1]

The ultimate result was dispiriting. The society achieved one spectacular *coup* in September 1769 when its members, led by Sir Robert Bernard, Horne, Sawbridge and Townsend, helped the corporation of Bedford to throw off the yoke of the Duke of Bedford by flooding the electorate with hundreds of honorary freemen, but any expectation that this might lead to a general revolt of boroughs against their patrons was disappointed.[2] Nor was it the kind of activity likely to endear the radical members of the society to their aristocratic allies. In the end, eighteen counties and twelve boroughs adopted petitions – barely enough to make a respectable showing and certainly insufficient to overawe the ministers.[3] The opposition's main parliamentary effort at the beginning of the 1770 session was an amendment to the address, demanding an enquiry into the 'unhappy discontents'. It was rejected by 254 votes to 138 – not an encouraging result. Their victory in contributing to the retirement of the first minister, the Duke of Grafton, redounded to the opposition's disadvantage since his successor, Lord North, was more resolute and capable.

Under the strain of disappointment, tempers began to fray. Beckford, serving his second term as Lord Mayor of London, was still the pacemaker in the spring of 1770. In March, presiding over a meeting of the liverymen in the Guildhall, he unburdened himself of his *political creed*, which included the usual attack on rotten boroughs and a demand for

[1] *Burke Corr.*, II, 66–7, 70, 76, 29; H. Walpole, *Memoirs*, III, 262.
[2] *The House of Commons, 1754–90*, I, 207; Journal of the fourth Duke of Bedford, *Cavendish Debates*, I, 622; *London Chronicle*, 7/9 September 1769.
[3] G. Rudé, 135 observes that the result was 'indeed impressive', but I think he has somewhat under-estimated the size of the national electorate. The agitation against the Cider Bill in 1763 had produced 23 petitions, and that from a particular region.

a more equal representation. The meeting then went on to adopt a remonstrance to the King couched in language of almost unprecedented ferocity. Neither Charles I's imposition of ship money nor James II's use of the dispensing power was, they informed the King, as dangerous as the 'secret and malign influence' in his reign which had deprived the people of their dearest rights. The House of Commons no longer represented the nation and the only remedy was the dismissal of ministers and the dissolution of Parliament.[1] When the matter was raised in the House of Commons, the Rockinghams were obviously embarrassed by the violence of the remonstrance and a resolution condemning it passed with a massive majority. A few days later, at a public banquet, Beckford tried without success to persuade Rockingham to endorse a reform programme.[2] The following week he and Horne were only just prevented from making their resentments public at an open meeting of the Middlesex freeholders: 'they lay the whole of this mischief to the Rockingham party', reported Calcraft to Chatham.[3] The publication in April of Burke's pamphlet, with its emphasis on the virtues of the nobility, widened the breach still more. Sawbridge's sister, Mrs Macaulay, dashed off an answer to this 'pernicious work', dismissing Burke's remedies as mere palliatives. The Rockinghams in turn were exasperated with their headstrong allies. By August, Burke was describing the 'bill of rights people' as 'a rotten subdivision of a faction amongst ourselves, who have done us infinite mischief by the violence, rashness and often wickedness of their measures'. The alliance was in ruins and so were the Rockinghams' ambitions of a speedy return to power. There was not 'the least glimmering of hope', Burke told his leader bluntly at the end of the year.[4]

Meanwhile the Society had also run into difficulties. The death of Beckford in June 1770, less than a month after his well-publicized retort to the King at an audience,[5] deprived it of a spokesman who made up in audacity what he lacked in subtlety. Robert Morris, the secretary, resigned in August, overworked and disillusioned: petitions and remonstrances having been tried without effect, he hinted darkly that 'operations of a different nature' were needed if the 'noble resentment of an injured

[1] *Gent. Mag.* (1770), 108–12.
[2] Horne to Junius, 31 July 1771, *The letters of Junius*, ed. C. W. Everett, 231–2.
[3] 29 March 1770, *Pitt. Corr.*, III, 435–6.
[4] *Burke Corr.*, II, 150, 176.
[5] After submitting a second remonstrance on behalf of the London liverymen, Beckford told the King that 'whoever has already dared...by false insinuations and suggestions to alienate Your Majesty's affections from your loyal subjects in general, and from the City of London in particular...is an enemy to Your Majesty's person and family, a violator of the public peace, and a betrayer of our happy constitution, as it was established at the glorious and necessary revolution'. *Gent. Mag.* (1770), 218. Beckford had never been a member of the society, presumably because of his personal dislike of Wilkes.

people' was to be vindicated.[1] Meanwhile there were ominous signs of an impending breach between Wilkes and some of his leading supporters. In October Sawbridge attacked instructions to the Westminster members to impeach Lord North as 'nugatory, ridiculous and ineffectual', though they had Wilkes' blessing. Worse still, by the new year Horne and Townsend were out of all patience at Wilkes' lack of interest in everything but his personal cause and his resentment at the employment of the Society's funds for any other purpose: it was intolerable, insisted Townsend, that Wilkes' liberal way of life and contempt of money should be 'a charge upon the prudent and industrious'. In April 1771 a 'violent altercation' led to Horne moving the Society's dissolution on the grounds that it had become 'nothing more than a source of personal quarrel'. Defeated by 26 votes to 24 he seceded to form a new *Constitutional Society*, taking with him Townsend, Sawbridge, Richard Oliver, Sir Robert Bernard, Sir Francis Delaval, Wray, Charles Turner, George Bellas, and the Society's new secretary, Boddington.[2] Acrimonious exchanges between the two groups filled newspapers for much of the summer, with *Junius* intervening on Wilkes' side.

The desire to prove that they were the genuine reformers appears to have stimulated each side to new endeavours. Sawbridge moved in the House for leave to introduce a bill for shorter Parliaments – his own preference, he stated, would be for annual: the ministry voted it down in silence by 105 to 54. It was small consolation that Chatham, five days later, declared himself a convert to triennial Parliaments.[3] The surviving members of the Society for the Supporters of the Bill of Rights adopted in June an eleven-point programme, which included annual Parliaments, a place bill, bribery legislation, and 'a full and equal representation of the people in Parliament'. Candidates for every borough and county in the kingdom were to be asked to pledge themselves to these objects. But little was done to ensure that these were other than pious hopes. 'The resolutions', *Junius* told Wilkes in September, 'are either totally neglected in the country, or, if read, are laughed at, and by people who mean as well to the cause as any of us.'[4] Wilkes' main energies were directed to building up his political position in the city of London: elected an Alderman while in prison in 1769, he became Sheriff in 1771, and Lord Mayor in 1774.

The general election of 1774 provided an opportunity to test the progress radicalism had made, and the Society duly reissued its appeal of 1771 asking for pledges from candidates. Its main achievement was to con-

---

[1] Letter dated 6 August 1770, *Political Register*, VII, 216–18.
[2] *London Chronicle*, 1/3 November 1770, 17/19 January and 9/11 April 1771.
[3] *Parl. Hist.*, XVII, 223. Chatham was a spent force.
[4] Letter of 7 September 1771.

solidate its metropolitan base. At the dissolution, radicals of various persuasions had held six of the ten metropolitan seats:[1] after the election the number had risen to seven, the loss of Sir Robert Bernard's seat at Westminster being cancelled by the gain of a seat for the city, and by Wilkes' own unopposed return for the county of Middlesex.

But outside the London area, the response was negligible. Robert Sparrow, Sir Robert Bernard's brother-in-law, was one of the members returned for Bedford, but was ousted on petition. Sir Watkin Lewes, a member of the Society, was defeated at Worcester in a riotous and confused contest; Mawbey, who had taken a prominent part on behalf of Wilkes, lost in Surrey; a radical challenge to the sitting members at Newcastle was beaten off without difficulty. Though candidates sympathetic to reform were returned elsewhere, the only clear victory for provincial radicalism was at Bristol, where Henry Cruger, an American, publicly pledged himself to receive his constituents' instructions and was returned top of the poll. The number of county contests was indeed the highest for forty years, but only in Surrey does radicalism seem to have been an issue. In Warwickshire, however, the result demonstrated the changing nature of society. The freeholders of Birmingham, which though a town of 50,000 persons was unrepresented, made a deliberate and successful attempt to capture one of the county seats for their own use, defeating a country gentleman whose father had been returned unopposed for forty years – a foretaste of the time, sixty years later, when they would take the further step of seeking representation for themselves. Judged by the result of Sawbridge's motion for shorter Parliaments in 1775, now an annual event, the movement for reform had come to a halt: Wilkes' assistance in the short debate could not prevent it from being rejected by almost two to one.

Wilkes himself made but one substantial effort on behalf of parliamentary reform, and its failure may be regarded as the end of this phase of radicalism. In March 1776, in a careful and sober speech, he moved for a more equal representation of the people. His argument was derived mainly from James Burgh's *Political disquisitions*, published in 1774–5. He outlined the defects of the representation, untouched since the days of Charles II, 'notwithstanding the many and important changes which have since happened'. The decayed boroughs must be amputated and the great new towns brought into the representation. For the first time for decades Cromwell's reform of the electoral system was mentioned with

[1] Trecothick, Oliver and Bull for London (the latter two returned at by-elections in 1770 and 1773); Glynn for Middlesex; Bernard elected at Westminster in 1770, and Mawbey sitting for the borough of Southwark. Radicalism in this election is examined in detail by I. R. Christie, 'The Wilkites and the General Election of 1774', reprinted in his *Myth and reality in late-eighteenth-century British politics and other papers.*

admiration and approval. But the most remarkable passage in Wilkes' speech was one which pointed the way towards manhood suffrage:[1]

> The meanest mechanic, the poorest peasant and day-labourer, has important rights respecting his personal liberty, that of his wife and children, his property, however inconsiderable, his wages, his earnings, the very price and value of each day's hard labour, which are in many trades and manufactures regulated by the power of Parliament ...Some share, therefore, in the power of making those laws, which deeply interest them, and to which they are expected to pay obedience, should be reserved even to this inferior, but most useful, set of men in the community. We ought always to remember this important truth, acknowledged by every free state, that all government is instituted for the good of the mass of the people to be governed; that they are the original fountain of power, and even of revenue, and in all events the last resource.

Only Lord North bothered to reply, pointing out how painful and hazardous amputations could be, but presuming that the honourable gentleman was 'not serious'. Not a voice was raised on Wilkes' behalf and, without a division, the proposal was rejected. Three months later, Wilkes' overwhelming defeat, for the second time running, in a contest for the city Chamberlainship showed to what extent radical enthusiasm had waned. In an agonized outburst, Wilkes turned to rend his erstwhile supporters: 'no longer worthy of the name of freemen, they are sunk into tame, mean vassals, ignominiously courting and bowing their necks to the ministerial yoke...We are ripe for destruction.'[2]

*   *   *   *

Tactical mistakes contributed a certain amount to the collapse of the first reform movement. It relied too much upon one man, and that man neither a serious nor determined reformer. Its impetus came, less from changes in society, than from a series of dramatic, but to some extent fortuitous, incidents. It was weakened by the feuds and animosities among the city radicals – though these were often the product rather than the cause of misfortune. It was too closely identified in its later stages with the American question, and when war came it suffered from the patriotic backlash: the same mistake was to be repeated with France twenty years later. Organization was weak. There was no systematic attempt by the Society for the Supporters of the Bill of Rights to send out speakers, to

---

[1] *Parl. Hist.*, XVIII, 1295–6. The argument follows very closely that of Burgh, I, 37–8. It echoes the views of the Levellers, for example John Lilburne's *The charters of London*: 'the poorest that lives, hath as true a right to give a vote, as well as the richest and greatest'.

[2] *Annual Register* (1776), 154.

provide for a regular supply of pamphlets, to organize local branches or to coordinate a campaign.[1] It was so slow to adopt a programme of reform that it missed the peak of excitement in 1768 and 1769: by the time it found a platform, the worsening colonial situation stole much of its thunder.

But too much emphasis on these marginal factors may obscure the truth that what the radicals were attempting was, at that time, impossible. Indeed, there was an almost ludicrous disparity between the size of the changes they hoped to effect and the resources they commanded. Parliamentary reform, with frequent elections, a wider franchise and secret ballot, meant a major change in the political and social structure of the country. Even in constitutional states, changes of this magnitude can be brought about only by massive pressure outside Parliament and resolute action inside. In the 1770s neither condition existed. There was little support in the country. The unrepresented towns made no stir. In many of the larger boroughs, where some response was hoped for, the old members had been returned unopposed in 1774. In the smaller boroughs the voters were either uncomprehending or hostile. At Cricklade, where Wilkes went in 1775 to support the candidature of his friend, Samuel Petrie, an hour's canvass was enough to convince him that 'Wilkes and Liberty will not do here: I see it must be hard money'.[2] In Parliament, the Rockinghams, the only substantial opposition group, had no patience with radical reform: an alliance between Beckford and Almon, with their hatred of the *grandees*, and the Marquis of Rockingham and Duke of Portland was bound to be uneasy. Even the terrible *Junius* was something of a paper tiger. He could remind his readers menacingly enough that a throne gained in one revolution might be lost in another, but his basic motive, as Horne perceived, was no more than to *vex* the King, while in reform the furthest he would go was shorter Parliaments – the abolition of rotten boroughs seemed to him fraught with danger.

To escape from this *impasse* there were two possibilities, which the radicals neither took nor appear to have seen. They could have scaled down their proposals to modest proportions, jettisoning the extreme suggestions, in the hope of engaging support among the country gentlemen, many of whom were prepared to consider shorter Parliaments and bribery legislation but jibbed at secret ballot and manhood suffrage.[3]

[1] *Junius* urged in vain the need to form societies throughout the country in his letter of 7 September 1771.
[2] John Cannon, 'Samuel Petrie and the borough of Cricklade', *Wiltshire Archaeological Magazine*, LVI (1956), 373.
[3] Sawbridge at least tried to appeal to the country gentlemen in 1771 when he moved for shorter Parliaments, arguing that they would eliminate bribery. 'From whence did bribery spring? Not from country gentlemen. They are sure of being chosen without any such scandalous practice…Now it is well known that country gentlemen are the

Alternatively they could have tried to enlist the support of the labouring classes to augment the inadequate pressure that the middle classes could bring to bear. Ingredients for such a policy were not completely lacking.[1] But to advocate a radical programme without any attempt to gain the support of the people most likely to benefit was to play at politics. Indeed, one does feel that the radicals, almost as much as their adversaries, accepted that politics was a game played by the select few. Beckford was certainly no firebrand in this respect. In May 1768 he denounced the seamen on strike as 'men (who) want more money for less labour done', and urged the House of Commons to unite in the face of common danger: 'they who raise mobs raise the Devil, and when they have raised him they know not how to lay him again'.[2] Such thoughts were never far from the governing class. Even Horace Walpole's desire to see a national outcry at the dismissal of his dear friend Conway was mitigated by the consideration that 'there is nothing so difficult as to make the people go far enough, and prevent their going too far'.[3]

Nevertheless, the movement was far from being a total failure.[4] True, it did not achieve its main objectives. Sawbridge's motion for shorter Parliaments was heard each year in bored indifference and rejected without debate. Even Wilkes' much vaunted victory in 1782, when the House of Commons voted to expunge from their Journals the resolution declaring his incapacity to serve was a personal triumph of limited significance. But the by-products of the campaign were not inconsiderable. First was a notable extension of the power of the press. The carefully arranged clash between the House of Commons and the city of London in 1771, in the course of which the Lord Mayor, a supporter of the Bill of Rights, was sent to the Tower, resulted in the House abandoning the struggle to preserve the secrecy of debates.[5] It would be difficult to exaggerate the

best support of the constitution, as they know the wants and grievances of their constituents. What then is more desirable than triennial parliaments, which will necessarily bring them into the House?...What more proper...than short parliaments, composed of country gentlemen.' *Parl. Hist.*, XVII, 179–82.

[1] A pamphlet of 1768 begged Beckford to intervene on behalf of the coal-heavers. *Monthly Review*, XXXIX, 327. The success of the Methodists showed that it was possible to stir and interest the masses. Indeed, there was fear in high places at the beginning of the movement that it would take a revolutionary direction.

[2] *Cavendish Debates*, I, 10.

[3] *Memoirs*, II, 2–3.

[4] G. S. Veitch's judgements in *The genesis of parliamentary reform* seem to me a little harsh. See also C. Robbins, *The eighteenth-century Commonwealthman*, 320 for the view that their achievements were 'as slight as that of their predecessors'.

[5] Treated by P. D. G. Thomas, 'John Wilkes and the Freedom of the Press (1771)', *Bulletin of Institute of Historical Research*, XXXIII (1960) 86–98; 'The beginnings of parliamentary reporting in newspapers, 1768–74', *English Historical Review*, 74 (1959); A. Aspinall, 'The reporting and publishing of the House of Commons debates, 1771–1834', in *Essays presented to Sir Lewis Namier*, ed. R. Pares & A. J. P. Taylor.

importance to reformers, who could only hope to succeed by bringing popular pressure to bear on a recalcitrant Parliament, of being able without hindrance to publicize votes and speeches in the House. At this time the reformers were unable to exploit the advantage they had gained, but when, forty years later, Sir John Nicholl spoke of the vast increase in the influence of the popular branch of the constitution he attributed it to 'the free publication of debates in Parliament'.[1] In addition, the collapse of the government's prosecution against the printer of *Junius*' letter to the King paved the way to a more liberal interpretation of the law of libel, though the position was not finally established until Fox's Libel Act of 1792.[2]

Secondly, the organization of the movement, however defective, pointed the way to the future: Wray, Sawbridge and Mawbey were founder-members of the Society for Constitutional Information, set up in 1780, and the improved techniques of that organization were in part derived from lessons learned in the earlier campaign. John Horne Tooke and Major John Cartwright, who were to take such prominent parts in the reform movement in the years ahead, became interested in the problem during the Wilkite struggle. Thirdly, the movement produced in James Burgh's *Political disquisitions* and Cartwright's *Take your choice* two classic restatements of the case for reform. Fourthly, George Grenville's election act, pushed through shortly before his death in 1770, was a useful advance towards a less partisan treatment of election petitions and suggests a growing sensitivity inside Parliament to public opinion.[3] Lastly, Beckford's campaign against bribery helped to produce action against some of the more flagrantly corrupt boroughs. New Shoreham was reformed in 1770 by opening the franchise to the freeholders of the hundred of Bramber after an election dispute had revealed the existence among the voters of a *Christian Club*, formed to sell the borough to the highest bidder. Hindon and Shaftesbury, threatened with the same treatment after the election of 1774, were able to escape, but Cricklade in Wiltshire joined Shoreham as a reformed borough in 1782.[4] Though this type of reform

---

[1] *Parl. Debs.*, 1st series, vol. XXXVI, 751.
[2] The issue was whether the jury must confine itself to the mere fact of publication, leaving the judge to decide whether the matter was libellous. John Almon was one of the printers prosecuted. The question was fought again in the case of the Dean of St Asaph's in 1783.
[3] 10 George III c. 16. It provided for petitions to be heard by select committees, specially chosen, instead of the whole House. This was another measure strongly supported by country gentlemen. On the third reading, Sir William Bagot, a Staffordshire Tory, declared that 'the effect of all this would be of restoring the representation to the natural interest of the country, the landed interest'. *Parl. Hist.*, XVI, 919. In 1774 radicals and Tories united to defeat the government and make the bill perpetual, Sawbridge, Glynn, Townsend, Mawbey, Crosby and Oliver voting with Bagot, Newdigate, Sir James Long, Sir John Hynde Cotton and the Drakes of Amersham.
[4] 11 George III c. 55 and 22 George III c. 31.

was moderate rather than radical, strengthening the influence of the
country gentlemen, the impetus clearly came from the agitation of the
1760s.[1] Much of the indignation expressed was certainly synthetic – the
House appeared to find bribery by nabobs more heinous than that
committed by country gentlemen – yet the reforms were the first breach
in the monolithic structure of the old representative system. At long last
the ghost of Oliver was laid.

[1] The Shoreham petition was the first to be heard under the new procedure of the
Grenville Act.

4

Mr Wyvill's Congress[1]

To understand the next phase of the agitation for reform, it is necessary
to distinguish three campaigns – however much they were inter-related
in practice. One was the campaign for moderate parliamentary reform,
organized by Christopher Wyvill, and having as its main objective a
substantial increase in county representation. The second was the more
radical movement, which revived and gained new impetus, with John
Jebb, John Cartwright and the Duke of Richmond taking over the work
of Beckford, Sawbridge and Wilkes. The third campaign, and the only one
to achieve any immediate success, was the agitation for economical reform,
championed above all others by Edmund Burke.

By late 1779 the plight of the Rockinghams was desperate. Paradoxically
the weakness of the administration did not seem to impart any vigour to
opposition, and each languished at the same time. Though the Rockinghams had soon repented of their flirtation with extra-parliamentary forces
in 1769–70,[2] the alternative lines of action had been far from encouraging.
Negotiations for coalition had broken down. In the winter of 1776–7 they
had tried the effect of a secession from Parliament without the public
being noticeably perturbed.[3] They could wait for military disaster to drive
the last nail into the coffin of the government, but there was no guarantee
that even in defeat the King would turn to them.

In this dilemma they continued with routine opposition criticism,
attacking the government for ineptitude, waste and corruption, and calling
for reforms to preserve the balance of the constitution. Since 1770 with the
publication of *Thoughts on the present discontents* and William Dowdeswell's
motion for a bill to disfranchise revenue officers, they had been committed
to some kind of economical reform. In April 1770 Dowdeswell had moved
without success a long motion imploring the King to direct his servants

---

[1] 'Mr Wyvill's Congress' was George III's description in 1781 of the coordinating body
for parliamentary reform. *The correspondence of King George the third*, ed. Sir J. Fortescue,
v, no. 3291. The word 'Congress' had, of course, painful implications.
[2] For a characteristically languid attitude towards popular participation, see the letter
by Walker King, later private secretary to Lord Rockingham, in *Burke Corr.*, IV, 167.
Speaking in November 1779 of associations, he wrote: 'Nothing would be so likely to
make the people, what one can not say they have hitherto in the smallest degree been,
a part of opposition. It is a sort of appeal to their judgement that flatters their vanity,
and gives them...all the ardour of self-consequence, and the strength of connection.'
[3] G. H. Guttridge, *English whiggism and the American revolution*, 89–93; Burke to
Rockingham, 6 January 1777, *Burke Corr.*, III, 311–14; Lord Albemarle, *Memoirs of
Rockingham*, II, 304–9.

to 'practise that economy which will tend most to the honour and dignity of his Majesty's crown...and the content of his people'.[1]

The Rockingham interest in economical reform arose directly from their diagnosis of the political situation and from their own predicament. How was it that with debaters as accomplished as Burke and Fox and propertied supporters as respected as Sir George Savile and Lord John Cavendish, they were in danger of becoming a permanent opposition, constantly deluded by hope? It was not enough to blame the King's hostility, for they had not even won the confidence of the House of Commons. Might it not be that the influence of the crown had grown so prodigiously that the independence of the House of Commons had been destroyed? Yet by judicious reform the number of placemen and pensioners might be reduced, the political balance restored, and victory obtained. Thus, at one and the same time, economical reform provided the Rockinghams with a programme and an explanation of past failures.

It had other manifest advantages. A proposal to eliminate waste and extravagance was sure to appeal to voters groaning under wartime taxation. It could appeal strongly to country gentlemen, with their deep-rooted suspicion of the executive and their anxiety to rid themselves of borough competition from Treasury-supported candidates.[2] It was a policy that would be difficult for the government to oppose directly. Best of all, it was a modest reform, in no way raising fundamental questions – a pruning not an uprooting. Indeed, it might well obviate the need for parliamentary reform.

In the later 1770s the public became more receptive to this issue. The reforms of Necker in France attracted much attention and lost nothing in the telling. In April 1777 the King was obliged to reveal accumulated debts of £600,000 and to ask the Commons to increase the civil list grant by £100,000 p.a. The opposition enjoyed a field day, openly insisting that the money had been spent in purchasing a corrupt majority in Parliament. 'Is there no feeling for the suffering of this impoverished country?' demanded Wilkes – scarcely the most austere of financiers. Barré, Shelburne's lieutenant, took the opportunity to repeat his standard diatribe against wartime profiteers, 'a certain race of animals who were daily increasing in this country, called Contractors'. Though the augmentation was granted, the King's feelings were not spared: the increase,

---

[1] *Parl. Hist.*, XVI, 924–6.
[2] Burke devoted a long passage in the *Thoughts* to this argument, and used it against triennial Parliaments – that no private purse could match government competition every three years. Sir John Molesworth, speaking in support of Dowdeswell's proposed bill, said that if it passed he hoped to see 'more of my country neighbours in this House'. *Parl. Hist.*, XVI, 835.

he was told by the Speaker, was 'great, beyond Your Majesty's highest expense'. When Richard Rigby imprudently challenged the Speaker's remarks, a resolution by Fox approving them passed without a division.[1]

This promising line of attack was followed up in subsequent sessions with considerable success. In March 1778, Thomas Gilbert, acting independently, moved for a special tax of 25% on the salaries of all placemen for the duration of the war: in committee it passed by 100 votes to 82, and the government succeeded in defeating it at a later stage by only 6 votes. A fortnight later Barré moved for and obtained a committee to enquire into public expenditure: Lord North did not venture to oppose. In April the ministry suffered two more narrow escapes. Its tax on inhabited houses was carried by only 77 votes to 70.[2] A week later Sir Philip Jennings Clerke moved for a bill to exclude government contractors from the House: despite North's objections leave was granted and the bill read a first time. When the government rallied its forces, three weeks later, it was rejected on the committee stage by only two votes. In February 1779 the same bill was introduced, leave being granted by 158 votes to 143, but was defeated in committee by 165 to 124. In the debate on the 1779 budget Burke followed up the chase after contractors, describing them as persons who cared nothing for their country, but 'wished only to suck her inmost vitals, to feast on her entrails, and finally glut their all devouring maws on her lifeless cadaver'.[3]

In the autumn of 1779 the leaders of the opposition, casting round as they usually did for some plan of campaign before Parliament met, perceived, with some surprise, evidence of widespread public discontent. 'The blisters begin to rise', wrote Burke, 'and there are signs of life in the body.'[4] Richmond's prophecy of February 1777 was in process of being fulfilled – 'I have so very bad an opinion of my countrymen that I believe nothing will move us but being obliged to *pay*.'[5] Even so, Rockingham's

[1] *Parl. Hist.*, XIX, 103–87, 213–14, 227–34.

[2] *CJ*, XXXVI, 888; Fortescue, vol. IV, no. 2276. Strictly speaking the vote was on an opposition amendment to exempt houses paying less than £10 p.a. rent.

[3] *Parl. Hist.*, XX, 824. These attacks were certainly better supported than censures on the ministry's main policies. Fox's resolution of February 1778 that no more of the Old Corps be sent out of the kingdom (tantamount to abandoning the prosecution of the American war) was rejected by 259 to 165. Direct motions in April to end the war and recognize American independence found the opposition divided and were not pressed to a vote. For a more dispassionate view of contractors than Burke's, see N. Baker, *Government and contractors: the British treasury and war supplies, 1775–1783*.

[4] *Burke Corr.*, IV, 158.

[5] Albemarle, II, 309. Supplies annually rose from £6½ millions in 1775 to 12 millions in 1777, 21 millions in 1780 and 25 millions in 1781. Though most of this expenditure was financed by loans, the interest repayments necessitated additional taxation each

battle-orders were distressingly vague. The first day, he wrote, should be
devoted to 'much activity and *general censure*, and if *all* the opposition can
agree upon any particular *specific points*...they should be announced and
proceeded on immediately'.[1] Accordingly the Rockinghams contented
themselves with an amendment to the address, calling for 'new councils
and new counsellors'.

* * * *

It is clear that the widespread demand for economical reform which made
itself heard in the last few months of 1779 was less a spontaneous national
reaction than a belated reward to the Rockinghams for their efforts to
kindle into flame embers that had been dully glowing for years. When
success came, it found them unprepared. Two years before, Richmond had
urged Rockingham to draw up specific proposals for reducing the influence
of the crown and to insist upon them when summoned to power. No such
plan was ready.[2]

The initiative in the new movement came from a small group of
Yorkshire country gentlemen who met on 25 November, the day of the
opening of the parliamentary session, at the home of General George Cary,
and agreed on the need for economical reform. The driving force was
Christopher Wyvill, an Anglican clergyman of large estates.[3] In the course
of the next few days they circularized friends and neighbours, demanded
a county meeting, and made the first cautious approaches to the parliamentary opposition. The Rockinghams had little choice but to adopt the
cause as their own, though there were aspects of the matter which gave
concern. Wyvill's scheme envisaged a network of associations throughout
the country to force reform through Parliament if necessary: the revolutionary implications of such a policy were not lost on Lord Rockingham.

year. The Land Tax was raised from 3*s* to 4*s* in the £ in November 1775. The subsequent annual *increase* in taxation was as follows:

1776	£73,000	1779	£482,000
1777	£237,000	1780	£701,000
1778	£336,000	1781	£814,000

[1] Rockingham to Burke, 3 November 1779, *Burke Corr.*, IV, 163-4.
[2] The editor of volume IV of Burke's *Correspondence*, 171 n. 3, suggests that a meeting
of opposition members on 27 November prepared resolutions on economical reform:
this would have been before they could have heard of the Yorkshire enterprise. But it
seems to me more likely that the resolutions referred to were concerned with Ireland.
The presence of Burgoyne at the discussion suggests Irish matters, and the opposition
moved censure motions in the Lords on 1 December and the Commons on 6 December.
It may also be noted that Thomas Townshend, present at the discussion of 27 November,
spoke in the Irish debate of the 6th. Lord John Cavendish in debate (*Parl. Hist.*, XX,
1301) denied having heard of Burke's scheme before 29 November.
[3] For Wyvill, see N. C. Phillips, 'Country against court: Christopher Wyvill, a Yorkshire champion', *Yorkshire Archaeological Society Journal* (1962), 588-602; and I. R.
Christie, *Wilkes, Wyvill and reform*.

Secondly, Wyvill seems from the beginning to have regarded economical reform as no more than a preliminary to parliamentary reform. The raising of that issue would be most unwelcome. But for the time being, these were distant dangers.

In Parliament, the opposition hastened to make the most of its new-found popularity. Richmond moved as early as 7 December for a reform of the civil list establishment, dwelling much on the French example: 'while our inveterate enemy was adopting the wise system of economy, this country was daily plunging deeper into boundless extravagance'. Rockingham, supporting him, brought out the old constitutional arguments: the continual majorities that supported the crown on all questions demonstrated how widespread influence had become. A week later Burke gave notice of detailed proposals which he claimed would save the country £200,000 p.a., and cut off an amount of influence equivalent to fifty members of Parliament.[1]

During the Christmas recess, the movement out of doors gained momentum. The city of London voted on 17 December its thanks to those lords who had supported the call for economy. On 30 December the Yorkshire meeting took place. A petition was adopted declaring that 'rigid frugality' was indispensably necessary, and demanding a complete reform of expenditure before any new taxes were levied. A committee of sixty-one was charged with correspondence and association with other interested bodies. Four days later the Hampshire freeholders held a meeting at Winchester and followed suit. Middlesex, which had been caught in the middle of a somewhat unprofitable agitation of its own, abandoned it in favour of the Yorkshire lead.[2] The city of York soon followed the county, its member claiming that almost every elector had signed the petition. At Bristol, the corporation disregarded an appeal to ignore the 'general infatuation...a manoeuvre politically adopted...to embarrass government', and voted by 19 to 4 to join the campaign.[3] By the end of the spring, 26 counties and 11 cities had taken up the issue.

The signal for the parliamentary battle to begin was given by Sir George Savile on 8 February when he presented the Yorkshire petition. Though he stressed the moderation, the respectability and the wealth of the petitioners, he was not above threatening ministers: 'this petition is not presented by men with swords and muskets...The request of the petitioners is here so reasonable that they cannot but expect that it will be granted; but should it be refused...here I leave a blank.' North made a characteristically cool reply, noted the intimidation, and advised the House to judge the petition strictly on its merits. The opposition set-

---

[1] *Parl. Hist.*, xx, 1255–66; 1293–1305.
[2] *The House of Commons, 1754–90*, eds. L. B. Namier and J. Brooke, I, 334.
[3] *Bonner & Middleton's Bristol Journal*, 5 February 1780, letter by A. B.

piece went off well, though the occasion was somewhat marred by an intervention from Lord George Gordon that true reformation ought to begin with religion and that action against the Papists was essential. In the Lords there was a long debate on a proposal by Shelburne for a committee to enquire into public expenditure. Rockingham dutifully reiterated the message of Burke's *Thoughts*: from the beginning of the reign there had been an intention 'to govern this country...through the influence of the crown'. He was at pains to establish the independence of the petitioning movement – 'it originated in the spontaneous propositions and communications of the independent and honest part of the people of all descriptions'. Shelburne's motion was lost by 55 votes to 101.[1]

When the opposition's plans at length made their appearance they were seven in number. Five were Burke's bills, of which the chief was for the reform of the civil establishment, with the suppression of many useless offices; Dowdeswell's measure for the disqualification of revenue officers was resurrected and sponsored by John Crewe; Sir Philip Jennings Clerke presented for the third time his bill to exclude government contractors.

North conducted a skilful campaign in the hope that the hurricane, given time, would blow itself out, offering direct opposition only when it could not be avoided. Barré's demand for a commission of accounts was accepted, issued its first report in November 1780, and, according to a recent commentator, produced some effective reforms.[2] When Sir George Savile moved for a statement of all places and pensions, North agreed to the first part and objected to the second on the grounds that it would expose to public ridicule poor unimportant pensioners of the crown. He carried his amendment by two votes. The Contractors' bill was allowed to pass the Commons without a division, only to be destroyed in the Lords. Crewe's bill to disqualify revenue officers was met head on in the Commons and defeated on the second reading by 224 votes to 195.[3]

The centre of the parliamentary struggle was Burke's scheme. His main proposals were to provide for the royal household by contract, and to abolish a number of sinecure offices, chief of which were the third Secretaryship, the Board of Trade, the Clerks of the Green Cloth, and the Treasurer, Cofferer, Comptroller and Master of the Household. The first clause of the main bill, to abolish the office of third Secretary, was defeated on 8 March by 208 votes to 201; the proposal to abolish the Board of Trade was carried by 8 votes; but when the motion to abolish the post of Treasurer of the Chamber was rejected by 211 to 158, Burke declared his indifference to the fate of the remainder of his proposals.

---

[1] *Parl. Hist.*, xx, 1318–65, 1370–83.
[2] J. E. D. Binney, *British public finance and administration, 1774–1792*.
[3] *CJ*, xxxvii, 624, 634, 698, 717–18, 727, 735–7; Horace Walpole, *Last journals*, ii, 371; *Parl. Hist.*, xxi, 414–57.

The bill, abandoned by its parent, was finally knocked on the head on 23 June.

The difficulties which the particular proposals had encountered persuaded the opposition to make one more attempt to rally support by returning to the general principle, and on 6 April Dunning carried by 233 votes to 215 his motion that the influence of the crown had increased, was increasing and ought to be diminished. The hollowness of this famous victory was demonstrated as soon as the House resumed discussion of specific propositions. In the debate on Crewe's bill a week later, several members who had voted for Dunning's motion explained that they did not regard themselves as bound to support particular measures, and gave their votes for government. North had weathered yet another storm.

It is unlikely that the sponsors of the original Yorkshire campaign were surprised at the outcome of their endeavours. They had little faith in a House of Commons which they regarded as corrupt and subservient. Consequently a scheme of association outside Parliament had been one of their objectives from the outset. The need for some such national organization had been argued by reformers like Burgh and Jebb, and the success of associations in America and Ireland in extorting concessions was added encouragement. The Yorkshire freeholders had instructed their committee to 'prepare a plan of an association, on legal and constitutional grounds, to support the laudable reform'.[1] This could mean anything or nothing. Some county meetings found it lukewarm. Devon was reported to have declared for arms.[2] Middlesex specifically included in its resolutions the demand for a national association. On the other hand, Suffolk, Northumberland, Herefordshire, Derbyshire and Wiltshire, though petitioning, refused to associate.

As early as December 1779, Frederick Montagu had warned Rockingham that the cause of economical reform might be endangered by the scheme of association: 'I have constantly objected to that idea, as the name would appear alarming to moderate persons.'[3] His misgivings were justified. In the course of the following month correspondents in many newspapers attacked associations as seditious, and a well-supported Hertfordshire protest declared that they would lead to Insurrection, Confusion and Anarchy. Though Wyvill made public in February a letter he had written which established that he would entertain nothing that was not 'pacific and conformable to law and the constitution', his critics were

---

[1] The association movement is discussed in a number of publications, chief of which are E. C. Black, *The Association*; H. Butterfield, *George III, Lord North and the people 1779–80*; I. R. Christie, 'The Yorkshire Association, 1780–4: a study in political organisation', reprinted in his *Myth and reality in late-eighteenth-century British politics*.
[2] Walpole, *Last journals*, II, 361.
[3] 28 December 1779, Rockingham MSS., quoted E. C. Black, 43.

by no means assuaged. 'Mr Wyvill may be a *well-meaning*, good sort of man', wrote *Pacificus* in a London newspaper, 'but it is no very uncommon thing for *well-meaning*, good sort of men to be made the dupes of ill-designing, factious demagogues.'[1] Nor could Wyvill's declaration obscure the fact that some of his political allies were less moderate than he. John Jebb, a leading member of the Westminster committee, was on record that a national association could consider itself a sovereign body, and might constitutionally, if it chose, declare the House of Commons dissolved.[2] A correspondent in the *General Evening Post*, in a letter which received wide publicity, echoed his views: nothing would be gained by carrying on 'the old farce of petitioning for what we know a corrupt ministry will never grant, nor for the purpose of trusting to the obstinacy of an un-feeling k—g for redress'. The petitioners must obtain redress themselves, and form a national convention 'with the full powers to enforce such regulations'.[3] To counteract the effect of such militancy, some of the supporters of reform adopted the most seemly language: the mayor and burgesses of Nottingham addressed their petition to a '*British* House of Commons, with that respect which is due to the appointed guardians of our rights...honoured with so great a trust'.[4] But the damage was done. When Wyvill summoned his meeting of deputies in London for March 1780, fewer than half of the petitioning bodies sent representatives. Sir Fletcher Norton, Speaker of the House of Commons, spoke for many moderate reformers when invited by Charles Fox to state his opinions:[5] 'Although he approved of the petitions, he totally disapproved of the committees and associations. If they were not illegal, they were, in his opinion, extremely improper, and might terminate in consequences which every good man, upon cool reflection, would wish to avoid.' The opponents of reform were not slow to play upon these fears. Lord Nugent, dubbed 'the old rat of the constitution' by Lord George Gordon, retorted that a rat 'always cautiously avoided gnawing through the sides of the vessel: it never made a hole which would endanger the ship'.[6] When, in June 1780, Lord George Gordon's Protestant Association erupted in a burst of violence that handed London over to the mob for a whole week, the supporters of government considered their case proven.

*   *   *   *

Under cover of the economical reform campaign, the agitation for parliamentary reform revived. The Duke of Richmond, influenced by John Cartwright, hoped in the summer of 1779 that the Rockinghams

[1] Wyvill's letter to Dr Hunter, 7 January 1780, Wyvill, III, 174 was reprinted in the *General Evening Post*, 19 February. *Pacificus* is in 29 February/2 March 1780.
[2] *An address to the freeholders of Middlesex*, 20 Dec. 1779, 15, quoted Butterfield, 192.
[3] 10 January 1780.
[4] *CJ*, XXXVII, 581.
[5] *Parl. Hist.*, XXI, 265.
[6] *Parl. Hist.*, XXI, 407-8.

would embrace parliamentary reform as their immediate objective. To Walker King he expounded a plan for annual Parliaments, manhood suffrage, equal electoral districts together with sweeping administrative reforms, and a scheme of association to accomplish the task.[1] Instead the party took up economical reform, and Rockingham himself was most anxious that the issue of parliamentary reform should not be raised. Many of his supporters, including Burke and the Cavendishes, were hostile: even among those who approved, there was vast room for disagreement over the mode and extent.

There was however little chance that parliamentary reform could for long be ignored. Even before the first meeting of the Yorkshire freeholders an elector from that county had insisted that the 'evil complained of' went deeper than economical reform could touch and called for an attack on the borough influence of the nobility.[2] The Middlesex and West-minster radicals were at first remarkably restrained, anxious no doubt not to jeopardize a promising beginning: at their meetings on 7 January and 2 February they carefully excluded extraneous matters and followed the Yorkshire lead. Others were less patient. At the Wiltshire meeting on 27 January William Jones, a friend of Shelburne, warned that without parliamentary reform any concessions might easily be revoked, and Shelburne himself drew attention to Chatham's approbation of additional county members.[3] The first major break-away came when Wyvill assem-bled his conference of deputies at the St Albans Tavern in March. It included many men publicly pledged to parliamentary reform – James Townsend and Brass Crosby, surviving members of the Supporters of the Bill of Rights, Lord Mahon who had contested Westminster as a radical in 1774, Thomas Brand Hollis heir to Thomas Hollis, as well as Jebb and Cartwright. After days of debate they produced a programme that totally changed the direction of the movement, declaring in favour of 100 additional county members, annual Parliaments, equal electoral areas and tests for candidates. This platform was then remitted to the county associations for approval. 'The deputies from the several county commit-tees...seem to have traversed beyond the bounds of their commissions', commented one observer.[4]

Already Rockingham was sounding the tocsin. To Pemberton Milnes, a Yorkshire supporter, he unburdened himself on 28 February 1780 in an uncharacteristically long letter attacking 'some vague and crude proposi-tions' that had come to his notice. While not denying that shorter Parlia-

[1] Walker King to Burke, 5 November 1779, *Burke Corr.*, IV, 165–8. It is clear from the letter that the conversation with Richmond referred to took place several weeks earlier.
[2] A Yorkshire Freeholder, 28 December 1779, quoted *General Evening Post*, 10 January 1780.
[3] Report of the General Meeting of Wiltshire, Wyvill, I, 108 ff.; *Bonner and Middleton's Bristol Journal*, 5 February 1780.   [4] *General Evening Post*, 25/8 March 1780.

ments and a more equitable representation were desirable, he argued with considerable acumen the tactical case against departing from the issue of economical reform:

> The fair conclusion to be drawn (when the men *who are eager for shortening the duration of Parliament* cannot as yet agree amongst themselves whether annual triennial and quinquennial parliaments *should be substituted*) is that the matter is by no means ripe for them to call upon a candidate for a declaration. It seems to me that the idea of calling for a declaration of support for a *more equal representation* is also, as yet, very premature...Some persons, I know, by the expression of a *more equal representation* mean *little more* than the abolishing *what are called the rotten boroughs*; some of these persons think that these boroughs should be taken away from their possessors *without any compensation* (as being unconstitutional); some allow that the possessors should be compensated. Some persons think that the seats for these boroughs should be filled up by additional members from their respective counties; others think that like *Shoreham* the seats should be filled up by the voices of the persons resident within certain neighbouring districts. Others think, that many of the great, important towns of trade and manufactures...should fill up the parliamentary vacant seats...What a situation will every honest, conscientious candidate be in when he is called upon to declare most solemnly upon his honour that he will be for *shortening the duration of Parliament* and for a *more equal representation* when he cannot form a guess what specific proposition it is on either of these points.

As soon as the outcome of Wyvill's conference was known, Rockingham wrote again urging that triennial parliaments were preferable to annual, and that the addition of one hundred county members ought not to be accepted before the distribution had been worked out.[1]

The reception of the conference's proposals by the first three associations to consider them bore out all Lord Rockingham's fears. They bolted three different ways. Westminster's committee, under the chairmanship of Fox, adopted the proposals in their entirety, though the subsequent general meeting at Westminster Hall in April committed itself only to shorter Parliaments.[2] Yorkshire adopted an intermediate position. Lord

---

[1] Albemarle, II, 395–400, 402–6.
[2] The position was rather complicated. A sub-committee under Sheridan was appointed and declared for annual Parliaments. The main committee, with Fox in the chair, accepted the suggestion, but a further sub-committee of Fox, Sheridan and Fitzpatrick was appointed to prepare resolutions for the general meeting. They changed the recommendation to shorter Parliaments only, and this the general meeting accepted. Meanwhile the first sub-committee's report had been published in the newspapers, and a later report, *London Courant* 15 July, pursued a full-blooded radical line.

John Cavendish's appeal not to depart from the original issue was ignored, but the committee came out in favour of triennial rather than annual elections. The Wiltshire freeholders on 28 March insisted on keeping to the question of economical reform, and took no further part in the campaign of association.[1]

Parliamentary reform had been refloated once more, but at the cost of contributing to the failure of economical reform. 'If a torrent is divided into three channels,' Walpole had written prophetically, 'not one of the three will carry a great mass of tide along with it.'[2] Left behind also was a residue of mistrust and recrimination between the leaders, Wyvill against Rockingham, Rockingham against Shelburne, Richmond against Fitzwilliam, Jebb against Wyvill.[3] Faced with a movement so riven, Wyvill paused for consolidation.

Wyvill's decision not to call another conference for the time being opened the way for the radicals to take up the running, with the powerful Westminster committee well to the fore. The report of its second sub-committee, under the chairmanship of Thomas Brand Hollis, was more radical than anything yet to appear, denouncing property as 'the grand enchantress of the world'. If Hollis and his friends meant more than a fine flourish, here indeed was a challenge to the assumptions on which the 1688 settlement was based, for Locke had put the preservation of property as the 'chief and great end' of civil government. To the proposals for manhood suffrage, annual Parliaments and equal electoral areas were added secret ballot, payment of members and the abolition of the property qualification, thus anticipating by more than fifty years the programme of the Chartist movement. A detailed scheme of redistribution, in relation to population, awarded 46 seats to Yorkshire, 45 to Middlesex, 30 to Wales, 22 to Norfolk, 21 to Devon and Durham, and 18 to Kent, Lancashire, Somerset and Suffolk.[4]

The radical drive was strengthened in April 1780 by the establishment

---

[1] Of the 12 counties that had participated in the conference, 5 associated on the full programme (Yorkshire, Middlesex, Essex, Surrey and Devon); 3 more agreed to associate only on economical reform (Bucks., Dorset and Hertfordshire); 4 others would not associate at all (Sussex, Hunts., Kent and Gloucestershire). Cheshire joined Wiltshire in disbanding its committee.

[2] *Last Journals*, II, 379.

[3] Wyvill thought Rockingham had deluded him over the Yorkshire meeting of 28 March; Shelburne thought Rockingham had been too cautious; Richmond and Fitzwilliam clashed in the Westminster committee; Jebb thought Wyvill too dependent on the politicians, and Wyvill thought Jebb utterly impractical. Wyvill, vol. I, pp. xvii–xviii; Christie, 'The Yorkshire Association, 1780–4', 102–4, 133–4; Fitzmaurice, *Life of Shelburne*, II, 67–72.

[4] Minute Book, Add. MS. 38593, ff. 16–19, 38–44. Printed in Wyvill, I, 228–43. The report was presented in May and published after the Gordon riots in July.

of the Society for Constitutional Information.[1] The founder members included Cartwright, Jebb, Brand Hollis, and Sheridan, whose interest in politics was developing fast: they were soon joined by Mawbey, Sawbridge and James Townsend, veterans of the Wilkite campaign, and by Granville Sharp, whose persistent pamphleteering in favour of annual Parliaments helped to push public opinion in that direction. Their object was to build up a solid body of public support by the systematic production and distribution of pamphlets and broadsheets. Though the extreme views of the Society were often an embarrassment to its moderate allies, it was a distinct advance on the old Society for the Supporters of the Bill of Rights, being far more devoted and methodical in its endeavours.[2] In its very objectives was a recognition of a more realistic time-scale, an acceptance that the task of accomplishing reform might be slow and laborious. It was more positive than the Rockinghams, who were prepared to wait upon but never hasten public opinion: the Society for Constitutional Information understood that public opinion does not emerge, but needs to be, if not produced, at least prompted.

Although the Society's work imparted a little vigour into the campaign it did nothing to heal the breaches. Wyvill's willingness to accept triennial Parliaments in the interests of political unity seemed to many radicals a dereliction of principle. Thomas Day's *Speech to the Essex county meeting*, of which the Society printed 3000 copies, contained a sharp attack on the Rockinghams: 'are heaven and earth and hell to be moved...not that the great causes of all our miseries may be removed...but that one garrison may evacuate the place and another march in...I have never yet heard of an aristocracy, from ancient Rome to modern Venice, that was not the universal tyrant and inquisitor of the species.'[3] Two parliamentary attempts which were the counterpart to all this activity did nothing but reveal the divisions among reformers. On 8 May 1780 Sawbridge moved for the tenth time his motion on annual Parliaments. His only comfort could be that, though rejected by 182 votes to 90, a good deal more interest was aroused than on the previous occasion, when only 8 members had troubled to support him and 32 to oppose. But though the debate was more spirited, the opposition paraded its disunity. Barré and George Byng supported the motion, and Fox rose to explain, rather lamely, why

[1] The best account of the Society is in E. C. Black, ch. v. The Society's minutes are extant among the papers of the Treasury Solicitor. Its origins seem to be Cartwright's suggestion for a Society of Political Enquiry, which he discussed in 1778 with Richmond, Abingdon and others. Cartwright, I, 120–1.
[2] There was a full-time paid secretary, and publications were to be distributed free of charge. The initial subscription to the Society was one guinea. They began by producing 4000 copies of Cartwright's *Declaration of those rights of the commonalty of Great Britain without which they cannot be free*, with a second edition of 10,000 copies a month later.
[3] Quoted Butterfield, 295.

he had changed his mind. Lord John Cavendish and Thomas Pitt spoke against, and Burke devoted a major oration to the task of extirpating the new heresy. 'Popular election', he declared bluntly, 'is a mighty evil.' Stripped of its oratorical and philosophical trimmings, his argument was simple – that frequent elections would enable the crown to wear out private fortunes. Triennial elections, no less than annual, would bring disaster to the constitution, indeed, to civil society. 'What will be the consequence of triennial corruption, triennial drunkenness, triennial idleness, triennial law-suits, litigations, prosecutions, triennial frenzy, of society dissolved, industry interrupted...morals vitiated and gangrened to the vitals.'[1]

Burke's challenge to the radicals was taken up by another prominent member of the opposition, the Duke of Richmond, who wrote to Burke for a copy of the speech so that he could refute it point by point. Of all things in the world, replied Burke, he wished to avoid a public controversy with Richmond: the radicals were not worth it, they were 'very despotic persons', constantly employed in deriding the Rockinghams as 'a *faction*'.[2] But Richmond pressed on, determined to test opinion, and on 3 June moved for leave in the House of Lords to introduce a reform bill. His timing could not have been more unfortunate. While he spoke, Lord George Gordon's supporters were in almost unchallenged command of the streets of London, burning and looting, and their lordships, some of whom had been manhandled by the populace the previous day, were in no mood for reform. Leave was refused without a division.[3] The session, which at times had seemed so full of promise, ended with the opposition in total disarray.

*   *   *   *

Throughout 1781 reform in all its aspects languished, partly under the shadow of the Gordon riots, partly because hopes of a military victory in America had not been finally crushed. The general election of 1780 had made little difference to the attitude of the House of Commons.[4] The Rockinghams duly presented their three main reform measures in the new session, and each was rejected by a substantial majority. The Society for Constitutional Information had fallen on hard times and was too short of ready money to undertake many publications. Wyvill summoned a second meeting of his congress in the spring of 1781, but the response was disappointing: only one new county, Nottinghamshire, joined in, and at least eight associations dropped out. A body composed of 9 counties and

[1] *Parl. Hist.*, XXI, 594–615.   [2] *Burke Corr.*, IV, 235–8.
[3] The basis of Richmond's bill was manhood suffrage, annual elections and equal electoral areas. Richmond's interest in reform is discussed in A. Olson, *The radical Duke, Career and correspondence of Charles Lennox, Third Duke of Richmond*, chapter iv.
[4] I. R. Christie, *The end of North's ministry*, ch. ii; idem, *Wilkes, Wyvill and reform*, 116–20.

2 boroughs could hardly claim to speak for the nation. The conference agreed that the presentation of legislation for reform should be postponed 'to a more favourable, but, they trust, not a very distant season'.[1]

The surrender of Lord Cornwallis at Yorktown in October 1781 changed the whole political situation, spelling doom for Lord North's administration. After the misunderstandings of the spring of 1780 Rockingham had resisted all efforts to edge him into any commitment to parliamentary reform, but in the negotiations that followed North's resignation in March 1782 he insisted on economical reform as a *sine qua non*, and its implementation formed the main activity of his short ministry. With North's following in temporary disorder, the legislation passed without much difficulty.[2] On the coat-tails of economical reform went through the bill to extend the right of voting at Cricklade to the neighbouring hundreds.[3]

Modern historians who have examined the economical reform legislation in detail are sceptical whether it dealt that 'good stout blow to the influence of the crown' that Fox had anticipated.[4] Crewe's Act may have caused government managers anxiety in a few constituencies, but it is doubtful whether its operation deprived the ministry of more than one or two seats at the subsequent general election. Clerke's Act could be evaded by transferring contracts to friends or relatives. Burke's Civil Establishment Act, less ambitious than the 1780 version, was not completely satisfactory: the Board of Trade had to be re-established in 1786, and a third secretaryship was recreated in 1793 for Dundas as Secretary for War. Burke's belief that he had imposed such tight financial controls that the crown would be unable to find money for corrupt purposes was certainly too sanguine: at the general election of 1784 the King borrowed £24,000 from a banker, some of which went to defeat Burke and his political allies. Nor did it prevent the accumulation on the civil list

[1] Wyvill, I, 339. There was a long debate on 8 May on a petition presented by Savile, which triggered off a discussion of the propriety of associations. See also Wilberforce's comment in R. I. & S. Wilberforce, *The life of William Wilberforce*, I, 20.
[2] The Contractors' Bill and the Civil List reform passed the Commons without a division; Crewe's bill was carried by 87 to 12. In the Lords the main opposition came from Thurlow, the King's man in the cabinet, but all three passed with comfortable majorities.
[3] It is clear that the Cricklade reform was a party matter. Samuel Petrie, one of the candidates at the 1780 election and the instigator of the legal actions which followed, was a reformer and a friend of Wilkes, and in Parliament it was supported and opposed on a party basis. A bill brought in by Lord Mahon to curtail the expense of county elections by allowing the sheriff to move the poll ran into difficulties and had to be withdrawn. *Parl. Hist.*, XXIII, 101–9.
[4] D. L. Keir, 'Economical reform, 1779–87', *Law Quarterly Review*, I, 368–85; B. Kemp, 'Crewe's Act, 1782', *English Historical Review*, LXVIII (1953), 258–63; I. R. Christie, 'Economical reform and "the influence of the crown", 1780', *Cambridge Historical Journal*, XII (1956), 144–54; J. Norris, *Shelburne and reform*; J. E. D. Binney, *British public finance and administration, 1774–92*; E. A. Reitan, 'The civil list in eighteenth-century British politics: parliamentary supremacy versus the independence of the crown', *Historical Journal*, IX (1966), 318–37.

account of further debts, which had to be presented to Parliament in 1784 and 1786. In direct terms, therefore, the reforms probably had little effect on the crown's position. The weakening of royal power during the next fifty years, which improved substantially the chances of effecting a reform of Parliament, owed more to the increasing complexity of public business, a persistent series of economies and reductions, the rise of party and the growth of an informed public opinion than it did to the Rockinghams' measures. In a more general sense, however, the campaign was of importance. The attack on sinecures, even if not pressed by the Rockinghams with much vigour where their own interests were concerned, helped to prepare the way for a more utilitarian concept of government. The separation of the personal expenses of the monarch from the public expenses of the state made easier the transition to a less politically-active monarchy. Finally, the reports of the commissioners of public accounts, with their clear statements of proper principles, laid the foundation for the comprehensive financial and administrative reforms undertaken by William Pitt.

Wyvill wasted little time in exploiting the changed situation. Superficially the position looked promising. Three members of the Marquis of Rockingham's cabinet were pledged to parliamentary reform – Fox and Shelburne, the two Secretaries of State, and Richmond, the Master of the Ordnance. In addition the 1780 general election had brought into the House of Commons two new members of Parliament, Pitt and Sheridan, each speedily establishing a parliamentary reputation, and sympathetic to reform. Even Rockingham was prepared to concede that if the members of the cabinet could 'settle some plan that should unite the opinions of the public, he should by no means hold himself bound to resist it'.[1] Wyvill decided that a new mass campaign could not be organized until 1783: in the meantime, to keep the issue before the public, he persuaded Pitt to move for a committee on parliamentary reform.

The debate of 7 May 1782 was the first serious discussion of the question in Parliament. The difficulty of deciding what measure of reform to recommend was overcome by moving merely for a select committee to investigate. Pitt's tone was moderate. It was not innovation but 'recovery of constitution' that he advocated: no man had greater reverence for the constitution than he had, but they must take care that enthusiasm did not destroy it, by refusing to remove its defects 'for fear of touching its beauty'. The main opposition came from his cousin, Thomas Pitt, 'the dragon of Old Sarum'. Equal representation had never been the principle of the constitution – or Yorkshire and Rutland would never have been given the same number of seats. The proper function of Parliament was to act as a balance against the crown, and this the Commons had been

---

[1] Richmond to Shelburne, 21 March 1782, quoted Olson, 191.

able to do only because of the aristocratical weight of property it contained. William Pitt's caution in committing himself to no specific proposal was turned to disadvantage:

> Should we receive the proposition we should launch into a sea that has no shore; it is a general enquiry, without anything defined or specific as its object; it opens an inquisition into the state of every borough...whilst it holds out to the public an expectation which you neither mean to satisfy, nor ought to satisfy, nor could satisfy...It is whether we shall think it expedient to open a general shop to receive all the projects of the wildest of the projectors.

A combination of the conservative Rockinghams with Lord North's friends was sufficient to reject the motion by 161 votes to 141 – a majority which, as subsequent events proved, was deceptively small.[1]

The next move, announced at a meeting of reformers at the Thatched House Tavern on 18 May, was to resume petitioning, but this time with parliamentary reform as the avowed object: at the end of the campaign Pitt was to test opinion in the Commons once more. Much thought was devoted to the form of the petitions. A general commendation of reform, though it would help to unite supporters, would leave the way open to sinister interpretations. Wyvill was anxious for a general statement only, but he had difficulty keeping his supporters in line. The Yorkshire committee, meeting in November, urged the addition of one hundred county members, the abolition of fifty of the most 'obnoxious' boroughs,[2] shorter Parliaments, the extension of the county franchise to copyholders,[3] and reform of the Scottish electoral system.[4] Yet another issue arose when some boroughs wished to include a protest against the oligarchical character of their local government.

The response to Wyvill's initiative was not impressive. Several of the replies indicated that the steam was going out of the issue. From Gloucestershire Sir George Onesiphorus Paul reported that the activities of the Society for Constitutional Information and the Westminster Committee

---

[1] *Parl. Hist.*, XXII, 1416–38.
[2] By 'obnoxious' was not necessarily meant those with the smallest electorate, but those under Treasury control. One reason for adopting this proposal was to meet the objection that the addition of 100 county members would produce an overlarge House of Commons.
[3] This had been a bone of contention for many years, the celebrated Oxfordshire election of 1754 having turned on the issue. Copyholders were expressly excluded from the franchise by 10 Anne c. 23, but since some of them were men of substance the law was not always obeyed. In any case the complications of tenure could be enormous. But it was a curious anomaly that a copyholder worth £600 p.a. could be elected to Parliament but had no vote. After the Oxfordshire contest, the exclusion of copyholders was reiterated by 31 George II c. 14.
[4] The Scottish reform movement is discussed in chapter five below. Wyvill had good reason to support it since so many Scottish members were at the command of government.

had alarmed many former sympathizers. From Norfolk and Hertfordshire came similar tidings of declining enthusiasm. In the end, only 12 English counties submitted petitions, less than half the number that had demanded economical reform in 1780. The reply from the boroughs was better, with 23 petitioning instead of 11, but the addition of places like Penryn, Launceston, Lyme Regis, Lymington and Chester was poor consolation for the lack of interest shown by Bristol, Newcastle, Nottingham and Hull, which had taken part in the former campaign. It was significant too that the adversaries of reform were recovering their spirits. The Mayor of West Looe retorted that the unanimous opinion of his corporation was that it would be 'highly improper to make any alteration in the constitution... which we have always respected as the most perfect that any country was blest with'; the Mayor of Poole explained that 'we think ourselves better employed in supporting the present laws than we should be in lending any assistance to new model the constitution of Great Britain'; the Mayor of Petersfield told Wyvill bluntly that 'you and your association will do much injury to Old England'.[1]

In one other respect Wyvill was also unlucky. The political situation, on which so much depended, had taken a turn for the worse by the time his campaign got under way. The resignation of Lord North, much against the King's wish, cast doubt on the proposition that the crown was dangerously strong. At the same time the end of the war held out some prospect of relief from taxation and persuaded some electors that drastic measures might not, after all, be necessary: it would, thought Wyvill, 'add new obstructions to the work of reformation'.[2] The formation of the coalition between Lord North and Charles Fox in the spring of 1783 did not, in itself, alter the situation as far as parliamentary reform was concerned: the new allies agreed that it should remain an open question, and indeed there is little else Fox could have done since it was an open question within the Rockingham party itself.[3] But William Pitt had taken up an attitude of open hostility towards the coalition, and there was therefore less chance that his proposals would be considered strictly on their merits.

The nature of those proposals remained a mystery until the day of the debate. The metropolitan radicals, now formed into the Quintuple Alliance,[4] hoped that he would once more move for a committee of investigation, so that Richmond's plans for annual Parliaments and manhood suffrage would not be ruled out. Wyvill was convinced that such

---

[1] Wyvill, IV, 241–7, 257, 254–5; II, 97–8. [2] Wyvill, IV, 289.
[3] For a contrary opinion, see Black, 104, and Christie, *Wilkes, Wyvill and reform*, 176–9. There was not enough strength in the reform movement to make it the overriding issue in political life.
[4] A confederation of the radical reformers of London, Westminster, Southwark, Middlesex and Surrey. The moving spirit was Jebb. See E. C. Black, 84.

a course would be disastrous, and in a meeting with Pitt on 5 May 1783, two days before the debate, he put the case for the Yorkshire position. He found Pitt determined to avoid 'any matter that could give offence'. The most he was prepared to suggest was the addition of a hundred county members and the disfranchisement of such boroughs as should be proved guilty of corruption in future.[1]

Pitt's second motion for reform attracted much more attention than his first. The gallery of the House of Commons was full and a large number of members present for the debate. He began with the obligatory eulogy of the constitution: 'there was no form of government, on the known surface of the globe, that was so nearly allied to perfect freedom'. He was resolved utterly to repudiate manhood suffrage.[2] Nor could he accept the abolition of rotten boroughs which he feared 'could not be removed without endangering the whole pile'. Hence, his proposal for the addition of at least 100 county members, with the gradual elimination of corrupt boroughs should it be necessary to keep down the total numbers. Thomas Powys, the independent member for Northamptonshire, opening the attack, agreed that this was the least objectionable of all the expedients suggested. But it would certainly not satisfy the reform movement. It was remarkable that the great towns did not find their lack of representation a grievance sufficient to make them petition. George Byng, the member for Middlesex, drew attention to the petition from Tower Hamlets, which paid £34,000 in land tax and had no representation: Cornwall, in comparison, paid £14,000 and had 42 members.[3] The centre-piece of the debate was the return of Lord North to his best form. He denied that the American War showed that the wishes of the people could not make themselves felt:

It was the war of the people...nor did it ever cease to be popular until a series of the most unparalleled disasters and calamities caused the people...to call out as loudly for peace as they had formerly done for war. Had the constitution been so disordered as the reformers would persuade us that it is, how comes it to pass that the voice of the people prevailed against the influence of the crown?...the history of my political life is one proof which will stand against and overturn a thousand wild assertions that there is a corrupt influence of the crown which destroys the independence of this House.

He could by no means approve the addition of 100 county members: 'the addition of one hundred, or even fifty, county members,

---

[1] Wyvill, IV, 2–5.
[2] His remarks at this point were so unconvincing that it is charitable to presume that he was pandering to the prejudices of his fellow members. He observed that all who voted for unsuccessful candidates would remain slaves. This is an argument, not against manhood suffrage, but against majority decisions of any kind, and applied equally to the unreformed system.   [3] *Sic.* Cornwall had of course 44 members altogether.

would give a decided superiority to the landed interest over the commercial'.

North's last remark focussed attention on one of the weaknesses of Pitt's proposition. At a time when the beginnings of industrialization were creating the new manufacturing towns, it was peculiarly inappropriate to add to the county representation. In the pre-debate interview, Wyvill had warned him of this danger. 'What struck me most forcibly, as an objection to adding an equal number of members to the small as well as the great counties was this: in the small counties the interest of powerful families is found most prevalent...therefore adding as many to the small counties as to the large would in a much greater degree strengthen the aristocracy, who are already too powerful in this country.' Wyvill was under the impression that he had persuaded Pitt to announce that the county augmentation must be in due proportion to the importance of the county, but there was no reference to it in the reports of Pitt's speech, and it would have been at variance with his insistence that the details should be decided later.

The rest of the debate was enlivened by an offer from Thomas Pitt to sacrifice his borough of Old Sarum as a gesture of goodwill, and by a typically robust speech against the motion by Richard Rigby, a survivor of the old Bedford party. He laughed at the resolutions of the Constitutional Society and Quintuple Alliance: 'the honest gentlemen who composed those meetings, and gave them ridiculous names, only deceived themselves. They thought the attention of all the world was as much engaged in the question of parliamentary reform as they were, when in fact scarce anybody else thought or cared about the matter.' When the House divided, Powys' motion for the order of the day was carried by 293 votes to 149. In the year that had elapsed since Pitt's previous motion, the reform vote had increased by 8, the anti-reform by 132.[1]

The result was a stunning blow to the reformers. 'My defeat', wrote Pitt to his mother, 'was much more complete than I expected.'[2] Wyvill was unwilling to blame Pitt for the disaster, though he regarded his attitude as cautious in the extreme. 'The majority of the people had not petitioned for the reformation of Parliament', he conceded, 'and they who had petitioned could not agree to recommend any specific mode whatever. The counties and the capital aimed at schemes of reformation so widely different that there was hardly a probability of their acting in concert again; and the zeal of the capital for the principle of universal suffrage in this respect may be deemed a disadvantage to the cause.'[3] It was clear that the 1782 vote had been totally misleading and that the movement for reform of Parliament had a long road to travel.

*   *   *   *

---

[1] *Parl. Hist.*, XXIII, 826–75.
[2] 15 May 1783, Earl Stanhope, *Life of William Pitt*, I, 121.   [3] Wyvill, IV, 288–9.

The remainder of the fifteenth British Parliament was scarcely conducive to reform. The animosities arising from Fox's India Bill and the way in which it was defeated swept aside all other considerations. It was a tactical mistake on Wyvill's part to allow an unsupported Yorkshire petition to go forward in January 1784. North remarked that a single petition, after years of agitation, hardly suggested a widespread demand for constitutional innovation.[1] Worse still, Wyvill allowed himself to be drawn from his principle of neutrality and took an active part in the spring of 1784 in enlisting support for Pitt. The result was predictable. Many of the coalition's supporters severed their connection with the Yorkshire Association. Though he considered reform necessary, wrote Sir Watts Horton, he would not abandon other principles which he thought more material – 'I mean, supporting the dignity and authority of that most essential branch of the constitution, the representative body of the people of England, against the overstrained prerogative of the Crown.'[2] Wyvill had the satisfaction during the general election of helping to eject Lord John Cavendish from his bastion at York, and secured the ignominious withdrawal of the Rockingham candidates for the county, but the price was great. After 1784 the Yorkshire Association, the driving force behind the reform movement, ceased to meet.

For a few months it looked as if Wyvill's gamble in pinning his hopes to Pitt might succeed. His new ally, now first minister, was returned at the general election with a massive parliamentary majority and the prospect of power for years to come. Better still, in December 1784 he pledged himself to bring forward a plan of reform the following session, and to support it honestly and boldly, *'as a man and a minister'*.[3] Conscious of his own rise to power, he was at pains to ensure that he would not be stabbed in the back by royal influence, unconstitutionally exerted. 'There is but one issue of the business', he warned the King, 'to which he could look as fatal...that is the possibility of the measure being rejected by the weight of those who are supposed to be connected with government.' The King's reply made no attempt to conceal his lack of enthusiasm for reform but promised not to confide his opinion to anyone – 'indeed on a question of such magnitude, I should think very ill of any man...who would suffer his civility to any one to make him vote contrary to his own opinion'.[4] But obtaining a grudging promise of neutrality from the King was only part of Pitt's problem. Many of his colleagues lamented that he had become involved in such an enterprise. His own secretary to the Treasury, George Rose, refused all appeals to support the measure, and tendered his

---

[1] *Parl. Hist.*, XXIV, 347–52; *Gent. Mag.* (1784), I, 125.
[2] Wyvill, IV, 384–5.   [3] Wyvill, IV, 433 ff.
[4] Quoted D. G. Barnes, *George III and William Pitt, 1783–1806*, 125–7. See also J. Ehrman, *The younger Pitt*, chapter ix.

resignation instead.[1] Lord Courtown, Comptroller to the Household, Robert Manners, equerry to the King, and Sir George Howard, Commander-in-chief, were prevented from voting against it, but could not be prevailed upon to support it.[2]

Wyvill's part in the preliminary campaign proved equally difficult. Indefatigably he wrote round to his collaborators, warned them that this was '*the crisis of the cause*', and urged them to rouse their own localities in a mass campaign. 'All the reformers are stirring', wrote Robert Smith jubilantly.[3] The reality was quite different. Only two counties and ten boroughs sent in petitions – one-third the number that had moved on the previous occasion, and a sorry contrast to the sixty places that had just petitioned against the government's Irish commercial propositions.[4]

The proposals Pitt put forward on 18 April 1785, drawn up in close consultation with Wyvill, were the most detailed submitted to Parliament at that date. Thirty-six of the most decayed boroughs were to be encouraged to surrender their seats voluntarily by the offer of monetary compensation: their representation would then be transferred to the counties and the metropolis. The populous unrepresented towns might be given seats at a later date if further boroughs chose to relinquish their rights. Copyholders in counties were to be enfranchised, and closed corporations, such as Bath and Bury St Edmunds, would be allowed to abandon their exclusive franchise. The proposals, Wyvill estimated, would add some 99,000 to the electorate – an increase of some 30%. The whole measure, insisted Pitt, would be 'final and complete'.

Pitt was not unprepared for the turn the debate took as soon as he sat down. A week earlier John Robinson had reported conversations with government supporters on the subject:[5]

> I find them in general very much against meddling with it in any shape, fearing to open a door to confusion...The idea of voting a large sum of money to accumulate for the purpose of purchasing boroughs, as talked of, appears to be much disliked, it will be greatly contested, and I cannot avoid mentioning to you that I think you will find almost insuperable difficulties in carrying this.

Though Wilberforce and Henry Dundas tried to come to Pitt's rescue, the absence of support in the country played straight into the hands of Lord North: had the unrepresented towns not been totally indifferent, he

---

[1] *The House of Commons, 1754–90*, III, 376. [2] *Ibid.*, III, 485.
[3] R. I. & S. Wilberforce, I, 77.
[4] Manchester, for example, subscribed 55,000 signatures against the commercial propositions, but showed no interest in reform. The petitions came from Yorkshire, Notts., York, Launceston, Gt Yarmouth, Scarborough, Newcastle-on-Tyne, Norwich, Hull, Lyme Regis, King's Lynn and Morpeth. *CJ*, XL.
[5] 9 April 1785, Abergavenny MSS.

observed, 'surely this would have been the time for them to make their exertions, when they were informed that the right honourable gentleman would support their claims, "both as a man and a minister",' and when they were taught to believe that all England, with one voice, would second their application...Well might he say with the man in *The Rehearsal*, 'what horrid sound of *silence* doth assail mine ear'.[1] Henry Bankes and John Rolle, two of Pitt's closest supporters, declared against him, and in the division lobby the government's troops deserted in droves. Less than half the office-holders in the administration voted for the measure. Two of the five members of Pitt's own Treasury Board withheld their support.[2] Of the six members of the Board of Trade, not one voted with him, and two of them even spoke against.[3] The leaders of the Rockinghams, Fox, Fitzpatrick, Sheridan and Burgoyne, all deeply committed to reform, gave him support, but many of the opposition rank and file saw no reason to exert themselves to prepare a triumph for a man they distrusted and disliked.[4] The waning enthusiasm among the country gentlemen at large was reflected in the declining support from the knights of the shire, 39 of whom had supported the motion in 1783 and only 28 in 1785. A small crumb of comfort may have been that the new members of Parliament were significantly more sympathetic to reform than the old: 44% of them voted with Pitt as against 26% of the old members.[5] Nevertheless he went down to defeat by 248 votes to 174 and the hopes of reform vanished for a generation.[6] 'Terribly disappointed and beat', wrote Wilberforce next day: 'called at Pitt's; met poor Wyvill.'[7]

*   *   *   *

In the moment of disaster Wyvill blamed the disunity of the reform movement. His irritation with the metropolitan reformers is not hard to understand. In their excitement, often under the influence of dissenting or unitarian principles, they had sketched out and adhered to proposals some of which, like secret ballot and manhood suffrage, would take a century or

---

[1] *Parl. Hist.*, xxv, 458.
[2] John Buller, sr., and Lord Graham.
[3] Lord Frederick Campbell and Lord Mulgrave spoke against, influenced perhaps by the doyen of the Board, Charles Jenkinson; the other three members were James Grenville, Thomas Harley and C. W. Boughton Rouse. Of the six members and secretary of the Board of Admiralty, three supported Pitt and four did not.
[4] Of 39 members who supported reform in 1783 but not in 1785, no less than 22 were coalitionists. Of the 34 members who had not voted in 1783 but supported reform in 1785, only 5 were coalitionists. The figure 34 includes 7 who paired off in favour of reform.
[5] By 'new member' I mean one of the 163 who had not sat in the previous Parliament.
[6] Wyvill wrote later that by 1787 'the nation had become indifferent to all questions of reform, and the hope of success, in that temper of the public, was quite extinguished'. Wyvill, IV, 61.
[7] R. I. & S. Wilberforce, I, 78.

more to achieve, and others, such as annual Parliaments and church dis-establishment, which have never been implemented. In doing so, they undoubtedly helped to spoil his chances. Their retort was that his limited programme, based on property rights, was hardly worth the effort, and that he trusted too much to his political alliances: 'our business', wrote Jebb, 'is with the people; and the people's business is to do their own business. No present or future idol will do it for them.'[1] Each side saw half of the problem. Wyvill understood that reform would never get through the House of Commons without the coordinated support of a powerful parliamentary group – in the end it was as a government measure that reform triumphed: Jebb saw that without a massive popular following parliamentary attempts would founder. Nevertheless, disunity was no more than a contributory factor. In matters of this weight and importance, it is fruitless to expect unanimity, and one can hardly think what great reform would have been effected had it first been necessary for all good men to agree.[2]

Later commentators have shared Jebb's doubts on the sincerity of the parliamentary leaders. Of Fox, Professor Black wrote that his principles were shallow and that he 'personally killed the movement in 1785': Pitt's conduct is explained by his ambition – 'when the popular cause suited him... he used it: otherwise he did not'.[3] These criticisms make too little allowance for the genuine political difficulties that existed: nor do they distinguish between front-rank politicians and political crusaders, such as Wyvill, Wilberforce and Shaftesbury, who could afford to dedicate them-selves to one cause. Of Pitt, Wyvill wrote that he would certainly make parliamentary reform 'the great object of his political life'.[4] It was both too much and too little to ask. Pitt had to work with anti-reformers, just as Fox and Shelburne did, because there were not enough dedicated reformers to go round. Pitt was unable to make reform a government measure, just as Fox had been unable to make it a coalition, or even a Rockingham, measure.[5]

---

[1] J. Disney, *Memoir of Jebb*, quoted E. C. Black, 211.

[2] Lord Mahon, with much experience of public life, reminded Wyvill in 1786: 'can we expect unanimity upon such questions, even amongst those who call themselves our friends?' Wyvill, IV, 547.

[3] *The Association*, 128–9. The reference to Fox is his vote with a majority of reformers at the Thatched House Tavern in May 1785 that Pitt's proposals could not be considered 'a substantial improvement of the constitution'. Professor Black wrote that 'that vote killed moderate constitutional reform'. I think it was already dead and that the Thatched Tavern scene was no more than an unseemly fracas at the funeral.

[4] Wyvill, IV, 465.

[5] Their defence was the same. Fox declared at the time of his coalition with North that 'without this sense of the people explicitly declared, it will not be in the power of any administration, however friendly to the measure, to carry it'. Quoted I. R. Christie, *Wilkes, Wyvill and reform*, 178. Pitt explained later that 'he was at a loss to conceive

The Fox–North coalition, wrote Professor Black, was disastrous to the reform movement, and 'split the extra-parliamentary movement at the one time when it possibly had accumulated sufficient support among the politically effective orders of society to carry the day'.[1] This is hard to believe. The extra-parliamentary movement was already split: indeed, it was born split. The anti-reformers had a majority in the House of Commons, and in the country reform sentiment waned with the end of the war. It is not easy to reconcile Professor Black's comment with his subsequent observation that 'the great mass of the nation was unconcerned'.[2]

Here, indeed, was the root cause of the movement's failure, and one which Wyvill fully recognized: Pitt, he wrote later, had been 'most shamefully deserted by the majority of those counties who had so loudly demanded that reformation'.[3] Sending Pitt into action so ill supported was like pushing an infantryman over the top without a rifle. The truth is that outside London and Yorkshire the movement's support was feeble and spasmodic, depending too much upon a handful of collaborators. The mass of the labouring people played no part at all, despite occasional attempts by the Society for Constitutional Information to kindle their interest.[4] The middle-class elements outside London scarcely stirred. What kind of case could Pitt or Fox make in Parliament for the urgency of reform when Manchester, Birmingham, Leeds and Sheffield did not trouble to ask for redress? Even the support which Wyvill could tap among his fellow country gentlemen suffered from two grave weaknesses. Many were less interested in reform than in expressing discontent and warding off heavier taxation; others, prepared to consider a mild reform which might improve their chances of a parliamentary seat, drew back when they realized that it could not stop there.

One must doubt whether at any stage, for all Wyvill's efforts, his movement was within range of success. Even had some measure of reform passed the House of Commons, there were still the Lords to deal with – emboldened by their intervention against Fox's India Bill and by no means bereft of their powers. Nor can it be certain that the King would have given his consent.[5] The determination to overcome such powerful constitutional obstacles is not much in evidence.

where they had learned that he would never make part of a cabinet any one member of which should be hostile to a parliamentary reform: perhaps it would be absolutely impossible ever to form such a cabinet.' *Parl. Hist.*, XXIV, 350–1. Pitt failed in 1785 to have reform adopted as a cabinet measure.
[1] Pp. 104, 128.   [2] P. 129.
[3] Wyvill, IV, 542; V, 68.
[4] For example, by the publication in 1782 of Sir William Jones' pamphlet *The principles of government in a dialogue between a scholar and a peasant.*
[5] I. R. Christie, *Wilkes, Wyvill and reform*, 177 refers to a claim by Shelburne that the King in 1783 had given his approval for a county augmentation. But the claim was made in 1792 and must be regarded as dubious.

Nor, among the causes of failure, must one neglect the campaign mounted by the opponents of reform and conducted at times with skill and vigour. The divisions among reformers were exploited to good effect and their occasional absurdities used to discredit the whole movement. 'I would wish to ask of our parliamentary reformers', wrote one fairly unsophisticated pamphleteer, 'how far they mean to go, and when and where a stop is to be put to the proposed changes?'[1] In particular, the demand for annual Parliaments, which Granville Sharp so sedulously propagated, was a millstone round the reformers' necks. Their opponents were able without much difficulty to show that their appeal to historical precedent was misleading and that the implementation of annual Parliaments must promote riot and disorder.

Other writers developed particular points. Soame Jenyns, in *Thoughts on a parliamentary reform*, observed that the complete elimination of influence from the House of Commons would render majorities haphazard and government impossible – a fair point at a time when many were unwilling to accept the alternative of party discipline. Josiah Tucker, Dean of Gloucester, worked on the dislike of London, discernible in the seventeenth century and by no means extinct today: a numerical representation would give that swarming capital a predominant bloc vote. 'Overgrown cities', he concluded, 'are the seats of faction and sedition, and the nurseries of anarchy and confusion.'[2]

The doctrine of virtual representation was employed against reformers less frequently than one might have expected, perhaps because the American troubles had taken the shine off that argument. More commonly found is the suggestion that the machinery of representation was less important than the end-product – a distinguished and honest House of Commons; that the pocket boroughs, by providing a refuge on occasions for men such as William Pitt, Burke, Fox, Barré and Dunning, contributed to a vigorous political life. Suspicion of democracy ran deep. Manchester and Leeds were reminded that they were spared the horrors of election brawls and election orgies, and Tucker began one pamphlet with the remark that democratic logic must lead to votes for women – the bare mention of which was 'an insult to common sense'.[3]

The opponents of reform also charged their adversaries with subversion. This was not always without foundation. Some of the reformers had certainly shown delight at American successes; others toyed with the idea of armed resistance. In *The principles of government in a dialogue between a gentleman and a farmer* Sir William Jones emphasized the right of citizens to bear arms: privately he wrote to Cartwright in May 1782 that

[1] *Thoughts on equal representation*, quoted *Monthly Review*, I (1783), 445–7.
[2] *Treatise concerning civil government*, 258–9.
[3] *Four letters on important national subjects*, 55.

England would never be a people 'in the majestic sense of the word unless two hundred thousand of the *civil* state be ready, before the first of next November, to take the field, without rashness or disorder, at twenty-four hour's notice'.[1]

The defects of Wyvill's campaign are not hard to perceive. He and his friends rarely attempted to explain to the public what practical advantages were to be expected from a reform of Parliament or to relate it in any way to the aspirations of social groups. Though the prominence in the reform movement of dissenters of various descriptions might have suggested what could be accomplished by harnessing specific grievances to the cause of reform, little effort was made to do so. Nevertheless the movement had achievements to its credit and represented an advance on that of Wilkes' day, being more restrained, mature and better organized. From the very beginning, in 1779, radicals and moderates alike recognized the importance of persuasion and propaganda, even if their products were often arid and unconvincing. Discussion of reform was moved from general principles to practical proposals, and politicians of the first rank brought into collaboration.

Wyvill's own importance lay not in the field of ideas, where his very derivativeness was an undoubted asset, but as a tactician and organizer. He was one of the first reformers not to be disconcerted when the walls of Jericho refused to fall at the opening blast. The use of county meetings to express opinion was, of course, nothing new. But Wyvill attempted to remedy the weakness of the county meeting – that it was better suited to make protests than to conduct a sustained campaign – by his system of committees of association to carry on the work in the meantime. The comparative novelty of this proceeding was one reason for the deep suspicion with which many contemporaries regarded it. In 1795 Lord Lansdowne, in a debate in the House of Lords, commented on the new methods of mobilizing public opinion: 'their mode of proceeding, by association and affiliation, was a discovery of as much moment in politics, as any that the present century has produced in any other science'.[2] Though, on this occasion, he attributed this political revolution to the Paineite radicals, Lansdowne must have known that the real author, for good or ill, was Christopher Wyvill.

[1] *The letters of Sir William Jones*, ed. G. Cannon, II, 547.
[2] *Parl. Hist.*, XXXII, 534.

5

The Irish and Scottish reform movements: bright bayonets and inflexible perseverance[1]

From the Scottish Bishops' war and the Irish rebellion of 1640, which helped to precipitate the English civil war, to the granting of Catholic Emancipation in 1829 after the county Clare election, the affairs of the three kingdoms were inextricably linked. The achievement of parliamentary reform in any of the three countries was certain to have the most important consequences for the other two.

The political situation in Ireland towards the end of the American war was quadpartite and potentially unstable. The dominant group was the nobles and gentry of the Anglican ascendancy, possessing the greater part of the landed property of the country and a near monopoly of political power. Though most of them were related to English aristocratic families and many of them had estates in England also, they were aware that the interests of the two countries did not necessarily coincide, and were anxious to acquire as much freedom of action in Ireland as possible. Their militancy was tempered however by the reflection that they were in a precarious position amidst an alien population, and they were unwilling totally to antagonize England lest they should, on some occasion, need her protection. The great majority of the population was Catholic Irish, submissive and apathetic after decades of relegation to an inferior political, economic and social position, venting their miseries and frustrations in occasional outbursts of savage agrarian violence. In the larger towns, however, middle-class Catholics had made some progress in recent years in commerce,[2] and a measure of their advance was the establishment in 1760 of a Catholic committee, to represent their interests. The position of the third group, the Presbyterian dissenters, was more complex. By an act of 1704 anyone holding military or civil office was to qualify by taking the sacrament after the mode of the Established Church. Rigorously applied this would have excluded Presbyterians from both the Irish Parliament and the municipal corporations. In practice the oath was not

[1] The Rev. John Harvey of Donegal was captain of a Volunteer company: his motto was 'Moderation and bright bayonets'. *HMC Charlemont*, 1, 164. The annual meeting of the burgh reformers in Scotland in 1790, after a series of disappointments, called for 'inflexible perseverance'. *Caledonian Mercury*, 7 August 1790. The phrases seemed to me to catch something of the difference between the Irish and Scottish movements.
[2] M. Wall, 'The rise of a Catholic middle class in eighteenth-century Ireland', *Irish Historical Studies*, XI, no. 42 (1958).

demanded from members of Parliament and a few Presbyterians usually took their seats. They were however excluded from corporations and played only a minor role in Irish political life. In 1780, by one of the first measures of the Irish revolution, the ban was removed, though their Anglican opponents were so solidly entrenched that few Presbyterians were able to take advantage of it. The last element in the political scene was the Castle administration, appointed by and responsible to the English government, and dedicated to its interests. By and large English governments wanted an Ireland that was quiet and orderly, offered no commercial rivalry, and afforded no encouragement to foreign invaders.[1] Political life in Ireland was febrile but artificial. Contests in the counties were frequent but they were fought out by a tiny segment of the population.[2] Debates in the Irish House of Commons were often brilliant, but they were largely irrelevant – not engaging on the executive machinery, like some high-powered engine with nothing to drive. Political decisions were made for Ireland, not in Dublin, but by the English cabinet in London.

The Irish representative system contained most of the blemishes of the English and a good many special ones of its own. In the thirty-two Irish counties, which returned two members apiece, aristocratic domination was even more marked than in England, and dislike of the nobility is to be found repeatedly expressed in pamphlets and newspapers. The 117 boroughs contained examples as strange as Gatton, Malmesbury or Dunwich in England. Most of them were seventeenth-century creations, designed to consolidate the Protestant Ascendancy. Many of them were no more than straggling villages, and some, such as Bannow and Harriston, were without habitation of any kind. In the corporation boroughs with no freemen, some 55 in number, political life was almost totally extinct. Lord Ely, patron of three such boroughs in county Wexford, carried rationalization to its logical conclusion, and made the same thirteen persons serve as the corporation for each of the boroughs.[3] In other boroughs, the institution of honorary freemen had been taken to such lengths that there were no resident voters at all: the entire electorate of Kinsale in county Cork was resident in Ulster, on the patron's northern estates, while only 2 of the 150 voters of Dingle lived in the town;

[1] After examining the attitude of the Rockingham, Shelburne, Portland and Pitt administrations towards Irish problems, I find it difficult to quarrel with Charlemont's assessment – 'Where is the English party that is not, more or less, hostile to the constitutional and commercial interests of Ireland.' *HMC Charlemont*, I, 15. Burke was even more bitter. He had never known any English government, he remarked, 'influenced by any passion relative to Ireland than the wish that they should hear of it and of its concerns as little as possible'. *Corr.*, VII, 290.
[2] According to my calculation there were contests in at least 25 of the 32 Irish counties at the general election of 1783: there were of course very few contests in the boroughs.
[3] The boroughs were Fethard, Clonmines and Bannow.

Monaghan and Newton were said to have but one resident elector and Charlemont none at all.[1]

Three major considerations rendered these defects of the representative system comparatively unimportant. For the greater part of the century, until the Octennial Act of 1768, Irish Parliaments lasted the full length of the reign: consequently the Parliament summoned in 1727 at the accession of George II continued until 1760 with no intervening general election. Secondly, the Irish Parliament was, until 1782, a subordinate one: while the English Parliament had the right to legislate for Ireland, all legislation passed at Dublin required the approval of the English privy council. Thirdly, the greater part of the Irish population, being Catholic, had no share whatever in the representation: throughout the whole eighteenth century no Catholic could sit in either House, and between 1728 and 1793 no Catholic was permitted to vote.[2]

Until the American war there was no sustained campaign for Irish parliamentary reform. The defenceless state of the country and the threat of invasion led in 1778 to the foundation of the Volunteer movement, which grew so rapidly that by 1780 no fewer than 40,000 men were under arms. The political situation was at once transformed and the English government watched developments with considerable uneasiness. The Volunteers' first venture into politics was strikingly successful. On 4 November 1779 the Dublin Volunteers paraded on College Green with field guns labelled 'Free Trade or this': a month later Lord North rose in the English House of Commons to announce substantial commercial concessions. In the spring of 1780, when Wyvill's first petitioning campaign was gathering strength in England, Lord Buckinghamshire wrote to Hillsborough that 'the conduct of some of your English counties may be inconveniently infectious'.[3] But when the Volunteers took up political agitation in earnest they turned towards legislative independence rather than parliamentary reform. Mass meetings of the Ulster Volunteers in February 1781 and 1782 passed resolutions demanding the abolition of Poyning's Law and the establishment of an independent Irish Parliament. 'If you delay, or refuse to be liberal', the Duke of Portland warned Rockingham's cabinet, 'government cannot exist here in its present form, and the sooner you recall your lieutenant and renounce

[1] *Letter to Henry Flood on the present state of the representation of Ireland*, 1783, p. 8. Essential reading on the Irish representative system is E. M. Johnston, *Great Britain and Ireland, 1760–1800*, together with the second volume of E. Porritt, *The unreformed House of Commons*.

[2] There is some doubt whether the act of 1 George II c. 9 originated this disqualification or merely confirmed it. J. G. Simms, 'Irish Catholics and the parliamentary franchise, 1692–1728', *Irish Historical Studies*, vol. XII, no. 45 (1960), argues that until 1728 Catholics had voted.

[3] Quoted E. Johnston, 290.

all claim to this country the better.'[1] In May 1782 the cabinet agreed to concede.

Demands for a parliamentary reform began to be heard in the summer and autumn of 1782. In July Sir Edward Newenham, the member for Dublin county, moved for leave to introduce a bill for a more effectual representation, but it was not followed up. A little later, the freeholders of Meath petitioned for legislation against non-residence in boroughs.[2] An appeal to the Volunteer movement to take up the cause of reform came from Francis Dobbs, a lawyer, in his pamphlet, a *History of Irish affairs from 12 October 1779 to 15 September 1782* (pp. 161–2). But the attention of the nation was fixed on the renunciation of English legislative and judicial authority, and not until that was settled by the passage at Westminster of a special act of renunciation in 1783 did reform come to the fore.[3]

The task of arousing public interest in the question was undertaken with great success by a writer contributing to the *Dublin Evening Post* under the pseudonym, *Molyneux*.[4] His first effort, on 2 January 1783, was an eye-catching table on the front page giving details of borough patronage throughout Ireland, and appealing to the people of Ireland to join their endeavours to those of William Pitt. This was followed by a revised and corrected table later the same month drawing attention to the 'melancholy truth that about *one hundred* men in Ireland have *greater influence* in our House of Commons than all the *independent* freeholders of the kingdom'.[5] A series of letters in successive months drove home the argument. Without parliamentary reform, he insisted in March, the constitutional gains of the previous two years would remain in jeopardy: 'men who could vote, *not two years since*, against the expediency of declaring our legislative independency, could vote *two years hence* for rendering their legislative again dependent' – a reasonable forecast of what was to happen in 1800.[6] Under this stimulus, a campaign began to take shape. On 15 February the Clogher Volunteers denounced the undue influence of landlords and on 1 March a meeting in Cork of the Munster Volunteers declared in favour

[1] *Memoirs and correspondence of Charles James Fox*, ed. Lord J. Russell, I, 417.
[2] *CJI*, X, 378; XI, 197.
[3] Irish fears that the renunciation had not been complete were roused first by a wild speech from Lord Abingdon and then by a judicial ruling of Lord Mansfield. The renunciation act was 23 George III c. 28. One outcome of the agitation was to re-establish the reputation of Henry Flood and prepare the way for the important role he was to play in the reform campaign.
[4] Presumably the pseudonym was borrowed from William Molyneux (1656–98), the correspondent of John Locke and member for Dublin University, an ardent advocate of Irish legislative independence.
[5] *Dublin Evening Post*, 25 January 1783.
[6] 25 March 1783. *Molyneux*'s other letters can be found under 4 February, 18 April, 13 May, 27 May and 12 July.

of a parliamentary reform. By 17 March 1783 reform had become 'the very favourite topic of the day'.[1]

The Munster Volunteers' lead was followed in July by the delegates of forty-five companies assembled at Lisburne, who agreed to summon an Ulster meeting at Dungannon for September, and instituted a committee of correspondence to draw up proposals. The committee, under the chairmanship of Lt Col. Sharman, sought the advice of the leading reformers in England and Ireland: 'we are young in politics', they confessed engagingly. In particular, they emphasized that the favourite remedy of moderate reformers in England – the augmentation of the county representation – might be peculiarly inappropriate in Ireland, where aristocratic domination was so marked a feature.[2]

The replies received – from Charlemont and Grattan in Ireland, and Pitt, Jebb, Cartwright, Price, Effingham, Richmond and Wyvill in England – form a handbook of advanced opinion. Wyvill's reply, predictably, was the most constructive and systematic, Pitt's the briefest. Some of the issues were quickly despatched. Only Cartwright showed any sympathy for secret ballot, which he had been told worked to advantage in South Carolina: the rest repudiated it as evasive and unmanly. There was general approval of annual, or at least triennial, Parliaments, and a grudging acceptance of the need to pay compensation to dispossessed borough owners. But the critical question was the fourth – whether the right to vote should be extended. Wyvill and Price would have limited it to persons possessing some property; Effingham approved of manhood suffrage in theory, but would accept a scot and lot suffrage if it commanded wider support; Richmond, Jebb and Cartwright came out for complete manhood suffrage. Richmond's reply showed that he, at least, had considered how sufficient support was to be mobilized. Manhood suffrage, he argued, was tactically advantageous: 'all other plans that are of a palliative nature have been found insufficient to interest and animate the great body of the people, from whose earnestness alone any reform can be expected. A long exclusion...has rendered the great mass of the people indifferent whether the monopoly that subsists continues in the hands of a more or less extended company.'

---

[1] 'A barrister', *Hibernian Journal*, 14–17 March. It is possible of course that I have been taken in by a stage army, and that *Molyneux* and 'a barrister' are Francis Dobbs in disguise.
[2] *Proceedings relative to the Ulster Assembly of Volunteer Delegates*; Wyvill, III, 49–55. The committee proposed eight questions. (1) Should boroughs where the right of election was vested in a few be disfranchised and the county representation increased (2) should the House of Commons be more than 300 in number (3) was an increase in county representation desirable (4) should the right of voting be extended (5) should secret ballot be introduced (6) should parliaments be of shorter duration (7) should compensation be paid for disqualified boroughs (8) what mode of reform would the recipient recommend considering the nature of Ireland?

Even more important than the class issue was whether the vote should be given to Catholics, and here the correspondents showed clearly that they knew they stood on treacherous ground. Wyvill, who declared for complete equality, added a postscript recognizing that a propertied franchise must mean Catholic inferiority: in any case there could be no question of their admission to Parliament. The other replies were similar in tone, striking a brave attitude and modifying it on reflection. Richmond insisted that nothing short of evident danger to the state could justify religious discrimination, and added: 'but unacquainted as I am with the state of Ireland, it is impossible for me to know the present temper of the roman catholics there; and those only who are on the spot can judge how far exclusions of this sort are necessary'. Price followed suit: 'why should not a papist be attached to the liberties of his country as well as a protestant, *if he is allowed to share in them*' – but at the last minute the trumpet quavered and he finished feebly – 'there may be stronger objections to this than I am aware of'. Jebb and Effingham took refuge in the observation that only the Irish themselves could have the necessary information for a correct judgement of the problem.

Lt Col. Sharman's committee had thus been given clear advice on every issue save the vital one. But of greater immediate moment were the replies received from the leaders of Irish opinion. Lord Charlemont, a most cautious man and the commander of the Volunteer army itself, advised them to adopt no specific propositions but to submit the whole matter 'earnestly, warmly and respectfully' to the wisdom of Parliament: above all, they should avoid giving the appearance of dictating as a body of armed men. Grattan's opinion, privately confided to Charlemont, was equally moderate: 'there is another difficulty which I am sure you feel as I do. The repetitions of Dungannon meetings will alarm Parliament, as if the delegates were coming in place of the legislature...At the same time, I acknowledge that the business of a more equal representation might have little chance unless taken up by the people.' This was in marked contrast to Jebb's plea that the reformers should on no account petition Parliament, which implied submission, but present their demands boldly. It remained to be seen which course of action would be adopted.[1]

[1] Charlemont and Grattan's letters are in *HMC Charlemont*, I, 112–15. The rest were printed in many English, Irish and Scottish newspapers, and subsequently issued in two pamphlets, *A collection of letters which have been addressed to the volunteers of Ireland on the subject of a parliamentary reform*, London, 1783, and *Proceedings relative to the Ulster Assembly...on a more equal representation*, Belfast, 1783. Since these pamphlets are not easy to obtain, it might be helpful to indicate other places where the letters may be found. Wyvill: Wyvill, III, 79–82; *Dublin Evening Post*, 30 September; Price: *DEP*, 25 September, *Edinburgh Advertiser*, 24/8 October; Jebb: *DEP*, 27 September, *Saunders News Letter*, 10 and 14 October; Effingham: *DEP*, 11 October, *Saunders News Letter*, 14 October; Richmond: *DEP*, 4 October, *Saunders News Letter*, 3 and 4 October, *Edinburgh Evening*

The Dungannon meeting on 8 September 1783 attracted much attention. Five hundred representatives from 278 Volunteer corps took part, including fifteen members of Parliament, with the Earl of Bristol, Bishop of Derry, attending as a delegate from the Derry corps. The main decision was to invite the other provinces to join in a National Convention to assemble in Dublin on 10 November. The convention was to be asked to endorse a detailed programme of reform, including annual Parliaments, secret ballot, the abolition of decayed boroughs, augmentation of the county representation and anti-bribery legislation. The county franchise was to extend to forty-shilling freeholders and to owners of any kind of property worth £20 p.a. or more: the borough franchise should in addition extend to persons paying £5 p.a. in rent. On the vexed question of Catholic Emancipation, the meeting played safe by leaving it to such catholics as the Convention should deem 'proper objects for that great trust'.[1]

The reformers had embarked on a course which might well lead to a direct clash with the Irish Parliament. Charlemont took an extremely grave view of the prospects which, he thought, indicated a 'fatal convulsion'. The English government was also alarmed. 'I want words to express to you', wrote Fox to the Lord Lieutenant Northington 'how *critical* in the genuine sense of the word I conceive the present moment to be.'[2] Northington was less anxious. The rivalries and antagonisms latent in the movement, suitably stimulated, would be sufficient to render it harmless: his aim was to 'perplex its proceedings and create confusion in their deliberations'. In other words he intended to play the Catholic card, and hoped that it might be possible to embroil the Convention with the House of Commons.[3]

Northington's machinations were remarkably successful. The opening of the Convention was splendid and imposing, accompanied by military parades and the firing of cannon: the newspapers gave its proceedings the widest publicity. But from the very outset its deliberations were dogged by dissension. There was marked antagonism between Charlemont, elected President, and the Earl-Bishop, impatient at his caution. On the second day, as soon as real business commenced, the Castle administration showed its hand. General George Ogle informed the assembly that he had

Courant, 22 October. Richmond's reply was subsequently reprinted in pamphlet form as *Letter to Lt Col. Sharman*, copies of which were distributed by the Society for Constitutional Information in November 1783.
[1] Wyvill, III, 94–6. According to Charlemont, the committee brought forward a resolution in favour of Catholic equality, which was rejected. The statement above I take to be a compromise resolution. The matter is discussed in P. Rogers, *The Irish Volunteers and Catholic Emancipation, 1778–93*, 96–8.
[2] *HMC Charlemont*, I, 121; Russell, II, 163–4.
[3] Northington to Fox, 17 and 30 November, Russell, II, 175–6, 185.

a letter from Lord Kenmare, the acknowledged leader of the Catholics, stating that they made no claim to participation in the franchise. Though the Catholic committee immediately denied that this was the case and Kenmare himself wrote to disavow the letter, the damage was done. Many of the moderate delegates jumped at the chance of avoiding an embarrassing and acrimonious controversy. One delegate was quoted as observing that since the great object was parliamentary reform, 'he wished that religion had not been mentioned. From the papers on the table there was a difference of opinion in the roman catholics on the subject. How can we decide, when they themselves are divided?'[1] To the dismay of the Earl-Bishop and the Catholic sympathizers, it was agreed to shelve the question. The main business of drawing up proposals was handed over to a sub-committee, on which Henry Flood was the dominant influence, and on 29 November the Convention instructed him to present them at once to the House of Commons, resolving not to adjourn until the fate of their plans was known.[2]

The trial of strength between the Convention and Parliament which Northington had hoped to engineer was thus brought about by the action of the Convention itself, and Flood, in the uniform of a volunteer, hurried from the Rotunda to the Parliament House to move for a reform bill. All decayed boroughs were to have their boundaries extended to include the neighbouring parishes, after the fashion of the Shoreham and Cricklade reforms; Protestant leaseholders worth £10 p.a. were to have the vote; there were to be measures against non-residence; Parliaments were to last for not more than three years, and placemen were to be excluded from the House.[3]

There was little chance of the bill being discussed on its merits. The debate was tumultuous in the extreme. Government supporters had already decided that their best line was to refuse permission to proceed on the grounds that the bill's presentation was unlawful and intimidating. Barry Yelverton, the Attorney-General, declared that he would not sit there 'to receive propositions at the point of the bayonet', and Denis Daly warned his fellow members that 'while an armed assembly is sitting in the capital, your debate is not free'. Leave to introduce the bill was refused by 158 votes to 49, and for good measure the majority proceeded

---

[1] *Volunteer Journal*, 17 November. Kenmare's disavowal is in *Hibernian Journal*, 26/8 November. The *Dublin Evening Post*, 18 November carried the Catholic committee's assertion that it alone was competent to represent Catholic views. There is a full discussion in Rogers. The attitude originally attributed to Kenmare was not dissimilar from the one he adopted in 1792. See *Burke Corr.*, VII, 6 n. 1.

[2] For the Convention, see *History of the proceedings of the Volunteer delegates*, Dublin, 1784, and *HMC Charlemont*, I, 123–7. For hostile comments, see letters to Lord Buckinghamshire in *HMC Lothian*, 421–6. The Bishop of Cloyne's letter should be dated 29 November.   [3] Wyvill, III, 94–107.

to express its 'perfect satisfaction' with the constitution. 'It is the universal opinion', exulted Northington, 'that this day has given a most complete defeat to the Volunteers and to their Conventional Assembly.'[1]

At the first show of resistance, the Convention appears to have been nonplussed. It reverted to Charlemont's original plan and sent the proposals to the counties for comment so that they could be resubmitted free from the taint of military intimidation. The response in the spring of 1784 showed how widespread was the demand for reform, with 22 of the 32 counties and 11 boroughs forwarding petitions in support of it.[2] But the Irish House of Commons was adamant. Liberals who deplored the exclusion of the Catholics joined forces with the defenders of the established order to attack reform. John Monck Mason, member for St Canice, ridiculed the petitioners for having sought the assistance of 'every meddling priest and every political mountebank whose names they had read of in the English newspaper, whom they rendered the arbiters of the Irish constitution'. When Flood moved the second reading in March 1784, he was defeated by 159 votes to 85.[3]

Though the Volunteer movement was henceforth in decline, the summer of 1784 was an anxious one for the new Lord Lieutenant, the Duke of Rutland. There were widespread disturbances as the Catholics began to play a more active part, joining the movement in considerable numbers and reaching an understanding with some of the Presbyterians. There was much talk of French intervention and the government seriously contemplated arresting Newenham and the Earl-Bishop on charges of high treason. Grattan denounced the folly of drilling 'the lowest classes of the populace': the Volunteers had once been 'the armed property of Ireland. Were they to become the armed beggary?'[4] Support for the reform movement among the gentry and propertied classes fell away sharply and a national congress summoned for October 1784 met with a limited response. That the reform movement did not collapse completely was primarily due to hopes that Pitt might be willing to introduce some measure as a government proposal. This the Duke of Rutland strove to prevent: an erstwhile member of the Society for Constitutional Information, he was not the only Lord Lieutenant to suffer a sea-change on the voyage from Holyhead. To Pitt he wrote that though the Irish

---

[1] *Parl. Reg.* II, 226, 263; Russell, II, 186; J. Barrington, *Historic memoirs of Ireland*, II, 202. Johnston prints the division list on Flood's motion, pp. 391–401. Forty-one county members were in Flood's minority and only fourteen against.

[2] *CJI*, XI, part ii. Dublin submitted two petitions and there were petitions against from Co. Down and Kilkenny. Other estimates have been strangely at odds. Porritt, II, 243 thought there were thirteen petitions; Lecky, VI, 347 thought they came from twenty-six counties.

[3] *Parl. Reg.*, III, 47–8.

[4] *The speeches of Henry Grattan*, ed. H. Grattan, I, 212.

electoral system did not bear 'the smallest *resemblance to representation*, I do not see how quiet and good government could exist under any more popular mode'. Pitt's reply was to warn him not to commit the administration unequivocally against reform. 'Government', retorted Rutland, 'cannot embark in the measure without the risk of absolute ruin... If you admit Catholics to vote, your next parliament will be composed of papists; and should your reform only go to increase the number of protestant voters to the exclusion of the Catholics, I am convinced the latter would run into rebellion... In short, it would in my opinion be little less than lunacy for government here to involve itself with a question of so dangerous a tendency.' Rutland was strongly supported in the English cabinet and in January 1785 Lord Sydney wrote to inform him that if the question was again raised, he should endeavour to postpone any decision until it had been debated and decided at Westminster.[1] Pitt's defeat in April 1785 necessarily killed any chance of government action in Ireland, and when, ten days later, Flood rose to move for leave to present a bill, his cause was hopeless: 'I know the fate of reform in another country, and it has been told me in private, and will doubtless be urged here against any attempt at a reform now. But men who are enemies to a reform catch at any occurrence to oppose it.' The debate on the second reading was unanimated and turned mainly on whether the country at large wished for reform. Monck Mason made the traditional attack on 'factious agitators'; William Brownlow remarked that the 'greater the necessity of a reform, the less is the probability of it being carried'. Flood tried his hardest to shed the *damnosa hereditas* of the Convention: 'you have said the people have been seditious about it, and now you say they have no wish for it. When it was introduced before you objected to it, because it was, you said, on the point of a bayonet. It was an imaginary bayonet, like the imaginary dagger of Macbeth; but why did that dagger alarm him? Because his soul was filled with conscious guilt.' Flood's rhetoric, however charming, turned few votes, and the bill was rejected by 112 votes to 60. It is sufficient comment on the limits of that legislative independence Ireland had achieved in 1782 to note that the effective decision was still made in England.[2]

*   *   *   *

The Scottish reform movement might have been designed as a stark contrast to the Irish. Where the Irish movement was tempestuous and flamboyant, a thing of handsome uniforms and sparkling eloquence, the

---

[1] *Correspondence between William Pitt and Charles Duke of Rutland*, ed. John Duke of Rutland, 17, 32, 45, 79; *HMC Rutland*, III, 147–8, 161. The absence of any reference to reform in the Lord Lieutenant's speech at the opening of the session was commented on by Flood and others. There was much discussion of Wyvill's letter containing Pitt's promise to support reform as a man and a minister. *Parl. Reg.*, IV, 19–42.

[2] *Parl. Reg.*, V, 150–68, 188–96.

Scottish was sober, deliberate and restrained, the product of lawyers' disquisitions in Edinburgh coffee-houses. While the Irish delegates rushed from their Convention to urge their claims on the House of Commons within a matter of hours, the Scottish reformers built up their movement with such patient circumspection that at times it seemed to have expired in the process. The difference was, perhaps, one of national temperament, but more of tactics. The Scots had no Parliament sitting in Edinburgh to be overawed by a show of force. Nor had they a Volunteer movement and the English government was extremely anxious that they should not have one.[1]

The Scottish representative system was by far the most narrow and oligarchical of the three. In England perhaps one in ten of the male population had the right to vote; in Ireland, despite the exclusion of the Catholics, it was about one in twenty; in Scotland it was certainly less than one in a hundred.[2] Several of the Irish counties had substantial electorates: Down, the largest, had 6000 voters, and Antrim, Cork and Tyrone 3000 or more. By contrast the average for the Scottish counties was less than a hundred voters, and some, like Buteshire, Nairnshire and Cromartyshire, had fewer than twenty. While the electorate of Dublin in 1780 was 4000 that of Edinburgh was 33 – the members of the corporation. Henry Dundas, opposing reform in 1782, admitted that if anywhere needed it, it was 'the place from whence he came'.[3]

The Scots, like the Irish, were slow to awake to the issue of parliamentary reform. As late as July 1782 a well-informed Englishman, by no means hostile to reform, could write that it had not appeared that the Scots were at all dissatisfied with their representation.[4] In 1779 and 1780, while the campaign for economical reform was building up in England, the Scots were preoccupied with the threat of popery. There was no Scottish petition for economical reform: instead, in March 1780, Glasgow submitted a petition on behalf of its eighty-five societies, claiming to represent 12,000 people, against any concessions to the Catholics. There were of course other reasons for Scotland's slowness to respond. England was still regarded by most Scots as remote: even the Scottish Protestants were lukewarm about cooperation with their English brethren. In the

---

[1] There was considerable agitation on the subject in 1782 and Lord Graham, the member for Richmond, presented a bill for a Scottish militia. He was obliged to withdraw it. *The House of Commons, 1754–90*, eds. L. B. Namier & J. Brooke, II, 527.

[2] These figures are of course approximate. For the Scottish electorate, see above p. 28, the English see p. 30. The Irish electorate I take to be about 66,000, of whom 50,000 were county voters: this is based on Johnston, appendix B. In 1793 Dr Duigenan in the Irish House of Commons was of the opinion that the electorate did not exceed 60,000. *Parl. Reg.*, XXII, 101.

[3] *Parl. Hist.*, XXII, 1434.

[4] William Enfield, reviewing in *Monthly Review*, LXVII, 137. The owner of the University of Bristol copy has noted sourly in pencil: 'it has not appeared that England is'.

field of politics years of anti-Scottish propaganda by the Wilkites must have left some mark. When the Scottish movement came it was an almost totally indigenous one. The underlying cause was, however, similar to that in England – a growth in national prosperity and sophistication. 'The progress of improvement in agriculture, manufactures and commerce', wrote a newspaper correspondent in 1783, 'have been more rapid in the last thirty years than for centuries before.'[1] Scotland's distinguished cultural and intellectual life in the age of Hume, Adam Smith and Robertson contrasted strangely with her political sluggishness.

As in Ireland, the beginnings of the reform movement seem to be traceable to a pamphlet. On 27 March 1782 was published *An address to the landed gentlemen of Scotland*, complaining that the spread of fictitious and nominal voting in the Scottish counties was rendering elections a mockery: 'we might soon expect to see the meetings of elections for members of Parliament filled with the footmen, postilions, cooks, pimps and parasites of these mighty superiors'.[2] The remark struck home. Correspondents in Scottish newspapers took up the theme, and at the end of the following month a meeting of the freeholders of Inverness-shire declared that the practice was 'subversive of the freedom of election'. In May and June 1782 the freeholders of Elginshire and Caithness followed suit and appointed commissioners to consult with other counties on the question.[3]

The practice complained of had been a bone of contention in Scotland for many years. The franchise in the Scottish counties was extremely complex. The right to vote was possessed by freeholders of land of forty shillings 'of old extent' held of the crown, and by the owners of land held of the crown and rated for taxation at £400 Scots – that is, £33.6.8 English.[4] There were two evident defects. The definition 'of old extent'

---

[1] 'A burgher of Aberdeen', writing in the *Aberdeen Journal*, 16 June. See also Theophrastus' account of the advances in manners and travel between 1763 and 1783, *Edinburgh Evening Courant*, 7 January 1784. For a modern assessment of Scotland's economic progress in the period, see R. H. Campbell, *Scotland since 1707: the rise of an industrial society*. H. W. Meikle, *Scotland and the French Revolution*, 86–7 draws attention to the increase in newspapers at this time.   [2] B.M. 114. g. 53.
[3] *Aberdeen Journal*, 22 and 29 April 1782; *Caledonian Mercury*, 29 July 1782.
[4] Acts of the Scottish Parliament, VIII, 353 (1681). In addition the act enfranchised creditors in possession, mortgagees ('proper wadsetters'), apparent heirs and life-renters. A later act gave the vote to husbands on behalf of their wife's freehold. Sutherland had a special franchise which allowed vassals of the Earl to vote. For the definition of a 'proper wadset', see Porritt, II, 83. A helpful article is Sir James Fergusson, '"Making interest" in Scottish county elections', *Scottish Historical Review*, XXVI (1947), 119. A clear account of the reformers' grievances is given in a letter from Norman Macleod to Charles Grey, 30 November 1792, printed as an appendix by E. Hughes, 'The Scottish reform movement and Charles Grey, 1792–4', *Scottish Historical Review*, XXXV (1956), 39–41. A mass of information can be gathered from *View of the political state of Scotland in the last century*, ed. C. E. Adam.

was so archaic that only a few wealthy landowners qualified in each county. Secondly, as the competition for seats increased after the Act of Union, the practice had grown up of creating fictitious or nominal votes by sub-dividing property on behalf of trusted friends or dependents. The holders of these legal properties were known colloquially as 'parchment-barons' and might have votes in several counties. Acts in 1714 and 1734 to prevent splitting proved totally ineffective. The act of 1734 laid down a series of questions designed to verify whether the tenure was genuine or for electoral purposes: these the voters were required to answer before taking the oath and being enrolled.[1] The result was merely to disqualify the scrupulous and put a premium on lying. In the Ayrshire contest of 1774, in which Sir Adam Fergusson stood against David Kennedy, five of the latter's voters jibbed at the oath and he was defeated: it was said later that while three dragoons dared not take the oath three clergymen on Sir Adam's side were less squeamish.[2] Laurence Hill's canvass of the Scottish electorate in 1788 contains many conjectures – 'may or may not swear', 'doubtful if he will swear', 'will not like the oath', and so on.[3] Each general election produced its crop of contests decided by fictitious voting. The Cromarty contest of 1768 was followed by a legal action, the result of which was held to demonstrate that nominal votes could not be challenged at law.[4] In 1785 it was asserted that only 16 of the 92 voters of Inverness-shire had property within the county, and only 21 of Linlithgowshire's 57.[5]

The initiative of the three northern counties resulted in a meeting in the Prince's Street coffee-house on 5 August 1782, attended by representatives from 23 of the 33 shires. This drew up for consideration two bills – the first for the abolition of life-rent and wadset voting, and the second to reduce the qualification to £200 Scots.[6] These proposals were then sent to the county meetings for further discussion. The agitation in the counties stimulated in turn a movement for reform in the royal burghs of Scotland. The *Edinburgh Advertiser*, 2/6 August, contained the following appeal:

> In this time of political reform, when the counties are employed in cutting off fictitious votes and restoring the constitution, it is much to be wished that the inhabitants of the towns of Scotland would form associations for the same laudable purpose. How absurd it is...for

---

[1] 7 George II c. 16. A further unsuccessful attack was made on the problem in 1743 by 16 George II c. 11.
[2] *The House of Commons, 1754–90*, I, 472; *Aberdeen Journal*, 29 April 1782. For another example of nominal voters refusing the oath see the Linlithgowshire election of 1784.
[3] *View of the political state of Scotland in the last century.*
[4] *The House of Commons, 1754–90*, I, 476. A bill to forbid fictitious voting foundered in 1775.
[5] *CJ*, XL, 1110.
[6] B.M. 8142, f. 15 (3).

a junto of twenty or thirty men to elect a member of parliament, when even this junto is not chosen by the people at large, but elect and re-elect themselves *ad infinitum*.

Coupled with complaints against the oligarchical nature of the parliamentary franchise were accusations that the local magistrates, being unaccountable to the citizens, diverted public funds to their own pockets. As long ago as the reign of Charles II a commission had been appointed to investigate the allegations.[1]

Slowly life was breathed into the new movement. 'How ridiculous is it', wrote *Lucius Junius Brutus* in December 1782, 'that the almost unheard of towns of Inverury, Kintore, Rothesay, etc. should send a member to Parliament; while the flourishing boroughs of Leith, Greenock, Port Glasgow, Paisley, Borrowstounness send none.'[2] The most influential of the reform propagandists was Thomas McGrugar, an Edinburgh advocate, who, under the pseudonym of *Zeno*, claimed the franchise for those men 'in the middle ranks of life who generally constitute the majority of every free community'. His second letter commented on the re-election of Henry Dundas, Lord Advocate, for Edinburghshire on 2 January 1783 for the fifth successive time without opposition: 'if such is an election...can we, the citizens at large, be said to enjoy *civil liberty?*'[3]

Wyvill, hearing of the burgeoning Scottish movement, hastened to include a reference to the need for Scottish reform in the recommendations of the Yorkshire committee in November 1782, and opened up a correspondence with the citizens of Glasgow. But his hopes for massive support from across the border came to nothing. Feeling was against any close alliance with the English reform movement and even Wyvill must have thought the Scots tepid. The Provost of Glasgow returned a civil reply and agreed that it was an anomaly that in a thriving town of some 100,000 persons only the 30 members of the corporation should have the vote, but his main concern seems to have been that decorum should be preserved – the legislative should at all costs be treated with 'delicacy, moderation and attention'.[4] Only the boroughs of Montrose, Dumbarton and Irvine joined in the petitioning campaign in the spring of 1783.

The failure of Pitt's motion in May 1783 seems to have cast a blight on the Scottish movement. The proposals for county reform ran into hardening resistance. Opponents argued, with some plausibility, that the dis-

---

[1] A. Fletcher, *A memoir concerning the origin and progress of the reform proposed in the internal government of the Royal Burghs of Scotland*, 7–8.
[2] *Edinburgh Advertiser*, 24/7 December 1782.
[3] *Edinburgh Evening Courant*, 15 January 1783.
[4] Wyvill, II, 82–5. This was certainly different from the attitude of some of the Irish reformers. The *Volunteers Journal* of 14 November 1783 declared the absurdity of expecting redress from a 'CORRUPT, PROSTITUTE PARLIAMENT' and threatened it with the 'Vengeance of an INJURED AND LONG INSULTED NATION'.

qualification of fictitious votes would deprive some counties of almost all their electors, while the protagonists of reform seem to have been reluctant to press their proposals for the enfranchisement of the £200 Scots free-holder.[1] The electors of Renfrewshire declared against the bills, and in October 1783, reversing its decision of the previous year, the Edinburgh-shire head court came out against reform.[2] The Elginshire association carried its opposition to Lord Fife to the polls at the general election of 1784 but its chairman and candidate was badly beaten and his subsequent legal action and petition to Parliament were equally unsuccessful. Petitions from four counties were submitted to Parliament in 1785, but they were too late to support Pitt's motion, and there appears to have been no follow up.[3]

The burgh reform movement was of sturdier growth. The Merchant Company of Edinburgh, which had taken the lead in the spring of 1783, soon dropped out, but McGrugar was able to organize an association of Edinburgh citizens which made contact with similar groups in the other burghs. In March 1784 a convention at Edinburgh was attended by representatives from 33 of the 66 royal burghs. A committee appointed to consider two bills, one dealing with municipal and one with parliamentary reform, came to the conclusion that it would be premature to present them without more information from individual towns. But replies came in very slowly, and the defeat of Pitt's motion in 1785 persuaded them to abandon parliamentary reform in favour of internal reform, presumably in the hope that it would meet with less resistance. Another convention, in October 1785, attended by 49 representatives, resolved to hold annual meetings in August until reform was granted.[4]

In 1787 the reformers decided that the time had come for an appeal to Parliament. A preliminary statement emphasized that parliamentary re-form was no longer an issue: their case was 'manifestly distinguished from the reform that had been sought and denied in England'. A memorial stated their complaint with great clarity:

> The Magistrates and town-councillors in the Royal Boroughs of Scot-land are the governors of the police of the towns and the administra-tors of the common property; yet these men are totally unconnected

---

[1] See the interesting exchange between Sir Adam Fergusson and James Boswell at the Ayrshire meeting of October 1782. The latter described the Scottish county system as 'a representation of shadows'. *Edinburgh Advertiser*, 19/22 November 1782.

[2] *Edinburgh Advertiser*, 2/6 May, 3/7 October 1783.

[3] *The House of Commons, 1754–90*, I, 479–80; *CJ*, XL, 1109–10, 37, 464, 574, 767, 814.

[4] *Edinburgh Evening Courant*, 27 and 31 March 1784; *Caledonian Mercury*, 21 April 1783; *Edinburgh Evening Courant*, 19 and 22 October 1785. Reports of the successive annual meetings are in the *Caledonian Mercury* for 19 August 1786, 16 August 1787, 23 August 1788, 20 August 1789, 7 August 1790, 11 August 1791. See also Fletcher, 19–32.

with the burgesses whose common affairs they administer. They are self-elected into office; derive no power from the citizens; are not subject to their control in matters of public police; and are not in any respect accountable to them for the application of the public money.[1]

But the reformers found considerable difficulty in persuading any leading politician to take their cause under his wing. After George Dempster, Dundas, Beaufoy, Wilberforce and Pitt had declined, their committee sounded out Fox, who passed the matter on to Sheridan: 'he will bring it forward in all its force', Fox assured them. But Sheridan's parliamentary campaign had the impetuosity of a slow bicycle race.[2] The first move in the House of Commons was delayed until May 1787, when Dundas carried the adjournment without difficulty, arguing that the matter was too important to be debated at the end of the session and in a very thin house. The impact of forty-six petitions from the royal burghs the following year was wasted because Sheridan took action even later, and had to content himself with asking leave to present a bill so that the public could become acquainted with its contents. The 1789 attempt was later still, and Dundas, who had taken on the role of chief objector, was able to insinuate that grievances so listlessly pursued could not be very serious. In 1790 nothing whatever was attempted, perhaps because Sheridan and his friends were too busy preparing for the general election. A growing uneasiness can be detected in the report of the annual general meeting for August 1790: 'the delay in bringing forward the business in Parliament was well accounted for, and the consideration of having prudently attended to the proper circumstances and season in which the motion should be made with the best effect, rather than to gratify the solicitude of the public when it was not likely to answer any beneficial purpose, was happily illustrated'. The meeting also insisted that its proposals had 'not the remotest intention' of altering the constitution of the country, 'which they hold in the highest veneration'. In 1791, when Sheridan resumed his endeavours, he defended himself rather lamely from the accusation that the business had 'not been taken up with all the earnestness to which it was entitled'. The exchanges between Sheridan and Dundas had, by this time, become almost ritualized: Dundas objected to the matter being brought forward so late in the session, and Sheridan was easily persuaded

---

[1] Wyvill, III, 27–34. The opponents of burgh reform insisted that magistrates could be brought to account by the Convention of the Royal Burghs. That ancient institution had waged a counter-campaign against reform. But a test case over the burgh of Dumbarton in 1786 resulted in the decision that neither the Convention nor the Court of Exchequer had any jurisdiction. T. Pagan, *The convention of the royal burghs of Scotland*, 97–8; Fletcher, 51–7.
[2] Unfortunately the Sheridan MSS., which contained materials on the burgh reform movement, appear to have been destroyed in a bonfire. Info., C.R.O., Dorset. W. Sichel, Sheridan's biographer, saw them in the early years of the twentieth century.

to adopt Fox's advice to postpone the matter for yet another year. His 1792 oration was however a good deal more animated than usual, largely because he abandoned his unpromising subject in favour of a rhapsody on the French Revolution, which, he assured an incredulous House, had 'infused its benign influence through all our avocations of life; it mingled with the light which we enjoyed; it floated in the air which we breathed'. On Scottish burgh reform its benign influence was less evident, and the motion was defeated by 69 votes to 27.[1]

*   *   *   *

Neither bright bayonets nor inflexible perseverance had produced any concession. Superficially the Irish seem to have had the better chance. For the first time since the English civil war reformers had arms in their hands. But the threat constituted by the Volunteer Movement was effectively neutralized by the attitude of its commander, Lord Charlemont, equally unwilling to form an alliance with the Catholics or to entertain the use of force. Indeed, it is clear from his own remarks that his primary aim was the preservation of public order rather than the achievement of parliamentary reform, and one can understand the Earl-Bishop's irritation with him. But even if the threat of violence had been sufficient to force the Irish House of Commons to give way, there were more formidable obstacles to overcome. The Irish House of Lords, where the Castle administration was always strong, would resist. The King, with his deep-rooted fear of Catholicism, might refuse his consent. Most of all, the English government would certainly have been reluctant to see any measure of reform implemented, and the outcome might well have been to bring about the union of the two countries fifteen years before it was effected.

The difficulties facing the Scots were in some ways even more disheartening. They were well expressed in a letter to Charles Grey from Norman Macleod, the member for Inverness-shire, in 1792:[2]

> Kept out of view by your greater mass so as never to make our concerns be the principal objects even to our own representatives, at a distance so as not to make our cries be heard in the capital which alone awes an arbitrary government; our laws and our customs different so as to make our grievances unintelligible...We have suffered the misery which is perhaps inevitable to a lesser and remote country in a junction where the governing powers are united but the nations are not united.

[1] *Parl. Hist.*, XXVI, 1214–17; XXVII, 631–5; XXVIII, 221–6; XXIX, 636, 1183; *Caledonian Mercury*, 7 August 1790. The Lord Advocate, Robert Dundas, sponsored a bill in 1792 to improve the accounting in royal burghs, but the reformers denounced it as totally inadequate, and it was eventually dropped. Fletcher, 119–21. For the revival of interest in 1792, see N. Macleod to Grey, 4 July and 13 August, Grey MSS.

[2] Quoted E. Hughes, *Scottish Historical Review*, XXXV (1956), 35.

One advance had perhaps been made. The reformers in each country seem to have mastered the technique of fostering and directing a public opinion.[1] But they were hardly any nearer to the solution of their main problem – how to bring public opinion to bear, how to turn a demonstration into an instrument of political change, what to do when an unreformed Parliament rejected their proposals. Many suggestions were canvassed. Jebb's hope that it might be possible to by-pass Parliament by a revolutionary national convention was no more than fanciful. *Molyneux*, just before the Irish general election in the summer of 1783, had discussed the possibility of establishing a reform association which would buy up parliamentary seats and put supporters into them.[2] It was never attempted. Some wished to petition the King to use his prerogative to disqualify decayed boroughs: others suggested that *quo warranto* proceedings should be brought against delinquent boroughs. Other proposals included a non-importation agreement or a national refusal to pay taxes: 'Oh for some glorious Hampden to set a bright example to the nation', sighed the *Volunteer Journal*.[3]

From the years of failure and frustration two conclusions might perhaps have been drawn. The forces demanding reform could not hope to succeed until strengthened by the support of the labouring classes in England and Scotland, and by the Catholics in Ireland.[4] To obtain this support, the middle classes would have to make concessions: this they would do only when they became convinced of the truth of Richmond's proposition that without a mass following they would achieve nothing. Secondly, it was clear that they must obtain the assistance, if possible, of a governing party, or one which had a chance of governing. The Scottish experience served to show that the help of an opposition party was not necessarily a blessing:[5] the Irish, that the support of individuals – even when the individual was first minister – was not enough. The most sanguine reformer must have come to realize that the way ahead would be hard: how hard he had yet to learn.

[1] This is an area where exact proof cannot be supplied and the use of so many pseudonyms in the newspapers makes it easy for the historian to be deceived about the amount of interest aroused. But it scarcely seems coincidental that in each country a notable pamphlet, followed by a sustained newspaper campaign, got the movement on its feet. One has the feeling that in all three countries in this period a public response was fairly easy to raise and extremely difficult to sustain. Perhaps it still is.
[2] *Dublin Evening Post*, 13 May 1783. The suggestion was worked out in more detail in a pamphlet, *An address to the people of England and Ireland...more particularly adapted to the electors of the county of Limerick*.
[3] Quoted R. B. Macdowell, *Irish public opinion, 1750–1800*, 102.
[4] The Catholics in Ireland were of course also the labouring classes, but they were excluded from the franchise *as* Catholics. Otherwise Protestant reformers would not have objected to middle-class Catholics having the vote.
[5] It is only fair to add that the Scottish reformers were aware of this, and turned to Sheridan and the opposition only when it was evident that the supporters of administration would not help them.

6

Reformers' nightmare

Reformers' nightmare began as the sweetest of dreams – that a neighbouring land, long an adversary, flattering Britain by imitation, had flung off the yoke of absolutism, and established a moderate constitutional monarchy. From its influence reformers everywhere would draw new inspiration and new strength. 'I have lived', Richard Price told the Revolution Society in November 1789, 'to see the rights of men better understood than ever; and nations panting for liberty which seemed to have lost the idea of it. I have lived to see thirty millions of people, indignant and resolute, spurning at slavery and demanding liberty with an irresistible voice...And now, methinks, I see the ardour for liberty catching and spreading; a general amendment beginning in human affairs.'[1] These generous sentiments were reciprocated from across the channel in the most handsome terms. The Patriotic Union of Lille replied to the address of the Revolution Society in the language of intellectual homage: 'it must be owned, gentlemen, that in politics, you are the instructors and examples of the whole world. It is among you, yes, it is in your favoured isle that Liberty, everywhere attacked and trampled upon by Despotism, has formed a sacred asylum'.[2] It is not difficult to understand why many English reformers, derided for years by their fellow countrymen as cranks and eccentrics, should have been knocked off balance by such adulation.

First to move to exploit the changing situation was the Society for Constitutional Information. Since the collapse of the previous reform campaign it had busied itself chasing members in arrears and supporting miscellaneous good causes – prison reform, abolition of the slave trade, changes in the libel law, and the like. Now it followed up Price's lead, declared its conviction that a pure and equal representation would 'progressively take place in the several communities of Europe, and gradually extend over the globe', and urged its chairman, Henry Flood, to test

[1] *A Discourse on the love of our country*, a sermon preached on 4 Nov. 1789 to the Revolution Society, Earl Stanhope in the chair, 6th ed., pp. 49–50. The Revolution Society, composed mainly of dissenters, commemorated the Glorious Revolution of 1688 with an annual dinner. In the course of his remarks Price, a member of the Society for Constitutional Information, referred to the inadequacy of the representation as the main defect of the settlement – 'in truth, our fundamental grievance'.
[2] G. S. Veitch, *The genesis of parliamentary reform*, 129–30. Veitch did a great deal of work on the relations between the English and French societies, and his book is still extremely useful on that side.

opinion in Parliament once more.[1] But fast though the Society moved, events moved faster. Reports, coming in from France in the autumn, of murders and atrocities convinced many observers that the revolution was unlikely to limit itself to moderate constitutional reform, and the more excitable began already to fear the total overthrow of law and order. When Parliament reassembled in January 1790, after a recess of more than five months, this anxiety was soon in evidence. In the debate of 9 February on the army estimates, Burke made the first of his public onslaughts on the whole tendency of the revolution in France, comparing it disadvantage-ously to the Glorious Revolution of 1688. The declaration of the rights of man was, he insisted, no more than a 'digest of anarchy', and he warned the House that in England, 'some wicked persons had shown a strong dis-position to recommend an imitation of the French spirit of reform'.[2] Though a breach with Fox was averted, Sheridan rose to the bait, and an angry exchange with Burke ended in the latter renouncing all political connection. Three weeks later, the debate on Fox's motion to repeal the Test and Corporation Acts confirmed that opinion was hardening against reform of any kind. The previous year a similar motion had been rejected by the narrow margin of 122 votes to 102: this time Fox went down to defeat by 294 votes to 105.[3]

Flood's speech on 4 March 1790 was without question one of the most impressive made in support of reform up to then. The developments in France had put the problem into a totally different context, and introduced a new urgency. What had formerly been a fringe subject was fast becoming the central issue of political life. His specific proposal was for the increase of 100 members, to be elected by the resident householders in each county. The objection that this would render the House of Commons too large could be met by requiring the smaller boroughs to give up one of their two representatives. 'On this principle', explained Flood, 'I introduce four hundred thousand responsible citizens from the middle ranks of the people to fortify the constitution, and to render it impregnable.' The policy of defensive reform was, for the first time, clearly enunciated: 'I am no friend to revolutions...I am, therefore, a friend to timely reform.' The doctrine of virtual representation Flood treated with little respect. The American troubles, he reminded the House, 'began with virtual represen-tation and ended in dismemberment...Virtual parliaments and an inadequate representation have cost you enough abroad already; take care that they do not cost you more at home, by costing you your constitution.'

---

[1] E. C. Black, *The Association*, 209; C. B. Cone, *The English Jacobins*, 88.
[2] *Parl. Hist.*, XXVIII, 356, 358. Lord Stanhope produced a pamphlet in reply to Burke's strictures entitled *A Letter from Earl Stanhope to the Rt. Hon. Edmund Burke*. It is summarized in G. Stanhope & G. P. Gooch, *Life of Charles, third Earl Stanhope*, 89–93.
[3] *Parl. Hist.*, XXVIII, 41, 452.

Direct hostility to the motion was declared immediately by William Windham, Burke's disciple, who expressed dismay that a cause he had hoped dead had proved only to be sleeping. From his speech reformers might have guessed something of what was in store for them during the rest of the decade: 'Truly sorry am I to observe that swarms of these strange impracticable notions have lately been wafted over to us from the continent, to prey like locusts on the fair flowers of our soil. . . What would recommend you to repair your house in the hurricane season?' Pitt insisted that he was still a firm and zealous friend to reform but thought the time so unsuitable that he would move the adjournment, and though Fox came to Flood's support, it is clear that he too regarded the motion as inopportune. In the face of this reception, Flood withdrew.[1]

The reformers chose to ignore signs of the gathering storm. A joint meeting of friends to a parliamentary reform at the Crown and Anchor in April 1790 affirmed defiantly that it was 'peculiarly a proper time' to bring forward proposals, and a month later that the apostacy of 'the most ostentatious advocates' of reform should not be permitted to dampen the cause.[2] Almost total lack of success in the general election in mid-summer did not abate their enthusiasm, and on 14 July they held a monster banquet at the Crown and Anchor to celebrate the anniversary of the storming of the Bastille. Stanhope again was in the chair, and the 650 guests included Sheridan and several other members of Parliament. Amid the usual ecstatic toasts, Horne Tooke seems to have kept a rather cooler head than his companions, and perceived the danger of identifying the reform cause too completely with the French Revolution: when he attempted to suggest that the British constitution was fundamentally sound and stood only in need of repair while the French had to be totally reconstructed, he was shouted down.[3] Fraternal greetings were sent to the National Assembly in France, whose president replied in glowing terms: 'when shall we see that happy day in which governments shall be distinguished only by their humanity and good faith? It is to men like you, my Lord, and to the worthy members of your society that it is reserved to hasten this new revolution.' Such language was easily misunderstood, and confirmed the worst fears of the opponents of reform. 'This is the state of things', wrote Richard Burke, echoing his father's opinions, 'that excites the warm and tender passions, the sweet sentimental love and admiration of our English enthusiasts for liberty.'[4]

---

[1] *Parl. Hist.*, XXVIII, 452–79.
[2] The meeting was under the auspices of the Society for Constitutional Information and the Revolution Society. C. B. Cone, *The English Jacobins*, 89 thought that this meeting, fixed for 23 April, had been abandoned, but it is clearly the one reported in Wyvill, II, 564.
[3] *State Trials*, XXV, 389–91.
[4] *Life of Charles, third Earl Stanhope*, 95–6; *Burke Corr.*, VI, 126.

The rancour developing between reformers and their critics was immeasurably increased by the publication in November 1790 of Burke's *Reflections on the French Revolution*, followed five months later by the most notable reply, Paine's *The rights of man*. In many ways it was tragic that opinion should be polarized by these two books, equally brilliant and equally extreme. From his private correspondence it seems clear that what moved Burke most were reports of the treatment in France of the nobility and clergy, and the plight of the many refugees.[1] Sentiments of pity flowing strongly from an emotional man coincided with his deepest political instincts in favour of an aristocratic form of government. In the most passionate and celebrated section of his book Burke mourned the passing of the age of chivalry, and another key section was that in which he defended the nobility of France, 'the graceful ornament of the civil order...the Corinthian capital of polished society'. What had they done, he asked, 'that they were to be driven into exile, that their persons should be hunted about, mangled and tortured, their families dispersed, their houses laid in ashes, that their order should be abolished, and the memory of it, if possible, extinguished...?' Titles, retorted Paine coldly, were but nicknames – 'the thing is perfectly harmless in itself, but it marks a sort of foppery in the human character which degrades it'.[2]

Burke's book began with a sardonic attack on the Society for Constitutional Information, which he insisted on treating as a kind of charitable institution: 'it was intended for the circulation, at the expense of the members, of many books, which few others would be at the expense of buying...Whether the books so charitably circulated were ever as charitably read, is more than I know.' Paine, a member of the Society since 1787, replied with a detailed comparison between the new French and the old British Constitutions:[3]

> The constitution of France says, That every man who pays a tax of sixty sous *per annum* (2*s*. 6*d*. English) is an elector. What article will Mr Burke place against this? Can anything be more limited, and at the same time more capricious than the qualifications of electors are in England?...The French constitution says, That the number of representatives for any place shall be in a ratio to the number of taxable inhabitants or electors. What article will Mr Burke place against this? The county of Yorkshire, which contains nearly a million of souls, sends two county members; and so does the county of Rutland, which contains not an hundredth part of that number...Is there any principle in these things?

[1] See Burke to Windham, 27 February 1789, *Burke Corr.*, VI, 24–6, and H. W. Meikle, 69, n. 3.
[2] *The rights of man*, ed. H. B. Bonner, 46.
[3] Pp. 38–9.

The first part of *The rights of man* was inflammatory enough – 'the most seditious pamphlet ever seen but in open rebellion', thought Horace Walpole – but the second part, published in February 1792, broke completely new ground, with a sketch for a social and political revolution. Monarchy and aristocracy, Paine predicted, would not survive seven years longer in any enlightened European country. His proposals included payment of members, graduated income tax, family allowances, old age pensions from the age of fifty, and a public works programme. But most alarming of all to people of property was the undeniable strain of class hatred in Paine's references to the aristocracy and the monarchy. The Duke of Richmond, he reminded his readers, 'takes away as much for himself as would maintain two thousand poor and aged persons', while of the Hanoverian dynasty he wrote: 'it has cost England almost seventy millions sterling to maintain a family imported from abroad, of very inferior capacity to thousands in the nation; and scarcely a year has passed that has not produced some mercenary application. Even the physicians' bills have been sent to the public to be paid.'[1]

Though Paine had little faith in simple parliamentary reform, many were delighted at such a champion. The Society for Constitutional Information recommended his book to the nation, and one enthusiast wrote to taunt Burke on the 'magnificent answer' he had provoked.[2] Certainly Paine captured the interest of vast numbers of the labouring classes, who had remained indifferent to the mild proposals of Wyvill or the arid constitutionalism of Major Cartwright. By providing the missing link between parliamentary reform and social and economic progress Paine demonstrated how a mass response might be effected. But the price paid was enormous. Paine's work seemed a triumphant justification of those who had argued that parliamentary reform would be but the prelude to social revolution and that the moderates would never be able to control their wild men. For a generation the cause of reform was inexorably linked with godless republicanism and the total overthrow of established society.[3] It was the signal for many of the middle class sympathizers to disembark. Worst of all, Paine tied the reform movement to the juggernaut of the French Revolution at precisely the moment when events were shaping to produce a direct clash between Britain and France. By doing so he ensured that the force of patriotism would come to the aid of those resisting change.

One immediate consequence of the frenetic controversy of 1791 was the foundation of a series of radical reform clubs, organized by working men.

[1] Pp. 205, 216.
[2] *State trials*, XXIV, 281; Henry Wisemore to Burke, 16 April 1791, *Burke Corr.*, VI, 246–7.
[3] Paine was in fact a deist as his later publication *The age of reason* made clear, but the distinction was little regarded.

One of the first, established late in 1791 under the name of the Sheffield Society for Constitutional Information, began by publishing a cheap edition of Paine's book, and within a few months was claiming more than two thousand members. 'Tradesmen and artificers' was the description they gave of themselves a little later.[1] With the arrival in the reform movement of this new element came a significant change of interest: less was heard about the merits of the Anglo-Saxon constitution and more about the living conditions of the poor. The aim of the Society, said one of its secretaries, was 'to show the people the reason, the ground of all their complaints and sufferings; when a man works hard for thirteen or fourteen hours of the day, the week through, and is not able to maintain his family'.[2] Into the writings of the period came the note of class antagonism. 'While the rich enjoy almost all the benefits', wrote one pamphleteer, 'the poor undergo all the labour. The rich, in many instances, have little to do but to give orders, or to sign their names, and sometimes not even that.'[3]

The Sheffield Society's arrangement into divisions was copied by its more famous counterpart, the London Corresponding Society, founded by the shoemaker Thomas Hardy and seven other members in January 1792. The membership fee of one shilling, followed by a penny a week, was in pointed contrast to the five guineas *per annum* demanded by the Society for Constitutional Information. The new London society made rapid progress, and in August 1792 distributed *gratis* copies of a demand for reform, with a social programme obviously derived from Paine.[4] Though not all the members of the new working men's clubs were as sober and dedicated as Francis Place later maintained, their stamina, endurance and capacity for organization distinguished them sharply from the riotous followers of John Wilkes, a generation earlier.[5]

More moderate advocates of reform watched these developments with uneasiness, lest the imprudence and zeal of the new recruits should injure the cause. In April 1792 a group of members of Parliament

---

[1] In their petition of 1792. *Parl. Hist.*, xxx, 775–6.
[2] William Broomhead's evidence at the trial of Thomas Hardy in 1794. *State Trials*, xxiv, 630.
[3] G. Dyer, *The complaints of the poor people of England*, 1793.
[4] 'Soon then we should see our liberties restored, the press free, the laws simplified, judges unbiassed, juries independent, needless places and pensions retrenched, immoderate salaries reduced, the public better served, taxes diminished, and the necessaries of life more within the reach of the poor, youth better educated, prisons less crowded, old age better provided for, and sumptuous feasts at the expense of the starving poor less frequent. Look not upon this, dear countrymen, as an enthusiastic vision.' *State Trials*, xxv, 590–2.
[5] See E. P. Thompson, *The making of the English working class*, 183, and Gwyn Williams, *Artisans and sans-culottes: popular movements in France and Britain during the French Revolution*.

among the Foxite opposition formed their own association – part ally and part rival to the radical societies. The leaders of the Society of the Friends of the People were Lauderdale and Buchan in the peerage, and Charles Grey, Sheridan, Francis, Thomas Erskine, Lambton and Whitbread in the Commons. George Tierney, not then an MP, was one of the joint treasurers: Fox, for tactical reasons, did not join.[1] With a subscription of $2\frac{1}{2}$ guineas and a cautious process of nomination there was little danger of infiltration by the labouring classes, and the policy adopted was deliberately moderate, calling merely for a more equal representation and more frequent elections. Of their opponents the Friends declared – 'they will not innovate, but they are no enemies to gradual decay'.[2] On 30 April 1792 Grey gave notice in the House of Commons that he would move for reform next session, and Tierney began work on a summary of the state of the representation which was to prepare public opinion.[3]

Though Grey disclaimed any sympathy for those who intended to 'promote confusion and excite mischief', his reception by the House was hostile. Pitt replied that Grey and his associates were connected with persons whose aim was not reform but 'the overthrow of the whole system of our present government...all, all might be lost by an indiscreet attempt'. Burke declared that there were men in the country who made no scruple of alliance with 'a set in France of the worst traitors and regicides that had ever been heard of – the club of the Jacobins'. Windham supported Burke, but reserved his deepest fears for his private correspondence:[4]

I can consider it as nothing but the first big drops of that storm, which having already deluged France is driving fast to this country...Sup-

---

[1] The question of the motivation of the Friends of the People is discussed in H. Butterfield, 'Charles James Fox and the Whig Opposition', *Cambridge Historical Journal*, IX (1949). He pointedly denies that the Friends were alarmed at the growth of radical organizations, relying on the remark in their Address about 'general tranquillity'. But their argument in the Address is somewhat conflicting, for it continues that if, in the general tranquillity, there is 'some mixture of discontent...we wish it to be considered by men whose judgement has been formed or enlightened by experience, and whose actions are most likely to be directed by prudence'. By 30 April, when Grey raised the matter in the House of Commons, the defensive element was even more to the fore: 'the times were critical and the minds of the people agitated' – only a timely and temperate reform could avoid the danger of 'civil commotion'. Further evidence on the foundation of the Society is given by L. G. Mitchell, *Charles James Fox and the disintegration of the Whig party, 1782–94*, 176–7.

Fox's lack of enthusiasm for raising the issue at this time may be gauged from his letter to Fitzwilliam quoted by Butterfield, 297.　　[2] Wyvill, III, appendix, 128ff.
[3] E. C. Black shows that Tierney's work was largely a summary of T. H. B. Oldfield's *History of the boroughs*, published in 1792. This was a detailed work, produced under the auspices of the Society for Constitutional Information, and destined, like Burgh, to become a mine of information for reformers. Professor Black gives much interesting biographical information on Oldfield in appendix A. One might perhaps add that Oldfield had acted as secretary to the Westminster Association in 1783/4.
[4] *The Windham Papers*, ed. Lord Rosebery, I, 100–5.

pose someone should take it into their head to write a work addressed
to the labouring people, exposing to them the iniquity of that system
which condemns half the world to labour for the other, and pleading
for such a partition of goods as may give to every one a competence
and leave to none a superfluity?

Windham was not alone in seeing the position of his class in jeopardy.
From Switzerland Gibbon wrote during the same month to remind his
correspondent of the fate of the monarchy and nobility in France: 'they
are crumbled into dust; they are vanished from the earth. If this tremen-
dous warning has no effect on the men of property in England, if it does
not open every eye and raise every arm, you will deserve your fate.'[1]

The Friends of the People soon discovered how disagreeable it was to
be moderate in a world running to extremes. Denounced by many of their
colleagues as traitors to their own class, they were simultaneously mocked
by the radicals as patronizing and half-hearted. The Sheffield Society was
as respectful as though Paine had never written, and assured the Friends
that its members looked up to them as 'our leaders and directors in this
great and necessary business', but the Society for Constitutional Information, conscious of its role as elder society, approached 'its new brethren'
with unsolicited and offensive advice:[2]

It is not the first time that members of that House have professed
themselves reformers. It is not the first time that they have entered
into popular associations; but should they, on this occasion, prove
faithfully instrumental in effecting a substantial reform...it *will* be
the first time that the nation hath not found itself in an error, when it
placed confidence in associated members of parliament for the recovery of the constitutional and inestimable rights of the people.

Above all, warned the Society for Constitutional Information, the Friends
must lay aside 'all aristocratic reserves', and work with the cooperation
and understanding of the people for the implementation of their rights,
'in their full extent'. This was by no means what the new Society had in
mind. They replied bluntly that they, too, would not permit delicacy to
inhibit frankness, deplored the 'indefinite language of delusion' employed
by the Society for Constitutional Information, and repudiated any connection with a body that had endorsed the doctrines of Paine. Though
relations between the Friends and the London Corresponding Society
were rather warmer, and Hardy subsequently paid handsome tribute to the
assistance he had received, by the end of the year they were at odds over
the declarations of sympathy sent by the London Corresponding Society
to the new French Convention.

[1] Gibbon to Lord Sheffield, 30 May 1792, *Letters*, ed. J. E. Norton, III, 258.
[2] Wyvill, III, appendix, 150.

These animosities between fellow reformers were the struggles of men fighting in the condemned cell. The 'season of general tranquillity' which the Friends had claimed to detect in the spring of 1792 did not last long. The attack on the Tuileries in August was followed in quick succession by the hideous excesses of the September massacres, the abolition of the monarchy, and the Convention's announcement that it would assist all peoples struggling to achieve liberty. Opinion in England shifted rapidly. John Reeves' *Association for the preservation of liberty and property against republicans and levellers*, founded on 20 November, evoked an ecstatic response. Branches were formed in town after town. Middle-class audiences interrupted theatrical performances with protracted singing of *God save the King* and *Rule Britannia*, while the labouring classes, sometimes with a little gentle encouragement, burned Tom Paine in effigy. December 1792 witnessed a frenzy of loyalty as relations between France and Britain approached breaking point. The readers of one Bristol newspaper were regaled with a 'Constitutional Song', which, if not poetic, was fervent:[1]

> Why let them who are friends to PAINE
> Sound his ignoble merit;
> We Britons ever will maintain
> A loyal English spirit.
>
> *Chorus*
> Let every loyal subject sing
> Long stand our constitution;
> While England has so GOOD a KING
> We want no revolution.

William Cowper spoke for many who had at first welcomed the Revolution when he commented in January 1793 on the execution of Louis XVI: 'I will tell you what the French have done. They have made me weep for a King of France, which I never thought to do, and they have made me sick of the very name of liberty, which I never thought to be.'[2]

The Friends of the People found their position increasingly uncomfortable. Events in France, wrote Tierney in October 1792, had made 'one party here desperate and the other drunk. Many are become wild republicans who a few months back were moderate reformers, and numbers who six weeks ago were contented with plain old-fashioned Toryism have now worked themselves up into such apprehensions for the fate of royalty as to be incapable of distinguishing between reform and treason'.[3] Lord

[1] *Sarah Farley's Bristol Journal*, 15 Dec. 1792.
[2] Cowper to William Hayley, 29 January 1793, *Correspondence*, ed. T. Wright, IV, 363–4.
[3] Tierney to Grey, 20 October 1792, quoted G. M. Trevelyan, *Lord Grey of the Reform Bill*, 60.

Stanhope was sure that no move for reform ought to be made, and Wyvill wrote in January 1793 that it would be 'ruinous' to summon a county meeting to petition.[1] Yet Grey was pledged to make the effort. If not, warned the Scottish reformer, Lord Daer, 'many will consider it almost treachery in you and your friends'.[2] Without hope the Society decided to press on. But by the time Tierney's *Report on the state of parliamentary representation* was ready for publication in February 1793, the French government had declared war.[3] A ragged fusillade of petitions, mostly from Scotland, anticipated Grey's motion, but it was difficult to maintain that any widespread demand for reform existed.[4] Grey did his best to shake off the curse of France when he opened the debate on 6 May – 'it was impossible that any set of men who had not actually lost their senses should ever propose the French revolution as a model for imitation' – but it was to no avail. 'His honourable friend', retorted Windham, 'might open the door, but would he be able to shut it?' Windham's question, in various guises, dominated the debate, and in the division Grey was beaten by 282 votes to 41.[5]

*　　*　　*　　*

In the meantime, for some reformers, the ordeal had already commenced. First to suffer, in July 1791, were the middle-class dissenters of Birmingham, terrorized for three days by a 'Church and King' mob that the magistrates either could not or would not suppress. It is not difficult to understand why many dissenters favoured reform and felt a good deal of sympathy for the French Revolution. The defeat of their own efforts to force repeal of the Test and Corporation Acts in 1787, 1789 and 1790 persuaded many that they had nothing for which to hope from an unreformed Parliament: at the same time, French non-Catholics had been granted complete religious equality under the new constitution.[6] In all, three meeting houses and some dozen private residences were attacked. Though the most recent investigation has suggested a strong class element

[1] Stanhope to Wyvill, 18 September 1792, *Life*, 121; Wyvill to Capel Lofft, 6 January 1793, Wyvill, v, 105–6.
[2] 17 January 1793, Grey MSS., quoted E. Hughes, *Scottish Historical Review*, xxxv (1956), 26–41.
[3] Tierney was primarily concerned to demonstrate the extent of patronage in the representative system. His report claimed that 257 members for England and Wales were returned by 11,075 voters. 71 peers, 91 commoners and the Treasury were said to nominate or influence the returns of 306 of the 513 English and Welsh members. Wyvill, iii, appendix, 189–251.
[4] There were 36 petitions in all, 24 from Scotland. Some of the unrepresented towns, such as Birmingham, Huddersfield and Dunfermline, showed interest, but no county petitioned, and the overall response was tiny. The Sheffield petition was rejected as derogatory to the dignity of the House of Commons, and a petition from Norwich, signed by 3700 persons, was disqualified as a printed submission. *CJ*, XLVIII, 724–5, 729–31, 735–43; *Parl. Hist.*, xxx, 775–86.   [5] *Parl. Hist.*, xxx, 787–925.
[6] Article X of the Declaration of the Rights of Man, and the decree of 24 Dec. 1789.

in the riots, it remains true that the original provocation was a dinner held by reformers to celebrate the anniversary of the storming of the Bastille, and that none but dissenters suffered.[1]

Action in some form against Thomas Paine was to be expected, and by his spirited attack upon hereditary monarchy and aristocracy, he may be said to have courted it. The government made no move against Part One of *The rights of man*, and instituted proceedings against Part Two only after cheap editions had been brought out, aimed not at 'the judicious reader' but the masses. In May 1792 a royal proclamation against seditious writings, hotly debated in Parliament, was presumed to be directed at Paine, and the following month he was indicted on a charge of seditious libel. Whatever slight chance there was of his acquittal was certainly removed by a letter addressed by Paine from Paris to the Attorney-General, expressing contempt for the decision of the court, and asking: 'is it possible that you or I can believe, that the capacity of such a man as Mr Guelph, or any of his profligate sons, is necessary for the government of a nation?' Thomas Erskine, conducting the defence in Paine's absence, strove to show that there was no attack on the rights of property, and that Paine's polemics were within the bounds of legitimate controversy, but the jury excused the Attorney-General from the need to reply, and found Paine guilty.

The full weight of the growing loyalist reaction was first felt not in England but in Scotland, where a vigorous parliamentary reform movement had grown up in the course of 1792, just as the old burgh reform movement was expiring.[2] Though many of the Scottish organizations called themselves Friends of the People, they had more in common with the London Corresponding Society than with Grey and his associates. Henry Dundas, Home Secretary and Pitt's chief lieutenant, on a prolonged visit to Scotland in the autumn, was most alarmed at what he found. Societies were spreading rapidly, disturbances were not uncommon, and that most of the reformers expressly repudiated violence was taken merely as evidence of hypocrisy. In November Dundas reported

[1] R. B. Rose, 'The Priestley Riots of 1791', *Past & Present*, no. 18 (1960), pp. 68–88. The most celebrated victim was Joseph Priestley, whose library and scientific equipment was destroyed, along with many memoranda and notes. Priestley had provoked resentment by some incautious remarks about putting gunpowder under the old building of error and superstition. W. Hutton, *History of Birmingham*, 422. The text of an inflammatory handbill circulated in Birmingham is printed in the *Annual Register* (1791), chronicle, 29. Denounced by the reformers as a forgery, it carries some conviction: F. W. Gibbs, *Joseph Priestley*, 197–8 suggests that it may have been by William Stone, one of the Hackney dissenting group. A motion in the House of Commons by Whitbread for an enquiry was rejected. *Parl. Hist.*, XXIX, 1431–64.
[2] The burgh reformers had for the most part little respect for the radicals. See A. Fletcher, *Memoir*, 126–9; *Autobiography of Mrs Fletcher*, 65; Minutes of the first general convention, printed as appendix A by Meikle, 261–6.

that it would soon become necessary to augment the armed forces available, and the royal proclamation of December 1, calling out part of the militia, was justified by reference to the Scottish situation.[1] There is little doubt that the government somewhat overestimated the danger on this occasion. Dundas and Pitt seemed embarrassed at the paucity of the evidence to support the proclamation, while Lord Daer admitted to Grey that the number of declared friends to reform was 'contemptible'.[2] But later, in December, the summoning of a reform convention in Edinburgh gave further cause for alarm. The following month began a series of trials for sedition or seditious libel, remarkable chiefly for the freedom with which the judges expressed their own views. At the trial of three young men, accused of attempting to suborn some of the garrison of Edinburgh Castle, Lord Henderland declared of the reform clubs: 'I like not their names. The Friends of the People, and a Club for Equality and Freedom! What occasion for such associations, with such names? Are not the people protected in the enjoyment of their constitutional rights, and in reaping the fruits of their industry?' Braxfield, the Lord Justice Clerk, followed this up with the observation that the low-born had no right to a share in the representation: 'the landed interest alone should be represented in Parliament, for they only hae an interest in the country'.[3]

These were but the preliminaries to the sensational trials later in the year that went far towards smashing the Scottish reform movement. Thomas Muir, an Edinburgh lawyer aged 27, had taken a prominent and militant part in the general convention of December 1792. In August 1793 he was charged with sedition. The trial itself was a monstrous farce. The main accusations were that Muir had exhorted people to read Paine, and that at the convention he had been responsible for the reception of treasonable communications from the United Irishmen. Muir objected in vain to the jury, every member of which belonged to the Goldsmith's Hall Association, a loyalist club. The court made no attempt at impartiality. On the indictment, Lord Swinton observed that it was such as he had never before heard, with hardly a line that would not warrant a charge of high treason. Muir conducted his defence with considerable ability, though calling attention to the anomalous position of Pitt and Richmond – 'shall what was patriotism in 1782 be criminal in 1793?' – was more likely to irritate than persuade. Of Muir's attempts to organize a petition to Parliament for manhood suffrage, Braxfield commented: 'Mr Muir might have known that no attention could be paid to such a rabble. What right had they to representation?' In examining the question,

[1] Meikle, 95; *Parl. Hist.*, XXX, 1–80.
[2] Pitt to Dundas, 4 December 1792, Stanhope, II, 176–7; *Scottish Historical Review*, XXXV (1956), 34.
[3] *State Trials*, XXIII, 12, 43.

Braxfield told the jury, there were 'two things you should attend to, which require no proof. The first is, that the British Constitution is the best in the world...Is not every man secure in his life, liberty and property?' But Braxfield's most disreputable remark was reserved until the end. Sentencing Muir to fourteen years transportation, he confessed that expressions of support for the defendant from onlookers in court had had 'no little weight with him when considering of the punishment Mr Muir deserved.' From this sentence there was, under Scottish law, no appeal.[1]

The following month, Thomas Fyshe Palmer, a Unitarian minister, was sentenced to seven years transportation for seditious practices. The crown witnesses admitted that Palmer had advised against publishing an inflammatory address and had tried to moderate certain passages, but the prosecution construed this as a 'demonstration of the criminality of his intention', and the court took a similar view.[2]

In the early months of 1794 there were several more prosecutions arising out of the holding of reform conventions. The rejection of Grey's motion in 1793 encouraged the more militant elements, and a national convention was summoned in Edinburgh during October. The London Corresponding Society, the Society for Constitutional Information and the Sheffield society all sent delegates, and there were representatives from the United Irishmen. After the meeting had declared itself a British Convention and appointed a secret committee to act in case of emergency the authorities broke it up and placed the secretary, William Skirving and the two London Corresponding Society delegates, Maurice Margarot and Joseph Gerrald under arrest. Charged with sedition, they were each given sentences of fourteen years transportation. For what purpose, demanded Skirving's prosecutor, had the convention assembled? 'For the purpose of obtaining universal suffrage; in other words, for the purpose of subverting the government of Great Britain.'[3] Of the five transported, only Margarot lived to see Britain again.[4]

There was a tragi-comical postscript to the sedition trials. Deprived of all responsible leadership, the remnant of the Scottish reform movement fell under the influence of Robert Watt, who appears to have enrolled as a government informer, only to suffer a genuine conversion to the cause.[5] During 1794 he evolved an absurd plan to manufacture pikes, seize

---

[1] *State trials*, XXIII, 117–238. For a rather different view of the trial, see W. Ferguson *Scotland 1689 to the present*, 256–8. The trials were debated at considerable length i both Houses of Parliament. *Parl. Hist.*, XXX, 1298–1308, 1346–53, 1449–61, 1486–1576.
[2] *State trials*, XXIII, 237–382.   [3] *State trials*, XXIII, 486–7.
[4] Skirving and Gerrald died in Australia in 1796; Muir escaped and made his way to France, where he died in 1799; Fyshe Palmer died in 1802 on his way home.
[5] At the trial of Thomas Hardy, Gibbs put forward an alternative view that Watt was trying to reinstate himself as an informer by creating and then unmasking a sensational plot. *State Trials*, XXIV, 1146.

Edinburgh Castle, and establish a provisional revolutionary government. When the total of finished weapons had reached fourteen pikes and two battle-axes, the government swooped. Charged with high treason, Watt was convicted in October 1794, and executed the following month.

The government's decision to take strong action against the English societies seems to have been prompted in part by the success of the London Corresponding Society's new policy of open-air meetings, and in part by the decision to organize an English convention in the summer of 1794.[1] In May Habeas Corpus was suspended, and the government arrested seven members of the London Corresponding Society, including Hardy its secretary and John Thelwall, its best orator, and six members of the Society for Constitutional Information, including John Horne Tooke, but excluding Cartwright.

The debates in the House of Commons on the suspension of Habeas Corpus were among the fiercest of the century, the small Foxite opposition dividing against the bill time and time again. The evidence of letters and addresses, produced by the committee of secrecy to justify the proceedings, were dismissed by the opposition as known to everyone through newspaper publication, while the new evidence suggesting attempts by some societies to procure arms was not strong. Pitt opened the debate with an attack on the doctrine of the Rights of Man which even Burke could scarcely have exceeded:

> That monstrous doctrine, under which the weak and ignorant, who are most susceptible of impression from such barren, abstract positions, were attempted to be seduced to overturn government, law, property, security, religion, order and everything valuable in this country, as men acting upon the same ideas had already overturned and destroyed everything in France.

On the third reading, Grey retaliated with an uncharacteristically passionate attack on Pitt himself as the grand apostate: 'William Pitt, the reformer of that day (1782) was William Pitt, the prosecutor, aye and persecutor too, of reformers now.' If it were criminal to declare that no reform was to be expected from Parliament without pressure by the people, he avowed it as his own conviction. If belief in universal suffrage was in itself seditious, why was the Duke of Richmond not under lock and key?[2]

Of the thirteen arrested, only three were brought to trial. The first was Hardy, charged at the Old Bailey with high treason. Charles Grey, who

---

[1] There had of course been prosecutions of individuals at an earlier stage, notably of John Frost, an attorney member of the Society for Constitutional Information, sentenced in May 1793 to six months gaol for declaring in a coffee-house that he was for equality and no King.
[2] *Parl. Hist.*, XXXI, 497–605.

attended the trial, was convinced that the fate of all reformers turned on the verdict: 'if this man is hanged', he wrote to his future wife, 'there is no safety for any man...and I do not know how soon it may come to my turn'.[1] The prosecution's case made up in quantity for any defects in relevance: the attorney-general's opening speech lasted nine hours, and the trial went on for eight days. The evidence about arms could not be brought home to Hardy, and in any case amounted to very little.[2] More damaging were letters exchanged with some of the provincial societies. The Stockport Society of the Friends of Universal Peace had certainly urged a convention, with the implication that it could overrule Parliament,[3] while the Society for Political Information at Norwich had addressed to the London Corresponding Society a question that was either very naive or very disingenuous: 'it is desired to know whether the generality of the societies mean to rest satisfied with the Duke of Richmond's plan only, or whether it is their private design to rip up monarchy by the roots and place democracy in its stead?' Yet however seditious these observations might be they afforded justification for a prosecution of their authors rather than the recipient who, as secretary of a society, was scarcely to be held responsible for letters addressed to him. In reply the London Corresponding Society had advised their Norwich friends to 'above all, be careful to preserve peace and good order among you; let no dispute be carried to excess; leave monarchy, democracy and even religion entirely aside'. Prosecuting counsel thought this a far less specific disavowal of violence than was called for, but the jury must have taken a different view, for they found Hardy not guilty after a very short recess.[4]

The trial of Horne Tooke a fortnight later attracted if anything more attention, since he was a gentleman, a man of letters, and had been a well-known political figure since the days of Wilkes and Liberty. The fourth day of the trial saw a parade of reformers, past and present, Fox, Cartwright,

[1] Quoted Trevelyan, 85.
[2] Defence counsel dismissed it as a 'miserable case...This array preparing against the government of the country...had for its support no more than three dozen of pikes; and I do not know whether it was an order, or only a conversation about an order, for sixty muskets, for the Lambeth Association, and three or four French knives'. *State Trials*, XXIV, 1136, 1148. It is only fair to add that pikes, which do not sound very formidable to modern ears, were the mainstay of the Irish rebellion in 1798, and proved very effective against cavalry.
[3] 'Does it appear probable', wrote the Stockport Society, 'that the odious laws which we complain of will be abolished any other way? Can the grievances arising from the aristocracy be redressed while the House of Lords retains its present authority in the legislature?' The second was a very pertinent question, as the events of 1831–2 were to show. *State Trials*, XXIV, 388.
[4] Henry Crabb Robinson, then a 19-year-old clerk in a Norwich office, recalled that he had been too excited to work during the trial and celebrated the verdict by running around the streets, 'knocking at people's doors and screaming out the joyful words'. *Diaries*, I, 27.

Sheridan, Wyvill, Francis and Stanhope sharing the witness box with Pitt and the Duke of Richmond, subpoenaed by the defence and subjected to some very harassing questioning by Horne Tooke. Despite the affliction of a remarkably bad memory, Richmond could recall that he had once been a member of the Society for Constitutional Information, and Pitt admitted attending a convention in May 1782 composed of persons representing groups or societies associated for the purpose of seeking a parliamentary reform.[1] Though the prosecution unearthed many extravagant and imprudent addresses and resolutions, it was quite unable to sustain the charge of treason, and Horne Tooke was in turn acquitted. Thelwall, the third to be tried, was acquitted after a trial of only one day.

Each side had some reason to be satisfied with the outcome of the English treason trials. The reformers could take comfort from the fact that the more wild accusations against them had been shown to be without foundation: their opponents could retort that the acquittal of Hardy and his associates demonstrated the excellence of that very constitution of which they had been so scornful. Certainly it was an ironic contrast between the situation of Hardy, acquitted in England after a fair trial, and of Thomas Paine, imprisoned without trial for more than ten months in France, and, according to his own account, saved from the guillotine by the merest chance.

Despite the acquittal of the defendants, the prosecutions struck a deadly blow at the reform societies. The Society for Constitutional Information seems never to have recovered from the seizure of its papers in May 1794. The Friends of the People survived a little longer. After a year of inactivity, they met again in May 1794 and adopted a detailed plan of reform,[2] which Grey eventually presented to the House of

[1] Pitt was most reluctant to concede that it was more than a meeting, but ultimately took the witness box a second time to admit that it was composed of persons 'delegated from different county meetings, and several cities and towns'. *State Trials*, xxv, 394.

[2] The scheme was based on proposals discussed between Wyvill and Francis for several months. It provided for the purchased redemption of rotten boroughs; extra seats for London and some counties; representation for Sheffield, Birmingham, Manchester and Leeds; two seats each for Glasgow, Edinburgh and Aberdeen; simultaneous polling; payment of members; a franchise extending to copyholders in the counties and all householders paying tax in the boroughs. It was estimated that this would produce an electorate of about 1¼ million. Wyvill, v, pp. xvi–xviii, 256–302. Grey's motion was intended to test opinion in the new Parliament, elected in 1796. If the reform proposals were accepted, but not otherwise, Grey would have suggested shortening the term of Parliament to three years. One feature of the debate was a suggestion by Lord Hawkesbury that reforms of the Cricklade and Shoreham type had rendered comprehensive reform unnecessary. The point was taken up by Sheridan, but neither he nor Hawkesbury seemed very clear how many boroughs had been reformed in this way. The debate also saw the first speech on reform by Sir Francis Burdett, returned at the general election for Boroughbridge, and destined to represent Westminster as a radical for thirty years. Grey's motion was lost by 256 votes to 91. *Parl. Hist.*, xxxiii, 644–734.

Commons in 1797. But by the beginning of 1796 they too were defunct.[1] The London Corresponding Society battled on alone, and indeed enjoyed a brief revival in mid-1795, mainly as a result of the acute distress that the war was causing among the poorer classes. But a series of large open-air meetings alarmed the government once more. A meeting near Copenhagen House, Islington, on 26 October 1795 was followed three days later by an ugly demonstration when the King went to open Parliament: alarmist rumours insisted that he had been shot at, perhaps by a wind-gun, and the government turned to further measures of repression.[2] By the Treasonable Practices Bill any persons expressing views calculated to bring into contempt the King, government or constitution might, at the second offence, be transported for seven years. The Seditious Meetings Bill forbade assemblies of more than fifty persons without prior notice, and gave authority to magistrates to disperse the onlookers if seditious observations were being made. As a blow to Thelwall's colourful and popular lecture series, all lecture rooms were required to be licensed. With unconscious humour, article xviii added that these provisions did not apply to the two Universities.

Fox and his friends waged a desperate struggle against the two bills. In the most deliberate fashion, he warned the government that if the legislation passed he would advise his fellow subjects that obedience to the law was no longer a moral duty but a mere question of prudence. Reference in a speech to the existence of rotten or pocket boroughs might well be regarded as bringing the constitution into contempt, and thus justifying banishment to Botany Bay. In the House of Lords even Thurlow, one of the least liberal of lawyers, was disturbed at the very wide powers granted to magistrates by the bills – there would be 'an end at once to all discussion with a view to parliamentary reform'. These objections, powerfully reinforced by protest meetings and petitions, made no headway, and both bills passed by overwhelming majorities.[3]

The London Corresponding Society tried to carry on, advising its members how they could comply with the terms of the acts, but the continued suspension of Habeas Corpus allowed the government to hold

---

[1] The Friends protested against the repressive legislation of late 1795, made a rather feeble attempt to transform their society into something more vigorous at the beginning of 1796, and expired. See the unpublished Manchester M.A. thesis by P. J. Brunsdon, 'The Association of the Friends of the People, 1792–6', pp. 230–1.

[2] Pitt admitted subsequently that the missile which shattered the glass of the state coach was only a stone. *Parl. Hist.*, XXXII, 522.

There had been earlier disorders in the summer in London and in Sheffield, where deaths had occurred. See reports to the Duke of Portland in Portland MSS., PwF 3934, 3937–40 and 3943.

[3] *Parl. Hist.*, XXXII, 244–556. According to Wyvill, V, 307, 62 towns and 9 counties petitioned against the bills, and 33 towns and 7 counties in favour. The vote on the second reading of the Seditious Meetings Bill was 213–43, and on the third reading of the Treasonable Practices Bill 226–45.

suspects at will, and they made wide use of their powers.[1] In 1797 the tax on newspapers was raised from 2*d* to 3½*d*, and the following year the government augmented its control with an act extending the powers of magistrates against blasphemous or seditious newspaper items.[2] Meanwhile the naval mutinies and the rebellion of the United Irishmen made the country less willing than ever to contemplate change.[3] 'It cannot be much worse', wrote one dejected reformer to Grey in March 1798.[4] The Whig parliamentary opposition seceded from a House of Commons in which they felt they could serve no purpose. The papers of the London Corresponding Society were seized in April 1798 on suspicion of collaboration with the Irish rebels, and the final banning of the Society in July 1799 by the act against illegal combinations was supererogation on the part of government.[5]

Throughout the country the ministry's measures against the national reform organizations and their leaders were supported by the zeal of local magistrates in detecting and bringing to justice their own malcontents. At Salisbury, in December 1792, a bookbinder, John Richardson, was arrested for drinking health to Tom Paine, though the subsequent assizes dismissed the case as too trivial to be heard.[6] Others were less fortunate. At times of acute tension, rash topers, incautious printers, imprudent news-vendors and bill-stickers could expect lengthy terms of imprisonment, often accompanied by the pillory. In addition there were the penalties exacted from reformers by the heavy social and economic pressure of the loyalist majority. Though Thomas Hardy was acquitted, his wife was terrified by a mob into a miscarriage and death. Thomas Walker, cotton merchant and founder of the Manchester Constitutional Society, survived an attack on his house in 1792 and a charge of high treason in 1794, only to be driven into bankruptcy a few years later. The Duke of Newcastle dismissed Cartwright from his commission in the Nottinghamshire Militia. Henry Erskine, though too temperate to join the Friends of the

---

[1] John Courtenay, speaking against the renewed suspension of Habeas Corpus in December 1798 asserted that 70 to 80 persons had been arrested the previous year without any attempt to bring them to trial. He was not challenged. See also E. P. Thompson, 147, note 2.

[2] That the law was already fierce may be gauged from a case cited in debate by Tierney and not denied of a printer charged, among other things, with impugning the sincerity of Pitt. *Parl. Hist.*, XXXIII, 1419.

[3] The Irish government secured an admission from the Irish rebels after their defeat that the agitation for parliamentary reform had been a 'mere pretence' to cover insurrection. T. Pakenham, *The year of liberty*, 290.

[4] Quoted Brunsdon, unpublished M.A. thesis, Manchester University, 'The Association of the Friends of the People, 1792–6', 240.

[5] An act for the more effectual suppression of societies established for seditious and treasonable purposes, 39 George III c. 79. It also banned all other corresponding societies.

[6] *Salisbury Journal*, 10 December 1792.

People, was deprived by his colleagues of the Deanship of the Faculty of Advocates at Edinburgh for protesting against the Treasonable Practices and Seditious Meetings bills. Stanhope's marriage to Pitt's sister was not enough to save him from the wrath his reform activities provoked: in the summer of 1794 his private secretary was arrested for high treason, and a few weeks later his town house was set on fire by loyalists celebrating Lord Howe's naval victory. Some gave up the unequal struggle and followed Priestley across the Atlantic to settle in America. Others recanted. Thomas Brimble of Keynsham in Somerset, sentenced to six months imprisonment for seditious remarks, gave three cheers for King and Constitution while in the pillory, and was rewarded with a collection. John Hooton of Lancaster, in similar circumstances, issued a public statement, which hardly sounds like his own unaided composition: 'Too late I have experienced the folly of men placed in humble stations in life attempting to subvert good order and create anarchy by speaking disrespectfully of the establishments of their country.'[1] Most reformers shut their mouths and waited. By the end of the century, William Pitt presided over a country in which opposition had been beaten into submission.

* * * *

The consensus of historical opinion has always been that Pitt's measures were excessive.[2] Certainly the evidence of insurrectionary intent discovered by the ministers was derisory – the planting of a few trees of liberty, one hare-brained scheme to seize Edinburgh Castle, and the manufacture of a few dozen pikes and daggers. It gave Horne Tooke considerable pleasure at his trial to point out that the Society for Constitutional Information had a balance of only ten pounds with which to overthrow established government.[3] Nor can it be doubted that many innocent persons suffered, nor that many who were technically guilty were punished out of all proportion to the gravity of their offence.

But such a formulation is scarcely fair to the government, which saw little and suspected much. Heavy sentences were not limited to political offences but were part of the whole legal code of the day. Judged against the backcloth of massacres and executions taking place across the water, enthusiasms and gestures that were merely naive took on a sinister and lurid colour. Pitt and his colleagues knew what store some of the French leaders set on political collaboration in Britain, and the course of events

---

[1] *Bristol Gazette*, 4 April and 2 May 1793.
[2] See, *inter alia*, G. S. Veitch, *The genesis of parliamentary reform*, pp. ix–x, 341–2; J. R. M. Butler, *The passing of the great Reform Bill*, 21; R. Birley, *The English Jacobins from 1789 to 1802*, 23–33; J. H. Rose, *William Pitt and the Great War*, 193; C. Grant Robertson, *England under the Hanoverians*, 366; G. D. H. Cole, *The Life of William Cobbett*, 4; J. S. Watson, *The reign of George III*, 361.
[3] *State Trials*, xxv, 86.

on the continent, where Belgian, Rhenish, Dutch and Swiss radicals welcomed the French advance, did nothing to soothe their fears.

It is not possible to make more than a crude estimate of feeling in the country, which fluctuated according to economic and political circumstances: nor can one offer more than a guess as to what proportion of reformers were potential revolutionaries. Burke declared in 1796 that of the 'British public' – that is, the 400,000 informed and articulate citizens – about one-fifth or some 80,000 were 'pure Jacobins' and would not scruple to call in French assistance if they had the chance.[1] But this was an *ex-cathedra* utterance, not susceptible to proof, and one can have little faith in Burke's judgement. Of more concern, perhaps, to the government was how many of the less prosperous citizens might rally to a French invasion. What evidence there is suggests that it might not be wise to put the figure too low, at least in London and some of the larger towns. The cheap editions of Paine's *The rights of man* sold in vast numbers, and though it would be rash to presume that everyone buying a copy was or became a dedicated Jacobin, one must remember on the other hand that many copies were read by several people. One of Paine's biographers believed that no fewer than 200,000 copies had been sold by 1793.[2] The London Corresponding Society, at its peak, may have had a membership of 10,000, though many of these would be in arrears of subscription.[3] The open-air meetings of the Society in 1794 and 1795 were certainly on an unprecedented scale: the attendance at the Copenhagen House in October 1795 was said to be 150,000, and the *Annual Register's* estimate of the crowd that gave so hostile a reception to the King in the same month was 200,000. Most of the demonstrators may have been interested more in the price of bread than political convulsion, but of such discontents are revolutions made. The following year, at the general election, Horne Tooke, who presumably attracted few votes save from radical reformers, polled 2819 at Westminster, against 5160 for Charles Fox and 4814 for Admiral Gardner. These figures must be considered in the context of the small number of police and troops available to maintain law and order.

Nor should sympathy for the reformers blind us to the fact that their ranks undoubtedly included republicans and revolutionaries. The famous episode in the House of Commons when Burke flung a dagger on the floor was regarded by his critics as a characteristic charade. But the daggers were not figments of his imagination. He was in possession of evidence that several thousands stamped 'Rights of Man' had been ordered from a Birmingham firm. Dr William Maxwell, who ordered them, was an

[1] *Letter I on the overtures of peace.*
[2] M. D. Conway, *Life of Paine*, I, 346. An even larger figure is suggested by P. S. Foner, *The complete writings of Thomas Paine*, II, 910.
[3] E. P. Thompson, 152–4.

ardent Jacobin, and left soon afterwards to enlist in the French army. Since the two countries were not, at that time, at war his actions were not illegal, yet the government's anxieties are easily understood.[1] Nor were all the broadsheets and pamphlets in circulation of a restrained and constitutional nature. Baxter, a member of the London Corresponding Society, is said to have passed on mock play bills:[2]

A new and entertaining farce called

LA GUILLOTINE

or GEORGE'S HEAD IN THE BASKET!

Dramatis Personae

Numpy the Third by Mr Gwelp

(being the last time of his appearing in that character)

In the debates on the Seditious Meetings Bill, Lord Mornington quoted from a publication disseminated just before the attack on the King's coach, containing a homily on the guillotine:[3] 'An instrument of rare invention. As it is the custom to decapitate and not hang kings, it is proper to have this instrument ready to make death easy to them supposing a necessity of cutting them off...England and France have had regular turns in executing their kings. France did it last.'

The reformers denounced such publications as the work of *agents provocateurs*, and this may have been the case. The popular organizations were undoubtedly riddled with spies and informers. 'Citizen Groves', a prominent member of the London Corresponding Society's secret executive, was a government agent, furnishing regular reports of meetings, as was Lynam, member of the committee established to revise the Society's constitution.[4] Fabricated evidence was common enough. The case against Thomas Walker in 1794 collapsed when the crown's chief witness broke down and was subsequently given two years gaol for perjury.[5] But in view of the excitable language which some of the societies used, it is asking a lot to presume that every such publication was a forgery or provocation. John Binns, a very active member of the London Corresponding Society in its

---

[1] *Parl. Hist.*, xxx, 189; *Burke Corr.*, vii, 331–5. Maxwell's activities are discussed in an unpublished London Ph.D. thesis by W. A. L. Seaman, 'British Democratic Societies in the period of the French Revolution', pp. 219–22. Pitt is reported to have said, on hearing of the dagger plot, that 'probably, by this time tomorrow, we may not have a hand to act or a tongue to utter'. W. N. Massey, *History of England during the reign of George III*, iv, 3, n.c, 45 n.k.

[2] *State Trials*, xxiv, 682–3.

[3] *Parl. Hist.*, xxxii, 332.

[4] E. P. Thompson, 134–5; R. Birley, 24.

[5] Under cross-examination Thomas Dunn gave the memorable reply, 'I went there when I was intoxicated, the same as I am now'. *State Trials*, xxiii, 1153.

later days, admitted in his memoirs that many of its leading men hoped for the overthrow of the monarchy and the establishment of a republic.[1]

The Society of the Friends of the People was particularly indignant at what they believed to be a deliberate attempt by Pitt to smear them with extremism. 'You look for our principles not in our declarations', objected Francis, 'but in the supposed views and projects of other men, whose views and projects, if any such exist, we have expressly renounced and disclaimed.'[2] Yet even the Friends were not quite as immaculate as Francis may have wished. Their membership included not only Cartwright, Capel Lofft and Brand Hollis, who were certainly advocates of manhood suffrage rather than moderate reform, but others who were far more extreme. Six signed their names to a subscription to send supplies to the French in November 1792, and several of the Friends of the People attended a dinner in Paris the same month, at which the toasts included 'the speedy abolition of hereditary titles and feudal distinctions in England'.[3] John Nicholls, another Friend of the People, signed the address of the Society of Constitutional Whigs, which declared the 'highest veneration' for French achievements and hinted that, if reform failed, revolution would have to be tried.[4] In his old age, Grey himself confessed that some members of the Society had held views widely different from his own, and were persons 'with whom it was not safe to have any communication'.[5]

It is in this heated atmosphere of bravado and rhetoric, suspicion and innuendo, that the reaction of the government must be placed. Its conviction that the whole social order was in jeopardy made it unwilling or

---

[1] J. Binns, *Recollections*, 45. It is of course possible to argue of the later years that repression drove reformers into conspiracy, but in 1792 the radicals had only themselves to blame if their fellow citizens regarded their loyalty as suspect. In October 1792 the London Corresponding Society, in an address to the French, declared: 'Let German despots act as they please, we shall rejoice at their fall…with unconcern therefore we view the Elector of Hanover join his troops to traitors and robbers.' The Society for Constitutional Information, not to be outdone, wrote to the National Convention of France: 'After the example which France has given, the science of revolutions will be rendered easy…it would not be strange if, in a period far short of what we should venture to predict, addresses of felicitation should cross the sea to a National Convention in England.' If their fellow countrymen misunderstood these sentiments, so did the French. The Popular and Republican Society of Apt replied – 'one may then say with reason that kings are ripe and ready to fall'. *State Trials*, XXIV, 313, 317–18, 319.
[2] *Parl. Hist.*, XXIX, 1340.
[3] A list of the Friends of the People is given as an appendix by P. J. Brunsdon in his thesis entitled 'The Association of the Friends of the People, 1792–6'. For the subscription list, see p. 79. The dinner is described by J. G. Alger, 'The British colony in Paris, 1792–3', *English Historical Review*, 13 (1898). Among the Friends certainly attending were John Hurford Stone, who took the chair, Robert Cherry and Lord Edward Fitzgerald.
[4] Brunsdon, 109.
[5] C. Grey, *Some account of the life and opinions of Charles Second Earl Grey*, 11.

unable to distinguish between speculative opinion and downright conspiracy. 'I trust in the mercy of God', Burke beseeched Pitt, 'that you
may never be led to think that this war is, in its principle, or in any thing
that belongs to it, the least resembling any other war.' To Windham he
wrote, a little later, that it would be shameful 'if Mr Fox's guillotin
. . .should come to our doors, without our having a previous struggle for
our necks, and for what ought to be far more precious to us'.[1]

Professor Alfred Cobban, in a much-read book, denied that the ruling
classes believed property to be threatened, and wrote that the 'panic of
property' was more in evidence in the writings of historians than in those
of contemporaries.[2] This is, in my judgement, seriously misleading. It is
certainly true, as Professor Cobban argued, that anarchy rather than
socialism was seen as the menace, but it was a commonplace assumption
that anarchy must lead, in turn, to spoliation.

Windham and Burke may, if one chooses, be regarded as obsessive in
their fears for property, but they did not stand alone. Supporters of
government and moderate reformers alike agreed that property was at
stake. The intention of Horne Tooke, insisted prosecuting counsel at his
trial, was to preach hatred of the rich, 'in which description seem to be
included all that had any property. . .it was endeavoured to excite those
who had nothing to aim at taking that which other men possessed': if
these notions were not checked, it would be difficult to say what property
was safe.[3] Wyvill and Francis used similar arguments to justify moderate
reform. 'If Mr Paine should be able to rouse up the lower classes', wrote
Wyvill, 'their interference will probably be marked by wild work, and all
we now possess, whether in private property or public liberty, will be at
the mercy of a lawless and furious rabble.' Francis argued that manhood
suffrage, by 'placing power in the hands of indigence', must lead to
expropriation, since 'power and property cannot be separated long'.[4] The
very success of John Reeves' *Association for the preservation of liberty
and property* suggests that many substantial citizens thought both in
danger.

It is not difficult to trace whence these apprehensions arose. Attacks
upon property as an institution were not an uncommon feature of enlightened thinking, particularly in France. Jean Jacques Rousseau in 1753
in *The origin of inequality* had maintained that property originated in the
successful imposture of the first man to enclose a piece of land, say '*This*

---

[1] *Burke Corr.*, VIII, 331 and 345. 'I vote for this bill', Burke had said in his dagger speech,
'because I consider it the means of saving my life and all our lives from the hands of
assassins.' Fanny Burney testified that Burke spoke on the French Revolution with the
vehemence of a man defending himself against murderers, and he left instructions that
the position of his grave should not be revealed lest it be despoiled by Jacobins.
[2] *The debate on the French Revolution*, 17.
[3] *State Trials*, XXV, 35.   [4] Wyvill, V, 23, 281.

is mine', and find 'people simple enough to believe him.' In a commentary on the American Indians, Morellet wrote that 'the most human nations, the gentlest, have always been those among whom there was nothing of property', and Mably agreed with him that property was the source of division and hatred. These views were certainly known in advanced circles in England, since Morellet corresponded with Shelburne, and Daniel Eaton, the publisher of *The rights of man* quoted approvingly from Mably. Similar ideas were propagated in England by William Godwin, a close friend of Thelwall and of Thomas Holcroft the dramatist.[1] Book VIII of Godwin's *Enquiry concerning the principles of political justice*, which came out in 1793, was devoted to the question of property which, Godwin maintained, ought to belong to the person 'who most wants it, or to whom the possession of it will be the most beneficial'. Though these arguments would be familiar only to the intellectual minority, other writers carried them down to a wider audience. Mary Wollstonecraft, Godwin's wife, in one of the most successful replies to Burke's *Reflections*, wrote scathingly of the Englishman's birthright as nothing more than the security of property – 'behold, the definition of English liberty'. Paine followed this up a year later with the assertion that when the rich plundered the poor of their rights, 'it becomes an example to the poor to plunder the rich of their property'. Thomas Spence, that strangest of reformers who peddled his own tracts from a barrow, asked how mankind could enjoy liberty if landlords were allowed to remain? These sentiments were disseminated among the poorer classes by leaflets and posters. 'Papers are dispersed against property', noted Wilberforce in his diary for 29 October 1795, 'prints of guillotining the King and others'.[2] In November 1792 it was reported from Scotland that the peasantry was convinced that a division of property would take place, and General Lambton was said to have been told by Sunderland strikers that his estates would soon be in their hands.[3]

The point is of some consequence. If the propertied class was convinced that manhood suffrage would lead to expropriation, their resistance to it would be, under any circumstances, tenacious in the extreme. The French Revolution added a dimension of terror, but it did not change the basic issue.

[1] Holcroft was one of the reformers arrested in 1794 with Hardy and Horne Tooke but was not put on trial, rather to his chagrin since he had an heroic speech prepared.
[2] *Life*, II, 113. Some of these were presumably the pamphlets quoted by Mornington in the debate of 17 November 1795. 'The landed property of the country was originally got by conquest...and as those public robbers, who had so obtained its possession, had shown no moderation in the use of it, it would not be fit to neglect the precious opportunity of recovering their rights...and if the aristocracy rose in resistance let the people be firm and dispatch them, cutting them off root and branch.' *Parl. Hist.*, XXXII, 332.
[3] Meikle, 99, n. 1; E. P. Thompson, 103.

It has for so long been a commonplace of British historiography that the French Revolution delayed reform in this country for a generation that to challenge or even question that assumption may seem foolhardy. Yet it is less self-evident than has been accepted. It presumes that the reform movement was in a promising position in 1789 until the shadow of the Revolution fell across it. We have seen that it was not. The Yorkshire Association was extinct, the Society for Constitutional Information dormant, and the reformers in despair. Professor Cobban wrote that reform proposals, 'which before the revolution had met with a moderate and open-minded reception, withered in the hard climate of the new Toryism'.[1] But it had not been the candour of the opponents of reform that had impressed Daniel Pulteney when he witnessed the debate of 1785: Pitt, he reported, was heard with great interest, 'but with that sort of civil attention which people give to a person who has a good claim to be heard, but with whom the hearers are determined to disagree'.[2] Sawbridge, too, would have been surprised to learn that his annual motion had been accorded a dispassionate hearing.[3]

Such a judgement also begs the question what sort of reform might have been implemented had there been no French Revolution. The most that seems possible is a limited reform of a few delinquent boroughs, on the Shoreham principle, or possibly the adoption of the Wyvill scheme for an augmentation of the county representation. Though such changes could not permanently have satisfied the middle classes, they might well have served to postpone a more comprehensive measure.

No one could, of course, deny that the excesses of the Revolution introduced an element of bitterness and provided sticks with which to beat the reformers. Yet the English ruling class did not need a French Revolution to teach them that reform carried a threat to their political supremacy – they had understood that as long ago as the Putney debates

---

[1] P. 30.   [2] *HMC Rutland*, III, 202.

[3] The need to examine evidence on this subject rather critically may be demonstrated by one striking example. In his *Memoirs* Sir Samuel Romilly wrote of his bill in 1808 to abolish the death penalty for pickpockets: 'If any person be desirous of having an adequate idea of the mischievous effects which have been produced in this country by the French Revolution...he should attempt some legislative reform on humane and liberal principles. He will then find, not only what a stupid dread of innovation, but what a savage spirit it has infused into the minds of many of his countrymen...It is but a few nights ago that, while I was standing at the bar of the House of Commons, a young man, the brother of a peer, came up to me and breathing in my face the nauseous fumes of his undigested debauch, stammered out, "I am against your bill – I am for hanging all...there is no good done by mercy. They only get worse. I would hang them all up at once." One would hardly guess from Romilly's evidence that the bill in question went through all its stages in both Houses without a division and received the royal assent within six weeks of its introduction. One must be on guard against the insidious and flattering suggestion that there are no English bigots save those produced by foreign contamination.

– and it is hard to believe that, but for the French Revolution, they would have given way gracefully. There is more than a little truth in the reply made by the London Corresponding Society in 1792 when they were rebuked by the Friends of the People for their imprudent correspondence with the French: 'as to our address to the French national convention, we imagine it best to say no more about it at present, only that if it has furnished pretexts to designing men, it has only saved them the trouble of seeking excuses elsewhere; but such men, even without our aid, would have been at no loss'.[1] And one must not forget that in 1819, when next the ruling class turned to repression to maintain its position, there was no foreign terror to serve as an excuse.

G. M. Trevelyan, in his celebrated biography of Charles Grey, suggested that Fox's decision in 1792 to cast his lot with the Friends of the People was a momentous one which 'enabled England, many years after his own death, to obtain Reform without Revolution'.[2] Such a claim can hardly be disproved, yet it may be doubted. It draws the thread of historical causation uncomfortably tight and exaggerates the influence that any man, even a Fox, can wield from the grave. At the very least the credit must be shared with others – with Grey himself, with William Cobbett, who did so much to persuade the poorer classes to seek redress through patient agitation and not commotion, or even with that much-derided figure, Addington, who demonstrated in his short premiership that repression need not be a permanent feature of government. The argument that the mass of the people refrained from revolution because they trusted Fox's successors to do them justice is a little indulgent to Whiggism, and ignores a number of more prosaic factors, such as the improved economic conditions in the 1820s. Nor is it safe to presume that had Fox turned his back on reform, not one of his colleagues would have taken up the cause.

Part of the difficulty in assessing the impact of the French Revolution on English politics is that its influence was twofold and conflicting. In its early stages the Revolution gave an enormous stimulus to reform, kindling enthusiasm in groups that had never before shown interest. But this, in turn, stimulated repression, which succeeded in snuffing out the reform movement. Historians have tended to write as though the absence of a French Revolution would have meant no obstruction to reform without taking into account that, in the same way, it would have meant no initial encouragement to reform.

The events of 1789–99 point a somewhat different moral – that the reform movement languished not because it was caught in the backlash of

---

[1] *State Trials*, XXIV, 400.
[2] *Lord Grey of the Reform Bill*, 44. Fox was doubtful what role there could be for him in a Pitt-dominated administration, but though his refusal may have been less disinterested than Trevelyan implied, it does not invalidate the argument.

revolution but because of its own weakness. It waited not upon tranquillity but upon urbanization. The growth of each new town added to those who, emancipated from the conformist pressures of village life, were free for the first time to take part in political activity.[1] With towns came numbers and anonymity. We have seen Dean Tucker attacking cities as hotbeds of radicalism.[2] Thelwall, on the opposite side politically, welcomed them: 'whatever presses men together is favourable to the diffusion of knowledge and ultimately promotive of human liberty. Hence every large workshop and manufactory is a sort of political society, which no act of Parliament can silence.'[3] But though the census of 1801 revealed that nearly a quarter of the population of England were urban dwellers, a close examination shows that, with the exception of London, the towns were still of modest size. If it is true that 150,000 persons assembled for the Copenhagen House meeting, it must have been an impressive sight; yet there was not another town in Britain that could produce such a meeting, even if every man, woman and child was a Jacobin and attended.[4]

Under these circumstances the task of constructing a coalition capable of carrying reform was bound to be difficult. That a coalition would be needed one could scarcely doubt. Not only did the middle-class reformers need all the help they could get in so formidable a struggle, but there were important tactical considerations. Moderate reformers stood to gain from the activity of radicals who, by posing to the ruling class a far more unpleasant alternative, might reconcile them to the need for judicious concessions. Some of the reformers at least were aware of this aspect. In *Politics from the people*, Daniel Eaton quoted from Mably that 'in revolutions enthusiasts are necessary, who in transgressing all bounds, may enable the wise and temperate to attain their ends'.[5] This role could be undertaken only by the urban radicals. Hence one must doubt the validity of E. P. Thompson's suggestion that an alliance of Wyvill's country gentlemen with the other reformers might have won substantial con-

---

[1] They were also free for the first time to decide whether or not they wanted to attend church: hence the fall in religious attendances.
[2] P. 96 above.
[3] *Rights of nature*, I, 21, 24, quoted E. P. Thompson, 185.
[4] With over one million inhabitants London equalled the whole of the rest of the urban population in that it was the equivalent of the next seventy towns put together. For this purpose a town is taken to be 5000 people or more. The population of England according to the census was 8,331,000. After London came Manchester 84,000, Liverpool 78,000, Birmingham 73,000, Bristol 64,000, Leeds 53,000, Plymouth 43,000, Norwich 37,000, Bath 32,000, Portsmouth 32,000, Sheffield 31,000, Hull 30,000, Nottingham 29,000, Newcastle 28,000, Leicester 17,000. Bradford-on-Avon, Wiltshire, was still larger than Bradford, Yorks. Wales was almost completely rural, with only three towns of more than 5000 in a population of half a million: Cardiff had only 1870 inhabitants.
[5] Quoted H. Collins, 'The London Corresponding Society', in *Democracy and the labour movement*, ed. J. Saville, 120.

cessions.[1] This seems to me to exaggerate the enthusiasm felt by the gentry for parliamentary reform. Wyvill, it is true, had moved from economical reform to county augmentation and thence to franchise reform, but at every stage he had left behind part of his following, until in the 1790s he was a leader without an army. The animosities between radicals and moderates in the 1780s and 1790s showed how hard it would be to maintain a working agreement for any length of time. They therefore emphasize the achievement of the men who in 1830 forged such an alliance and held it together in the critical months that followed.

[1] P. 178.

7

The aloe of reform

'He argues well for the future hopes of mankind from the smallest beginnings, watches the slow, gradual, reluctant growth of liberal views, and smiling sees the aloe of reform blossom at the end of a hundred years.'[1]

By a strange irony, at precisely the moment when ministers seemed to have scotched parliamentary reform, they were forced into steps that were bound to revive the issue and to cast doubt on the sacrosanct nature of the ancient constitution. The rebellion of 1798 convinced them that only a complete legislative union would ensure that Ireland did not continue to be a threat to England's security.

The final shape of the proposals for Union was dictated by two principal considerations – to avoid giving a handle to English reformers to reopen the question and to ensure the passage of the bill through the Irish Parliament. On the first point, Pitt was adamant: any new agitation of the question of parliamentary reform would be attended by 'infinite danger'.[2] Consequently there could be no change in the franchise for the Irish constituencies, since any discrimination against close boroughs must have implications for England as well. For practical reasons the number of Irish members at Westminster could not exceed 100, and even this, in the opinion of some, would produce an unmanageable House of Commons. The need to appease important parliamentary interests dictated that each of the 32 Irish counties should retain its two seats and this in turn necessitated a drastic reduction in borough representation, since a mere 36 seats remained to accommodate the 117 cities and boroughs formerly represented at Dublin. Schemes of alternating representation or groupings on the Scottish pattern were dropped in deference to borough patrons, who much preferred to be bought out altogether than retain only a share in a borough. Consequently, under the scheme as finally presented, no fewer than 84 of the smaller boroughs lost their representation, the survivors being chosen according to the contribution in taxes.[3]

[1] This is William Hazlitt's description of Francis Jeffrey, editor of the *Edinburgh Review*, in one of the more charitable sketches in *The Spirit of the Age*. The original version of Jeffrey's *bon mot* is presumably in his letter to Horner, 25 January 1811, printed in H. Cockburn, *Life of Jeffrey*, II, 132.
[2] Pitt to Isaac Hawkins Browne, 7 February 1799, *HMC Lonsdale*, 148–9.
[3] Ireton's principle was thus resurrected after 160 years. A list of the reprieved boroughs, with their population and taxation positions, is given in Porritt, II, 517. Thirty-two members of the Irish peerage were to sit in the House of Lords.

In presenting the proposals to the English Parliament in April 1800, Pitt was at pains to separate English and Irish reform, and went further than ever in repudiating his past. The slightest change in the constitution would, he declared, be an evil, 'even if the times were proper for experiments'. Fox and the majority of his supporters were still in secession, and the main opposition came from Grey. The addition of 100 members had, he recalled, been one of the chief objections offered to Pitt's earlier schemes in the 1780s: the logical measure in 1800 was to disfranchise some forty of the smallest English boroughs, scale down the numbers of the Irish representatives, and keep the House at its existing size. This would be no speculative reform, but a preservation of the essential features of the constitution. Grey's motion was defeated by 34 votes to 176 after Lord Hawkesbury, later prime minister,[1] had launched a vigorous counter-attack. Contrary to common assertion, he argued, the popular element in the constitution had increased: the decline in the value of the forty-shilling freehold had produced a vast addition to the county electorate, while the growth of population meant that there were thousands of voters in some boroughs where previously there had been but hundreds.[2]

The issue which Fox expected to be the greatest embarrassment to ministers gave no trouble at all. From the beginning it was obvious that without compensation to dispossessed patrons the measure would never get through an Irish House of Commons. Such compensation was open to the gravest objection as the use of public money to bribe persons to renounce an influence they should never have had. 'It must', Fox confided to Fitzpatrick, 'be almost equally disagreeable to both reformers and anti-reformers...to sell directly and avowedly the influence a man has upon others was reserved for these times.'[3] But Fox's absence from Westminster allowed Pitt to slip through unscathed. When General Walpole asked from what fund the compensation was to be paid, Pitt replied tersely that 'there was no intention to bring forward any such proposition'. Later that summer, £1,400,000 was allocated for compensation from the Irish revenues, £45,000 going to Lord Ely for the loss of his three Wexford boroughs. Porritt charitably presumed that Pitt must have meant that no proposition would be brought forward *in the English Parliament*.[4]

Reformers could hardly be expected to ignore the advantage which Pitt had handed them. Tierney and Benjamin Hobhouse pointed out that this precedent robbed ministers of one of their favourite arguments

[1] Robert Banks Jenkinson, 2nd Earl of Liverpool, prime minister from 1812 until 1827.
[2] *Parl. Hist.*, xxxv, 39–150. I have tried to show, pp. 40–2 above, that, by and large, Hawkesbury's argument was faulty.
[3] Russell, III, 295–6.
[4] Porritt, II, 509. A complete list of the disfranchised boroughs, with patronage and compensation, is in *The correspondence of Charles, First Marquis Cornwallis*, ed. C. Ross, III, 321–4.

against reform, 'for could there be', asked Hobhouse, 'a greater innovation than the destruction of the close boroughs and a compensation
allowed to the proprietors?' In the House of Lords, Holland asked
with what decency a reform could any longer be refused the people
of England?[1]

Though the weakness of the reformers prevented them from doing
more than score a few debating points, in the long term the union of the
kingdoms worked in their favour. Irish Catholics had been given the vote
in 1793, and it was at first mooted that the union would be followed by
complete emancipation, granting the right to sit in Parliament and to hold
public office. Indeed, such an understanding was a powerful inducement
for both Irish Catholics and Protestants to support the union, since the
latter would be able to neutralize their embarrassing problem by placing
Catholic MPs in a permanent minority at Westminster. It is scarcely to be
doubted that, at the same time, English Catholic and Protestant dissenters
would have been relieved from their remaining disabilities. The issue of
religious minorities would then have been separated from the issue of
parliamentary reform. But the intervention of the King in 1801 and the
subsequent resignation of Pitt made the fulfilment of Catholic Emancipation impossible, and left the problem to fester for a further twenty-
eight years. When at length the issue of emancipation had once more to be
faced, it was inextricably bound up with reform, and by splitting the anti-
reform forces, it permitted the decisive break-through.

In a more direct sense, too, the Union assisted reform. In 1800, Grey
and many of his friends assumed that the presence of 100 Irish members
at Westminster must make their task more difficult. Arguing from the
notorious cupidity of the members of the Irish Parliament and the docility
that the Scots had shown at Westminster since 1707, Grey feared that the
new recruits would act as a government bloc, 'a regular band of ministerial
adherents', who would stifle reform.[2] He misjudged the situation. The
Whigs were not destined to be in opposition for ever, and in the critical
division of 1831 when the second reading of the Reform Bill was carried
by one vote, Grey's government was saved by the Irish members, after
the Scottish and English members had provided a majority against
reform.

*   *   *   *

Though there was no immediate prospect of a revival of the reform movement, the years after the Union afforded some slight indications that the
tension was relaxing. William Pitt, now regarded by reformers as their
arch-enemy, resigned over Catholic Emancipation in February 1801, and
his successor, Henry Addington, was more conciliatory. With the advent

---

[1] *Parl. Hist.*, xxxv, 152, 155–6.   [2] *Ibid.* 71.

of peace the suspension of Habeas Corpus was allowed to lapse, and a number of state prisoners were released. Though the peace of Amiens lasted a mere eighteen months, it provided a valuable cooling-down period, and the war, when it was resumed against Napoleonic France in 1803, was more patriotic, less ideological and less divisive in character.[1]

Major Cartwright, irrepressible as ever, even convinced himself in 1801 that the time was ripe for a new initiative, though he was quite unable to convince anyone else. Horne Tooke and Thomas Hardy were markedly less active after their escapes in 1794, and Lord Stanhope, to whom Cartwright wrote in February 1801, replied bluntly 'success is not likely to attend your laudable plans'.[2] Undeterred, Cartwright addressed a public appeal to Wyvill, calling for a new society to promote manhood suffrage. Wyvill replied with a long argument in favour of a more limited franchise, wished the new venture well, but refrained from specific offers of help.[3] Cartwright, nothing if not versatile, then resumed his attempts to interest the government in his multifarious schemes – for a Temple of Naval Celebration, the conservation of forests, a flying drawbridge, and a peculiarly efficient pike to be known as the Britannic Spear.

The general election of 1802, though not as dramatic as Cobbett suggested,[4] provided further evidence that for the reformers the worst was over. In two open constituencies they scored remarkable victories. In Middlesex, Sir Francis Burdett, who had taken a prominent part in the struggle to obtain decent treatment for reformers in prison, beat the sitting member into third place.[5] An even more sensational result was at Norwich, where Windham, one of the most determined opponents of reform, lost the seat he had held since 1784 to William Smith, a radical dissenter – 'King-Killer Smith' according to his adversaries – and had to

[1] Lord Holland wrote of Addington that he had 'assuaged' the wounds inflicted by Pitt's administration, and Robert Southey declared that the 'internal pacification' was of greater importance than the peace. Quoted P. Ziegler, *Addington*, 153.
[2] Cartwright, I, 295–6. Horne Tooke had been returned to Parliament in February 1801 as the member for Old Sarum on the interest of his friend Lord Camelford. He was subsequently disqualified as a clerk in holy orders. His stay in the House of Commons was unremarkable and he made no attempt to raise the issue of reform.
[3] Wyvill, IV, 559–76. Wyvill's later career is treated by J. R. Dinwiddy, 'Christopher Wyvill and Reform 1790–1820', *Borthwick Paper*, no. 39.
[4] In his *Political Register*, 24 July 1802, Cobbett, then in his anti-reform phase, claimed to discern a spirit of hostility to all established authority. 'It is not, as heretofore, a contest between such a gentleman and such a gentleman, but between the high and the low, the rich and the poor. In many places, at least, almost all the rich are on one side, and all the poor on the other.' His evidence was a little thin for such apocalyptic pronouncements. The riots at Nottingham he regarded as the work of a 'republican revolutionary mob', and of Kent he wrote that the 'triumph of Jacobinism' was complete.
[5] The voting was George Byng 3848, Burdett 3207, William Mainwaring 2936. Burdett's election was declared void on petition.

take refuge in the Marquis of Buckingham's pocket borough of St Mawes. A 'Jacobin triumph' was Thomas Grenville's description.[1]

Another election result of importance was at Aylesbury, Wilkes' old seat, and an inhabitant householder borough with a long-standing reputation for corruption. The petition of the defeated candidate, alleging gross bribery, was not heard until early in 1804, when one member was unseated. The election committee reported that its investigations had revealed systematic bribery in the borough: fearing an undisputed return, a number of voters had brought in a third candidate, from whom they demanded 'Christmas boxes', despite the fact that it was high summer. The chairman of the committee, Sir George Cornewall, then moved for a bill to eliminate corruption in future by extending the franchise to the freeholders of the three neighbouring hundreds, on the lines of the earlier reforms at Shoreham and Cricklade.

For a variety of reasons the bill made unexpectedly good progress. Its introduction coincided with a severe political crisis as the Addington ministry disintegrated, and the government was in no shape to offer determined resistance. Some of the more sophisticated opponents of comprehensive reform had also realized that changes of this kind could be used to turn the edge of radical attack. This, apparently, is how Sir John Newport saw it, for he argued repeatedly that the bill would 'disarm' the extremists – 'would the House leave it in the power of every pretended reformer to say that they were either unwilling or had not within themselves the power to reform?' Opposition in the Commons came from those who objected with candour that if bribery were to be punished in this way, 'there would scarcely be a borough in the empire secure from violation'. On the motion for engrossing the bill, it was carried by 154 votes to 126. In the House of Lords the most vigorous opposition came from the new Lord Chancellor, Eldon, embarking on a long career of resistance to change, and objecting that the principles on which the bill was based were similar to those of the corresponding societies. Lord Grenville retorted that pragmatic reform was preferable to speculative reform, and that nothing would encourage corresponding societies more than an obdurate refusal to contemplate change of any kind. After Hawkesbury, translated to the Lords in 1803, and Lord Grosvenor had supported it, the bill passed its second reading by 39 votes to 7.[2]

---

[1] *HMC Fortescue*, VII, 71, 97, 99. The poll was Robert Fellowes 1515, Smith 1427, Windham 1339, and Frere 1318. A letter in Buckingham, III, 205–6 suggests that Smith's support was not all political. Smith, first returned for Sudbury in 1784, was a wealthy Foxite, an erstwhile Friend of the People, and had been active in seeking repeal of the Test Act and the abolition of the slave trade. He had close connections with the Hackney dissenting group. He is the subject of a recent biography by R. W. Davis, *Dissent in politics, 1780–1830: the political life of William Smith M.P.*

[2] *Cobbett's Parl. Debs.*, I, 1011–16; II, 143–30*, 387–91, 395, 396–7, 513–18, 681–3; *CJ*, LVIII, 53; LIX, 121, 176, 178, 204, 209–10, 261, 265, 268. The act was 44 George III c. 60.

The outcome showed how insubstantial were the fears of Lord Eldon,[1] and why so many of the landed classes found this kind of reform attractive. At the first election under the revised franchise, the constituency was contested between a Cavendish and a Grenville, neither of which families could be said to suffer from under-representation in the unreformed parliament. At no stage in the debates was the question of transferring the seats to one of the large industrial towns raised.

*   *   *   *

Gradually, almost imperceptibly, in the course of the later 1800s, the issue of reform revived, until in 1809 it dominated the parliamentary session. The impeachment of Melville and the death of Pitt in January 1806 removed two of the stoutest props of the old order. The Ministry of All the Talents, which succeeded Pitt's administration, raised hopes in some quarters: Fox, Grey and Erskine were of the cabinet, Fitzpatrick was Secretary at War and Sheridan Treasurer of the Navy. But the presence in the cabinet of Grenville, Windham, Sidmouth, Fitzwilliam, Spencer and Ellenborough was a guarantee that parliamentary reform would not be undertaken, and the only move in that direction came as an individual venture from Tierney, who did not join the government until after Fox's death. In March 1806 he introduced a measure to curb election expenses by prohibiting the conveyance of voters to the poll by candidates. Denounced on all sides as a bill that would, in effect, disfranchise a large number of voters, it was defeated on the third reading by 42 votes to 17.[2]

Radicals were soon disillusioned with the Talents. Indirectly however the short administration may have helped to promote reform. Its greatest achievement, the abolition of the slave trade, as well as providing a further example of private interest yielding to public good, was evidence that the mood of the country was not what it had been in the 1790s, when Wilberforce was told that people connected abolition with 'democratical principles' and would not hear of it.[3] Secondly, the circumstances of their dismissal ought to have clarified the predicament of the Whigs, reminding them that royal influence was a dubious method of retaining political power and opening their eyes to the need for an approach to the people. The reluctance of their leaders to draw such conclusions stemmed partly from their continued faith in the Prince of Wales, whose advent to power

[1] They seem to have been shared by the King who, in an unrestrained outburst in September 1804, condemned the passing of the Aylesbury bill and declared he hated all reforms. *Correspondence of George, Prince of Wales*, ed. A. Aspinall, v, 113.
[2] *Cobbett's Parl. Debs.*, VI, 371, 425, 505, 955; VII, 336, 571. Cobbett attacked the bill in the *Political Register* for 15 and 29 March, and a letter defending it appeared on 19 April. Tierney's biographer dismissed it as 'singularly futile'. H. K. Olphin, *George Tierney*, 103–5.
[3] R. Coupland, *Wilberforce*, 213.

could not in the course of nature be long delayed, and partly from their aristocratic disdain. It was, after all, Grey himself who, when the Talents was in the process of formation, explained to his brother-in-law Whitbread that his business connections made it impossible to offer him a place.[1] Such a party would embrace popular causes with some misgiving. To the radicals, of course, there was no difficulty. *Alured*, writing in Cobbett's *Political Register*, insisted that Fox had missed a golden opportunity by not nailing his colours to reform, and warned his surviving colleagues against 'patriotic lingerers' overtaken by death.[2] Major Cartwright saw the problem in the same light, writing in June 1808 to urge William Smith to join forces in a new petitioning campaign:[3]

> I confess I see no good to be done by any other means – certainly not by coalitions or ministries in which the Whigs are to have a share. We have had them both, and what was the benefit? Reformation and a restored constitution we have not had. If the Whig leaders would for a season forget that ignis fatuus expediency, which for half a century past has led them into nothing but deserts and quagmires, and seek the only means of strength, public confidence...they might do their country great good, even yet.

But Cartwright was a reform crusader, not a Whig politician. There was little evidence in 1808 that reform commanded great public support or could become the key to unlock the door to power.[4] And, unlike Cartwright, the Whig leaders would need to make sacrifices. Nothing but despair would induce the patrons of Malton and Higham Ferrers, of Buckingham and St Mawes, of Bere Alston and Newport, to throw in their lot with reform. Nevertheless, as reverse followed reverse in the dreary years ahead, as their Tory opponents tottered constantly and fell never, the more enterprising Whigs began to edge towards the people.

Pointing the way ahead to the faltering Whig leaders were new groups, inside and outside Parliament. Of growing importance were the journalists and newspaper editors who, in the early years of the nineteenth century, demonstrated a new vigour and independence.[5] From 1806 onwards William Cobbett, once the hammer of the Jacobins, put his weekly *Political*

---

[1] To Grey, Whitbread wrote: 'I thought you felt very strongly my want of Birth...In the sequel of that conversation we talked about trade, which you appeared to think disqualified me from every high situation.' R. Fulford, *Samuel Whitbread, 1764–1815, a study in opposition*, 148.

[2] 20 September, 18 October 1806.

[3] Cartwright, I, 357–8.

[4] Wyvill, for example, acquitted the Talents of any deceit over reform, admitting that there was 'general apathy on all that concerns Liberty'. Quoted Dinwiddy, 16.

[5] I. R. Christie, 'British newspapers in the later Georgian Age', in his *Myth and reality in late-eighteenth-century British politics* points out that growing circulation meant less dependence on government subsidies.

Register behind the cause of reform. Appealing to a more prosperous readership was the *Edinburgh Review*, founded in the same year as Cobbett's paper by Sydney Smith, Francis Jeffrey, Francis Horner and Henry Brougham:[1] concerned at first with purely literary questions, it took an increasingly political stance from 1807 onwards.[2] The following year it was joined by a more radical weekly, Leigh Hunt's *The Examiner*, started specifically to promote the cause of reform.[3] The renewed interest was found in Parliament also. Though some of the old leaders – Grey, Tierney and Sheridan – had lost much of their enthusiasm, a new and more militant group was emerging, soon to be known as the *Insurgents* or *Patriots*. Their leader was Sir Francis Burdett, a protégé of Horne Tooke and a Wilkes *manqué*, thrust by the 1807 Westminster election into a prominence he found difficult to sustain.[4] Though urban radicalism was clearly the driving force of the new movement, traces of the old Tory attitude can be detected in their suspicion of the executive, hatred of placemen, accusations of corruption, and, at times, a hankering after royalism.[5]

[1] The *Political Register* was first issued in January 1802, the *Edinburgh Review* in October.

[2] The issue for July 1807 contained an attack by Jeffrey on Cobbett's inconsistencies, and an article of July 1808, on Fox's *History of James II*, took the opportunity to deplore the extent of government patronage and the cult of authority: 'it is now at least ten years since Jacobinism was prostrated at Paris, and it is still longer since it ceased to be regarded with anything but horror in this country. Yet the favourers of power would still take advantage of its name to shield authority from question.' In the following number, an article on Don Pedro and the French Usurpation gave great offence by claiming that resistance to French domination in Spain had come not from the aristocracy, but from the mob: 'a lesson to all governments – a warning to all oligarchies – a cheering example to every people'. One result of the Don Pedro article was the hiving-off of the Tory contributors to found the *Quarterly Review*.

[3] *Autobiography*, ed. R. Ingpen, I, 192–5; G. D. Stout, 'The political history of Leigh Hunt's Examiner', *Washington University Studies*, New series, no. 19.

[4] Burdett's main ally among the Whigs was Samuel Whitbread, the brewer, MP for Bedford since 1790. Other important radicals were W. A. Madocks, son of the lawyer, returned for Boston in 1802; Thomas Creevey, the diarist, of obscure origins, returned for Thetford in 1802; Peter Moore, son of a clergyman and erstwhile nabob, returned for Coventry in 1803; Lord Cochrane, the sailor, returned for Honiton in 1806 after two elections in which Cobbett played a prominent part – in 1807 he joined Burdett in the Westminster representation; George Knapp, grocer, returned for his native Abingdon in 1807; G. L. Wardle, returned Okehampton, 1807. They received a good deal of support from Romilly, himself the son of a jeweller. It is perhaps significant that several of them were of less exalted origins than most Whig members. Sympathizers among the aristocracy and gentry included Lord Folkestone, Lord Archibald Hamilton, Lord Althorp, W. H. Lyttelton and Coke of Norfolk. For Westminster politics, see J. M. Main, 'Radical Westminster, 1807–20', *Historical Studies (Australia and N. Zealand)*, 1966; G. Wallas, *Life of Francis Place 1771–1854*; M. W. Patterson, *Sir Francis Burdett and his times*; E. P. Thompson, *The making of the English working class*, ch. 13.

[5] Burdett in June 1809 lamented that the crown was not still possessed of its prerogative of granting or withholding representation, and Cobbett argued that the House of Commons should have no say in the choice of ministers. The *Edinburgh Review*, in its

The excitement of the dismissal of the Ministry of All the Talents, with two general elections within eight months, the continued ill-success of the war and the increasing burden of taxation, all led to a quickening of political interest from 1807 onwards. In the course of his attack upon Cobbett in July 1807 Francis Jeffrey conceded that there was abroad a general spirit of discontent: 'we can see, as well as Mr Cobbett, the seeds of a revolution in the present aspect and temper of the nation'.[1] Cartwright, everlastingly snuffing the air, decided that the time was ripe for another attempt. After he had failed to persuade Burdett, Cobbett or Folkestone to bring forward a reform bill he had drafted, he turned, in the autumn of 1808, to plans for a monster reform banquet. There was little response. Wyvill refused to take the chair, pleading age and infirmity, and the parliamentary Whigs held aloof. But in January 1809 the situation was dramatically transformed when G. L. Wardle, one of the radical group, levelled charges against Mrs Anne Clarke, mistress of the Duke of York, alleging that she had used her position to sell commissions in the army. The House of Commons resolved to investigate the matter and for weeks the attention of the country was 'occupied in discussion with prostitutes and with swindlers'.[2] The resultant revelations produced a storm of popular indignation: scores of angry petitions demanded the rooting-out of corruption and the institution of economical reform, while the House of Commons' refusal to support Wardle's address calling for the Duke's dismissal was interpreted as evidence that the opinions of the country were not represented in Parliament. As in 1780, economical reform acted as first-stage rocket to put parliamentary reform into orbit: 'there is no evading any longer those discussions about sinecure places and the reform of Parliament', wrote Horner in May 1809.[3]

But even in the changed circumstances of 1809 the task Cartwright had set himself – to reconcile the radicals and the parliamentary Whigs – was fraught with difficulty. Samuel Whitbread, one of the ablest of the opposition, was induced to attend a Westminster Hall meeting in March and a livery dinner in April, and Cobbett rejoiced in the acquisition: 'it shows that he has broken through the cursed trammels of faction: that he is at last weary of an association with the Sheridans and Fitzpatricks'.[4] Cobbett's joy was premature, for events showed how isolated Whitbread himself was. Grey at once declared their political connection to be at an

---

article on Parliamentary Reform in July 1809, took them to task for such 'glaring absurdities'. Yet there was a certain logic in both suggestions. Burdett thought that the royal prerogative might provide a way of outflanking an unreformed House of Commons; Cobbett distrusted a corrupt House of Commons too much to want to see it choosing ministers.

[1] *Edinburgh Review*, X (1807), 421.   [2] *HMC Fortescue*, IX, 279–80.
[3] *Memoirs of Francis Horner*, ed. L. Horner, 218.
[4] *Political Register*, 1809, I, 504.

end, Grenville wrote deploring Whitbread's appearance at 'proceedings which attract so much attention', and even the radicals continued to treat Whitbread with suspicion.[1] On 1 May 1809 Cartwright was able to put on his postponed banquet at the Crown and Anchor: Burdett was in the chair, and the 1200 guests included six other members of Parliament.[2] But as a demonstration of convivial unity it was a signal failure, and the few moderates present must have felt they had entered a lion's den. William Smith was 'all but hissed' when he tried to warn the company against over-optimism: Robert Waithman, a leading London radical, fell upon him and accused the Whigs of never supporting reform except to torment the government of the day. Capel Lofft, a veteran reformer from the days of Wilkes, attempted to defend the memory of Fox, and was shouted down with cries of 'Give us a song, a song': wisely he went home and next day began turning his intended observations into a pamphlet. 'A precious scene it was', wrote Henry Crabb Robinson, 'neither prudence nor sense in what was done or said. Rank fanaticism, unthinking democracy, fit for the mob.'[3]

Public indignation was sufficient to oblige each parliamentary group to pay some heed to it, and at every stage the differences between Whigs and radicals revealed themselves. On 17 April, when the radicals moved for a general enquiry into abuses, the Whigs jibbed: Tierney thought the charge far too vague to be fair, while Ponsonby, in an unusually fierce speech, attacked those who maintained that government and opposition were equally obnoxious – 'that we are all knaves and rogues alike'.[4] The government's reply was to introduce a bill to prevent the sale of offices. Thomas Creevey, one of the militants, attacked it savagely as a piece of window-dressing: 'it was absolute nonsense...for the House to spend their time in considering abuses in the commissioners of the lottery ...when they knew, and when the public knew, that the greatest of all abuses was constantly practised by every secretary of the Treasury, in buying and selling seats in Parliament'.[5] Perceval, as a matter of course, challenged Creevey to produce his evidence, and thus paved the way for W. A. Madocks, another radical, to bring forward specific charges against the ministers on 11 May. Castlereagh was accused of bringing pressure to bear on Quintin Dick, the member for Cashel, to resign his seat after he had intimated that he could not bring himself to vote in favour of the Duke of York. This was cutting near the bone, and the Whig leadership refused to join in the hunt, Ponsonby arguing that

[1] R. Fulford, 251–4.
[2] Cartwright, I, 392; M. Roberts, *The Whig party, 1807–12*, 246–8. The MPs were Cochrane, Wardle, Smith, Brand, Madocks and George Byng.
[3] *Crown and Anchor Proceedings*, 22–4, 36–8; Reminiscences of Henry Crabb Robinson, I, 417–18, Dr Williams' Library; Capel Lofft, *On the revival of the cause of reform*.
[4] *Cobbett's Parl. Debs.*, XIV, 62. [5] *Ibid.* 116.

since everyone recognized that these were routine practices it would be disreputable to 'take advantage' of the present ministers. Though the opposition mustered 85 votes against 310, Tierney, Ponsonby and Sheridan abstained.[1]

Though as a harassing tactic the charge against Castlereagh failed, it afforded the radicals a propaganda feast, and was an indication of a shift of attitude in public life. To most members still, nothing seemed more honourable and decent than that a man whose political views had undergone a change should tender his resignation to the patron, whether a private individual or the Treasury, and they regarded the attack on Castlereagh as spiteful and underhand. The minority, but a growing one, argued that this was to put private responsibility above duty to the public. Pushed to its logical conclusions, the radical attitude would dissolve that intricate network of patronage and obligation on which the old system, politically and socially, rested. Grey and the moderate Whigs seem instinctively to have understood that more was at stake than a mere parliamentary victory, and made common cause with the Tories. That the radicals did not invariably adhere to their own rigorous standards may be seen from the case of Francis Horner, the economist, and one of the eighty-five to join in censuring Castlereagh. Having lost his seat at the general election of 1812 he was offered another by the Marquis of Buckingham on no condition 'saving that which of course, you would feel it just to admit, namely, to resign whenever your politics should differ from the person who has the means of recommending you to the seat'. Horner accepted, and in April 1813 was returned for the pocket borough of St Mawes.[2]

The chief effort of the moderate Whigs was the introduction of a bill by John Christian Curwen, the member for Carlisle, to prevent the sale of seats by requiring an oath from members that money had not changed hands. 'For the first time', he declared, 'the people call out for Reform, without instigation, and purely on their own persuasion of its necessity.' As first introduced, Curwen's measure would considerably have weakened the influence of the Treasury: it was in consequence heavily contested at every stage, and amended almost out of recognition. Though by no means a radical measure – one of Curwen's claims for it was that it would strengthen the representation of the landed interest – it produced a series of debates that laid bare the working of the unreformed system. A few members were prepared to court unpopularity and reject it out of hand.

---

[1] *Ibid.* 486–527.
[2] *Memoirs*, 272. When William Pitt, a man of conscious principle, was offered a seat for Appleby in 1780 by Sir James Lowther, he wrote to his mother: 'No kind of condition was mentioned, but that if ever our lines of conduct should become opposite, I should give him an opportunity of choosing another person. On such liberal terms I could certainly not hesitate to accept the proposal.' Stanhope, I, 46–7.

Windham delivered a sustained defence of the existing position against 'the artificers of revolution':

> A number of persons are accordingly in a constant state of active search, prying about among the establishments, and winding round like a wood-pecker round a tree, in the hopes of finding some unsound part into which they can strike their beaks and begin to work: but not like the honest wood-pecker, who is only in search of the grubs and worms on which to make a meal, and is at least indifferent as to the fate of the tree. They on the contrary only take the grubs and worms for their pretext, and have for their ultimate object to open a hole, into which the wet and the rot may enter, and by which the tree, the British oak, (a beautiful shaft of I know not how many load, and the growth of ages) may decay and perish.

The only way to eliminate the abuse of influence, Windham argued, was to eliminate the influence itself: but did members really believe that property should not have influence? The vast majority of 'jobs', of which the radicals so loudly complained, came not from the government corrupting the people, but from the people importuning their members to get them: 'the people in all quarters, and by all opportunities, are preying upon the public, and then making it the reproach of the government that it has not the power to prevent them'. To stamp out corruption and jobbery in every single instance, it would be necessary to arm the government with powers intolerable in a free society.

Spencer Perceval, leading the ministry in the Commons, was not prepared to offer such heroic defiance. First the proposed oath was struck out, and then the measure was amended so that it did not apply to posts or offices, save where 'express' corrupt agreements could be produced in evidence. Perceval's objections were not unreasonable: the condemnation of 'implied agreements' was so vague that it might disqualify from appointment anyone who had electoral influence, however well suited to the post. Many of the bill's supporters insisted that these amendments made nonsense of the measure: if straight cash transactions were to be ruled out, inducements by honours, dignities and offices would be of enhanced importance, and these were, by definition, in the gift of government. Nevertheless, it passed its third reading by 98 votes to 83.[1]

---

[1] *Cobbett's Parl. Debs.*, xiv, 353–80, 617–20, 717–84, 837–51, 899–905, 924–8, 975–87, 990–1015. Perceval's attitude is set out in a long letter to the Speaker, printed in *Diary and correspondence of Charles Abbot, Lord Colchester*, ii, 188–92, and is discussed in Denis Gray's biography, *Spencer Perceval: the evangelical prime minister, 1762–1812*, pp. 208–12. He was afraid that, since the activities of the Treasury would be under close scrutiny, the bill might harm its influence more than that of individuals. The Speaker was also keenly interested in the bill and one of his observations was quoted by radicals with great approval: 'the question now before us is no less than this – whether the seats

One feature of the debates was the animosity between Whigs and radicals. The latter made no secret of their contempt for the bill: Burdett suggested that it might more properly be called 'a bill for the better prevention of the detection of corruption', and Folkestone even moved an amendment to add to the title 'and for promoting a monopoly thereof to the Treasury by means of patronage'. The Whigs counter-attacked with equal vigour. Tierney, whose relations with Burdett had been soured by Westminster electoral disputes, derided him as a 'political sea-gull, screaming and screeching and sputtering about foul weather, which never arrived'.[1]

In the course of the debates on the bill, Burdett declared his intention of moving for parliamentary reform. It was now the chance of the Whigs to gain their revenge. Burdett put his motion towards the end of the session, and in a thin House: it was not easy to find fresh matter for debate, and he relied upon Tierney's work of 1793 for his evidence. The franchise was to go to householders, each county was to be subdivided according to the incidence of taxation, elections were to be held at the same time, and Parliaments were to be of 'constitutional duration'. Burdett's claims on behalf of his proposals were sanguine to a degree – it would provide the 'remedy for all our grievances':

> No bribery, perjury, drunkenness nor riot; no 'Wealthy Brewer', as was humorously described, who, disappointed of a job, takes, in consequence, the 'independent line', and bawls out against 'Corruption';[2] ... no ill blood engendered between friends and relations – setting families at variance, and making each county a perpetual depository of election feuds and quarrels ... no possibility of false votes – no treating – no carrying out voters – no charges of any kind – no expense, legal or illegal – no contested elections.[3]

Perceval had an easy task in picking off Burdett's excesses, and it was left to W. A. Madocks to rescue the motion with a forceful supporting speech.

in this House shall be henceforth publicly saleable – a proposition at the sound of which our ancestors would have startled with indignation'. Cobbett's view is given in Letter no. 4 to the people of Hampshire, *Political Register*, 10 June 1809, and the bill is also discussed in the *Edinburgh Review*, vol. 17, February 1811.

In its final form, 49 George III c. 118, provided for a fine of £1000 and disqualification for any member shown to have given money, or to have been party to an express agreement to provide an office, place or employment, in exchange for his election. The main effect was to make people more careful, at least for a few years. Thomas Croggon was sent to Newgate in 1813 for election malpractices at Tregony, but in 1821 Lord John Russell stated that Curwen admitted that the bill had been 'totally inefficacious' and had never been put into effect. *Parl. Debs.*, xxv, 810–11; *Parl. Debs.*, 2nd series, v. 609.

[1] *Cobbett's Parl. Debs.*, 1st series, XIV, 775.
[2] One in the eye for Whitbread. The rapprochement had broken down again.
[3] *Cobbett's Parl. Debs.*, XIV, 1053–4. A good many of Burdett's old Tory prejudices are on show in this diatribe.

He agreed in deploring universal suffrage, and wished the representation to be based upon property: that was why he found it absurd that Gatton, Midhurst or Old Sarum should have as many members as the whole of the landed property of Yorkshire. How could the House refuse a vote to the copyholder worth £1000 p.a., yet give it to the fields and stones of the burgage boroughs? The debate was by no means animated, none of the main opposition speakers took part, and abandoned by the moderate Whigs Burdett went down to defeat by 15 votes to 74.[1]

Though the Commons was in recess from June 1809 until January 1810 radicals and Whigs took to the journals and newspapers to continue their warfare. Jeffrey devoted a complete article in the July number of the *Edinburgh Review* to the subject of parliamentary reform, singling out for attack those who degraded what could be a useful medicine by pushing it as a 'quack's panacea'. The crippling burden of taxation came neither from corruption nor from inadequate representation but from the war, which the people had supported with enthusiasm. That there was a general desire for reform, Jeffrey did not deny, but it should be moderate: some aristocratic influence was necessary, some inequalities desirable. The pages of Cobbett's *Political Register* in the second half of 1809 were thick with denunciations of the *Edinburgh Reviewers* as 'mere temporizers, soothing the country under its present afflictions'.[2] Jeffrey returned to the theme in January 1810 in an article on the state of parties which reiterated orthodox Whiggism. Democratical principles had made such progress that the nation was in grave danger of dividing into extremes, royalists against democrats. 'Between these stand a small but most respectable band... the old constitutional whigs of England... every hour the rising tides are eating away the narrow isthmus upon which the adherents of the constitution are stationed.' Though Jeffrey's attitude remains patrician – the Whig leaders are advised to 'become the patrons' of the people in order to conciliate and restrain them – there is some recognition of the urgency of the situation, and a greater willingness to see changes made. The abolition of some of the rotten boroughs has become necessary, some extension of the franchise should be undertaken. 'The people', Jeffrey concludes, 'have far more wealth and far more intelligence now than they had in former times; and therefore they ought to have, and they must have more political power. The danger is not in yielding to this swell, but in endeavouring to resist it.'[3]

* * * *

[1] *Ibid.* XIV, 1041–71.
[2] Vol. XVI, p. 549. See also *ibid.* 348–50, 444–9, 449–57, 547–54, 596–603, 677–9, 769–73.
[3] Sydney Smith, one of Jeffrey's fellow contributors, thought his analysis hysterical: 'there never was so wrong an exposition of the political state of any country...I believe you take your notions of the state of opinion in Britain from the state of opinion among the commercial and manufacturing population of your own country; overlooking the

What chance was there of the Whig leadership accepting the advice of the *Edinburgh Review* and moving closer, however diffidently, to the popular movement? It was not out of the question. Whiggism, at least in the hands of Charles Fox, had been a fairly elastic creed.[1] The *Insurgents* certainly tried to force their hand as soon as the new session of Parliament opened in 1810. On 30 January London presented Wardle with the freedom of the city in a gold box. The freeholders of Middlesex submitted a petition for reform on 8 February, and the following day a large meeting of the Westminster voters, attended by Burdett, Cochrane, Creevey and Lord Archibald Hamilton, adopted another petition which, to put salt on Grey's tail, was based on the very words he had used in May 1793.[2] In April, a dispute between Burdett and the House of Commons on a point of privilege led to his arrest and incarceration in the Tower for the remainder of the session. Though this much-publicized clash caused great excitement and supplied the radical press with a good deal of ammunition, it did doubtful service to the cause of reform. By providing a diversion at the critical moment it helped to save Perceval's ministry from the wrack of the debate on the Walcheren fiasco; the spectre of mob violence antagonized many moderates, and Burdett threw away his demagogic opportunities by disappearing quietly from the Tower by water after his supporters had prepared a mammoth demonstration to celebrate his release.

But it is doubtful whether, under any circumstances, Fox's successors would have embraced radicalism. In the Commons, Ponsonby was cautious and tentative, while Tierney, who followed him as leader, was already on record as saying that no widespread demand for reform existed.[3] The two leaders in the House of Lords, Grenville and Grey, vied with each other in timidity, with victory going narrowly to the former. In March 1809 Grenville confided to his brother that though reform might not, under certain circumstances, be undesirable, the danger of innovation was so acute that 'it must be resisted and everything leading to it however plausible in itself must be as much as possible checked and discountenanced'. In December 1809 his battle-plan for the next parliamentary campaign was to keep the troops together to take advantage of 'any change

great mass of English landed proprietors, who, leaning always a little towards the Crown, would still rally round the constitution and moderate principles, whenever the state of affairs came to be such as to make their interference necessary.' *Letters*, ed. N. C. Smith, I. 186.
[1] See, for example, Fox's remarks in favour of democracy in the debate of 1797 on Grey's reform proposals: 'it gives a power of which no other form of government is capable...because every individual feels that he is fighting for himself and not for another...'. *Parl. Hist.*, XXXIII, 715.
[2] It began, 'That in a petition presented to the House by Charles Grey, Esquire in 1793...'. *CJ*, LXV, 81–2; Creevey, I, 128.
[3] *Cobbett's Parl. Debs.*, XIV, 509.

of circumstances that may arise. And this, as it seems to me, will best be
done by our abstaining (at least by my abstaining) from taking any very
active part, or even habituating myself to any frequent attendance in
Parliament; because such activity and attendance would, I fear, almost
inevitably lead to disunion.'[1]

Grey was in full agreement with the policy of masterly inactivity. Even
Curwen's bill – the main Whig enterprise of the 1809 session – he thought
imprudent. In the spring of 1810 he watched helplessly as his leaderless
forces squandered their opportunities. Whitbread was once more giving
trouble, associating with Waithman, Wardle and the city radicals at
a public dinner in the Burdett cause. Turning over in his mind whether it
would be better to avow the split or to secede once more from Parliament
(thus allowing him to spend even more time at his beloved Howick),
Grey came to the conclusion that perhaps 'the principles on which we
act' should be declared to the public. But what were they? He had the
gravest doubts of the wisdom of bringing forward any plan of reform.
By May 1810 he was in despair – 'more in the dumps', reported one
observer, 'and more enraged against his own friends, and the general
conduct of opposition, than you or I could have been'.[2]

On 13 June, under guise of a motion on the state of the nation, Grey
delivered himself of a declaration of intent – a statement of Whiggism at
its most insipid, passionate only in its detestation of those 'mischievous
and misguided men' who sought to attain reform by 'public clamour'.
He would not deny that his own enthusiasm for reform had run low
– perhaps he no longer saw 'in the same high colouring the extent of the
evil sought to be redressed'; nor did he think, 'notwithstanding all we
every day hear', that there was any general disposition towards reform.
Nevertheless, should that day come, 'whenever this great question shall
be taken up by the people of this country seriously and affectionately
...there will then be a fair prospect of accomplishing it'. With this
ringing non-commitment reformers had to be content. If others would do
the work, would educate and inform the people, though not by clamour,
Lord Grey would know where his duty lay.[3]

Without any blessing from their leaders, other Whigs had taken up the
running. On 21 May 1810 Thomas Brand, member for Hertfordshire and
a close political friend of Whitbread, moved for a committee to consider
the question of reform. Eschewing all philosophical and speculative
approaches, he proposed only the remedy of grievances. His franchise
suggestions were modest – to extend the vote in the counties to copy-

[1] Grenville to Thomas Grenville, 27 Mar. 1809, Add. MS. 41853, f. 8–9; Buckingham,
IV, 404–5. The Rockingham tradition lived on.
[2] Fremantle to Temple, Buckingham, IV, 445; *HMC Fortescue*, X, 26–9.
[3] *Cobbett's Parl. Debs.*, XVII, 565.

holders and in the boroughs to householders contributing to parish expenses. He would deprive decayed boroughs of their representation and transfer it to populous places, though with compensation, as an act of grace, to the patrons. Elections were to be triennial, and a place act should exclude from the House of Commons holders of office without responsibility. The English system was to apply to Scotland.[1]

The chief opposition to Brand's motion came from George Canning in an excitable and undistinguished speech, dwelling much on the excesses of the French Revolution. Whereas Brand had argued that to reject reform would court military government to hold down the people, Canning retorted that to grant it would promote military government by way of democracy and anarchy. Either way the future looked bleak. A more perceptive speech came from Davies Giddy, the member for Bodmin, who did not see how the balanced constitution could survive a democratic reform of the representation: the House of Commons would be so completely identified with the people and so directly under their control that it must gradually absorb the whole power of the state, while the two other branches of the legislature sank into insignificance.[2] Burdett was still in the Tower and only Wardle of the radical group intervened in the debate, being accorded a rough hearing. The most significant development was that Ponsonby and Tierney, while deploring any extreme measures, conceded that the 'sensible and reflecting' part of the community was now in favour of reform. Brand's motion was supported by 115 votes against 234 – the largest vote for reform since Pitt's motion of 1785. The inclusion among the minority of eighteen knights of the shire showed that the cause of reform, however far it still had to travel, was once more respectable.[3]

Brand's motion and Grey's declaration, though far from satisfactory to the radicals, suggested that the Whigs might still be persuaded or pushed into committing themselves to a reform policy.[4] In the course of his reply to the debate, Brand pledged himself to bring forward the motion again and again. Major Cartwright devoted the later months of 1810 to a lengthy pamphlet, *The comparison, in which are considered mock reform, half reform and constitutional reform*, thoughtfully sending a copy to Brand: 'should you detect any fallacy in my reasonings', he wrote innocently, 'the

---

[1] Brand's proposals were not dissimilar to Grey's in 1797, and were more moderate than Burdett's, which had included a uniform franchise and equal electoral areas. Brand's suggestion of compensation to borough patrons was also totally unacceptable to radicals.
[2] It is doubtful whether this was so much a glimpse of the future as a recollection of the seventeenth-century past, when the House of Commons, in the name of the people, had overthrown monarchy and Lords.
[3] *Cobbett's Parl. Debs.*, XVII, 123–64.
[4] Lord Holland had to defend Grey from the strictures of the seventeen-year-old Lord John Russell. *Early correspondence of Lord John Russell*, ed. R. Russell, I, 135–9.

communication of your observations will greatly oblige'.[1] Undiscouraged by his previous experience he decided early in 1811 to organize another reform banquet. It was a thankless task. Francis replied bluntly that it was hopeless, and Cobbett warned Cartwright that he would get nothing from the Whigs but '*double-dealing*'.[2] Brand attended a preliminary meeting in March and promised to bring thirty sympathizers a week later. In the event only three came, of whom two subsequently withdrew. According to Cartwright, Brand was warned by his colleagues that they would give him no support on parliamentary reform unless he broke off his liaison with the radicals, and there is no reason to doubt his testimony.[3] Consequently the grand dinner took place at the Freemason's Tavern on 10 June 1811 with the moderate reformers conspicuously absent: they were, complained Cartwright, 'as shy as if asked to handle a serpent'.[4] Cartwright and his friends next proceeded to turn themselves into a stage army. After he, Cochrane, Wardle and the others had feasted in public in June as the Society of Friends to Parliamentary Reform they were transmogrified the following year into the Union for Parliamentary Reform. A good many of the same faces appeared in the Hampden Club, mooted in May 1811, and holding its first meeting on 20 April 1812. Dedicated to the principle that those who paid taxation were entitled to representation, its members set about dining their way to victory. With a rule that every member must be worth at least £300 p.a. in landed property, it was unlikely to pose a very serious challenge to the upper classes.[5] Never has an institution done less to earn its posthumous fame. The formidable assiduity of Cartwright was not enough to persuade the members to show more than the most desultory interest, and its one service to the cause of reform was to provide Cartwright with a respectable address from which to undertake his evangelism. Politically it fell between two stools. The gentlemen of substantial property were frightened off by the well-known radical names: the mass of the people showed no interest at all.[6]

[1] Cartwright, I, 404. Brand's version was, of course, half-reform. Of Grey's intentions towards the cause, Cartwright wrote that they were 'so delicate, so faint, so evanescent, so equivocal, a man must have good eyes and close attention to find them out'.
[2] Cartwright, II, 4; *Political Register*, 1811, XIX, 897.
[3] Letter to the Marquis of Tavistock, *Political Register*, 1811, XIX, 1516–21.
[4] Cartwright, II, 5. George Byng attended, and his moderate speech was received with disapproval.
[5] *Reports of the Hampden Club*, B.M. 8135, f. 19. This is a compilation of its addresses, together with manuscript additions, by Thomas Cleary, the secretary and Cartwright's man-of-business. Cleary wrote an autobiography, could find no publisher, and eventually passed the collection over to Joseph Hume.
[6] Dinwiddy, 24. Cobbett was preaching constantly in his newspaper against clubs and associations, and the experience of government spies and agents had made many working men wary of reform politics. Some of their efforts went into the early trades union movement, some into Luddism, and a certain amount into conspiratorial political activity.

The Whigs, as a party, held aloof from the marches and counter-marches. Throughout much of 1811 and 1812 they comforted themselves with the expectation that their patron, the Prince Regent, installed in power by the permanent insanity of the King, would place them in office on their own terms – thus rendering any approach to the people unnecessary. Not until February 1812 were they finally disabused. Emerging from the protracted negotiations with the suspicion that another long haul might be just beginning, their interest in popular causes stirred fitfully once again. Brand's motion for reform, which had been repeatedly postponed in 1811, was refurbished and presented to the House on 8 May 1812. On this occasion Brand's scheme was to proceed by easy stages, the first of which was to obtain permission for a bill to enfranchise copyholders in the counties: this was to be followed by bills to curtail bribery, to repeal the Septennial Act, and to redistribute seats.[1]

For the 'half-reformers' the debate was disastrous. Brand and Lord Tavistock, proposer and seconder, were glum and defensive: the former admitted to having expected a larger attendance of his own political friends; had it been a party question it might have been better supported. A dubious consolation to Brand might have been the excellence of the speeches in opposition to his motion. No longer could reform be jeered out of court. Unfortunately the refutation came chiefly from the Gren-villite wing of his own party – from William Elliot, Lord Milton (Fitz-william's heir), and J. W. Ward, the member for Wareham and future Foreign Secretary. Elliot launched the attack with a lively debating speech: Birmingham, Leeds and Sheffield were unrepresented, but would anyone say that they were less prosperous than Hull, York or Bristol? Never had there been fewer petitions for reform, never had its advocates been more divided among themselves: 'they scarcely got together at the Crown and Anchor Tavern, or at the Freemason's Tavern, before they began to dispute upon their respective plans. How would his honourable friend propose to reconcile these discordant opinions? How could he conciliate that great patriarch, as he was called, of reform, Major Cartwright?' But the dominant speech of the debate was a long and prepared statement by J. W. Ward. He began by protesting against the ludicrous exaggerations of the radicals, who spoke of English government as though it were on a par with that of Spain or Turkey. Yet the fact was that for a century the country had increased in prosperity, and the last two decades, in particular, had been 'years of the most rapid, visible and essential improvement':

I am perfectly well aware that it is bad reasoning to say that because we have a good constitution now, because the people are tolerably happy... therefore no attempt ought to be made to improve the con-

[1] *Cobbett's Parl. Debs.*, XXIII, 99–161.

stitution...But as often as we hear those exaggerated and mischievous statements of the public grievances...so often must we be permitted to remind them of their real condition...that we enjoy a measure of tranquillity and happiness unknown to any other country in this stormy and disastrous age.

Reform could never be experimental – it was irreversible, it was final:

They call upon us, sir, to put off from shore in search of what they tell us is a more genial climate and a more fertile soil, but if we do so, let us at least not forget that it is under this inexorable condition, that we shall never return, even if upon our arrival we find that this promised land of theirs is cursed with irremediable barrenness and perpetual storms.

As for the argument strongly urged by Brand and the *Edinburgh Reviewers*, that the Whigs should occupy the middle ground of politics on this question, Ward denied that any such ground existed:

I must own that of this moderate party, so limited in their wishes, and consequently so easily to be contented, I am not able to see any very evident traces. That it exists I do not deny, but that it exists in any considerable number I utterly disbelieve. On the contrary, in all the most numerous meetings that have been held for the purpose of agitating this question...the idea of moderate reform has not been mentioned at all, or mentioned only to be reprobated and disclaimed.

These home-truths from a political colleague were not the only wounds Brand had to suffer. Ponsonby supported him, indeed, but with a listless and timid speech: the whole question of reform was a delicate one. Perceval, winding up the debate in the last speech he made before his assassination, remarked cheerfully that his own objections had been admirably put by the opposition itself, and limited himself to a defence of his administration. In the division lobby the reform vote dropped to 88, 27 less than it had been on Brand's first motion in 1810, and 53 fewer votes than it had attracted when the matter was first proposed by the young William Pitt thirty years earlier. Judged strictly by numbers in the House, the movement was going backwards fast. The extent of Whig apathy can be gauged from the fact that the following month, on a straight party question, they mustered 164 votes.[1]

The fate of Brand's second motion seems to have persuaded the moderates to abandon any attempt in Parliament for the time being, and the trend of the following months confirmed their decision: the murder of

[1] *Cobbett's Parl. Debs.*, XXIII, 99–161. The vote of 164 was on Wortley's motion on the negotiations for a new administration, *ibid.* 465.

Perceval, the Luddite riots in the summer, and the crescendo of the long war, starting with Napoleon's invasion of Russia, drove the issue into the background. Cartwright, his policy of conciliation in ruins, decided to stump the country, and at the age of 72 began the first of his tours of England: a 'travelling reformist' was a new thing, observed the editor of the *Morning Post* primly.[1] But although Cartwright returned with armfuls of petitions, it was to no avail. The flame of 1809 burned lower and lower, flickered, and went out. Once again the reform movement had revealed itself to be short-winded – to be too dependent on chance events and spectacular incidents. The scandal over the Duke of York had been enough to provoke public excitement but not to sustain it. The meeting of the Hampden Club in December 1814 mustered three members, and it was agreed to defer business until March: at that meeting only one member was in attendance – predictably the Major himself. 'Week after week, month after month, year after year rolls on', wrote one disillusioned member, 'and we still continue in the same torpid state in which we at first set out...the sooner it is consigned to the tomb of the Capulets the better.'[2] As for the Whigs, 'they may stand', wrote Cobbett, 'until they turn to stone'.[3]

[1] Cartwright, II, 46.   [2] *Ibid.* II, 86, 105–6.
[3] *Political Register*, XXI, 29 February 1812.

8

Whig dilemma

On 15 July 1815 Napoleon was on board the *Bellerophon*, Louis XVIII was back in the Tuileries, and the long war was over. For a generation it had dominated political life. Charles Grey, a young man of 29 at its outbreak, was 51 when it ended; Lord John Russell, a five-months-old baby when the French declared war, was a man of 23 at the close, and had been for two years a member of Parliament. At home and abroad, the world had changed, almost out of recognition, and in many respects the position of the opponents of reform had been weakened. In France, absolutism was gone for ever. Swedes, Poles and Norwegians all had new or reformed constitutions: even the Prussians had the repeated promise of a constitution. No longer was it self-evident that Britain was in the vanguard of progress, a favoured isle of liberty in a world of despotism.

In Britain the changes were, if anything, even more profound. Ward's speech against Brand's motion in 1812 had shown an awareness of the extraordinary expansion of the economy that had taken place since the later 1780s and had, in the words of Colquhoun in 1814, 'excited the wonder, the astonishment and perhaps the envy of the civilised world'.[1] Ward had used it as evidence that parliamentary reform was not necessary, but there was another side to the coin. The industrial developments had also brought distress and even ruin to some areas and occupations, and the million or more persons on poor relief could not be expected to share Ward's satisfaction at the 'tranquillity and happiness' of the country. The growing contrast between the fortunate many and the unlucky few served to sharpen the edge of conflict, to develop feelings of class interest, and to add new urgency to the reform issue. Indeed, in the immediate post-war years the sufferings of certain sections of the labouring poor were so acute that it was a question whether they would retain any confidence in the possibility of improving their lot by peaceful means. 'The evil which I apprehended', wrote Sir James Mackintosh, the Whig politician, looking back on the turbulent year of 1819, 'was the alienation of the working classes from the proprietors and the constitution.'[2] But perhaps on a long-term view an even greater danger to the unreformed system was the rapid growth in influence of the middle classes. Though they had played a relatively small part in any of the previous reform agitations, perceptive politicians realized that they were a powerful force waiting to be harnessed.

[1] Quoted H. Perkin, *The origins of modern English society, 1780–1880*, 2.
[2] Mackintosh to Russell, 12 January 1820, *Early correspondence*, I, 210.

'The public feeling is becoming very strong', wrote James Abercromby to Tierney in 1818: 'it seems to me to result from the diffusion of knowledge and wealth among the middle classes...who are determined to assert their power and to have some share in the government of the country.'[1]

The immediate post-war years were some of the most sombre in modern British history. The sudden drop in government spending, depressed foreign markets, the return of demobilized troops and a series of poor harvests helped to produce the most widespread distress. Exports, which in the last year of war had reached the record level of £50 million, slumped to £35 million by 1819, and took twenty years to recapture their former position. The cost of poor relief rose from just over £4 million in 1801 to almost double in 1818. The pages of the *Annual Register* for 1816 are full of reports of distress and discontent from all parts of the country. In Staffordshire the closure of several large ironworks put hundreds out of employment and reduced one family at least to living on cabbage-stalks; at Halstead in Essex the collapse of the cloth industry left 2012 out of a population of 3279 in receipt of poor relief, and a riot in sympathy with machine-breakers in May 1816 was suppressed with the utmost difficulty after the local cavalry had charged repeatedly in vain. At Bideford, the populace attempted to prevent a ship sailing with a cargo of potatoes; Midland colliers marched on London with loads of coal, placarded 'Willing to work, but none of us will beg'; the agricultural labourers of Suffolk took for their slogan 'Bread or Blood'.[2]

A succession of disorders over the next five years struck terror into the upper classes. The Luddite burnings and the agricultural rising of the summer of 1816 was followed by the Spa Fields riot, the march of the Blanketeers, the Derbyshire rising of June 1817, and, after some improvement in 1818, by Peterloo and the Cato Street conspiracy. The government preached resignation and practised repression. 'The present distress of the country', Lord Sidmouth told Samuel Bamford, brought before the privy council on a charge of treason, 'arises from unavoidable circumstances.'[3] The *Bath Journal* exhorted 3000 Radstock miners, attempting

---

[1] Quoted H. K. Olphin, *George Tierney*, 183–4.

[2] *Annual Register* (1816), chronicle, 110–12, 76, 68–9, 99, 67; *Report of the select committee on the poor laws*, 1817, pp. 83, A. J. Peacock, *Bread or blood*, gives a vivid account of the riots in East Anglia, as a result of which 40 persons were sentenced to death. In Somerset, Radstock miners borrowed the East Anglian slogan and added 'Hunt for ever' when they attempted a strike in March 1817: they told the magistrates that they wanted full wages and that they were starving. *Annual Register*, 1817, chronicle, 15–17.

J. R. Poynter, *Society and pauperism*, 276–7 warns against untypical examples, but in general agrees that the post-war distress was such as to threaten the very structure of society, p. 223.

[3] *Autobiography of Samuel Bamford*, II: *Passages in the life of a radical*, 148.

a strike against wage-cuts, to shun blasphemous publications and 'look to their masters as their best friends'.[1] Repression took the form of a repeat performance of the 1790s, with the Spencean Philanthropists taking over the role of the Paineite radicals. Once more spies were set to work, committees of secrecy produced evidence of plots from their little green bags, Habeas Corpus was suspended, the sedition laws strengthened, and a series of treason trials instituted. The uneasy feeling of having seen the whole thing before is enhanced by a second 'pop-gun' plot and fresh allegations of the manufacture of pikes. At times hatred and fear between the classes rose to an unprecedented level. The Spa Fields meeting was heralded by hand-bills declaring: 'Four millions in distress...Half a million live in splendid luxury...Death would now be a relief to millions.'[2] A committee of secrecy, set up by the House of Lords, complained that 'the landholder has been represented as a Monster which must be hunted down'.[3] The spectre of a concerted attack upon property reappeared. Robert Southey, surveying events from his refuge at Keswick, thought that it had become 'no longer a question between Ins and Outs, nor between Whigs and Tories. It is between those who have something to lose, and those who have everything to gain by a dissolution of society.'[4] Though Southey wrote with all the agitation of the converted Jacobin, by 1819 his opinion was shared by one of the most bland and level-headed Whigs. Sydney Smith wrote that if trade did not soon improve, 'there will be a war of the rich against the poor'.[5]

* * * *

Want and taxation proved to be as reliable allies to reform as they had been in the past: when, in the summer of 1816, Burdett and Cartwright sent out on behalf of the Hampden Club an appeal for renewed petitioning, the response was immediate and overwhelming.[6] Hampden Clubs and Union Clubs sprang up in all parts of the country and began proselytizing their neighbourhoods. They borrowed little from their London prototypes save the names, being groups of labouring men, contributing a penny a week, and meeting in cottages, pubs and dissenting chapels – a re-

[1] 6 March 1817.
[2] *State Trials*, XXXII, 86.
[3] *LJ*, LI, 41.
[4] *Life and correspondence*, IV, 360. See also 147 and 220, where he expresses fears of a *bellum servile*.
[5] Smith to Jeffrey, 23 September 1819, *Letters*, I, 338.
[6] *Reports of the Hampden Club*. Cartwright had of course issued appeals with monotonous regularity. This was one on 18 May 1816, endorsed at a general meeting of the club on 15 June. Place's Westminster committee took up the theme in August, Add. MS. 27809, f. 18, and Cobbett gave strong support.

incarnation of the working class associations of the 1790s.[1] The object of the appeal was to coordinate a new campaign and a conference was summoned to take place in London early in 1817. As usual, disagreement was not long in appearing. Burdett and Cartwright were willing to moderate their demands in the hope of obtaining some parliamentary support from the Whigs, and Cobbett was at first inclined to agree with them, but Henry Hunt, orator of the Spa Fields meetings and the newest fiery meteor in the movement, would not hear of compromise. On 22 January 1817, a few days before the opening of the parliamentary session, the conference assembled at the Crown and Anchor, with some seventy persons present – the first convention of reformers in England since the 1780s.[2] The differences of opinion could hardly have been better publicized. Burdett pointedly absented himself. When Cobbett moved for the acceptance of a householder franchise, Hunt opposed him and, supported by Bamford, carried the day overwhelmingly for the full programme of manhood suffrage and secret ballot.[3] But the following session, the conference adjourned to the King's Arms, Palace Yard, where it was agreed to leave the details of the bill to Burdett's judgement.[4] The method was to be mass-petitioning, 'the main-spring', exulted Cartwright, 'for the destruction of the machinery of the borough-faction'.[5] A further refine-

---

[1] The London Hampden Club had, as we have seen, almost expired though Cartwright had a little money in hand which he used to subsidize the new clubs. The London Union Society, according to a petition presented by its secretary Thomas Cleary to the House of Lords, had held no meetings since 1813. *Parl. Debs.*, 2nd series, XXXV, 474–7. The organization of the Middleton Hampden Club, founded 1816, is described in S. Bamford, II, 8–11. The best general account of these clubs is in H. W. C. Davis, *The age of Grey and Peel*, ch. viii, being based on his specialist work 'Lancashire reformers 1816–7', published in the *Bulletin of the John Rylands Library*, vol. 10, no. 1.

D. Bythell, *The handloom weavers*, gives a salutary reminder that it is easy to exaggerate the support for these clubs.

[2] The proposed conference of the London Corresponding Society in 1794 had been frustrated by government action. There is a lively account of the 1817 meeting by Bamford, II, 15–17. Cartwright was in the chair. To avoid the law against organizations with local branches Hunt insisted that those attending were not delegates but 'deputies from petitioning bodies for parliamentary reform', and that the conference had no permanent existence. *CJ*, LXXII, 103.

[3] Perhaps not quite the full programme, since some clubs advocated votes at eighteen. See the petition from Ripponden, Yorks., *CJ*, LXXII, 79. I do not remember seeing female suffrage mentioned in any petition at this time, but women were allowed to participate at some meetings. There is a pleasant description of the scene at Lydgate when Bamford suggested that women should vote: 'the women, who attended numerously on that bleak ridge, were mightily pleased with it, and the men being nothing dissentient, when the resolution was put, the women held up their hands amid much laughter; and ever from that time females voted with the men at the radical meetings'. Bamford, II, 165.

[4] MSS. notes on the 22 January meeting, *Reports of the Hampden Club,* confirmed by *Political Register*, 13 September 1817. Hunt's account is in his *Memoirs*, vol. I, p. ix and vol. III, 421.

[5] Cartwright, II, 139.

ment was to provoke a debate on each petition as presented, which was easily done by employing language so offensive that the government was almost bound to move its rejection.

The new parliamentary session opened in an atmosphere of great tension. On its return from Westminster, the Prince Regent's coach was attacked and the glass shattered, some said by stones, others by an air-gun. Two committees of secrecy, set up to investigate the disorders, reported in the most lurid terms, running together the Spencean Philanthropists, the Hampden Clubs and the Union Clubs in one grand conspiracy to destroy 'the present frame of society': parliamentary reform, the committees insisted, was no more than a pretext and cloak for these machinations, which had made the most alarming progress.[1] It was some comfort that 'few, if any, of the higher orders' had been infected, but even there, one could not be too careful, and the following month the Vice-Chancellor of the University of Cambridge closed down the newly-formed Union society, despite its offer to eschew political debates.[2]

With Burdett disgruntled at the extremism of the Hampden Club conference, the parliamentary bombardment was entrusted to Cochrane, whose bitter experiences had made him more radical than ever.[3] He opened on the second day with a fierce petition from Bristol, Henry Hunt's stamping-ground, said to be signed by nearly 16,000 people: the House of Commons, it asserted, was no more than the tool of 'an ever-grasping and tyrannical oligarchy of borough-mongers'. After a confused debate, the government decided to swallow its pride – there was nothing 'so disrespectful' to the House as to justify refusing it, thought Vansittart – and it was allowed to lie on the table. Cochrane then produced an even more insulting petition from Quick, in Yorkshire, which Canning denounced as a direct incitement to rebellion. Brand, while deploring the extremists, intervened to protect the rights of petitioning, and after another long wrangle, it was rejected by 135 votes to 48. Six more petitions followed.[4]

This was merely the prelude to several weeks of ordeal by petition. At the next sitting Burdett presented one from Halifax, alleging that hundreds of parliamentary seats had been usurped by peers and borough-despots and that the laws of the land were being enforced by the bayonet. After yet another long debate the House determined to receive it, and Burdett produced three other petitions from the same town. By the end of February, more than one hundred petitions had been brought forward, hours of parliamentary time consumed, and the House had grown accustomed

[1] *Parl. Debs.*, 1st series, xxxv, 411–19, 438–47.
[2] D. A. Winstanley, *Early Victorian Cambridge*, 25–7.
[3] He was expelled the House in July 1814 after being found guilty of criminal conspiracy in connection with the Stock Exchange scandal, and was re-elected for Westminster the same month. He insisted on regarding himself as a political victim.
[4] *Parl. Debs.*, 1st series, xxxv, 78–99.

to hearing itself described in the most unflattering terms. The Lord Mayor and Aldermen of London warned them that they had ceased to represent the feelings, the opinions or the interests of the people; the inhabitants of Kilmarnock observed that seats in the House were notoriously bought and sold like tickets for the opera; the petitioners from Spitalfields, London, improved on the image with a metaphor drawn from their own neighbourhood – seats were 'bought and sold like cattle-stalls at Smithfield'; the subscribers from Bolton assured them that, unless they mended their ways, the people, goaded beyond endurance, would look forward to the final crisis.[1]

Fugleman of the campaign was Cochrane, in the final stages of his political career, appearing in the House every night 'like a busy trader, with his commodities under his arm'.[2] Behind the scenes Cartwright, at the age of 76, worked incessantly, despatching draft petitions and organizing meetings. The climax of this stage of the campaign came on 3 March 1817 when Burdett announced his intention of presenting nearly six hundred petitions, which he claimed represented almost one million people. For some time members waded among petitions. After an adjournment to examine and sort them, the Speaker reported that 468 were printed and therefore unacceptable, 43 were identical with previous petitions which had been rejected as insulting, and only 13 were unexceptionable. By 58 votes to 6 the House upheld the Speaker's ruling.[3]

Meanwhile, Whigs quarrelled with radicals and radicals with each other. Henry Brougham, living down an earlier flirtation with manhood suffrage, launched fierce attacks on extremists who deluded the people: Bamford, listening to his first debate in the Commons, was appalled at the 'dead set' Brougham made against the Crown and Anchor men. Grey confessed that he had no hope of seeing reform in his lifetime, and blamed Cartwright and Cobbett for it. Burdett complained, with some justice, that Hunt was overbearing and dictatorial; Cochrane insisted that Burdett had not given him adequate support. Cobbett, temporarily in America, helped to keep the pot boiling with attacks on Burdett as a trimmer, a toady and a ranter. Burdett distrusted Place as a government spy; Place distrusted Hunt as an 'ignorant turbulent mischief-making fellow'; Hunt distrusted everybody – he would 'mix with no committee, or any party: he will act by himself'. The advocates of reform, remarked Burdett, 'acted towards each other with the hostility of different sects of religion'.[4]

---

[1] *CJ*, LXXII, 16, 36, 42, 64, 79.   [2] *Parl. Debs.*, 1st series, XXXV, 362.
[3] *CJ*, LXXII, 128–9, 155–6; *Parl. Debs.*, 1st series, XXXV, 859–63, 991–1004; *Diary and correspondence of Charles Abbot, Lord Colchester*, II, 605–7.
[4] *Parl. Debs.*, 1st series, XXXV, 84, 365–7, 374–5, 377; Bamford, II, 28; Grey to Wyvill, 10 April 1817, quoted J. R. Dinwiddy, 'Christopher Wyvill and reform, 1790–1820', *Borthwick Paper*, no. 39, 29; M. W. Patterson, *Sir Francis Burdett and his times*, II, 424–7; Wallas, *Life of Place*, 119, 124–5, 129.

After these intensive preliminaries, Burdett moved on 20 May 1817 for a select committee on reform. It could hardly be any longer maintained that the people were indifferent to the subject. Petitions from the un-represented towns – Manchester, Birmingham, Bradford, Leeds, Sheffield, Bolton, Halifax, Wolverhampton, Blackburn – were supported from some of the country areas, where the agricultural depression was causing hardship – from the freeholders of Cornwall, the gentry of Monmouth, the sheriff of Kent. The journeymen tailors of London declared that they had never previously meddled in political matters but were now obliged to do so by the unprecedented distress. Never, claimed Thomas Brand, had the people expressed more emphatically their demand for reform. On the government side, Sir John Nicholl made a sharp attack on Cartwright as 'the great manager and oracle of parliamentary reform', but the main defence was left, as on previous occasions, to J. W. Ward, who had recently crossed the floor. The agitation, he maintained, was the outcome of temporary hardship: two years previously, reform had scarcely been mentioned, nor would it be two years hence, if trade improved. Whatever inequalities the representation possessed they were certainly not, as Burdett seemed to think, the product of recent years: one would search in vain for a time when Rutland was as big as Yorkshire, or Gatton as prosperous as Bristol. As for the moderate reform advocated by Brand and Brougham, it had no support outside the ranks of the Whig aristocracy. The Whigs, as usual, were divided. Plunket, Milton and William Lamb spoke against, Brand, Tierney and Brougham in favour. In the division, Burdett lost his motion by 77 votes to 265.[1]

Though it contained a certain amount of window-dressing, the petition-ing movement of 1816–17 was a prodigious effort, demonstrating how far the political education of the working class had progressed. In the days of the younger Pitt, thirty or forty petitions were considered impressive: the 1817 parliamentary session saw more than 700 petitions presented from over 350 towns. Though some of them were limited to twenty signatures, others ran to thousands.[2] An analysis of their geographical origin[3]

[1] *Parl. Debs.*, 1st series, XXXVI, 704–812.
[2] See, for example, Norwich, Manchester (30,000 claimed) and Hampshire (20,000 claimed). *Parl. Debs.*, 1st series, XXXV, 203, 234, 362.
[3] Straight geographical analysis is complicated by the fact that several towns petitioned more than once. But a rough indication of the distribution of the petitions can be gained by dividing the country into areas, each town to count as one unit. This means equating Spoondon with Manchester, but it is the best one can do. Total of towns, 346.

Midlands	87	West Country	6
Lancs. & Cheshire	76	East Anglia	6
Scotland	65	Ireland	3
Yorkshire	52	Wales	nil
London & Middlesex	24	Elsewhere	27

The Midlands divides into Leics. 28, Derbyshire 25, Notts. 22, elsewhere 12.

demonstrates that the nucleus of the petitioning campaign was the textile areas, Lancashire, Yorkshire, and the three midland counties of Leicestershire, Nottinghamshire and Derbyshire. Major Cartwright's tour of Scotland in 1815 had been a great success, and for the first time that country, so often the despair of earlier agitators, played an important part in a British campaign. Wales and Ireland remained, by contrast, unevangelized. There was modest support in Birmingham and the West Midlands, a disappointing response from London, and elsewhere only lonely outposts – Church Stretton and Ludlow in Shropshire, Brading in the Isle of Wight, St Ives in Huntingdonshire. Though there was much prompting by Cartwright and the organizers, and certain phrases appear constantly, in other petitions one can hear the authentic voice of the Regency working class. Of the degree of misery in certain areas, there can be no question. Great numbers, petitioned Bolton, 'find themselves under the necessity of labouring sixteen hours out of the twenty four, without being able to procure half a sufficiency of food or of fuel for the use of their families, without having one farthing which they can lay out in the purchase of cloaths, or being able to lay by one farthing for the payment of rents'. More tersely, the petitioners of Irvine, in Ayrshire, described themselves as 'little better than living spectres or animated skeletons'. There was much bitterness towards pensioners and sinecurists, 'an army of locusts' on the nation. Of Spencean influence there is little trace, unless a petition from the village of Wylye, near Salisbury, was thinking in those terms when it demanded half an acre of land for every adult male. Many places, on the other hand, specifically disavowed violence, none more emphatically than Middleton in Lancashire, where Bamford's influence can surely be traced: 'the petitioners now know, from the numbers executed in the year 1812 for rioting, that the legal way is to petition the legislature for the redress of their grievances, and the inhabitants of those districts are not so destitute of honesty and ability, as to suffer themselves to die of hunger without stating their grievances; that if want of knowledge had prevented the people adopting the course they have pursued, their unparalleled distress would have led to riot, murder, and executions; this is not an idle assertion but is well known to almost every man in the country'.[1]

The failure of this great campaign to make any impact on the House of Commons demonstrated cruelly the weakness of the radicals' position and the realities of the political situation. At the end of six months sustained effort, supported by all the vigour of the new radical press,[2] Burdett had

---

[1] *CJ*, LXXII, 64, 134, 121, 118.

[2] In November 1816 Cobbett had begun printing his leading article as a twopenny pamphlet: the success of his 'Address to the Journeymen and Labourers of England', and 'Letter to the Luddites' was enormous. In 1817 his efforts were augmented by Thomas Wooler's *Black dwarf*, T. Sherwin's *The republican*, and William Hone's

found 11 fewer supporters than Brand in 1812, while his adversaries had increased their vote by 50. Whig support in the country might, as Ward said, be feeble, but their parliamentary strength was enough to give them, in effect, a veto on radical reform. Attempts to bullock through by sheer weight of popular numbers were doomed to fail.

Granted that the radicals were in a difficult position, their lack of constructive political thinking was glaring. Cartwright, of course, was certain that once the people had spoken, success must follow: how exactly he did not enquire. 'The Major', wrote Place not unfairly, 'had no doubt whatever that the plan would amaze the world, oust the ministry and produce an immediate reform.' Another suggestion came from the poet, Shelley, improbably disguised as *The hermit of Marlow*: this was for a kind of reform-in at the Crown and Anchor, to be attended by all supporters, at which a measure would be thrashed out and put to the nation in a referendum. But even with the *Hermit* sanity kept breaking in, and he added, sagely – 'a certain degree of coalition among the sincere friends of reform...is indispensable to the success of this proposal'. Cochrane, as a member of Parliament, had some better idea of the odds the radicals were facing, and suggested to the Hampden Club on 12 June 1816 that they might spend more time on ways and means and less on constitutional disputes. The Hampden Club, understandably, shied away from such strange thoughts: even so, Cochrane's suggestion that they might bring down the government by renouncing luxuries (thus inflicting a mortal wound on the revenue) was neither the most practical nor tactful proposal in 1816 when the mass of the people was finding difficulty in keeping body and soul together. Finally, the inhabitants of St George's, Hanover Square, in their petition, declared bluntly that if the Commons did not meet their wishes they would 'most certainly resist paying taxes': the House, even more bluntly, flung out the petition without a division.[1]

At the end of the debate on Burdett's motion, George Tierney pointed the moral: 'it had been the fate of parliamentary reform to suffer deeply from the madness and insolence of the advocates who had lately espoused it. They foolishly and presumptuously imagined that they could carry that great question exclusively of all persons of rank and influence in the country. This doctrine had been inculcated at public meetings by an individual (Hunt), who though he had attacked the Whigs, now found that

---

Reformist's register. See A. Aspinall, *Politics and the press, 1780–1850.* In 1816 Oldfield took the opportunity to bring out a second and enlarged edition of his *History of the boroughs* under the title *The representative history of Great Britain.*
[1] Add. MS. 27809, f. 33; P. B. Shelley, *A proposal for putting Parliamentary reform to the vote*; *Reports on the Hampden Club*; *CJ*, LXXIII, 67; *Parl. Debs.*, 1st series, XXXVII, 418.

without them he could do nothing.'[1] To radicals, no doubt, Tierney's remarks were smug, patronizing and unpalatable. Nevertheless, they were true, and Burdett, for one, was beginning to understand.

*   *   *   *

The ball was once more at the feet of the Whigs and once more they fell over it. Although for convenience the historian is forced to divide reformers into moderates and radicals, the Whig opposition in the 1810s embraced a vast variety of views, from the Grenvillites, who disliked any comprehensive reform, to the 'Mountain' some of whom were sympathetic to manhood suffrage and annual Parliaments.[2] In the spring of 1817 there were signs that the Grenville wing might be breaking away – as the radicals had hoped for years: Grey and Grenville took pointedly different lines on the green bag revelations, and there were rumours in April that the Grenvilles had actually joined the government.[3] In fact they did not do so until 1821, and as long as they maintained even tenuous links with the opposition, they were a deterrent to the adoption of a reform policy. But disregarding the Grenvilles, who did not constitute numerically a large proportion of the party, there were other Whigs whose attitude to reform was far from enthusiastic. Fitzwilliam and his son, Lord Milton, Devonshire, Spencer and Carlisle were all opposed, in varying degrees. Lord Holland, Fox's 'young'un', thought universal suffrage the 'wildest fancy' that could enter anyone's head, did not deny that some improvement in the representation was possible, but was afraid the time was not ripe.[4] In the Commons, Ponsonby, the ostensible leader, had 'great *doubts*' on this, as on most subjects: he will as usual, wrote Tom Grenville laconically, 'be led by those whom he is considered as leading'.[5] George Tierney, his successor, had a better political head, but lacked the standing and perhaps the stamina to force reform on the party, while Brougham, main protagonist of reform after the death of Whitbread, was too distrusted to carry the party with him.

Nevertheless, it was not easy for the more enterprising Whigs to sit still under the radical lash. Francis Place, in the prospectus he wrote for Hone's new paper, turned with savagery on 'our *hereditary* guardians ...Do *they* call public meetings? No, *not* they. They *call* no meetings,

---

[1] *Parl. Debs.*, 1st series, XXXVI, 810–11.
[2] Discussed in A. Mitchell, 'The Whigs and Parliamentary Reform before 1830', *Historical Studies (Australia and New Zealand)*, 12 (1965), pp. 22–42.
[3] *Parl. Debs.*, 1st series, XXXV, 573–8, 583–4; *HMC Fortescue*, X, 423. Grenville concurred with the view of the secret committee that 'the name of parliamentary reform was now employed to cover projects of the most visionary nature, which, if successful, must inevitably terminate in the destruction of the constitution of this country'.
[4] A. Mitchell, *The Whigs in Opposition, 1815–30*, 15–17; *Parl. Debs.*, 1st series, XXXV, 420–4.
[5] *HMC Fortescue*, X, 421.

they *attend* no meetings, they do all they can to *prevent* meetings. They would have all *quiet*, quiet as death.'[1] The news in January 1817 that Burdett and his associates had hundreds of petitions to unleash on Parliament stimulated some Whigs to try to snatch the lead: Waithman and the Lord Mayor of London, Alderman Wood, organized a reform banquet on 17 January and came out for triennial Parliaments, much to Cobbett's disgust, but the committee of secrecy reports seem to have stunned the moderates, and they attempted little in the parliamentary session. Under these circumstances, Grey had some excuse for marking time. Agreement on the question he thought was hopeless: it should be left to individual judgements, and in the House of Lords he reiterated that parliamentary reform could not be considered a *sine qua non*.[2]

The 1818 session was a repetition *diminuendo* and did nothing to clarify the Whig dilemma. A slight improvement in trade took much of the sting out of the agitation: though the number of radical petitions was greater than ever, the total of signatures was appreciably smaller, the novelty had gone, and there was little parliamentary interest.[3] The Whig effort was feeble and dispirited. In May, Sir Robert Heron moved for triennial Parliaments. The House was bored and fractious and, after a short debate, threw out the motion by 117 votes to 42. To compound for their own shortcomings the Whigs proceeded to expose those of the radicals. When the following month Burdett moved a string of 26 resolutions, framed in conjunction with Jeremy Bentham, and culminating in a demand for annual Parliaments, manhood suffrage, secret ballot and equal electoral areas, not a man stirred to help him save Cochrane, and the motion was defeated by 106 votes to nil.

It is doubtful whether Bentham's intervention in the controversy, though received by Burdett with rapture, was of any immediate service.[4]

---

[1] Add. MS. 27809, f. 51–2. Place's remarks were attacked by Southey in his article 'Rise and Progress of Popular Disaffection', for the *Quarterly Review*, vol. 16, January 1817. The sarcasm seems to have been wasted on the Whigs, for when Brougham launched his moderate newspaper in the summer of 1817 it was called *The Guardian*. It ran for only a few numbers. A. Aspinall, 299–306.

[2] Grey to Holland, 17 January 1817, quoted Mitchell, *The Whigs in opposition*, 17; *Parl. Debs.*, 1st series, xxxv, 428.

[3] There were 1570 petitions but most of them had only twenty names. This was because many petitioners were afraid that the government would prosecute under an act against tumults and disorders passed just after the Restoration, 13 Charles II c. 5. Romilly denied that the act applied. *Parl. Debs.*, 1st series, xxxvii, 752–3. Bristol provided 437 petitions, Leeds 248, Scotland 128, Sheffield 72, Halifax 70, Bath 64, Todmorden 60, Middlesex 49, Birmingham 48, Westminster 41, Manchester 35, Warrington 29, Preston 29 and London 24.

[4] Bentham's work was entitled *Plan for parliamentary reform in the form of a Catechism ...showing the necessity of radical and the inadequacy of moderate reform.* Burdett was at his most fatuous: 'Bentham and Burdett, the alliteration charms my ear'. Patterson, II, 463.

The fearful jargon he employed in his treatise must have rendered it unintelligible to all but the most pertinacious; his demonstration of the inevitability of 'democratic ascendancy' confirmed many waverers in their worst fears; while his advocacy of secret ballot and the vote, not only for females but for criminals, lunatics and bankrupts, though to his admirers evidence of the rigour of his logic, to most others seemed bookish cranki-ness.[1] Nevertheless, his work demanded a refutation from the Whig theoreticians of the *Edinburgh Review*, and in December 1818 Sir James Mackintosh addressed himself to the task. He endorsed dutifully Grey's position that reform ought not to be 'an article in the original contract of any party'. Bentham's commendation of universal suffrage was totally unacceptable since it would lead to 'a permanent animosity between opinion and property'. But Mackintosh's illustration was not, perhaps, the most felicitous: 'Does any man doubt that the establishment of universal suffrage among emancipated slaves would be only another word for the oppression, if not the destruction, of their former masters?...The principle is applicable in some degree in all communities...The labouring classes are in every country a perpetual majority.' On the other hand, Mackintosh was uneasy about a uniform franchise based on property which, by excluding the lower classes from that share in the representation they possessed, would make their inferior status too explicit. A one-class representative system would be an evil, yet, concluded Mackintosh, if it were inescapable 'we must indeed vest it in the middling classes; both because they possess the largest share of sense and virtue, and because they have the most numerous connections of interest with the other parts of society'.

There was nothing very positive in Mackintosh's article, yet it suggested the way in which some of the Whigs were moving in an attempt to escape their difficulties. If comprehensive franchise reform was ruled out, the only avenue was gradual redistribution by the disqualification of corrupt boroughs. Carried through on a sufficient scale it might turn the edge of the radical attack. It would call the bluff of those who constantly affirmed that they would remedy defects in the constitution when proved, and by forcing the opponents of the proposal to defend, or at least palliate, corruption, would place them at a disadvantage. The Cornish boroughs, from their number and notoriety, were peculiarly susceptible to such treatment.

At the general election of 1812 a contest for Helston had been brought before the House and sent, in the normal way, to an election committee. Helston was a borough which on many occasions in the past had engaged the attention of the House and was a fair specimen of the idiosyncrasies

[1] Curiously enough he drew a line at women MPs. The *simplification principle* seems to have faltered.

of the old system. In the 1780s it looked as though it might become extinct, since the right of voting was confined to members of the old corporation, of which only one, Richard Penhale, survived – an old gentleman of nearly eighty. This danger was averted in 1790 by the House switching the franchise to the new corporation in the nick of time. After the 1812 contest the election committee, by a majority of 11 votes to 3, resolved to bring the state of affairs in the borough before the House, which was then told, what everyone already knew, that the Duke of Leeds was patron of the borough, that he exerted an undue influence on the returns, and that he paid the annual poor rate for the borough. Curwen's Act was recent enough to make this revelation a source of embarrassment to some members and a motion was put to institute a prosecution of the Duke. Government was able to defeat this by 55 votes to 52, but at the price of allowing a bill to be introduced to reform the borough by extending the franchise to the neighbouring hundred. Though Lord Tavistock and William Smith urged that the seats should be transferred to Yorkshire instead, Brand commended the measure as a safe way of effecting reform. The House of Lords then rejected it in three successive years, and in 1816 it finally foundered. In a debate on the third presentation of the bill, however, the first minister, Lord Liverpool, expressed agreement with the principle, the more so since he was opposed to comprehensive schemes of parliamentary reform.[1]

The 1818 general election was followed by another hunt after delinquent boroughs. Two admirable specimens were found in the west country. Penryn, reported to the House in February 1819, had narrowly escaped reform in 1807, when Sir Christopher Hawkins, one of the candidates, who had contracted for voters at 24 guineas a head, was ordered to be prosecuted.[2] Of Barnstaple, reported the following month, Oldfield had written in 1816: 'if any borough in the country is more corrupt than another it is this'.[3] In 1819 the charge of bribery was levelled against Sir Manasseh Masseh Lopes, a Spanish Jew and an ideal villain, who was alleged to have spent £3000 in corrupting the electors. Bills to reform both boroughs were introduced and began to make progress through the House. But in the meantime an even better example was unearthed at Grampound in Cornwall. No petition had been received, but in March 1819, as a consequence of the election, Sir Manasseh had been convicted of bribery at the Exeter assizes, fined £1000, and sent to gaol for two years.

---

[1] S. Toy, *The history of Helston*; T. H. B. Oldfield, *The representative history of Great Britain*, III, 154–86; *The House of Commons, 1754–90*, I, 229–30; *Parl. Debs.*, 1st series, vols. XXV–XXXI, XXXIII–XXXIV; *CJ*, LXIX–LXXI; *LJ*, XLIX–L. Liverpool's interest in the matter while a member of the lower House as Lord Hawkesbury has been mentioned in chapter six.

[2] *CJ*, LXII, 354.

[3] *Representative history*, III, 300.

Lord John Russell accordingly moved on 5 July 1819 for the House to give the matter its attention next session.

The struggle over Grampound went on for several years and became a test case. One advantage in attacking this borough was that with a legal conviction no doubt could be expressed as to the bribery, and the issue could be fought as one of principle. To many of the Whigs a great attraction of the proposal to effect reform by the piecemeal transfer of seats was that it did not raise the question of a national franchise, and Mackintosh in the *Edinburgh Review* commended Russell's scheme as combining 'the prudence of a statesman with the enlarged views of a philosopher'.[1] But the limitations of Russell's approach were considerable. Even if the general principle that hopelessly delinquent boroughs should lose their representation were accepted, one could not expect more than two or three boroughs to be dealt with in each Parliament. In addition, it would only catch certain classes of borough: the inhabitant householder and freeman boroughs of the Honiton and Barnstaple type, where bribery was open and squalid, might well lose their representation, and with them an area of popular influence would vanish; but the snug corporation and burgage boroughs, where influence was seemly, would remain uncontested, undenounced, and undisturbed.

Parliament reassembled in November 1819 in the shadow of Peterloo, the Prince Regent's speech tracing seditious proceedings which aimed 'at the subversion of the rights of property and of all order in society'. On 14 December, Russell moved for a bill to reform Grampound, expecting to be beaten: 'the violent will not care for it', he wrote, 'and the other side will throw it out'.[2] It was not, he assured the House, a general plan for reform, but a practical measure for remedying specific abuses. All boroughs guilty of gross corruption should lose their representation either to the new towns or to some populous counties, and Grampound should be forthwith disfranchised. To the amazement of nearly all observers, Castlereagh rose for the government as soon as the motion had been seconded and congratulated Russell on his moderation: the principle that delinquent boroughs should lose their representation had already, he thought, been accepted by the House, and would meet with his 'cordial cooperation'. He would certainly put no difficulty in the way of a bill to reform Grampound. In view of this unexpected harmony, Russell accepted Tierney's advice to withdraw his motion, and content himself with leave to introduce a bill.[3]

Castlereagh's response took not only the Whigs by surprise but many

[1] Vol. 34, article of Nov. 1820 on the speech of Lord John Russell on 14 Dec. 1819, p. 468.   [2] *Early Correspondence*, I, 208.

[3] *Parl. Debs.*, 1st series, XLI, 1091–1122; J. Russell, *Recollections and suggestions, 1813–73*, 1st ed. 39–41.

of his own side. Behind it one can detect the conciliatory approach of Liverpool. He had frequently been on record in the House of Commons as approving the gradual modification of the electoral system in this way, and there is evidence that he had given particular consideration to the government's attitude towards Grampound.[1] That liberalization of the Tory party, which was of such importance for the future and with which Peel has most commonly been credited, has been traced back to Liverpool, and his attitude on this question is a telling illustration.[2]

The new-found cordiality did not last. Castlereagh had been careful not to pledge himself to any particular scheme. Since the hundreds adjacent to Grampound were already plentifully supplied with borough representation, the formula that had been employed for Shoreham, Cricklade and Aylesbury was clearly unsuitable. The issue was therefore whether Grampound's seats should go to augment the representation of a county, or whether the opportunity should be taken to bring one of the great industrial towns, such as Leeds, into the system. Lord Liverpool was insistent for the former: the landed interest was 'the stamina of the county' and its predominance must be maintained.[3] J. W. Croker, secretary to the Admiralty, tried to convince him that, contrary to appearances, the enfranchisement of the industrial towns would be a less democratic step: there were, he argued, only eight unrepresented towns with a population of more than 20,000, whereas the principle of adjusting county representation in the search for equality would be almost unlimited in operation. Liverpool remained unpersuaded, and the government's attitude was that the seats should go to Yorkshire, by which means several unrepresented towns would be indirectly enfranchised.[4]

Debates on Russell's bill were long and complicated, its passage being interrupted by the death of George III and the consequent general election. Widespread acceptance of the principle of disqualification was accompanied by great divergencies in detail. In February 1821 a proposal to give Grampound's seats to the neighbouring hundreds was easily defeated, and the more dangerous one to give them to Yorkshire rather than Leeds was beaten by 126 votes to 66. Russell's difficulties were by no means over. On the committee stage, the franchise for the new borough

---

[1] Add. MS. 38458, f. 273; 38370, f. 63.

[2] The general work is W. R. Brock, *Lord Liverpool and liberal toryism, 1820–7*. The author was not specifically concerned with Liverpool's attitude towards electoral reform.

[3] The phrase was used in one of Liverpool's earliest speeches in the Commons in 1793 on Grey's reform motion. *Parl. Hist.*, xxx, 811.

[4] *The correspondence and diaries of John Wilson Croker*, ed. L. J. Jennings, I, 135–7. I have assumed that the memo, Add. MS. 38370, f. 63 is the gist of Croker's proposal, though it does not seem to be in his handwriting. The eight towns were Manchester, Birmingham, Leeds, Sheffield, Bolton, Paisley, Preston and Stockport. Croker's argument was faulty since new towns would qualify decade by decade.

had to be decided. Russell's original proposal had been to give the vote to householders paying a rent of at least £5 p.a., which would have produced an electorate of some 8000. This was modified before the bill was presented to a £10 franchise. Lord Milton's proposal in committee for a scot and lot franchise was rejected, but Stuart Wortley, with Castlereagh's support, carried an amendment for a £20 franchise, which would have had the effect of reducing the electorate to between 2000 and 3000. Russell abandoned the measure in disgust, and Stuart Wortley guided it through its third reading. In the Lords, Liverpool gave it a cautious welcome and defended it against Lord Chancellor Eldon, but carried an amendment giving the seats to Yorkshire. Russell, in the Commons, accepted the amendment rather than lose the whole bill. In 1826, therefore, when the act came into operation, the county of York returned four members, and for the first time for nearly three hundred years a parliamentary borough had lost its representation through delinquency.[1]

Edward Porritt in *The Unreformed House of Commons* laid great emphasis on the Grampound affair. It was the first time that representation had been transferred from one part of the country to another, and in that respect it was a significant innovation. 'It does little, but promises much', wrote Sir Robert Heron in his diary in December 1819.[2] But the subsequent modification of the bill did a good deal to mitigate its importance, and in the end Russell's approach turned out to be not the highroad to reform but a *cul de sac*. The treatment the Whigs had received convinced Russell and others that there was little to be gained by conciliatory gestures, prepared the way for their acceptance of a comprehensive programme of reform, and reminded them of the dangers they could anticipate from the House of Lords. For the Tories it was one more chance missed of reducing the growing pressure for reform by an agreed non-party policy of phased withdrawal from exposed positions.[3]

*   *   *   *

One difficulty in assessing the importance of the Grampound case is that it coincided with Peterloo, and there can be little doubt that the latter

---

[1] Maidstone was deprived of its representation during the reign of Mary for complicity in the Wyatt rebellion.

[2] Sir R. Heron, *Notes*, 110. This is a rare volume, printed but unpublished. There is no copy in the British Museum, but the Grantham Public Library has a copy, with manuscript additions, apparently in Heron's hand. Heron's observation was made before it was understood that Castlereagh would not support the transfer to Leeds: there was much bitterness on the point, and Castlereagh was accused of backsliding.

[3] The opponents of the bill did not see it like that and they may, of course, have been right. They argued that the grant to Leeds would whet the appetite of other unrepresented towns, and result in an unseemly pursuit of other delinquent boroughs. Peel, in a letter to Croker of 23 March 1820 hazarded the guess that if reform could not be resisted, Whigs and Tories would unite to carry a moderate measure.

made a far greater contribution to that shift in public attitude which one can trace in the early 1820s. The immediate effect of Peterloo was, of course, to harden entrenched positions and exacerbate class antagonisms – yet one has the feeling that once the initial fright was over the upper classes gazed into the abyss and recoiled at the prospect of unending strife they saw before them. The early months of 1819 had been disturbed and anxious. The recovery in trade that had made 1818 a relatively quiet year was not sustained, and Hunt and his friends were soon stoking the fires of radical protest. 'We anticipate at no distant period a general rising', wrote five Lancashire magistrates to the government at the beginning of July.[1] A new departure was the holding in unrepresented towns of elections for 'legislative attorneys' – a move unintelligible to the Whigs as a legal absurdity, but a brilliant means of dramatizing the reform issue.[2] For taking part in such an election at Birmingham in July 1819 Cartwright was charged with conspiracy to traduce and vilify the constitution, and subsequently fined. A meeting later the same month in London resolved that, since Parliament was not properly elected, the protestors would not consider themselves bound by the laws of the land after 1 January 1820. Early in August, the Manchester reformers advertised a meeting to follow Birmingham's example. Warned by the magistrates that it was illegal, they substituted a less provocative meeting to be called for 16 August with Henry Hunt as the principal speaker. It was at this meeting, in St Peter's Field, that the clash between the yeomanry and the crowd left 11 people killed and more than 400 injured.[3] The Prince Regent at once congratulated the yeomanry on their attention to duty, and when Parliament reassembled the government brought forward the six 'gag acts' to control the situation. That the ministers were seriously alarmed is without question. In October 1819 Lord Sidmouth confided to

[1] *Parl. Debs.*, 1st series, XLI, 230–1.
[2] That it was conceived as such and was not, as some Whigs seemed to think, the product of proletarian ignorance is clear from remarks made at the Birmingham meeting by George Edmonds: 'the effect to be produced is not in the House but in the country and upon public opinion...It is very difficult for people to reason upon abstract questions. The present proceeding supplies a fact...This is doing something, and something which, from its novelty, as well as its justice, will excite a very general sensation throughout the country.' *State Trials*, new series, I, 794. Grey dismissed the proceedings as 'insane'. *Parl. Debs.*, 1st series, XLI, 9.
[3] I have put the matter as dispassionately as possible. Bamford, an eye-witness, insisted that it was an unprovoked attack by the cavalry on a good-humoured crowd: Castlereagh, in the House of Commons, maintained that the troops were first attacked with stones and brickbats, and fired on with pistols. Bamford, II, 205–8; *Parl. Debs.*, 1st series, XLI, 95–6. Estimates of the casualties varied wildly. Mine are taken from G. M. Trevelyan, 'The number of casualties at Peterloo', *History* (1922), based on the Metropolitan Relief Committee's detailed report. The most recent works are D. Read, *Peterloo* (1958) and R. Walmsley, *Peterloo, the case reopened* (1969). It is also commented on in E. P. Thompson, *The making of the English working class*.

a friend, who was inclined to doubt the extent of sedition, that the reports coming in every day were 'frightful', while the Duke of Wellington was greatly exercised lest several cannon, lying on the beach at Aldeburgh, should be seized by the radicals: 'the possession of them would give occasion to a triumph...and it was not at all clear that they could not and would not use these cannon if they knew how to set about it'.[1] Nor was the government alone in its fears. Grey seems to have succumbed to a moment of sheer terror when he warned his radical friend, Sir Robert Wilson, that if Hunt and his supporters gained power, 'I shall not precede you many months on the scaffold'.[2]

Even before Peterloo some Whig politicians, alarmed at the danger signals, were urging that the party should move to conciliate the popular mood. To Francis Jeffrey, Smith wrote in July that, sooner or later, Parliament must be reformed: 'I am doubtful whether it is not your duty and my duty to become moderate reformers to keep off worse.'[3] Peterloo, the following month, gave new impetus, and Tierney told Grey in September that the party must seize the initiative and come out in favour of reform as soon as Parliament reassembled.[4] Still Grey hesitated, writing sadly to Brougham that though it had sometimes occurred to him to try once more the middle ground, the hope was delusive.[5] Holland complained that the party was crumbling for want of activity.[6] Indeed, so slow was Grey's response that there was even the possibility that he would be overtaken on the road by the more enterprising of the Tories: 'do not you think', wrote Peel to Croker in March 1820, 'that the tone of England ...is more liberal – to use an odious but intelligible phrase – than the policy of the government?...It seems to me a curious crisis – when public opinion never had such influence on public measures, and yet never was so dissatisfied with the share it possessed. It is growing too large for the channels it has been accustomed to run through...Can we resist – I mean not next session or the session after that – but can we resist for seven years reform in Parliament?'[7] Later the same year the *Edinburgh Review*, in an article commending Russell's scheme of reform, also discerned a change of mood. Many of the Whig opposition, it asserted, were thoroughly tired of their wilder associates, and on the Tory side there was a growing conviction that the time had come for 'a more conciliatory approach'.[8]

Few things are harder for an historian than to say at which moment

---

[1] *Memoirs of Robert Plumer Ward*, ed. E. Phipps, II, 17, 41.
[2] Add. MS. 30109, f. 56.
[3] *Letters*, I, 330–1. See also Smith to Edward Davenport, 3 January 1820.
[4] Olphin, 210–11.
[5] *Life and times of Henry Brougham*, by himself, II, 343.
[6] A. Mitchell, 141.
[7] Croker, I, 170. [8] Vol. 34, November 1820.

a campaign or movement changes from a crusade to become an accepted creed – unless it is to say why. Perhaps it is wrong to look for a precise point of time, yet with many protracted struggles – for women's suffrage or the abolition of capital punishment – one has the impression that suddenly, often within a surprisingly short period, resistance crumbled. It seems less the result of rational argument – in the sense that new evidence or expositions are brought forward – than the growth of a feeling on all sides that the thing is, after all, inevitable. It would be foolish to deny that in the later 1820s the opponents of parliamentary reform remained numerous, active and formidable, yet stage by stage they were forced on to the defensive: the arguments that had carried the day so easily in the past no longer held conviction. Such is the feeling conveyed by one of Canning's speeches on the subject in 1822 when he advised Russell to ponder what he was doing and what its effect would be: 'if, however, he shall persevere, and if his perseverance shall be successful...his be the triumph to have precipitated those results – be mine the consolation that to the utmost, and the latest of my power, I have opposed them'. It is the speech of a man who knows in his heart that he is fighting for a lost cause.[1]

In 1820 and 1821 began that tiny shift of pebbles that anticipates the avalanche, as, one by one, members began to announce their conversion to reform. Pascoe Grenfell and Alexander Baring declared their change of heart in the debate of 31 January 1821: a month later, that assiduous opponent of reform, J. W. Ward, who had once declared that a motion for reform produced in him the same sensations as 'a motion for a revolution', admitted that the great towns stood in need of representation. Even the Whig magnates began to move. 'The Duke of Devonshire has declared for reform', noted Creevey in January 1821, while Lord Milton made his conversion public in April: 'the great mass of the middle classes of society are in favour of reform'.[2] In 1822 Croker wrote that 'at tables where ten years ago you would have no more heard reform advocated than treason, you will now find half the company reformers'.[3]

Slowly Lord Grey began to respond to the changing situation. In January 1820 he remained of the opinion that he would not see reform carried in his lifetime. At the end of the same year, he wrote to Lord Holland that he could not reach any satisfactory conclusion on whether the party ought to commit itself to reform: 'the more I write and the more I think, the more I involve myself in doubt and perplexity'. In a letter to Fitzwilliam, he acknowledged the tactical case for a Whig pledge: 'calculating, as the new administration must, on the inveterate hostility of the

[1] *Parl. Debs.*, 2nd series, VII, 136.
[2] *Parl. Debs.*, 2nd series, IV, 223–4, 226–7, 591–2; V, 436–8; Creevey, II, 6. Mitchell, 167, n. 3 gives other examples.   [3] Croker, II, 52.

court, and its determination to trip them up on the first favourable opportunity, public confidence alone could support them'. His renewed commitment to 'a complete and total change in the system of government', of which reform should be a 'principal feature' was announced to the public at a meeting in Northumberland in January 1821, and a year later he wrote to Holland that 'nibbling at reform' would not do.[1]

The first real test of the new Whig policy came in April 1822 when Lord John Russell, abandoning the gradualism of the Grampound approach, moved to deprive the one hundred smallest boroughs of one member each and to distribute the seats to the counties and the unenfranchised towns. His main argument was evidence, taken from the *Elector's remembrancer*, that the representatives of the smaller boroughs were disproportionately inclined to support government. The Whigs were still soundly defeated by 269 votes to 164, but the reform support was the largest since Pitt in 1785, and Russell exulted at the presence in his lobby of three converts, believed to be worth a million. 'In the days when it was said that Reform threatened property', he commented later, 'such substantial support was worth a great deal.'[2] The *Annual Register* thought that the minority's strength afforded 'more rational hopes of ultimate, though remote, triumph' than could have been entertained for more than thirty years.[3]

*   *   *   *

No sooner had the Whigs, after agonies of circumspection, embarked on the vessel of reform than it ran aground. For years Castlereagh and Liverpool had insisted that the country's distress was only temporary and would cure itself. From the autumn of 1820 onwards the improvement in trade was sufficiently obvious to allow Sydney Smith to twit his Whig friends: 'there seems to be a fatality which pursues us', he wrote in October, 'when, oh when, shall we be really ruined', and the following year he told Edward Davenport to 'learn to look the prosperity of the country in the face and bear it as well as you can'.[4] The new Chancellor

---

[1] Grey to Lambton, 3 January 1820, S. J. Reid, *Life and letters of the first Earl of Durham*, I, 129; Grey to Holland, 6 December 1820, Trevelyan, appendix A, pp. 372–3; Mitchell, 154–5, 167–8. Grey was adept however at hedging his bets, and after his Northumberland declaration, he continued that whether reform should be pressed 'as an indispensable object in the first place...is a question which, like every other question of a public nature, must be determined by considerations of expediency at the time'. *Tyne Mercury*, 16 January 1821. But reform was a *sine qua non* again in 1822 when he discussed with Brougham the possibility of the Whigs taking office after the death of Castlereagh: they should 'stipulate for some plan on a moderate principle with a pledge to resist anything more'. Brougham, *Life and times*, II, 444. Grey's political opponents were not the only people to be bewildered by his subtleties and reservations.
[2] *Parl. Debs.*, 2nd series, VII, 51–141; J. Russell, *Recollections and suggestions*, 47.
[3] Vol. 64 (1822), 78–9.   [4] *Letters*, I, 366, 379.

of the Exchequer, appointed in the cabinet reshuffle after the suicide of Castlereagh in 1822, was so successful in the next three years that he acquired the nickname 'Prosperity' Robinson.[1] With the developing boom, interest in reform waned once more. The London Hampden Club, never a very solid institution, tottered out of existence, one secretary decamping, the next sued by the printer for outstanding debts.[2] In September 1824 died old Major Cartwright, eighty-four years of age, and still not in sight of the promised land: tedious, importunate, pedantic, often absurd, he redeemed everything by his pertinacity and self-sacrifice.[3] In the same year Thomas Wooler was forced to close down his newspaper, reproaching the reformers that 'what their enemies asserted and the *Black dwarf* treated as a calumny, that they only clamoured for bread', had proved to be true.[4]

The declining interest in the country was not long in making itself felt inside Parliament. In the spring of 1823 Russell, buttressed by petitions from several county meetings, moved a motion almost identical with that of 1822. One of the knights of the shire for Somerset, Sir Thomas Lethbridge, announced his conversion on the grounds that reform should be taken out of the hands of factious demagogues and effected by 'men of high character'. Russell declared that the final issue was no longer in doubt – 'the great stream of public opinion flowed on' – but the debate was dull and the adverse majority greater than before. In 1824 he apologized for not bringing forward the motion again as promised – the time was not expedient though he would do so the following session. In 1825 nothing was attempted. The Whigs began to shuffle. Reform could never be a 'bond of party', explained Tierney in May 1824, and early in 1825 Lord Lansdowne commented that prosperity had 'driven reform out of the heads of the reformers'.[5]

---

[1] See W. D. Jones, *Prosperity Robinson, the life of Viscount Goderich, 1782–1859* (1967).
[2] *Reports of the Hampden Club*, Cartwright's circular of June 1819 and Thomas Cleary's statement of February 1822.
[3] The most recent works on Cartwright are by N. C. Miller, 'John Cartwright and radical parliamentary reform, 1808–19', *English Historical Review*, 83 (1968) and John Osborne, *John Cartwright* (1972).
[4] Quoted J. H. Rose, 'The unstamped press, 1815–36', *English Historical Review*, 12 (1897), 718.
[5] *Parl. Debs.*, 2nd series, VIII, 1260–89; XI, 721, 756; Mitchell, 182. Tierney's declaration came in answer to an unkind question from Canning: 'were they or were they not pledged to parliamentary reform? The country at least believed so'. Canning's question revealed that many Whigs did not seem to know whether they were or not.

9

A strange and agitated sea

'We seem to be in a shattered boat, and in a strange and agitated sea, without pilot, chart or compass.'[1]

In the early summer of 1827 the prospects for parliamentary reform looked anything but good. The country evinced very little interest,[2] while the juxtaposition of political events seemed to have wiped out all the painful progress made since the end of the Napoleonic war. That one of the ablest and most outspoken of the opponents of reform, Canning, should be at the head of the ministry in succession to the stricken Liverpool was bad enough, but that he should be joined or supported by Brougham, Tierney and Burdett was worse. Worst of all was that the concessions seemed all to have come from the Whig side of the new coalition. Whereas Canning did not yield one inch in his resistance to reform – he would oppose it, he told the Commons, to the end of his life under whatever shape it assumed – the Whigs were ready to trim.[3] It was natural enough that those Whigs who had gone into partnership with Canning should deny that their party had ever been committed to reform, but Russell and Grey, who held aloof, joined them in minimizing the pledges of the past. Few things could have been more dispiriting to ardent reformers than Russell's intervention in the debate of 3 May 1827:[4]

> He himself, some few years since, had expressed his wish that the whole of the party...should unite to promote the cause of parliamentary reform; but it then appeared not only that most of the

[1] Lord Sidmouth to Pellew, early 1829, *Life and Correspondence of Henry Addington, 1st Viscount Sidmouth*, ed. G. Pellew, III, 426–7.
[2] From January 1824 to the early summer of 1827 there were only 5 petitions on reform, from London, Edinburgh, Rochdale, Tewkesbury and Oldham. Russell repeated his motion on 27 April 1826, previous to the general election of that year, and was beaten by 247 votes to 124. 'A great triumph against the Reformers', noted one observer: Buckingham, II, 300.
[3] Canning set out his terms in a memo to Lansdowne, 23 April 1827: 'all the existing members of the cabinet are united in opposing the question of parliamentary reform, and could not acquiesce in its being brought forward or supported by any member of the cabinet'. *The formation of Canning's ministry, February to August 1827*, Camden Society, 3rd series, vol. LIX, 124, 158, 190–1. Though Lansdowne did not join the ministry, the terms remained the same. See also the protest of Lord Althorp in *Memoir of John Charles, Viscount Althorp, third Earl Spencer*, ed. D. le Marchant, 215–16.
[4] *Parl. Debs.*, 2nd series, XVII, pp. 543–4. Peel expressed surprise that the Whigs were so keen to shrug off reform: 'that question certainly was with those hon. gentlemen a common bond of connection', *ibid.* 524.

leaders were desirous that it should not be made a party question, but that the whig party, if they should come in as a party, would be opposed to it...This fact he mentioned to show that it could not be justly imputed as a crime to any person...to have taken office on the present occasion without having stipulated that parliamentary reform should be made a party question...The very last time he had mentioned the question in the course of the last session, he had declared that that would be the last occasion of his doing so. And why had he made that declaration? Because he found a great lukewarmness on the subject throughout the country.

Even Grey, who might have been expected to include among his reasons for not joining the new ministry the question of reform, did not do so. Though he objected to the uncertainty over Catholic Emancipation and expressed distrust of Canning's foreign policy, he went out of his way to support his wandering colleagues in their contention that parliamentary reform was 'not a question to which they are pledged, nor on which the party to which they belong are agreed'. There was not sufficient support in the country to make it the *sine qua non* of any administration: in any case, he concluded, it was well known that he was himself withdrawing more and more from political life.[1] With Grey in opposition, reneging on his former commitments, deserted by some of his most able colleagues, confronted by Canning aged fifty-six, the crown hostile, the country indifferent, it would have taken some foresight to see him, three years thence, at the head of a reforming ministry. Meanwhile the gloom and disunity in the ranks of the reformers was suitably publicized at their annual dinner at the Crown and Anchor on 24 May, which degenerated into a shambles, amendments and reproachful speeches accompanying every toast. Cobbett behaved, according to Hobhouse, 'like a madman ...he drank several glasses of wine during his first speech against Burdett, and subsequently he gesticulated furiously, and shook his fist at us, called us bad names, and swore tremendously'.[2]

In the end, however, the situation developed in a way that few could have predicted to ease the path of reform. The split among the Tories turned out to be deeper and more enduring than among the Whigs. Canning's death, within months of taking the Treasury, removed an opponent and prepared the way for Whig reunification, while the mood of liberalism, growing since the early twenties, placed increasing strain on Tory consciences and Tory loyalties.

Though the Whigs continued to deny that they were pledged to comprehensive reform, they were prepared to promote gradual change.

[1] *Parl. Debs.*, 2nd series, XVII, 731–3.
[2] Lord Broughton, *Recollections of a long life*, III, 195–7.

Russell maintained his watch over electoral corruption, and in November 1826, five months after the general election, his brother William wrote pointing out Sudbury as a suitable case for treatment.[1] But the choice eventually fell upon Penryn and East Retford, brought before the House by their election committees in the course of Canning's brief ministry. At Penryn, several times threatened with the wrath of the Commons, the voters were said to have been regaled with a 'breakfast' worth 24 guineas a head to them: at East Retford the market price was 40 guineas, and several pubs had been kept open for months before the election, serving free beer from six a.m. until midnight or later. Russell succeeded in carrying against Canning an amendment that Penryn's seats should go, not to the neighbouring hundreds in Cornwall, but to Manchester, and it was his intention to move that the East Retford representation be transferred to Birmingham. Wellington's administration gave the matter considerable thought in the spring of 1828. The Duke's inclination, supported by Lord Bathurst, was to give all the seats to the neighbouring hundreds: the Canningites, led by Huskisson, wanted some of the seats to go to the great towns, and Dudley thought all four should be transferred. Croker argued in favour of a compromise – that Penryn's seats should go to the towns, but East Retford's should be given to the hundred of Bassetlaw in Nottinghamshire: thus the balance between the landed and commercial interests would be maintained, the door not slammed on gradual reform, yet the *ultra* Tories not outraged.[2]

Croker's suggestion was the one ultimately adopted by ministers. In the Commons the Whigs protested fiercely against the proposal to extend the franchise to Bassetlaw hundred, on the grounds that it would present two seats to the Duke of Newcastle, whose interest was paramount there, and thus strengthen aristocratic influence. Peel carried the day by 157 votes to 121, but his compromise was wrecked by the House of Lords, which flung out the Penryn bill without a division. Of the preamble to the bill, which declared that it was expedient to enfranchise Manchester 'on account of the increased wealth and population', Lord Salisbury observed that 'in that single sentence were embodied the wildest doctrines of radical reform'.[3] The Whigs then tried without success to persuade Peel to salvage something of his compromise by agreeing that the East Retford representation should go instead to Birmingham, but when the bill received the royal assent, just before the 1830 election, it was in the form of an extension to the hundreds.

[1] *Early correspondence*, I, 252.
[2] W. H. L. E. Bulwer, *The life of Henry John Temple, Viscount Palmerston*, I, 234–5, 253; Croker, I, 409–11; Lord Ellenborough, *A political diary, 1828–30*, ed. Lord Colchester, I, 63–4; See also the account in N. Gash, *Mr Secretary Peel: the life of Sir Robert Peel to 1830*, 469–70.
[3] *Parl. Debs.*, 2nd series, XIX, 1450.

The fate of the Penryn and East Retford bills was a fresh warning to reformers of the opposition they must expect from the House of Lords. But it was becoming evident that in the Commons a majority realized the need to bring the great towns into the representation, even if the Tories were still unwilling to make it a point of principle and commit themselves to systematic action. In addition the debates helped to rekindle interest in the country at large. Charles Tennyson, leading for the Whigs on the East Retford bill, made a powerful plea on behalf of Birmingham, drawing attention to the large number of private acts of Parliament which had to be steered by the county members, the local rate of £55,000, and the town's estimated capital of some ten million pounds. A public meeting called in the town in 1827 expressed great satisfaction at the prospect of representation, and was the forerunner of Thomas Attwood's Birmingham Political Union, founded in December 1829.[1] Manchester, where the political tradition ran deeper, needed less awakening. Archibald Prentice, editor of the *Manchester Times*, was a seasoned campaigner, and had published a calculation showing that the aggregate population of 100 small parliamentary boroughs was less than that of the single unrepresented parish of Manchester. The Penryn bill brought about unwonted collaboration between the local Tories, Whigs and radicals, and a joint committee was established in 1827 to lobby for representation. Sheffield, too, petitioned for inclusion in February 1830, asserting that a town of 80,000 inhabitants had 'a just claim to be directly represented by deputies of its own choice'. Many of these new claimants were men of wealth and importance in their communities, often drawn from the ranks of the employers, and convinced that their economic interests demanded direct representation. Attwood himself was a banker; the secretary of his committee, Joseph Parkes, was a solicitor, and the son of a factory owner; G. F. Muntz, who presided over the first meeting of the Birmingham Political Union, was a copper manufacturer. At the Manchester meeting for representation in 1827 the first resolution was moved by H. H. Birley, a cotton manufacturer, who had been at the head of the local yeomanry when they had charged the crowd at Peterloo eight years before. The Leeds petition in 1830 was specifically said to come from the 'bankers, merchants, manufacturers and others'. The time was past when the prospect of election riots was sufficient to deter men of property from seeking representation – when it could be written of Manchester that 'nothing could be more fatal to its trading interest, if it should be incorporated and have representation in Parliament'.[2] Prentice commented

[1] Place MSS., Add. MS. 35148, ff. 16–26.
[2] James Ogden, *A description of Manchester by a native of the town*, 1783, quoted in J. M. Main, 'The Parliamentary Reform Movement in Manchester, 1825–32', an unpublished Oxford B.Litt. thesis. Mrs Arbuthnot put the old-fashioned view when she wrote that 'in practice, nothing can exceed the folly of giving members to these populous

on the chance the Tories missed of appeasing these powerful local interests: 'fortunately our expectations were disappointed – fortunately, because if ministers had possessed even the left-handed wisdom of cunning, they would have granted the Penryn seats to Manchester one year, and East Retford seats to Birmingham in another, and thus have spread over fifty years the demolition effected at once by the 1832 bill'.[1]

In another but less direct way the East Retford bill promoted reform. William Huskisson, who served as leader of the House in the Goderich and Wellington ministries, was opposed to general reform, but supported the inclusion of the great towns, which would, in his view, establish a strong defensive position – 'early arrangements with a friendly power often prevent capitulations'. If no gesture of conciliation was made, he predicted a great stimulus to the reform agitation, with the prospect of annual confrontations.[2] Consequently, on 19 May 1828, when Peel carried the government's motion for Bassetlaw hundred, Huskisson voted with the minority, causing something of a sensation. Early next morning he submitted to Wellington his resignation which was promptly – even avidly – accepted. In this case, East Retford was only the last straw: the *ultra* Tories had for some years been uneasy at the drift towards liberalism, and viewed Huskisson and his associates with great suspicion. But out with Huskisson went William Lamb, Palmerston, Dudley and Charles Grant – a realignment of forces that helped to clarify the confused situation brought about by the collapse of Liverpool, and produced a more emphatically Tory administration.[3]

Finally, 'the battle of Retford' triggered off by accident the whole question of Catholic Emancipation. Charles Grant's successor at the Board of Trade was William Vesey Fitzgerald, who sat for county Clare. In July 1828 he offered himself for re-election on taking office and was resoundingly defeated by Daniel O'Connell, an avowed Catholic and, as the law stood, incapable of taking his seat. The government was faced, not only with the possibility of a new Wilkes controversy, but with the serious danger of civil war. That the Protestant Dissenters had earlier that year been relieved of their remaining civil disabilities by the Repeal of the Test

towns. It causes riots and loss of lives and property at every election, and it is not needed, for the great merchants get returned for the rotten boroughs, and can attend to the interests of their town much better than if they were obliged to pander to the passions of an interested mob.' *The journal of Mrs Arbuthnot, 1820-32*, ed. F. Bamford and the Duke of Wellington, II, 173.

[1] A. Prentice, *Historical sketches and personal recollections of Manchester*, 300–10; *CJ*, LXXXV, 96, 405–6; A. S. Turbeville & F. Beckwith, 'Leeds and parliamentary reform, 1820–32', *Publications of the Thoresby Society*, XLI, part i. See also D. Read, *The English provinces*, ch. iii.

[2] *Parl. Debs.*, 2nd series, XIX, 915–44; XXI, 1087–97; XXII, 341–8.

[3] For a Canningite view of the crisis, see Palmerston's journal, printed Bulwer, 253–76. A Wellingtonian view is Ellenborough I, 110–32.

and Corporation Acts made it even harder for the government to stand firm against the Catholics. Wellington and Peel resolved to give way, the legislation was pushed speedily through Parliament in the spring of 1829, and Catholic Emancipation, a Whig pledge since 1807, was finally effected by a Tory government. But the price paid was the total alienation of part of its following, outraged at what they deemed a betrayal of the Church of England.

Catholic Emancipation was the battering ram that broke down the old unreformed system. The Glorious Revolution of 1688 had been a settlement in both church and state: time and time again Burke, North and Pitt had insisted that the two must stand or fall together. Now a breach had been made in the Anglican supremacy, and Catholics could enjoy all but a few of the highest offices of state. It was, declared Lord Falmouth, a measure revolutionary in its implications. 'I have never been a reformer; but upon what principle will you resist reform when you have made a radical reform at the fountain head? Upon what principle will you talk of preserving the tree of the constitution, when you have laid your axe to the root?'[1] Ever since the seventeenth century, religious toleration and parliamentary reform had gone hand in hand. At times it had seemed that the Protestant Dissenters might prove to be the spearhead of reform in their own efforts to obtain redress, and they had played a very active part in the agitation before the French Revolution. But though a force to be reckoned with in many constituencies, especially in East Anglia and parts of the West, their status of quasi-toleration did not allow them to capture a seat and use it as a lever. The enfranchisement of the forty-shilling freeholder in Ireland in 1793 had placed a weapon of vast potential in Catholic hands. That they were slow to exploit it is an indication of the tenacity of the Protestant ascendancy, but within three years of the founding of the Catholic Association in 1823 they had gained electoral successes that pointed the way to the future.[2]

Although repeal of the Test and Corporation Acts preceded Catholic Emancipation by a year, the impact was much smaller. Memories of the 1640s when the Church of England had been humbled by the Dissenters were overlaid by James II's attack on behalf of the Catholics in the 1680s and by the subsequent history of Jacobitism. Nor did the repeal of the Test and Corporation Acts do more than remove a theoretical grievance, since the practice of annual indemnification had been long established. Catholic Emancipation, on the other hand, affected the reform issue in many ways. It was accompanied by an act to disqualify the forty-shilling Irish freeholders by raising the county franchise to a £10 freehold – a safeguard which the government deemed essential if the main bill was

---

[1] *Parl. Debs.*, 2nd series, XXI, 223.
[2] The best account is G. I. T. Machin, *The Catholic question in English politics, 1820–30*.

to pass: the result was that no fewer than 200,000 freeholders lost the right to vote, and the electorate was reduced in some Irish counties to derisory numbers. At one stroke was destroyed an argument against reform that had done service for many years – that the multi-patterned franchise was a thing of such exquisite balance and deftness that it should on no account be disturbed. Reformers were quick also to notice the success the Catholic Association had achieved. By union and organization, declared Attwood in May 1829, 'the Irish people have lately obtained a glorious and bloodless victory'.[1]

Most of all, Catholic Emancipation dealt damaging blows to two institutions that stood in the path of reform – the crown and the Tory party. It was widely known that George IV was under great pressure to refuse his consent to the measure, and he was inclined, like his father, to appeal to his coronation oath. In the end, with much heart-searching, he gave way. The moral was clear: a resolute government could anticipate with some confidence that the crown could be forced to swallow parliamentary reform as well. The Tory party also emerged from the crisis seriously weakened. The hatred of many Tories for Wellington and Peel as the leaders who had betrayed them was intense. Oxford University rejected Peel when he offered himself for re-election in favour of Sir Robert Inglis, the Anglican champion, and sent him scurrying to one of the western boroughs that Sir Manasseh Masseh Lopes had managed to hold in the midst of his electoral misfortunes; the Duchess of Richmond, a furious *ultra*, kept in a glass case a number of stuffed rats, upon which she bestowed appropriate names; as for the Duke of Wellington, he deserved hanging, wrote one partisan in private, while the public strictures of Lord Winchilsea led to a duel in Battersea Fields.[2] Though the administration carried on, its survival was precarious, and the absence of ministerial talent in the House of Commons was a source of constant embarrassment to Peel.

The effect on the Whigs was to increase the chance of their embracing reform, since for decades Catholic Emancipation had been the fig-leaf they had used to cover their political nakedness. Now they must look for another. On the Tories, the effect was the reverse, since to follow up repeal of the Test and Corporation Acts and Catholic Emancipation by yet another affront to the Tory conscience would be excessive, even for Wellington. Indeed, the curious ferocity of the Duke's disavowal of reform in November 1830 must in part be attributed to the events of the spring of 1829.[3] But some of the *ultras* reacted quite differently. In the House of

---

[1] Speech of 8 May 1829 at Birmingham printed as a pamphlet, *The distressed state of the country*.   [2] Arbuthnot, II, 257; Greville, I, 196–8; Machin, 180.
[3] See Mrs Arbuthnot's comment that Peel was afraid he 'would be thought shabby if he lent himself again to a measure he had hitherto opposed'. Arbuthnot, II, 398.

Lords, Winchilsea announced that whatever doubts he had previously entertained on the reform question had been removed by the behaviour of the Tory leaders:[1] in the House of Commons, Lord Blandford, who had previously shown little interest in anything but the preservation of game, announced himself an instant convert to radical reform and gave notice of a motion he intended to move on the subject. The carrying of Catholic Emancipation in the teeth of a vast number of hostile petitions demonstrated, in his view, that the reformers were right in asserting that Parliament did not represent the wishes of the people. Without a sweeping reform, a new Catholic party, solidly based on the Irish constituencies, might improve its position by buying up close boroughs and establish such a phalanx in the House of Commons that would enable it to dominate the state. Eccentric though he unquestionably was, there was a certain wild logic in Blandford's position, nor, in view of developments in the 1880s, can his glimpse of a nightmare future be utterly dismissed. Hitherto the pocket boroughs had been an invaluable aid to governments, mainly Tory, in their opposition to radical and dissenting pressure: should they become the means of undermining what was left of the citadel of Anglicanism, they must go. In Blandford's mind, the Church of England took precedence over all other loyalties. Once before, in 1688, the Tories had faced a similar agony of choice, when the crown, to which they were devoted, attempted to use its prerogatives to subvert their Church. Now Blandford called to his colleagues to sacrifice the old parliamentary settlement in order to save the old religious settlement.

On 18 February 1830 he unfolded to an astonished House of Commons a plan of reform to cheer the hearts of the Bromleys and Hynde Cottons of one hundred years before.[2] It was, thought Howick, 'a mere schoolboy's declamation...such a tissue of nonsense as never was seen'.[3] Almost every proposal aired in the previous century was brought forward and displayed, so that Blandford's speech became a kind of compendium of reform. The rotten boroughs should be abolished and their seats transferred to the counties and populous towns; the septennial act should be repealed; members of Parliament were to receive pay once more; no persons holding place or office of profit under the crown were to sit in Parliament; copyholders were to be enfranchised; the property qualification for burgesses was to go, together with the legislation against persons in holy orders (passed in 1801 to get rid of the embarrassment of Horne Tooke); non-resident voters were to be disqualified; the Scottish repre-

---

[1] *Parl. Debs.*, 2nd series, xx, 933.
[2] He had previously raised the matter on 2 June 1829 with the remark that others seemed to have abandoned the task of reform they had once set themselves. His motion that the existence of the decayed boroughs was disgraceful to the House was rejected by 114 votes to 40. *Parl. Debs.*, 2nd series, xxi, 1672–89.
[3] Journal of 3rd Earl Grey, Grey MSS., Durham.

7

sentation reformed; and a general scot and lot franchise introduced. Members had some difficulty in framing their replies to such a bombardment. Sir Robert Wilson admitted that he had been suspicious of Blandford's hasty conversion, taking it to be a mere instrument of revenge on the Tory leadership, but was now satisfied; Horace Twiss thought the motion was intended to be a mockery of reform – 'a snake in the grass'. Ultimately his motion was defeated by 160 votes to 57. As an attempt at reform it could hardly be taken seriously, though it helped to stir up interest, and even the modest support given to Blandford by a handful of *ultras* boded ill for the future of Wellington's government.[1]

Up to this point the renewed interest in Parliament had come about largely because of the party situation and was in advance of opinion in the country. As late as May 1829 a member could refer in debate to 'the now almost forgotten and ill-omened cause of reform'.[2] But with the onset of a very severe recession in the winter of 1829/30, the position began to change. The King's Speech, at the beginning of February, admitted distress, but insisted that it was partial, and advised extreme caution in proposing remedies.[3] It was not long before the reform agitation began to revive. In July 1829, under O'Connell's auspices, a London Radical Association was founded. Of greater importance were the discussions in Birmingham in December 1829 which led to the foundation of the Birmingham Political Union the following month at a meeting said to be the largest ever held inside a building. The new organization was essentially moderate and middle class in character: they would seek reform, Attwood confided to Hobhouse, upon 'the conservative principle...he was convinced that the whole people of England were essentially aristocratic'.[4] In March 1830 the Metropolitan Political Union in London was far more radical, with Hunt and O'Connell joined by the stalwarts of the unstamped press campaign, Hetherington and Carlile. These efforts were augmented by a grand speaking tour of Cobbett's in the winter of 1829/30 and the spring months of 1830. Most remarkable of all were indications that bitterness over Catholic Emancipation coupled with distress was forcing farmers and landowners to reconsider long-held prejudices. 'Country gentlemen, magistrates, and even clergymen appear in

---

[1] *Parl. Debs.*, 2nd series, XXII, 678–725. Blandford's draft bill is given on pp. 726–52. There was confusion about the voting. The *Parl. Debs.* give it as on an amendment by Brougham, but *CJ*, LXXXV, 70 as on the original motion. Broughton, IV, 9 confirms the *CJ* version.

[2] *Parl. Debs.*, 2nd series, XXI, 1070.

[3] The subsequent debate showed how precarious events had made the government's majority. Sir Edward Knatchbull and Blandford, on behalf of the *ultras*, moved an amendment that the distress was 'general': it was defeated by only 55 votes. According to Hobhouse, the government was saved by 28 Whigs, who voted with them on the grounds that the *ultras*' behaviour was factious. Broughton, IV, 7–8.

[4] Broughton, IV, 28.

the parts of demagogues', wrote the *Examiner* in January 1830.[1] At Worcester a county meeting was said to have voted a petition linking distress and reform with 'scarcely a dissentient voice', and the Hampshire meeting at Winchester was said to be unanimous for parliamentary reform.[2] By April 1830 Lord Eldon, whose House of Commons career stretched back to the time Pitt had been a reformer, thought the portents more alarming than in the 1790s: 'the sacrifice of the Test Act', he wrote to his brother, 'and the passing of the Roman Catholic Emancipation Bill have established a precedent so encouraging to the present attempts at revolution under name of Reform that he must be a very bold fool who does not tremble at what seems to be fast approaching'.[3]

Blandford's motion prodded the Whigs into activity once more. On 23 February, Lord John Russell moved for a bill to give representation to Manchester, Birmingham and Leeds – a proposal, he insisted, least open to the charge of being wild and visionary. These three towns, he maintained, could be enfranchised without opening the flood-gates, since they were the capitals of their respective industries – an argument on which the presence of an unwanted petition from Sheffield cast some doubt. Huskisson supported him, suggesting that the cases of Penryn and East Retford had demonstrated the improbability of piece-meal reform succeeding. Once again Russell was defeated, but the division – 188 votes to 140 – showed that the tide was flowing for reform. The trickle of conversions went on. In a debate on the East Retford bill a fortnight later, Sir Christopher Cole, the member for Glamorgan, deserted the government, explaining that he would be ashamed not to give an independent vote on a matter of such importance, and Robert Bransby Cooper, who had voted against Russell's motion, declared that the time had come for ministers to take reform into their own hands.[4] Inside the government, Croker urged the same policy – let the Grampound seats be withdrawn from Yorkshire and used with Retford to enfranchise Leeds, Sheffield, Manchester and Birmingham. But political subtlety was scarcely the strong suit of the administration: both Wellington and Peel carried pragmatism to extreme lengths, and neither showed much desire to come to terms with reform. Nor did Goulburn, their Chancellor of the Exchequer, who perceived 'great danger' in advancing one step in that direction. The East Retford bill, still grinding its way through the parliamentary machinery, was the ministry's sole concession to persons dissatisfied with the state of the representation.[5]

---

[1] Quoted in H. Jephson, *The Platform*, II, 47.   [2] *Bristol Gazette*, 11 and 18 March 1830.
[3] Quoted Trevelyan, 206.   [4] *Parl. Debs.*, 2nd series, XXII, 1324, 1326.
[5] Croker, II, 54–5; *Parl. Debs.*, 2nd series, XXII, 348. Peel even had to fight hard to save the East Retford bill after the death of George IV warning the cabinet that he would not be able to oppose general reform 'if we do not show a disposition to punish individual cases of corruption'. Ellenborough, II, 315.

Perhaps ministers were encouraged in their obduracy by the fate of a motion for radical reform introduced in May 1830 by O'Connell. Russell confessed himself embarrassed by the demand for manhood suffrage: it would make it impossible, in the long run, to maintain equal rights to unequal things. Only a handful of radicals voted with the *ultras* Blandford and C. N. Pallmer, and O'Connell lost by 319 votes to 13. Russell's subsequent proposal to extend the representation to a considerable number of manufacturing towns was rejected by 213 votes to 117 – a sharp setback compared with his motion of February, and confirming, perhaps, the point made in debate that moderate reform flourished when radical reform was not there to blight it.[1]

With the government in poor shape and the pressure for reform growing in the country, the Whigs began to scent victory – 'they seem to think that they are capable of making an administration', wrote Croker scornfully.[2] In March 1830 a group of some forty Whigs, perceiving that their lack of leadership in the Commons since Tierney gave up the thankless task ten years earlier might have contributed to their ill success, offered to place themselves under the orders of Lord Althorp, the least brilliant but most agreeable of their natural leaders. Even so, they were far from becoming a determined opposition, since the first consequence of their action was that Althorp 'succeeded in stopping the factious attacks preparing against the government, and in obtaining for it an honest, discriminating support'.[3] But a new element entered the situation the following month as the seriousness of George IV's illness became apparent. With the prospect of the ban on their employment being lifted after so many decades, the Whigs became noticeably less cordial towards the ministry. A similar transition may be traced in the attitude of Lord Grey who, by the end of April, found politics sufficiently promising to warrant leaving Northumberland and making an appearance in the Lords. Far from waiting patiently in the wings for his moment of historical destiny to arrive,[4] he had spent much of 1829 and early 1830 impatiently expecting an offer to join Wellington's government. On 26 June the King died, and from Wellington four days later came not an invitation but notice of the

---

[1] *Parl. Debs.*, 2nd series, XXIV, 1254. Russell mentioned Macclesfield, Stockport, Whitehaven, Sunderland, Cheltenham, Brighton, Bury, Bolton, Wolverhampton, Birmingham, Dudley, Leeds, Wakefield, Sheffield, and North and South Shields, in addition to Edinburgh, Glasgow and Belfast. The omission of Manchester was presumably an oversight. Russell had quickly abandoned his pretence that enfranchisement could be confined to the three great towns, and this may have cost him some parliamentary support. But more likely it was guilt by association with O'Connell.
[2] Croker to Fitzgerald, 3 May 1830, Croker, II, 58.
[3] *Althorp*, 246. For further evidence of these meetings and the disunity demonstrated, see Lord Howick's journal for 3 and 6 March, Grey MSS.
[4] Trevelyan, 215. 'It was in the year 1830 that the change began, for which Grey, all too patiently perhaps but very faithfully, had been waiting as the signal for his own action.'

dissolution of Parliament. To the indignation of some noble lords, Grey now revealed that his real opinion was that the ministers were 'incompetent to manage the business of the country'.[1] On 24 July, after the East Retford bill had at last gone through all its stages, Parliament was dissolved and a general election called.[2]

* * * *

In many respects the election of 1830 was unremarkable. The number of contests was not unduly high – some 83 in England compared with 89 in 1826.[3] Nor was there a significantly large number of new members returned – 175 against 171 at the previous election.[4] There was, as usual, hardly a stir in Wales, where 19 of the 24 sitting members were returned for their previous constituencies, most of them without the trouble of a contest, and scarcely more excitement in Scotland. Though there were important changes in the English counties, 62 of the 82 previous occupants were back in their seats when Parliament reassembled in November.

From the earliest returns however it was clear that, in those places where it could be expressed, opinion was running strongly against Wellington's administration. Peel and his relatives fared particularly badly. Abandoning the undignified refuge at Westbury in favour of a seat on the family interest at Tamworth, he shunted his brother William on to a pocket borough at Yarmouth, Isle of Wight; but Jonathan Peel was beaten at Norwich and Edmund Peel at Newcastle-under-Lyme. George Dawson, Peel's brother-in-law, lost his seat for the county of Londonderry and was brought in for the Treasury borough of Harwich. John Wilson Croker, belatedly paying for the support he had given to Catholic Emancipation, was forced out of his seat for Trinity College, Dublin, and made his election for the obscurity of Aldeburgh.

Reform gained a dramatic victory in Yorkshire, where Henry Brougham, with no local interest whatever, made a triumphant return after an extensive speaking tour.[5] Lord Fordwich, an avowed advocate of reform,

[1] *Parl. Debs.*, 2nd series, xxv, 728. Ellenborough retorted that Grey's remarks came with a bad grace. 'Adverting to the noble Earl's conduct since the formation of the present government, to his almost entire confidence in the wisdom of its measures...it was with the deepest feelings of personal regret that he had heard the noble earl's words tonight...that he considered the existing government incapable of conducting the business of the country with advantage.'
[2] The third reading was on 21 July, and it received the royal assent on the 23rd, when the King attended to dissolve Parliament.
[3] The 1830 figures were 9 county polls and 74 borough polls. For 1818 and 1820 the totals were 93 and 73. These figures are of course approximations.
[4] The new members in 1830 were as follows: England 122, Wales 5, Scotland 12, Ireland 35. For 1826 I have accepted the figures given by the *Gent. Mag.* II, 72–6, which may not be completely accurate. They break down as England 125, Wales 5, Scotland 12, Ireland 29.
[5] N. Gash, 'Brougham and the Yorkshire election of 1830', *Proceedings of the Leeds Philosophical and Literary Society*, vol. VIII, part i; A. Aspinall, *Lord Brougham and the Whig Party*, 174–8.

won a hard-fought struggle at Canterbury; in Suffolk, Thomas Sherlock Gooch, who had held the seat for twenty-four years, was, in Cobbett's unkind phrase, 'hooted down as a common nuisance'; while *The Times* described the attempt to overthrow the Grosvenor interest at Shaftesbury, though unsuccessful, as 'the most extraordinary movement which has been made for the last half-century in the West of England'. In the English counties, the government suffered severe setbacks: of the seventeen new county members who took part in the decisive division of 15 November 1830, fifteen voted against the ministers. Planta, surveying the havoc, was obliged to protest that these matters were 'utterly unmanageable' by anything the Treasury could do.[1] Government successes to offset these misfortunes were few and far between, though Lord John Russell lost his election at Bedford by one vote and had to fall back on the family borough of Tavistock. After no more than two days polling, Greville remarked that no candidate would 'avow that he stands on government interest, or with the intention of supporting the Duke's ministry'.[2] On 13 August, with most of the results in save for some Irish and Scottish seats, Croker wrote:[3]

> Not one man elected in any *contested* place (except I believe Bristol) on ministerial principles. Whigs and Ultra Tories and Radicals and reformers and economists were everywhere successful against those who stood on the government interest. I know this is not the light in which the Treasury views the returns, but I see in them the seeds of the most troublesome and unmanageable Parliament since that of 1640 which overturned the monarchy and beheaded the monarch.

The government put a brave face on things, claimed a small improvement, and may even have believed it.[4] *The Spectator*, on the other hand, put government losses at between forty and fifty. Brougham, for the opposition, dashed off a hasty pamphlet, insisting that in the open constituencies, of 236 seats available only 79 fell to ministerialists against 141 to persons

[1] Joseph Planta to Peel, 18 August, Add. MS. 40401, f. 130.
[2] C. C. F. Greville, II, 20.
[3] Quoted A. Aspinall, ed., *Three early nineteenth century diaries*, introduction, xxiii. At Bristol Richard Hart Davis, a ministerialist, held his seat, but the chief election issue was anti-slavery rather than reform. By the 'Treasury view' Croker presumably meant Planta, who compiled a comforting list of sixteen 'gains in populous places' as against twelve losses. Add. MS. 40401, f. 139. Unfortunately many of the gains were illusory while the losses were certain. Of the 16 'gains' only 7 voted with the government on 15 November: of the 12 'losses', 9 divided with opposition and 3 were absent.
[4] Mitchell, *The Whigs in opposition, 1815–30*, 232–3 quotes a series of estimates. Planta reported on 23 August a net gain of 20 (Add. MS. 40401, f. 138): there were then 56 more results to come in. Mitchell (p. 232, n. 6.), quoting from the Apsley House papers, put Planta's final estimate at 22.

in 'avowed opposition'.[1] These widely divergent views make it difficult to say precisely what was the outcome of the election. It has been hailed as the moment when public opinion came of age, when the props that had supported administration for so long finally collapsed.[2] For years patronage secretaries had complained that there was not sufficient pasture for the parliamentary sheep, nor enough government boroughs for all the key men. Certainly the 1830 election appears to be unique in that government did not even improve its position, yet the political situation was too confused for a clear moral to emerge. It is hard to say what the effective strength of the government was in the spring of 1830, while the three months that elapsed between the election and the opening of the parliamentary session in November permits at least the possibility of a last-minute swing of opinion among elected members.[3]

Of equal importance were the negotiations that Wellington was conducting in the hope of strengthening his ministry. For months Peel had complained that he was left almost single-handed to defend the government in the House of Commons. With the attitude of the Whigs hardening rapidly, overtures were directed at the Canningites. A tentative discussion in July broke down when Melbourne pitched his terms absurdly high, declaring that he would only come in with Huskisson and Grey. Negotiations were resumed with more vigour in September soon after Huskisson's death at the opening of the Liverpool and Manchester railway. This time the approach was to Palmerston who, in an interview with the Duke, demanded a complete reconstruction of the ministry, with room found for Grey and Lansdowne, as well as his Canningite colleagues.[4] Wellington found the terms unreasonable, but persistent rumours continued that the government might itself introduce a measure of reform: in that case, Grey confided to Holland, he would feel obliged to offer his

---

[1] Brougham's work was entitled *The result of the general election, or what has the Duke of Wellington gained by the dissolution?* It was reviewed at length in the *Edinburgh Review* vol. 52 of October 1830 by its author, who pronounced it 'of great and admitted force'. A government reply, *Observations on two pamphlets (lately published) attributed to Mr Brougham*, attempted a refutation. For a private exchange on the interpretation of the results, see Brougham, *Life and Times*, III, 55–9.

[2] A. S. Foord, 'The waning of "The influence of the Crown"', *English Historical Review*, 62 (1947).

[3] It is not even certain that Wellington would have been defeated had the vote on reform taken place on 16 November 1830. The *ultras* were said to have decided to abstain. B. T. Bradfield, 'Sir Richard Vyvyan and the Country Gentlemen, 1830–1834', *English Historical Review*, 83 (1968).

[4] The best account of these negotiations is in Palmerston's journal, printed Bulwer, I, 361–4. There were two approaches to Palmerston – one at the end of September, and a second at the end of October. Further discussion is in A. Aspinall, 'The last of the Canningites', *English Historical Review*, 50 (1935), and C. Flick, 'The fall of Wellington's government', *Journal of Modern History*, 37 (1965).

support.[1] In the end, however, the Duke resolved to try to recapture the confidence of the *ultras* instead. Mrs Arbuthnot, reflecting Wellington's own optimism, believed that the failure of the negotiations, 'and the hostility that will necessarily ensue, will bring back our Tory party'.[2]

There seems little doubt that the question of reform played an important part in the negotiations, despite Mrs Arbuthnot's assertion to the contrary.[3] On 3 October Lord Rosslyn, a well-informed observer, told Ellenborough that reform had made a coalition impossible, and a month later Sir Henry Hardinge confirmed that the Canningites had 'at once started the difficulty of reform, which put an end to the negotiation'.[4] After the Duke had made his categorical declaration against reform, the Canningites took an even firmer line, and Croker concluded an interview with Palmerston by demanding: 'are you resolved or are you not to vote for parliamentary reform? I said, "I am." "Well then", said he, "there is no use in talking to you any more on this subject." '[5]

Parliament assembled on 2 November for the King's speech amid widespread disorders in the southern counties as a consequence of acute rural distress. In Kent, the *Annual Register* reported, 'night after night new conflagrations were lighted up by bands of incendiaries: corn-stacks, barns, farm-buildings, live-stock were consumed indiscriminately'.[6] Brougham brought the political pot to the boil with a declaration that he would move for parliamentary reform a fortnight later. In the Lords, Grey took up the same theme and warned ministers that if they neglected to introduce reform, they would be obliged to yield to expediency what they had denied to principle, as they had done over Catholic Emancipation. It was in reply to Grey's observations that Wellington delivered his

[1] Grey to Holland, 19 September and 17 October 1830, Add. MS. 51555, ff. 477 and 480; Grey to Princess Lieven, 15 September and 7 October 1830, Princess Lieven, II, 89–90, 104. See also Lord Tavistock to G. W. Russell, 6 October 1830, *Letters to G. W. Russell, 1817–45*. This was privately printed and I have not found a copy in the British Museum: the Cambridge University library has one.

[2] Arbuthnot, II, 396. This was just a week before Parliament assembled. Later she told Greville that the opposition would be beaten on reform, 'people will return to the government and we shall go on very well'. Greville, II, 56.

[3] Arbuthnot, II, 370, 396. 'Lord Palmerston did not say one syllable upon *policy* or *principles*; it turned entirely upon *places*.'

[4] Ellenborough, II, 381, 418. A third approach through Littleton, referred to in C. S. Parker, *Sir Robert Peel*, II, 163–6, seems to have been a solo effort. Littleton maintained that if the government would promote moderate reform the Canningites would join.

[5] Bulwer, I, 364.

[6] P. 149. E. J. Hobsbawm & G. Rudé, *Captain Swing*, has now replaced J. L. & B. Hammond, *The Village Labourer*, as the best account of these riots. G. Rudé, 'English rural and urban disturbances, 1830–1', *Past & Present*, no. 37 (1967), concludes that they had little political significance.

astonishing statement that under no circumstances would the government bring forward reform:[1]

> He was fully convinced that the country possessed at the present moment a legislature which answered all the good purposes of legislation, and this to a greater degree than any legislature ever had answered in any country whatever. He would go further and say that the legislature and the system of representation possessed the full and entire confidence of the country...He would go still further and say that if at the present moment he had imposed upon him the duty of forming a legislature for any country, and particularly for a country like this, in possession of great property of various descriptions, he did not mean to assert that he could form such a legislature as they possessed now, for the nature of man was incapable of reaching such excellence at once; but his great endeavour would be to form some description of legislature which would produce the same results ...Under these circumstances he was not prepared to bring forward any measure of the description alluded to by the noble lord...and he would at once declare that, as far as he was concerned, as long as he held any station in the government of the country, he should always feel it his duty to resist such measures when proposed by others.

In his anxiety, perhaps, to shake off the charge of opportunism, he had committed the supreme blunder of leaving himself no room for manoeuvre: he had made the redoubt so secure that it became, not the refuge of his followers, but their prison. The next night, Sir George Murray, the colonial secretary, amid opposition cheers, dissociated himself from so extreme a position, and even the adoring Mrs Arbuthnot was forced to contemplate the possibility that the Duke had gone too far.[2] Publicly, the government continued to exude confidence – 'they talk of a majority of 76 on the reform question', Grey told Princess Lieven – but privately they were more subdued. At cabinet on the 9th, there were gloomy reports of defection on reform – 'the Staffords, young Hope, Lord Talbot, the Clives very unwilling to vote against it, thinking the public feeling so strong'. Peel brushed aside Ellenborough's suggestion that the Duke's declaration was not as categorical as it seemed: verbal quibbling would not do, 'It was "Reform or No Reform"'.[3]

---

[1] *Parl. Debs.*, 3rd series, I, 37–8, 52–3.
[2] *Parl. Debs.*, 3rd series, I, 168, 175–6. Greville thought the Duke's speech 'violent and uncalled-for...an act of egregious folly...I found the town ringing with his imprudence'. Greville, II, 56. Countess Granville wrote that 'even his own people hold the language that the sooner he goes the better'. *Letters of Harriet, Countess Granville*, ed. F. L. Gower, II, 64.
[3] Princess Lieven, II, 116; Ellenborough, II, 426.

Peel was, of course, right. The Duke's speech had had the effect of polarizing politics – which, indeed, was what had been intended. But the advantage did not fall to Wellington, who split his friends and united his opponents. He made the Whigs, by contrast, seem more of a reform party than ever they had been, and they were able to bask in the enjoyment of that rarest of political pleasures, an outrageously bigoted adversary.

The scene was now set for a grand confrontation when Brougham's motion for reform was to come before the House on the 16th. It did not take place. The day before, Sir Henry Parnell moved for a select committee to investigate civil list expenditure, and after an unremarkable debate, government was defeated by 233 votes to 204. The following day ministers, some at least not without relief, tendered their resignations.[1]

Though one cannot entirely rule out the possibility that the ministry might have scraped a majority had it faced Brougham's motion, it is hardly likely that that majority would have been sufficient to ride out the storm that was bound to follow. The vote on 15 November was not on an issue of major importance: nevertheless it was decisive enough, and there was little to encourage the Duke to continue. No fewer than forty-seven of the English county members had voted with opposition against only fifteen in the government ranks, while the new members, on whom Planta had put a good deal of reliance, proved a sad disappointment.[2] If the Duke's declaration had been intended to rally the *ultras*, it failed of its purpose: thirty-three of them voted with opposition and only eight with government.[3]

In retrospect the Duke was inclined to put much of the blame on the revolution in France, which 'occurred at the very moment of the dissolution of Parliament'.[4] Such an explanation was more attractive than an admission that he had miscalculated the mood of his own country. Professor Gash has shown that the July revolution can have had little effect on the elections, most of which were concluded by the time the

[1] According to le Marchant, ministers were so unprepared for defeat on this question that at first the Duke thought the majority of 29 was in his favour and expressed disquiet at its inadequacy. *Three diaries*, 1-2. Mrs Arbuthnot wrote of Peel after the defeat, 'I never saw a man so delighted'. Arbuthnot, II, 402.

[2] On 23 August, Planta classified 134 newly elected members as 79 'known to be friends', 45 opponents and 10 doubtful – that is he expected them to divide roughly 2-1 for government. In the event, of the 175 new members, 81 voted with opposition, 47 with government, 43 were absent, 3 were absent opposition, and 1 was dead – i.e. roughly 2-1 against government. The new Irish members were particularly hostile, voting 16-4 against. The matter is discussed in A. Macintyre, *The Liberator*, 12-16. The Welsh members were as usual conspicuous by their absence and the Scots voted 7-2 with government. Planta's list is Add. MS. 40401, f. 139.

[3] Taking Planta's list of 37 moderate *ultras* and 25 violent *ultras* as the basis of the calculation. For a different basis, see Aspinall, introduction, xxv.

[4] Wellington to Maurice Fitzgerald, 26 December 1830, *Despatches, correspondence and memoranda of the Duke of Wellington*, new series, VII, 382-3.

news of the overthrow of Charles X came through.[1] There remains however the possibility that public opinion was powerfully swayed in the
months of September and October before Parliament met. On such
a question it is unwise to be categorical, but it is unlikely that the impact
of events was wholly in favour of reform, particularly after the developing
crisis about Belgium had revived old fears of French revolutionary
aggrandisement. Certainly Palmerston was not alone in thinking that
events abroad might have strengthened the Duke's position. 'There is no
answering for the absurdity of mankind', he wrote to Littleton, 'and it is
not impossible that all these convulsions on the continent...may be, with
many well-meaning men, a reason for giving their support.'[2]

On 17 November 1830, for the first time, a ministry pledged to parliamentary reform assumed office. Grey took the earliest opportunity in the
Lords to acknowledge the need for reform and his 'anxious wish to
regulate that reform in such a manner as to restore confidence and satisfaction upon the part of the people'.[3] At long last the Whigs had attained
power and principle.

[1] 'English reform and French revolution in the general election of 1830', *Essays presented to Sir Lewis Namier*, ed. R. Pares & A. J. P. Taylor.
[2] 25 September 1830, Hatherton MSS., quoted A. Aspinall, *Lord Brougham and the Whig Party*, 181. See also Buckingham, I, 45.
[3] *Parl. Debs.*, 3rd series, I, 607.

10

Revolution by due course of law

'It will be what Mr Hume calls "a bloodless revolution". There will be, there can be, no resistance. But we shall be destroyed one after the other... by due course of law.'[1]

One of Lord Grey's first acts upon taking office was to empower a committee of ministers to draft reform proposals. The chairmanship went to Grey's son-in-law, Lord Durham, long an advocate of reform: his bill of April 1821, including provisions for triennial Parliaments, equal electoral areas and a ratepayer franchise, had been far too extreme for his fellow Whigs, and he was still one of the most radical in the party.[2] Lord John Russell was not a member of the cabinet but his previous exertions in the cause of reform gave him a claim to consideration, and he was the obvious man to present the measure in the Commons should the leader of the House, Althorp, be thought inadequate. The third member, Lord Duncannon, as well as being closely connected with the great Whig families, was a sound party man, an experienced whip, and of a conciliatory nature. The fourth, and most surprising choice, was Sir James Graham, who had only recently come to the fore as a parliamentarian and a reformer: he had useful contacts with the Canningites, whose attitude would be of critical importance.[3] For Brougham no place was found on the committee, though he had a draft reform plan in his pocket;[4] nor were any of the *ultras* included, though Richmond is said to have been considered.[5]

At the same time Grey provided the committee with its terms of reference. The reform was to be large enough to satisfy public opinion and 'to afford sure ground of resistance to further innovation'.[6] It was to be

[1] Wellington to Melville, 30 May 1831, Despatches, VII, 451.
[2] Parl. Debs., 2nd series, V, 359–453 and appendix ciii–cxxvii. His reform activities before 1830 are discussed at some length in C. W. New, Lord Durham, 54–8, 68–71.
[3] Graham's reputation in the House was established in the spring of 1830 by a series of speeches in favour of retrenchment. He declared in favour of 'moderate but effective reform' at an election dinner in August, and in October was urging Grey to make a declaration against nomination boroughs. J. T. Ward, Sir James Graham, 85–8; Russell to Grey, October 1830, Grey MSS.
[4] Printed in J. Roebuck, History of the Whig ministry of 1830, I, 420–2, and commented on in C. W. New, Life of Henry Brougham to 1830, 412–14. For Brougham's jealousy of Russell, see Tavistock to G. W. Russell, 5 November 1830, Letters to G. W. Russell, 1817–45.
[5] J. Russell, Recollections and suggestions, 1813–73, 68–9.
[6] This account is not Grey's but was given by Graham to Roebuck in 1851, and is printed as an appendix to chapter five in C. S. Parker, Life of Sir James Graham. There is

based on property and existing franchises – that is, from the very beginning Grey ruled out any question of manhood suffrage, as his speech of 22 November had made clear.[1] Lastly, the existing territorial divisions were to be maintained – thus Durham was warned that proposals for equal electoral areas, such as he had put forward in 1821, would not be entertained.[2]

The first meeting of the committee of four seems to have been held at Durham's house on 11 December, within a month of the Whigs taking office.[3] It considered two drafts, submitted by Russell and Althorp, labelled plans no. 1 and no. 2.[4] Between the two was much common ground. Each envisaged a substantial disqualification of decayed boroughs, on the basis of their population figures. Russell proposed that some fifty boroughs with populations of less than 1400, should lose both members, and that another fifty, with populations between 1400 and 3000, should lose one – making about 150 disqualifications in all. Althorp contented himself with suggesting the disqualification of one hundred seats.[5] They agreed that some 42 seats should be allocated to the large unrepresented towns, including London. In the new boroughs, Althorp wanted the £10 householder enfranchised: Russell, more cautiously, wanted £15 p.a. or jury service as the basis.[6] Althorp proposed the disfranchisement of all out-

however nothing in Grey's writings at variance with it, and its general tenor corresponds with Grey's observations in his letters to the King, for example 'the great desideratum therefore is to make an arrangement on which we can stand, announcing our determination not to go beyond it'. *Grey and William IV*, 1, 65.

[1] 'I do not support, I never have supported universal suffrage and annual parliaments, nor any other of those very extensive changes which have been, I regret to say, too much promulgated in this country, and promulgated by gentlemen from whom better things might have been expected.' *Parl. Debs.*, 3rd series, 1, 606. The tone of these remarks encouraged a widespread belief that the reform would be a cautious one.

[2] Russell later announced that one reason for rejecting equal electoral areas and proportional representation was the number of seats it would give to London. *Letter to the electors of Stroud on the principles of the reform act*, 1839.

[3] The following account of the committee's proceedings is based largely on the minutes and memoranda in the Grey MSS. at Durham. It is strange that Trevelyan, in his research for the life of Grey, 'failed to find any trace of these minutes'. Appendix E, 'The framing of the Reform Bill', p. 381.

[4] Russell's draft was printed in his *Essay on the English constitution and government*, 3rd edition, 1865, pp. xxxvi–xxxviii. Althorp's suggestions are printed in C. W. New, *Lord Durham*, 116. There is a valuable chapter in this book on the preparation of the bill, but New was inclined to disparage Russell in order to boost Durham.

[5] These were clearly meant to be no more than sighting shots. Althorp's previous opinions may be traced in his contribution to debate of 28 May 1830, where he spoke in favour of triennial parliaments and the ballot. *Parl. Debs.*, 2nd series, xxiv, 1230–2.

[6] In the existing boroughs, Althorp's proposal was that the £10 householder should have the vote where less than a certain proportion of the inhabitants were electors. Russell's was for £10 p.a. or jury service. The jury service franchise would have meant £20 p.a. rental and £30 p.a. in Middlesex. This complex question is discussed in Russell's letter printed New, *Lord Durham*, 120–1. These proposals meant, of course, the abolition of the corporation boroughs like Bath, Buckingham and Bury St Edmunds by opening up the franchise.

voters: Russell wished to see copyholders and leaseholders of 21 years or more given the county vote. Althorp added that he presumed the ballot must be given up, and it does not seem to have been discussed at this stage. In addition, at its first sitting, the committee considered suggestions for a complete reform of the Scottish representative system,[1] and a plan by Graham to provide polling districts in the county constituencies.[2] The first step was to order the preparation of lists showing the population of all boroughs and counties, and all unrepresented towns over 10,000, according to the 1821 census.

As soon as this information was available, the proposals began to take shape in a draft bill. Fifty boroughs were listed in an appendix one to lose all representation, ranging from Bramber with a population of 98 to Weymouth with 2269;[3] a second appendix listed a further 54 boroughs to lose one member, the largest being Bridport, with a population of 3742.[4] A third appendix suggested 6 towns to be given two members, and 22 to have one.[5] Appendix four proposed six seats to go to the unrepresented parts of the metropolis, viz. two for Marylebone, two for Tower Hamlets and two for Brixton. Appendix five dealt with the counties: of these 22, with populations above 200,000, were to have two extra seats, while a further 7, with populations between 150,000 and 200,000, were to have one additional member.

In the course of the committee's deliberations, changes were made. The number of boroughs to be totally disqualified was increased from 50 to 61 by raising the ceiling to 2000 inhabitants, thereby transferring 9 from appendix two, and adding Buckingham and Seaford which had been overlooked in the first draft: these, the ministers argued, were essentially the nomination boroughs, and too small to be redeemable. Appendix two was reduced from 54 to 47: Wenlock was dropped, Lyme Regis, Cockermouth and Sudbury brought in, and the ceiling fixed at 4000

---

[1] Plan no. 4, Grey MSS. Plan no. 5 was also concerned with Scottish reform, and was attributed to Loch. This was presumably James Loch, elder of the two brothers, MP St Germans 1827–30, Wick Burghs 1830–52. His conversion to reform was noted by Countess Granville, *Letters*, II, 62.

[2] Plan no. 3, Grey MSS.

[3] Weymouth was rather an exceptional case since it shared four seats with Melcombe Regis. The latter, with a population of 4252, kept its two seats.

[4] There are several omissions in the list, and Appleby which, with a population of 824, should obviously have been in appendix one, was tucked in towards the end of appendix two. It was presumably a hasty compilation to show roughly the effect which different definitions would have.

[5] Two seats were to go to Manchester, Birmingham, Leeds, Sheffield; Greenwich, Deptford and Woolwich together, and Sunderland and Wearmouth together. The single-member towns were to be Tynemouth and the Shields, Brighton, Swansea and Merthyr Tydvil, Bolton, Whitehaven, Workington and Havington, Blackburn, Stockport, Aston, Wolverhampton, Sedgeley, Dudley, Macclesfield, Kidderminster, Warrington, Huddersfield, Bradford, Halifax, Gateshead, Cheltenham, Frome, Bilston and Wakefield.

inhabitants.[1] The number of seats available for redistribution was thereby increased to 168. The suggested allocation of these seats was 34 to the unrepresented towns, 8 to London, 5 to Scotland, 3 to Ireland, and 1 to Wales, with another 55 seats to go to the county constituencies.[2] The House of Commons was therefore to be reduced by 62 members to a total of 596.

The Scottish representation was to be substantially remodelled.[3] The cumbersome system of alternating counties was to end: instead, 12 counties were joined in pairs, the other 22 being allocated one member each.[4] The archaic franchise based on superiorities was to be replaced in the counties by a £10 ownership or a £50 copyhold on a minimum of 19 years: in the towns, occupants of £10 houses were to have the vote.[5] Edinburgh and Glasgow were to have two members each, and Aberdeen, Paisley, Dundee, Leith and Greenock one. The group of Fife towns known as Anstruther burghs, with an aggregate population of less than 6000, was to be totally disqualified: the remaining thirteen groups, with some slight adjustments, were to retain one member apiece, who was to be directly elected.[6]

By contrast the Irish system, completely refashioned in 1800 and modified in 1829, suffered little further change. It was first proposed to award her three additional seats, to go to Belfast, Limerick and Waterford: this was ultimately raised to five, the two extra seats going to Galway and Trinity College, Dublin.[7] The introduction of the £10 franchise in the Irish towns produced many small electorates, but the addition of the £10 leaseholder in the counties led to a considerable increase on the 1829 electorate.

[1] Russell gave an account of these changes in his *Essay*, xxxix. C. W. New, *Lord Durham*, 118, was severe on Russell, insisting that the account was 'quite incorrect'. It was, in fact, substantially true. Professor New was at fault himself in assuming that appendix one of the committee's report was identical with schedule A of the first bill.
[2] The proposal in appendix five was modified. Instead of counties over 200,000 getting 2 more seats, and between 150,000 and 200,000 one more, the 27 largest counties were all to get two more. From the original list of counties to be given one more, Dorset (population 144,499) and Buckinghamshire (134,088) were demoted. The last seat went to the Isle of Wight.
[3] The Scottish and Irish changes were incorporated in separate bills, the fate of which depended on the English. Since these are discussed very fully in N. Gash, *Politics in the age of Peel*, ch. 2, I have dealt with them summarily.
[4] The paired counties were to be Peebles and Selkirk, Dumbarton and Bute, Elgin and Nairn, Ross and Cromarty, Orkney and Shetland, Clackmannan and Kinross. This was a considerable modification of plan no. 4, which had suggested as pairings Ross and Cromarty, Bute and Dumbarton, Caithness and Sutherland, Nairn and Elgin, with Kinross and Clackmannan to join with the tongue of Perthshire.
[5] Plan no. 4 had envisaged a town franchise of £20 p.a.
[6] These arrangements were subsequently modified when three more seats were allotted to Scotland, making a total of 53. The counties of Peebles and Selkirk, Dumbarton and Bute were given separate representation. Anstruther burghs were reorganized and reprieved, Leith became part of a group of burghs, while Perth became a constituency in its own right.
[7] Trinity College, Dublin had already one seat.

The more controversial proposals, concerning the ballot and the duration of Parliaments, were raised towards the end of the committee's work. Opinion in favour of secret ballot had made rapid progress, even among Whig reformers, since Bentham had raised the matter in 1817. Four years later George Grote, in his first publication, argued the case for it in opposition to the ideas expressed by Sir James Mackintosh in the *Edinburgh Review*.[1] A more extensive statement of the case for the ballot appeared in July 1830 when James Mill contributed a long article to the *Westminster Review*,[2] and it was recommended in many petitions in the course of 1830 and 1831. Radicals maintained that it was essential if the influence of property was to be destroyed and aristocratic predominance overthrown: otherwise manhood suffrage would be both nullified and discredited by gross bribery. Durham was an avowed supporter of the ballot: more surprisingly, Althorp also favoured it, though not expecting to see it adopted.[3] But when raised in the committee the proposal prospered and was carried, against the 'earnest advice' of Lord John Russell.[4]

The recommendation of the ballot carried important implications for the urban franchise. The committee had resisted the temptation to discriminate between voters in the old and new boroughs, and had resolved on a uniform franchise of £10. This had already caused Russell uneasiness, lest it place power in the hands of persons 'open to the influence of bribery and beer'. To Durham he wrote:[5]

> Elections carried by money, treating & an appeal to low passions, will produce such disorder, and such disgust, that an arbitrary monarchy will sooner or later be the consequence. Our object should be rather to place the power of choice in men of property and intelligence, who will exercise it with honesty and discrimination...If you give up all the close boroughs and place the franchise too (low), you can never again raise it...Where you retain a franchise it may be right to fix it at £10, but if where you have a franchise to give, you give it to scot-and-lot householders, you run the risk of creating more evils on the one side, than you put down on the other.[6]

---

[1] The British Museum does not appear to have a copy of Grote's *Statement of the question of parliamentary reform*, but it is summarized in *The minor works of George Grote*, ed. A. Bain, ch. 1. Mackintosh's article in the *Edinburgh Review*, vol. xxi (1818), was itself a commentary on Bentham's *Catechism*.

[2] In his famous *Encyclopaedia Britannica* article on government, James Mill had concealed his advocacy of the ballot, apparently for tactical reasons. J. Hamburger, *Intellectuals in politics*, 5.   [3] Plan no. 2, Grey MSS.

[4] Russell, *Essay*, XLI. The evidence is discussed in J. R. M. Butler, *The passing of the Great Reform Bill*, 181, n. 2.

[5] Undated, but clearly written before the question of the ballot was raised in committee. C. W. New, *Lord Durham*, 120–1.

[6] The letter explains that £10 p.a. was usually the lowest rent at which a householder was assessed for poor rate, so the £10 franchise was, in effect, scot and lot.

The decision on the ballot prompted Russell to reopen the question of the franchise, and the committee agreed to recommend the higher limit of £20 – presumably to mitigate the effect of the ballot, and to increase the chances of the bill being accepted by cabinet and Parliament.[1]

The last major discussion was on the duration of Parliaments. Though the case for annual Parliaments had lost ground since it had been a shibboleth of the reformers, there was considerable support for some shortening of the period. Grey had himself suggested triennial Parliaments in his 1797 proposals, and in May 1830 Althorp had admitted that he was in favour. In the committee, the proposal for triennial Parliaments was made by Durham and resisted by Russell: it was then agreed to recommend quinquennial Parliaments by way of compromise.[2]

That part of the committee's recommendations most likely to win approval in the House of Commons was concerned with the regulation of elections – to render them less noisy and time-consuming, and, above all, to curb the ever-increasing expense. For generations this had been a favourite topic in the House. As recently as 1828 an act had passed limiting polls in boroughs to eight days and providing for several polling places if necessary.[3] The most effective limitation on cost was the provision that non-residents should lose their right to vote: at one stroke was ended the situation whereby dozens of freeholders and freemen of boroughs could enjoy a septennial visit home at the expense of the parliamentary candidates. Secondly, a severe restriction on the duration of polls aimed to introduce regularity and economy: the committee's suggestion was that two days should be the maximum in both boroughs and counties.[4] The provision of up to fifteen different polling places in the counties would reduce transport costs: it was estimated that no voter should be more than fifteen miles from a polling booth. Lastly, the systematic registration of voters was intended to do away with protracted legal wrangles at the polls – wrangles which had given employment to generations of attorneys.[5]

At no stage does the question of compensation to dispossessed borough patrons seem to have been discussed, though such compensation had been

[1] *Early Correspondence*, II, 53.
[2] Russell's views had changed since 1819 when he had thought triennial parliaments desirable. *Parl. Debs.*, 1st series, XL, 1496.
[3] This was 9 George IV c. 59, piloted by Colonel Thomas Davies. In 1774 a bill had been introduced to permit several polling places in counties, and in 1788 a measure for the registration of county voters had reached the statute book, only to be repealed the following year before it had taken effect. *Parl. Hist.*, XVIII, 53–4; Porritt, I, 26–8.
[4] In accordance with Russell's scheme no. 1 which had suggested a two-day limit for towns. I do not know why C. W. New, *Lord Durham*, 122 said that the committee recommended 3 days in boroughs and 6 in the counties.
[5] Based on a bill brought forward in 1828 by Althorp and Graham, which had foundered.

part of Pitt's plan in 1785, and had, of course, been given at the Union with Ireland. In part this was an indication of the extent to which public opinion had changed in the meantime – in part, also, perhaps the impossibility of finding funds on the scale needed.

The committee's deliberations completed, the draft was forwarded to Grey on 14 January 1831 with an exposition of the principles upon which the reform was based. The committee had been satisfied with no 'bare redemption' of its pledge, but had aimed at a 'permanent settlement', which would 'remove at once, and for ever, all rational grounds of complaint from the minds of the intelligent and independent portion of the community'. Unwittingly the members of the committee paid tribute to the work of Cartwright, Cobbett, Burdett, and Hunt in forcing their hands. Their proposals, they claimed, would no longer render the reform agitation 'subservient to the designs of the factious and discontented': 'By pursuing such a course we conceive that the surest and most effectual check will be opposed to that restless spirit of innovation which...aims in secret at nothing less than the overthrow of all our Institutions and even of the Throne itself.' The last flourish was perhaps intended as a useful debating point when the time came to lay the recommendations before the King.

It was by no means certain that the cabinet, when it met on 24 January, would swallow the dose prescribed by its committee. Four of the thirteen ministers might be expected to give broad approval: Durham and Graham were themselves cabinet members, while Althorp and Grey had been in close touch with the committee's thinking throughout. Brougham, the new Lord Chancellor, was publicly pledged to reform, though his soreness at having so important an issue taken out of his hands might make him inclined to find fault. Lansdowne and Holland, the Whig grandees, had never shown more than a languid interest in reform. Several of the other ministers would have much explaining to do. Richmond, the *ultra*, had taken a prominent part against the disqualification of the Irish freeholders in 1829 on the grounds that it provided a dangerous precedent to subvert the constitution: the elective franchise, he told the Lords on one occasion, was a species of property and entitled to protection like any other.[1] Goderich's last public utterance on the subject had been that though he approved the enfranchisement of Birmingham, he was no 'theoretical reformer'.[2] The rest of the Canningites had been equally unenthusiastic until recently. In 1828 Palmerston declared that he supported the East Retford bill not as a friend to 'reform in principle', but as 'its decided enemy';[3]

---

[1] *Parl. Debs.*, 2nd series, XXI, 584–5, 410–12, 721–5. He was twitted on his change of heart in 1831. *Parl. Debs.*, 3rd series, III, 33.
[2] *Parl. Debs.*, 2nd series, XXV, 1289.
[3] *Ibid.* XIX, 1538.

Melbourne, looking back on the period 1828–30, confessed that his opinion had been 'against reform altogether'.[1]

One of the first decisions of the cabinet was to strike out the proposal for the ballot. Grey himself disapproved: 'my opinion is against this', he wrote in the margin of his own copy of the committee's report, and it transpired subsequently that it was totally unacceptable to the King, who saw it as 'inconsistent with the manly spirit and the free avowal of opinion which distinguish the people of England'.[2] Nor would it have been easy to carry such a measure through the Commons: when O'Connell had tested opinion in March 1830 by moving that the ballot should operate in the new Bassetlaw constituency, he had been beaten by 179 votes to 21.

At the same time, the cabinet made a decision which, if adhered to, could well have meant the shipwreck of the whole scheme. The committee must have realized that the ballot would almost certainly not be acceptable: it is therefore probable that it was proposed, together with the £20 franchise, to facilitate a tactical compromise, from which the £10 franchise might emerge. The middle-class radicals, whose opinions Durham had been sounding out through Colonel Leslie Grove Jones, had made it clear that they would prefer a high franchise with ballot to a lower one without. They were now in danger of getting neither the ballot nor the lower franchise, since the cabinet struck out the ballot but retained the £20 qualification. This would certainly have produced strange consequences. In Bristol, for example, the electorate would have been cut, according to one computation, from more than 5000 to 2719: in newly enfranchised Birmingham, the electorate would be a mere 1500 out of a total population of 85,000, and in Manchester 1212 out of 142,000.[3] It is very doubtful whether a scheme so watered down would have evoked the response necessary to drive it through in the face of tenacious opposition.

It dawned rather belatedly on members of the cabinet how severely the £20 qualification would curtail the electorate. On 13 February, only a fortnight before the bill was due to be presented to the House, Russell sent Durham an agitated letter, observing that the retention of the £20 franchise without the ballot would make the measure 'a mark for all the noisy and turbulent advocates of popular rights'. In some of the boroughs that were to retain one member, there were hardly any £20 voters to be found – 14 only at Wilton, 7 at Amersham, 1 at St Germans and none at all at Downton. 'We should be accused of creating new close or corrupt boroughs', confessed Russell. He had at length realized that the population

[1] *Papers*, ed. L. C. Sanders, 118. The remaining two members, Charles Grant and Carlisle, had both served under Canning.
[2] Grey MSS.; *Grey and William IV*, 1, 96–7; Grey to Lansdowne, 15 January 1831, Grey MSS.
[3] P.P. 1830–1, no. 202 x 9. See also the pamphlet *What will be the practical effect of the Reform Bill?*

figures were not a reliable guide, since the parliamentary boundaries frequently did not coincide with the parishes. Amersham, with a population of 2612, had only 25 £10 householders in the parliamentary borough, and Downton, with 3114 population, had no more than 9 £10 voters.[1]

It was undoubtedly disconcerting to discover that the basis of the computations was suspect, and the cabinet had no alternative but to patch things up as best it could. The borough franchise was perforce lowered to £10. Even then there was a considerable number of schedule B boroughs that would not be able to muster a respectable electorate, and it was agreed in those cases to call in voters from the immediate neighbourhood to make up a total of 300. The patches on the bill could not be hidden, and it was said that Croker, on discovering the discrepancy between borough and parish populations, was convinced that the bill could never pass.[2] Thus one of the most notable features of the reform, the £10 franchise, came about, less as an act of principle than as the outcome of an administrative muddle, with Grey, at least, reluctant to make the change.[3]

Nor were these the only blemishes in the bill. The drafting was done in a rush. On 17 February Graham wrote urgently to Grey that he anticipated disaster if the bill was not examined minutely, clause by clause.[4] Even so, absurdities escaped detection. The borough of Bewdley was placed in schedule B, to lose one member, and the arithmetical calculations made accordingly, without anyone realizing that it had only one member to lose. The town of Wakefield was left out of the first draft by a similar oversight. The bill was not ready in time for the parliamentary session, and Russell found himself with some awkward apologies to make.

There was very little determined opposition in cabinet to the basic provisions of the scheme. Palmerston, though uneasy, seems not to have offered much objection at this stage. A threat of trouble came from Brougham, who confided to Althorp his dislike of the proposal to abolish the nomination boroughs, which would deprive government of the means of introducing to Parliament young men of talent and distinction. 'On this point I cannot give way', wrote Grey to Durham, suspecting Brougham of trimming to the King's opinions.[5] The cabinet prepared for battle at its next meeting, but Brougham chose not to press the point. To Hobhouse, Tavistock confided as 'a most inviolable secret' that Brougham was the only cabinet minister who thought the bill was going too far: 'however,

[1] Grey MSS. Russell himself provided the examples quoted. The last two, it will be noted, were for £10 householders, not £20.
[2] Russell, *Recollections and suggestions*, 92.
[3] This is assuming the validity of the King's remark that he would 'with Earl Grey, greatly prefer the higher qualification'. *Grey and William IV*, I, 111.
[4] J. T. Ward, 102–3.
[5] 24 January 1831, Lambton MSS., quoted C. W. New, *Lord Durham*, 129.

like a clever old lawyer, now that the measure is resolved upon, he takes care to have it given out he originated it'.[1]

Lastly there was the task of gaining the King's approval. Grey handled William with considerable skill, possibly because he shared so many of his fears: his constant theme was the need for sensible moderate men to construct defences against the wild ones. On 16 January the King observed that two proposals he would deplore were any shortening of the duration of Parliament or any increase in the number of members: in reply Grey pointed out, with some satisfaction, that there would be a *decrease* in membership. As for the quinquennial proposal, it was of 'comparatively inferior importance', and the cabinet agreed to waive it – whether in deference to the King's opinion is not clear. On other points, the King's views were moderate Tory, but malleable: the ballot was anathema, and he would gladly see a raising of the county franchise, since the forty-shilling freehold had become diluted over the years. This Grey could not concede, but comforted William with the assurance that the continuation of the existing franchise would 'operate rather favourably than otherwise for the landed interest'. By the end of their exchanges, Grey had convinced the King that the measure was a thoroughly aristocratic one.[2]

On 30 January Grey went to Brighton for an audience and exposition, and was delighted at his reception. 'He was particularly pleased', Grey advised Durham, 'with your report, and entirely concurred in the statement, so powerfully and clearly made in it, of the necessity of doing something, and that that something should be effectual and final.'[3] Graham, to whom Durham imparted the glad tidings at once, expressed great relief: 'I was in a state of most powerful anxiety, full of gloomy forebodings, when your note arrived...if the King be with us, the battle is won.'[4]

The preparation of the bill had been accomplished with surprisingly little trouble. No minister had resigned, nor, as far as we know, had any threatened to do so. The Canningites, in particular, had changed sides with hardly a backward glance. The rest of the bill's passage was not to be as smooth.

* * * *

The cabinet was at great pains to secure the secrecy of their proposals, and very little information seems to have leaked out to its opponents. Most commentators believed that it would be a limited measure, abolishing a few of the more notorious rotten boroughs, enfranchising one or two large towns, and giving the vote to copyholders. 'The general fear', wrote le Marchant, 'was that it would not go far enough and thus please nobody.'[5]

---

[1] Broughton, IV, 82.
[2] C. S. Parker, *Sir Robert Peel*, II, 178.
[3] S. J. Reid, *Life and letters of Lord Durham*, I, 244.
[4] C. W. New, *Lord Durham*, 131.   [5] *Three diaries*, 12.

Throughout the country the ministerial declaration for reform evoked an enormous response. Political unions on the Birmingham model sprang up in dozens of towns. Their attitude towards the government was half ally, half gaoler: 'if the Whigs intend to realise their promises', wrote Joseph Parkes of Birmingham, 'they cannot object to strong demonstrations: if they mean to break their vows, it is wholesome to remind them of them'.[1] As the day approached, petitions poured into the House of Commons from all parts of the kingdom:[2] on the Saturday before Russell moved for leave to introduce the bill, the House was obliged to arrange a special sitting to receive them. 'There was scarcely a spare room, closet or corner, near or about the lobby', wrote one observer, 'that was not occupied with bundles of reform petitions. When the House assembled, the seats were so covered with bundles of petitions that, in many instances, the members found it difficult to find sitting-room for themselves.'[3]

Russell's somewhat low-keyed speech on 1st March, outlining the ministry's plans, was received with dismay by the moderates, jubilation by the radicals, and fury by the Tory opposition. Of several staunch reformers, le Marchant wrote that 'they were like men taking breath immediately after an explosion'. Creevey, on the other hand, long an advocate of sweeping changes, was delighted: 'my raptures with it increase every hour, and my astonishment at its boldness... What a coup it is! It is its *boldness* that makes its success so certain.'[4]

The Tory opposition had previously agreed not to resist the introduction of the bill, so that members under constituency pressure could discharge their consciences while defeating the bill at a later stage. To this resolution they adhered, though the consequence was that they got off to a somewhat faltering start. Sir Robert Inglis and Sir Charles Wetherell, two of their most doughty champions, were too narrow and legalistic to be completely effective. Inglis, opening for the opposition, attacked Russell's claim that the measure restored the representation to its original basis in population,

---

[1] Quoted D. Read, *The English provinces, c. 1760–1960: a study in influence*, 88.
[2] The total number of petitions presented between October 1830 and April 1831 appears to be about 3000, the vast majority of which were in favour of reform. More than 1600 were presented to the Commons, with a further 200 or so on Scottish reform: the Lords received another 1000 or so. Bearing in mind that, at the same time, there were also several thousand petitions for the abolition of slavery, one could scarcely ask for a more dramatic indication of the growth of a public opinion since the eighteenth century. The number of petitions for and against Catholic Emancipation was greater than either. In comparison, the movement in favour of economical reform in 1780 produced 38 petitions, and was regarded as impressive: even the addresses in support of Pitt in 1784, probably the most widespread expression of opinion to that date, numbered no more than 200. See John Cannon, *The Fox–North coalition*, 186–7. Whereas in the eighteenth century, petitions with 5000 signatories were remarkable, and more than 1000 formidable, in 1831 there were petitions of 21,000 from Birmingham and Edinburgh, more than 30,000 from Glasgow, 17,000 from Leeds, and 12,000 from Manchester and Bristol.
[3] *Glocester Journal*, 5 Mar. 1831.   [4] *Three diaries*, 13; Creevey, II, 221.

and demonstrated, with some triumph, that few of the decayed boroughs could ever have been populous – an argument which, as later speakers remarked, would have been devastating in a society of antiquarians but was of no great comfort to Manchester and Birmingham. Horace Twiss, who followed Inglis, compounding no doubt for being the son of an actress, launched a most maladroit onslaught upon the middle classes – 'shopkeepers and attorneys, persons of narrow minds and bigotted views, now to be called in to counsel the nation'. Not until the third day of the debate, when Peel made his long-awaited intervention, did a speaker on the Tory side rise to the importance of the occasion. Indignantly he brushed aside Palmerston's assertion that, had Canning lived, he might well have changed his mind on reform. He took also the earliest opportunity to repudiate Twiss' remarks about the middle classes, 'sprung, as I am, from those classes, and proud of my connection with them'. In a passage that carried weight with the House, Peel pointed out that the small boroughs, which it was intended to disfranchise, had been represented by men of the calibre of Burke, Pitt, Fox, Sheridan, Canning, Tierney, Brougham, Romilly and others. But the fatal objection to the proposals was that, by destroying the representation of the lower classes, they wrecked the fine balance of the constitution and severed all communication between the legislature and that class of voters above pauperism yet below the ten pounds franchise. Nor should the ministers delude themselves that such a reform could be final:

> No doubt you cannot propose to share your power with half a million of men without gaining some popularity – without purchasing by such a bribe some portion of goodwill. But these are vulgar arts of government; others will outbid you, not now, but at no remote period – they will offer votes and power to a million of men, will quote your precedent for the concession, and will carry your principles to their legitimate and natural consequences.

The government had sent through the land the fireball of agitation: 'no one can now recall it'.[1]

The most eloquent and sustained defence of the government's measures was by Macaulay, whose speech marked him out as a man of the future. Doing battle on what the Tories thought their strongest ground – that the bill was revolutionary in character – Macaulay argued that it was, on the contrary, the best possible guarantee against revolution, by bringing over to the side of security and stability the power of the middle classes. How could the existing system be said to be based on property when it excluded so much wealth and intelligence? 'It is government by certain detached portions and fragments of property...preferred to the rest on no rational

[1] *Parl. Debs.*, 3rd series, II, 1090–1128, 1180, 1134, 1330–56.

principle whatever.' The growing alienation of the people from the legislature was neither the product of the recent revolution in France, as many Tories maintained, nor any passing infatuation:[1]

> This alarming discontent is not the growth of a day or of a year... Who flatters himself that he can turn this feeling back? Does there remain any argument that escaped the comprehensive intellect of Mr Burke, or the subtlety of Mr Wyndham? Does there remain any species of coercion which was not tried by Mr Pitt or by Lord Londonderry? We have had laws. We have had blood. New treasons have been created. The press has been shackled. The Habeas Corpus act has been suspended. Public meetings have been prohibited. The event has proved that these expedients were mere palliatives. You are at the end of your palliatives... The danger is terrible. The time is short. If this bill should be rejected, I pray to God, that none of those who concur in rejecting it may ever remember their votes with unavailing regret, amidst the wreck of laws, the confusion of ranks, the spoliation of property, and the dissolution of social order.

In the course of the seven days of debate the government sustained some reverses. Though Hume, Hobhouse and Burdett, on the radical side, gave them warm support, Hunt, newly elected for Preston, expressed disgust. Few speeches gave more comfort to the Tories than his declaration that the bill would give no satisfaction to the poorer classes: 'when they heard the nature of the measure proposed, and the arguments by which some persons supported it, they would not view it with much gratification'.[2] Inevitably, too, the bill proved too strong for some government followers. Charles Wynn, the secretary-at-war, confessed that he was not prepared for so great a sacrifice, and tendered his resignation. Alexander Baring, William Duncombe and Lord Seymour announced in turn that they could not vote with the ministers: the bill, said Duncombe, was revolutionary and tyrannical. Croker's speech on the fourth day also succeeded in causing the ministers some harassment. With some justice he complained that Russell had offered no explanation why the population figures of 2000 and 4000 had been taken for schedules A and B: it was purely arbitrary. Why was Downton, with only 9 £10 householders, to keep one member, while Buckingham, a county town with eight times as many qualified voters, was to lose both? Why was Calne, with fewer than 5000 persons, to retain two seats, while Bolton, Blackburn, Brighton and

---

[1] *Parl. Debs.*, 3rd series, II, 1190–1205.
[2] Hunt seems to have been much irritated by Macaulay's speech. A month later his objections were even stronger. The people, he insisted, felt deluded by the bill. 'They thought that they should have got something for themselves by it; that they were going to get meat or clothes cheaper by it; but when they found it would have none of these effects, they were naturally disappointed at the whole measure.' *Parl. Debs.*, 3rd series, II, 1208–17; III, 1245–6.

Tyneside, with more than 20,000, had to be content with one? Was it not strange that the borough that just made its escape from schedule B, with a population of 4005, should be Malton, belonging to Lord Fitzwilliam, a Whig magnate? How could a settlement incorporating such anomalies ever be permanent? 'No wonder the noble lord (Russell) was so sore last night when we asked him a question or two about returns.'[1]

But, in the face of these difficulties, ministers were fortified by the growing evidence, which their opponents scarcely disputed, that the bill had been welcomed with open arms by the country at large. The fortnight between leave being granted to introduce the bill and the debate on the second reading gave ample time for the mood of the country to express itself, and when the discussion was resumed the opponents of reform were noticeably more subdued. Sir Richard Vyvyan, a leader of the *ultras*, in moving the rejection of the bill, pledged himself to introduce some kind of reform, thereby throwing over Wellington completely. Charles Grant, a cabinet minister, was quick to point the moral: 'the question as to Reform or no Reform, then, I consider is absolutely decided, and the question we are now called upon to decide is not whether we are to have reform, but what ought to be the nature of that reform, and at what time we should adopt it'.[2]

Despite nine days of debate, it remained far from clear what the outcome of the postponed division on 22 March would be. While the Tories were aware that the tide was running against them, they were greatly heartened by a vote on the timber duties four days earlier, in which ministers were left in a minority of 46. Russell, summing-up for the government in a House jammed tight with members, reverted to Macaulay's argument about revolution. Opponents of the bill, he argued, had made much of the danger of concessions. Was there no counter-danger in resisting popular claims? Had not Charles X of France fallen because he set his face against concession of any kind? At three minutes to three in the morning, the Tories trooped out into the lobby, members betting with each other on the result. They returned 301 strong, against 302 for the ministers:[3]

> We set up a shout that you might have heard to Charing Cross, waving our hats, stamping against the floor, and clapping our hands.

[1] *Parl. Debs.*, 3rd series, III, 81–107.   [2] *Parl. Debs.*, 3rd series, III, 665.
[3] Macaulay to Thomas Flower Ellis, 30 March 1831, *Life & letters of Lord Macaulay*, ed. G. O. Trevelyan, I, 206–9.
   The bill, as has often been observed, was carried by the Irish members, who divided 55–37 in its favour: the English members divided 229–237 against. The English county members supported government 53–27.
   The *ultras*, having had their fling by overthrowing Wellington, returned to the fold. Of the 62 identified by Planta as *ultras*, 50 voted in opposition and only 9 with government. Of the 33 who had voted against Wellington on 15 November 1830, 25 rejoined the Tories in opposition. Aspinall, *Three diaries*, p. xxix takes a wider definition of *ultra*, but his conclusions are broadly the same, that is of some 140, 111 voted against the bill.

The tellers scarcely got through the crowd: for the House was thronged up to the table, and all the floor was fluctuating with heads like the pit of a theatre. But you might have heard a pin drop as Duncannon read the numbers. Then again the shouts broke out, and many of us shed tears. I could scarcely refrain. And the jaw of Peel fell; and the face of Twiss was as the face of a damned soul; and Herries looked like Judas taking his necktie off for the last operation. We shook hands, and clapped each other on the back, and went out laughing crying and huzzaing into the lobby. And no sooner were the outer doors opened than another shout answered that within the House. All the passages, and the stairs into the waiting rooms, were thronged by people who had waited till four in the morning to know the issue. We passed through a narrow lane between two thick masses of them; and all the way down they were shouting and waving their hats, till we got into the open air. I called a cabriolet, and the first thing the driver asked was, 'Is the bill carried?' 'Yes, by one.' 'Thank God for it, Sir.'

* * * *

Whether the Whigs had any rational grounds for their joy may be doubted. True, they had escaped immediate shipwreck, but the probability, in view of such a slender majority, was that the bill would be chopped to pieces in committee. It would, in that case, become a question whether the King was prepared to grant a dissolution and allow Grey to augment his force by an appeal to the public. The King had already warned Grey, in most emphatic terms, that he was not.

As early as January, in his conversations at Brighton, Grey had been made aware of the King's strong dislike of a dissolution. The matter was not raised again until the government's defeat on the timber duties on 18 March cast serious doubt on their hopes of obtaining a majority on the second reading of the reform bill. On 20 March, the King replied that he regarded it as his 'sacred duty' to resist any such recommendation, and the following day his private secretary confided to Grey that, in his judgement, the King's decision was 'final and conclusive'. This impression was reinforced by a letter from the King himself recording all his deepest fears if a question on which there had been so much 'popular clamour' were to be put to the electorate:[1]

this country would be thrown into convulsion from the Land's End to John O'Groat's house: miners, manufacturers, colliers, labourers, all who have recently formed unions for the furtherance of illegal purposes, would assemble on every point in support of a *popular*

[1] *Grey and William IV*, I, 154–83.

question, with the declared object of carrying the measure by intimidation. It would be in vain to hope to be able to resist their course or
to check disturbances of every kind, amounting possibly to open
rebellion.

Trapped between a hostile House of Commons and a recalcitrant
monarch, ministers were in a most awkward position. Palmerston urged
substantial modifications in the measure – otherwise there was no reasonable chance of it being carried.[1] But the changes which Russell announced
on 18 April, when he opened the committee stage of the bill, were of
a marginal character. Five boroughs, where the population had proved
on investigation to be greater than at first assumed, were moved from
schedule A to schedule B, and another seven were taken out of schedule B
and reprieved altogether.[2] Eight more towns with populations above
10,000 were to be given one member, and to keep the balance right, eight
more seats were allotted to counties of more than 100,000.[3] The total
number of members of Parliament would then be 627, a decrease of 31
on the existing House. The right to vote was to be extended to sixty year
leaseholders of £10 value in the counties, to the sons and apprentices of
existing freemen in the boroughs, and to the occupiers of warehouses.[4]
These alterations did little to mollify the opponents of the bill. General
Gascoyne moved a carefully-devised amendment that the representation
of England and Wales should not be diminished, and the government was
defeated by 299 votes to 291.[5]

A cabinet next morning decided to make a formal approach to the King
for a dissolution. For a day the fate of both bill and ministry hung in the
balance as the King pondered his reply. Ministers were perhaps fortunate
in that the particular issue on which they had been defeated – against any
increase in the total membership of the House – was one where the King's
private views coincided with their own. The King had also had a month

[1] Palmerston to Grey, 8 April 1831, Grey MSS.
[2] Buckingham, Malmesbury, Okehampton and Reigate were moved to schedule B, and
Aldborough and Boroughbridge joined to keep one member; Leominster, Morpeth,
Northallerton, Tamworth, Truro, Westbury and Wycombe were reprieved. At Leominster, for example, the 1821 census had given the population as 3651, classifying
separately the townships of Broadward and Ivington at 321 and 674 respectively. It was
accordingly placed in schedule B. By the revision all three were treated as part of the
parliamentary borough and a population of 4646 returned.
[3] Bury, Oldham, Rochdale, Salford, Stoke, Wakefield, and Whitby were added, and the
boundaries of Halifax adjusted. An extra seat was given to Berkshire, Bucks., Cambs.,
Dorset, Herts., Herefordshire, Oxon., and Glamorgan.
[4] The latter change was necessary, explained Russell, because otherwise large manufacturers in Manchester and Liverpool, living outside the boundaries, would have no
vote.
[5] Of the 15 members who voted for the second reading of the bill but joined Gascoyne,
11 were county members.

to reflect on Lord Durham's argument that disorder was more likely should reform be abandoned than at a general election.[1] On 21 April, with great reluctance, the King gave way, though stipulating that if the government won the election, the bill was on no account to be made more radical. Desperate last-minute attempts by the opposition to place obstacles in the way of a dissolution were brushed aside, and, amid extraordinary scenes in both Houses of recrimination and reproach, Parliament was brought to an end.[2]

The result of the general election was almost a foregone conclusion. In the open constituencies, Tory candidates went down like ninepins. Anyone who had taken a prominent part against the bill was a marked man. General Gascoyne lost the seat at Liverpool he had held since 1796. Sir Robert Wilson, a radical member for Southwark since 1818 and personal friend of Lord Grey, withheld his vote from government on Gascoyne's amendment, and was bundled out with the rest. 'The great *smash*', wrote Mrs Arbuthnot, 'has been among the Ultra-Tories': of their eight county members, only one survived the debacle.[3] The seven English county members who had supported the government on the second reading, but switched votes on Gascoyne's amendment, all lost their seats.[4] Old established interests that had dominated shires and boroughs for generations were swept away in the storm. The Lowther empire collapsed, leaving Lord Lowther himself without a seat in the House of Commons; the Beauforts lost the seat in Gloucestershire they had commanded since the days of George II; the Manners family was ousted in Leicestershire and Cambridgeshire; the Duke of Newcastle lost control in Nottinghamshire; in Worcestershire the Lygons were beaten for a seat they had held without either interruption or challenge since the beginning of the American war, 55 years before. The position in the large boroughs was no better. Dover, in defiance of the Duke of Wellington as Lord Warden, returned two reformers on the first day of the election; at Bristol, two Whigs were elected for the first time for more than fifty years; the Earl of Warwick failed to hold his own borough, and Lord Exeter lost

---

[1] *Grey and William IV*, I, 193–5.
[2] In the Commons there was an attempt to postpone supplies, and ministers were again defeated, by 164 votes to 142. Greville described the scene in the Lords, where Londonderry had to be held down by his friends, as 'as much like the preparatory days of a revolution as can well be imagined'. In the Commons, there was 'wild confusion'. William Bankes 'looked as if his face would burst with blood; Peel stormed; the Speaker was equally furious'. Greville, II, 139; Broughton, IV, 105. There is a long account in Brougham, *Life and times*, III, 111–18.
[3] Keck (Leics.), Patten (Lancs.), Bankes (Dorset), Vyvyan (Cornwall), Duncombe (Yorks.), Knatchbull (Kent) and Heathcote (Hants.) all lost their seats; only Mandeville (Hunts.) was in the new Parliament.
[4] Acland (Devon), Fane (Oxon.), Keck (Leics.), Mundy (Derbyshire), Palmer (Berks.), Patten (Lancs.), Powlett (Durham).

a seat at Stamford to Charles Tennyson, the reformer. 'Everywhere our friends seem to be beaten with ease', wrote Ellenborough, and Greville concluded that, in the Commons, the bill was as good as carried.[1] 'England is gone perfectly mad', declared Mrs Arbuthnot, surveying these disasters.[2]

Though the Tory party was far from decimated, it was almost completely shut off from popular support: never had the charge that it was a mere *borough faction* looked more convincing. Only six of the English county members could be relied upon. Of its English strength of some 187 members,[3] no fewer than 165 represented boroughs doomed under schedules A and B, or with less than 400 voters, while another 4 sat for the universities – i.e. more than 90%. The Tories managed to capture both seats in only one county – Shropshire – while the Whigs swept 35 English counties.[4] The only town with an electorate of more than 600 where the Tories could claim both members was Sudbury, a by-word in corruption, and disfranchised thirteen years later. The extent to which the Tory party was driven back to the decayed boroughs may be judged from the fact that the total electorate they could claim to represent (allocating to each member the full number of voters in his area) was some 50,000: the four Whig members for Yorkshire might, by a similar computation, claim to represent 100,000 voters.[5] In the last analysis, the living part of the representative system confronted the dead part.

Crumbs of comfort for the Tories were not easy to find. They took some satisfaction from the failure of an attempt to oust Lord Chandos in Buckinghamshire, though this was only a defensive victory. More piquant was the defeat of Lord Palmerston at Cambridge University: there might still be need for schedule A boroughs, jeered Sir Robert Peel, to provide accommodation for the foreign secretary. But in general the Tories could do little save comfort themselves with the wry reflection that never had the old system shown itself more responsive to public opinion than when it stood on the brink of extinction.

*   *   *   *

As soon as the result of the general election became apparent, attention turned to the House of Lords. Expressing dread of a direct clash between the two Houses, the King wrote on 28 May urging Grey to consider modifications which, while not affecting the principle of the bill, would indicate 'a disposition to conciliate'. Grey dealt with the intervention

---

[1] *Three diaries*, 90; Greville, II, 144.   [2] Arbuthnot, II, 421.
[3] Based on the second reading division of 6 July 1831, *Parl. Debs.*, 3rd series, IV, 907–19.
[4] The shared counties, Westmorland, Bucks., Huntingdonshire and Monmouth, were among the smallest in the kingdom. Compare the position with the Tory triumph of 1841 when they won 124 out of 144 English county seats. R. Blake, *The Conservative party from Peel to Churchill*, 44.
[5] More than 23,000 persons voted in the Yorkshire election of 1807.

briskly: frankness, he replied, forced him to observe that, in his judgement, 'no concessions that could be made, short of a total destruction of all the beneficial effects of the bill, would satisfy those by whom it has hitherto been most violently opposed'.[1] Of possibly greater concern to Grey was a threatened cabinet revolt, Palmerston, supported by Lansdowne and Goderich, canvassing once more the return to a higher franchise. Grey, Althorp and Durham stood out firmly against the suggestion, arguing that it was more likely to alienate the House of Commons than mollify the Lords, and their views carried the day.[2] Consequently the bill, as presented by Lord John Russell on 24 June, was little different from the first. Downton and St Germans were moved from schedule B to A, on the grounds that neither could supply a respectable electorate: Penryn and Sandwich, on the other hand, were reprieved by uniting them with the larger towns of Falmouth and Deal respectively.[3]

The new bill was given its second reading on 6 July 1831 by a handsome majority – 367 votes against 231. There was much acrimonious scuffling over the use made of the King's name during the election campaign and the propriety of giving pledges, but the greater themes were almost exhausted. Macaulay added to his reputation with a second oration, which Littleton thought the most powerful he had ever heard.[4] Attacking the Tory argument that the country had prospered under the old system, Macaulay insisted that it had prospered by accepting change and reform. The present danger was that 'society was outgrowing our institutions':[5]

> Let us contrast our commerce, wealth and perfect civilisation, with our Penal Laws, at once barbarous and inefficient...Here we see the barbarism of the thirteenth century coupled with the civilisation of the nineteenth, and we see too, that the barbarism belongs to the government, and the civilisation to the people. Then I say that this incongruous state of affairs cannot continue; and if we do not terminate it with wisdom, ere long we shall find it ended by violence.

Sir Charles Wetherell argued that in towns such as Bristol, of which he was Recorder, the £10 householders were no better than paupers: it was beneath the dignity of a member of Parliament 'to solicit votes in the lazaretto', words that were remembered when he visited the town in his

---

[1] *Grey and William IV*, I, 275, 279.
[2] Palmerston to Grey, 25 April, 14 May, Grey MSS; *Three diaries*, 98; S. J. Reid, 260–1.
[3] The term for leaseholders, paying £50 p.a., was reduced from 14 to 7 years. The government was much embarrassed by an oversight whereby, in order to qualify for the borough vote, rents were to be paid twice-yearly. This, it was discovered, would disfranchise thousands. Opposition found the affair sinister, and scoffed at the ministers' explanation of 'inadvertence', but Althorp, writing presumably without guile to his father about the 'scrape' they were in, pleaded genuine ignorance. Althorp, 325.
[4] *Three diaries*, 100.   [5] *Parl. Debs.*, IV, 773–83.

judicial capacity three months later. Peel, in a bright and vigorous speech, took up Macaulay's remarks, and denied that the House was behind the spirit of the times – indeed, over Catholic Emancipation, it was clearly in advance of public opinion. He felt no guilt at having voted in 1828 against enfranchising Manchester and Birmingham: if public demand was as great as they were assured, and only *the bill, the whole bill and nothing but the bill* would suffice, it was clear that such a modest reform could never have stemmed the tide.[1]

The House then suffered in the wilderness of the committee stage for forty days. Member after member for the doomed boroughs rose to pay valedictory and sometimes truthful tributes to the probity of their constituents, while Croker snapped at the heels of ministers on points of detail.[2] From this ordeal the bill emerged relatively unscathed. The borough of Saltash, against the wishes of government, was transferred from schedule A to B, but Althorp had conceded that it was a doubtful case. At a later stage, ministers admitted the justice of complaints that Wales had been shabbily treated, and agreed to add a member to the counties of Carmarthen and Denbigh: to keep the balance equal, two more towns were enfranchised – Ashton-under-Lyne and Stroud. On two issues the opposition was formidable. They made a very plausible case for using the 1831 census, the results of which were just becoming available, as the basis of computation, instead of condemning boroughs on out-of-date evidence. This would have placed ministers in some difficulty by raising at least a *prima facie* case for reconsidering more than twenty boroughs in schedules A and B.[3] Russell and Althorp resisted strongly, and with success. They were less fortunate however on a matter of even greater importance concerning the county franchise. Sibthorp, the member for Lincoln, and Lord Chandos moved that tenants-at-will renting property of £50 p.a. should be given the vote.[4] Althorp opposed, arguing

---

[1] *Parl. Debs.*, IV, 861, 871–93.
[2] Croker's indefatigability and grasp of detail deserve recognition. His speciality was anomalies. Why should Calne, paying only £650 in taxes, be spared, yet Dorchester, paying £2100, find itself in schedule B? Why did Sunderland, with a population of 33,000, merit 2 MPs, but Bolton, with 44,000, only one?
[3] According to my calculations, some 11 boroughs in schedule A had since 1821 increased over the 2000 population mark, and 10 of the schedule B boroughs over the 4000 mark. The schedule A boroughs were Appleby, Bedwyn, Bishop's Castle, Brackley, Downton, Eye, Milborne Port, Newtown, St Germans, Wareham and Wendover: the schedule B were Ashburton, Bridport, Chippenham, Clithero, Cockermouth, Grimsby, Liskeard, Marlow, St Ives and Sudbury. Russell's retort was that the 1831 returns had been influenced by knowledge of the pending bill – 'in some places, the people had poured into the boroughs for one night in order to swell the return'. *Parl. Debs.*, IV, 1265.
[4] Sibthorp had given prior notice of his intention to move, and was extremely indignant at Chandos forestalling him. Sibthorp's later claim to remembrance was his fanatical opposition to the Great Exhibition of 1851, which he was convinced must lead to revolution.

that it must greatly increase the influence of the landlords, but admitted that his own constituents were in favour of it. Deserted by many of their usual supporters, government was defeated by 232 votes to 148 – a majority too large to allow hopes of reversing it. After the third reading had been carried by 346 votes to 235 – a slight falling-off in the government's majority, Russell, accompanied by two hundred 'godfathers', presented the bill, on 22 September 1831, to the House of Lords.

Their lordships could hardly complain that they had been left without guidance at this critical juncture. The political unions, newspaper editors and pamphleteers bombarded them with suggestions, many of them of a pointed nature. Lord Chancellor Brougham, thinly disguised as the anonymous author of *Friendly advice most respectfully submitted to the Lords*, reminded them of the time in 1649 when their House had been voted useless and dangerous; another observer threatened them with inclusion in schedule A.[1] 'I cannot believe', declared the author of *What will the Lords do ?*, 'that a body of staid, sober, wealthy, elderly gentlemen, fathers too of large and affectionate families, should, for the sake of an opinion, meditate a proceeding so nearly approaching to a political *felo de se*.'[2] They should bear in mind, warned Macaulay, the fate of the French aristocracy: 'have they ever seen the ruins of those castles whose terraces and gardens overhang the Loire? Have they ever heard that from those magnificent hotels, from those ancient castles, an aristocracy, as splendid, as brave, as proud, as accomplished, as ever Europe saw, was driven forth to exile and beggary...to cut wood in the back settlements of America – or to teach French in the schoolrooms of London.' From the other side came appeals to do their duty like men, and throw out the bill. 'In what crisis of public affairs', asked Croker, 'will it ever be permitted to the peers to exercise their deliberative functions if it be denied to them now? or are they henceforward to understand that they must confine their independence to amending a Turnpike Act.'[3]

This chorus did not make it easier for the Tory leaders to decide how to use the majority they commanded in the House of Lords. To set up a government against the existing House of Commons was clearly impossible. Yet there was little prospect that the King would grant another dissolution, and still less that the country would not return an emphatic reform majority if he did.[4] Greville hoped for a negotiated compromise with Lord Grey; others wished to trim slightly by allowing the bill to reach committee before knocking its brains out. But a dinner party at the Duke's house on 21 September, enlivened by the late arrival of Lords

---

[1] *Annual Register* (1831), 254.
[2] P. 17.
[3] *Parl. Debs.*, VII, 309, 354–5.
[4] Peel's diagnosis is in Parker, II, 189–90.

Kenyon and Eldon, spectacularly drunk, resolved to oppose the second reading and take the consequences.[1]

The debate in the Lords lasted five days. For the government the important contributions were a three-hour *tour de force* by Brougham, primed with port, and the winding-up speech by Grey himself, in which he denied, once again, that the bill would injure the landed interest. Wellington found the albatross of his declaration against all reform too much to bear and was quite ineffective, leaving Harrowby and Lyndhurst to put the opposition's main case. The Archbishop of Canterbury, whose speech was attended to more for the light it threw upon the Bishops' intentions than for its intrinsic merit, fell back upon that nostrum of the weak-minded, 'a union of parties', but declared himself against the bill. By a majority of 41, of whom 21 were bishops, it was rejected. 'An honourable and manly decision', thought the young Gladstone, down from Oxford to attend the debates.[2]

* * * *

The situation was near to deadlock. Grey would neither resign nor abandon reform, yet the size of the majority ruled out the possibility of creating enough peers to carry the bill. When the House of Commons met, the following week, Althorp announced the government's determination to introduce, as soon as possible, a bill on the same principles and equally efficient.[3] Such a formula, which Grey and the cabinet deemed necessary to soothe opinion in the country, did not leave much room for manoeuvre. Yet some modification, some gesture of conciliation, was essential if the third reform bill was to escape the fate of the second. In the course of the next few weeks, therefore, there was much lobbying of individual peers and bishops, and a good deal of discussion of alterations which, though not fundamental, might appease some opponents and afford others a dignified excuse for reconsidering their position.

On 20 October, Russell submitted to Grey a memorandum on 'possible changes'.[4] The most acceptable would be to abandon or remodel schedule B, perhaps cutting it to as few as twenty boroughs. Russell conceded that the population returns had been shown to be an inadequate basis for the

[1] Greville, II, 198, 202–4; *Three diaries*, 131–2; J. S. Wortley to Lady Wharncliffe, in Wharncliffe, II, 84, 86; Wellington's memo of 22 September and letter to Northumberland 23 September, *Despatches*, VII, 530–3.
[2] *Parl. Debs.*, 3rd series, VII, 928–1026, 1133–1205, 1334–8; VIII, 67–132, 188–343; *Three diaries*, 127–9, 140–5; Greville, II, 207–8; *Correspondence of Charles Arbuthnot*, ed. A. Aspinall, 147–8; J. Morley, *Life of Gladstone*, book I, chapter iii.
[3] *Parl. Debs.*, 3rd series, VIII, 458–62; the form of words to be employed had been carefully considered by the cabinet. See Althorp to his father, 10 October, Althorp, 355, and Grey to Palmerston, 10 October, printed in *Grey and William IV*, I, 375–8. The editor of the latter suppressed the name of the recipient, but the original is in the Grey MSS. [4] Grey MSS.

8

decisions made. There was also 'great objection' to the increased representation for London, which might be transferred instead to the adjoining counties. Palmerston and Richmond were urging some accommodation with the more moderate Tories, and on 16 November Palmerston was able to bring about a meeting between Grey and Lord Wharncliffe. Grey insisted that the essential and immutable features of the bill were the disfranchisement of the decayed boroughs, the representation for large towns, and the £10 franchise. He admitted that he was uneasy about the schedule B provisions, agreeing that the proposed constituencies were, in some cases, scarcely adequate, and that the opposition's dislike of single-member boroughs was well founded.[1] He was also willing to consider arrangements to retain the existing number of English members of Parliament. Wharncliffe, on his side, expressed strong objection to the London representation and to the provision whereby freeholders dwelling in towns were permitted to vote at county elections. At this stage each man appeared to think that there was a possible basis for negotiation. But the cabinet, to which Grey reported, was less accommodating. On 19 November, Grey, Richmond and Palmerston were outvoted on a proposition to defer summoning Parliament until after Christmas: instead the new session was to begin on 6 December – a decision which Palmerston interpreted as an attempt to discourage further negotiation.[2]

Consequently, when Wharncliffe resumed the discussions the following week, submitting his own memorandum, he found Grey markedly less responsive: 'he had evidently (along with the moderate members of the cabinet) been bullied and overruled by the violent ones', wrote Lady Wharncliffe.[3] Although a second interview took place on 29 November, Wharncliffe wrote the following day, after consultation with Harrowby, that there was insufficient agreement to form the basis of any understanding. Ministers were dubious whether Wharncliffe could, in any case, carry more than a handful of supporters with him, for Peel, Wellington, Herries and Croker were resolute against any treating with the enemy.

[1] The latter was a point Peel had made forcibly in the House of Commons, maintaining that the two-member constituencies allowed for the representation of minorities and permitted compromises. His proposal was rejected by 182 votes to 115. *Parl. Debs.*, 3rd series, v, 405–33.

[2] A memorandum of Grey's discussion with Wharncliffe is printed as appendix B to volume one of *Grey and William IV*. The marginal comments by Wharncliffe seem to have been transposed. Palmerston's comments to Grey are in two letters of 18 and 20 November, Grey MSS. Palmerston complained that Melbourne had betrayed the negotiations by voting for an early meeting of Parliament – 'every week would have been so much gained'. Melbourne, *Papers*, 140–5. Melbourne seems not to have been shown the memorandum and had to be briefed by his brother. The cabinet meeting of 19 November is described in Lord Holland's Journal, Add. MS. 51868, ff. 215–18. See also, Wharncliffe, ii, 95–9; Greville, ii, 217–26; *Three diaries*, 145–8; Brougham, iii, 140–1.

[3] Wharncliffe, ii, 97. Lord Wharncliffe's memorandum is appendix C to volume one of *Grey and William IV*.

These were by no means the worst of the difficulties that beset Lord Grey in the two months between the rejection of the second bill and the introduction of the third. The decision of the House of Lords triggered off riots and disorders in many parts of the country, and there was an alarming growth of militancy in the political unions. Members of the peerage were hooted and assaulted, and their windows broken. At Nottingham, the castle of the Duke of Newcastle was burned; at Derby, the gaol was demolished; and at Bristol, the mob was in command for three days, while the Mansion House, Gaol, Custom's House and the Bishop's Palace were destroyed and their contents looted: a grand piano is said to have changed hands for four shillings, with no questions asked, and the Bishop's wine sold on College Green at a penny a bottle.[1] A monster meeting of the Birmingham Political Union resolved to pay no taxes if the bill was defeated, and in London a National Political Union held its first meeting on 31 October, under the presidency of Sir Francis Burdett.[2] 'The crisis is arrived', wrote Ellenborough that day, and, in an hysterical moment, Peel began stockpiling arms for the defence of his property at Drayton Manor.[3] Ministers were acutely aware that radical militancy could lead to a widespread reaction against reform among the middle classes: indeed, some of their opponents claimed that such a movement was already discernible. Grey, Melbourne and Althorp used their influence to moderate the activities of Burdett and Attwood, but on 22 November, in the face of preparations for arming and drilling the Birmingham Political Union, the government was obliged to issue a proclamation declaring all associations assuming a power of action independent of the civil magistrates illegal and unconstitutional.[4]

---

[1] The most spectacular of these disorders, the Bristol riots, still await an authoritative investigation, for which there is ample material. My surmise is that the demonstration against Sir Charles Wetherell was certainly a reformers' enterprise, but that the political element in the riots that followed was small. Many of the rioters appear to have been very young lads, some at least inflamed by liquor. That this was the version the respectable reformers were anxious to propagate does not mean that it was not correct. In 1835 J. Ham wrote to Francis Place, who was collecting materials for an account, begging him to stress the efforts made by the Bristol Political Union to discourage violence: 'be particular in stating that the affair began politically and ended criminally, and by different sets of persons'. MSS. letters, Bristol Reference Library, B 24936.

[2] For Birmingham, see A. Briggs, 'The background of the Parliamentary reform movement in three English cities, 1830–2', *Cambridge Historical Journal*, 10 (1952), and H. Ferguson, 'The Birmingham Political Union and the government, 1830–1', *Victorian Studies*, 3 (1960). For London, see D. J. Rowe, 'Class and political radicalism in London, 1831–2', *Historical Journal*, 13 (1970), and the same author's edition of documents, *London radicalism, 1830–43*, published by the London Record Society.

[3] *Three diaries*, 153; Parker, II, 190–2. Croker replied sensibly that Peel's proposal for 'counter associations for the purpose of defence' must mean civil war.

[4] J. R. M. Butler's rather severe strictures on Grey over his treatment of the unions seem to me to miss the point. He wrote, pp. 314–15, of his 'helpless alarm in the face of the unfamiliar', and that 'Attwood, Place, Doherty and Cobbett knew more of the real

Grey was also having considerable trouble holding his cabinet together. Althorp, exhausted after his exertions in the Commons, took the defeat in the Lords hard, and thought they ought to resign: 'indeed', he wrote to his father, 'I am inclined to think...that this is the only mode of carrying Reform. I think reform will never pass the House of Lords unless it is brought forward by its enemies, as the Catholic question was.' Palmerston was irritated at the immediate pledge of an equally efficient bill. Russell got himself into a scrape when, in answer to an expression of thanks from the Birmingham Political Union, he described the opposition to the bill as 'the whisper of a faction': under pressure in the Commons, he admitted that he did not deny the constitutional right of the Lords to reject the bill. In the middle of the negotiations with Wharncliffe, Sir James Graham suddenly declared that, unless the cabinet at once demanded a pledge from the King to create the necessary peers, he would resign: in which case, observed Althorp, 'our days are numbered'. No sooner had Graham been pacified than Durham returned from his visit to the continent, waxed indignant at the compromises that had been mooted in his absence, and, at a cabinet meeting described by his host Lord Althorp, launched 'the most brutal attack on Lord Grey I ever heard in my life, and I conclude will certainly resign'. That he changed his mind was not for his colleagues an unmixed blessing.[1]

The main alteration in the bill, as presented by Russell on 12 December 1831, was the remodelling of schedule B, which had been considered during the discussions with Wharncliffe and then persisted with, despite objections by Palmerston, Melbourne and Russell.[2] The number of towns to lose one member was reduced from 41 to 30, and, as a counter-weight to the restored influence of the gentry, 10 of the newly enfranchised towns were awarded a second seat.[3] There were two features of this change that

history of the country in those years than did Grey or Melbourne or Peel'. It is an odd suggestion that the opinions of ordinary people are necessarily more real than those of a cabinet. Grey might have known less of feeling in the country, but he had a superior grasp of feeling in Parliament. The core of the problem in 1831–2 was not so much the organization of public support, as the method of using that force to unpick the parliamentary lock. I think Butler underestimated the need for subtlety in handling the King and the waverers.

[1] Althorp, 354, 370–2, 374–5; Palmerston to Grey, 9, 10, 11 October, Grey to Palmerston 10 and 14 October, Durham to Grey 11 October, Holland to Grey 10 October, Grey MSS.; *Parl. Debs.*, 3rd series, VIII, 594–646; *Early Correspondence*, II, 25–6; J. T. Ward, 115–17; Lord Holland's Journal, Add. MS. 51867, f. 178, 51868, ff. 230–6.

[2] Palmerston to Grey, 29 November 1831, Grey MSS.

[3] Five towns were added to schedule A, viz. Aldborough, Amersham, East Grinstead, Okehampton and Saltash; 5 were taken away, viz. Eye, Midhurst, Petersfield, Wareham and Woodstock. 12 were added to schedule B, viz. Calne, Christchurch, Dartmouth, Eye, Horsham, Midhurst, Morpeth, Northallerton, Petersfield, Wareham, Westbury and Woodstock; 23 were taken from schedule B, viz. Aldborough, Amersham, Bodmin, Bridport, Buckingham, Chippenham, Cockermouth, Dorchester, Evesham, East

might appease Tory critics. Among the 11 reprieved boroughs were the county towns of Bodmin, Buckingham, Dorchester, Guildford and Huntingdon, whose demotion had been regarded as peculiarly hard: it also meant a net reduction of 20 in the number of single-member boroughs, which the Tories disliked. Radicals, on the other hand, could take pleasure in the substantial increase in the new urban representation. The restructuring also meant that the House of Commons would suffer no diminution of numbers, and met another Tory objection. The census of 1831 was taken as the basis for the computations, and it was conceded that disqualification should not depend upon population alone, but on a combination of houses and taxation.[1] A further concession was the decision to perpetuate the freeman qualification in the boroughs.[2] In detail, too, there were some consolations for the opposition. Many of the points they had argued most vehemently in committee were yielded, and in particular the borough of Calne, patronized by the cabinet minister Lansdowne and represented by the obnoxious Macaulay, was downgraded to schedule B. With some justice Croker claimed that the new bill was 'a great triumph for me and for our party', and reflected ruefully that his researches had done a good deal to make reform more equitable and less objectionable.[3]

The divisions in the House of Commons were a foregone conclusion and the interest was whether there would be any response to the olive branches. Though it may appear surprising that such relatively minor changes should either sway or be expected to sway votes, it must be remembered how much the battle had shifted since Wellington's declaration a year earlier, that almost everyone now agreed that some reform was necessary, and that most Tories admitted that the nomination boroughs would have to go. Peel, Croker, Inglis, Vyvyan and Wetherell were as relentless as ever, but Sandon, Clive and Chandos were moderate in tone. The division on the second reading certainly reflected the waning excitement – 112 fewer members took part than in the division of 6 July – but the increase in the government's majority from 136 to 162 proved that Grey's tactics had not been wholly without success.[4]

Grinstead, Guildford, Honiton, Huntingdon, Lymington, Maldon, Marlborough, Marlow, Okehampton, Richmond, Saltash, Sudbury, East Retford, Wallingford.

The 10 towns to be given a second seat were Bolton, Brighton, Bradford, Blackburn, Macclesfield, Oldham, Stockport, Stoke, Halifax and Stroud. In addition, Monmouthshire received another seat, and Chatham was separated from Rochester, and given one seat.

[1] The formula for the new calculation is given in *Parl. Debs.*, 3rd series, IX, appendix, pp. 30–1, and in P.P. 1831–2, no. 44 xxxvi 185.
[2] Discussed C. Seymour, *Electoral reform in England and Wales*, 28–35.
[3] Croker, II, 140–1.
[4] The voting was 324–162. Palmerston reported to Russell, 16 Dec. 1831 that Lord Clive and his brother would absent themselves from the second reading in response to 'the temperate and conciliatory tone in which you had spoke the other night'. *Early Correspondence*, II, 27–8.

The shift in opinion, though encouraging to the ministers, was far from providing evidence that the new bill would get through the House of Lords. Consequently, the question of the creation of peers came to the fore again. The decision was an extremely nice one. Wharncliffe and Harrowby, on behalf of the waverers, insisted that, provided the government did not make peers, they could turn enough votes to carry the second reading. But they could offer no categorical pledges, and many reformers suspected that the vast majority of Tory peers would stay with Wellington, and fight *à l'outrance*. Durham and Brougham led the militants in the cabinet, who were for forcing the issue at once, rather than relying on the assistance of avowed enemies. But even if the King could be cajoled or bullied into making forty or fifty peers, the violence of the tactic – which many of the cabinet conceded would be akin to a 'revolutionary *coup d'état*' – would certainly consolidate the Tory opposition, and might well alienate previous government supporters.

The early months of 1832 were wretched ones for Grey and his colleagues, full of acrimony and uncertainty. Almost every member of the cabinet threatened resignation at one time or another, and Durham constantly. Even that phlegmatic man, Lord Althorp, confessed to Hobhouse that he felt like shooting himself. On 29 December 1831, Durham, in a long and cogent letter, demanded an immediate creation of peers: even if the government gleaned a majority for the second reading, which seemed unlikely, there was no guarantee that the bill would survive the committee stage intact. But though Durham dealt with the constitutional points trenchantly – the King had an undoubted and unfettered right to create peers, and it was for precisely this kind of state emergency that the prerogative existed – his belief that such action would not antagonize moderate supporters was more questionable.[1] The same day, Brougham wrote to Grey, arguing a similar case, and suggesting the immediate creation of up to fifteen peers as an earnest of intention.[2] On 2 January the cabinet debated the matter in full, and found itself almost equally divided.[3] By seven votes to five it was agreed to adopt a scaled-down version of Brougham's proposal, and ask the King to create a preliminary batch of eight to ten peers: any permanent increase in the size of the House of Lords was to be avoided by promoting the eldest sons of existing peers or the heirs collateral. The King replied that he disliked 'beating about the bush', and would much prefer one large creation than risk the need for a 'second edition'. This put Grey and his colleagues on the defensive,

---

[1] S. J. Reid, I, 270–5.   [2] Brougham, III, 151–8.
[3] Brougham was absent unwell. The more conservative five were Palmerston, Melbourne, Richmond, Lansdowne and Stanley; Durham, Althorp, Russell, Holland, Grant and Carlisle voted with Grey for an application to the King. Goderich and Graham, both militants, were also absent. J. R. M. Butler, 331; Brougham, III, 164–6, 454–6.

since they had little idea how many peerages would be necessary, and the King, not unnaturally, was reluctant to give them *carte blanche*. But on 15 January, after a further exchange of opinions, he agreed that, should it become demonstrably necessary, he would support them 'to the full exigency of the case'.[1]

Outsiders could not see what the difficulty was, nor why Grey hesitated. 'Everybody expects it as a matter of course', wrote Sydney Smith in his breezy way: 'I am for 40, to make things safe in committees.' Some weeks later, he resumed the attack: 'the greatest boldness is the greatest prudence...there is not a moment to lose...If you wish to avoid an old age of Sorrow and Reproach, create Peers.'[2] But Grey had personal, as well as tactical reasons for caution: not for nothing had he once declared that, in a crisis, he would 'stand by his order'.[3] To his son he admitted that a second defeat in the Lords would 'make his whole long political life a failure; but he must play the game his own way; that he was convinced a premature creation of peers, instead of securing the passing of the bill, would diminish the chances of its success'.[4]

As the third bill progressed through committee in the Commons and the day of confrontation in the Lords approached Grey was subjected to increasing pressure. On 9 March, Graham wrote urging a large creation of peers immediately, and the following day Althorp declared he was 'quite decided' for the same course, and determined otherwise to resign: 'if the bill be lost after a large creation of Peers, our characters are safe; but if it be lost without a creation of peers, every one of us in whom the country at present places confidence, will be utterly and entirely ruined in character'.[5] Durham, too, joined in the attack, and at a cabinet on 11 March presented four resolutions for debate: that a majority for the second reading could not be depended on, that it would be composed of persons hostile to the bill, that the committee stage was as important as the second reading, and that, consequently, an immediate creation of peers was essential. Grey won a remarkable victory. Insisting that the resource of making peers was best employed as a threat, and that if postponed until a defeat in committee they would have demonstrated patience and goodwill, he carried all but Durham with him. To the King's secretary he reported laconically the decision not to propose any creation before the second reading. Durham went home to tender his resignation as usual, and as usual was dissuaded.[6] Later that month, reports of more defections

---

[1] *Grey and William IV*, II, 112–13.
[2] 7 January and March 1832 to Lady Grey, *Letters*, II, 552, 554.
[3] *Parl. Debs.*, 2nd series, XVII, 1261. Speech of 13 June 1827 on the Corn Bill.
[4] Footnote by 3rd Earl Grey, *Grey and William IV*, II, 196.
[5] J. T Ward, 118; Althorp, 403–14.
[6] C. W. New, *Lord Durham*, 165–8; Broughton, IV, 194–9; *Grey and William IV*, II, 255; Durham to Grey, 12 March 1832, Grey MSS.

from the Tory ranks strengthened Grey's position, though it remained
conjectural what size the majority on the second reading would be. When
the bill was given its formal first reading in the Lords on 26 March,
Harrowby, Wharncliffe and the Bishop of London announced that they
would support the second reading, and the following day Grey's son told
Creevey that his father had received letters of support from six Tory peers,
thanking him for not resorting to a creation.[1] But against these encouraging signs were ominous indications that the King was becoming restive.
More and more he pressed on Grey the possibility of a negotiated settlement should the bill be rejected, and when Grey warned him that it might
be necessary to create some fifty or sixty peers, it was, he remarked,
'a fearful number'.[2]

The Lords' debate on the second reading, from 9 to 13 April, was the
last grand parliamentary inquest on the reform question. It was, however,
less concerned with the principles of the measure, about which little fresh
remained to be said, than with political tactics, Grey wooing the moderates
with diplomacy and conciliation while Durham terrified them with apocalyptic nightmares. It was true, Grey conceded, that there were anomalies
in the bill – the retention in the representation of many small boroughs
– but this was evidence of the government's reluctance to embrace equal
electoral areas and its desire to preserve the essential features of the old
constitution. Durham, on the other hand, vied with Macaulay to make
their lordships' flesh creep: 'are you prepared to live in solitude in the
midst of multitudes – your mansions fortified with cannon...and protected by troops of faithful, perhaps, but if the hour of danger come, useless retainers?' Harrowby came under sharp attack for his change of front
since the second bill: his speech of defiance on that occasion, observed
Mansfield, had apparently made more impression on others than on himself. Lord Wynford, in what he thought might well be his last speech in
that House,[3] declared that the mischief they would perpetrate by permitting the second reading could never be repaired, while Wellington
warned the waverers not to delude themselves that the government would
allow substantial amendments at the committee stage: how many concessions had all Wharncliffe's negotiations elicited? Harrowby retorted
that he was well aware that those who pursued a middle course would be
denounced by both sides: nevertheless, their Lordships would be imprudent a second time to defy the Commons on such a popular issue.
Grey, winding-up, allowed that he regarded neither the number of
56 disfranchised boroughs nor the £10 franchise as matters of essential

---

[1] *Parl. Debs.*, 3rd series, XI, 858–70; Creevey, II, 243. Lord Wharncliffe nearly missed
his cue and left Grey touting for custom: 'if any other noble lords wished to address
their lordships...he was anxious to hear their opinions'.
[2] *Grey and William IV*, II, 288–327.   [3] It was not.

principle, but gave clear warning that he would advise the creation of peers if necessary. Some 16 peers followed Wharncliffe's lead and switched votes, another 15 Tory supporters went absent, and the government's exertions persuaded 6 bishops to answer the call.[1] By a majority of 9, the second reading was carried, 184 against 175.[2]

Even at this late stage, the ultimate fate of the bill was far from clear. Seven of the government's slender majority were proxy votes, which could not be used in committee. After the successful vote on the second reading, the Waverers felt that their part of the bargain had been fulfilled and that further concessions must come from the ministers. They therefore hastily restored links with the main Tory opposition and began to concert plans for the amendments to be proposed in committee. The scheme hammered out, in consultation with Peel and Wellington, would have made substantial changes in the bill. They were prepared to accept the total abolition of the schedule A boroughs, but all the schedule B boroughs were to be preserved: as a consequence the augmentation of the new towns would be limited to twenty, with two members apiece, thus eliminating schedule D altogether. The proposed metropolitan increases were to be severely curtailed.[3] In those boroughs where a scot-and-lot franchise was in operation, it was to be continued, partly to demonstrate the principle of a non-uniform franchise, and partly to provide some element of lower class representation.[4] Borough dwellers would not be permitted to vote in the counties, which were to remain the undisputed preserve of the landed interest. Wellington was doubtful whether their forces would hold together in protracted committee debates and urged an immediate blow against the government by proposing the postponement of the disfranchising clauses until the extent of enfranchisement had been decided. Since

[1] The Waverers, that is peers who voted against the second bill but in favour of the second reading of the third were: Bradford, Harrowby, Wharncliffe, Coventry, Tankerville, De Roos, Gage, Gambier, Melros, Northwick, Ravensworth, Calthorpe (proxy), and the Bishops of Bath, Lincoln, Llandaff and Lichfield. The absentees were: Bath, Dudley, St Germans, Carbery, Duffrin, Ribblesdale, Skelmersdale, De Dunstanville, Stamford, Ross, the Archbishop of Tuam, and the Bishops of Cloyne, Cork, Leighlin and Peterborough. The 6 bishops who had not voted on the previous bill were the Archbishop of York, and Bishops of London, Chester, Worcester, Killaloe (proxy) and St David's (proxy). In all, 12 bishops voted with government and 15 in opposition.
[2] *Parl. Debs.*, 3rd series, XII, 1 463. Government held 56 proxies against 49 for opposition.
[3] Ellenborough, the spokesman for the Tories, did not mention this in his speech of 7 May, but it had been decided at a meeting on 2 May with Croker, Lyndhurst and Wellington. It was a point the Tories had pushed very strongly in the Commons on the committee stage of the bill and with some success, the government majority dropping to 80. *Parl. Debs.*, 3rd series, X, 915–60. Croker, in a letter to Lord Haddington, 7 April 1832, called the proposals for London 'a poisonous clause'. *Despatches*, VIII, 272–4.
[4] Peel carried this against Wellington who thought it too democratical. *Three diaries*, 236–7.

it was inconceivable that the Whigs would allow their bill to be changed in this fashion, these amendments implied a readiness to form a Tory administration, pledged to moderate reform.

When Grey opened the committee stage after a short recess, on 7 May, he ran straight into the ambush. He began with a gesture of conciliation, offering to waive discussion on the precise number of schedule A boroughs to be disqualified in order to allow each case to be decided on its merits. Lyndhurst then moved to postpone consideration of the disfranchisement clauses. Grey interpreted this correctly, not only as an attempt to take the conduct of the bill out of the hands of the ministers, but as an indication of major changes to come, and declared it quite unacceptable. The Waverers then rejoined their main corps, and, after a short debate, Grey found himself in a minority of 35, by 151 votes to 116. 'I was quite stupified', wrote one government supporter.[1]

The following day the cabinet formally tendered their resignations failing a creation of peers, and Grey and the Lord Chancellor went to Windsor to enforce this advice. After a 'very distressing interview', in which the King revealed his horror of creating fifty or more peers, he wrote next day accepting the resignations.[2]

* * * *

The success of their own stratagem seems to have taken the Tories by surprise. Despite all the consultations, the crisis found them unprepared and at odds with each other. The first difficulty was that the King, acting through Lyndhurst, made it plain that any government must undertake an extensive measure of reform[3] – otherwise there would be no prospect of

---

[1] Denis le Marchant, Brougham's principal secretary, in *Three diaries*, 241. The best account of the Tory deliberations is in Lord Ellenborough's diary, *ibid.*, 229–40. See also *Parl. Debs.*, 3rd series, XII, 676–733; Croker, II, 171–6; Wharncliffe, II, 139–42; Greville, II, 294–300. Theodore Martin, *Life of Lyndhurst*, 300, implied that the Tories did not intend to overthrow the government, but that Grey saw his chance and outmanoeuvred them, treating as a matter of principle what was merely a procedural difference: not surprisingly, Brougham, in retrospect, supported this interpretation, claiming that he and Grey at once perceived their advantage. *Life and Times*, III, 190–1. But Ellenborough's diary makes it clear that the intention was 'to put the ministers out'. *Three diaries*, 240. Nor would Grey's move, which Trevelyan considered remarkably adroit, have looked so subtle had Peel not wrecked the Tory plan by refusing to join the administration. There is a curious contrast between Trevelyan's belief that Grey outsmarted his opponents and the letters of Grey during the crisis, which he printed in appendix H. To Holland, on 14 May 1832, Grey wrote that he 'wished to God' the Tories would succeed in forming a government... 'never was a captive more desirous of escaping from prison than I am from my present situation': this hardly sounds like a man who is determined to secure his own recall. Le Marchant added that the Archbishop of Canterbury had assured the Tories that the King would not save Grey by creating peers.
[2] *Grey and William IV*, II, 394–6; Brougham, III, 191–4.
[3] There was some dispute as to the exact form of words used by the King in briefing

permanent tranquillity. But the fundamental problem was command of the House of Commons. Wellington's previous front bench had been piteously weak in debating talent – indeed, it was a major cause of the collapse of the ministry. There were no signs that the situation had improved, while the rapturous reception accorded Althorp when he announced the resignation of the ministers was a clear augury of Whig intransigence.[1] Even if the Tories could persuade the King to grant yet another dissolution, there could be little doubt that a Whig majority would be returned. The new leader of the House of Commons would need to be a man of nerve and resource.

The preliminary discussions served only to underline the difficulties. On 10 May Wellington and Lyndhurst urged Peel to accept office, and were met by an uncompromising refusal: he could have nothing to do with a ministry pledged to reform. The mortifications to which his change of front on Catholic Emancipation had exposed him were branded on Peel's memory: rather than bring in a reform measure, he had confided to a friend, he would be 'cut in pieces'.[2] Croker, Goulburn and Herries, the men of business of the previous Tory administration, took the same view, and though Sir George Murray and Sir Henry Hardinge, the Duke's old Peninsula comrades, volunteered for active service, they were of no political consequence. For that matter, it was no easier to find a commander-in-chief than subalterns. Harrowby was asked and refused; Wellington, ever-zealous, was willing to try until it was explained to him how much his stand against reform would compromise him as the leader of a reform ministry;[3] eventually – *faute de mieux* – it was agreed to approach Charles Manners-Sutton, Speaker of the House of Commons. The previous experiment of turning a Speaker into a first minister – that of Henry Addington – was not greatly encouraging, but the alternative was the triumphant return of the Whigs. Alexander Baring, the banker, was persuaded to serve as Chancellor of the Exchequer, and with Sir George Murray as leader of the House, the outlines of a possible ministry, however feeble, began to appear. But even before the first blows were exchanged, Manners-Sutton's sponsors began to entertain doubts: a two-hour garrulous harangue at the Duke's on Sunday 13 May convinced

Lyndhurst. Wellington's version, *Parl. Debs.*, 3rd series, XII, 996 is confirmed by Croker, II, 155, who had it straight from Lyndhurst.

[1] Althorp, Grey and Palmerston attempted to moderate the zeal of the back-benchers, arguing that no obstacles should be placed in the way of a Tory reform ministry.

[2] Diary of Lord Ellenborough, 10 Oct. 1831, *Three diaries*, 147. Hardinge commented to Mrs Arbuthnot, 18 Jan. 1832 that 'some of our friends having in short words *ratted* once on the Catholic question cannot afford to do so a second time'.

[3] Manners-Sutton spelled it out by refusing to serve under him: 'His Grace's avowed antipathy to *all* reform would afford an Opposition a colourable ground for suspecting all their propositions'. Croker, II, 161–2. Baring took the same line, being willing to serve under Manners-Sutton, but not under the Duke.

Lyndhurst that their new leader was a '*damned tiresome old bitch*'.[1] Worse still, Manners-Sutton would not commit himself until he saw how the House of Commons was likely to respond.

All this gave time for the counter-offensive to develop. In the Commons, Lord Ebrington moved on 10 May a motion expressing deep regret at the resignation of the ministry and urging the King to ensure the passage of the bill 'in all its essential provisions'. Peel countered with the conventional argument that this was an attempt to dictate to the monarch: the creation of peers would set a precedent that would make independent judgement impossible. Once again Macaulay emerged as the Whig champion, contending that it was absurd to suppose there could be no constitutional check on the power of the Lords. An obdurate monarch could be curbed by the withholding of supplies; an obdurate House of Commons by a dissolution – were the Lords alone to be beyond restraint? Why should members feel abhorrence at the creation of some fifty Whig peers yet take in their stride the flooding of the Lords by some two hundred Tory peers since the time of Pitt? How could men like Wellington, who had signed a solemn protest against the bill less than a month before, now step forward to take charge of it and see it through in all essentials? There was some slight falling away in Whig support, but Ebrington's motion went through by 288 votes to 208. Meanwhile petitions urging the House to postpone supplies until the bill was passed began to come in.[2]

Outside Parliament, reformers rallied their forces to face the crisis they had long anticipated, vying with each other in audacity. The Common Council of the City of London declared that bad advice had 'put to imminent hazard the security of the throne'; the Liverpool reformers announced that they would have 'more lords – or none'; while a meeting at Birmingham, under Attwood's direction, reminded Englishmen of their undoubted constitutional right to bear arms. Many threatened to pay no taxes until the bill passed. At a meeting in Regent's Park on Friday 11 May, Colonel Leslie Grove Jones declared that if necessary he was prepared to lead his fellow-countrymen to victory.[3] Francis Place concerted plans with representatives from Birmingham for armed resistance should the Duke form a ministry, and on Saturday 12 May hit upon his famous slogan,

---

[1] Greville, II, 305. I do not think there is any evidence to support J. R. M. Butler's suggestion in *The passing of the great Reform Bill*, 394, that the premiership was offered to Baring. The reference to him in Lyndhurst to Wellington, 12 May, *Despatches*, VIII, 308, is as *leader* of the House.

[2] *Parl. Debs.*, 3rd series, XII, 781–868.

[3] Add. MS. 27793, f. 203. Lady Wharncliffe, on the other hand, reported the Regent's Park meeting 'a complete failure...there were not above 3 or 4000 assembled, & generally quiet and goodhumour'd. Numbers were quietly drinking and laughing in public houses, & others walk'd away after they had heard a speech or two. In short nothing could be more *flat*.' Wharncliffe, II, 145.

'To stop the Duke – Go for Gold' – which was posted up on London walls within twenty-four hours. At the end of the week Croker was confronted in his village of Molesey by Manchester workmen, 'up to carry the bill'.[1]

In the meantime Manners-Sutton and his associates agreed that the fragile bark of the new ministry should undergo sea-trials in the House of Commons on Monday 14 May. The result was one of the most extraordinary debates in parliamentary history, in the course of which the vessel foundered without trace. Baring, on whom the government case rested (the Speaker still being in the chair), was quite unable to cope with the situation: his 'incompetency to conduct the House' was evident, remarked Peel later, while Baring himself confessed that he would 'rather face a thousand devils' than such a Commons. The opportunity for Manners-Sutton to declare himself never arrived. Instead, speaker after speaker lambasted Wellington for his change of front. Davies Gilbert told the House that, though he had voted against the second reading of the bill, it was 'perfectly absurd' that the Whigs should not pass it; Charles Wynn, who had been approached to take office in the new administration, agreed that the management of the bill should stay with its authors, while Sir Robert Inglis, the *ultra* Tory for Oxford University, delivered the *coup de grâce* when he declared that if Wellington had agreed to support the measure it would be 'one of the most fatal violations of public confidence that could be inflicted'. Baring floundered, then bowed to the inevitable. Perhaps Lord Grey and his colleagues might be reinstated – it would be 'much for the good of the country' if they were; the last thing he would desire was to form part of an administration to succeed Lord Grey; then, if the opposition refrained from pushing things to the limit, the creation of peers would not be necessary. Of Manners-Sutton and his aspirations not a word was said. It was, wrote one observer, perhaps the most complete triumph ever gained by one party over another within the walls of that House. When, after the debate, Manners-Sutton, Croker, Baring and Peel met at the Duke's, 'the Speaker's intended administration was dropped in silence'.[2]

All that remained was to arrange the terms of the King's surrender. On 15 May he wrote to Grey that a change of ministry might not, after all, be necessary: the negotiations were tedious, awkward and protracted, but the final issue was no longer in doubt. The King was anxious at all costs to avoid a creation of peers, while the more militant Whigs demanded that now they had the upper hand they should insist on an adequate

---

[1] *Annual Register* (1832), pp. 169–73; G. Wallas, *Life of Francis Place*, 295–323; Broughton, IV, 218–35; Croker, II, 169

[2] *Parl. Debs.*, 3rd series, XII, 905–80; Greville, II, 305–6; *Three diaries*, 251–7; Broughton, IV, 225–7; Croker, II, 164–7.

creation without delay. To the general public, unacquainted with the full extent of the Tory debacle, the situation seemed desperate, but the absence of an alternative government left the King with no cards in his hand, and on 18 May he was compelled to give Grey the assurance he wanted – that if the bill encountered further obstacles, sufficient peers would be created to carry it.[1]

The 'days of May' have been endowed with an heroic quality which a close examination hardly justifies. Place claimed that they ushered in a new era, since the 'knowledge and power of the people' had been so clearly demonstrated.[2] Wallas endorsed Place's view almost in full, and even Butler was inclined to take him at his face value.[3] But there is little doubt that the decisive factor was not the mobilization of public opinion, but Peel's refusal to serve. Had he been willing to do so, the prospects for a Tory ministry might, as Brougham later admitted, have been reasonably good.[4]

Many of the devices which Place tried to employ as deterrents were too late to influence events. The posters urging a run on the banks – which Place asserted had 'finished it' – were not printed until Sunday 13 May. The previous day, the Duke had confessed to Croker that they were in a 'fine scrape' and that he did not see how they were to get out of it.[5] Similarly, Place observed that between 8 May and 23 May no fewer than 290 petitions were presented to the House of Commons begging them to withhold supplies.[6] But by 14 May, when the Tories abandoned their attempt to form a ministry, the number of petitions actually received was four, two predictably from London, one from Manchester, and one from the Political Union of St Matthews, Bethnal Green. The truth is, that in a pre-railway age, it was almost impossible to mobilize opinion fast enough to have a bearing on a crisis of this brief duration. Indeed, it was even more difficult to stop the machine than to start it, and petitions demanding instant action were still rolling in on 13 July, some five weeks after the bill had become law.[7]

In his subsequent account of the crisis, Place insisted that plans were laid for armed resistance should the Duke take office, and his ally Joseph

---

[1] *Grey and William IV*, II, 406–37; *Parl. Debs.*, 3rd series, XII, 993–1094; Princess Lieven, II, 352–3.
[2] Add. MS. 27795, f. 27–30.
[3] E. Halévy also attached great importance to the outside pressure, *The triumph of reform*, 54–9.   [4] *Life and times*, III, 196.
[5] Croker, II, 157. That is to say, any idea of a Wellington ministry had been abandoned before Place began his counter-measures. There would not have been the same public feeling against a Manners-Sutton ministry, which would not have the military associations.
[6] Add. MS. 27794, ff. 58, 344, 347. Quoted Butler, 395, n. 3.
[7] According to my own check, the number of petitions presented to the Commons within the period Place mentioned was 167, with another 90 subsequently. *CJ*, LXXXVII, 304, 307–8, 311–488.

Parkes of Birmingham wrote that 'I and two friends should have *made* the Revolution, whatever the cost.'[1] It is not of course possible to demonstrate beyond disbelief that no rising could have taken place: certainly one member of Parliament was told by his constituents that 'people were tired of signing petitions and addresses – they wished to fight it out at once, and the sooner the better'.[2] But it is perhaps fortunate for Place's reputation that his plan was never put into effect. The proposed strategy was rather strange. The signal for resistance was to be given at Birmingham, where the people were to erect barricades, and 'await the result of the proceedings in London'.[3] But we are told by Wallas (p. 305) that 'not much in the way of an organised rising was intended for London. The part assigned to Place and his friends was to prevent the seven thousand troops near London being used to crush the movement in the midlands.'

Parkes also revealed that he had in his eye several potential commanders-in-chief, though why they were needed is not clear. With Colonel William Napier no contact had actually been made, but Parkes had obtained a parliamentary frank to cover the postage. Perhaps it was just as well that relations were not closer, for not only was Napier hardly the intrepid character Parkes took him for,[4] but his opinion of the radicals was low, and the idea of taking up arms 'with a Birmingham attorney and a London tailor against the Duke of Wellington' struck him as grotesque.[5] The second possibility was 'general Johnstone', probably a half-pay colonel and one-time radical member for Boston;[6] the third was a 'count Chopski, a Pole', who, having been driven out of his native land by the Russians, was regarded as an expert on revolutionary warfare.[7]

The most charitable explanation of these curious posturings is that they formed part of an elaborate bluff by Place and his friends to terrify the upper classes into submission. This thesis has been developed, with a wealth of illustration, in an interesting and scholarly work.[8] The author points out, for example, that Parkes' frank for Napier could have been obtained from any of his parliamentary acquaintances: by going to Tom Young, Lord Melbourne's private secretary, he must have been deliberately drawing the government's attention to his proceedings. But whatever its merits as a general explanation, the theory can hardly apply to the

---

[1] H. Grote, *The personal life of George Grote*, 78–80.
[2] *Three diaries*, 258–9.   [3] Add. MS. 27793, f. 141.
[4] Wallas quotes Napier's letter to his wife a few months earlier: 'I mean to go with the great stream, and if I can float, it will do for me. No dancing on breakers until I have a good safe lifeboat for you and the babes.'
[5] *Life of W. Napier*, ed. H. A. Bruce, II, 274–5.
[6] William Augustus Johnson, MP Boston 1820–6 and Oldham 1837–47. Occasional radical interventions in debate, where he is described as 'colonel Johnson' or 'Johnstone'.
[7] Count Joseph Napoleon Czapski.
[8] J. Hamburger, *James Mill and the art of revolution*.

May crisis. Place's contacts were with the Whigs. During the May days the initiative was, however temporarily, with the Tories, and there is no evidence that they knew of Place's preparations. Setting aside the possibility that the victor of Waterloo might not have been intimidated by 'Count Chopski' and his associates, he seems to have been too immersed in the parliamentary discussions to pay much heed to the external situation. Hence, Place and Parkes were in something of the position of two ants, perched on top of an elephant's head, and marvelling that the jungle fled from them in terror.

This is not to say that public opinion played no part in the resolution of the May crisis, but to doubt that it could be manipulated in quite the way Place intended. Its influence was exerted – and exerted with effect – on the King and Peel. The King had been so thoroughly persuaded of the need for a comprehensive reform that he made it a *sine qua non* of any government – thus bolting the door to an anti-reform Tory ministry. This, in turn, made it impossible for Peel and his immediate allies to serve. But it was the opinion of his political friends that concerned Peel rather than that of the general public. In other words, granted what most of the Tories now conceded – that the King's reading of the situation was correct and some measure of reform was inescapable – Peel had followed Wellington in placing himself in an untenable political position. Public opinion had done its work well before the May days – but in a more insidious and less melodramatic fashion than Place's account would suggest.

*   *   *   *

With the reinstatement of the Whigs,[1] organized resistance to the bill collapsed. Wellington and Lyndhurst led most of the Tories in absenting themselves from all further discussion, and a mere handful of Waverers, trapped by the logic of their position, attended the committee stages. The third reading was carried, after a short debate, by 106 votes to 22. Only a small number of commoners and even fewer peers troubled to witness the royal assent, given significantly *in absentia*, on 7 June 1832. Croker, that indefatigable critic of the bill, had already decided that a reformed House of Commons was no place for him. 'Our revolution is a sure, and not slow progress', he wrote to a friend, 'and every legitimate government in Europe will feel its effects. We have been for half a century the ark which preserved in the great democratic deluge the principles of social order and monarchical government. We are now become a fire-ship, which will spread the conflagration.'[2]

On 16 August 1832 Parliament was prorogued, in anticipation of the dissolution, and the members for the disqualified boroughs left St Stephens for the last time. There was hardly a borough in schedule A, however

---

[1] Technically they had never been out of office.   [2] Croker, II, 182.

decayed, that had not had, at some time, a moment of reflected glory. Tregony had started both Harley and Castlereagh on their parliamentary careers, and Ilchester had given refuge to Sheridan at the end of his. Wendover could boast John Hampden in the seventeenth century and Edmund Burke in the eighteenth. Sir John Eliot, scourge of the Stuarts, had sat for Newport and for St Germans. Bolingbroke came into Parliament as the member for Wootton Bassett, and his great rival, Walpole, was returned, at the same general election, for Castle Rising. The seven voters of Old Sarum had once been represented by the Great Commoner himself, while his precocious son owed his entry to the House to the Lowther interest at Appleby. William Pulteney had entered Parliament for Hedon, Canning for Newtown, Romilly for Queenborough. The great lawyers had leaned heavily on the pocket boroughs, Coke sitting for Aldeburgh, Blackstone for Hindon, Mansfield for Boroughbridge, Eldon for Weobley. It was of no consequence. The House was weary of reform and weary of business, and the last rites of a dying age were conducted with little sentiment. Indeed, the demise of the old system could hardly have been more casual. In its last debate, the unreformed House of Commons was counted out, on the motion of Henry Hunt, friend of the people and spokesman of the future. The symbolism, for once, seems unforced.

11

Interpretive

In this final chapter I want to attempt three things – to re-examine the question of causation to see whether it throws any new light on the problem posed in the introduction; to look at the consequences of the bill, as far as the historian can trace them, to see whether they matched the hopes and intentions of its authors; and lastly to put the bill into a more general historical perspective.

It is not surprising that historians should have found difficulty in reaching agreement on the Reform Act when contemporaries themselves were so divided. These differences of interpretation were to be found, not only between government and opposition, but within the same division lobby. Wellington, for example, considered the bill a dangerously democratic measure, while one of Peel's main objections was that the elimination of working-class representation would pave the way for a middle-class oligarchy. Lord Norreys, in debate on the first bill, objected that it would have the effect of giving 'a preponderance to the manufacturing interest', and was followed next evening by Sir James Scarlett, also against the bill, whose complaint was that it gave 'too decided a preponderancy to the land'.[1] The authors of the bill were no less divided. Grey insisted that it was an aristocratic measure and would preserve the position of the landed interest, but when Russell repeated the assertion in 1839, Brougham issued an indignant denial:[2]

> Surely you never could have said so... I am bound to give the statement a flat contradiction, if it is applied to the other authors of the measure... Both Lord Althorp and myself often said that the fault of the bill was its being too aristocratic, and especially we said this after the Chandos clause had been forced upon us... But instead of this proving our desire of strengthening the landed interest in Parliament, it rather proves the reverse.

In the same way, spokesmen for the bill repeated again and again that it was intended as a final measure, a maginot line against further democratic advance. Such was certainly how Grey saw it, and the drafting committee made it a main thesis. But it was as well for ministers that the Tories did not know of the letter Althorp had written to the committee, explaining

[1] *Parl. Debs.*, 3rd series, III, 675, 778–9.
[2] Russell's *Letter to the electors of Stroud on the principles of the Reform Act* produced Brougham's *Reply to Lord J. Russell's letter to the electors of Stroud.*

that he would not press the issue of the ballot because 'with such a reform as proposed, the people will have the power of taking what more they want'.[1]

Sometimes these differences of emphasis were the product of tactical considerations. It is understandable that Grey should stress the conservative side of the bill in his discussions with the King. Similarly, the difference between Norreys and Scarlett was explained by Russell as a desire to pick up votes from all and sundry.[2] Faced with the accusation in Parliament that they were selling the pass, it was natural that the Whigs should emphasize the finality of the settlement, more than they did in private. But one of the most important things to recognize in assessing the bill is the range of motive and opinion among members of the cabinet – to say nothing of their supporters in Parliament and in the country at large. Some of the more questionable interpretations of the measure seem to me to have arisen in part from a belief that the historian can say categorically 'what the Whigs wanted', from assuming a degree of unanimity greater than the evidence will support.

The 1867 Reform Act has been exhibited as a specimen of political change owing less to popular pressure than to the dialectic of party conflict.[3] Those attempts that have been made to sustain the point in relation to 1832 have met, in my judgement, with much less success. It would of course be difficult to deny the element of party advantage in the reform issue. The Whigs took up the cause partly because they despaired of finding alternative popular support, and once saddled with it they were acutely aware that on its successful implementation rested, not merely their immediate political prospects, but their larger hope of posterity: if the bill failed, remarked Althorp, they were 'dished for ever'.[4] Carlos Flick, in a recent article,[5] has argued that the fall of Wellington's government – and by implication the introduction of a reform bill – was brought about more by 'the product of regular party activity' than by extra-parliamentary factors.[6] In some ways this is doing little more than refurbishing the Tory argument, put by Wellington, that his government was overthrown by a 'political combination'.[7] There is one sense, of

---

[1] Plan no. 2, Grey MSS.   [2] *Parl. Debs.*, 3rd series, III, 799.

[3] M. Cowling, *1867: Disraeli, Gladstone and revolution: the passing of the second reform bill*. The author looked at the reform bill 'as an incident in the history of party', and remarks that 'there is a sociology of power as well as a sociology of protest'.

[4] Althorp, 416.

[5] 'The fall of Wellington's Government', *Journal of Modern History*, 37 (1965).

[6] I am not sure that the phrase 'regular party activity' is very illuminating at any time, but it seems more than a little suspect in the wake of the Catholic crisis. One might with equal plausibility suggest that Catholic Emancipation produced a good deal of irregular – i.e. unusual = party activity.

[7] *Despatches*, VII, 460. 'The truth is, that my government was broken up by a political combination.'

course, in which this is beyond dispute: governments often are broken up by political activity, and it is always possible to give a purely mechanistic account of their downfall. But if the suggestion is that Wellington's defeat should be seen solely as the outcome of a party manoeuvre, or that it can be considered in isolation from the movements of public opinion, it is peculiarly inappropriate. It is doubtful whether it is ever wise to try to detach specific factors in this way, but the crisis of 1832 seems a particularly unpromising example for such treatment. Indeed, it involved the interplay of so many factors, short-term and long-term, that it comes close to justifying Michael Oakeshott's contention that the only proper historical explanation is a complete account of the antecedent events.[1] Wellington's fall must be seen against the background of that progressively 'liberal mood' which Peel had perceived in 1820, and which was bound to place an increasing strain on the Tories as the defenders of the established order: the emergence of the *ultras* then appears not as the product of inept political tactics but as a predictable protest against 'the spirit of the age'.

One contemporary who despite his enthusiastic partisanship was capable of seeing the reform crisis in its wider setting was Macaulay, and it is this sense of the past leaning on the present that helps to account for the high level of excitement that his orations generated:[2]

> If ever there was in the history of mankind a national sentiment which was the very opposite of a caprice – with which accident had nothing to do – which was produced by the slow steady certain progress of the human mind, it is the feeling of the English people on the subject of reform. Accidental circumstances may have brought that feeling to maturity in a particular year or a particular month. That point I will not dispute for it is not worth disputing... Thinking thus of the public opinion concerning reform, I expect no reaction. I no more expect to see my countrymen again content with the mere semblance of a representation than to see them again drowning witches or burning heretics. I no more expect a reaction in favour of Gatton and Old Sarum than a reaction in favour of Thor and Odin.

To this the Tories retorted that the issue of reform had been almost dead in the mid-1820s and had been artificially revived by the Whigs for party advantage. This was perhaps to credit their political opponents with more enterprise than they usually demonstrated for the Whigs seem to have been, if anything, rather slow in perceiving the renewed interest in reform in 1830. But even if, for purposes of argument, we concede that

---

[1] *Experience and its modes*, 143. 'The only explanation of change relevant or possible in history is simply a complete account of change. History accounts *for* change by means of a full account *of* change.' I approve the theory: the practice is difficult in a normal lifetime.

[2] *Parl. Debs.*, 3rd series, VII, 307.

the reform bill was the product of the peculiar political juxtapositions of the year 1830, those juxtapositions were themselves, in great measure, the outcome of the reform problem. The secession of the Canningites in 1828 from the Tory government was on the issue of parliamentary reform. The revolt of the *ultras* was a consequence of the crisis over Catholic Emancipation, which was an aspect of the reform question,[1] and the most spectacular demonstration of *ultra* discontent was the flirtation of some of their number with reform. Finally, the inability of Wellington to strengthen his government in the summer and autumn of 1830 may be traced directly to disagreements over reform.

Nor does it follow that because the agitation withered in the mid-1820s the ground previously captured for reform was entirely lost. If, in the distress of 1830, men called for a reform of Parliament, this was in part the outcome of years of patient propaganda. Francis Jeffrey made the point when dealing with the taunt that the agitation of 1830, like previous ones, would run out of steam:[2] 'True, the cry for reform has formerly subsided; but has it not always revived; and, at every revival, been echoed from a wider circle, and in a louder tone?... Occasional causes there have been, no doubt, but the great exciting cause has been the spread of intelligence.'

It is the more remarkable that historians should have disputed the role of public opinion in the crisis since it was a factor – perhaps above all others – to which the ministers constantly referred, and not merely in their public utterances. 'My information', wrote Grey to Palmerston, when the latter had misgivings, 'leads me to believe that the middle classes, who form the real and efficient mass of public opinion, and without whom the power of the gentry is nothing, are almost unanimous on this question.'[3] Holland certainly concurred with this diagnosis, confiding to Grey that the King was insufficiently aware that 'if the great mass of the middle class are bent upon that method of enforcing their views, there is not in the nature of society any real force that can prevent them'.[4] Grey was, in fact, proud of his sensitivity to public opinion, regarding it as the chief criterion of statesmanship. To the Princess Lieven he wrote in May 1831 that, whatever Wellington's merits as a military commander, in public affairs he had shown himself as 'a man who does not understand the character of the times'.[5] The ministers may of course have been quite mistaken in their assessment of the public mood, but since they were themselves under the impression that they were bowing to irresistible pressure, it is hard to see on what grounds it can now be denied.

*   *   *   *

[1] That is being concerned with the qualifications of MPs and with the Irish franchise.
[2] *Parl. Debs.*, 3rd series, III, 77–8.   [3] 10 October 1831, Grey MSS.
[4] Holland to Grey, 5 November 1831, Grey MSS.
[5] Princess Lieven, II, 217–18.

The most persistent attempt to challenge the orthodox interpretation of the Reform Act as an intelligent concession by the upper classes is to be found in the writings of Professor D. C. Moore.[1] He has developed, with considerable elaboration, the thesis that the governing class, finding its position in danger, particularly from the spread of urban influence into the county areas, conducted a tactical regrouping which enabled it to survive the crisis with its strength unimpaired, and in some respects enhanced : its solution was to seal off the urban freeholders from the county constituencies and to buttress its domination there by the enfranchisement of tenant farmers under the terms of the Chandos amendment. 'The men who drafted the bill', wrote Professor Moore, 'were primarily concerned to correct the conditions from which they believed the demands for reform had arisen – not to yield to these demands.'[2]

That this argument has elements of truth I would not deny. The most ardent exponent of the 'concession' thesis would scarcely dispute that the upper classes made the best possible bargain for themselves, and that the eventual settlement was a compromise rather than a surrender. Grey and his colleagues insisted that an important principle of the bill was to maintain a balance between the rural and urban interests: hence when eleven of the schedule B boroughs were reprieved by the third bill an equivalent addition of ten seats was made to the towns.[3] But Professor Moore's main proposition rests upon the assumption that one feature of the bill – the exclusion of the urban freeholders from the county electorates – was the over-riding consideration of its authors. It was certainly one consideration. In the debate of 17 August 1831 Althorp admitted that 'one great object which they had originally in view in arranging the bill was to diminish the influence of towns in county elections'.[4] But too much should not be made

[1] 'The other face of reform', *Victorian Studies*, 4 (1961); 'Concession or cure: the sociological premises of the first Reform Act', *Historical Journal*, 9 (1966); 'Social structure, political structure and public opinion in mid-Victorian England', *Ideas and institutions of Victorian Britain*, ed. R. Robson; 'Political morality in mid-nineteenth century England', *Victorian Studies*, 13 (1969). A criticism of Moore's thesis, with a reply, by E. P. Hennock is in *Victorian Studies*, 14 (1971).
[2] *Historical Journal*, 9 (1966), pp. 44–5. In the wider sense, this is self-evidently absurd. We have seen Macaulay, Jeffrey and Grey testifying that the cause of reform was the growing wealth and intelligence of the middle classes. I do not think it could be profitably suggested that they hoped to reverse that trend. One might say that they were 'correcting the conditions' by restoring confidence in the system, but this is not what Professor Moore had in mind. His proposition was that the main cause was the spread of urban influence into the counties and that ministers sought to contain this by separating urban and rural constituencies, thereby making each area a 'homogeneous social community'.
[3] It was presumed that the restored seats in the small boroughs would fall into the hands of the gentry. For tactical parliamentary reasons it was important to insist on the balance of interests: a bill which manifestly favoured one at the expense of the other would probably not have passed.
[4] *Parl. Debs.*, 3rd series, VI, 182.

of this. In their correspondence, cabinet ministers were frequently reminding each other what the 'fundamental principles' of the bill were:
I have not seen one letter that refers to the question of urban penetration.[1]
A clause prohibiting urban freeholders from voting in the counties was
included in the first bill, and defended by Russell on the grounds that the
towns should not 'interfere' with the rural areas, but it was modified in
the second bill. Lord Holland noted in his journal that the decision to
modify was taken after a long cabinet meeting because ministers doubted
whether they could carry 'a provision so injurious to the rights of persons
connected with town population'.[2] Had the main consideration been to
preserve the sanctity of the counties at all costs, ministers would neither
have modified the clause, nor offered any opposition to the Chandos
amendment.[3]

In the first of his articles, Professor Moore propounded the argument
that voting in the counties was still deferential, the majority of electors
owing 'allegiance to an immediate social or economic superior'. Consequently the public opinion expressed so strongly in the 1831 general
election should be regarded as the opinion of the landed classes as
a whole – the natural leaders of the shires. With this I would agree, though
the evidence offered by Professor Moore is slight.[4] Since this county
opinion was expressed so emphatically in favour of reform, the bill must
have had the broad approval of the *ultras*, who were 'especially numerous
among the aristocracy and gentry', and must therefore have reflected their

---

[1] Almost invariably the abolition of the nomination boroughs is given top
priority.
[2] Add. MS. 51867, f. 79. The compromise meant that freeholders with property between 40 shillings and £10, who did not qualify for the borough franchise, could vote
in the county. Certain ministers objected that this would endanger the landed interest
but they were in a minority.
[3] Nor would they have insisted on the division of counties in the teeth of bitter Tory
opposition. Russell argued that by dividing counties the cost of elections would be
greatly diminished. The Tories objected that the effect would be to augment the influence
of the urban freeholders who would play a proportionately larger role in the reduced
county electorates. Sir Edward Sugden begged ministers to pause 'before they entirely
destroy the influence of the aristocracy over the elections for counties'. The theme was
taken up by Peel on 27 January 1832 and again on 1 February: in the Lords it was put by
Wharncliffe on 24 May 1832. See also Wynford to Wellington, 7 May 1832, *Despatches*,
VIII, 298–9.
[4] For example he constructs one argument from the voting pattern of the village of
Lowick in Northamptonshire where 'all the voters . . . polled for the anti-bill candidates'.
The unsuspecting reader would hardly guess, and is certainly not told, that the voters
in question totalled four: since one of these was the parson and another the parish-clerk
(traditionally Tory voters) the unanimity of the village is less remarkable than at first
sight. Similarly, Professor Moore relies on the Oxfordshire election of 1831 to disprove
the existence of party voting. Norreys, the Tory, stood single against two reformers. He
received 1316 votes, of which 996 were plumpers. I would have thought that, bearing in
mind the complicated network of friendship and patronage in a county, one could hardly
find a stronger example of party voting.

interests and fears. Lord Blandford is quoted as an example of a reforming *ultra*.[1]

To this interpretation there are three fundamental objections. First, it exaggerates both the *ultras'* enthusiasm for reform and their command of the situation. Blandford was too much of a political freak to represent anybody but himself. By the spring of 1831 the great majority of the *ultras* had come to understand that in wreaking vengeance on the Duke of Wellington they were in danger of sawing off the branch they sat on. They had consequently enlisted in the ranks of the opponents of reform. Since they were neither the framers nor even the supporters of the bill, to conjecture the intentions of the bill by inference from their behaviour is an unusually tortuous proceeding. If the bill really did represent *ultra* aspirations, somebody should have told them, because they were under the impression it did not. Secondly – in one of the strangest omissions I can recall – Professor Moore has neglected to mention that the *ultras* were utterly repudiated by the voters in 1831, so that whatever they represented, it could hardly be county opinion. Thirdly, he has attempted to combine his thesis that the county vote was still largely deferential with the opposite assertion that 'in many counties most freeholders were urban'[2] and that this was why the gentry was so anxious to exclude the towns. To maintain both propositions at once is a feat of some ingenuity.

The spread of urban influence into the counties is undoubtedly a phenomenon of some significance. It helps to explain the extraordinary victory of John Wilkes in Middlesex as early as 1768, and its repercussions can be traced in Warwickshire politics in the 1770s. In Yorkshire, Durham, Lancashire, Kent and Surrey it was also increasingly apparent. But to elevate it to the main preoccupation of the reformers is to give it an importance out of all proportion, and one which Professor Moore's evidence certainly does not sustain. He refers, for example, to the 'predominant power' which towns such as Cambridge and Birmingham exercised in their respective counties. At the 1830 election, out of 3717 county voters, 456 were from Cambridge borough: in 1831, 471 out of 3426 – a substantial number, certainly, but hardly a predominating power even if all the borough voters were on the same side. His second example – the Warwickshire election of 1820 – is curiously unlucky. Birmingham provided 399 voters out of a county total of 3122, and since the town voters did poll almost *en bloc*, giving 367 for Richard Spooner against only 32 for Francis Lawley, it provides an ideal test of Birmingham's power. So far from its

---

[1] I have done my best honestly to summarize Professor Moore's argument, though the diffuseness of the writing makes it a little difficult. I need hardly stress the importance of referring to the original articles.
[2] *Victorian Studies*, 1961, 23.

support being decisive, Lawley was elected by 2153 against 969 – a majority of well over 2 to 1.

In appendix five I have attempted to measure the extent of urban penetration of the counties in the period immediately before 1832. The result in no way bears out Professor Moore's belief that in many counties most freeholders were urban. Even where the proportion of urban voters relatively high, a cautious interpretation is needed. Some 22 % of the voters in Dorset in 1831 were urban, yet one can scarcely believe that it was the growth of Bridport, with 140 voters, or Sherborne with 102, that so alarmed the ministers in 1830 and convinced them that reform was necessary.

One important reason why the degree of urban penetration in 1830 was moderate is that in no less than sixteen towns, with the status of counties, the freeholders had no right to vote in the adjacent county. These were, by definition, towns of very considerable importance.[1] Newcastle was believed to have 968 freeholders, Norwich over 700, Coventry and Nottingham more than 600 each.[2] The exclusion from Gloucestershire of both Bristol and Gloucester meant that Tewkesbury was the largest town left in the county electorate. The treatment of these towns can be regarded as a further test of the ministers' intentions. Had they been determined, at all costs, to separate town and country, they would presumably have continued the exclusion of these sixteen towns, and quoted precedent to defend their action. Yet the first and second bills proposed that these towns should henceforth vote in the counties. The third bill enacted that the freeholders in those county boroughs who already voted in their own towns should continue to do so,[3] but left the others to vote in their respective counties.[4] If the problem of urban penetration loomed as large in the minds of the bill's authors as Professor Moore suggested, it is inconceivable that they should have missed such a chance to limit it. That many of the Whigs, as well as the Tories, would have liked to keep the counties uncontaminated, if it could be done without difficulty or controversy, can hardly be doubted;[5] but

---

[1] Bristol, Haverfordwest, Lichfield, Norwich, Nottingham, Carmarthen, Chester, Coventry, Exeter, Gloucester, Hull, Lincoln, London, Newcastle-on-Tyne, Worcester, and parts of York. Three other towns – Canterbury, Poole and Southampton – had the right to vote in their counties.

[2] P.P. 1831, no. 150 xvi 189.

[3] Bristol, Haverfordwest, Lichfield, Norwich and Nottingham.

[4] The difference between schedule H in the second bill and schedule G in the third.

[5] It must be remembered that ministers were also under pressure from their more radical supporters, anxious to include all town voters in the counties. In the debate of 20 August 1831, for example, Thomas Frankland Lewis and Lord Milton objected strongly to any proposal to exclude them. Milton complained of the false principle of 'dividing the country into two divisions, opposed to each other...it was absurd to attempt to separate their interests, and there was no fear that the town population could overpower the county constituency'.

that the question of urban penetration is the hidden clue to the whole meaning of the reform crisis is hard to credit.[1]

*　　*　　*　　*

Since a sociological analysis has yet to provide a wholly satisfactory explanation of the motivation of the bill, we must fall back on the more conventional evidence provided by private letters and public statements. The impression which these sources leave is that the ministers introduced reform primarily because they believed that the old system had lost the confidence of the country and could not go on. Grey was a reluctant reformer, moved mainly by the desire to restore public tranquillity, while Durham, Althorp and the more radical members of his cabinet welcomed the need for change. The solution, acceptable to both groups, was to strengthen the institutions of the country by bringing into the representation the prosperous middle class and to eliminate those features of the old system that had, over the years, brought it into disrepute. Hence Althorp's observation that the pillars on which the bill was based were the £10 franchise and the abolition of the decayed boroughs under schedule A.[2]

Grey's motives are the best documented and, since his instructions to the drafting committee defined the scope of the bill, the most important to establish. He was a cautious man who had witnessed, in his lifetime, the most violent convulsions throughout Europe. He was haunted by the fear of revolutionary disorders. His first important political step – the establishment in 1792 of the Friends of the People – had had, as a primary objective, the heading-off of radicalism. His actions in 1830 were, in effect, a repeat performance. To the Knight of Kerry he wrote of the great change that had taken place in Europe since 1815:[3]

> Everywhere, as far as I could form any judgement, this change required a greater influence to be yielded to the middle classes, who have made wonderful advances both in property and in intelligence... Without

---

[1] Since this section was completed, the exchange between Dr Hennock and Professor Moore in *Victorian Studies*, 1971 has appeared. I must resist the temptation to plunge into other people's controversies. Professor Moore tries to meet Dr Hennock's argument that, if the Whigs were determined to exclude urban freeholders from the counties they would not have modified their original clause, by retreating into a distinction between 'those (the Whigs) who, while wishing to exclude the borough freeholders from the counties... were constrained from making the exclusion complete by their reluctance to disfranchise the smaller borough freeholders', and 'those (the Tories) who, uncertain of their own influences in the communities the bill proposed to create, wished to enhance these influences by whatever means'. I render this as those to whom exclusion was desirable, other things permitting, and those to whom it was essential. But since those to whom it was essential were the opponents of the measure, I fail to understand why Professor Moore continues to regard exclusion as the major principle of the bill. To compound the confusion, Professor Moore then observes severely that 'their arguments (i.e. of the Tories) should not be used to describe the bill'. Indeed not.

[2] *Parl. Debs.*, 3rd series, VI, 688–90.　　　　　[3] Grey MSS.

some such concessions the change alluded to will lead rapidly to republicanism and to the destruction of established institutions.[1]

This was the constant theme of his correspondence with the King. In January 1831 he wrote, through Sir Herbert Taylor, that public opinion was 'so strongly directed to this question, and so general, that it cannot be resisted without the greatest danger of leaving the government in a situation in which it would be deprived of all authority and strength'.[2] His lack of zeal, at least initially, may be gauged from his remark to Althorp that 'when we took office we thought that a reform of Parliament could no longer be postponed'.[3]

Lansdowne was, if anything, even more lukewarm than Grey, sharing most of his misgivings but little of his political grasp. 'We must recollect', he wrote to Grey in January 1831, 'that we are legislating (and it is a misfortune that we are so compelled to legislate) in what may be called a "hot fit" on the subject of reform, excited by numberless foreign and domestic circumstances, much more than by a definite, fixed opinion on the merits of the measure.'[4]

Also on the conservative side of the cabinet were the ex-Canningites, Palmerston and Melbourne. Palmerston was a last-minute convert to the need for reform, and even then harboured so many reservations that Durham, on one occasion, described him as 'a thorough anti-reformer'.[5] Yet it was Palmerston's insistence on reform that had bolted the door against any reconciliation between Wellington and the Canningites in the autumn of 1830, and in the crisis over peer-making he had taken a firm stand. Melbourne was equally unenthusiastic. He had no great dislike for the old system and was too sophisticated to expect much from any change: 'it will be found not to be attended with any of the benefits expected from it', he had written, 'and then more and more will be required'. But his approach to politics was unashamedly pragmatic and he came to see that it would be folly to try to retain a system so universally condemned. He was not much in favour of reform, he told the young Victoria in his laconic way, but it had been 'unavoidable'.[6]

---

[1] Norman McCord, 'Some difficulties of parliamentary reform', *Historical Journal*, 1967, argues that no coherent middle class existed, and that it certainly did not possess the virtues of frugality, sobriety and altruism claimed for it by many reformers. He is more successful at proving the latter than the former, and indeed one may wonder why he should wish to deny the attributes if he is convinced that the class had no existence.
[2] *Grey and William IV*, I, 65–6.   [3] 11 March 1832, Grey MSS.
[4] 18 January 1831, Grey MSS.   [5] Durham to Grey, 11 October 1831, Grey MSS.
[6] Quoted M. G. Brock, 'The Reform Act of 1832', *Britain and the Netherlands*, ed. J. S. Bromley and E. H. Kossman, vol. 1. Mr Brock's article has also perceptive comments on Grey's attitude. Holland's motives may be judged by an entry in his journal in October 1831: 'our only motive for...remaining in office is that by retaining the confidence we may secure the tranquillity and subordination of the people'. Add. MS. 51867, f. 187–8.

The views of Palmerston and Melbourne, coupled with those of Grey and Lansdowne, demonstrate that there is much truth behind the traditional interpretation of the bill as a reluctant concession. But it is not the whole truth, for the more radical ministers, Durham and Althorp in particular, saw reform as a positive good rather than a choice of evils. Durham's impetuosity pushed him far beyond Grey, both in the proposals he would support and in the extent to which he would lead and not follow public opinion. In his early speeches he struck a note of class antagonism that must have made Grey uneasy. On 17 April 1821 he told the Commons: 'that this system works well in practice for honourable gentlemen opposite, their friends, their relations and their families, I cannot deny – the fact is unquestionably proved by a reference to the Place lists and Pension lists – but that it works ill for the country is as surely demonstrated by a view of its present state and condition'.[1] Ten years later, he argued that concessions to the middle classes were more a matter of justice than of political necessity. Those classes had shown themselves, he told the Lords, entitled to 'their fair share of political power', and on another occasion he went out of his way to repudiate the suggestion of political calculation:[2]

> If it be true...that there is a spirit of discontent abroad among the lower classes...if there be this spirit abroad (which I deny) I should like to know in what class will the supporters of the constitution find greater friends henceforward, or more steadfast allies, than among the middle classes?...The lower orders of the people have ever been set in motion by their superiors...From the multitude therefore we take the body from whence they derived their leaders, and the direction of their movements. To property and good order, we attach numbers...
> But I cannot make these observations without stating that I do not believe such a spirit exists as that which we have been told of. I believe ...that, of all the nations in the world, the lower orders of England would be least disposed to change for a theoretical republic or a pure despotism.

Examples of the differences of opinion and of emphasis between ministers might be multiplied, without advantage. Indeed, undue stress on the differences would run the risk of distorting the political context, for when the effective choice was, as Peel said, 'reform or no reform', politicians who saw it as dire necessity could collaborate wholeheartedly with others who saw it as an act of justice.

The general nature of the measure was dictated by Grey's determination that it should gratify public expectation and provide a satisfactory halting-

---

[1] *Parl. Debs.*, 2nd series, v, 383.
[2] Speeches of 13 April 1832 and 28 March 1831, *Parl. Debs.*, 3rd series, XII, 356; III, 1029.

place. This was necessary strategically and tactically. It reflected Grey's anxiety to prevent further radical advance, and it went some way to meet the criticism, which Grey knew from experience would be offered, that he was opening a gate he could not shut. Grey's boldness, which so surprised his supporters, was the boldness of conservatism, and Greville, an opponent, paid tribute to his good intentions in this respect: 'I believe they are conscientiously persuaded that this bill is the least democratical bill it is possible to get the country to accept.'[1] But the boldness of the measure had one further advantage. Though in motivation it was anti-democratic, in appearance it was democratic, and won for Grey the support of his own militants and the vast majority of radicals in the country.

In assessing Grey's policy it is therefore essential to recognize that his primary objective was to prevent a revolution. I have already expressed doubt of the chances of a successful rising in 1832. But this is not to say that the old system could have gone on much longer. If it is legitimate to postulate the same economic developments without the political changes, one can hardly see the old regime surviving the acute recessions of the 1840s. Even William IV, more inclined to Toryism than Whiggism, agreed that some reform was inescapable: 'the measure would, the King is satisfied, have been soon forced upon any government, however unwilling it might have felt to introduce it'.[2]

A further motive, which critics claimed to detect, was direct electoral advantage, particularly through partisan treatment of the disqualified boroughs. Disraeli, speaking many years later, asserted that it was generally accepted that a number of 'jobs' had been effected by the bill: 'its nominal object was to improve the representation of the people, its great substantial object was the consolidation of Whig power'.[3] Charges to this effect were certainly freely made during the debates. To disprove or substantiate them would require an investigation of minute detail and great tedium, but my impression is that in the exchanges ministers were usually able to justify their decisions.[4] It would not, in any case, have been easy to

---

[1] Greville, II, 204. [2] *Grey and William IV*, I, 266.
[3] Quoted Seymour, *Electoral reform in England and Wales*, 67.
[4] Seymour discussed this matter, pp. 64–8, and found the case against the Whigs not proven. But the examples he took are not always well chosen. There was nothing sinister in the reprieve given to Wycombe. It was included erroneously in the provisional schedule B because the population of Chipping Wycombe alone had been considered – viz. 2864: it was later realized that another 2735 persons lived in High Wycombe, which removed it from the danger zone. Durham to Grey, undated, B. 6, vol. III, Grey MSS. Similarly Calne was excluded from consideration at first because its population was 4549: only with the revised computation for the third bill did it come into danger. By establishing a new basis for the third bill the ministers conceded that their original calculations had been unreliable. The final order was based on Lieutenant Drummond's revised list of 120 boroughs. Granted that Drummond's information was a ccurate and that the basis of his calculation was sound (both of which Croker denied)

smuggle Whig goods past the watchful eye of Croker, and such accusations are hard to reconcile with Tory statements that the third bill had gone so far in meeting their objections that it was virtually their own measure. If the Whigs did rig the electoral system to their own advantage, it did not prevent a Tory landslide nine years later.

* * * *

The tendency of modern scholarship has been to question whether the Reform Act deserved the epithet 'Great'. This was in part a reaction to the more extreme claims made in the heat of debate and in part to the exuberance of some Victorian commentators. Erskine May wrote in 1861 that 'no law since the Bill of Rights is to be compared with it in importance – it conferred immortal honour on the statesmen who had the wisdom to conceive it', and Dicey in 1898 explained to his audience that the aim of the bill was 'to diminish the power of the gentry and to transfer predominant authority to the middle classes'.[1] Charles Seymour, in his pioneer study of the electoral consequences, published in 1915, sounded a warning note. While recognizing the importance of the act in initiating change, he pointed out that the power of the aristocracy was 'by no means destroyed', and that the act was 'but the beginning of the transformation' (p. 521). Later historians continued to minimize the extent of the alterations effected. A contributor to the *English Historical Review* in 1938 started his article with the bald statement: 'there are no grounds for asserting, as some have done, that parliamentary representation was fundamentally changed by the Reform Act of 1832'.[2] In 1953 Professor Gash observed that it would be wrong 'to assume that the political scene in the succeeding generation differed essentially from that of the preceding one'.[3]

A semantic discussion of the terms *fundamentally* and *essentially* would be wearisome, and the validity of much of this argument must at once be conceded. Lord North or Lord Liverpool would not have felt lost in the world of the Duke of Omnium. Greville, at the end of the first session of the reformed Parliament, remarked that it 'turns out to be very much like every other Parliament'.[4] Halévy, in a preliminary study of the personnel

there was no room for partisanship. In any case it would have tested the ingenuity of the finest intellect to devise a scheme that favoured the Whigs on all occasions. *Parl. Debs.*, 3rd series, IX, 652–7, 739–40; X, 536–7, 545–67; XI, 207–19. The revised and final edition of Drummond's list is in P.P. 1831–2, no. 44 xxxvi 185.

[1] *The Constitutional History of England since the accession of George III*, I, 357; A. V. Dicey, *Law and Public Opinion in England during the Nineteenth Century*, 2nd ed., 185. As late as 1913 J. A. R. Marriott, *England after Waterloo*, could refer to the period 1832–67 as 'the reign of the middle class'.

[2] S. F. Woolley, 'The personnel of the Parliament of 1833', *E.H.R.*, vol. 53.

[3] *Politics in the age of Peel*, introduction, x.

[4] Greville, III, 30.

of the 1833 Parliament, concluded that, like its predecessors, it was composed overwhelmingly of country gentlemen and aristocrats.[1] Subsequent analyses have merely confirmed that impression. Other historians have drawn attention to the perpetuation of a considerable number of nomination boroughs, the continuation or even extension of bribery and corruption until late Victorian times, the relatively small number of contests in the decades after 1832, and the maintenance by the gentry of their domination over the shires.

What is less clear is how these observations relate to the motives of the authors of the bill. Total and abrupt changes in the personnel of a ruling regime can be brought about only by revolutionary action. Since the authors of the bill wished neither for a drastic change of personnel nor for a revolution, the consequences in this area serve to demonstrate their competence as practising politicians rather than the reverse. Similarly, none of the ministers ever suggested that their object was to produce an increase in the number of contests: to observe therefore that the number of contests did not subsequently increase very rapidly may be a legitimate comment *per se*, but can hardly be used as implied criticism of the effectiveness of the bill.

The point needs to be made with some emphasis because in one of the most admirable commentaries on the electoral consequences of the measure, Professor Gash succeeded, in my judgement, in giving a seriously misleading impression. 'The continuity of political fibre', he observed, 'was tough enough to withstand the not very murderous instrument of 2 William IV c. 45.' It would not be the first time that doctors have been accused of attempting to murder their patients, but one would have thought it clear that the last thing Grey wanted was to see the old political system dead. It can scarcely be contended that Grey, of all people, wished to drive country gentlemen and aristocrats out of the House of Commons in order to replace them by manufacturers and radicals. The mere suggestion that the bill might inadvertently have promoted the growth of radicalism was enough to fill him with remorse. 'If I had thought', he wrote to Ellice in 1837 in reference to O'Connell, 'that the result of the Reform Bill was to be the raising of a new Rienzi, and to make his dictatorship and the democracy of the towns paramount...I would have died before I would have proposed it.'[2]

A brief examination of the redistributive and franchise provisions of the bill may serve to indicate how little the ministers intended to eradicate the old system and introduce democratic government.

It is certainly true that, although the act destroyed a large number of nomination boroughs, many survived. The ministers' hopes of bringing all boroughs up to a respectable minimum of 300 voters were not fulfilled,

[1] *The triumph of reform*, 62–4. [2] M. Brock, 185.

and no less than 31 of the remaining boroughs had electorates of 300 or below. At the registration of 1833, Thetford had only 146 voters, Reigate 152, Westbury 184, and Calne 191. As the 'ancient rights' voters died off, year by year, the electorate in some of these small boroughs dwindled still more: by 1860, Calne had sunk to 175, and Knaresborough from 278 to 266. A further 42 boroughs in 1833 had between 301 and 500 electors, including newly enfranchised towns, such as Frome with 322 voters, Kidderminster 390 and Whitby 422. But these consequences were certainly not unforeseen by the ministers. We have already noted Brougham's anxiety to preserve some nomination boroughs: Melbourne was of the same opinion, and Russell remarked on behalf of the government: 'at present there were very small boroughs to be saved from disfranchisement, and it was not therefore advisable to give all the towns with 10,000 inhabitants a member'.[1]

The same element of conservatism may be seen in the proposals for enfranchisement. Apparent anomalies are glaringly obvious. Despite the addition of 8 seats, London was still grossly under-represented.[2] This was quite deliberate, most of the Whigs sharing to the full the Tories' dislike of the teeming metropolis. It may also seem absurd that Doncaster, Croydon and Loughborough, with more than 10,000 inhabitants were left unrepresented, while Thetford with 3464 inhabitants and Marlborough with 3426 retained two members apiece. But the ministers had been determined from the outset not to build all things new: 'a regular arithmetical proportion of population' – to use Russell's phrase – would play into the hands of the radicals.[3] Hence the ministers maintained that population was only one consideration among several, and they reserved the right to give representation to particular industries and interests. On these grounds they defended their decision to enfranchise Frome, a centre of the West Country cloth trade, Whitby for its shipping interests, and Walsall – which Croker denounced as 'the Old Sarum of the Reform Bill' – as a flourishing manufacturing town.[4]

[1] *Parl. Debs.*, 3rd series, III, 1519.
[2] See Durham's speech of 22 May 1832 on the metropolitan districts, and the appendices printed in support when it was issued in pamphlet form. *Parl. Debs.*, 3rd series, XII, 1223–44.
[3] On another occasion he declared of the ministers that 'anomalies they found . . . and anomalies they meant to leave'. *Parl. Debs.*, 3rd series, III, 307.
[4] *Parl. Debs.*, 3rd series, V, 840; XI, 62–72, 43–62. Russell's explanation was as follows: 'there were different grounds for giving representation to different places, and, in some places, a number of reasons combine. These grounds, however, were principally three. One was to give representation to important seats of trade and manufactures. Another reason was, that it was desirable to bind bodies of people to our institutions . . . Another ground for enfranchisement was more general – that this House . . . might be improved by the presence of men qualified to bear a part in the discussion of the various questions that might come before the legislature.' This was so vague that it gave ministers a fairly free hand.

Thirdly, it has frequently been remarked that one consequence of the measure was to reduce the electorate in a considerable number of towns, and particularly to cut the working-class vote. Lancaster was reduced from some 4000 voters to hardly more than 1000, and Colchester from 2500 to 1099. In part this was the result of eliminating non-residence, to which ministers objected mainly on grounds of expense. But the reduction of working-class influence, if reprehensible, was certainly not inadvertent. Hunt and the Tories had made a particular point of drawing the attention of ministers to this probability. In introducing the third bill, Russell asserted that the Tories wanted a large lower-class electorate which they could suborn with beer and bribery while the radicals hoped to dominate it by specious promises. He then quoted evidence to show how few working men would vote in the new towns: 'out of 160 householders in the mill of Messrs C. Willans and son, Holbeck...not one will have a vote; out of 100 householders in the works of Messrs Taylor and Wordsworth... only one will have a vote'.[1]

With these considerations in mind, the comparative modesty of the changes inaugurated by the act becomes less startling. It did not institute a new political system because it was not intended to: it did not hand over power to the middle classes because it was not intended to. Seymour commented that 'both King and ministers overrated the changes that would take place' (p. 102). But we have, on the contrary, seen Grey persistently assuring the King that the bill would make the world safe once more for aristocracy by bringing auxiliaries to its support – it was to be 'such a reform as might be effectual for the removal of what is most complained of, without endangering the institutions of the country'.[2] The whole measure, he told the House of Lords, was based on 'a conservative principle'.[3] Brougham also placed on record a conversation in which he assured the King 'how little risk there was of *no* places being accessible, and explained as to several of the boroughs being sure to be in whole or part in the hands of powerful proprietors...He (the King) very distinctly said that *he* was quite clear the shock of the change was much over-rated, and that when once the bill was passed, things would slide into an easy and quiet posture as before.'[4] Nor can these remarks be dismissed as special pleading, designed to allay the fears of an elderly and anxious monarch. The theme of preservation and continuity runs through the whole bill, and if the outcome was to afford a new lease of life to aristocratic influence, it is

---

[1] *Parl. Debs.*, 3rd series, IX, 499. The £10 franchise was far from uniform in practice however because of local differences in rent. In London, a large proportion of the new voters were working class: in other towns, such as Leeds, the proportion was much lower.
[2] *Grey and William IV*, I, 81.   [3] *Parl. Debs.*, 3rd series, IV, 113.
[4] Minute of conversation with the King at Brighton, 28 November 1831, Brougham, *Life and times*, III, 145.

scarcely a surprising result to issue from a cabinet that was, as has been pointed out, overwhelmingly aristocratic in composition.

I have emphasized the underlying preservationist motives of the bill in order to suggest that the political system which emerged was by no means at variance with the authors' intentions. But a balanced assessment demands that we should not *underestimate* the degree of innovation. If Grey and his colleagues were surgeons, their knife cut deep. Lord Lansdowne, a member of the cabinet, had little idea of how the committee was approaching the problem and in January 1831 was at Bowood when Grey broke the news to him. His reaction was, he wrote, immediate and without discussion with any other person. He was stunned at the magnitude of the alterations proposed, which 'we must not conceal from ourselves will when carried effect the greatest change in the system of government in this country it has ever known except in times of violence'.[1] Many of the government's supporters were equally bewildered two months later as they listened to Russell unfolding the scheme: 'they are mad! they are mad!' shouted Charles Baring-Wall.[2] How nicely the ministers judged the situation must, of course, be a matter of opinion only. My own is that they erred, if anything, on the side of boldness – that they could not have carried a more radical measure and that they might have been able to meet the situation with one substantially more moderate.[3]

If it is right to point out how many small boroughs survived, one must also observe that, until March 1831, the total abolition of 56 boroughs would have seemed unthinkable. 'I see no objection', wrote Lord Hertford languidly, 'to a few large towns, even if the indefensible boroughs of Gatton, Old Sarum and Midhurst were to be got rid of.'[4] Against the small electorates in some surviving boroughs must be set the sizeable additions in the great towns brought in for the first time – 6726 voters in Manchester, 4172 in Leeds, 4000 in Birmingham and 3508 in Sheffield – together with a total of 33,885 from the four new metropolitan boroughs.[5]

[1] Lansdowne to Grey, 18 January 1831, Grey MSS.
[2] Broughton, IV, 87.
[3] There is an interesting discussion of the point in a letter from Lord Northampton to Holland, 24 November 1831, refusing to move the address: 'I believe that a much less *extensive* (I will call it neither *sweeping* nor *efficient* for this would prejudge the question) reform would have been received not only gratefully but contentedly by the country – would have passed without a dissolution, and would have prevented much of the evils of the present agitation...At the same time I look upon so extensive a reform rather in the light of a choice of *evils* than of advantage. The House of Commons as at present constituted has lost the confidence of the country. This is a fact too plain to be denied ...It is therefore a matter of *necessity* to reconstitute it and the objection that it is *dangerous* is overwhelmed by the answer, *it is necessary*.' Add. MS. 51837, ff. 144–5.
[4] Croker, II, 99. By January 1831 rumours of the sweeping nature of the changes proposed were beginning to trickle through, but Lord Hertford was in Italy and behind the times.
[5] Finsbury 10,309; Tower Hamlets 9906; Marylebone 8902; Lambeth 4768.

In contrast, the total electorate of the 56 boroughs in schedule A was less than 4000. A further large increase took place in those towns where the corporation had hitherto the exclusive right to vote: the electorate of Bath increased from 30 to 2853, that of Plymouth from 192 to 1461, Portsmouth from 49 to 1295, and Bury St Edmunds from 35 to 620.

To estimate the total increase in the electorate is far from easy, and there is some evidence to suggest that it may have been greater than is commonly supposed. The main difficulty is to form any reliable estimate for the decades before 1832, when there were no electoral registers and many constituencies went uncontested for long periods. The figure usually quoted puts the increase for England and Wales at between 47 and 50%.[1] This is however derived from an article published in a nineteenth-century journal, in which no evidence is given and which cannot be checked in any way.[2] In appendix four I have printed my own estimate, which suggests that the English county electorate in 1831 may have been about 188,000 with another 156,000 in the English boroughs. To the total of 344,000 must be added 22,000 for the Welsh electorate, giving an aggregate of 366,000. This would mean, if correct, that the increase in the electorate effected by the act was nearer to 80% than the 50% usually quoted, and would bring the figures rather closer to the ministers' own forecasts.[3]

* * * *

One of the most excellent investigations of the electoral consequences of the Reform Act was that by Professor Gash. But his preliminary observations on the political issues involved are not equally convincing. We are told that 'given the contemporary political assumptions accepted by both sides, the tories were in the right... Sooner or later all the major prophecies of the opposition came true... taken as a whole the tory case against the reform bill was an accurate analysis of the real consequences of reform'.[4]

[1] C. Seymour, 533; E. Halévy, *History of the English people*, III, 27; E. L. Woodward, *The age of reform*, 88; D. L. Keir, *The constitutional history of modern Britain, 1485–1837*, 403; C. O'Leary, *The elimination of corrupt practices in British elections, 1868–1911*, 14. J. A. R. Marriott, *England since Waterloo*, 99, put the increase at 455,000 which 'more than tripled the electorate', but he was merely using Russell's estimates in March 1831.
[2] J. Lambert, 'Parliamentary franchises, past and present', *The nineteenth century*, December 1889. Seymour used Lambert's figures in his own appendix I, and subsequent authors seem to have used them in turn on Seymour's authority.
[3] The electorate in 1833 is known from registration and was 652,777. The most dramatic change took place in Scotland. Though the redistributive alterations had been only marginal, the previous county and burgh franchises had afforded no basis at all for a revised representation. Consequently the £10 franchise sent the total electorate up from a mere 4500 to 65,000, and for the first time Scotland could claim some genuine form of representation. W. Ferguson discusses the Scottish Act in 'The Reform Act (Scotland) of 1832: intention and effect', *Scottish Historical Review*, XLV (1966), and warns that many defects and anomalies continued.
[4] *Politics in the age of Peel*, 3–4.

As a reminder that there was a respectable Tory case these remarks are salutary, though they do not succeed, in my opinion, in identifying that case well. In other respects they beg too many questions. Can the historian ever say, in matters of this degree of complexity, that a particular party was 'in the right'? Are the Tories to be congratulated on their political acumen when they were opposing all reform, or after the Whigs had educated them to the need for some reform? Does not the phrase 'sooner or later' glide over the supreme political difficulty – in that it is generally held that there is little choice over the direction of change and that what is at stake is normally the pace of change? If the Tories were right in predicting that reform would lead to consequences that both parties would regret, did not the Whigs understand that non-reform would lead to even more unpleasant consequences and quicker? Is there any evidence that the Tories were equipped to estimate the consequences of non-reform?

Professor Gash's commendation of the Tories for their 'accurate analysis' of the consequences of reform is somewhat at variance with the rest of his book. One of the things the Tories were agreed upon was that Whig reform must mean catastrophic alterations – 'a complete and entire change of our whole constitution', to quote Mrs Arbuthnot; the sweeping-away of 'the whole aristocracy of the country', in Alexander Baring's words.[1] Yet Professor Gash demonstrated, in careful and convincing detail, that the resultant changes were much less profound than had been anticipated. Indeed, in the same chapter (p. 28), he noted that 'what the Whigs expected to produce by the Reform Act was what in fact largely resulted. The strength and homogeneity of the aristocratic ruling classes ...remained substantially intact after 1832'.

Nor can his praise for the accuracy of Tory predictions be permitted to pass unchallenged. 'The succeeding century was to vindicate in an impressive fashion the correctness of their prophecies. On this high historical and philosophic plane, therefore, the Tory case against reform was irrefutable' (p. 9). I have not myself found the philosophic plane much in evidence in Tory speeches, and indeed they predicted so many things that a representative anthology of doom is hard to compile. Wellington, for example, did not believe there was a man in England 'who does not think that this Reform must lead to the total extinction of the power and property of this country'.[2] If we are to understand that this was an accurate glimpse of Victorian England – when national power was at its height and

---

[1] Arbuthnot, II, 414; *Parl. Debs.*, 3rd series, II, 1309.
[2] Wellington to Cowley, 15 July 1831, *Despatches*, VII, 469. This was not an isolated outburst. He told Ellenborough that the bill established a democracy, and confided to Mrs Arbuthnot that 'all property will become insecure, that the Funds will fall, the revenue not be paid, and that, when once we get into financial difficulties, our whole frame will be dislocated and destroyed'. *Three diaries*, 106; Arbuthnot, II, 417.

income tax 7*d* in the pound – some very substantial rewriting will be called for. Sir Richard Vyvyan was convinced that, if the bill passed, 'all the accumulations of the Savings Banks must be sacrificed in the general wreck…of course, if one description of property goes, all will go'.[1] To justify calling such nightmare visions an 'accurate analysis' demands more than one reference to menacing language towards property by Joseph Chamberlain some fifty years later. Croker thought that the consequences of reform must be 'No King, no Lords, no inequalities in the social system'.[2] One must have an Olympian view of contemporary society to believe that all this has come to pass.

In two important respects the forecasts of the Tories were accurate. They were right to maintain that the settlement could not be final. The explanation is not so much that the Tories penetrated the future in a way the Whigs could not, as that the Whigs were prohibited, for debating reasons, from admitting their own misgivings.[3] Secondly, Peel was right to argue that reform must augment the authority of the House of Commons against that of the other two branches of the legislature. Yet what he was predicting had, in great measure, already taken place, and it would be more accurate to say that reform endangered the *remaining* balance of the constitution than the *existing* balance. Reform, wrote Professor Gash (p. 5), was bound to 'deprive the constitution of the checks and balances implicit in the character of the House of Lords' – to paralyse it as an independent working feature of the constitution. But in fact the House of Lords had for decades been no more than an adjunct of the crown, and Blackstone's famous description of its independent balancing role was out of date before it was written.[4] Indeed, it might as plausibly be argued that reform was more a *consequence* of the decline of the power of the crown and House of Lords than a cause.

Professor Gash concluded this part of his argument with a bold aphorism, which has been much admired: 'what the Tories said was true, but what the Whigs did was necessary'. It is a captivating phrase, yet it contains an internal flaw. Both halves of the equation cannot be right because the most important thing the Tories said was that the reform bill was *not* necessary. 'I have attempted to show', declared Peel at the end of perhaps

---

[1] *Parl. Debs.*, 3rd series, III, 636. One need hardly add that the consolidation of savings banks was one of the features of their society of which Victorians were most proud.

[2] Croker, II, 113.

[3] As soon as the political situation changed, so did the arguments, and then Peel was remarking in the Tamworth manifesto that the Reform Act was a 'final and irrevocable settlement of a great constitutional question'.

[4] 'A body of nobility to support the rights of both the crown and the people by forming a barrier to withstand the encroachments of both', *Commentaries*, bk. 1, ch. 2. In the 1830s the House of Lords was in process of transformation from an adjunct of the crown to an adjunct of the Tory party.

his best speech against the bill, 'that there do not exist any such practical grievances...as would warrant us in incurring the risk of so extensive an alteration in the Constitution of the country as that proposed.'[1]

I have examined these arguments at some length because Professor Gash's work is justly influential, and because his observations lead, in my view, to a mistaken assessment of Lord Grey. One of the reasons for the tendency to downgrade the Reform Act is that the twentieth-century interest in electoral studies has induced scholars to approach it mainly in that light. If it is assessed purely as an electoral reform, it is natural enough to compare it with the acts of 1867, 1884 and 1918 and to remark upon the comparative modesty of the changes it wrought. But the provisions of the bill were less important than the *fact* of the bill, and it is as a *political* action that it must, ultimately, be considered. In this wider context the bill appears not only as the beginning of the transformation from one political system to another but also as the foundation achievement of modern conservatism. Lord Grey deserves a place of honour in the pantheon of the Conservative party, instead of the two brief mentions he receives from its latest distinguished historian.[2] Between Grey's attitude and Peel's there were – as Professor Gash rightly observed – few fundamental differences. There would have been fewer still had Peel not been knocked off balance by the Catholic crisis – so that, in this study, we have seen him at his least impressive as a politician. But where Grey sowed, Peel reaped. Despair is said by some to be the great theological sin: certainly it is the ultimate political sin. The real voice of conservatism is to be heard not in the doom-laden pronouncements of Croker, Wetherell, Inglis and Wellington, but in the reluctant concessions of Lord Grey. If the true conservative is one who suspects those who declare that the supreme crisis is at hand, resists invitations to die in the last ditch, and comforts himself with the unheroic virtues of patience and resilience, conscious that reform, like income tax, death duties and capital gains tax, may not be as deadly as it seems, Grey and the Waverers are in the direct line of ancestry.

These reflections lead me back to my original *point de départ* – J. F. Stephen's challenge to suggest any single great change that was not, in the last analysis, carried by fear. All such apothegms, if they are to convince, must do so at a rush: like bayonet charges they cannot hope to succeed in slow motion. It contains of course a good deal of truth and the brisk Johnsonian unsentimentality nearly carries all before it. But it is really no more than an attempt to reduce complex and involved matters to an over-simple formula. It does not distinguish whether force is explicit or implicit, yet the difference may well be important for the people concerned. It is a case where the last analysis is not necessarily very helpful. Nor could one

---

[1] *Parl. Debs.*, 3rd series, VII, 454.
[2] R. Blake, *The Conservative party from Peel to Churchill.*

easily maintain that the abolition of the slave trade, for example, was carried by the threat of force – in any realistic use of the term. I doubt whether it could seriously be argued that the emancipation of women in 1918 was the product of fear – though I am far from denying that it may have contributed.

It would certainly be unwise for any reformer to exaggerate the extent to which reasoned argument will assist his cause. More important is the existence of a large number of people, or an influential group of people, whose interests are served by the reform in question. Argument has a part to play, and an important part, in drumming-up support, but less in persuading opponents: it can reveal to a man his interest, but it cannot create it.[1] Bentham was by no means the most effective propagandist for reform, despite his redoubtable intellect, and there is truth in the remark that Edmund Cartwright, the inventor of the power loom, did more to promote reform than his brother John. A man is not easily argued out of his country house, his racing stables, his acres of parkland and his social superiority, as events in our own century have demonstrated. The point was made by one of the radicals in the 1790s when he warned his comrades that the struggle would be hard: 'it is not likely that they will tamely give up their sinecures, pensions, etc. which they have enjoyed for years'.[2]

Yet it is easy to be over-cynical. One weakness of Stephen's remark is that it takes no account of the response. If force is the *ultima ratio* of politics, it does not follow that the outcome must be concession. It might be defiance, and if the *ultras* had had their way, it would have been. Only through a consideration of European parallels can the full measure of Lord Grey's achievement be appreciated. The French upper classes clung to their privileges with such tenacity that they brought revolution on their heads: the Polish *szlachta* defended their constitutional rights so obstinately that their country was destroyed in the process. Under the guidance first of Grey, then of Peel, the English upper classes – albeit with acrimony and dissension – gave way, regrouped, and discovered that things were not as bad as they might have been. The innocent are sometimes more perceptive than the sophisticated: 'this will clip the aristocracy', wrote Lady Belgrave calmly on hearing the terms of the bill, 'but a good deal must be sacrificed to save the rest'.[3]

[1] A not dissimilar conclusion was reached by Ursula Henriques, *Religious toleration in England, 1787–1833*, 260–2: 'the Rational Dissenters hoped that reasoned argument would convert their opponents. In fact, argument merely stimulated their opponents to systematize their own case.'

[2] John Kay, quoted E. P. Thompson, *The making of the English working class*, 618.

[3] G. Huxley, *Lady Elizabeth and the Grosvenors: life in a Whig family, 1822–1839*, 98.

Appendix 1

Representation proposals 1648–53 related to taxation assessments

This appendix compares the proposals and provisions for representation between 1648 and 1653 with various taxation assessments to establish the degree of correlation. Neither the Irish assessment of 1641 nor the general assessment of June 1647 offer sufficient correlation to suggest that they could have been used as the basis of redistribution. The ship money assessments are taken from the appendix to M. D. Gordon, 'The collection of ship money in the reign of Charles I', *Transactions of the Royal Historical Society*, 3rd series, IV (1910). By Agreement 1 is meant the proposals submitted by Lilburne in 1648 and by Agreement 2 those submitted by the army officers to the Rump Parliament on 20 Jan. 1649. They may conveniently be found in D. M. Wolfe, *Leveller Manifestoes of the Puritan Revolution*, 291–303 and 331–50. The Rump proposals are those reported in January 1650 and printed in *CJ*, VI, 344–5. The provisions of the Instrument of Government can be found in S. R. Gardiner, *The Constitutional Documents of the Puritan Revolution*, 1625–60, no. 97. For convenience of analysis the material is printed in four sections.

Though there is no direct evidence that the ship money assessment was used as the basis for redistribution, the degree of correlation is quite high. By dividing the total assessment by the number of seats, one can reach a par figure for each county. Of the 40 counties, Agreement 1 gives 30 their par allocation to within one seat: the remaining ten are Herts., Surrey, Cheshire, Cumberland and Westmorland, which are over-represented, and Yorkshire, Wiltshire, Cornwall, Hants. and Northants., which are under-represented.

The possibility that the ship money assessment was used as the basis for redistribution is enhanced by a consideration of the proposals for additional borough representation in Agreement 2. Of 42 towns assessed for ship money at £150 or above, Agreement 2 gave representation to 38: the four excluded were Maidstone (£160), Cranbrook (£200), Lichfield (£150) and Grantham (£200). It gave representation in addition to eight other boroughs: Rochester (£80), Dorchester (£45), Taunton (£100), Oxford (£100), Cambridge (£100), Boston (£70), Berwick (£20) and Manchester (not separately assessed).

(1) *Ship money assessments in 1636 (including boroughs) compared with proposals for county representation in Agreements 1 and 2 (including boroughs)*

County	S.M. Ass. (£)	Ag. 1	Ag. 2	Comment
Yorkshire	12,000	16	20	
Devon	9000	14	17	
Somerset	9000	11	12	includes Bristol, separately assessed
Essex	8000	11	13	
Kent	8000	12	15	Ag. 2 includes 2 Cinque Ports
Lincolnshire	8000	11	13	
Suffolk	8000	11	13	
Norfolk	7800	11	14	
Wiltshire	7000	8	8	
Hampshire	6000	7	10	
Northamptonshire	6000	6	6	substantially underrep-resented
Gloucestershire	5500	8	9	
Cornwall	5500	6	8	
Middlesex	5000	8	6	excludes London
Sussex	5000	7	10	Ag. 2 includes 1 Cinque Port
Dorset	5000	6	8	
Buckinghamshire	4500	8	6	
Leicestershire	4500	6	6	
Shropshire	4500	6	7	
Berkshire	4000	7	6	
Hertfordshire	4000	8	6	
Lancashire	4000	7	7	
Warwickshire	4000	6	7	
Cambridgeshire	3500	5	6	excludes University
Derbyshire	3500	6	6	
Herefordshire	3500	5	5	
Nottinghamshire	3500	5	5	
Oxfordshire	3500	5	6	excludes University
Surrey	3500	7	7	
Worcestershire	3500	6	6	
Bedfordshire	3000	5	4	
Cheshire	3000	6	7	
Staffordshire	3000	5	6	
Northumberland	2100	4	6	includes Berwick
Durham	2000	3	4	
Huntingdonshire	2000	3	3	
Monmouthshire	1500	3	4	
Cumberland & Westmorland	1400	4	3+2	
Rutland	800	2	1	
Total	£186,600	275	308	

(2) *Ship money assessment of 1636 (excluding boroughs) compared with proposals in Agreements 1 and 2 for county representation (excluding boroughs)*

County	S.M. Ass. (£)	Ag. 1	Ag. 2
Yorkshire	10,800	13	15
Devon	7700	11	12
Suffolk	7600	10	10
Lincolnshire	7500	11	11
Somerset	7500	8	8
Essex	7400	10	11
Norfolk	6700	9	9
Wiltshire	6600	7	7
Kent	6300	11	10
Northamptonshire	5500	5	5
Hampshire	5400	6	8
Gloucestershire	4900	7	7
Cornwall	4800	6	8
Dorset	4700	6	7
Sussex	4600	7	8
Buckinghamshire	4400	8	6
Leicestershire	4300	5	5
Middlesex	3800	7	4
Lancashire	3800	7	6
Hertfordshire	3800	8	6
Shropshire	3500	5	6
Cambridgeshire	3400	4	4
Warwickshire	3400	5	5
Berkshire	3300	6	5
Derbyshire	3300	6	5
Oxfordshire	3200	4	4
Herefordshire	3200	4	4
Nottinghamshire	3100	5	4
Surrey	3000	5	5
Worcestershire	3000	5	4
Bedfordshire	2900	5	4
Staffordshire	2800	5	6
Cheshire	2700	4	5
Durham	1900	3	3
Huntingdonshire	1900	3	3
Northumberland	1400	2	3
Monmouthshire	1400	3	4
Cumberland & Westmorland	1400	4	3+2
Rutland	800	2	1
Total		242	243

(3) *General assessment of April 1649 compared with county representation suggested by the Rump in January 1650 and awarded by the Instrument of Government in 1653*

N.B. The general assessment incorporates borough assessments and the Instrument figures incorporate borough representation.

County	Gen. Ass. (£)	Rump	Inst.	Comment
Norfolk	4900	14	16	
Suffolk	4700	16	16	
Kent	4700	18	18	
Essex	4500	14	16	
Yorkshire	4000	24	22	
Devon	4000	20	20	
Somerset	3720	14	18	
Lincolnshire	3500	15	16	
Hampshire	2599	13	14	includes Isle of Wight 2
Wiltshire	2500	13	14	
Sussex	2450	14	14	
Gloucestershire	2300	8	9	
Middlesex	2300	6	6	excludes London
Surrey	2249	7	10	
Cornwall	2100	10	12	
Cambridgeshire	1889	8	7	excludes University: includes Ely 2
Northamptonshire	1800	8	8	
Hertfordshire	1800	6	7	
Shropshire	1700	8	8	
Dorset	1699	8	10	
Buckinghamshire	1650	9	8	
Worcestershire	1600	7	7	
Warwickshire	1600	7	7	
Herefordshire	1500	6	6	
Oxfordshire	1450	6	7	excludes University
Berkshire	1400	6	7	
Leicestershire	1400	6	6	
Bedfordshire	1200	6	6	
Lancashire	1200	12	8	
Derbyshire	1200	5	5	
Staffordshire	1200	6	6	
Nottinghamshire	1198	6	6	
Cheshire	1100	5	5	
Huntingdonshire	800	4	4	
Monmouthshire	600	3	3	
Rutland	350	2	2	
Northumberland	273	8	5	
Durham	185	4	3	
Cumberland	138	4	3	
Westmorland	92	3	2	
Total		359	365	

It is curious that the one correlation supported by literary evidence (Moyle's testimony), viz. between the general assessment and the Rump proposals, should be one of the least satisfactory mathematically.

(4) *Total ship money assessment for 1636 compared with the Instrument of Government county distribution (including boroughs)*

County	S.M. Ass. (£)	Inst.	Comment
Yorkshire	12,000	22	
Devon	9000	20	
Somerset	9000	18	includes Bristol
Kent	8000	18	
Essex	8000	16	
Lincolnshire	8000	16	
Suffolk	8000	16	
Norfolk	7800	16	
Wiltshire	7000	14	
Hampshire	6000	14	
Northamptonshire	6000	8	
Gloucestershire	5500	9	
Cornwall	5500	12	
Middlesex	5000	6	excludes London
Sussex	5000	14	
Dorset	5000	10	
Buckinghamshire	4500	8	
Leicestershire	4500	6	
Shropshire	4500	8	
Berkshire	4000	7	
Hertfordshire	4000	7	
Lancashire	4000	8	
Warwickshire	4000	7	
Cambridgeshire	3500	7	excludes University
Derbyshire	3500	5	
Herefordshire	3500	6	
Nottinghamshire	3500	6	
Oxfordshire	3500	7	excludes University
Surrey	3500	10	
Worcestershire	3500	7	
Bedfordshire	3000	6	
Cheshire	3000	5	
Staffordshire	3000	6	
Northumberland	2100	5	
Durham	2000	3	
Huntingdonshire	2000	4	
Monmouthshire	1500	3	
Cumberland & Westmorland	1400	3+2	
Rutland	800	2	

I have included this comparison because although there is no direct evidence that ship money assessments were used as a basis for the Instrument distribution, there is a considerable degree of correlation.

Appendix 2

Ship money assessments related to borough representation

This appendix attempts to show to what extent the representation of boroughs in the schemes of 1648, 1649 and 1653 could be justified by reference to their tax burdens. Since the monthly assessments of the Commonwealth treat few boroughs separately, I have gone back to the ship money assessments of 1636 to convey some idea of the boroughs' importance. Towns which had parliamentary representation in 1640 are printed in capital letters.

Town	S.M. Ass. (£)	Ag. 1	Ag. 2	Inst.	Comment
LONDON	14,000	8	8	6	
WESTMINSTER	1180	1	2	2	
BRISTOL	1000	2	3	2	
NEWCASTLE	700	1	2	1	
YORK	520	2	3	2	
NORWICH	500	2	3	2	
GLOUCESTER	500	1	2	2	
SHREWSBURY	456	1	1	2	
COLCHESTER	400	1	2	2	
SOUTHWARK	350	2	2	2	
EXETER	350	2	2	2	
BURY ST EDMUNDS	330	—	1	2	1635 assessment used
CANTERBURY	300	1	2	2	
KING'S LYNN	300	—	1	2	
COVENTRY	266	1	2	2	
CHESTER	260	2	2	1	
READING	260	1	1	1	
IPSWICH	240	1	2	2	
SALISBURY	240	1	1	2	
WORCESTER	233	1	2	2	
HEREFORD	220	1	1	1	
GT YARMOUTH	220	—	1	2	
LEICESTER	200	1	1	2	
NORTHAMPTON	200	1	1	1	
NOTTINGHAM	200	—	1	2	
Leeds	200	—	1	1	
GRANTHAM	200	—	—	1	
Cranbrook, Kent	200	—	—	—	not subsequently assessed
SOUTHAMPTON	195	1	1	1	
LINCOLN	193	—	1	2	

Town	S.M. Ass. (£)	Ag. 1	Ag. 2	Inst.	Comment
PLYMOUTH	190	1	2	2	
WINCHESTER	190	—	1	1	
DERBY	175	—	1	1	
MAIDSTONE	160	—	—	1	
CHICHESTER	150	—	1	1	
BARNSTAPLE	150	—	1	1	
LICHFIELD	150	—	—	1	
Durham	150	—	1	1	
HULL	140	1	1	1	
BEDFORD	140	—	—	1	
TIVERTON	130	—	—	1	
TOTNES	120	—	—	1	
PETERBOROUGH	120	—	—	1	
Hadleigh	120	—	—	—	
ST ALBANS	120	—	—	1	
Newark	120	—	—	—	
Newbury	120	—	—	—	
LUDLOW	102	—	—	1	
Birmingham	100	—	—	—	
Doncaster	100	—	—	—	Gordon prints 'Dorchester, Yorks.'
WARWICK	100	—	—	1	
ABINGDON	100	—	—	1	
OXFORD	100	1	2	1	
CAMBRIDGE	100	1	2	1	
TAUNTON	100	1	1	2	
MARLBOROUGH	100	—	—	1	
WINDSOR	100	—	—	—	
Oswaldston	90	—	—	—	
Kingston-on-Thames	88	—	—	—	
BODMIN	83	—	—	—	
AYLESBURY	80	—	—	1	1635 assessment; reformed 1804
LAUNCESTON	80	—	—	1	lost one seat schedule B 1832
DARTMOUTH	80	—	—	1	lost one seat schedule B 1832
Walden	80	—	—	—	
MALDEN	80	—	—	1	
Godmanchester	80	—	—	—	
ROCHESTER	80	—	1	1	
Sutton Coldfield	80	—	—	—	
BUCKINGHAM	70	—	—	1	
TRURO	70	—	—	1	
Padstow	70	—	—	—	
BOSTON	70	—	1	1	
BRIDGWATER	70	—	—	1	
BATH	70	—	—	1	
EVESHAM	74	—	—	—	
BEWDLEY	62	—	—	—	

Town	S.M. Ass. (£)	Ag. 1	Ag. 2	Inst.	Comment
DROITWICH	62	—	—	—	lost one seat schedule B 1832
PORTSMOUTH	60	—	—	1	
TEWKESBURY	60	—	—	1	
STAMFORD	60	—	—	1	
WELLS	60	—	—	1	
Torrington	60	—	—	—	
Basingstoke	60	—	—	—	
Henley	60	—	—	—	
PONTEFRACT	60	—	—	—	
MINEHEAD	60	—	—	—	abolished schedule A 1832
BEVERLEY	57	—	—	1	
HERTFORD	55	—	—	1	
GUILDFORD	53	—	—	1	
BRIDGNORTH	51	—	—	1	
Oswestry	51	—	—	—	
WYCOMBE	50	—	—	1	
Wokingham	50	—	—	—	
Chesterfield	50	—	—	—	
Bradninch	50	—	—	—	
ANDOVER	50	—	—	1	
HUNTINGDON	50	—	—	1	
RICHMOND	50	—	—	1	
DEVIZES	50	—	—	1	
WIGAN	50	—	—	—	
BRACKLEY	50	—	—	—	abolished schedule A 1832
Stratford-on-Avon	50	—	—	—	
Daventry	50	—	—	—	
PENRYN	48	—	—	1	
DORCHESTER	45	—	1	1	
South Molton	45	—	—	—	
LEOMINSTER	44	—	—	1	
EAST & WEST LOOE	43	—	—	1	abolished schedule A 1832
WEYMOUTH	40	—	—	1	
LYME REGIS	40	—	—	1	lost one seat schedule B 1832
PRESTON	40	—	—	1	
SALTASH	40	—	—	—	abolished schedule A 1832
LISKEARD	40	—	—	—	lost one seat schedule B 1832
HELSTON	40	—	—	—	lost one seat schedule B 1832
Bideford	40	—	—	—	
CORFE CASTLE	40	—	—	—	abolished schedule A 1832
Thaxted	40	—	—	—	
Burford	40	—	—	—	
Gravesend	40	—	—	—	
BANBURY	40	—	—	—	
MONMOUTH	40	—	—	—	

Town	S.M. Ass. (£)	Ag. 1	Ag. 2	Inst.	Comment
RIPON ·	40	—	—	—	
HIGHAM FERRERS	36	—	—	—	abolished schedule A 1832
BOSSINEY	36	—	—	—	abolished schedule A 1832
PLYMPTON	35	—	—	—	abolished schedule A 1832
SHAFTESBURY	35	—	—	—	lost one seat schedule B 1832
TREGONY	33	—	—	—	abolished schedule A 1832
Walsall	32	—	—	—	
STAFFORD	30	—	—	1	
SCARBOROUGH	30	—	—	1	
THETFORD	30	—	—	—	
EYE	30	—	—	—	lost one seat schedule B 1832
CHIPPENHAM	30				
OKEHAMPTON	30	—	—	—	abolished schedule A 1832
POOLE	30	—	—	1	
LANCASTER	30	—	—	1	
EAST RETFORD	30	—	—	—	reformed 1830
Yeovil	30	—	—	—	
ILCHESTER	30	—	—	—	abolished schedule A 1832
Axbridge	30	—	—	—	
Chipping Norton	30				
GRAMPOUND	29	—	—	—	reformed 1821
Penzance	28	—	—	—	
Kidderminster	27	—	—	—	
Blandford	25	—	—	—	
Berkhampstead	25	—	—	—	
LIVERPOOL	25	—	—	1	
WAREHAM	25	—	—	—	lost one seat schedule B 1832
NEWCASTLE-U-LYME	24	—	—	1	
Newport, Mon.	23	—	—	—	
BERWICK	20	1	1	1	
HEDON	20	—	—	—	abolished schedule A 1832
Langport	20	—	—	—	
MORPETH	20	—	—	—	lost one seat schedule B 1832
WOODSTOCK	20	—	—	1	lost one seat schedule B 1832
CARLISLE	20	—	—	1	
HARWICH	20	—	—	—	
Chipping Camden	20	—	—	—	
LOSTWITHIEL	20	—	—	—	abolished schedule A 1832
CALLINGTON	20	—	—	—	abolished schedule A 1832
WALLINGFORD	20	—	—	—	lost one seat schedule B 1832
BRIDPORT	20	—	—	—	
ARUNDEL	20	—	—	1	lost one seat schedule B 1832
BISHOP'S CASTLE	15	—	—	—	abolished schedule A 1832

Town	S.M. Ass. (£)	Ag. 1	Ag. 2	Inst.	Comment
GRIMSBY	15	—	—	1	lost one seat schedule B 1832
Kendal	15	—	—	—	
ORFORD	12	—	—	—	abolished schedule A 1832
ST MAWES	10	—	—	—	abolished schedule A 1832
CAMELFORD	10	—	—	—	abolished schedule A 1832
QUEENBOROUGH	10	—	—	1	abolished schedule A 1832
CASTLE RISING	10	—	—	—	abolished schedule A 1832
SHOREHAM	10	—	—	—	reformed 1771
ALDEBURGH	8	—	—	—	abolished schedule A 1832
Southwold	8	—	—	—	
NEWTON	7	—	—	—	abolished schedule A 1832
CLITHEROE	7	—	—	—	lost one seat schedule B 1832
WILTON	5	—	—	—	lost one seat schedule B 1832
APPLEBY	5	—	—	—	abolished schedule A 1832
DUNWICH	4	—	—	1	abolished schedule A 1832
Manchester	Not/ass.	—	1	1	
HONITON	Not/ass.	—	—	1	
CIRENCESTER	Not/ass.	—	—	1	
LEWES	Not/ass.	—	—	1	
REIGATE	Not/ass.	—	—	1	lost one seat schedule B 1832
SUDBURY	Not/ass.	—	—	1	
Halifax	Not/ass.	—	—	1	
EAST GRINSTEAD	Not/ass.	—	—	1	abolished schedule A 1832
AMERSHAM	Not/ass.	—	—	—	abolished schedule A 1832
GREAT MARLOW	Not/ass.	—	—	—	
WENDOVER	Not/ass.	—	—	—	abolished schedule A 1832
FOWEY	Not/ass.	—	—	—	abolished schedule A 1832
MITCHELL	Not/ass.	—	—	—	abolished schedule A 1832
NEWPORT, Cornwall	Not/ass.	—	—	—	abolished schedule A 1832
ST GERMANS	Not/ass.	—	—	—	abolished schedule A 1832
ST IVES	Not/ass.	—	—	—	lost one seat schedule B 1832
COCKERMOUTH	Not/ass.	—	—	—	
ASHBURTON	Not/ass.	—	—	—	lost one seat schedule B 1832
BERE ALSTON	Not/ass.	—	—	—	abolished schedule A 1832
CHRISTCHURCH	Not/ass.	—	—	—	lost one seat schedule B 1832
LYMINGTON	Not/ass.	—	—	—	
NEWPORT, IoW	Not/ass.	—	—	—	
NEWTOWN, IoW	Not/ass.	—	—	—	abolished schedule A 1832
PETERSFIELD	Not/ass.	—	—	—	lost one seat schedule B 1832
STOCKBRIDGE	Not/ass.	—	—	—	abolished schedule A 1832
WHITCHURCH	Not/ass.	—	—	—	abolished schedule A 1832
YARMOUTH, IoW	Not/ass.	—	—	—	abolished schedule A 1832

Town	S.M. Ass. (£)	Ag. 1	Ag. 2	Inst.	Comment
WEOBLEY	Not/ass.	—	—	—	abolished schedule A 1832
MILBORNE PORT	Not/ass.	—	—	—	abolished schedule A 1832
TAMWORTH	Not/ass.	—	—	—	
BLETCHINGLEY	Not/ass.	—	—	—	abolished schedule A 1832
GATTON	Not/ass.	—	—	—	abolished schedule A 1832
HASLEMERE	Not/ass.	—	—	—	abolished schedule A 1832
BRAMBER	Not/ass.	—	—	—	abolished schedule A 1832
HORSHAM	Not/ass.	—	—	—	lost one seat schedule B 1832
MIDHURST	Not/ass.	—	—	—	lost one seat schedule B 1832
STEYNING	Not/ass.	—	—	—	abolished schedule A 1832
CALNE	Not/ass.	—	—	—	lost one seat schedule B 1832
CRICKLADE	Not/ass.	—	—	—	reformed 1782
DOWNTON	Not/ass.	—	—	—	abolished schedule A 1832
GREAT BEDWYN	Not/ass.	—	—	—	abolished schedule A 1832
HEYTESBURY	Not/ass.	—	—	—	abolished schedule A 1832
HINDON	Not/ass.	—	—	—	abolished schedule A 1832
LUDGERSHALL	Not/ass.	—	—	—	abolished schedule A 1832
MALMESBURY	Not/ass.	—	—	—	lost one seat schedule B 1832
OLD SARUM	Not/ass.	—	—	—	abolished schedule A 1832
WESTBURY	Not/ass.	—	—	—	lost one seat schedule B 1832
WOOTTON BASSETT	Not/ass.	—	—	—	abolished schedule A 1832
ALDBOROUGH	Not/ass.	—	—	—	abolished schedule A 1832
BOROUGHBRIDGE	Not/ass.	—	—	—	abolished schedule A 1832
KNARESBOROUGH	Not/ass.	—	—	—	
MALTON	Not/ass.	—	—	—	
NORTHALLERTON	Not/ass.	—	—	—	lost one seat schedule B 1832
THIRSK	Not/ass.	—	—	—	lost one seat schedule B 1832

N.B. Five of the Cinque Ports were separately assessed in 1636 – Dover at £330, Sandwich at 250, Hastings 250, Romney 180 and Hythe 40. Agreement 1 ignored them all; Agreement 2 awarded three seats collectively to the Cinque Ports; the Instrument of Government gave 1 seat each to Dover, Sandwich and Rye. Of the 5 Cinque Ports not given representation in 1653, Winchelsea, Romney and Seaford finished up in schedule A and Hythe in schedule B; the fifth was Hastings. The Instrument also awarded 2 seats to the Isle of Wight and 2 to the Isle of Ely: the latter were in effect given to Wisbech, assessed at £180 in 1635. In 1659 Wisbech seemed reluctant to admit that a traditional Parliament had been summoned and returned John Thurloe: he very sensibly transferred at once to the University of Cambridge.

The above table makes, I suggest, three points:

(1) Despite special cases and anomalies, some of which can be explained or guessed at, it demonstrates the overall rationality of the reforms proposed and implemented.

(2) It reveals the tenderness towards the old parliamentary boroughs.

(3) It establishes the extent to which that part of the representation which was reformed in 1832 was in decay in the seventeenth century and was recognized as such.

Appendix 3

Contested elections 1701–1832

The following table attempts to record contested elections between 1701 and 1832. By a contested election is meant one where there is indisputable evidence that a poll was held. I have confined my enquiries to general elections since the search for by-election evidence would be an overwhelming task. The scarcity of newspaper sources makes it difficult to compile a satisfactory record for an earlier period.

The evidence on which the table is based has been taken from a large number of sources. H. S. Smith, *The Parliaments of England* (1844), printed many polls, to which a correspondence in *Notes and Queries*, 1892–4, initiated by W. W. Bean, made considerable additions. W. Speck, *Tory and Whig, the struggle in the constituencies* prints a list of polls 1701–15 as Appendix E. The two instalments of the *History of Parliament*, from 1715–54 and 1754–90, also have lists. These sources can be augmented by reference to local histories, newspapers, poll books, private correspondence, corporation archives, Commons Journals, parliamentary papers and specialized studies.

It is impossible to do more than surmize what proportion of polls have been recovered. My guess is that the figures for the counties are reasonably reliable, since a county contest was always an important event and few can have escaped notice. For the boroughs I should be surprised if the figures were not 75% complete. Polls that have not been traced are more likely to be in the early period when newspaper sources are more meagre, and it may therefore be anticipated that fresh evidence is more likely to confirm the trend towards a reduction of contests than to contradict it.

Since it is impossible to arrive at any complete picture except by collective endeavour, I should be glad to receive information of contests I have overlooked. But best of all would be for the Institute of Historical Research to compile a register of contested elections as a counterpart to its growing collection of poll books.

The evidence for the English counties is the most remarkable, showing that contests were common until 1734, with more than half the counties going to the poll at the general elections of 1705 and 1710. In mid-century there were then four elections, from 1741–61 inclusive, with very few contests. There was subsequently some increase in the number of contests, though there were considerable fluctuations and the very high number of contests for the early period is never repeated.

The English boroughs follow a similar pattern, more than half of them being contested in 1710 and at least 94 at the election of 1734. The period 1741–61 again sees a marked reduction in the number of contests, followed by a slight increase.

I have not been able to devote enough attention to my lists of Welsh and Scottish contests to justify including them in this appendix. Speck records Welsh contests for the period 1701–15, and both Welsh and Scottish contests can be traced in the *History of Parliament*, 1715–90. There does not appear to have been the same political activity in Wales in Anne's reign as in England: the period of greatest contests comes later, from 1715–41 inclusive. This is also the period of most contests in Scotland, with at least 20 in 1722 and 1734.

The general election with most contests was probably that of 1722, with 17 English counties, 110 English boroughs, 9 Welsh and 20 Scottish contests making a grand total of 156. Next comes the election of 1710 with a total of 143 (23, 104, 4, 12), and thirdly that of 1734 with 136 contests (13, 94, 9, 20). The election in the whole period with fewest contests was 1761, the first of George III's reign, with a total of only 57 (4, 42, 2, 9). The next lowest was 1747 with 61 (3, 48, 2, 8), and third came 1754 with 66 (5, 55, 4, 2). The fact that the period with fewest contests also happens to be that accorded the most intensive study may have contributed to produce a misleading impression of political sluggishness during the eighteenth century as a whole. Sir Goronwy Edwards in his presidential address to the Royal Historical Society in December 1964 ('The emergence of majority rule in the procedure of the House of Commons', *TRHS*, 5th series, xv) hazarded the guess in relation to the first half of the eighteenth century that there was 'already some reason to anticipate that its election pattern will be found not to differ in any fundamental way from the pattern worked out by Sir Lewis Namier for the latter half of the same century'. It is now apparent that this was a doubtful assumption. The reduction of the number of contests from 1722 to 1747 to almost one-third denotes a political change of very considerable importance.

(1) English counties – contested elections 1701–1832

Year	Bedfordshire	Berkshire	Buckinghamshire	Cambridgeshire	Cheshire	Cornwall	Cumberland	Derbyshire	Devon	Dorset	Durham	Essex	Gloucestershire	Herefordshire	Hertfordshire	Huntingdonshire	Kent	Lancashire
1831	×	·	×	·	·	×	×	·	·	×	·	×	·	·	·	×	·	·
1830	·	·	·	×	·	·	·	·	×	·	·	×	·	·	·	×	·	·
1826	×	·	·	×	·	·	·	·	×	·	·	·	·	·	·	×	·	×
1820	×	×	·	·	·	·	×	×	×	·	×	·	·	·	·	·	·	×
1818	·	×	·	·	·	·	·	·	×	·	·	·	·	·	×	×	×	·
1812	·	×	·	·	·	·	·	·	×	·	·	×	·	·	·	·	·	·
1807	×	·	·	·	·	·	·	·	·	×	×	·	·	·	·	×	·	·
1806	·	·	·	·	·	·	·	·	·	×	·	·	·	·	·	·	·	×
1802	·	·	·	×	·	·	·	·	·	·	·	·	·	×	×	·	·	×
1796	·	×	·	·	·	·	·	·	·	·	·	·	·	×	×	·	·	×
1790	·	·	·	·	·	×	·	·	×	·	×	·	·	·	·	·	·	×
1784	×	×	×	·	·	·	·	·	·	·	·	·	×	·	·	·	·	·
1780	·	·	·	×	·	·	·	·	·	·	·	·	·	·	·	·	·	·
1774	×	·	·	·	·	×	×	·	·	·	·	×	·	×	×	·	·	·
1768	·	×	·	·	·	·	×	×	·	·	·	×	·	·	·	×	·	·
1761	·	·	·	·	·	·	·	·	·	·	×	·	·	·	×	·	·	·
1754	·	·	·	·	·	·	·	·	·	·	·	·	·	×	×	·	×	·
1747	·	·	·	·	·	·	·	·	·	·	·	·	·	·	·	·	·	×
1741	·	·	·	·	·	·	·	·	·	·	·	·	·	·	·	×	·	·
1734	×	·	×	·	·	×	·	×	·	·	·	×	×	·	×	·	×	·
1727	×	×	×	×	×	·	·	·	·	×	·	·	·	·	×	·	×	·
1722	×	×	×	×	·	·	×	·	·	·	×	×	×	·	×	·	·	×
1715	×	·	·	×	×	·	·	·	·	·	·	×	×	·	×	·	×	·
1713	×	·	×	·	·	·	·	·	·	·	·	·	×	×	·	×	×	·
1710	×	×	×	×	×	×	·	·	·	·	·	×	×	×	·	×	×	·
1708	×	·	·	·	·	·	·	·	·	·	·	·	·	·	·	·	·	·
1705	×	×	×	×	×	×	·	·	·	·	·	×	×	·	×	·	×	·
1702	·	×	×	·	×	·	×	·	·	·	·	×	×	·	·	·	·	·
1701	·	·	×	·	×	·	·	×	·	·	×	×	·	·	·	·	×	·

Leicestershire	·	×	·	×	·	×	·	×	·	×	·	·	·	·	·	·	·	·	·	·	·	×	·	·	·	×	·	×	·
Lincolnshire	·	·	×	·	·	×	×	×	·	·	·	·	·	·	·	·	·	·	·	·	·	×	·	×	×	×	·	·	·
Middlesex	×	×	×	×	×	×	×	×	·	×	·	·	·	×	×	×	×	×	×	×	×	×	×	×	×	×	×	·	×
Monmouthshire	·	·	×	×	·	·	·	·	×	·	·	·	·	·	·	·	·	·	·	·	·	·	·	·	·	·	·	·	·
Norfolk	×	·	·	·	×	×	·	·	·	×	·	·	·	×	·	·	·	·	·	×	×	·	·	×	·	·	·	×	·
Northamptonshire	×	·	×	·	·	·	·	·	·	·	·	·	·	·	·	·	·	·	·	×	×	·	·	·	·	·	·	·	×
Northumberland	×	×	·	×	×	·	·	×	·	·	·	·	·	·	·	·	·	×	·	·	·	·	·	·	·	×	·	·	·
Nottinghamshire	×	×	·	×	×	×	×	×	·	·	·	·	·	·	·	·	·	·	·	·	·	·	·	·	×	×	·	·	·
Oxfordshire	·	·	·	·	·	·	·	·	·	×	·	×	·	·	·	·	·	·	·	·	·	·	·	·	×	×	·	×	×
Rutland	·	·	·	×	×	×	×	×	·	·	×	×	·	·	·	·	·	·	·	·	·	·	·	·	·	·	·	·	·
Shropshire	×	×	·	×	×	×	×	×	·	·	·	·	·	·	·	·	·	·	·	·	·	×	·	·	·	·	×	·	×
Somerset	×	×	×	·	·	×	×	·	·	·	·	·	·	·	·	·	·	·	·	×	·	×	·	·	·	·	·	·	·
Southampton	·	·	×	×	×	×	×	·	·	·	·	·	·	·	×	×	·	·	·	·	·	×	×	·	·	×	×	×	·
Staffordshire	×	·	×	·	×	·	×	·	×	·	·	×	·	·	·	·	·	·	·	·	·	·	×	·	·	·	×	·	·
Suffolk	×	×	·	×	·	×	×	·	×	·	·	·	·	·	×	×	·	×	·	·	·	·	·	·	·	·	·	·	·
Surrey	×	×	×	×	×	×	×	×	×	×	·	·	·	×	×	×	×	×	×	×	×	×	×	×	×	·	×	×	×
Sussex	×	×	×	×	×	×	×	·	×	×	·	·	·	×	·	·	×	×	×	×	×	×	×	×	×	×	×	×	·
Warwickshire	·	×	·	·	·	·	·	·	×	·	·	·	·	·	·	·	×	×	·	·	·	·	·	·	·	·	·	·	·
Westmorland	×	×	×	×	×	×	·	·	·	·	×	×	×	×	·	·	×	×	·	·	·	×	·	·	×	×	×	×	·
Wiltshire	×	×	·	·	×	×	·	·	·	·	·	·	·	·	·	·	·	·	·	·	·	·	·	·	×	×	·	·	×
Worcestershire	×	×	·	·	·	·	·	×	·	×	·	×	·	·	·	·	·	·	·	·	·	·	·	·	·	·	·	·	·
Yorkshire	·	·	×	×	×	·	×	·	·	×	·	·	·	·	·	·	·	·	·	·	·	·	×	·	·	·	·	×	·
Total	18	18	26	14	23	12	17	17	12	13	4	3	5	4	8	11	2	7	8	4	6	7	11	4	11	10	11	9	11

(2) English boroughs – contested elections 1701–1832 (arranged by counties)

	1831	1830	1826	1820	1818	1812	1807	1806	1802	1796	1790	1784	1780	1774	1768	1761	1754	1747	1741	1734	1727	1722	1715	1713	1710	1708	1705	1702	1701
Bedfordshire																													
Bedford		×									×		×	×	×	×		×			×	×	×	×	×		×		
Berkshire																													
Abingdon		×		×	×	×	×	×	×	×			×	×	×		×			×	×	×				×	×		×
Reading		×	×	×	×	×			×		×		×	×		×	×			×	×	×	×	×		×			
Wallingford			×	×	×									×			×			×	×	×	×	×	×				×
Windsor			×					×															×	×					
Buckinghamshire																													
Amersham	×																			×			×	×	×		×		×
Aylesbury							×	×						×						×			×	×	×		×	×	×
Buckingham																			×				×					×	
Wycombe											×											×						×	
Great Marlow	×	×		×	×				×			×	×	×			×			×	×		×	×	×	×	×	×	
Wendover		×	×									×							×	×		×	×		×			×	
Cambridgeshire																													
Cambridge			×	×	×								×	×							×		×			×	×		
Cheshire																													
Chester			×	×		×						×						×		×	×	×	×						
Cornwall																													
Bodmin											×	×		×	×			×	×		×	×				×			
Bossiney				×	×														×										
Callington			×	×	×				×						×			×	×			×							×

Camelford	·	·	·	·	·	·	·	·	×	·	×	·	·	×	·	×	×		×	·		·		×	×	·
Fowey	·	·	·	·	·	·	·	·	·	×	·	·	×	·	×	×	×		·	·		·		·	×	·
Grampound*	×	×	·	·	·	·	·	×	·	×	·	·	×	·	·	×	·		×	·		·		·	×	·
Helston	·	·	·	×	·	·	·	·	×	×	×	·	·	·	×	×	×		×	·		·		·	×	·
Launceston	×	×	×	×	·	·	·	·	·	×	×	·	·	·	·	×	·		×	×		·		·	×	·
Liskeard	×	·	·	×	×	·	·	·	·	×	×	·	·	×	·	·	·		×	·		·		·	×	·
East Looe	·	·	×	·	·	·	·	·	×	×	×	·	×	×	·	×	×		·	·		·		·	×	·
West Looe	·	·	·	·	·	·	·	·	·	×	·	·	×	·	·	·	×		·	·		·		·	×	·
Lostwithiel	×	·	·	·	×	·	·	·	·	×	·	·	·	·	·	×	·		×	·		×		·	×	·
Mitchell	·	×	·	×	·	·	·	·	·	×	·	·	·	·	·	×	·		×	·		·		·	×	·
Newport	×	·	·	·	×	·	·	·	·	×	·	·	×	·	·	×	·		×	·		×		·	×	·
Penryn	·	·	·	×	·	·	·	·	×	·	×	×	·	×	·	·	·		·	·		×		·	×	·
St Germans	·	·	·	×	×	×	·	·	·	×	·	·	×	·	×	×	×		×	·		·		·	×	·
St Ives	·	×	·	·	·	·	·	·	×	·	·	·	×	·	·	×	·		×	·		·		×	×	·
St Mawes	·	·	·	·	·	·	·	·	×	·	·	·	×	·	×	×	×		×	·		·		×	×	·
Saltash	·	·	·	×	·	·	·	·	×	×	×	·	·	·	·	·	·		·	·		·		·	×	·
Tregony	·	·	·	·	·	·	·	·	×	·	·	·	·	·	·	×	·		·	·		×		·	·	·
Truro	·	·	×	·	·	·	·	·	×	·	×	·	·	·	·	·	·		×	·		·		·	·	·
Cumberland	·	·	·	×	·	·	·	·	×	·	×	·	×	×	×	·	·		×	·		×		×	·	·
Carlisle	·	·	·	·	·	·	·	·	×	·	·	·	·	×	·	·	·		·	×		·		×	·	·
Cockermouth	·	·	×	·	·	·	·	·	×	×	×	×	·	×	×	·	×		·	·		·		·	·	·
Derbyshire	·	·	·	×	·	·	·	·	×	·	·	·	×	·	·	·	·		·	×		×		·	·	·
Derby	·	·	·	·	·	·	×	·	·	×	·	×	·	×	·	·	·		×	×		×		×	·	·
Devon	·	×	·	·	·	·	·	·	·	×	×	·	·	×	·	·	·		·	·		·		×	·	·
Ashburton	·	·	·	·	·	·	×	×	·	·	×	·	·	×	·	·	·		×	×		×		×	·	·
Barnstaple	·	×	·	·	·	·	·	·	×	×	·	·	·	×	·	·	·		×	×		·		×	·	·
Bere Alston	·	×	·	·	·	·	·	×	·	×	·	·	×	×	·	×	·		×	×		·		·	·	·

* disfranchised w.e.f. 1826.

(2) English boroughs (cont.)

Year	Dartmouth	Exeter	Honiton	Okehampton	Plymouth	Plympton Erle	Tavistock	Tiverton	Totnes	Bridport	Corfe Castle	Dorchester	Lyme Regis	Poole	Shaftesbury	Wareham	Weymouth & Melcombe Regis	Durham	Colchester	Harwich	Maldon
1831	·	×	×	·	×	·	·	·	×	·	·	·	·	·	×	·	×	·	×	·	·
1830	×	·	·	·	·	·	·	·	·	·	·	·	·	·	×	·	×	×	×	·	·
1826	·	·	×	×	×	·	·	·	×	·	·	·	·	×	·	·	×	·	·	·	×
1820	·	×	·	·	·	·	·	·	·	×	·	·	·	·	·	·	·	·	×	·	·
1818	·	×	×	·	×	·	·	·	·	·	·	·	·	×	·	·	×	×	×	·	·
1812	·	·	·	·	·	·	·	·	×	×	·	·	·	·	·	×	·	×	·	·	·
1807	·	·	·	×	·	·	·	·	·	·	·	·	×	×	·	·	×	·	×	·	×
1806	·	·	·	·	×	·	·	·	·	×	·	×	·	·	·	×	·	·	×	·	×
1802	·	×	×	×	·	×	·	·	·	×	·	·	·	·	×	·	×	×	·	×	×
1796	·	·	·	·	·	·	·	·	×	×	·	·	·	·	×	·	·	·	×	·	·
1790	×	×	×	×	×	·	·	·	·	·	×	·	×	×	·	×	·	·	×	·	·
1784	×	×	×	×	×	·	·	·	·	×	·	·	×	×	·	×	·	·	×	·	·
1780	·	·	×	×	×	·	·	·	·	×	·	×	×	×	·	×	·	·	×	·	·
1774	·	·	×	·	·	·	·	·	×	×	·	×	·	×	×	·	·	×	·	·	·
1768	·	×	×	·	·	·	·	·	·	·	×	·	×	×	·	×	·	·	×	·	×
1761	·	×	·	·	·	·	·	·	·	×	·	·	·	·	×	·	·	×	·	·	×
1754	·	×	×	·	·	·	·	×	·	·	·	·	·	×	·	·	·	·	×	·	×
1747	·	×	·	·	·	·	·	·	×	×	·	·	·	×	×	·	·	×	×	·	×
1741	·	×	·	·	·	·	×	×	·	×	·	·	·	·	×	·	·	·	×	·	·
1734	·	×	·	·	·	·	×	·	×	×	·	×	×	·	×	×	·	·	·	×	×
1727	·	·	×	·	·	·	·	·	·	×	·	×	×	×	×	×	×	·	×	·	·
1722	·	×	·	·	·	·	·	×	·	×	·	×	×	·	×	×	·	×	×	×	×
1715	×	·	×	·	·	·	×	·	·	×	×	·	·	×	×	·	·	·	×	·	×
1713	·	·	×	·	·	·	·	·	·	·	×	·	·	×	·	×	·	·	×	×	·
1710	·	×	×	×	·	×	×	×	·	·	×	·	·	·	·	×	·	×	×	·	·
1708	·	×	·	·	·	·	·	×	·	·	·	×	×	·	·	×	·	·	×	×	·
1705	·	·	×	×	·	×	·	·	·	·	×	·	·	×	·	·	×	×	×	·	·
1702	·	·	·	·	×	×	·	·	·	·	·	·	·	·	·	·	·	·	×	·	·
1701	·	×	·	·	·	×	·	·	·	×	·	×	·	·	·	·	·	·	·	·	×

Dorset — Bridport, Corfe Castle, Dorchester, Lyme Regis, Poole, Shaftesbury, Wareham, Weymouth & Melcombe Regis

Durham — Durham

Essex — Colchester, Harwich, Maldon

Gloucestershire
  Bristol
  Cirencester
  Gloucester
  Tewkesbury

Herefordshire
  Hereford
  Leominster
  Weobley

Hertfordshire
  Hertford
  St Albans

Huntingdonshire
  Huntingdon

Kent
  Canterbury
  Maidstone
  Queenborough
  Rochester

Lancashire
  Clithero
  Lancaster
  Liverpool
  Newton
  Preston
  Wigan

(2) *English boroughs (cont.)*

Year	Leicester	Boston	Grantham	Great Grimsby	Lincoln	Stamford	London	Westminster	Monmouth	Castle Rising	King's Lynn	Norwich	Thetford	Gt Yarmouth	Brackley	Higham Ferrers
1831	·	×	×	×	·	×	·	·	×	·	·	×	·	×	·	·
1830	·	×	×	×	·	×	·	·	·	·	×	×	·	×	·	·
1826	×	×	×	×	×	·	×	·	·	·	×	·	·	×	·	·
1820	·	×	×	×	×	·	×	×	×	·	×	·	·	×	·	·
1818	·	×	×	×	×	·	×	·	·	·	·	×	·	×	·	·
1812	×	×	·	×	·	×	×	·	·	·	·	×	·	×	·	·
1807	×	×	×	×	·	·	×	×	·	·	·	×	·	×	·	·
1806	·	×	·	·	×	·	×	×	·	·	·	×	×	×	·	·
1802	×	×	×	×	·	·	×	×	·	·	·	×	·	×	·	·
1796	×	×	×	×	·	·	×	×	·	·	·	×	·	×	·	·
1790	×	×	·	×	×	·	×	×	·	·	·	×	·	×	·	·
1784	×	×	·	·	×	·	×	×	·	·	·	×	×	×	·	·
1780	·	×	·	·	×	·	×	×	·	·	·	×	·	×	·	·
1774	·	·	·	·	×	·	×	×	·	·	·	×	·	×	·	·
1768	×	·	·	·	×	·	×	·	·	·	×	×	×	·	·	·
1761	·	·	·	·	×	·	×	·	·	·	·	×	·	×	·	·
1754	×	·	·	·	×	·	×	×	·	·	·	×	·	×	·	×
1747	·	×	·	·	×	·	×	·	·	·	×	·	·	·	·	·
1741	·	·	·	×	×	·	×	×	·	·	·	×	·	×	·	·
1734	×	·	·	×	×	×	×	·	·	·	·	×	·	×	·	·
1727	×	·	·	×	×	×	×	·	·	·	×	·	·	×	·	·
1722	×	×	×	×	×	·	×	·	·	×	·	×	·	·	·	·
1715	·	·	×	×	×	·	×	·	×	×	·	×	·	·	·	·
1713	·	×	·	×	×	·	×	·	·	·	·	×	·	·	×	·
1710	·	·	×	×	×	·	×	×	·	·	·	×	·	×	×	·
1708	·	·	·	×	·	·	×	×	·	·	×	×	×	·	·	·
1705	×	·	·	×	·	·	×	×	·	·	·	×	·	·	×	·
1702	·	·	×	·	·	·	×	×	·	·	×	×	×	·	×	×
1701	·	·	×	×	×	·	×	×	·	·	×	·	×	·	×	·

Leicestershire: Leicester
Lincolnshire: Boston, Grantham, Great Grimsby, Lincoln, Stamford
Middlesex: London, Westminster
Monmouthshire: Monmouth
Norfolk: Castle Rising, King's Lynn, Norwich, Thetford, Gt Yarmouth
Northamptonshire: Brackley, Higham Ferrers

	Northampton	Peterborough	Berwick	Morpeth	Newcastle-o-T	Newark	Nottingham	East Retford	Banbury	Oxford	Woodstock	Bishop's Castle	Bridgnorth	Ludlow	Shrewsbury	Wenlock	Bath	Bridgwater	Ilchester	Milborne Port
	×	·	×	·	·	×	·	×	×	·	×	·	·	·	×	·	·	×	·	·
	×	·	×	·	·	×	×	×	·	×	·	·	×	·	×	·	×	·	×	·
	×	·	×	·	·	×	×	×	·	×	×	·	×	×	×	·	×	×	×	·
	×	·	×	·	×	·	×	·	·	×	·	×	·	·	·	×	·	·	×	×
	×	·	×	·	·	·	×	·	·	×	·	×	·	·	·	·	·	×	×	×
	·	·	×	·	·	·	×	·	·	×	·	·	·	·	×	·	×	·	·	·
	·	·	·	·	·	·	×	×	×	·	·	·	·	·	×	·	·	×	·	·
	·	·	×	·	·	·	×	×	×	×	×	·	·	·	×	·	·	·	×	·
	·	·	×	×	·	·	×	×	·	×	×	×	×	·	·	·	·	×	×	·
	×	·	·	·	·	×	×	×	·	×	·	·	·	·	×	·	·	×	×	×
	×	·	·	·	·	×	×	×	·	·	·	·	·	·	×	·	×	×	×	·
	×	·	·	·	·	×	×	·	·	×	·	·	·	·	·	·	×	·	×	×
	·	·	·	·	×	×	×	·	·	×	·	·	·	·	·	·	·	×	×	×
	×	×	×	×	×	×	×	·	·	·	·	·	·	·	·	·	×	·	×	×
	×	×	·	×	·	·	×	·	·	×	·	·	·	·	·	·	·	×	×	·
	·	·	·	×	·	·	·	·	·	×	·	·	·	·	·	·	·	×	×	×
	·	·	×	·	·	×	·	×	·	·	·	×	·	·	·	·	·	×	·	·
	·	·	·	·	·	·	·	·	·	·	·	·	·	·	×	·	×	·	·	×
	·	·	·	·	×	×	·	·	×	·	·	×	×	·	·	·	×	×	·	×
	×	×	×	·	·	×	·	·	×	·	·	·	×	·	×	·	×	×	×	×
	×	×	·	×	×	×	×	·	·	·	×	×	×	×	·	·	×	·	·	×
	·	·	·	×	×	×	×	·	·	·	·	×	·	×	·	·	×	·	×	·
	·	·	×	×	·	×	×	·	·	×	×	×	·	×	·	·	·	·	·	·
	×	×	·	·	×	×	×	×	·	·	·	×	×	×	×	×	×	·	·	×
	×	·	·	·	·	·	×	×	·	·	·	×	·	×	·	·	×	·	×	×
	·	·	·	·	·	·	×	×	×	×	×	×	·	×	·	·	×	·	·	×
	×	·	·	×	·	·	×	×	·	·	×	×	·	×	·	·	×	·	×	×
	·	×	·	·	·	×	×	×	·	×	·	×	×	·	·	·	·	·	·	×

Northampton
Peterborough

Northumberland
  Berwick
  Morpeth
  Newcastle-o-T

Nottinghamshire
  Newark
  Nottingham
  East Retford

Oxfordshire
  Banbury
  Oxford
  Woodstock

Shropshire
  Bishop's Castle
  Bridgnorth
  Ludlow
  Shrewsbury
  Wenlock

Somerset
  Bath
  Bridgwater
  Ilchester
  Milborne Port

(2) English boroughs (cont.)

	Minehead	Taunton	Wells	**Southampton** Andover	Christchurch	Lymington	Newport	Newtown	Petersfield	Portsmouth	Southampton	Stockbridge	Whitchurch	Winchester	Yarmouth	**Staffordshire** Lichfield	Newcastle-u-Lyme	Stafford	Tamworth
1831						×		×		×			×				×	×	
1830		×	×					×			×					×	×	×	
1826		×	×					×			×					×		×	
1820		×					×		×	×		×					×	×	
1818		×					×			×				×		×	×	×	×
1812		×						×		×			×			×	×	×	
1807	×				×					×			×			×	×	×	
1806		×			×					×		×				×	×	×	
1802	×	×	×							×							×	×	
1796	×																		
1790		×						×		×	×		×				×	×	
1784						×												×	
1780			×						×	×	×						×		
1774		×		×			×	×	×	×						×		×	
1768	×	×	×	×			×	×					×				×		
1761	×			×						×				×					×
1754	×		×							×			×	×				×	
1747			×								×			×					
1741		×		×				×	×	×									×
1734			×	×				×		×		×		×			×	×	×
1727	×		×	×	×	×		×			×					×			×
1722	×	×	×		×				×			×				×		×	
1715	×	×	×					×	×	×	×	×	×	×	×	×	×		
1713	×			×			×		×		×					×		×	
1710		×	×		×	×			×			×				×	×	×	
1708									×							×		×	
1705						×	×	×								×		×	
1702		×		×					×							×			
1701				×															

Suffolk
 Aldeburgh
 Bury St
 Edmunds
 Dunwich
 Eye
 Ipswich
 Orford
 Sudbury

Surrey
 Bletchingley
 Gatton
 Guildford
 Haslemere
 Reigate
 Southwark

Sussex
 Arundel
 Bramber
 Chichester
 East Grinstead
 Horsham
 Lewes
 Midhurst
 Shoreham
 Steyning

Warwickshire
 Coventry
 Warwick

(2) *English boroughs (cont.)*

	1831	1830	1826	1820	1818	1812	1807	1806	1802	1796	1790	1784	1780	1774	1768	1761	1754	1747	1741	1734	1727	1722	1715	1713	1710	1708	1705	1702	1701
Westmorland																													
Appleby	·	·	·	·	·	·	·	·	·	·	·	·	·	·	·	·	×	·	·	·	·	·	·	×	×	×	·	×	×
Wiltshire																													
Great Bedwyn	·	·	·	·	·	·	·	·	·	·	·	·	·	·	·	×	·	×	·	×	×	×	·	·	·	×	×	·	×
Calne	×	×	·	·	×	×	×	×	×	·	·	·	·	·	·	×	·	·	·	×	×	×	×	×	×	×	×	·	×
Chippenham	×	×	×	·	×	·	·	×	×	·	×	·	×	×	×	×	·	·	×	×	·	·	×	×	×	·	·	·	·
Cricklade	·	·	×	×	·	×	×	×	×	·	·	·	·	·	·	×	·	·	×	×	×	·	×	×	×	×	×	×	·
Devizes	·	·	·	·	·	·	·	·	·	·	·	·	·	·	·	·	·	·	×	·	·	·	·	·	·	·	·	·	·
Downton	·	×	·	·	·	·	·	·	·	·	·	·	·	·	·	·	·	·	·	·	·	·	·	·	·	×	·	·	·
Heytesbury	·	·	·	·	·	·	·	·	·	×	×	·	×	×	×	·	×	·	·	·	×	·	·	×	×	·	·	×	·
Hindon	×	·	·	·	·	·	·	·	·	·	·	·	·	·	·	·	×	·	·	·	·	·	×	·	·	·	·	·	·
Ludgershall	·	·	·	·	·	·	·	·	·	·	·	·	·	·	×	·	×	·	·	×	×	×	×	·	×	·	×	·	×
Malmesbury	·	·	·	·	·	·	·	·	·	·	×	·	·	·	·	·	·	·	·	·	·	·	×	·	·	·	×	·	·
Marlborough	·	·	×	·	·	·	×	·	×	·	·	·	·	·	·	·	·	×	×	×	×	·	×	·	×	·	×	·	·
Old Sarum	×	×	·	·	·	·	·	·	·	·	·	·	·	·	·	×	×	×	×	×	×	×	×	×	×	×	×	×	·
Salisbury	·	·	·	·	·	·	·	·	·	·	·	·	·	·	×	·	·	·	·	·	·	·	×	·	·	×	×	×	·
Westbury	·	·	·	·	·	·	·	·	·	·	·	·	·	·	·	·	·	×	·	×	×	×	×	×	×	×	·	×	·
Wilton	·	·	×	×	×	·	·	·	×	×	×	×	×	×	·	×	·	×	×	×	×	·	·	·	×	×	×	·	·
Wootton Bassett	·	·	·	·	·	·	·	·	·	·	·	·	·	·	·	·	·	·	·	·	·	·	·	×	·	×	·	·	·
Worcestershire																													
Bewdley	·	·	·	·	·	·	·	·	·	·	·	·	·	·	×	·	·	·	·	×	·	·	×	×	×	×	×	·	·
Droitwich	·	·	·	·	·	·	·	·	·	·	·	·	·	·	·	·	·	×	·	·	·	·	·	·	·	×	·	·	·
Evesham	×	×	×	·	×	·	×	·	×	×	×	×	×	×	·	·	·	·	·	·	×	·	×	×	·	×	×	×	·
Worcester	·	·	×	·	×	×	·	×	×	×	×	×	×	×	·	×	×	·	×	×	×	·	×	×	×	×	·	·	×

Yorkshire
Aldborough
Beverley
Boroughbridge
Hedon
Hull
Knaresborough
Malton
Northallerton
Pontefract
Richmond
Ripon
Scarborough
Thirsk
York
Cinque ports
Dover
Hastings
Hythe
New Romney
Rye
Sandwich
Seaford
Winchelsea

Total 71 67 82 78 104 85 94 110 84 94 61 48 55 42 62 70 67 69 68 56 67 58 60 53 82 63 77 74 64

Appendix 4

Estimate of the English electorate in 1831

For the county computation, I have taken as the basis the highest poll recorded between 1800 and 1831. For the 9 counties where there were no contests in this period, or only token ones, I have assumed the increase in the electorate to be proportionate to the overall increase. Though a calculation on this basis will leave a number of freeholders unaccounted for, the number is unlikely to be great, since most of the polls continued ten or fifteen days. The objection to departing from this basis in favour of some form of assessment is twofold. Any 'estimate' is suspect, as sheriffs sometimes pointed out when replying to parliamentary enquiries, since it involves guesses at the proportion of voters unpolled and the proportion of invalid votes cast. Secondly, the figures for 1754 given by *The House of Commons 1754–90* are also based on the highest polls – for example in the Wiltshire by-election of 1772, 2925 persons voted and the electorate is put at 'about 3000'.

Total of 31 counties = 149,730.
1754 total for same counties was 141,000.
Increase was 8730 = 6.19%.
Overall increase of 6.19% on 1754 figures gives total of *188,250*.
So, county electorate for 1831 was roughly *188,250*.

The electorate for the English boroughs (excluding Oxford and Cambridge Universities) is even more difficult to compute and the results should be treated with the utmost caution. The figure given by Lambert (see above p. 259) was 188,391, from which I subtract 8391 for the Welsh boroughs, giving an electorate for England of 180,000. There is no way of checking this. But in 1831 the Returning Officers for the boroughs were asked to make their own estimates, and the replies were printed in P.P. 1831–2 (112) xxxvi 489. These give a total of 167,829. But this figure may also be too high. With a reform bill in the offing, Returning Officers had every incentive for submitting inflated estimates, and there is sometimes an odd disparity between the number of voters claimed and the highest poll recorded. The Returning Officer for Berwick added a note that the number of votes had seldom, if ever, exceeded that cast in 1826, viz. 860: nevertheless his estimate was 1135. At Wareham, a borough in certain danger of reform, the previous highest poll was said to be 20, Oldfield's estimate in 1816 was 120, yet the Returning Officer guessed at 338 voters: at Malton, where the previous highest poll was 456, the Returning Officer

Elections

County	1715	1754	19th century	Comment
Bedfordshire	2500	2000	2546	1826 election: 10 days poll
Berkshire	3000	3000	2194	1832 election: 7 days poll
Buckinghamshire	4000	4000	2593	1831 election
Cambridgeshire	2500	3000	3717	1830 election
Cheshire	5000	5000		no contests 19th century
Cornwall	2300	2500	2762	1831 election
Cumberland	4000	4000		token contests only
Derbyshire	4000	4000		token contests only
Devon	3000	3000	7793	1818 election
Dorset	2400	3000	3658	1831 election: 15 days poll
Durham	2300	3000	2712	1820 election
Essex	6000	6000	5318	1830 election: 15 days poll
Gloucestershire	3000	6000	5757	1811 election: 10 days poll
Hampshire	5200	5000	4300	1806 election
Herefordshire	3800	4000	3505	1818 election
Hertfordshire	3000	4000	2628	1805 election
Huntingdonshire	1500	2000	1743	1826 election
Kent	7000	8000	8848	1802 election
Lancashire	7000	8000		token contests only
Leicestershire	5000	6000	5420	1830 election
Lincolnshire	5000	5000	5598	1818 election
Middlesex	3000	3500	7000	1820 election: approximate total
Monmouthshire	2000	1500		no contests
Norfolk	6000	6000	7251	1802 election
Northamptonshire	4000	3000	4182	1831 election: 13 days poll
Northumberland	2000	2000	2985	1826 election: 15 days poll
Nottinghamshire	2600	3000		no contests
Oxfordshire	4000	4000	2934	1831 election
Rutland	600	800		no contests
Shropshire	4000	4000	2850	1831 election
Somerset	4000	8000	6300	1807 election
Staffordshire	5000	5000		no contests
Suffolk	5000	5000		token contests only
Surrey	3500	4000	3428	1826 election
Sussex	4000	4000	5348	1807 election
Warwickshire	3500	4000	3122	1820 election: 9 days poll
Westmorland	2000	2000	3455	1826 election: 9 days poll
Wiltshire	3000	3000	3736	1818 election: 8 days poll
Worcestershire	4000	4000	3140	1831 election
Yorkshire	15000	20000	23007	1807 election
	158700	177300	149730	

suggested 809. It is therefore safer perhaps to assume that the actual polling figures were harder to falsify than mere estimates. A series of Parliamentary Papers give this information, viz. P.P. 1830–1 (216) x 33; P.P. 1830–1 (216) x 53; P.P. 1831–2 (112) xxxvi 489; P.P. 1831 (141) xxxviii–xli. From these figures it is possible to work out a computation based on the highest recorded poll after 1800, augmenting the information where necessary by reference to the estimates. This gives a total of some 145,000. Striking an average between that figure and the estimates of the Returning Officers, I arrive at a total for the English boroughs of some 156,000.

My calculation for the total English electorate in 1831 is therefore:

Counties	188,250
Boroughs	156,000
	344,250

Appendix 5

Degree of urban penetration of counties before 1832

The following is an attempt to assess by an analysis of poll books the extent to which urban freeholders dominated the county constituencies in the period before 1832. The aggregate number of voters with freeholds in towns of more than 100 voters in all is given as a percentage of the total county poll. The figure of 100 is arbitrary and was adopted mainly for simplicity, yet towns of fewer than 100 voters were unlikely to swing county elections. It is not possible to compile a complete list. Five counties: Cheshire, Monmouth, Nottinghamshire, Rutland and Stafford-shire, were not contested at all in the period 1800–32, and in several others, such as Derbyshire, Lancashire, Shropshire and Suffolk, there were only token contests that would yield distorted results.

The evidence suggests that Professor D. C. Moore's statement that 'in many counties most freeholders were urban' is without foundation, and renders it hard to credit his contention that fear of urban penetration was an important ingredient in the thinking of the authors of the Reform Act. Great caution is needed in interpreting the figures. With an urban ingredient as high as 33% Cambridgeshire might be construed as a developing industrial county. In fact it was a county with several flourishing market towns and a university city in the midst of an unusually thinly populated countryside. As early as 1724 the six towns referred to in the table accounted for 25% of the total county vote.

County	Date of poll	Total vote	Urban %	Composition of urban vote		Comment
Middlesex	1802	6298	63	Westminster division	1059	Followed by
				Holborn division	750	Hackney 97,
				Finsbury division	430	Brentford 95,
				Isleworth	427	Tottenham 91,
				St George's in the East	280	Edmonton 83
				Bethnal Green	157	
				Shoreditch	146	
				Enfield	145	
				Whitechapel	141	
				Christchurch parish	126	

County	Date of poll	Total vote	Urban %	Composition of urban vote		Comment
Middlesex	1802	6298	63	Limehouse	116	
				Chelsea	111	
				East Smithfield	108	
Hampshire	1806	4338	34	Portsmouth 'liberty'	773	In 1705, the
				Southampton	212	same places,
				Gosport	195	plus Andover
				Portsmouth borough	185	with 132 voters
				Winchester	125	gave 23% urban
Surrey	1826	3428	34	Kingston	176	Followed by
				Farnham	173	Godalming 86,
				Chertsey	166	Camberwell
				Southwark	158	83, Wands-
				Rotherhithe	153	worth 67,
				Guildford	131	Lambeth 63
				Bermondsey	107	
				Dorking	101	
Durham	1820	2789	34	Sunderland	386	Followed by
				Durham	170	Stockton 92
				Gateshead	168	
				Barnard Castle	111	
				Darlington	105	
Cambridgeshire	1830	3717	33	Cambridge	456	In 1724 the
				Wisbech	248	same 6 towns
				Soham	155	accounted for
				Whittlesea	138	25% of the
				Ely	130	total poll
				March	100	
Kent	1802	8848	32	Canterbury	384	
				Maidstone	244	
				Dover	210	
				Deal	199	
				Ramsgate	195	
				Chatham	192	
				Margate	187	
				Folkestone	170	
				Faversham	170	
				Deptford	155	
				Rochester	141	
				Tenterden	124	
				Tunbridge	122	
				Greenwich	121	
				Sandwich	108	
				Cranbrook	107	

County	Date of poll	Total vote	Urban %	Composition of urban vote		Comment
Northumberland	1826	2985	30	Tynemouth	307	Newcastle had
				Alnwick	205	county status.
				Morpeth	150	Followed by
				Hexham	124	Corbridge 70,
				North Shields	117	Haltwhistle 63
Leicestershire	1830	5420	28	Leicester	777	
				Loughborough	217	
				Hinckley	150	
				Melton Mowbray	137	
				Ashby	108	
				Castle Donington	106	
Sussex	1820	4114	26	Brighton	331	In 1774
				Chichester	215	Brighton had
				Hastings	146	yielded only
				Lewes	145	24 votes.
				Worthing	136	During the
				Horsham	117	Reform
						debates a good
						deal of hostility
						was shown
						towards this
						mushroom
						town
Worcestershire	1831	3140	25	Dudley	278	Worcester had
				Kidderminster	196	county status.
				Bromsgrove	183	Followed by
				Kings Norton	136	Evesham 93,
						Pershore 85,
						Tenbury 80
Dorset	1831	3658	22	Portland	291	Followed by
				Poole	191	Wimborne 96,
				Bridport	140	Shaftesbury 91,
				Sherborne	102	Dorchester 54,
				Lyme Regis	101	Blandford 48
Yorkshire	1807	23007	22	Leeds	627	Unfortunately,
				Sheffield	596	the 1830 vote,
				Scarborough	295	which would
				Wakefield	292	have been
				Hull	259	more revealing,
				Sculcoates	253	was a token
				Beverley	248	poll only and
				York	239	cannot be
				Doncaster	207	used. Hull
				Whitby	206	proper had the
				Quick	180	status of
				Halifax	171	county

County	Date of poll	Total vote	Urban %	Composition of urban vote		Comment
Yorkshire	1807	23007	22	Pickering	166	
				Bradford	163	
				Dewsbury	151	
				Bridlington	137	
				Knottingley	128	
				Keighley	126	
				Easingwold	119	
				Pudsey	117	
				Ripon	116	
				Rotherham	107	
				Richmond	107	
Wiltshire	1818	3736	19	Salisbury	205	Followed by
				Trowbridge	172	Wootton
				Bradford-on-Avon	122	Bassett 94 and
				Westbury	116	Calne 82
				Warminster	110	
Warwickshire	1820	3122	18	Birmingham	399	Stratford-on-
				Warwick	168	Avon 92, Nuneaton 88. Coventry had county status
Hertfordshire	1805	2628	18	St Albans	158	Followed by
				Bishop's Stortford	116	Hertford 85
				Ware	106	
				Hitchin	103	
Norfolk	1817	7217	17	Great Yarmouth	681	Thetford 93.
				King's Lynn	319	Norwich
				Norwich	233	proper had county status
Devon	1818	7793	16	Plymouth	453	Exeter had
				Tiverton	194	county status.
				Crediton	147	Followed by
				Barnstaple	139	Bideford 95,
				Totnes	113	Ottery St
				Brixham	110	Mary 93,
				Dawlish	103	South Molton 90, Cullompton 90, West Teignmouth 82, Chudleigh 78, Topsham 78, Buckfastleigh 75, Ashburton 70, Honiton 64

County	Date of poll	Total vote	Urban %	Composition of urban vote		Comment
Buckinghamshire	1831	2593	16	Aylesbury Chipping Wycombe Chesham	207 117 101	Newport Pagnell 74, Olney 73, Princes Risborough 66, Buckingham 63
Huntingdonshire	1826	1743	16	Ramsey Huntingdon	142 135	
Essex	1830	5318	16	'London & Middlesex' Colchester	467 365	Poll book gives 'London & Middlesex voters' separately. Hence this computation is on a slightly different basis.
Northamptonshire	1831	4182	15	Northampton Wellingborough Rothwell Daventry	321 115 102 102	
Oxfordshire	1831	2934	15	Oxford Banbury	333 117	Witney 87, Chipping Norton 80, Watlington 76, Thame 70, Henley 68, Burford 68, Bicester 65
Gloucestershire	1811	5757	14	Tewkesbury St Philip's & St Jacob's (ex-Bristol) Stroud Cheltenham Minchinhampton	212 189 157 140 139	Both Bristol & Gloucester had county status
Berkshire	1818	1849	13	Reading Newbury	122 119	Abingdon 96
Herefordshire	1818	3505	12	Hereford Leominster	221 197	Ross 85, Kington 75
Bedfordshire	1826	2546	9	Bedford	225	Leighton Buzzard 95, Luton 94, Dunstable 71

County	Date of poll	Total vote	Urban %	Composition of urban vote		Comment
Somerset	1807	6300	9	Bath & Walcott	287	Wincanton 96,
				Frome	130	Glastonbury
				Wells	120	95, Shepton Mallett 92, Yeovil 91, Wellington 91, Martock 87, Bridgwater 83
Westmorland	1826	3427	9	Kendal	309	Kirkby Lonsdale 91
Cumberland	1831	2008	8	Whitehaven	163	Poll includes votes cast after Lowther's retirement & votes reserved for assessment. Followed by Penrith 91, Carlisle 68, Workington 64
Lincolnshire	1823	5391	7	Boston	155	Gainsborough
				Lincoln	103	93. Lincoln
				Louth	102	proper had county status

Appendix 6

Schedule A and B boroughs in 2 William IV c. 45

N.B. There were considerable changes between the lists announced by Lord John Russell on 1 March 1831 and those in the final act.

Schedule A		Schedule B
Old Sarum	Callington	Petersfield
Newtown, IoW	Newton, L.	Ashburton
Mitchell	Ilchester	Eye
Gatton	Boroughbridge	Westbury
Bramber	Stockbridge	Wareham
Bossiney	New Romney	Midhurst
Dunwich	Hedon	Woodstock
Ludgershall	Plympton Erle	Wilton
St Mawes	Seaford	Malmesbury
Bere Alston	Heytesbury	Liskeard
West Looe	Steyning	Reigate
St Germans	Whitchurch	Hythe
Newport, C.	Wootton Bassett	Droitwich
Bletchingley	Downton	Lyme Regis
Aldborough	Fowey	Launceston
Camelford	Milborne Port	Shaftesbury
Hindon	Aldeburgh	Thirsk
East Looe	Minehead	Christchurch
Corfe Castle	Bishop's Castle	Horsham
Great Bedwyn	Okehampton	Great Grimsby
Yarmouth, IoW	Appleby	Calne
Queenborough	Lostwithiel	Arundel
Castle Rising	Brackley	St Ives
East Grinstead	Amersham	Rye
Higham Ferrers	(56)	Clithero
Wendover		Morpeth
Weobley		Helston
Winchelsea		Northallerton
Tregony		Wallingford
Haslemere		Dartmouth
Saltash		(30)
Orford		

A note on further reading

GENERAL WORKS

There is no general account of parliamentary reform in this period. A. Paul, *Short parliaments: a history of the national demand for frequent general elections* (1883) is slight and polemical: J. Grego, *A history of parliamentary elections and electioneering* (1886) is largely anecdotal. The best account of the old system of representation is still E. & A. G. Porritt, *The unreformed House of Commons*, 2 vols. (1903), the first volume of which deals with England and Wales and the second with Scotland and Ireland. Detailed evidence on electoral matters can be gathered from *The parliamentary history of England to the year 1803*, ed. W. Cobbett, 36 vols. (1806–20), *The Parliamentary Debates*, ed. T. C. Hansard, *The Journals of the House of Commons*, and for the later period, from the *Parliamentary Papers*. T. H. B. Oldfield's volumes, *The history of the boroughs* (1792) and *The representative history of Great Britain and Ireland*, 6 vols. (1816) though tendentious contain much valuable information. Further evidence for particular constituencies may be found in the published summaries of controverted election cases, a list of which is printed by S. Pargellis & D. J. Medley, *Bibliography of British history: the eighteenth century, 1714–89* (1951), nos. 415 and 418. Modern works devoting much attention to electoral history are J. H. Plumb, *The growth of political stability in England, 1675–1725* (1967), G. Holmes, *British politics in the age of Anne* (1967) and W. A. Speck, *Tory and Whig: the struggle in the constituencies, 1701–15* (1970). For the mid-eighteenth century, Sir Lewis Namier, *The structure of politics at the accession of George III* (2nd ed. 1957) is essential. The volumes of the History of Parliament that have appeared so far are *The House of Commons, 1715–54*, ed. R. R. Sedgwick, 2 vols. (1970) and *The House of Commons, 1754–90*, ed. Sir Lewis Namier & J. Brooke, 3 vols. (1964). Much work remains to be done on the late eighteenth and early nineteenth centuries, though E. P. Thompson, *The making of the English working class* (1964) is illuminating on radical activity. Three older books, G. S. Veitch, *The genesis of parliamentary reform* (1913), H. W. C. Davis, *The age of Grey and Peel* (1929) and J. R. M. Butler, *The passing of the Great Reform Bill* (1914) are still of considerable value. Much evidence on radical reform can be gleaned from the works of S. Maccoby, *English radicalism, 1762–85: the origins* (1955) and *English radicalism, 1786–1832: from Paine to Cobbett* (1955) though they are ill-assorted and haphazard. Recent books which include studies of particular general elections are J. B. Owen, *The rise of the Pelhams* (1957); J. Brooke, *The Chatham administration, 1766–8* (1956); I. R. Christie, *The end of North's ministry, 1780–2* (1958); John Cannon, *The Fox–North coalition: crisis of the con-*

stitution, 1782–4 (1969) and D. Ginter, *Whig organization and the general election of 1790* (1967). The pamphlet literature on parliamentary reform is too vast to be listed: for the seventeenth and early eighteenth century many examples are to be found in the Thomason Tracts and the Somers Tracts: other references can be pursued in the British Museum Catalogue (1965), vol. 63, pp. 1049–97, 1300–16; vol. 65, pp. 3801–3912; vol. 200, pp. 123–6.

CHAPTER 1   ANARCHIE OR BLEST REFORMATION

Documentary evidence on the reform proposals and provisions may be found in S. R. Gardiner, *Constitutional documents of the Puritan revolution, 1625–60* (3rd ed. 1901); G. W. Prothero, *Select statutes and other constitutional documents* (1906); D. M. Wolfe, *Leveller manifestoes of the Puritan revolution* (1944); *Journals of the House of Commons; Acts and Ordinances of the Interregnum*, ed. C. H. Firth & R. S. Rait, 3 vols. (1911); and in the volumes of the *Calendar of State Papers, Domestic*. The Putney debates are best studied in A. S. P. Woodhouse, *Puritanism and liberty* (1938). Though the pamphlet material in the Thomason collection in the British Museum is voluminous, useful selections are published in D. M. Wolfe; in W. Haller, *Tracts on liberty in the Puritan revolution, 1638–47*, 3 vols. (1934); and W. Haller & G. Davies, *The Leveller tracts, 1647–53* (1944). Three important contemporary sources are *The journal of Sir Simonds D'Ewes*, ed. W. Notestein (1923); *The diary of Thomas Burton*, 4 vols. ed. J. T. Rutt (1828); *The memoirs of Edmund Ludlow*, ed. C. H. Firth, 2 vols. (1894). For a general narrative of the period, S. R. Gardiner, *History of the commonwealth and protectorate, 1649–56*, 4 vols. (1903) still holds the field. D. Underdown, *Pride's purge* (1971) is a good deal wider than its title suggests and is useful for events leading up to the Rump's dismissal. Among the many books on the Levellers, H. N. Brailsford, *The Levellers and the English Revolution* (1961); J. Frank, *The Levellers* (1955) and D. B. Robertson, *The religious foundations of Leveller democracy* (1951) are particularly useful. C. B. Macpherson, *The political theory of possessive individualism* (1964) is important, but should be read in the light of critical reviews, particularly P. Laslett, *Historical Journal*, vol. 7 no. 1. Articles bearing on electoral history in this period are J. H. Plumb, 'The growth of the electorate in England from 1600–1715', *Past & Present*, no. 45 (1969); Lady de Villiers, 'Parliamentary boroughs restored by the House of Commons, 1621–41', *English Historical Review*, 67 (1952); R. L. Bushman, 'English franchise reform in the seventeenth century', *Journal of British Studies*, vol. 3 no. 1 (1963); J. W. Gough, 'The Agreements of the People, 1647–9', *History*, N S, 15 (1931–2); V. F. Snow, 'Parliamentary reapportionment proposals in the Puritan revolution', *English Historical Review*, 74 (1959); Blair Worden, 'The bill for a new representative: the dissolution of the Long Parliament, April 1653', *English Historical Review*, 86 (1971); G. D. Heath III, 'Making the Instrument of Government', *Journal of British Studies*, 6 (1967); H. Trevor-Roper, 'Oliver Cromwell and his Parliaments', *Essays presented to Sir Lewis Namier*, ed. R. Pares & A. J. P. Taylor (1956).

CHAPTER 2   PUDDING TIME

The key book for this period is J. H. Plumb, *The growth of political stability in England, 1675–1725* (1967). The political background may be studied in D. Ogg, *England in the reign of Charles II*, 2 vols. 2nd ed. (1956) and *England in the reigns of James II and William III* (1955); G. Holmes, *British politics in the age of Anne* (1967); D. Marshall, *Eighteenth century England* (1962). A valuable book of documents is *The eighteenth century constitution, 1688–1815*, ed. E. N. Williams (1960) and B. Kemp, *King and Commons, 1660–1832* (1957) provides much interesting commentary. The events of 1688 are dealt with by J. Carswell, *The descent upon England* (1969) and M. Ashley, *The Glorious Revolution of 1688* (1966): the rather indulgent view of G. M. Trevelyan, *The English revolution, 1688–9* (1938) may be contrasted with L. Pinkham, *William III and the respectable revolution* (1954). The volume of essays *Britain after the Glorious Revolution, 1689–1714*, ed. G. Holmes (1969) is full of good things. For the Union with Scotland, see J. D. Mackie, *A history of Scotland* (1964), W. Ferguson, *Scotland 1689 to the present* (1968) and W. H. Marwick, *Scotland in modern times* (1964). Biographies which throw indirectly a good deal of light on the question of reform are K. H. D. Haley, *The first Earl of Shaftesbury* (1968); H. T. Dickinson, *Bolingbroke* (1970); A. Macinnes, *Robert Harley: puritan politician* (1970); J. H. Plumb, *Sir Robert Walpole*, v. 1, *The making of a statesman* (1956), v. 2, *The King's minister* (1960). For a summary of the social and economic changes of the period, G. E. Mingay, *English landed society in the eighteenth century* (1963). The up-holders of the Whig–Republican tradition are treated in C. Robbins, *The eighteenth century commonwealthman* (1959).

CHAPTER 3   A PARCELL OF LOW SHOPKEEPERS

The first two decades of George III's reign have been accorded much attention in recent years. G. Rudé, *Wilkes and liberty* (1962) is a valuable grass-roots study and should be read with I. R. Christie, *Wilkes, Wyvill and reform* (1962). J. Norris, *Shelburne and reform* (1963) though mainly concerned with economical reform has a chapter on the radical agitation of 1769. E. C. Black, *The Association: British extra-parliamentary political organization, 1769–93* (1963) explores more systematically a theme started by H. Jephson, *The platform: its rise and progress* (1892): Black has a particularly comprehensive bibliography. Wilkes himself has suffered much at the hands of popular biographers and a modern, scholarly life is overdue: until then, R. Postgate, *That devil Wilkes* (1930). The intentions of George III have received, perhaps, more than their fair share of comment: the controversy may be traced in L. B. Namier, 'King George III: a study in personality' (1953), printed in *Personalities and powers* (1955); R. Pares, *King George the third and the politicians* (1953); H. Butterfield, *George III and the historians* (1957); W. R. Fryer, 'King George III, his political character and conduct, 1760–84: a new Whig interpretation', *Renaissance and modern studies*, VI (1962); I. R. Christie, 'Was there a "New Toryism" in the earlier part of George III's reign', and the title essay in his *Myth and reality in late-eighteenth-century British politics* (1970). Three essential studies on the role of London are by L. S. Sutherland, 'The city of London in eighteenth century politics', *Essays presented to Sir Lewis Namier*, ed. R. Pares & A. J. P. Taylor; 'The city of London and the opposition to government, 1768–74', Creighton lecture, printed 1959; 'The city of London and the Devonshire–Pitt administration, 1756–7', Raleigh lecture, *Proceedings of the British Academy*, 46 (1960). The important question of the development of the press can be studied in R. R. Rea, *The English press in politics, 1760–74* (1963); A. Aspinall, 'The reporting and publishing of the House of Commons debates, 1771–1834', in *Essays presented to Sir Lewis Namier*; P. D. G. Thomas, 'John Wilkes and the freedom of the press, 1771', *Bulletin of the Institute of Historical Research*, 33 (1960); 'The beginnings of parliamentary reporting in newspapers, 1768–74', *English Historical Review*, 74 (1959).

CHAPTER 4   MR WYVILL'S CONGRESS

Much contemporary evidence is contained in C. Wyvill, *Political papers, chiefly respecting the attempt of the county of York . . . to effect a reformation of the Parliament of Great Britain*, 6 vols. (1794–1806) and F. D. Cartwright, ed., *The life and correspondence of Major Cartwright* (1826). Other prominent reformers are dealt with in J. Disney, *Memoirs of Thomas Brand Hollis* (1808); A. Stephens, *Memoirs of John Horne Tooke* (1813); J. Disney, *The works of John Jebb* (1787); A. G. Olson, *The radical Duke: career and correspondence of Charles Lennox, third Duke of Richmond* (1961); G. Stanhope & G. P. Gooch, *The life of Charles, third Earl of Stanhope* (1914). *The correspondence of Edmund Burke*, ed. T. W. Copeland is essential for the Rockinghams' attitude towards economical and parliamentary reform. The views of two sympathizers can be traced in J. Norris, *Shelburne and Reform* and J. Ehrman, *The younger Pitt: I, the years of acclaim* (1969). H. Butterfield, *George III, Lord North and the people, 1779–80* (1949) is useful for economical reform and the Yorkshire Association. E. C. Black, *The Association* and I. R. Christie, *Wilkes, Wyvill and Reform* must be used. Chief of many articles on this period of

304 *A note on further reading*

reform are H. Butterfield, 'The Yorkshire Association and the crisis of 1779–80', *Transactions Royal Historical Society*, 4th series, no. 29 (1947); I. R. Christie, 'The Yorkshire Association, 1780–84', *Historical Journal*, 3 (1960); N. C. Phillips, 'Yorkshire and English national politics, 1783–4', pamphlet (1961) and 'Country against court: Christopher Wyvill, a Yorkshire champion', *Yorkshire Archaeological Society Journal*, 40 (1962); E. A. Reitan, 'The civil list in eighteenth-century British politics: parliamentary supremacy versus the Independence of the Crown', *Historical Journal*, 9 (1966); I. R. Christie, 'Economical reform and "the Influence of the Crown"', *Cambridge Historical Journal*, 12 (1956).

CHAPTER 5   THE IRISH AND SCOTTISH REFORM MOVEMENTS

The Irish and Scottish reform movements have been somewhat neglected by historians and most of this chapter has been reconstructed from newspaper and pamphlet sources. For the narrative of Irish events: W. E. H. Lecky, *A History of Ireland in the eighteenth century* (1892). The Irish electoral system is described in detail by E. M. Johnston, *Great Britain and Ireland, 1760–1800* (1963), which supplements the account in volume two of Porritt. R. B. McDowell, *Irish public opinion 1750–1800* (1944) has the best account of the reform campaign, together with a strong chronologically-arranged pamphlet bibliography. It should be read in conjunction with M. R. O'Connell, *Irish politics and social conflict in the age of the American revolution* (1965) and P. Rogers, *The Irish Volunteers and Catholic emancipation, 1778–93* (1934). For some of the leading participants, see *Memoirs of the life and times of Henry Grattan*, ed. H. Grattan, 5 vols. (1839–46); W. Flood, *Memoirs of the life and correspondence of the Rt Hon. Henry Flood* (1838); W. S. C. Pemberton, *The Earl Bishop: the life of Frederick Hervey, bishop of Derry, earl of Bristol* (1925); M. J. Craig, *The Volunteer Earl: being the life and times of James Caulfield, first Earl of Charlemont* (1948).

Evidence on the Scottish electoral system can be obtained from the volumes of the History of Parliament, from volume two of Porritt, and from C. E. Adam, ed., *View of the political state of Scotland in the last century* (1887). Volumes II and III of C. Wyvill, *Political papers* contain letters on Scottish reform. A. Fletcher, *A memoir concerning the origin and progress of the reform proposed in the internal government of the Royal Burghs of Scotland* (1819) is essential. Biographies of the 'uncrowned King of Scotland' are H. Furber, *Henry Dundas* (1931) and C. Matheson, *The life of Henry Dundas, first Viscount Melville, 1742–1811* (1933). Much contemporary political comment can be found in *Letters of George Dempster to Sir Adam Fergusson*, ed. J. Fergusson (1934) and A. & H. Tayler, *Lord Fife and his factor, 1729–1809* (1925). Modern histories include J. D. Mackie, *A history of Scotland* (1964); W. H. Marwick,

Scotland in modern times: an outline of economic and social development since the Union of 1707 (1964); R. H. Campbell, *Scotland since 1707: the rise of an industrial society* (1965); W. Ferguson, *Scotland 1689 to the present* (1968); T. C. Smout, *A history of the Scottish people, 1560–1830* (1969). H. W. Meikle, *Scotland and the French Revolution* (1912) has introductory chapters on the political awakening of Scotland. Articles on electoral history include E. Hughes, 'The Scottish reform movement and Charles Grey, 1792–4: some fresh correspondence', *Scottish Historical Review*, no. 35 (1956); Sir J. Fergusson, '"Making interest" in Scottish county elections', *Scottish Historical Review*, no. 26 (1947).

CHAPTER 6 REFORMERS' NIGHTMARE

The most important printed source for this period is perhaps *A complete collection of state trials*, compiled by T. B. Howell (1816–28) which includes as evidence a large number of letters, addresses and resolutions: further documentary evidence is in G. D. H. Cole & A. W. Filson, eds., *British working class movements, 1789–1875* (1951). A preliminary study of the effects of the French Revolution can be made in A. Cobban, *The debate on the French revolution* (2nd ed. 1960). The pioneer work by P. A. Brown, *The French Revolution in English history* (1918) is still of value, as are G. S. Veitch, *The genesis of parliamentary reform* (1913) and R. Birley, *The English Jacobins from 1789 to 1802* (1924). E. C. Black, *The Association* has a particularly useful chapter on the Association for the preservation of liberty and property. The affairs of the London Corresponding Society may be traced in F. P. Thompson, *The making of the English working class* and in C. B. Cone, *The English Jacobins* (1968): there is also an article on the society by H. Collins in *Democracy and the labour movement*, ed. J. Saville (1954). The predicament of the Whigs is discussed in two recent books, F. O'Gorman, *The Whig party and the French revolution* (1967) and L. G. Mitchell, *Charles James Fox and the disintegration of the Whig party, 1782–94* (1971). G. M. Trevelyan, *Lord Grey of the Reform Bill* (1920) is important for the Society of the Friends of the People, which is further treated in H. Butterfield, 'Charles James Fox and the Whig opposition in 1792', *Cambridge Historical Journal*, 9 (1949). There is a summary of the important report of the Society of the Friends of the People on *The state of the representation of England and Wales* (1793) in *English historical documents*, vol. XI, ed. A. Aspinall & E. A. Smith, no. 167.

CHAPTER 7 THE ALOE OF REFORM

W. Cobbett's *Political Register* and the *Edinburgh Review* are two important primary sources for this period: the growing importance of the press can be studied in A. Aspinall, *Politics and the press, c. 1780–1850* (1949). On the radical side, G. D. H. Cole, *Life of William Cobbett* (1924); M. W.

Patterson, *Sir Francis Burdett and his times*, 2 vols. (1931); F. D. Cart-wright, *Life of Major Cartwright* (1826); John Osborne, *John Cartwright* (1972); G. Wallas, *Life of Francis Place, 1771-1854* (1925). On the Whig side, G. M. Trevelyan, *Lord Grey of the Reform Bill* (1920); S. Fulford, *Samuel Whitbread, 1764-1815: a study in opposition* (1967); H. K. Olphin, *George Tierney* (1934); H. Cockburn, *Life of Lord Jeffrey* (1852); *Memoirs and correspondence of Francis Horner*, ed. L. Horner (1843); R. W. Davis, *Dissent in politics, 1780-1830: the political life of William Smith M.P.* (1971). For some opponents of reform in this period, H. Twiss, *The public and private life of Lord Eldon*, 3 vols. (1844); G. Pellew, *The life and correspondence of Henry Addington, first Viscount Sidmouth*, 3 vols. (1847); D. Gray, *Spencer Perceval: the evangelical prime minister, 1762-1812* (1963); P. J. V. Rolo, *George Canning* (1965); C. J. Bartlett, *Castlereagh* (1966). Two excellent studies of the Whigs are M. Roberts, *The Whig party, 1807-12* (1939) and A. Mitchell, *The Whigs in opposition, 1815-30* (1967). For general political comment see *The letters of Sydney Smith*, ed. N. C. Smith, 2 vols. (1953) and *The Creevey Papers*, ed. Sir H. Maxwell, 2 vols. (1904).

CHAPTER 8   WHIG DILEMMA

The watershed of the post-war period, Peterloo, is best studied in D. Read, *Peterloo* (1958) and R. Walmsley, *Peterloo, the case reopened* (1969). An important primary source for the working-class agitation is S. Bamford, *Autobiography*: II, *Passages in the life of a radical* (reprint, 1967). E. P. Thompson, *The making of the English working class* must of course be consulted. Henry Hunt has yet to find a modern biographer: his own *Memoirs* (1820) written in Ilchester jail are unreliable. A stimulating revisionist essay on the Luddites is by E. Hobsbawm, *Labouring men: 2, the machine breakers* (1964). The East Anglian riots of 1816 are treated in A. J. Peacock, *Bread or blood* (1965) and the Spencean philanthropists receive some attention in J. Stanhope, *The Cato Street conspiracy* (1962). The general question of law and order is explored in F. O. Darvall, *Popular disturbance and public order in Regency England* (1934). There is still much of interest on the Hampden clubs in H. W. C. Davis, 'Lan-cashire reformers, 1816-7', *Bulletin of the John Rylands Library*, 10, no. 1 (1926) and in his general work *The age of Grey and Peel* (1929). A. Mitchell, *The Whigs in opposition, 1815-30* is the best secondary source for that party. For day to day comment, see *The early correspondence of Lord John Russell, 1805-40*, ed. R. Russell, 2 vols. (1913); *The Creevey Papers*, ed. Sir H. Maxwell; S. J. Reid, *Life and letters of the first Earl of Durham, 1792-1840*, 2 vols. (1906); C. W. New, *Life of Henry Brougham to 1830* (1961). For a Tory response, see *The correspondence and diaries of John Wilson Croker*, ed. L. J. Jennings, 3 vols. (1884). Recent articles on two veteran reformers are J. R. Dinwiddy, 'Christopher Wyvill and Reform, 1790–1820', *Borthwick Paper*, no. 39, and N. C. Miller, 'John Cartwright and radical parliamentary reform, 1808–19', *English Historical Review*, 83 (1968).

CHAPTER 9 A STRANGE AND AGITATED SEA

The period of the Catholic Emancipation crisis is rich in memoir material. *The Creevey Papers*, ed. Sir H. Maxwell continue and are reinforced by Lord Broughton, *Recollections of a long life*, 4 vols. (1909) and C. C. F. Greville, *A journal of the reigns of King George IV, King William IV & Queen Victoria*, ed. H. Reeve (1874–87). C. S. Parker, *Sir Robert Peel*, 3 vols. (1891) should be read in conjunction with N. Gash, *Mr Secretary Peel: the life of Sir Robert Peel to 1830* (1961). Wellington's views can be found in *Despatches, correspondence and memoranda of the Duke of Wellington*, ed. the 2nd Duke of Wellington (1867–80), but more revealing are the many informal remarks preserved in *The Journal of Mrs Arbuthnot, 1820–32*, ed. F. Bamford & the Duke of Wellington, 2 vols. (1950). Also useful on the Tory side are Lord Ellenborough, *A political diary, 1828–30*, ed. Lord Colchester, 2 vols. (1881) and *The correspondence of Charles Arbuthnot*, ed. A. Aspinall for the Camden Society, 3rd series, vol. LXV. *Three early nineteenth century diaries*, ed. A. Aspinall (1952) are indispensable. On the Whig side, see *Memoirs of John Charles, Viscount Althorp, third Earl Spencer*, ed. D. le Marchant (1876) and H. W. Bulwer, *The life of Henry John Temple, Viscount Palmerston*, 3 vols. (1870).

For the Catholic crisis, see G. F. A. Best, 'The Protestant constitution and its supporters', *Transactions Royal Historical Society*, 5th series, vol. 8 (1958); A. Aspinall, *The formation of Canning's ministry, February to August 1827*, Camden Society, 3rd series, vol. LIX; G. I. T. Machin, *The Catholic question in English politics, 1820–30* (1964). For the events of 1830, N. Gash, 'Brougham and the Yorkshire election of 1830', *Proceedings Leeds Philosophical and Literary Society*, vol. 8; N. Gash, 'English reform and French Revolution in the general election of 1830', *Essays presented to Sir Lewis Namier*; A. Aspinall, 'The last of the Canningites', *English Historical Review*, 50 (1935); C. Flick, 'The fall of Wellington's government', *Journal of Modern History*, 37 (1965); B. T. Bradfield, 'Sir Richard Vyvyan and the country gentlemen, 1830–1834', *English Historical Review*, 83 (1968).

CHAPTER 10 REVOLUTION BY DUE COURSE OF LAW

The main provisions of the Reform Act are given in *English Historical Documents*, vol. 11 (1959), ed. A. Aspinall & E. A. Smith, no. 303. Grey's instructions to the drafting committee are given in C. S. Parker, *Life and letters of Sir James Graham*, 2 vols. (1907). Russell printed his own preliminary draft in *Essay on the history of the English government and constitution* (3rd ed. 1865) and supplemented his account in *Recollections and suggestions, 1813–74* (1875). Althorp's preliminary draft is given in C. W. New, *Lord Durham* (1929). Brougham's own reminiscences, *Life and times of Henry, Lord Brougham*, 3 vols. (1871) are interesting but should be treated with caution. Grey's relations with the monarch were all-important and can be traced in *The correspondence of the late Earl Grey with H.M. King William IV*, ed. Henry, Earl Grey, 2 vols. (1867). Some of Grey's private thoughts are in *The correspondence of Princess Lieven and Earl Grey*, ed. G. le Strange, 3 vols. (1890). The narrative of events in J. R. M. Butler, *The passing of the Great Reform Bill* (1914) and G. M. Trevelyan, *Lord Grey of the Reform Bill* can now be greatly augmented by *Three early nineteenth century diaries*, ed. A. Aspinall and *The Journal of Mrs Arbuthnot, 1820–32*, ed. F. Bamford & the Duke of Wellington. For the negotiations with the Waverers, see also C. Grosvenor & Lord Stuart of Wortley, *The first Lady Wharncliffe and her family, 1779–1856*, 2 vols. (1927).

The extra-parliamentary agitation is dealt with in a number of works. G. Wallas, *Life of Francis Place* (4th ed. 1925) is rather uncritical and should be used with care. The Birmingham reformers are treated in C. M. Wakefield, *Life of Thomas Attwood* (1885) and J. K. Buckley, *Joseph Parkes of Birmingham* (1926). J. Hamburger, *James Mill and the art of revolution* (1963) emphasizes the role of the philosophical radicals. The agricultural riots of 1830 are examined in G. Rudé, 'English rural and urban disturbances, 1830–1', *Past & Present*, no. 37 (1967). J. L. & B. Hammond, *The village labourer* (1941) should be supplemented by E. J. Hobsbawm & G. Rudé, *Captain Swing* (1969). Documents on the London organizations are printed in *London radicalism, 1830–43*, ed. D. J. Rowe (1970) and the same author comments in 'Class and political radicalism in London, 1831–2', *Historical Journal*, 13 (1970). Outside London, see D. Read, *The English provinces, c. 1760–1960: a study in influence* (1964), and for more detailed studies A. S. Turbeville & F. Beckwith, 'Leeds and parliamentary reform, 1820–32', *Publications of the Thoresby Society*, 41 (1954); A. Briggs, 'The background of the parliamentary reform movement in three English cities, 1830–2', *Cambridge Historical Journal*, 10 (1950–2); H. Ferguson, 'The Birmingham Political Union and the Government, 1830–1', *Victorian Studies*, 3 (1959–60).

CHAPTER 11   INTERPRETIVE

An assessment of the effects of reform is best begun with C. Seymour, *Electoral reform in England and Wales* (1915) and continued with N. Gash, *Politics in the age of Peel* (1953) and *Reaction and reconstruction in British politics, 1832–52* (1965). A convenient summary is H. J. Hanham, *The reformed electoral system in Great Britain, 1832–1914*, Historical Association (1968) and the same author's larger work *Elections and party management: politics in the time of Disraeli and Gladstone* (1959) has much of relevance. J. R. Vincent, *Poll books: how the Victorians voted* (1967) is valuable. E. Halévy, *History of the English people: III, the triumph of reform* is a fading classic. G. B. A. M. Finlayson, *England in the 1830s* (1969) and A. Briggs, *The age of improvement* (1959) are both useful. Articles stressing continuity after 1832 are S. F. Woolley, 'The personnel of the Parliament of 1833', *English Historical Review*, 53 (1938) and D. G. Wright, 'A radical borough: parliamentary politics in Bradford, 1832–41', *Northern History*, 4 (1969). A recent contribution on Whig motives is John Milton-Smith, 'Earl Grey's Cabinet and the objects of parliamentary reform', *Historical Journal*, vol. 15, no. 1 (March 1972).

Index

STATUTES

Peers are entered under their titles, thus:
Abingdon, Willoughby Bertie, 4th earl of

Association for Supervision and Curriculum Development
1703 N. Beauregard St. • Alexandria, VA 22311-1714 USA
Phone: 800-933-2723 or 703-578-9600 • Fax: 703-575-5400
Web site: www.ascd.org • E-mail: member@ascd.org
Author guidelines: www.ascd.org/write

Gene R. Carter, *Executive Director;* Nancy Modrak, *Director of Publishing;* Julie Houtz, *Director of Book Editing & Production;* Leah Lakins, *Project Manager;* Georgia Park, *Senior Graphic Designer;* Circle Graphics, *Typesetter;* Dina Seamon, *Production Specialist*

All Web links in this book are correct as of the publication date above but may have become inactive or otherwise modified since that time. If you notice a deactivated or changed link, please e-mail books@ascd.org with the words "Link Update" in the subject line. In your message, please specify the Web link, the book title, and the page number on which the link appears.

ASCD Member Book, No. FY06-06 (April 2006, PCR). ASCD Member Books mail to Premium (P), Comprehensive (C), and Regular (R) members on this schedule: Jan., PC; Feb., P; Apr., PCR; May, P; July, PC; Aug., P; Sept., PCR; Nov., PC; Dec., P.

PAPERBACK ISBN-13: 978-1-4166-0332-0   ASCD product #105151
PAPERBACK ISBN-10: 1-4166-0332-8

e-books editions: retail PDF ISBN-13: 978-1-4166-0389-4; retail ISBN-10: 1-4166-0389-1
netLibrary ISBN-13: 978-1-4166-0387-0; netLibrary ISBN-10: 1-4166-0387-5
ebrary ISBN-13: 978-1-4166-0388-7; ebrary ISBN-10: 1-4166-0388-3

Quantity discounts for this book: 10–49 copies, 10%; 50+ copies, 15%; for 500 or more copies, call 800-933-2723, ext. 5634, or 703-575-5634.

Library of Congress Cataloging-in-Publication Data

Reeves, Douglas B., 1953-
   The learning leader : how to focus school improvement for better results / Douglas B. Reeves.
      p. cm.
   Includes bibliographical references and index.
   ISBN-13: 978-1-4166-0332-0 (alk. paper)
   ISBN-10: 1-4166-0332-8 (alk. paper)
   1. Educational leadership—United States. 2. Educational accountability—United States. 3. School improvement programs—United States. I. Title.

   LB2805.R42 2006
   371.200973—dc22

                                                                              2005034560

12 11 10 09 08 07 06   12 11 10 9 8 7 6 5 4 3 2 1

For Julie Reeves

The Learning Leader

How to Focus School Improvement for Better Results

Preface

A Funny Thing Happened on the Way to *The Learning Leader*

The working title for this book was *The Multiple Intelligences of Leadership*. The book was conceived more than 20 years after Howard Gardner's groundbreaking work in this field, and it seemed a natural extension of his work. Just as intelligence is expressed in a variety of different ways, I reasoned, so leadership also has multiple expressions. The term "multiple intelligences" was widely accepted by many readers and it seemed a natural—perhaps I should have said an easy and palatable—extension of Gardner's ideas to the present study of leadership. As I reviewed the literature, organized my previous research, and conducted a new study on the practical implications of leadership on student achievement and educational equity, I realized that there were two problems with the prospective "multiple intelligences of leadership." I had the wrong words and the wrong theory.

Having already agreed to address a distinguished national audience with the title *The Multiple Intelligences of Leadership*, I had two choices. I could gut it out and make it fit—after all, I am keenly aware of how soon books can be forgotten. Or I could confess to my

readers and listeners that I was wrong. While the theory of multiple intelligences may have application elsewhere in education, the linguistic, logical, and evidentiary contortions required to apply that term to leadership are hurdles too great to surmount. As a professor in research classes, I admonish my students that "we learn more from error than uncertainty" and extol the virtues of research in which one's presuppositions were contradicted by evidence. I also believe that students should test their ideas in a community of scholars and thoughtfully evaluate their criticism and praise. Well, now I get a taste of my own medicine. Although it is certainly true that there are discrete and multiple dimensions of leadership, I was dead wrong to attempt to apply the term "multiple intelligences" in this context. The good news, aside from the remote possibility that confession is good for the soul, if not the ego, is that the research reported in this book is important for leaders at all levels. By identifying both the roles and functions of leadership and, in a large-scale research project, linking those leadership roles and functions to student achievement and educational equity variables, we can provide valuable insights on what matters most for leaders from the individual school principal or department head to system superintendents to state and national policymakers.

The Complexity of Simplicity

There are two types of complexity in leadership research. The first is the contrived complexity that emerges from the use of pretentious terminology and laborious processes. Schmoker (2004) demolished some of the more popular practices that depend more on process than on substance. In *The Daily Disciplines of Leadership* (Reeves,

2002a, p. 99), I suggested that it was time we "saved strategic planning from strategic plans." Planning can be effective and necessary, but when the plan supplants the purpose, the entire enterprise is misguided. When planning meetings focus not on the issues of student achievement, teaching practices, and leadership decisions, but on competing definitions of what a goal or strategy or objective is, then common sense has ceded ground to consulting babble. Guskey (2005) left a meeting of adults who were heatedly debating such points and asked 10 students in the hallway what they thought. Their wise response: "Who cares?" Students intuitively know that complexity born of pretense is an unproductive waste of time, unlikely to lead to meaningful insights. In this book, we will consider new research that supports what Schmoker and Guskey have claimed: Exquisitely formatted planning documents are worse than a waste of time. They are in fact inversely related to student achievement. If educators and leaders are to achieve their goals of excellence and equity, then the keys are monitoring, evaluation, values, beliefs, and implementation—not one more stack of beautifully bound documents.

Our commitment to avoid the errors of dumb complication, however, must not lead to the second error of complexity, and that is the embrace of unwarranted simplicity. Peruse the leadership section of your bookstore, and the appetite for groundless simplicity is endless. Books with big print and wide margins promise that the secrets of successful leadership will be yours if only you learn the "seven easy steps" or "five secret principles" of your trade. The research base for these insights appears in many cases to be a séance in which the ghosts of Attila the Hun, Catherine the Great, Elizabeth I, Robert E. Lee, and George Washington have been conjured and asked their opinions on the matters of the day. These volumes and scores more

are unburdened by research or relevance, common sense, or conscience. Their solutions are offered in minutes and monosyllables, willing to tax their readers' wallets without taxing their minds. By coaxing readers to worship at the altar of a leader like P. T. Barnum, the publishers have accomplished their mission the moment someone has been seduced by the title and paid for the book. Like cotton candy, the simple solutions satisfy an immediate hunger for something sweet and simple, but provide nothing in the way of long-term sustenance.

The research in *The Learning Leader* proposes that we pursue the appropriate balance of complexity and simplicity, taking excursions into challenging interrelationships when necessary, but also taking pains to reduce multivariate relationships to images that can be conveyed clearly to every stakeholder. The introduction of Leadership Maps (Chapters 1 and 8) represents an effort to take some enormously difficult teaching and leadership practices and present them in a manner that can be used by anyone without benefit of advanced statistical analysis. Similarly, the use of network science and the concept of moving "from nodes to hubs" (Chapter 9) will build on some very complex theory and research in the mathematics of networks, without inflicting the details of the research in physics and mathematics on the reader.

As it is our goal certainly to help leaders provide laser-like focus on their most important actions and roles, we cannot arrive at that destination through biographical distortion, historical misrepresentation, personal war stories, or other platitudinous baloney. Someone must actually do the hard work of slogging through the data, assessing the intersection of tens of thousands of data points, comparing the results of quantitative and qualitative analyses, and filtering each

hypothesis through the multiple lenses of research, experience, and common sense. I will not take you though all the laborious processes that led to this study; however, we cannot simply jump to the conclusions. If leaders are to convey the information in this book successfully and persuasively throughout their organizations, they must understand not only the *how* of leadership effectiveness, but the *why* revealed in this research. Rejecting closely held and deeply believed hypotheses is not easy, but it is necessary. I am walking evidence of that proposition, as I could not have made important research findings had I been unwilling to reject my own hypotheses.

To lay the groundwork for the research and theory we will explore, consider the following propositions. First, the theory of multiple intelligences lacks the descriptive capacity to be applied successfully to leadership. I cannot expect the reader to reject these hypotheses if I am not willing to do the same. Second, the prevailing leadership mythology that generally embraces the unitary "heroic" leadership model is unsustainable, unsupportable, and dangerous to individual and organizational health. Third, the dimensions of leadership can be defined, assessed, and improved in a systematic manner. Fourth, organizational effectiveness is best served when leadership is distributed in such a way that the dimensions of leadership are supported by a whole team (Elmore, 2000). Fifth and most important, "messy" leadership—the practice of reviewing data, making midcourse corrections, and focusing decision making on the greatest points of leverage—is superior to "neat" leadership in which planning, processes, and procedures take precedence over achievement. The confession of error and the willingness to make decisive and public changes is essential not only for researchers and authors, but for leaders as well.

Intelligence: The Wrong Word for Leadership

The word "intelligence" is frequently misused, particularly in the context where it is most important, education. The *Concise Oxford Dictionary, 10th Edition* (2001), offers a simple definition for intelligence: "the ability to acquire and apply knowledge and skills." In this sense, Einstein experimenting with the space-time continuum, a teenager playing an electronic game, and an infant toying with blocks all exhibit intelligence. The same can be said of Pavlov's dog or invertebrates that learn responses to electric shocks. Such broad application of the term, however, gives us little descriptive power. If we say that Einstein, the teenager, and the infant are all "human" and unconsciously assume that they are all "intelligent," then the latter provides no more insight than the former. Once intelligence is the word we apply to the inchworm, then the word has no more descriptive clarity than saying that the inchworm is part of the animal kingdom. Indeed, the profligate manner in which the word "intelligence" is used suggests that it could be applied to some species of plants as well. This conception of intelligence, popularized by the symbol *g* (Brand, 1996; Spearman, 1927) allows us to state categorically that humans are more intelligent than other animals and, with the advent of intelligence tests in the early 20th century, that some humans are more intelligent than others. Indeed, it is easy to identify intelligence not as an individual trait but as a group trait. Perkins (1995) provides the valuable reminder that the results of many purported tests of intelligence are strongly influenced by the language of the test and the bias of the times, allowing the convenient conclusion that Italians and Irish, despised in the early part of the 20th century, were inferior to their Anglo-Saxon neighbors. Herrnstein and Murray (1996) made similar arguments, though certainly without

any racist intent, eight decades later. Their reluctant conclusion (with the subtext of "Don't shoot the messenger; we're just reporting the data.") was that there are long-term structural inequalities among ethnic groups that are linked to a unitary definition of intelligence.

The primary advocate of multiple intelligences (MI) theory is Harvard Professor Howard Gardner. Although many other scholars have added research to the field and a legion of educators has also popularized the theory, it is a long leap from theory to practical application (Sternberg et al., 2000; Perkins 2003; Kagan & Kagan, 1998; Armstrong, 2000; Gardner, 1999; McBrien, Brandt, & Brandt, 1997; Perini, Silver, & Strong, 2000). This leap is facilitated by redefining the word "intelligence," as Gardner does, to "a bio-psychological potential to process information that can be activated in a cultural setting to solve problems or create products that are of value in a culture" (Gardner, 1999, pp. 33–34). This definition certainly narrows the scope to activity among thinking and culture-producing animals, though by no means exclusively to *Homo sapiens*.

Gardner's personal writings are often circumspect and self-deprecating, fully acknowledging that his role in the generation of theory invites challenge and testing. His published correspondence on the matter (Kagan, Gardner, & Sylwester, 2002) offers some caveats that Gardner's disciples too frequently forget. For example, Gardner remarked,

> One of the frustrations of my involvement with MI theory is that too infrequently have critics read carefully enough to raise good questions and think them through. . . . Even if the intelligences represent a genuine scientific discovery, the ways in which they are developed, nurtured, and canalized are still an issue for culture, not biology. It is on this issue that I expect to work in the coming years.

It is very interesting that the originator of MI theory is still working on matters that many MI advocates regard as settled science. Gardner's theory in the beginning of the 21st century asserts eight intelligences, but he readily acknowledges that the number could be adjusted as research in the field proceeds. The eight intelligences suggested by Gardner include

- Bodily/kinesthetic
- Interpersonal
- Intrapersonal
- Linguistic
- Logic/mathematical
- Musical
- Naturalist
- Spatial

Other scholars, such as Sternberg and colleagues (2000), offered terms such as "practical" intelligence, while Goleman (1997, 2000; Goleman, Boyatzis, & McKee 2002) popularized "emotional" intelligence, and Covey (2004) claimed the existence of "spiritual" intelligence. Willingham (2004) humorlessly suggests that by Gardner's criteria for the establishment of intelligence, we could have a humor intelligence, memory intelligence, olfactory intelligence, near-space intelligence, and far-space intelligence, though I have neither the patience nor (dare I say it?) the linguistic intelligence to understand these circumlocutions. If we accept the notion that there are different ways of expressing problem-solving ability, then it is possible to expand the list of possibilities to an exponential degree. Think of the specialization within a single team sport, profession, or academic discipline and the possible nominees for alternative varieties of intelligence could seem endless.

Perhaps most tellingly, Gardner himself is astonishingly blunt about the casual use of the term "intelligence." In an address to the American Educational Research Association in April 2003 he said, "I am quite confident that if I had written a book called *Seven Talents* it would not have received the attention that *Frames of Mind* received."

When we shift the context from cognition to leadership, "intelligence" is an imprecise and unhelpful term. Gardner's alternative, "talent," is even worse, as it might lend credence to the bilious combinations of pseudo-history, psychobabble, and platitudes that pass for leadership advice on bookshelves. The failure of these terms is certainly not Gardner's fault, any more than the widespread misuse of his theories is his fault. His caveats, suggestions for research, and invitations for scrutiny fall on deaf ears if adherents are on a marketing mission. I am in no position to be judgmental on the matter, as I came perilously close to making the same mistake. However fortuitous the words "intelligence" or "talent" may be for marketing books for improved leadership skills, those terms are unhelpful in explaining how leadership practices are related to improved student achievement, organizational performance, and educational equity. There are, as I have suggested in earlier writings (Reeves, 2002a), multiple *disciplines* of and distinct *dimensions* of leadership, and it is useful to bear in mind the multidimensional nature of leadership when assessing and developing leadership. Thus, while my original conception of this book may have been flawed, the lessons learned are, I trust, valuable.

Introduction

What *The Learning Leader* Will Do for You

I love watching people select books. I always wonder what makes prospective readers linger on a title, briefly examine the cover of one and replace it on the shelf, then select another and flip through its pages for several minutes, and finally pick up another and take it home. Although my observations are hardly scientific, my strong suspicion is that the decision to select a book is made quickly—within a few seconds. The author must respond to every reader's questions:

Why me? I have specialized needs and I'm tired of the generic pabulum about education, learning, and leadership.

Why this book? Of all the books available on Amazon.com right now, 16,971 address leadership and 3,199 address leadership in education. What makes this book worthy of my time?

Will it work? Spare me the undocumented historical speculation or the "education lite" aphorisms. I need substance, evidence, and practical application.

If you ask direct questions, you deserve direct answers.

Why you? If you are a leader or educator in a complex organization, then you have already concluded that the myths of the singular heroic leader and teacher are unsatisfying and fundamentally flawed. You know that the complexities of your organization and the enormity of your responsibilities demand performance, not platitudes. You want a solid intellectual framework that acknowledges the work of other researchers, but you want a new insight that will provide intellectual rigor and organizational energy. Above all, you want the answer to challenges that are facing you right now. You have an immediate need to improve communication within your organization, enhance staff morale, and increase performance at the individual and organizational levels. You are modest enough to know that you cannot achieve the objectives alone, but you are confident enough to know that one person can serve as a catalyst for the entire organization.

Why this book? There are many excellent books on leadership, and well over 100 other scholars are cited in the following pages. But there is also a lot of tripe masquerading as leadership insight. If you and other leaders and educators in your organization apply the lessons of this book, it will change your professional practices in profound ways. From conducting strategic planning, to running meetings, to evaluating projects, teams, and individuals, to organizing your leadership team and involving parents and community members, the Leadership for Learning Framework will help you reconceptualize your role and that of your colleagues. You will simultaneously discover strengths and acknowledge limitations, and you and your organization will be more resilient, less stressed, and more successful.

Will it work? The Leadership for Learning Framework is the result of extensive fieldwork and research. As I have done in my previous

19 books, I use authentic cases and real data. This book introduces a new and previously unpublished study that is the result of a detailed analysis of student achievement, teaching practices, and leadership planning for approximately 300,000 students in more than 290 schools. This is in addition to previous research and fieldwork from all 50 states and Canada, as well as my work in Africa, Asia, Europe, and the Middle East. In other words, this is not ivory tower theory or abstract musings. Leadership for Learning is a framework for success, not a silver bullet or a feel-good reassurance that all is well. The framework will encourage those who are discouraged because it provides specific guidance for the most difficult schools, and it will challenge complacent schools to differentiate between being effective and being lucky.

What is the Leadership for Learning Framework? Consider the diagram in Figure 1.1 (Reeves, 2002a). On the vertical axis is the "Achievement of Results." If you have high results, you are effective; if you have low results, you are ineffective or so goes the conventional wisdom. But such a superficial analysis does not distinguish between those who achieved high results through luck and through professional effectiveness. On the horizontal axis are the "Antecedents of Excellence," those observable qualities in leadership, teaching, curriculum, parental engagement, and other indicators that assist in understanding how results are achieved.

Educators in the upper left quadrant, the Lucky quadrant, teach students who achieve high results, probably true before these students walked into school in the morning. These teachers and leaders are unable to link their professional practices to results because they do not know how their practices influence achievement. In these demoralizing environments, there is so much self-congratulatory backslapping and protestations of "excellence" that the inhabitants of the

1.1 — The Leadership for Learning Framework

Achievement of Results	**Lucky** High results, low understanding of antecedents Replication of success unlikely	**Leading** High results, high understanding of antecedents Replication of success likely
	Losing Low results, low understanding of antecedents Replication of failure likely	**Learning** Low results, high understanding of antecedents Replication of success likely

Antecedents of Excellence

Lucky quadrant fail to recognize that a doll, television, computer game, or superior teacher could all achieve similar reading test results if these students are already reading fluently when they walk in the door of a 1st grade classroom. These Lucky schools treat their best teachers shabbily, because they do not recognize their extraordinary qualities. Those who choose the path of least resistance, who prefer popularity over effectiveness, or who decimate a forest with worksheets will achieve results similar to those who work their hearts out, analyze individual student results, challenge their high-achieving students, and encourage and coach their lowest-performing students. When challenges arrive, however, student achievement plummets. Lucky is nice while it lasts, but in a changing environment, lucky isn't enough.

In the lower left quadrant are the Losers. These leaders engage in stunningly self-defeating behavior by doing the same thing and expecting different results. Not only do they have low results on the

vertical axis, but they are clueless about the antecedents of excellence on the horizontal axis.

The best example of this behavior I have recently encountered was a middle school in which more than 80 percent of the students were not reading on grade level. When I asked the leadership team how much time had been devoted to reading in the previous year, they replied, "Thirty-seven minutes every day." Now, however, they were equipped with data that showed the error of their ways. Surely it would be obvious to the most casual observer that they needed to change their curriculum, schedule, and teaching practices, right? I innocently inquired, "So, now that we know how serious this situation is, how much time will you be spending on reading next year?" The stunning response: "Thirty-seven minutes every day."

Leaders and teachers who say, "I'll do whatever is needed in order to improve student results, as long as we don't have to change the schedule, modify the curriculum, improve teaching practices, or alter leadership behavior," are in the Loser quadrant. I might as well tell my physician that I am committed to losing 30 pounds as long as I can maintain a diet of fried chicken and martinis, sleep through my exercise class, and have a tailor who will adjust the waistband of my pants.

I have previously written about "belligerent indifference" (Reeves, 2001a) and have, not surprisingly, received some hostile responses to my use of the phrase. What better terminology is there for professionals who persist in leadership and teaching practices that are not working? We will not lure, cajole, bribe, or persuade people in the Loser quadrant to move to the right side of the matrix. We can only jolt them into a moment of extraordinary discomfort with this simple but profound question: "Is it working?" The Loser's answer is, at the very least, honest: "I don't know." Implicit in this

confession is the absolution that performance failures must be the fault of anyone except themselves. The fault for poor performance, if it lies anywhere, is with the students, their parents, their ethnicity, their culture, their environment, their peer group. It is anything except the professional conduct of the leaders and teachers involved in their education. This is the path of determined impotence and selected "victimhood." At the very least, it represents a decidedly unpleasant way to lead a professional life. At the worst, this attitude characterizes the classic "blame the victim" mentality, in which the assaulted student deserves punishment for dressing provocatively, the poor student reaps the seeds of indolence, and the illiterate student has chosen the path of irresponsibility and failure.

Blaming students and their families for poor achievement is a very small step removed from blaming the rape victim for the assault or the unemployed for their poverty. In the latter case, the victims deserved their fate due to lack of effort, planning, and preparation; in the former case the victims deserved their fate due to their choice of apparel or boyfriends, or their choice of education and professions. Shouldn't the readers of fashion magazines have known that the advertisers conflated sex appeal with irresistible enticement? Shouldn't the steelworkers of the 1960s have known that their jobs would be exported? Shouldn't the computer programmers of the 1990s have known that the doors of economic opportunity would evaporate with the speed with which information travels from corporate headquarters in New York to programming centers in Asia? This is not a polemic about trading policies or women's fashions, but only an observation that trade policies do not render hardworking and well-trained workers incompetent dolts who deserve homelessness any more than fashion trends render aspiring models punching bags who deserve abuse. No one chooses failure, and the presumption

that failure is a choice is deeply rooted in the need to elevate blame over responsibility.

The preceding paragraphs do not mean very much unless the remainder of this book offers a constructive solution. Fortunately, a significant body of research, including new research, suggests that there is hope. The primary conclusions of that research are as follows:

1. *Leadership, teaching, and adult actions matter.* This is not aphoristic pabulum, but statistical truth. While it is true that demographic variables are directly linked to student achievement, it is also true that adult variables, including the professional practices of teachers and the decisions leaders make, can be more important than demographic variables.

2. *There are particular leadership actions that show demonstrable links to improved student achievement and educational equity.* Our research suggests, for example, that excessive emphasis on school improvement plans is misplaced unless those plans are associated with very specific elements:

   - *Inquiry:* the degree to which leaders correctly analyze the underlying causes of deficiencies and successes in student achievement and equity. Successful inquiry attributes the causes to adults in the educational system—teachers, school leaders, and policymakers. Unsuccessful inquiry attributes causes to students. In other words, "blame the victim" is not only morally reprehensible but statistically untrue.
   - *Implementation:* the degree to which the specific elements of school improvement processes are implemented at the student and classroom levels. Successful planning processes recognize

that implementation is never a binary variable that leads to the unenlightening report that "We implemented the program" or "We did not implement the program." Rather, effective implementation is a continuous variable in which leaders recognize that there are degrees of successful implementation that are subject to quantitative and narrative description.

- *Monitoring*: the degree to which the implementation and frequency of an initiative is strongly associated with improvement and equity. While the Total Quality Management movement of the 20th century and its predecessor, the Taylorism movement of the 19th century, have given monitoring and measurement a sometimes unsavory reputation, the present study reminds us that plans without monitoring are little better than wishes upon stars. It is important to distinguish carefully between appropriate and insightful monitoring and monitoring that equates to a compliance drill for external authorities. The former, in the educational context, can be described as assessment, while the latter is testing. Assessment is designed to improve teaching and learning, provide immediate feedback for students and teachers, and focus on specific objectives. Testing, by contrast, is designed to provide an evaluation with feedback that is typically late, unfocused, and destructive. While there is a broad consensus that many classrooms are "over tested" as a result of a cascade of national, state, and district tests that are devoid of practical classroom insights, I would suggest that those same classrooms are woefully "under assessed."

3. *Leadership is neither a unitary skill set nor a solitary activity.* The Leadership for Learning Framework engages a variety of skills and

people throughout the organization, whether or not their official job titles suggest a leadership role.

Now that we have our framework, let us consider how Leadership for Learning can work for you.

Note: If you are conducting a book study with your colleagues, you can download a free book study guide at www.MakingStandardsWork.com, www.LeadAndLearn.com, and www.ascd.org and also find free access to information needed to apply the lessons from this book to develop your own Leadership Map.

– 1 –

The Results Paradox

Pop Quiz: Name America's most innovative company. The executives running *Fortune* 500 companies are asked to do just that each year, and the number one answer three years running surprised a lot of people (but not their peers). The majority voted for Enron.

(Neff & Citrin, 1999)

Lessons from Enron

No organization is more emblematic of spectacular failure than Enron, a company that started as a modest utility and then built a castle in the air based on a combination of illusory innovation and criminal fraud. Not only were employees duped, losing their life savings while insiders bailed out; sophisticated observers also were utterly taken in by the ruse. The quotation at the opening of the chapter was not written by Enron's publicity agents, but was typical of the adulation accorded to Enron by business journalists and professors as recently as two years before the company's bankruptcy. How can such smart people do such dumb things? This is the question that

1

leaders and stakeholders in every area of public life have asked in the wake of the financial scandals, governmental failures, and educational policy debacles in the first years of the 21st century.

Analytical intelligence, prized by business schools and policy-makers, created the illusion of invincibility. But as the aptly entitled *The Smartest Guys in the Room* (McLean & Elkind, 2003) dramatically illustrated, superior analytical intelligence gave us the Enron scandal. With complexity masquerading as intelligence, Enron's executives and consultants devised a vast array of transactions whose most telling feature was that they were not part of the corporation's reported financial statements. While the transactions hid a growing mountain of debt, the apparition of success continued. An uncritical business press and a bevy of academicians happily contributed to the fantasy, publishing stories, case studies, and books lauding the "creativity" of Enron.

Supported by the conviction that "numbers don't lie," a society thirsting for easy measurement equated short-term profits and a soaring stock market price with genuine business success. By such logic, other elements of society equate test scores with educational excel lence, just as a growing legion of Americans associate weight loss by any method with health. But as educators and parents, we know that some teenagers lose weight by diet and exercise, while other teens achieve the same objective with anorexia and drug use. We know that some schools achieve higher test scores with profound improvements in teaching and leadership practices, while others abuse the system. If the only objective is improved test scores, it's much faster and easier to have underperforming students drop out of school than to craft effective intervention programs for them. As Enron taught us, riches and notoriety come more quickly through manipulation than through innovation and hard work.

If we are to learn from our mistakes, then we must begin our journey with an acknowledgment that we have an educational Enron waiting to happen if we fail to recognize that the demands of leadership are more complex than intimidating students and teachers into short-term test score gains. We have a nutritional Enron waiting to happen if we pursue weight loss at the expense of rational health practices. Every organization has a leadership Enron waiting to happen if it maintains a myopic focus on results without considering how those results are achieved.

The Limits of Results

This book is not a screed against testing or a suggestion that focusing on results is inappropriate. Rather, the central thesis of the book is that results can be improved through applying a comprehensive framework such as Leadership for Learning. Conversely, results are diminished when we focus only on the fraction of the Leadership for Learning Framework that deals with results. One of the foremost advocates of a focus on results, Mike Schmoker, recently noted the imperative of leadership actions:

> When you truly want better results for students, you don't just stare at the
> data and display some colorful charts. You don't just talk about what the kids
> are doing. You display courage and you are willing to do unpopular things.
> The only schools that truly get results are the ones who say, "I know that the
> 'buffer,' as Elmore calls it, serves to protect teachers from outside inspection
> or scrutiny. Nonetheless, I'm going to inspect and scrutinize, and I'll encourage
> my colleagues to do this as much as they can themselves. I'll ask the
> uncomfortable questions, make sure certain things are happening, and confront
> the people who are not doing them. I'll do it as tactfully and painlessly

as possible, but if the good things are not happening, there will be a confrontation." (personal interview, December 2, 2004)

Schmoker is not sanguine about the prospects of such a confrontation occurring. He concluded:

> We have to shock the system. We have a duty to expose the system where it is clearly ineffectual. If enough people say the emperor has no clothes, we make real progress. But as things are now, we don't even pretend to improve most of our schools; we only talk about it.

Schmoker's pessimism is not the isolated despair of a travel-weary consultant. Recently, I interviewed the director of curriculum and instruction for a purportedly high-performing school system. With all the students affluent and none speaking a language other than English at home, one might expect them to best their urban counterparts who are plagued by poverty, mobility, and early illiteracy. The smugness of the faculty was shocking, particularly in view of a disturbing trend in the data that clearly showed the "great" performances in elementary school, due in large part to students who entered kindergarten already reading, had diminished by middle school. The curricular anarchy that is the culture of this system allows poor performance to be clouded by economic advantage and parental involvement, at least for the first 11 years of a student's life. After that, these leaders can blame hormones, television, and Nintendo—anything except taking personal responsibility for leaders in the system that lack the will to confront a culture in which the care, comfort, and convenience of the adults are elevated over the interests of children.

What is necessary is that we challenge dominant notions of leadership success and then provide a practical and effective alternative framework. The Results Paradox (Reeves, 2005) states:

The more myopic the focus on results, the lower the probability that the
results will improve. An important corollary is this: A myopic focus on process
rather than results yields neither improved results nor improved processes.
Only a comprehensive focus . . . leads an organization to achieve an optimal,
multifaceted view of both results and the antecedents of excellence. (pp. 4-5)

The Limits of Intelligence

While Enron vividly demonstrated that raw intelligence is an insufficient condition for leadership success, the dissatisfaction with
analytical intelligence as a leadership characteristic is hardly new.
Howard Gardner (1993) suggested more than 20 years ago that the
traditional view of intelligence as a unitary element, commonly
called g, for general intelligence, is inadequate.

Sternberg and his colleagues (2000) have provided an enormous
research base to support the contention that practical intelligence is
distinct from analytical intelligence, and the former is vital to survival
in any walk of life. Yet, even while some school curricula were adjusted
to provide a nod to the notion of multiple intelligences, the prevalence
of analytical intelligence remains predominant in graduate schools and,
in particular, in leadership training programs. Even the foremost exponent of emotional intelligence, Daniel Goleman (1995; Goleman,
et al., 2002), relies almost exclusively on quantitative analytical techniques to make the argument that emotional intelligence is associated
with more variation in financial success. The "emotional versus analytical" view of leadership fits neatly into the "right brain versus left
brain" hypotheses that are now entering their sixth decade of popularity. But despite the incessant talk about a broader view of intelligence,
the prevailing practices in leadership training, development, and evaluation that favor general intelligence are inadequate.

The Leadership for Learning Framework

The practical alternative that addresses both the results paradox and the limitations of analytical intelligence is the Leadership for Learning Framework. My initial conception of this framework (Reeves, 2002a) suggested the four quadrants displayed in Figure 1.1. The vertical axis reflects results, typically measured in the educational context as student test scores. The horizontal axis displays the leader's understanding of the "Antecedents of Excellence," those measurable indicators of leadership, teaching practices, curriculum, parental involvement, and other factors that influence results. As the matrix suggests in the upper left corner, if there are high results

1.1 — The Leadership for Learning Framework

Lucky High results, low understanding of antecedents Replication of success unlikely	**Leading** High results, high understanding of antecedents Replication of success likely
Losing Low results, low understanding of antecedents Replication of failure likely	**Learning** Low results, high understanding of antecedents Replication of success likely

Achievement of Results

Antecedents of Excellence

are accompanied by low understanding of the antecedents of excellence, the leader is not good but merely lucky. Such results are unlikely to be replicated. If the results are low and the antecedents of excellence are poorly understood, then we are doomed to a losing cycle of repeating the same actions and expecting different results. This quadrant of the matrix describes innumerable schools and entire systems where leaders will jump on every bandwagon and pursue every fad, but steadfastly refuse to make fundamental changes in scheduling, assessment, grading, personnel assignments, and leadership practices. They will change everything except, of course, those things that matter most for the results they want.

The focus of this book is the right side of the matrix, the Leading and Learning quadrants. In the lower right quadrant, the "Learner" has not yet achieved desired results but nevertheless possesses deep insights into the antecedents of excellence. This is the leader who will look and dig deeply into the data, rather than blaming the students or expressing bewilderment like the "Loser." While the Loser says, "It beats me—it must be the kids," the Learner says this:

> I've analyzed the data deeply, and here are my preliminary conclusions. First, although our average scores are disappointing, I've noticed that we have exceptional success in some isolated areas. Mr. Jasper's 4th graders excel in geometry, and Ms. Fitch's 2nd graders made enormous gains in vocabulary. I've conducted some extensive observations of both their classes and noted that they are engaging in some remarkably different teaching and classroom assessment practices. Our collective challenge is to conduct a treasure hunt and find other pockets of excellence and then determine how we can identify, document, and replicate these practices.

The Leader enjoys the optimal combination of high results and deep understanding of the antecedents of excellence, yet is perpetually seeking opportunities to improve. "Even if more than 80 percent of our students are meeting state standards, we still have a lot of work to do," the Leader says. "Not only do we need to work on the 15 to 20 percent of our students who are not yet proficient, but we clearly need to provide a higher level of challenge for those students for whom our state standards are a floor, not a ceiling."

– 2 –

Challenging Leadership Myths
Hope for the Exhausted Leader

The late psychiatrist M. Scott Peck opened one of the most insightful books of the last century, *The Road Less Traveled* (1985), with one of the best opening lines of any literary work: "Life is difficult." So could it be said of leadership, and were authors and publishers willing to substitute parsimony for palliatives, barrels of ink and thousands of trees could be spared. Peck's insights were not the stuff of popular psychology in which just the right belief system would solve one's problems. Rather, he noted that humans struggle with conflicting errors that range from neuroses to character defects. While we may become informed by studying the lives of the heroes and saints of history and legend, we are ultimately better served by acknowledging our weaknesses and confronting them. This is decidedly more challenging than "Three Easy Steps to Happiness" but represents a rare breath of intellectual honesty in the self-help genre.

Readers of this book are, I trust, similarly exasperated with simple solutions. They are willing to accept a challenge but cannot avoid the siren song of "It's really easy—just follow these steps. . . ." Leaders are particularly vulnerable to such an enticement after a challenging

day in which, they conclude, "It just shouldn't be this hard." As Peck reminds us, it *is* this hard. Humans, and the organizations in which they operate—families, corporations, schools, governments—are complex, simultaneously offering opportunities for heroism and cowardice, the peak performer and sluggard, loyal soldier and traitor, deacon and demon. These disturbing combinations of contradictory traits are found in leaders as well. Enron, the object lesson of the previous chapter, was a source of creativity and ingenuity, yet at the same time it spawned fraud and economic catastrophe.

Enron is hardly the only example of leadership mythology leading to disastrous results. Such preposterously wrong analyses should make every leader challenge the postulate that states: "If you emulate history's successes, then you too will be rich and famous." Well, perhaps they got the "famous" part of the equation right. As I write this chapter, Bernard J. Ebbers, former chief executive officer of WorldCom, has been convicted of nine counts of fraud (Searcey, Young, & Scannell, 2005). While the full 25-year sentence may not be served, for the 63-year-old former high-flying CEO, it may be a life sentence. Even had he been found not guilty, his defense—"I was a clueless victim who didn't understand the details"—was hardly the hallmark of the executive image Ebbers had cultivated just a few years ago. Whatever happens on appeal, it would be difficult to reconcile the alternatives of guilty guile and innocent idiocy with the following profile by the same experts who were duped by Enron:

Until late 1997, Bernard J. Ebbers was a well-kept secret outside the telecommunications industry. True, he had, through a series of more than 40 acquisitions, turned WorldCom into a billion-dollar company. And yes, he had made WorldCom the fourth-largest phone company in the United States, behind AT&T, MCI, and Sprint. But being fourth in the telephone industry is much

like being fourth in the American auto industry—it does not help you much when most people can only name the top three competitors.

And then Ebbers changed all that in one fell swoop. He acquired MCI Communications Corp. for $43 billion. The MCI takeover transformed MCI WorldCom into

- The second-largest U.S. long-distance carrier,
- One of the world's largest Internet companies, and
- A major international force in the telephony market.

This is none too shabby for a company run by a transplanted Canadian . . . who prefers cowboy hats and blue jeans to pinstripes and silk ties.

(Fennell, 1997)

By such logic, Henry McCarty, more popularly known as Billy the Kid, "transformed" the banking industry through shrewd acquisitions and uncanny business acumen. In the context of leadership literature, the aspiring bankers of the 19th century would be better advised to emulate the strategies of Billy the Kid than those of J. P. Morgan. Prevailing leadership mythologies are stunningly uninformed by the cautionary tales of Enron and WorldCom. Unburdened by history or logic, they persist in their enthusiastic but unearned claims. These include historical models and their self-contradictory themes, and a host of propositions that conflate facileness with facility.

The hope provided by this chapter is not another "solution" to leadership challenges, but the certainty that our inability to follow these models is neither a failure of character or effort, but rather a weakness inherent in the models themselves. Rather than fix leaders who are broken, we must redefine the leadership challenge in a way

that recognizes the complexities of leadership and leaders. In one of the few sports analogies that can be used throughout the world, we expect leaders to perform simultaneously as the goalie and the scorer, but fail to consider that no one would watch a World Cup match where such a preposterous dual assignment took place.

Historical Models

Historical models of leadership are hardly new. Herodotus and Thucydides warned us, respectively, that the record of history is inherently biased, written as it is by the victors, and that the oratorical abilities of leaders must not be confused with their character, wisdom, and other essential leadership abilities. We have much to learn from the great, not-so-great, and disastrous leaders of the past. In the historical and philosophical writings of Will and Ariel Durant (1933, 1935) and the masterpiece of historical synthesis by Jacques Barzun (2001), there is a treasure trove of historical insight and genuine scholarship. There are timeless truths about leadership, loyalty, honesty, motivation, and betrayal. The same could be said of the histories of the ancient world and the plays of Shakespeare, as well as the great novels of the African, Occidental, Oriental, South American, and native worlds. In legend and myth there is truth as well as fiction. It is not only the gods, heroes, and animal spirits who display courage and cowardice, fearlessness and fecklessness, inspiration and indolence. These themes are as instructive for today's leaders as they were for those of past millennia.

More recently, we can find insight in the biographies of John Adams (McCullough, 2002), Washington (Ellis, 2004), Mandela (Smith, 2004), King (Bennett, 1992), and Churchill (Jenkins, 2001), to name a few. These works provide a nuanced view, illuminating

strengths and weaknesses, victories and defeats. But the term "scholarly research" cannot be applied fairly to a raft of recent publications that are, to put it charitably, speculative, facile, ill informed, and stunningly devoid of either evidence or analysis.

Leading the pack is a volume, slim in every sense of the word, by Wess Roberts, Ph.D., entitled *Leadership Secrets of Attila the Hun* (1990). In a triumph of marketing, guile, and reverent worship at the altar of P. T. Barnum, the publisher and author have become wealthy, as the book has sold more than 486,000 copies. Company presidents and, alas, school superintendents have ordered copies of the book for each of their subordinate managers, based, I hope, on the cleverness of the title rather than the drivel between the covers. The author's expertise, it turns out, is in executive project management rather than history, but ignorance of the facts does not restrain him from earnest speculation.

In fact, Attila the Hun helped to define the term "barbarian" through his indiscriminate campaign of rape, murder, and plunder. Will Durant, who was criticized for scholarship that was too "light" in 10,000 pages of footnote-laden work, provides the following description of the real "secrets" that Attila offers to today's leaders:

> In 451 Attila and half a million men marched to the Rhine, sacked and burned Trier and Metz, and massacred their inhabitants. All Gaul was terrified; here was no civilized warrior like Caesar. (Durant, 1950)

What's next from Roberts? Perhaps even his publisher will blush at "Leadership Secrets of Saddam Hussein" and "The Wisdom of Adolf Hitler." The list of historical models is endless, but at least leaders who seek more than platitudes for guidance will find such faux historical analysis less than enlightening. Even less noxious

historical figures have entered the public market as leadership models and, depending on one's point of view, then Ulysses S. Grant, Robert E. Lee, Elizabeth I, Catherine the Great, and other heroes are subjects for the proposition that whatever is old is wise, and whoever is dead will very likely not correct the assertion of contemporary biographers.

Analytical Models

I am a quantitative methodologist. According to the creed of my profession, truth lies in numbers. Two and two is four, and the square root of 100 is 10. But as a one-time statistics professor, I was forced to acknowledge that perhaps the most important lesson I imparted to my students was that not everything that counts can be counted, not everything that can be observed can be expressed in quantitative terms. While a regression coefficient can express the statistical relationship between demographic factors and student achievement, only a narrative analysis will explain why some students and teachers defy the odds and perform at an exceptionally high level despite the prevalence of poverty, special education, second languages, or other factors that in statistical terms are associated with low student achievement. An analytical model would call these extraordinary students and teachers "outliers," while an inclusive leadership model would inquire what we can learn from them.

Perhaps the best illustration of the limits of analytical models is the work of educators of the 20th century (Coleman, 1966) and economists of the 21st century (Rothstein, 2004b) who make the error not permitted of first year students in statistics, the conflation of correlation and causality. The Coleman report concluded that 90 percent of the variation in student achievement is associated with the level of the education of the mother of the student. This "Blame

Mom" thesis has been widely embraced for the past 40 years by those who would assert that parents, families, and circumstances beyond the control of schools provide an insular safety net for teachers, administrators, and board members who conveniently claim that the factors most directly associated with student achievement are ingrained in students long before the children arrive in school. This is the logic of the physician who says, with the most sincere sigh, that "I might have saved the patient, but her genetic history and her past few years of deliberate and self-inflicted neglect have brought her to this state—I can only deliver the autopsy report, as it is too late to provide meaningful help to this hopeless patient."

Certainly a study of statistical relationships is important to understanding any phenomenon. Smoking has a positive statistical association with lung cancer and other ailments; frequent exercise is negatively associated with stroke and heart disease; nonfiction writing is positively associated with higher student performance in mathematics, science, and social studies; high percentages of students in poverty are negatively associated with student achievement. In each case, further inquiry is necessary. The question that leaders must address is not a statistical one but one requiring judgment and insight.

In the case of smoking and cancer, one could have heeded the cautionary notes of Tobacco Institute scientists who, quite correctly, dismissed the association between smoking and lung cancer as "only a correlation." Thoughtful leaders might consider the principle of comparative risk. "What is the risk if the Tobacco Institute is right and the medical warnings are wrong?" What would be the impact if we reduce tobacco use and years later it turns out that we didn't need to take such a step? Perhaps the impact would be an economic loss to the tobacco industry, along with the unpleasant prospect of dealing with cranky family members and coworkers who were withdrawing

from nicotine addiction. What would be the impact if we fail to reduce tobacco use and years later it turns out that we should have taken steps to reduce consumption of this dangerous practice much earlier? The answer, we now know, is clear: hundreds of thousands of totally avoidable, gruesome, lingering, and painful deaths not only for smokers but for coworkers and cohabiters who inhaled decades of secondhand smoke. "Only a correlation" indeed.

In the case of poverty and student achievement, it is easy to succumb to the fatalistic thesis proclaimed on the cover of some of the nation's leading educational publications that "even the best schools cannot close the equity gap" (Rothstein, 2004a). Educational leaders could subscribe to what I have called the "Potted Plant Theory of Leadership," perhaps best described as determined impotence. This is represented by the deliberate choice to surrender leadership initiative and eviscerate the hopes and aspirations of students and committed teachers. After all, the reasoning goes, since demography is destiny, there is nothing educators and leaders can do except witness the inexorable destruction of the lives of another generation of students as demographic influences take their toll. There is an alternative to the Potted Plant Theory, and that is an exploration of what statisticians call confounding variables. Confounding variables are those factors that affect the interaction between two variables (Kachigan, 1986). In the current example, there is no doubt of the negative statistical association between student poverty and achievement, as Figure 2.1 indicates.

The problem with two-variable correlations, of course, is that they insinuate that there is only one cause and one effect. Years of studying statistics reveal the following dose of common sense: Life is multivariate. The central challenge of leadership is also the intellectual challenge of statistical analysis. We must know more than the

interaction between variables. Every time we are confronted with
the apparent association between two variables, we must ask

- What other variables are in the equation?
- Which variables are most important?
- What is the sequence of the variables?
- Which variables are most subject to our influence and which
  variables are intractable?

2.1 — Poverty and Student Achievement

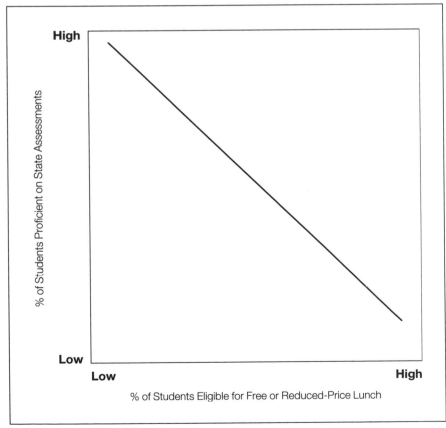

Continuing with the example of the relationship between student achievement and poverty, researcher Robert Ingersoll (2003) forces us to confront two realities, the first encouraging and the second decidedly ugly. The first reality is that teaching quality matters; it is a decisive variable associated with improved student achievement. Ingersoll is hardly the only researcher to reach this conclusion. Kati Haycock of The Education Trust, with extensive support from Linda Darling-Hammond of Stanford University, conclusively finds that although demographic variables influence student achievement, teacher quality trumps them all, and by a decisive margin. Her conclusion (in the most incisively titled academic article in recent memory, "Good Teaching Matters . . . A Lot") was that "we have chosen to focus . . . on what all of the studies conclude is the most significant factor in student achievement: the teacher" (Haycock, 1998, p. 3).

The first conclusion, that teaching quality is an important influence on student performance, is encouraging. After all, this is a variable that educational leaders and policymakers can influence. But the second conclusion is decidedly more distressing. No matter how much we improve the quality of teachers, we allocate this precious resource in a perverse manner, giving the most effective teachers to economically advantaged students and denying those teachers to impoverished students. Although there are wonderful examples of exceptionally effective teachers in high poverty schools (just as there are examples of ineffective teachers in economically advantaged schools), these are the exceptions that test the rule portrayed in Figure 2.2. In general, as Ingersoll reminds us, the more likely a school is to contain high-poverty students, the less likely it is to contain high-quality teachers.

Look carefully at this chart and then back at Figure 2.1, and then explain which variable is most important. Does poverty really have

the greatest impact on student achievement? Or is a stronger variable educational policies that systematically assign the best teachers to those students who need them the least, and deny those teachers to students need them the most? There are, fortunately, also exceptions to this rule. As Figure 2.3 indicates, there are some systems where the relationship between student poverty (as measured by the percentage of students eligible for free or reduced-priced lunch) and student achievement is negligible.

2.2 — Poverty and Teacher Quality

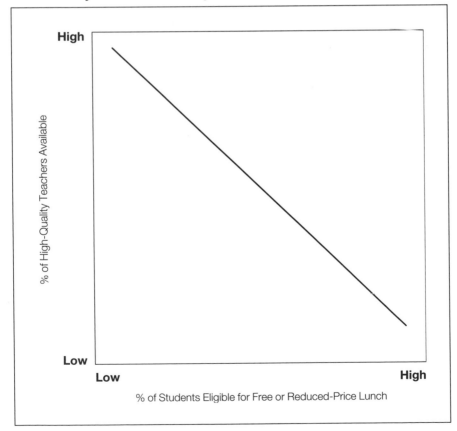

Figure 2.3 is not an idealistic version of the future but a statistical fact. In some cases, it represents the performance of an entire school system, such as Wayne Township in Indianapolis, where high-poverty schools regularly perform as well as low-poverty schools. In other cases, it represents only part of a system, and in still other cases, it represents student performance on some tests but not others, as is the case with Cobb County in the metropolitan Atlanta area. The common theme is the false assertion that demography is destiny, that "even the best schools cannot close the achievement gap." In fact, schools and entire school systems can close the achievement gap. The only question is whether the leaders and policymakers have the will to do so.

There is more to the student achievement and educational equity equation than the allocation of teacher quality; although this particu-

2.3 — Poverty and Student Achievement in High-Performance Schools

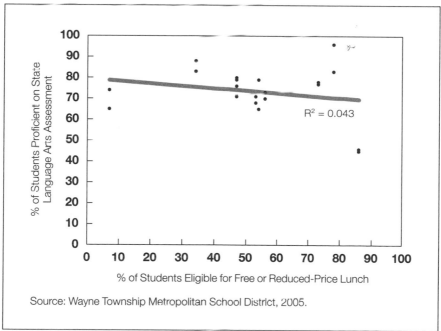

Source: Wayne Township Metropolitan School District, 2005.

lar variable is certainly a major step in the right direction. Allocation of resources, along with parent involvement, systematically high expectations verified by common assessments, and a host of other leadership practices are necessary to ensure equity. Analytical models can shed light on these matters, but accurate statistical analysis alone is insufficient for pursuing educational goals.

Relationship Models

When readers see the word "relationship," it can conjure up a variety of images, ranging from the "Mars and Venus" oppositional relationships popularized by John Gray (1992) and theatrical variations on the same theme, such as "Defending the Caveman," the hilarious one-man show written by and starting Rob Becker. There are also serious scientific studies of relationship models and leadership effectiveness. The pioneer in this area is Daniel Goleman (1995), who popularized the term "emotional intelligence." His applications to leadership are compelling, particularly when he synthesizes a substantial body of evidence that suggests emotional intelligence has a relatively stronger influence on leadership effectiveness and organizational results than do traditional measures such as analytical ability (Goleman et al., 2002).

There is an emerging school of research, known as Positive Organizational Scholarship (Cameron & Caza, 2004), that explicitly values the primacy of interpersonal relationships as a key to organizational effectiveness. The promise of intersecting two things that Freud claimed that we most need—work and love—is appealing, but it is a chimera. Every reader can recall examples that challenge the relationship model, such as the relationship master who ultimately failed to confront necessary realities and sacrificed organizational

success, or the relationship-impaired boss who saved the organization and was, if belatedly, revered by her colleagues for taking a tough but unpopular stance.

It is a very short step from valuing positive relationships to being so conflict averse that the leader is trapped by the relationship model and becomes unwilling to engage in conflict, inside or outside the organization. The organization is thus left defenseless to fail under the onslaught of internal strife or external attack.

The "One Thing" You Need to Know

Marcus Buckingham, formerly of The Gallup Organization, is the author of several blockbuster books on leadership and management. Following the international bestsellers, *First, Break All the Rules* (Buckingham & Coffman, 1999) and *Now, Discover Your Strengths* (Buckingham & Clifton, 2001), his latest contribution to the genre is *The One Thing You Need to Know . . . About Great Managing, Great Leading, and Sustained Individual Success* (Buckingham, 2005a). Buckingham leads the reader through a number of "controlling insights," the central organizing principles that help the reader to synthesize both large-scale research and Buckingham's individual case studies.

Without a hint of irony, the author helps us to understand that there are many things one needs to know about successful management, leadership, and individual success. Among the most important things is that we cannot do it alone. However talented and extraordinary great leaders and managers may be, one of their more common practices is the creation of a team with complementary strengths. Whether scheduling clerks in a drugstore, reorganizing the purchasing department of a multinational retailer, or leading complex scientific

enterprises, the "one thing" that leaders need to learn is that there is never "one thing." Whether the organization includes five people or 50,000 people, the complexities of human motivation will defy any attempt to take a one-size-fits-all approach to leadership.

Moreover, although Buckingham defines the "need for authority" as one of the human universals uniting all societies irrespective of geographic or cultural boundaries, the list of leadership imperatives that he provides inexorably leads to one of two directions. The first is a return to the historical perspective, where we mythologize the perfect leader. As the opening of this chapter indicated, the principal flaws of such an analysis are that historical mythology is inaccurate and, more to the point, the mythologized leaders are conveniently dead. This makes rigorous analysis and verification of assumptions challenging at best. The second alternative is the subject of the remainder of this book: We cannot do it alone. The essential challenge of the leader is not attaining perfection but acknowledging imperfection and obtaining complementarities. Rather than developing what they lack, great leaders will magnify their own strengths and simultaneously create teams that do not mimic the leader but provide different and equally important strengths for the organization.

$-3-$

Architectural Leadership
Why You Cannot Do It Alone

Since the publication of the Leadership Performance Matrix in my book *Assessing Educational Leaders* (Reeves, 2004c), the primary criticism of the matrix has been that exemplary performance on every dimension of leadership is impossible. That is precisely the point. Just as Waters, Marzano, and McNulty (2003, 2005) suggest in their meta-analysis of studies of leadership effectiveness, a variety of leadership practices are associated with positive educational effects. The Leadership Performance Matrix suggests that exceptional abilities in data analysis, staff motivation, and public communication are all essential for the effective leader. The task of the leader is to create an organization that is exemplary in every dimension and not engage in behaviors suggesting that a single person bears the burden of exemplary performance in every area. Indeed, data from The Gallup Organization on exceptional leadership (Buckingham & Clifton, 2001) are parallel to the findings from Perkins's research on intelligence (1995, 2003): strength in one area is not necessarily a predictor of strength in another. In fact, building on an existing strength in a diverse leadership team is superior to forever attempting to fix one's weaknesses.

The Wisdom of the Group

The landmark and counterintuitive research summary of David
Surowiecki's *The Wisdom of Crowds* (2004) makes it clear that leadership decision making is more accurate and less risky when entrusted
to a diverse group than to a single individual, even when that
individual has significant expertise. I replicated Surowiecki's findings
in field research with educational leaders and found substantially
similar results. In a roomful of leaders who are quite convinced that
their own perception, judgment, intelligence, and gamesmanship are
sufficient for success, I will ask participants to answer a straightforward question, such as the distance on that particular day between
the Earth and the moon, taking into account the elliptical orbit of
the moon and all the other variables in the universe that influence
this calculation. At first they seem overwhelmed, but then they
apply themselves to the task, some with sound reasoning and others
with spectacularly misguided logic. Nevertheless, the result every
time—bar none—is that the average of the group estimate is superi-
or to almost all of the individual estimates.

Then I ask something that is far more reasonable: estimate the
distance from your present location to my home near Boston. This
challenge is presented to an audience that represents an extraordinary
amount of academic learning. Almost always there is someone who
will say, "I just made that drive with my family last summer—I *know*
this!" But without exception, the average estimate of the group is
superior to the estimates from individuals who claim to know the
answer. In one group, several participants gamed the system by calling
their offices (perhaps inspired by the TV show *Who Wants to Be a
Millionaire*). The friends provided help, with a theoretical accuracy to
one-tenth of a mile. Nevertheless, the average of the group continued

to best the answers of all but the most lucky, conniving, and, in only a few cases, diligent individual members of the group. Surowiecki's insight, that the group is smarter than the individual, is important not only on trivial matters such as estimating distances in outer space or on the North American continent, but on critical matters such as the prices of vital commodities or the future leadership of the nation.

This is a difficult lesson for readers who believe in the myth of leadership as a heroic and solitary enterprise. There are times when the former description applies, but solitary efforts were of little benefit to our Cro Magnon predecessors, and they are not the source of our successes today. We survive as a species and as leaders of organizations not due to solitary efforts but due to organizational and collaborative success. Part of the mythology of the lone leader is a misunderstanding and misquotation of Charles Darwin. When you think of Darwinism, what is the first phrase that comes to mind? My guess is that your instantaneous reaction was "survival of the fittest." It is, after all, what every properly trained student knows, but as is so frequently the case, what every student knows is wrong. A few dictionaries get it right, at least in broad brushes. The *Concise Oxford Dictionary, 10th Edition* (2001), defines Darwinism as "the theory of the evolution of species by natural selection." This definition, however, leaves too much to chance. Let Darwin speak for himself: "It is not the strongest of the species that survive, nor the most intelligent, but the most responsive to change" (Darwin, 1859/2005).

The Leader as The Architect

In *The Daily Disciplines of Leadership* (Reeves, 2002a, p. 12), I examined a myriad of alternative definitions for leadership and found them

to be ponderous, unfocused, and unnecessarily complex. Many of these definitions also perpetuated the leadership mythology that elevated leaders on a pedestal and assumed that, with just enough study, seminars, and charisma, organizational miracles would naturally follow. Finding these definitions as unsatisfying as ill-conceived historical analogies to Attila the Hun, I offered an alternative definition: "Leaders are the *architects* of individual and organizational improvement." The architectural metaphor has some important implications.

Consider the Temple of Concord in Sicily. It has endured more than 2,500 years in a hostile environment. The Carthaginians from Africa, the Athenians from Rome, and the Romans from Italy all laid siege to this area over the years, and yet while the Parthenon in Athens crumbled and the Coliseum in Rome faded away, the Temple of Concord remains remarkably intact. Try to envision this amazing structure in your mind. Columns seem to rise to the sky, more than 150 feet high. The peaked tops exude grace and style. Despite the hostile surrounding, the temple conveys an aura of peace. Open on all sides, its firm foundation welcomes all who choose to enter. Careful observers note that the columns supporting the structure are more closely spaced than those of similar structures in Africa, Greece, and Italy—structures that have long since fallen apart. In contemporary organizational theory, the Temple of Concord was "meant to last." Here is the question I would like you to consider: What did the architect do? This was an enormous feat of leadership—the creation of a structure that has endured approximately 2,500 years. The condition of the structure is remarkable. This building was clearly not a "quick fix" to appease short-term demands; but it was built to last. The creativity is extraordinary with a picture hardly doing justice to the immensity of the scale or the detail of the design. The logistical challenges were enormous, from transporting the intellectual conception

from Greece to Sicily to quarrying the rock to preparing the soil in rocky and hostile terrain, to laying a foundation that would support thousands of tons for centuries, to the communication that involved expert seamanship, engineering, communication, and execution. The architect was clearly a visionary genius, but one conclusion is inescapable: No architect ever built a temple alone. Whether it is the Temple of Concord or the temple of student achievement, the temple of educational excellence or the temple of educational equity, even the most skilled and hard-working architect cannot build the temple alone.

The architectural definition of leadership helps us to understand that vision is a necessary but insufficient condition for effective leadership. Leadership must, in the words of the brilliant leadership theoretician Richard Elmore (2000), be "distributed." Distributed leadership is not merely an exercise in participatory democracy, nor is it the popular but ineffectual therapeutic brand of leadership in which the earnest but incompetent leaders assure followers that they "hear" us or "feel" for us, but otherwise blithely ignore our wishes. Distributed leadership is based on trust, as well as the certain knowledge that no single leader possesses the knowledge, skills, and talent to lead an organization, any more than the genius who designed the Temple of Concord had the ability to build the structure alone. Leadership literature is rich with descriptions of essential traits for successful leaders (Marzano, 2000; Marzano, Pickering, & Pollock, 2001; Reeves, 2004c; Waters et al., 2005). The overwhelming demands of these volumes lead us back to the architectural definition of leadership: no single person can achieve the essential demands of leadership alone.

To amplify Elmore's definition of distributed leadership, I would add the term "complementary" leadership. In practical terms for

educational leaders, we must acknowledge that effective leaders should have expertise in instruction, data analysis, and motivation, among many other qualities. But in reality, the leader who is a master in curriculum and instruction may lack some skills in emotional intelligence, just as the leader who displays empathy, social awareness, and other emotional intelligence skills may not be an expert in data analysis. The challenge of educational organizations is not to make these leaders into perfectly complete beings by filling in their deficiencies, but rather to create an environment in which the leaders are empowered to create complementary teams. Although no single leader will possess every dimension of effective leadership, the team will surely do so. The incentive for the complementary leader, therefore, is not to hire and retain clones who make the senior leader feel good, but rather to hire and retain complementary leaders—people with different skill sets, intelligences, and behavioral characteristics.

To extend the architectural metaphor of leadership, we must consider the role of the architect in making connections among all the participants in a complex project. The architect of the Temple of Concord knows how all the pieces of the puzzle fit together and can skillfully assemble the diverse talents to do the work: the laborers quarrying and transporting the stone, the stone masons, the engineers who planned how to move tons of material into perfect position, the foundation workers, and the acrobat who placed the final piece on the topmost cornice.

Architectural leaders in education similarly make connections. These are the school leaders who know that it is essential to include bus drivers and cafeteria workers in professional development sessions on student discipline and motivation, because the school day for many students begins on the bus or at breakfast, not in the classroom.

These are the leaders who include custodians and administrative assistants in professional development for reading groups, and when they say that everyone in the building will focus on literacy, they mean every single adult and child in the building. Such leaders do not view educational accountability as something done "to" teachers only in the grades and subjects that are required for standardized testing. Architectural leaders know that every class is an opportunity for students to engage in creativity, literacy, project management, personal responsibility, teamwork, and a host of other skills that will contribute to their success. In schools led by architectural leaders, everything is connected, and there is no such thing as a "nonacademic" class, assembly, or experience. The faculty is not divided between those who are accountable and those who are not. Every certified and noncertified staff member supports a common focus on improving teaching and learning.

The final element of the architectural analogy is also revealed in the description of the Temple of Concord. Think of the enormous challenges that this architect faced. Traveling over rough seas, landing on a rugged coast, scaling difficult terrain, the architect faced colossal environmental challenges. Working in Sicily, an island at the crossroads between Carthaginian conquerors from Africa, Roman defenders from the European mainland, and Greek explorers whose historical pendulum swung between empire and city-state, the architect of the Temple of Concord was required to surmount enormous human challenges within cultures that were sometimes harmonious but frequently hostile. The financial and physical costs of transforming a barren hillside into a temple that endured for millennia can scarcely be imagined. These efforts can also be seen in the overwhelming challenges that are the daily business of educational leaders.

Thus far we have explored leadership strategies that are ineffective and vacuous, from the historically erroneous sanctification of Attila the Hun to the sloppy generalizations and offensive gender stereotypes associated with "Mars and Venus." In the next chapter, we will explore the dimensions of leadership so that the most essential leadership skills, preferences, and practices can help you face your most important challenges.

-4-

The Dimensions of Leadership

The demands of leadership almost invariably exceed the capacity of a single person to meet the needs at hand. Even the most successful and iconic leaders of the past century—Churchill, Roosevelt, Mandela, Thatcher, Gandhi, and King—were not complete leaders. Although Churchill and King may go down in history as two of the 20th century's most successful communicative leaders, their performances as either analytical or relational leaders are undistinguished. Mandela and Gandhi were deeply reflective leaders, seeing their own place in the context of the struggles of millions, but neither showed distinction in systems leadership. In the context of education, many leaders seem less inclined to grasp the architectural vision of leadership that was posited in Chapter 3 and more likely to embrace the faux composite historical models in which the leader is simultaneously the great communicator, analyst, and a master of reflection. From such mythology are born the unrealistic expectations of communities, colleagues, and leaders themselves. Even the best of the lot frequently think of themselves as a failure because of their inability to attend three events simultaneously.

This chapter is not about identifying leadership failures or destroying historical figures. Rather, the focus of this chapter is to explain the dimensions of leadership in a way that allows leaders to capitalize on their strengths and take a complementary approach to their weaknesses. We need not fantasize about Churchill's missing analytical skills or engage in fruitless presumption that Gandhi was a master of systems thinking in order to appreciate their exceptional leadership qualities. Similarly, leaders with prodigious analytical and confrontational talents have made enormous contributions to government, education, and business, even though those leaders lacked abilities in communication and introspection. Great leaders are not mythological composites of every dimension of leadership. Instead they have self-confidence, and without hubris they acknowledge their deficiencies and fill their subordinate ranks not with lackeys but with exceptional leaders who bring complementary strengths to the organization.

The dimensions of leadership in the following paragraphs represent a wide range of leadership characteristics and skills. A good case can be made that these complementary dimensions are particularly important for educational leaders. Although these dimensions can form the basis for thoughtful self-assessment and organizational evaluations of leaders, such assessments must be used with care. A deficiency in one dimension of leadership is not necessarily a prescription for improving that apparent failing, but rather a suggestion that the leadership team should be broadened to include complementary dimensions. Unfortunately, the vast majority of contemporary leadership evaluations fall into one of two extremes, either omitting many of these dimensions or including all of them in a fruitless pursuit of perfection. In one recent study, we found that almost 20 percent of educational leaders had never been evaluated in their current position,

and more than half of the remaining 80 percent received evaluations that were ambiguous, inconsistent, and unrelated to their most important responsibilities (Reeves, 2004c). The dimensions of leadership are neither a checklist of things to accomplish nor a scale of perfection against which leaders measure themselves. Rather, these dimensions describe components of leadership that are necessary in every leadership team, but rarely present in a single leader. Leaders need not, indeed they cannot, *be* every dimension themselves, but they can and must ensure that every leadership dimension is provided by some member of the leadership team.

Visionary Leadership

"The last thing IBM needs right now is a vision." Louis Gerstner (2002, p. 68) famously said this at the beginning of his turnaround at IBM. Gerstner, credited with saving IBM from oblivion, clearly had run out of patience with traditional strategic planning and "visioning" exercises. The leader, faced with a crisis, needed to make some profoundly important decisions about products, markets, and people, and then he had to flawlessly execute those decisions. Gerstner's implication was that the concept of creating a vision was a squishy relic of the last century, when favorable economic conditions allowed leaders to indulge in such frivolities. Gerstner relented, however, and acknowledged the need for a dramatic change in vision for IBM. Without this profound change in direction, the company might have joined others on the technology scrap heap. The first obligations of leadership are articulating a compelling vision and linking clear standards of action that will accomplish the vision. This approach applies to tasks small and large, from respecting the time of colleagues by

starting and ending meetings on time to keeping commitments and meeting goals. Success is not an ephemeral concept, but it is clearly described. Every team member knows every day what the word "success" means and how it has been achieved.

Visionary leaders are not grandiose, as their visions are more likely to be the blueprints of the architect than the uncertain and cloudy visions of the dreamer. Great visionary leaders challenge the status quo with terminology that is clear and vivid. Perhaps half of the readers of this book remember the Berlin Wall, the dividing line between the Communists of the East and the promising democracies of the West. When President Reagan encouraged his Soviet counterpart to "Tear down this wall!" it was a vision that few had conceived since the end of World War II, yet within years it was realized. In earlier generations Thomas Paine and the anonymous authors of *The Federalist Papers* created a vision not as a skeleton, but as a living and breathing democracy, equipped with bones, muscle, sinew, and flesh. Centuries earlier, the authors of The Magna Carta envisioned a world of laws, and both Hammurabi in the ancient East and Hebrew schools in the ancient West believed that a society based upon justice, mercy, and walking humbly with one's god (Micah 6:8) would survive long past those societies whose gods were rife with covetousness, greed, and self-aggrandizement.

By definition, vision contemplates the future, and the future inevitably involves uncertainty, change, and fear. Therefore, visions that are fuzzy and described in a haze of mystic reassurance have a counterproductive effect. "My vision is of infinite possibilities, global expansion, and unlimited horizons," the leader claims. "But what does that mean?" followers inevitably ask. Unfortunately, the foot soldiers who are supposed to be inspired by a vision rarely express their doubts in a manner that reaches senior leadership. As a result, vision

statements, like many traditional strategic planning processes, remain a fiction of the executive suite and have little practical importance outside the confines of the annual offsite retreat, where leaders are safely isolated from organizational realities. Indeed, I would question the excessive formality and awkward phrasing that committees bring to vision statements. The cynicism that abounds in organizations, with few employees trusting their leaders, frequently stems from the gulf between the ordinary details of daily organizational life and the earnest protestations of leaders as seen in vision statements (Kouzes & Posner, 2000, 2003a, 2003b).

The organization need not be this way. Leaders can use vision to build trust rather than break it if they are willing to let their rhetoric give way to reality and allow their vision to become a blueprint rather than public relations baloney. Effective visions help individuals understand that they are part of a larger world and also reassure them of their individual importance to the organization. Equipped with an effective vision, the leader can respond in a consistent and coherent way to these questions:

- Where are we headed as an organization this year?
- Where will we be three to five years from now?
- What parts of our organization will be the same, and what will change?
- Will there still be a place for me in the future?
- How will my work change?
- What will I need to learn in order to be more valuable to the organization in the future?
- Why will I still want to be a part of this organization in the future?

The answers to these questions are personal and are communicated in dozens of moments of truth and in informal contacts between leaders and colleagues throughout the year. Formal annual reports and after-dinner speeches may address these issues in a general way, but vision must be communicated by leaders throughout the organization in personal encounters. Some visions in educational organizations are decidedly scary, particularly for people who may feel that their skills and abilities are not part of the leader's vision.

Consider this statement: "We will be a learning organization, using cutting edge technology to deliver world-class educational opportunities for our students." What does that mean to the literature teacher who associates computers with plagiarism, fragmentary speech patterns, and emotional isolation? What does that mean to the finance clerk and personnel specialists who have seen a growing workload with no increases in staff? While technology will play a role in the vision of most organizations, there is a better way to communicate the impact and meaning of that vision. As an alternative to the formal vision statement, consider this conversation:

> Jean, you've got a great future here. Your integrity and work ethic are terrific, and the way that you collaborate with your colleagues is a real model for others. You've probably noticed that we're using a lot more technology now than when you first came here, and I see us moving in that direction in the future. Technology will never replace human intelligence and creativity, but we've got to use every technology tool we can, including some new ones that neither one of us has learned yet, to serve our stakeholders. With your abilities and advanced technology, I can see you doing great things in the future. I'd like to support you in some professional development to build your technology skills. What do you think about it?

Visionary leadership, in sum, may include the big picture, but it is insufficient for giving meaning and substance to a vision. Commitment depends upon knowing one's personal role in the vision and seeing a clear path to how to get there.

Relational Leadership

When talk turns to human relationships and emotional intelligence in some leadership circles, eye rolling and finger tapping are the most obvious signs of impatience with the soft side of organizational life. There has been a great deal of uninformed blather written and said about these subjects, and some of it is not only wrong but destructive. In education in particular, the presumption that self-esteem is a characteristic to be nurtured and developed in students and adults has morphed into a justification for narcissism, insulating people from honest feedback that is necessary for improved performance. In an important article entitled "Exploding the Self-Esteem Myth," Baumeister, Campbell, Krueger, and Vohs (2004) concluded after a review of multiple studies, "We have found little to indicate that indiscriminately promoting self-esteem in today's children or adults, just for being themselves, offers society any compensatory benefits beyond the seductive pleasure it brings to those engaged in the exercise." These are hard words indeed for educational leaders who have been force-fed a gospel that says high self-esteem is the root of success and low self-esteem is the root of problems ranging from employee disengagement to teenage drug abuse. This conclusion might be welcome news for pathological jerks who have been complaining for years that faculty meetings are not group therapy, administrators are not therapists, and the workplace is not your

family. "The firings will continue," they might add, "until morale improves." Surely there is a middle ground between leadership by Barney the dinosaur and leadership by Attila the Hun. Relational leadership does not depend on false affirmations provided in vain attempts to build the self-esteem of subordinates, but rather on the trust and integrity that are at the foundation of any enduring relationship.

Interestingly, the foremost expert on emotional intelligence, Daniel Goleman, makes the case for relational leadership in strikingly cold and analytical terms. Citing a mountain of research including long-term longitudinal studies of organizational effectiveness, Goleman and colleagues (2002) conclude that relationship skills account for nearly three times as much impact on organizational performance as analytical skills do. Casciaro and Lobo (2005) found that those who lack relationship skills, the "competent jerks" in the words of the researchers, have negative influences on the organization despite their technical prowess, because so few people in the organization can stand to work with them. Kouzes and Posner (2000, 2003a, 2003b) find that in studies of more than 1 million leaders, the trust and credibility that stem from meaningful relationships are essential for leadership success. Researchers differ on how to approach the challenges of emotional intelligence and relational leadership. Some, like Goleman, assert vigorously that specific relationship skills can be taught and learned. Others differ, asserting that someone with good relationship skills can likely be taught technical skills, whereas someone deficient in relationship skills will likely have some difficulty learning the nuances and intuitive practices that are associated with building and maintaining successful relationships. In other words, you can send a jerk to charm school, but at the end of the day, he's still a jerk.

Tolerating jerks and a climate of incivility has a tangible as well as emotional cost. Gardiner Morse (2005) suggests that the costs of uncivil climates, including time wasted avoiding malcontents, worrying about their actions, and, worst of all, looking for other jobs, could exceed $50,000 per employee per year across all industries in the United States. An astonishing amount of turnover, which creates huge costs in training, lowers productivity, and creates poorer service quality, is due to people leaving toxic work environments. What can relational leaders do? You might want to listen to your own colleagues describe the elements of the effective relational leader, but the following list is a good start: listening without interruption or prejudgment, respect for confidentiality, and genuine empathy achieved through deliberate inquiry.

Relational leaders listen to their colleagues *without interrupting or prejudging* their statements. Tape a meeting or phone call with a subordinate and confront the data. How many times did each of you speak? Interrupt? Ask for clarification before coming to a judgment? Leaders frequently ascend to their positions because they are good communicators, or at least it appears that way. They make wonderful presentations to community groups and governing boards. When they talk to colleagues, they do so with conviction and enthusiasm. They are accustomed to hearing applause rather than questions and challenges. They are far more comfortable "communicating" through talking rather than listening. When senior leaders experience decades of positive reinforcement for such one-sided communication, it is little wonder that so few leaders understand the value of listening. Every leader needs a Nathan, the only member of King David's entourage who was willing to publicly confront the king when he was wrong.

Relational leaders respect confidences, never betraying a secret or private conversation. The only exceptions are when the leader has a legal obligation to reveal a confidential conversation, such as when there are allegations of child abuse, employee harassment, or other illegal activities.

Relational leaders practice empathy through deliberate inquiry. They don't say, "I know just how you feel," because, in fact, they do not know how others feel. Recognizing this, relational leaders ask their colleagues directly about what gives them great joy and what causes them heartache. They follow the advice of Marcus Buckingham (2005b) and provide the unique attention, feedback, and support that each colleague needs. Some employees need to be heard in a one to one setting, while others would be nervous and feel put on the spot in such an environment. Some colleagues would appreciate recognition before a group, while others would find the attention embarrassing and threatening to their peer relationships. Some employees appreciate recognition for their daily technical expertise, while others prefer recognition that is rare, unusual, and reserved for exceptional performance. Unskilled relational leaders presume that the rest of the world is a reflection of themselves, and they motivate, reward, and communicate in the way that reflects their own preferences. If they are comfortable with technical jargon, they pour it on their colleagues, presuming that people are impressed rather than bewildered by it. If they find financial rewards motivating, they presume that colleagues should be grateful for a raise or improvement in benefits, despite evidence that their colleagues find personal appreciation more rewarding. If relational leaders organize their lives in bullet points sent through e-mail, they communicate that way, even if they discover that some colleagues prefer rich and

vivid descriptions of expectations rather than bullet points that strike them as brusque and demeaning.

Some leadership literature states that using relational practices is situational: appropriate when things are going well but out of line in times of high anxiety. Some experts argue that high degrees of direction and a commanding presence are required for an organizational turnaround (Goleman, 2000; Hersey, 1985; Hersey & Blanchard, 1977). There is little evidence, however, that chameleons make great leaders or, for that matter, that leaders are capable of transforming their personal preferences in communication and management style as organizational life changes. On the contrary, when the going is particularly tough, budgets are cut, layoffs are imminent, public scrutiny is high, and the pressure seems nearly unbearable, then the skills of the relational leader are particularly important. This is especially true in education, where more than 80 percent of teachers leaving highly challenging schools reported that a higher salary would not have kept them there (Johnson & Duffett, 2003). In organizations of all types, public and private, large and small, for-profit and nonprofit, relationships—particularly with leaders—are one of the single greatest predictors of employee performance, satisfaction, and turnover (Buckingham & Coffman, 1999).

Relational leaders exhibit genuine passion for their mission and the people around them. When does the turnaround leader have time for passion? The direct answer is every single day. Passion, respect, civility, and gentility require not only time but genuine interest. In the midst of the most hectic organizational turnaround, babies will be born, relatives will fall ill, couples will become engaged, and couples will break up. In other words, the emotional lives of colleagues will continue whether or not the organization recognizes that there is life outside of work. The leader with relational intelligence stops—with

surprising alacrity—to divert attention from the organization to the person, to transfer attention from the ensemble to the soloist. While passion does not appear on the balance sheet, it is surely the asset that matters most for leaders and followers alike, and passion is most wisely invested by leaders in human relationships.

Systems Leadership

In my discussion of Leadership Maps later in Chapters 8 and 9, I refer to the dots marking the intersection of performance and leadership decisions as "nodes," a term chosen because of its association with the science of networks. Nodes represent complex connections, and understanding these complex interactions is at the heart of systems thinking. With the addition of a single variable (team member, supplier, creditor, customer, patient, service provider, student, investor, or interest groups), the number of systematic interactions increases exponentially. In fact, we can plot the relationship between the increase in nodes and system complexity as shown in Figure 4.1.

This chart reflects the potential complexity for only seven nodes, but consider the interactions for which most leaders are responsible. You could list a couple dozen and not depart from the confines of the instructional staff of a school. But systems leaders also understand how bus drivers, administrative support staff, cafeteria workers, finance specialists, and a host of other people influence student achievement and core organizational objectives. They know, for example, that bus drivers who understand and apply lessons on student motivation and discipline will deliver students to school on time, safely, and ready to learn. Systems leaders know that an error by a finance clerk who is right 99.5 percent of the time can destroy the morale and effectiveness

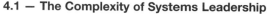

4.1 — The Complexity of Systems Leadership

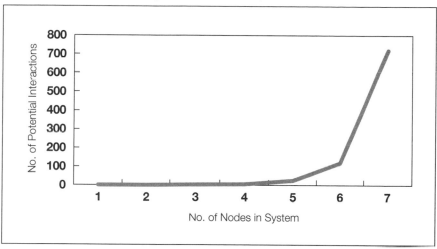

of five classroom teachers in a district with 1,000 employees. What is the level of complexity if the leader considers only 20 nodes and their possible interactions? Consider Figure 4.2. The first column lists the number of nodes, and the second column lists the number of interactions, calculated by the quantity of nodes minus one, and that number is multiplied by each smaller number in the number system down to 1. For example, in a network of three nodes, there are two potential interactions (3 minus 1 = 2, and 2 multiplied by 1 = 2). In a network of four nodes, there are six potential interactions (4 minus 1 = 3, and 3 times 2 times 1 = 6). With just a few more nodes, the complexity is staggering.

Although all interactions are not equally important, there are far more interactions than many leaders acknowledge. Only a handful of school leaders, for example, require central office departments to post and share data in a transparent manner with the same diligence that is required of schools. When they do, the community sees, for

4.2 — Complexity Beyond Seven Nodes

Number of Nodes	Potential Interactions
1	0
2	1
3	2
4	6
5	24
6	120
7	720
8	5,040
9	40,320
10	362,880
11	3,628,800
12	39,916,800
13	479,001,600
14	6,227,020,800
15	87,178,291,200
16	1,307,674,368,000
17	20,922,789,888,000
18	355,687,428,096,000
19	6,402,373,705,728,000
20	121,645,100,408,832,000

example, how energy savings, food service quality, bus safety, and the talent pipeline provided by the human resources department all contribute to the mission of the organization. The leader with systems intelligence must take the time to understand each interaction and its impact on the entire system, and then communicate this complexity in a manner that enables each member of the organization to understand and consistently use these important interconnections. This practice recalls the concept of the leader as architect who is able to make complex connections and master thousands of details in blueprints, yet build a temple that is masterful in conception and design and elegant in the simplicity of its steps, columns, and roof.

Thus systems leadership is not merely about complexity but about an even greater challenge: simplicity. This book is not the forum for a

rant on the irrelevance of many graduate school leadership programs, though Levine and his colleagues (2005) have given us a splendid and long overdue start. Equipped with many advanced degrees and years of bad intellectual habits from writing dissertations, the graduates of educational leadership programs are sometimes skilled at rendering simple subjects complex, substituting jargon for plain speech. It is far more difficult to take something that is complex, such as systems leadership, and make it simple. For example, despite the apparent overwhelming complexity in Figure 4.2, network connections can be surprisingly direct.

This idea is at the heart of the theory of Six Degrees of Separation, which was popularized by a Broadway play but is in fact based on experiments performed by psychology professor Stanley Milgram at Harvard almost 40 years ago. Using humans as a network and selecting what seemed to Milgram to be locations galaxies apart, Kansas and Massachusetts, the researchers sent letters to randomly selected people in Wichita and asked them to forward the letter to someone they knew "on a first name basis" who might know the target person in Cambridge. The participants' packets were equipped with 200 forwarding letters, based on the best estimate of the number of forwarded mailings that would be required to make the journey. The average number of actual times that letters were forwarded: 5.5. Though the Broadway play mischaracterized the research to suggest that everyone in the world is separated by only six people, and Milgram's research has been challenged on many counts, more contemporary reviews suggest that even in the most complex of network interactions (Barabási, 2003), six degrees of separation may be eerily close to the mark.

Before I was acquainted with the Milgram and Barabási research, I had postulated the Rule of Six (Reeves, 2002a) as my best estimate of the maximum number of priorities on which a leader could focus,

noting that those who claimed to have dozens of "priorities" in fact had none. Because every leader has far more than half a dozen people, tasks, projects, and constituencies all clamoring for priority treatment, the task of the systems leader is to know which of those competing factors have the greatest leverage. For example, we will learn later that some elements of teachers' professional practices, such as focusing on nonfiction writing and immediate feedback, have a disproportionate impact on student achievement across a wide variety of subjects.

Therefore, while it is folly for a leader to claim to monitor all effective teaching practices, it is malfeasance to abdicate the responsibility and monitor none of them. The pilot of the small private airplane in which I am now flying has 29 gauges in front of him—I just counted—along with a radar screen, navigation equipment, and a bank of radios. While he may conduct an occasional instrument scan, as pilots are trained to do, he focuses most of his attention on this particularly turbulent flight on his attitude indicator, compass, and altimeter. When we are in the clouds and have no external visual references, we need to know if we are flying right side up, in the right direction, at the altitude where we promised the air traffic controller we would be, and safely away from other aircraft. The pilot also keeps an eye on the gas and oil pressure, and before landing, he also will check the light that confirms our landing gear has been deployed. The other gauges may be interesting, but even in perfect weather they do not command the attention of the pilot as much as those six indicators. An educational leader faces an array of information that is at least as complex as that faced by the pilot, in conditions that can seem even stormier on a good day. Systems leaders know the six indicators to watch, the nodes in their network with the greatest leverage, and the warning signs that will help them avoid catastrophe and eventually travel safely to their destination.

Reflective Leadership

Adrenaline is not enough for the long-term systemic changes that effective leaders must create. New leaders typically bring with them the benefit of the doubt and at least a brief honeymoon, while the constituencies that decided to offer the leader the job all hope that their bet was correct. Emotional intensity, commitment to a vision, goodwill, and sheer intensity can sustain the performance of leaders, athletes, and fugitives for only so long. Every marathon runner knows that while emotions are important, in the long run, it is preparation, monitoring signals, and making midcourse corrections and occasional changes in pace that are essential not only for victory but for simply finishing the race. After a couple of marathons, mountain ascents, and many leadership endeavors, I have learned that during the course of any major initiative, the leadership team must stop, take stock, and impose order on chaos. This deliberate approach includes the celebration of short-term milestones ("One mile down, just 25 to go!"), analysis of disappointments ("If the weather doesn't change within 20 minutes, we will need to abandon the climb"), and an intensive reflection on lessons learned ("The price of hydration is planning for pit stops").

Reflective leadership is rarely among the characteristics associated with the mythological leaders who never recognize obstacles or consider retreat, and always seem to win through sheer guts and determination. Myth yields to history, however, and reflection trumps bravado. Pulitzer Prize–winning historian David McCullough in his brilliant book *1776* (2005) reminds us that, though George Washington was undeniably heroic and brave, his most decisive move during the Revolutionary War involved the safe retreat from New York. The colonists' extraordinary victory in Boston was achieved with hardly a shot being fired, as stealth, positioning, and intelligence led

the British to sail out of Boston Harbor in haste, after having enjoyed domination of the town with naval and land forces that had been superior to those in rebellion. Likewise, Winston Churchill recognized obstacles and responded to them with strategy rather than bravado. While Churchill (1974) is justly famed for his oratorical encouragement to victory and unwillingness to give in to the enemy—"Never, never, never, never"—the historical record shows that one of the decisive moves early in World War II was the 1940 evacuation of Dunkirk. Without this strategic retreat, the D-Day offensive in June of 1944 may never have happened. Both Washington and Churchill, it turns out, had extensive experience with the values of waiting, being silent, retreating, and executing circuitous routes to victory, as historians Joseph Ellis (2004) and Roy Jenkins (2001) have documented in detail. Indeed, even a mythological hero such as Odysseus had years of reflection for every moment of victory.

Reflective leaders take time to think about the lessons learned, record their small wins and setbacks, document conflicts between values and practice, identify the difference between idiosyncratic behavior and long-term pathologies, and notice trends that emerge over time. Kathy Whitmire, former mayor of Houston and president of the U.S. Conference of Mayors, encourages leaders to reflect on their proud moments. "Don't stop after naming the first three or four obvious accomplishments or joys of your life," Whitmire counsels. "Continue until you have named two dozen sources of pride, or more. Then review the list to see what values come up again and again, and you will see a pattern begin to emerge" (Whitmire, 2005). One particularly interesting tool is the 10+ Journal published by Because Time Flies (http://www.journal10.com). The unusual format of this journal lists the same day of the year on 1/10th of a page, so that the reflective leader can observe many years of observations on the same

date. Another leadership journal (Reeves, 2002a) asks the leader to focus on these essential questions:

- What did you learn today?
- Whom did you nurture today?
- What difficult issue did you confront today?
- What is your most important challenge right now?
- What did you do today to make progress on your most important challenge?

Reflection is so important for leaders because of the gulf between the theoretical abstractions of academic leadership development programs and the daily lives of leaders. Indeed, one of the nation's premier leadership training organizations, the Center for Creative Leadership, acknowledges that "people do not develop the capacity for leadership without being in the throes of the challenge of leadership work." Participating in leadership roles and processes is often the very source of the challenge needed for leadership development. Leadership roles and processes are full of novelty, difficulty, conflict, and disappointments. In other words, leadership itself is a development challenge. Leading is, in and of itself, leading by doing (Van Velsor & McCauley, 2004). Noel Tichy, one of the foremost leadership experts who has considered leadership in multiple contexts, including academic, business, nonprofit, and for-profit organizations, encourages leaders to literally write their leadership story. "Stories are a powerful tool for engaging people emotionally and intellectually and for leading them into the future," Tichy says. "Successful leaders must have teachable points of view about ideas, values, energy and edge. It is through stories, however, that they tie them together and teach and energize others to move from the present into a winning future" (Tichy & Cohen, 1997, p. 42).

A leadership journal need not require an exceptional commitment of time nor must it become a maudlin exercise in therapeutic self-revelation. Objective statements, such as those in response to the questions noted above, can seem mundane in isolation, but they are quite revealing over time. Although journaling is, in general, an intensely private activity, the reflective leader knows when personal revelation can have a profound impact. In my own case, some of my toughest leadership decisions have been prompted by a review of journal entries that forced me to recognize that I had attempted the same solution for a particular problem on several occasions, and unsurprisingly, the results did not improve with such a stagnant approach. My reflections forced me to recognize that conditions were not changing, people were not changing, and results were not changing—all because my leadership decisions and actions were not changing. Reflection forced me to admit that I had been as resistant to change as the others whom I had accused of being resistant and insufficiently enthusiastic to my favored initiatives. Reflection, in brief, forces leaders to climb down from the mythological perch, admit our human foibles, and get real.

Collaborative Leadership

At first, the phrase "collaborative leadership" appears to be an oxymoron. Collaboration implies shared decision making and a willingness to concede one's own agenda, while leadership requires asserting a vision, accomplishing a mission, and where necessary and appropriate, exerting authority and making unilateral decisions. President Eisenhower was fond of telling the tale of a meeting in which his staff unanimously supported an idea that Eisenhower opposed. The President said, "The vote is 15 ayes and one nay—

the nays have it." While there surely are times in the lives of most leaders for such single-minded decision making in the face of near-universal opposition, the complexity of life in large and small organizations requires that we recognize some essential truths that mandate a collaborative approach:

- Employees in any organization are volunteers. We can compel their attendance and compliance, but only they can volunteer their hearts and minds.
- Leaders can make decisions with their authority, but they can implement those decisions only through collaboration.
- Leverage for improved organizational performance happens through networks, not individuals. If the only source of inspiration for improvement is the imprecations of the individual leader, then islands of excellence may result and be recognized, but long-term systemwide improvement will continue to be an illusion.

In fact, decision making takes place at three levels in every organization. Level I allows for individual discretion. In schools, teachers enjoy wide discretion in choosing their teaching practices. Despite pervasive claims of micromanagement and teacher-proofing lessons, one need only watch three different classrooms of the same grade level and same subject to note significant differences in practice, interaction, questioning techniques, feedback, and assessment. In fact, to a greater degree than we might think in an era of standards, curriculum content varies widely from one classroom to the next. Level II decisions are made collaboratively: teachers and administrators seek common ground. Level III decisions are made unilaterally by leaders, and they usually are issues involving safety and values. After

all, the decisions to have fire drills, cafeteria hygiene, and gun-free schools are not matters of discretion, nor do they require a great deal of collaboration. When the issue is safety, a "command and control" orientation may be a matter of life and death.

While this three-level decision structure seems logical to most people, surveys of teachers and administrators throughout North America reveal a striking trend. The surveys included more than 2,000 teachers and administrators from more than 60 school systems, including urban, suburban, and rural schools. Two parochial school systems were also represented in this survey. When asked to identify which levels of decision making are most common, the results, as reflected in Figure 4.3, show that the micromanagement stereotype holds sway. The vast majority of respondents believe that the majority of decisions are those at Level III, where the leader unilaterally makes the decisions. "It's their way or the highway," the respondents seemed to say of their leaders.

4.3 — Perceptions of Decision Making

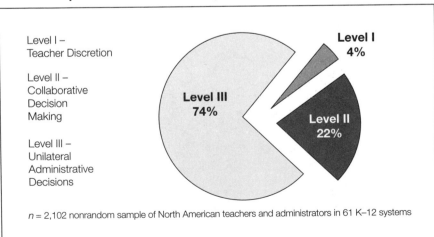

Level I –
Teacher Discretion

Level II –
Collaborative
Decision
Making

Level III –
Unilateral
Administrative
Decisions

Level I
4%

Level III
74%

Level II
22%

n = 2,102 nonrandom sample of North American teachers and administrators in 61 K–12 systems

I then asked the respondents to list those decisions over which they knew teachers exercised discretion based on their own professional experience—the real Level I decisions. Similarly, I asked them to list those actual decisions that were the result of teacher and administrative collaboration. Finally, I asked them to list those decisions that were Level III decisions made unilaterally by administrators, with neither collaboration nor discretion by teachers. The results were surprising in many respects. First, the actual decision-making structure is the opposite of the stereotype, with discretionary decisions by teachers representing the plurality of actual decisions in schools. As Figure 4.4 indicates, 39 percent of actual decisions listed by respondents were those made on a discretionary basis by teachers; 34 percent of the decisions they identified as collaborative, and the lowest percentage, 27 percent, were the Level III top-down administrator decisions.

4.4 — Actual Decision-Making Structure

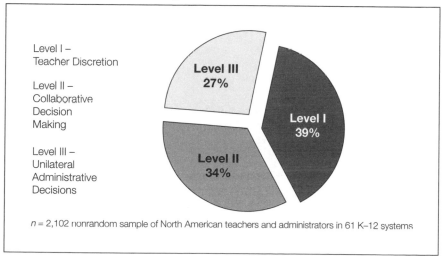

Level I –
Teacher Discretion

Level II –
Collaborative
Decision
Making

Level III –
Unilateral
Administrative
Decisions

Level III
27%

Level I
39%

Level II
34%

n = 2,102 nonrandom sample of North American teachers and administrators in 61 K–12 systems

Surprisingly, the actual data were consistent. The responses from quite diverse groups, including groups of teachers alone (without administrators) and groups of administrators alone (without teachers) all had the same sequence of decision-making frequency and uniformly defied the stereotype.

The point of this research is that just as leadership nostrums that are too simple to be true probably are, our own stereotypes about the leadership environment in which we work every day are also suspect and should be subject to challenge. There are times when each decision-making level is important, but the finding that most decisions in schools are either collaborative or discretionary decisions involving teachers is encouraging. Given the demands for training the next generation of leaders, the development of collaborative teams will be particularly important, as Van Velsor and McCauley (2004) conclude

> As we worked more with the same organizations over time and with multiple leaders in the same unit or organization, we became attuned to the limitations of an exclusive focus on individual development. Individual leaders can no longer accomplish leadership tasks by virtue of their authority or their own leadership capacity. Instead, individuals and groups need to carry out the leadership tasks together in a way that integrates differing perspectives and recognizes areas of interdependence and shared work. For organizations or other collectives to experience sustained leadership over time—to have a sense of direction and alignment, to maintain commitment to the collective work, particularly when dealing with difficult problems that require organizational change—they need more than well-developed individuals. They need well developed connections between individuals and deeper and more meaningful relationships around shared work. They need to form and deepen relationships within communities and across the boundaries between groups and collectives. They need to develop the capacities of collectives for shared sense making and for change. They need to get better at integrating the

learning into a unified sense of purpose and direction, new systems, and coherent shifts in culture—that is, to enact leadership together through the connections between individuals, groups, and organizations. (p. 21)

Analytical Leaders

Just as there is danger in greatly elevating analytical intelligence over every other intelligence, there is also danger in minimizing the importance of raw intellect and problem-solving ability. Leaders must consider the interaction of many complex variables, challenging facile conclusions and simple solutions. Even as technology is broadly disbursed and using computers is no longer just for nerds, the prototypical analytical leader in education is the master of budget details, assessment scores, and statistical data; he is apparently the smartest person in the room and is not afraid to let everyone else know it. Facts end arguments, and opinions fade away against the mountain of evidence, or so the stereotype goes. Analysis and collaboration are, in this stereotype, at opposite ends of the continuum. However, Boston Consulting Group leaders Philip Evans and Bob Wolf (2005), drawing on studies of groups such as computer programmers and automobile engineers, found that even in an intensely analytical environment, collaboration was at the heart of group success. Indeed, the most daunting analytical challenges required, rather than avoided, the greatest levels of collaboration.

The best analytical leaders are not masters of answers but rather persistent questioners. Their questions require the admission of ignorance, not the assertion of knowledge. As incongruous as it may seem, analytical leaders are so aware of the multivariate nature of life, systems, and organizations that they can be the engine that drives

collaboration. Return to the world of the prototypical analytical leaders, automotive engineers:

> Toyota engineers are famously drilled to "ask why five times" to follow a chain of causes and effects back to a problem's root. This is not a vapid cliché about thinking deeply. Quite the contrary, in fact. The precept's merit is precisely in its superficiality. Saying that B causes A is simplistic—all the complexities of multiple interactions boiled down to a single cause and effect. But the chain of thought required to discover that C causes B, and D causes C, quickly takes you into a new domain, probably someone else's. So rather than concoct complex solutions within their own domains, engineers must seek simple ones beyond them. "Doing your why-whys," as the practice is known, is not about depth at all—it's about breadth. (Evans & Wolf, 2005, p. 100)

If we extend this analogy to education, then the analytical leader is the one who will challenge assertions about student demographics being the cause for student achievement. If there are intervening variables, such as teacher quality, and we learn that students who are white and wealthy have a disproportionate quantity of teachers with the greatest experience and deepest subject matter expertise, then the analytical leaders will speak the truth. Similarly, analytical leaders inquire as to how the educational system treats males and females, students with English as a primary language and students who are learning English, students who are white and students who are brown and black. Analytical leaders speak the uncomfortable truths: Poor students do not exhibit low academic achievement because they are poor but because of the way that we treat poor children. Female students do not lag in science and math because they are female but because of the way that we treat female students. What commentators call an "ethnic gap" is, in fact, a teaching gap, a curriculum gap, and an expectations gap. Just as a computer programmer alone cannot

fix a bug, and an automotive engineer cannot independently recall a dangerous design flaw, so, too the analytical leader will require extraordinary collaboration skills to apply and distribute the lessons that inquiry and analysis can provide.

Communicative Leadership

Jim Collins (2001) was surprised to find that the "Great Communicator" theory of leadership was not supported by the evidence in most cases. Although some effective leaders are especially effective in oral communication, the majority of the most effective leaders in Collins's study were neither glib nor articulate. Their other leadership skills more than made up for this deficit. Of equal importance, however, is the comparison group of ineffective leaders that Collins studied which included many leaders who were distinguished more by their ability to articulate their ideas than by their ability to put them into action for the benefit of stakeholders. Nevertheless, communication is a skill that every complex organization demands of its leadership team. Although traditional written and oral communication skills are part of the repertoire of an effective leader, voice mail, Web casts, and e-mail are essential to allow the leader to create personal communication for a wide audience. Leaders underestimate the power of personalized communication and overestimate the effectiveness of hierarchical communication. During the course of every major change initiative I have witnessed the words "I wish I knew what was going on" are at the root of failures in translating leadership intent into action. At the start of each week, I give my staff a "Monday minute" that provides kudos, condolences, announcements, and encouragement. The wise limitations of our voice mail system

prevent me from rhetorical excess, as a kind voice will remind me after 180 seconds that I have exceeded the permissible limit for a message. But at least once a week, all my colleagues know, on the same day at the same time, what is happening at the Center for Performance Assessment. I also answer (without exaggeration) close to 500 e-mails every week. Some e-mails are mundane, organizational requirements of daily life, but some e-mails are from former students in China and Africa, or from people who found my e-mail address through books, articles, or colleagues, and feel the need to reach out and ask a question. Many e-mails are from graduate students, teachers, school leaders, and board members, asking specific questions about issues that represent their immediate needs. I do my best to answer each message, hoping that, as happened recently in the Dallas–Fort Worth airport, someone will stop me within hearing distance of my spouse and say, "I can't believe that you answered my e-mail. Thanks!" as we rush off to our respective flights.

There is a distinctly nontechnological side to effective communication. I still write personal thank-you notes to every client and every employee, and I encourage every leader to do the same. Disregard your apprehension about your penmanship or concerns that in the Internet era your personally signed notes will be regarded as old-fashioned. The power of gratitude, recognition, and appreciation is extraordinary. What letters and cards do you keep? My stash of letters and cards includes, amazingly, not only those I have received from friends, loved ones, and revered leaders, but also letters I have written and that were returned to me years later by parents and teachers. In the 21st century, you can communicate with millions of people at once, but the power of personal communication, voice to voice, pen to paper, heart to heart, is undiminished by technology. Communicative leaders are simultaneously high tech and high touch,

maximizing their reach through technology, as they optimize their effectiveness with the encouragement, appreciation, and nurturing that only a personal handshake, hug, note, or the spoken word can provide.

Thus far we have explored an extraordinary range of leadership research, strategies, and typologies. Our goal, however, is not complexity and bewilderment, but action and implementation. In the next chapter we will learn how to take school leadership from planning to performance.

– 5 –

What Matters Most
From Planning to Performance

The Myths of Planning

There is a new religion spreading like wildfire in school systems and state departments of education. The religion is "Documentarianism" and, with missionary zeal, its adherents believe that with just the right school improvement plan, or the right format, or with all the boxes completed in all the right places, the deity to whom they pray will grant educational miracles. Perhaps because it is easier to monitor two-dimensional planning documents than it is to review the implementation of initiatives in the complex, real world of schools, regulatory authorities at all levels appear to be consumed with documentary compliance. As a personal matter, I believe in tolerance and religious freedom, right up to the point that one person's religion tramples on the freedom of another. If the followers of Documentarianism were merely proponents of a quirky belief who wore funny hats and danced around campfires, then I could tolerate their belief systems and expect them to tolerate mine. But Documentarianism is not merely an innocuous personal belief system.

This devotion to plans and procedures not only destroys forests with its endless printed documents but, as the evidence will show, it also harms student achievement. That's the bad news.

The good news is that the same research studies that debunk Documentarianism also provide some insights into leadership practices that are strongly associated with improvements in student achievement and educational equity. Moreover, although the statistical association between student demographic characteristics and student achievement remains strong, educational leaders need not remain helpless victims in the fight for educational equity and improvement in student achievement. Several new research studies, including one published here for the first time, provide clear evidence that when it comes to achievement and equity, planning and processes are less important than implementation, execution, and monitoring.

The Virtues of "Ugly" Plans

Before considering the leadership factors that are most associated with improved achievement and equity, let us consider the relative merits of "pretty" versus "ugly" planning documents. Imagine two principals, both of whom approach their superintendent with planning documents a couple of months after the beginning of the school year. The first principal is equipped with a plan that meets every format requirement, with every "i" dotted and every "t" crossed, every box filled in, and every blank completed. The format of this pretty plan is as perfect as the day it was downloaded from the Internet or copied from a colleague, whose format had received the blessing of the high priests of Documentarianism. Neatly packaged in plastic pocket protectors, the plan is untouched by human hands and

uninformed by the changing reality of the students and faculty in the school. By any description, it is pretty. The second principal approaches the superintendent with a decidedly ugly plan. The pages are dog-eared and smudged, with some elements crossed out and others added in the margins. With a note of apology, the leader equipped with the ugly plan explains:

> I'm sorry this is a bit of a mess, but since my leadership team wrote this plan a few months ago, we have had changes in student population, changes in our faculty, and new student achievement data. We've had to modify some goals and add others. We have changed our schedule to meet some serious student needs, and we have had to add some intermediate objectives so that we can continuously monitor our progress and be aware of continuing changes during the school year. In fact, I can't promise you that this document won't change again in the months to come as we attempt to monitor our progress and make midcourse corrections.

With whom should the superintendent be more pleased? The research in this chapter suggests that when it comes to planning documents, ugly beats pretty, provided that ugly is not a reflection of wanton messiness, but rather thoughtful consideration of the continuous updates and modifications that make planning documents correspond to reality. Most importantly, ugly surpasses pretty when it comes to the most important variable of all: student achievement. Figure 5.1 reflects a composite of 25 student achievement variables (see Appendix A for a complete list) in the Planning, Implementation, and Monitoring (PIM) study. More details and findings about this study will be presented later in this chapter. However, one particular finding should be at the forefront of our consideration because it flies in the face of the conventional wisdom that supports an emphasis on document format, reviews, and compliance. As shown in Figure 5.1,

the vertical axis represents the percentage of students who scored proficient or higher on a variety of assessments, from elementary to high school, including language arts, math, science, and social studies. The large sample size includes more than 280,000 students and almost 300 schools. Each of the school improvement plans was scored on 17 separate indicators, one of which was adherence to format requirements. The stunning finding is that the "prettiness" of the plan—conformity to format requirements—is inversely (or should we say perversely?) related to student achievement.

The Prichard Committee (2005) concurred with the PIM study's finding that format quality is not nearly as helpful as the Documentarians would have you believe. In their review of successful high-poverty schools in Kentucky, researchers found that these schools achieved great success through a common set of professional and leadership practices, but low scores on conforming with planning format requirements. Other studies that we

5.1 — Inverse Relationship Between Plan Format and Student Achievement

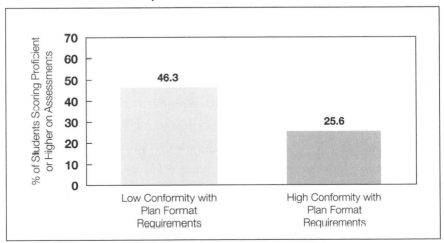

will explore later in this chapter find significant associations between student achievement and monitoring, implementation, and execution of school reform initiatives, but they are silent on the virtues of written plans. Every policymaker and administrator must ponder these questions:

- How much of our time, energy, and resources have been devoted to compliance with planning format requirements rather than direct observation of monitoring, implementation, and execution?
- If our goal is student achievement, why do we invest so much effort in compliance requirements that are not only unhelpful to this objective but counterproductive?

While planning documents may be requirements mandated by federal, state, and local authorities, they are insufficient to improve student achievement and educational equity. As the evidence will show, it's all about monitoring, implementation, and execution.

The PIM Study

PIM is an acronym for Planning, Implementation, and Monitoring. The data for this study were provided by Nevada's Clark County School District, one of the largest school systems in the United States. With over 280,000 students, Clark County is also one of the fastest-growing school districts and changes every year in size and complexity. Now a "majority-minority" district, with a majority of its students who are members of ethnic minorities, Clark County includes schools that have some of the nation's highest-performing

students and schools in challenging urban settings that contain profoundly disadvantaged students. Despite this complexity, the district leaders have provided a coherent and consistent planning and accountability system. This structure provides an extraordinary opportunity for educators and school leaders throughout the world to ask this question: When the external variables—governance, budget, union agreements, policies, and planning requirements—are constant, then which variables are most related to improvements in student achievement and educational equity? This question is at the heart of the PIM study.

Data Sources

The school system provided data on student achievement, school demographics, and copies of school plans. The Center for Performance Assessment supplied data on the analysis of school plans based on a scoring rubric created by the center. In creating this rubric, we relied on a combination of the requirements from the state of Nevada and its school district leadership, as well as a substantial research foundation regarding planning, implementation, monitoring, and student results. Although every school in the district was following the same format, district policies, and state mandates, we found significant differences among schools with regard to format, content and, most importantly, implementation and monitoring of school plans.

Reliability

The scoring rubric (see Appendix A) was subjected to an internal assessment of inter-rater reliability, with a double-blind check for consistency. When separate evaluators assessed more than 100 plans

using the same rubric and without knowledge of the scores of other evaluators, consistent results were achieved more than 80 percent of the time. Initially, some elements of the building plan scoring rubric exhibited poor reliability, with consistency scores as low as 36 percent. In these instances, the rubrics were revised and subsequent tests for consistency resulted in inter-rater reliability percentages ranging from 80 to 100 percent. Then all building plans were rescored with the revised evaluation instrument. By the conclusion of the study, every element of the building plan scoring rubric had consistency of greater than 80 percent.

Validity

The contents of the planning documents are largely governed by state and federal policy. The implicit assumption in creating these regulatory requirements and in planning research at large is that the content and format of the plan are related to what it purports to achieve. A "valid" plan that claims to improve achievement and equity would include actions that are, in fact, related to increases in achievement and equity. As this study shows, sometimes that it is true, and sometimes it is not. Although the study reveals that some elements of building plans are strongly related to student achievement, it is also clear that some elements of building plans are related neither to achievement nor to equity.

Correlations Analysis

There are undeniable limitations in any analyses that rely upon associations (correlations) between variables. Correlation is not causation. Some associated things are causal, such as thunderclouds and rain. Other things may be associated but not logically linked from

cause to effect. For example, just because cold weather in New England precedes the taciturn mood of Bostonians in January, this does not mean that the former causes the latter. Additionally, there are almost always multiple causes and multiple effects in the study of any human, organizational, or public policy phenomenon. In other words, life is multivariate. To illustrate this principle with an important educational example, there is a widely observed correlation between high poverty and low achievement, and a facile analysis would conclude that the former is the exclusive cause of the latter. However, there is an almost equally strong correlation between high poverty and a high proportion of teachers who lack the knowledge and skills to be effective in the classroom (Prince, 2002).

Another limitation of correlation analysis is that there are always outliers—those cases that do not conform to the general association implied by the correlation. For example, while there is a strong association between effective teaching and a teacher's strong content knowledge, virtually every reader can recall the subject matter expert who failed as a teacher, as well as the gifted educator who was less than expert in a subject. Similarly, there are 95-year-olds who smoke like a chimney and enjoy good health, but few physicians would use the exception to dispute the correlation between tobacco use and poor health. In many cases, however, outliers can be profoundly informative.

Although I readily acknowledge the shortcomings of correlation analysis, we apply it in the present study because of two very significant advantages. First, correlation studies often precede determination of causation. During the 1950s and 1960s, the American Tobacco Institute claimed that the correlation between cigarette smoking and cancer was "only a correlation" and therefore not important enough to change public policy. In the context of

education, early studies of the relationship between nonfiction writing and improved scores in math, science, and social studies were dismissed by some as "only a correlation." Causation can be established only by random assignment of subjects to control and experimental groups, or so the claim goes. But no one has ever been randomly assigned to smoke cigarettes as part of an experiment, and it would represent a breach of professional ethics for a teacher or researcher to randomly give some students fewer opportunities to develop literacy skills in a science class in order to conform to one researcher's model of causation. In fact, when the same correlation appears in multiple circumstances, the inference from correlation to causation can begin.

Second, and most importantly for this study, correlation analysis can suggest insights that are useful to leaders, teachers, and researchers. Even without definitive causation, the strong and consistent correlation between student writing and student success in a variety of areas has been responsible for giving teachers and school leaders the insights necessary to make profound and meaningful changes in classroom assessment techniques. Those changes have frequently been associated with strong gains in student achievement, even as the research remains imperfect. In the PIM study, there are correlations between specific elements of building plans and student achievement that can give school leaders insight into how to focus their efforts as they revise and improve their school plans. They need not wait for perfect research or randomized trials, as no principal will ever be randomly assigned to engage in poor planning and implementation practices. Indeed, we can use what we know now: improving the quality of planning, monitoring, and implementation is strongly associated with improvements in student achievement.

Research Context

This research did not occur in a vacuum. In particular, two recent research studies offer striking confirmation of the PIM research. The Stanford University Center for Educational Policy (Oberman & Symonds, 2005) makes clear that even when plans are governed by state policy, frequent monitoring is a particularly important variable influencing student achievement and equity. As Figure 5.2 shows, frequent monitoring of data is associated with a greater likelihood of closing the equity gap.

In a meta-analysis of educational leadership studies, Tim Waters, Robert J. Marzano, and Brian McNulty (2005) identified 21 leadership characteristics associated with student achievement, only three of which were associated with immediate and sustained change. These characteristics were ideals and beliefs (comparable

5.2 — The Impact of Frequent Monitoring on Achievement and Equity

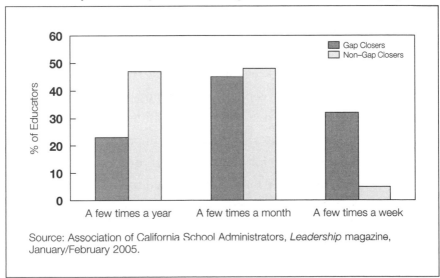

Source: Association of California School Administrators, *Leadership* magazine, January/February 2005.

to the Inquiry variable in the PIM study), monitoring and evaluation (comparable to the variables found in the PIM study and the Stanford study), and the application of research-based strategies (also identical to a central PIM finding). The meta-analysis therefore provides abundant and independent confirmation of the PIM finding, and it also strongly suggests that of all of the behaviors leaders are called upon to master, only a relative few have great influence.

My approaches to this research, including my analysis of the relationships among student achievement, leadership decisions, planning documents, monitoring, implementation, and the professional practices of educators, were significantly influenced by the work of DuFour, Schmoker, and others (DuFour, Eaker, & DuFour, 2005; Fullan, 2005; Schmoker, 2001; Waters, Marzano, & McNulty, 2005; White, 2005a, 2005b). My previous work on the impact of teaching and leadership (Reeves, 2002c, 2004a, 2004b), along with numerous client case studies as cited in Focus on Achievement and other resources found on the Web site of the Center for Performance Assessment (www.MakingStandardsWork.com), have also informed this study.

Limitations of the Study

Every research project has limitations, and this one is not exempt from many sources of human error. Although every precaution has been taken by the test vendors and district office to ensure the accuracy of data, we know that there are potential errors in scoring individual student tests and reporting those results. Moreover, even when data are accurately collected and analyzed, there will be cases when the results of standardized tests do not accurately reflect the achievement of students. This is particularly true for students with

developmental disabilities and students with limited English proficiency. These potential errors will affect the dependent variables—the
"effect data"—in this study. Although we have taken pains to evaluate
and improve our coding procedures for evaluating school plans, we
worked only with words, not people. Neither principals nor teachers
had the opportunity to explain their plans or elaborate upon the
written words in their documents. Therefore, even when our coding
is perfectly accurate, we will undoubtedly miss some important
insights, explanations, and elaborations that a more extensive study
(and one that might have taken years to produce) would have provided. We acknowledge these potential limitations, while noting
that these are precisely the conditions under which most state and
district document reviews take place. Nevertheless, we believe that
the results of the study provide valuable and time-saving insights for
administrators and teachers. The PIM study is certainly not the last
word on the relationship of school plans and student achievement,
but it is fair to say that this study, even with its limitations, provides
useful assistance to leaders at all levels. Acknowledgment of limitations, therefore, does not vitiate the value of the study but rather
allows the reader to conduct a mental risk/reward analysis. Openly
acknowledging the risks of error is clearly outweighed by the rewards
of saving time, streamlining planning, and improving implementation
and monitoring of school plans.

Student Achievement and Demographic Characteristics

In education, studies of schools with high poverty rates, high minority
populations, high second-language learners, and high achievement

levels have led to some important insights about specific leadership and teaching practices that mitigate the influence of demographic characteristics (Reeves, 2004b). However, these examples do not diminish the importance of student nutrition, health care, housing, and other factors directly associated with student learning (Rothstein, Rothstein, & Lauber, 2003). This is not an either/or controversy. It is a superficial and inaccurate conclusion to claim "even the best schools can't close the race achievement gap" (Rothstein, 2004a, 2004b). In fact, there are schools and districts where the statistical relationship between student achievement and poverty is close to zero. It is equally superficial and inaccurate, however, to claim that because some schools and districts have been successful in mitigating the influence of poverty, school leaders and society in general should neglect factors associated with poverty, race, and class.

Although the magnitude of the relationship between free or reduced-price lunches varies from one subject and from one grade to another, the districtwide data clearly indicate that higher levels of poverty are associated with lower levels of student achievement. Similar correlations are evident between high percentages of students who have been identified as English language learners and low percentages of students who score proficient or higher on achievement tests. To a substantially lesser degree, there is some association between schools with higher percentages of special education students and low percentages of students who score proficient or higher on achievement tests. When all district assessments are taken into account (the PIM study considered 25 assessments of student learning, ranging from early elementary to high school, including language arts, science, social studies, and mathe-

matics), the impact of student characteristics on achievement is as follows:

Poverty (Free/Reduced Lunch): $R^{2*} = .53$
English Language Learners: $R^2 = .53$
Individualized Education Plan: $R^2 = .13$

It must be noted that as a general rule, using an average of regression coefficients is not as accurate for summarizing data, as there are many available multivariate approaches such as structural equation modeling, factor analyses, multivariate analysis of variance, and other approaches that may help to identify the relative impact of different variables on student achievement. For the purposes of this book, however, the data presented thus far make it clear that there is an association between student characteristics and student achievement. Thus the remaining question for school leaders is this: Given that we cannot change student characteristics before children walk into school, what can we do once they are entrusted to our care?

Two key conclusions emerge from the PIM data. First, while the relationship between demographic factors and the percentage of students who score proficient or higher is consistently negative for the entire district, the relationship between demographic factors and the gains from 2003 to 2004 in schools is negligible.

$*R^2$ is an indication of the relationship between two variables. A value of 1.0 would yield a perfect relationship. For example, a gain in one unit of student wealth is related to a gain of one unit of student achievement. A relationship of zero indicates that there is no relationship between the two variables. R^2 is the square of Pearson's r. For a more detailed explanation of applications and cautions concerning correlation and regression coefficients, see *The Daily Disciplines of Leadership* (Reeves, 2002a, pp. 63–67).

Second, researchers are frequently so intent on looking for relationships that we fail to recognize the importance of the *absence* of a relationship. The following statistics may be the most important inference from the data thus far. When the issue is the impact of student characteristics on *gains* in student performance, the following relationships are telling:

Poverty (Free/Reduced Lunch): $R^{2*} = .00$
English Language Learners: $R^2 = .00$
Individualized Education Plan: $R^2 = .01$

While it is true that student characteristics influence student proficiency, it is absolutely not true that student characteristics influence the opportunity for school leaders and educators to influence *gains* in student achievement.

Inquiry: How Analysis of Causes Influences Performance

"What causes student achievement?" Ask your colleagues this question, and the conversation will take one of two decidedly different turns. Either the responses will be about adults in the school or about the children. When the responses are about the adults, the purported causes of student achievement will include such factors as curriculum, feedback, assessment, expectations, multidisciplinary lessons, engaging lessons, multiple opportunities for success, and writing and reading across the curriculum. When the responses are about the students, the purported causes of student achievement include poverty level of students, ethnicity of students, home language of students, and parent monitoring of schoolwork.

Here is the curious finding of the research: If you believe that adults make a difference in student achievement, you are right. If you believe that adults are helpless bystanders while demographic characteristics work their inexorable will on the academic lives of students, you are right. Both of these statements become self-fulfilling prophesies. Consider Figure 5.3. The vertical axis represents the percentage of students scoring proficient or higher on the same 25 assessments discussed previously, including a range of grade levels and subjects. The "inquiry" score represents the degree to which the leadership team of the school expressed a belief that the causes of student achievement were associated with adult or student variables. A high inquiry score indicated that the leadership team took personal responsibility for student achievement, associating the causes of achievement with adult variables. A low inquiry score indicated that the leadership team theorized that student achievement was principally caused by student demographic characteristics. In the words of one school improvement plan (not in the PIM study), "student achievement declined because of a decrease in the percentage of Caucasian students." Even the word "diversity," which most schools intend to be a source of pride, has become a code word for victimhood of adults, as in "We have a lot of diversity in our student population, so you have to understand. . . ." As Figure 5.3 illustrates, such self-fulfilling prophesies tend to be correct.

Rosenthal and Jacobson (1968) created the classic studies on the influence of expectations on student achievement. Their hypothesized "Pygmalion Effect," named after the George Bernard Shaw play *Pygmalion*, suggested that even when two groups of students had similar characteristics, the high expectations of a teacher caused students to rise to those expectations. Conversely, the low expectations of a teacher resulted in students falling to

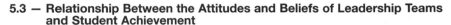

5.3 — Relationship Between the Attitudes and Beliefs of Leadership Teams and Student Achievement

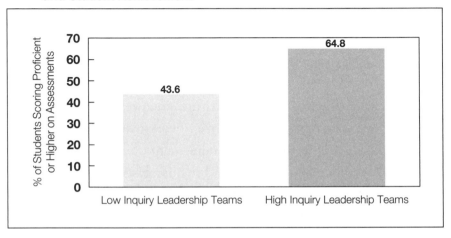

those lowered expectations. The PIM research suggests a Pygmalion Effect for adults. A high inquiry score indicates that when adults expect that teachers and leaders are associated with student achievement, then the adults and students rise to those expectations. A low inquiry score suggests the converse.

One might reasonably ask, "If the job of educational leadership is not about student achievement, what in the world is it about?" Universities, governmental entities, and grant-providing organizations might inquire, "If researchers in educational leadership are not investigating the relationship of leadership activities to student achievement, what in the world are they doing?" The methodology is different, but readers should note that when meta-analytic techniques (Waters et al., 2003, 2005), system-level analysis (Oberman & Symonds, 2005), and a large-scale study considering a direct analysis of student achievement (the PIM study) come to strikingly similar conclusions, then we are far beyond the speculation, personal

narratives, and war stories that dominate too much of the field of educational research.

Implementation and Monitoring

Once the leadership team and faculty are empowered with a sense of efficacy and the conviction that their work matters, they can proceed confidently to the heart of implementation and monitoring. They are beyond document drills and the paralysis of analysis, and they can use data to inform their daily work as educators and leaders. Figure 5.2 compares the data-monitoring practices of the two groups of teachers, those who successfully close the achievement gap and those who don't.

Characteristics of effective monitoring include not only frequency but also the specification of the levels of implementation. One of the more destructive and costly myths in contemporary educational circles is the "Legend of the Silver Bullet." This is the misplaced belief that the adoption of just the right program, brand name, or method (all claimed as proprietary by someone) will lead to better student achievement. Curiously, they all claim to be supported by scientifically based research, even though subsequent investigations reveal ambiguity. The "Foolproof Reading System" worked in some schools, but did not in others. The "Can't-Miss Math Program" succeeded one month and fell flat the next. The source of such inconsistencies is hardly a mystery, as the cause of success in improving student achievement is not the brand name of the product but the degree of implementation by the teacher. The latest 21st-century curriculum with poor implementation doesn't stand a chance, while the 19th-century classic, *McGuffey's Reader*, will succeed in the hands of a talented and thoughtful teacher,

supported by a leader with time, high expectations, professional development, and plentiful collaboration. Teaching and leadership, not brand names, are the salient variables in this equation.

Professional development is certainly important for success, but leaders and teachers must be skeptical consumers. Guskey (2000a) reminds us that the goal of professional development is neither entertainment nor popularity but a direct impact on professional practice and, ultimately, improvements in student achievement. Professional development must be based on research-based strategies. The research suggests that when professional development efforts are focused on a few key elements, such as improving classroom feedback, assessment practices, and cross-disciplinary nonfiction writing, the yield in student achievement is significantly greater than when professional developers yield to the "flavor of the month" approach in which fads replace effectiveness.

– 6 –

Transforming Research into Action

Why do I do it? Why do I travel more than a quarter million miles a year? Why do I sleep in motel rooms with bullet holes in the door? Why do I spend more time traveling from Indianapolis to Boston, normally a trip of about an hour and a half, than I would traveling from Boston to Paris? Why do I miss the choral performances of my own 6th grader so that I can read the portfolio of another 6th grader thousands of miles away? There is only one answer, and one that I hope my children will some day appreciate. Those 6th grade students are making history. Almost a decade ago, I documented the success of the "90 90 90" schools (Reeves, 2004b). These were schools in which 90 percent of the students were eligible for free or reduced-price lunches, 90 percent were members of ethnic minorities, and 90 percent met or exceeded state academic standards. Now we are seeing "100 100 100" schools in which 100 percent of students are eligible for free or reduced-price lunches, 100 percent are members of ethnic minorities, and 100 percent score proficient or higher not only in state reading tests but also in assessments of math, science, and social studies. Abstract research and theory would not sustain me in

the travails of travel in the 21st century, but the 100 100 100 schools will give me energy that people half my age would envy. This chapter is about what works, and I hope that it will invigorate every reader as much as it does me.

Is It Working?

Let us begin with the raw data. Norfolk Public Schools in Virginia has the following demographic characteristics:

- 80 percent of students receive free or reduced-priced lunch
- 68 percent minority student enrollment
- 40+ languages

Between 1998 and 2005 not a single child in the school system, to the best of my knowledge, has changed his or her ethnic identity. Not a single child has won the lottery. Few if any children have adopted different languages at home. In other words, this story is not about changes in children or their families, nor is it a story about changes in demographic characteristics. This is a story about changes in teaching, leadership, and learning. While demographic characteristics remained the same, student achievement rose dramatically. Again, let the data speak.

In 1998, only 11 percent of the elementary schools in Norfolk contained more than 50 percent of students who scored proficient or higher on the state's English/Language Arts assessments. In 2004, 84 percent of the elementary schools achieved that distinction, and in 2005, 100 percent of the elementary schools in the district were fully accredited. They not only had 50 percent of students meeting or

exceeding state standards in English/Language Arts, but these students also met state requirements in math, science, writing, and social studies. In 1998, none of the middle schools in this district had more than 50 percent of students meeting state English/Language Arts requirements, and six years later all the middle schools met this requirement. In addition, the district more than tripled the number of middle school students taking advanced math courses in middle school. In 1998, only one out of six high schools had more than 80 percent of students passing state English graduation requirements, and six years later every high school in the system achieved this distinction. Moreover, some high schools had more than 90 percent of students passing external exams in chemistry and biology (Simpson, 2003), while the dropout rate remained an astonishingly low 0.5 percent for the district— one of the lowest high school dropout rates of any urban system in the nation. The students didn't change. They were still ethnically, linguistically, and economically diverse. But something profound did change—the commitment of the leaders and teachers in this district to make a difference in the lives of students.

The Norfolk example is not unique. Wayne Township, a high-poverty and high-minority school system in Indianapolis, Indiana, has also made remarkable gains in the past six years. Their highest poverty schools are scoring record gains in student achievement, even as the student population reaches record percentages in poverty and second-language students. The statistical relationship between student poverty and student achievement in this district is .01 percent—meaning that, unlike most national statistics, it is impossible to predict the achievement of students based on the poverty level of their schools. On the contrary, one of the most consistently high-performing schools in Wayne Township is a school with the highest concentration of students eligible for free or reduced-price lunch. These

schools and school systems have been transformed in the past half-decade by remarkable leadership at all levels. Schools throughout the world—in California and Cairo, Mississippi and Missouri, New York and New Mexico—are applying the same techniques. This is not the story of a singularity—a great teacher, a great principal, or a great superintendent. This is the story of distributed leadership (Elmore, 2000; Fuhrman & Elmore, 2004) and architectural leadership (Reeves, 2002a). Whether you serve a public, private, or charter school, these strategies can work for you.

What are the trends in schools with the greatest gains in achievement and equity? First, they embrace holistic accountability (Reeves, 2002c). The Leadership for Learning Framework introduced in the first chapter suggested that accountability as a mere litany of test scores is inherently insufficient. Great accountability systems include causes and effects, and holistic accountability precisely provides such a system. Wayne Township received the Magna Award from the American School Boards Association in recognition for their accountability system, and Norfolk has been a finalist three times for the Broad Prize for the finest urban education system in the nation, and they finally won the award in 2005. Accountability is at the heart of this recognition, but in every instance of success, accountability is more than a list of scores. Rather, accountability includes the actions of adults, not merely the scores of students.

Second, these schools included consistent nonfiction writing assessments in every subject. The impact of nonfiction writing on student achievement is hardly a new research finding (Reeves, 2001b, 2002a, 2004e; Calkins, 1994; Darling-Hammond, 1997b). Nevertheless, because writing and evaluating writing are such time-consuming and demanding activities, many schools resist the expansion of writing to academic disciplines outside of language arts.

However, the evidence is clear—when students engage in more nonfiction writing that includes editing, collaborative scoring, constructive teacher feedback, and rewriting, student achievement improves. The impact of nonfiction writing on student achievement is manifested not only in language arts but also in math, science, and social studies. Nonfiction writing is also effective in improving performance on writing tests and extended response items, as well as on multiple-choice tests. When students write, they are engaged in thinking, reasoning, and analysis. Consider what Mel Levine (2002) says about writing:

> I think that the very fact that writing is so complex justifies its leading role in a curriculum. By writing, a kid learns how to mesh multiple brain functions, and ultimately that's something you need to do well whatever you do to earn a living. In a sense, the act of writing helps build and maintain the brain pathways that connect diverse functions, such as language memory, and motor control. In other words, writing is a great way for a kid to practice getting his act together.
>
> Writing also serves as a platform for systematic thinking and a means of problem solving, two more abilities needed in any career. (pp. 7–8)

Perhaps best-selling author Stephen King (2002) said it best when he posited that writing is "thinking through the end of a pen." The relationship of writing and thinking explains why I receive letters from art teachers, band leaders, and athletic coaches, all of whom testify to the power of writing as a device to improve student performance. Their testimonials are powerful. One said, "I wasn't very happy with you a few years ago when my principal required that we spend time during our practices on writing. But we just won a state competition, and I think that part of our success is that my students think about—that is, they write about—how they play and what they are doing.

When they think better, they play better." In brief, successful schools do not use writing as a diversion from math, science, music, or football. Rather, they proceed with the conviction that if these subjects are worthy of thinking, then they are worthy of writing.

Some important clarifications are necessary here. The most effective writing is nonfiction—description, analysis, and persuasion with evidence. Journals, although much in vogue, are not adequate if journaling is an academic code for "nobody will look at the work, so the rules don't apply." The most effective writing is a process in which teacher feedback is respected and students use that feedback to rewrite. Teacher evaluations are not a final word on student writing but an encouragement to higher levels of performance. The emphasis on nonfiction writing is not accidental. In one review I conducted of elementary school writing portfolios, I found a 90:1 ratio of fiction to nonfiction writing. This conforms to my personal experience volunteering as a writing teacher every week. Left to their own preferences, students will write poetry (preferring in many cases the most elementary of forms such as the acrostic), fiction, and personal narratives. These students receive high praise for their work, earning honor roll grades in writing. As they enter secondary school, the students are challenged to describe, analyze, compare, contrast, and persuade. Confronted with unfamiliar writing genres, the students who thought of themselves as excellent writers are frozen with fear, facing unfamiliar requirements. The journey from "excellent writer" to writer's block is measured in moments, not because the students lack the ability to write, but because they were emotionally and psychologically blindsided with the unexpected requirement to engage in nonfiction writing.

Part of the aversion of some educators to nonfiction writing and the preference for fiction is the idea that nonfiction writing is boring

and fiction is entertaining and engaging. Tell that to the kindergartner who is watching a butterfly emerge from a cocoon or to the 3rd grade student who watches with amazement as a tadpole becomes a frog. Tell that to the middle school student who feels passionately about issues ranging from school uniforms to world peace to animal rights. These students ache to engage in rich, descriptive, persuasive, and analytical writing. Writing with the rigor, thinking, and analysis that is required in nonfiction writing is engaging, exciting, and fun.

The third characteristic of schools that have achieved significant success is the use of frequent common assessments. This is, without a doubt, the least popular recommendation to make in any school. It is nearly an article of faith that students are overtested and that if teachers devote too much time to testing, then teachers will not have time to teach.

Both of these widely accepted contentions deserve a second look. With regard to the assertion that schools are overtested, we can respond in the affirmative only if the terms are correctly defined. Schools are, indeed, overtested if we define tests as summative, evaluative, provided at the end of the year, and accompanied by feedback that is woefully late and inherently useless. By such a definition, we are overtested. But schools are underassessed. Assessments, in contrast to tests, are formative, provided during the year, designed to improve teaching and learning, and accompanied by immediate feedback. In Norfolk, for example, feedback on their frequent common assessments (the interval is never less frequent than quarterly, and in some schools assessment takes place every other week) is typically provided the day after the assessment and, in some cases, on the same day. Assessment results include not only the scores for each student but a detailed item and cluster analysis. Teachers can use the results of assessments to plan instruction for the next week. In

contrast, many school systems are engaging in a regime of formative assessments that are viewed as nothing more than a compliance drill for a central office mandate. Such efforts are an expensive and inefficient waste of time, money, and energy. To be effective, the frequent common assessments used by the most successful schools are not isolated events but integral parts of the teaching, leadership, and learning cycle. Assessment informs teaching; leadership provides the time and resources for teachers to respond to assessment results; and students use assessment feedback as a series of cues for improved performance.

The fourth criterion for schools that have made great strides in achievement and equity is immediate and decisive intervention. Imagine a faculty meeting in your school that takes place two or three weeks after the beginning of the school year. The topic of the meeting is a question: Do we know the names, the faces, and the stories of students who are in danger of failure nine months from now? The inevitable answer is that we know. We *know* who cannot read the textbook. We *know* who cannot write the lab reports. We *know* who lacks the time management, project management, and study skills to complete the tasks that are essential for classroom success. Therefore the only relevant question is whether we have the will to apply that knowledge to meet the needs of our students.

Successful schools do not give a second thought to decisive and immediate interventions, including changing schedules, providing double classes for literacy and math, requiring homework supervision, breaking down major projects into incremental steps, and otherwise providing preventive assistance for students in need. Schools that fail to engage in decisive intervention—and at the time of this writing that is the vast majority of schools—always claim not to have the resources or time to provide successful intervention strategies. Yet

these same schools always manage to find the time, resources, and energy to deal with high failure rates. They cannot provide a double period of math this year, but they can inevitably provide extra sections of math for the 60 percent of students who failed the first time around. They cannot provide an extra reading course for students now, but they can devote untold sums for summer and after-school reading programs. By such logic, they could not take time to fill the car with gas before crossing the desert, but they could afford a chartered jet to take them from the middle of the desert to an oasis after they have been stranded in the middle of the desert.

Intervention, particularly at the secondary level, is typically opposed on two grounds. First, decisive intervention is opposed by those who fear tracking and homogenous grouping. After all, if we provided an extra math class or a required reading class, then students participating in the intervention classes might be disproportionately members of minority, ethnic, and second-language groups or would overrepresent students who are economically disadvantaged. That may be true. But the logic of denying these students needed help does not stand up well to further scrutiny. After all, is it true that students who come to school without vaccinations are more likely to be poor than rich? That is clearly the case, yet no responsible health official would hesitate to give poor children vaccinations for fear of the social stigma that might be attached to these children being in the "vaccination group." Similarly, contemporary aversion to grouping does not protect disadvantaged students, but perpetuates their disadvantages. Because we will not admit that a 9th grade student reading at a 6th grade level needs additional assistance, we doom that student to freshman failure, increasing the likelihood that the student will repeat classes in the 10th and 11th grades and, ultimately, drop out of school. However sympathetic and enlightened the aversion to

9th grade intervention may appear, it is a prescription for deadly social policy. Just as the student who is denied a vaccination is at a greater health risk later in life, the students who are denied immediate and decisive intervention also suffer risks—including health risks and economic risks—associated with school failure.

The second level of opposition to immediate and decisive intervention comes from those who believe that a preference for literacy and math over other subjects will diminish a focus on science, social studies, and elective courses. In fact, the opposite is true. When students fail a basic literacy or math course, they repeat it, effectively eliminating the opportunity for that student to take other courses later. Most importantly, when students drop out of school, they never take elective or advanced courses. The logic is straightforward. Do you want to have more elective and advanced courses? So do I. When do those elective and advanced courses take place? Typically in 11th and 12th grade. What is the best way to increase the participation in elective and advanced courses? Increase the number of 11th and 12th grade students. How do we increase the number of 11th and 12th grade students? Decrease the number of 9th and 10th grade failures.

In the most successful schools in Norfolk and Wayne Township, leaders and teachers did not hesitate to provide three hours of literacy instruction every day—typically two hours in reading and one hour in writing. In grades 6 through 10, they provided double and even triple classes in literacy and math when necessary. When students are drowning, they do not need a lecture on the theory of aquatics—they need a life preserver.

The final characteristic of schools that are making dramatic strides in improving educational achievement and equity is the constructive use of data. Rather than being tools for rating, ranking, sorting, or humiliation, data displays in these schools are celebrations of teacher

effectiveness. Recognizing the futility of districtwide or schoolwide averages, these schools publish the data for each class—teacher by teacher, class by class. They find that some teachers have a zero equity gap, while others have a large one. Some teachers have excessive referrals for discipline, while other teachers with the same students manage their classrooms well. Some teachers have ESL and special education students performing on a par with regular education students, while other teachers experience enormous gaps in student performance. The most effective data analysis technique used by leaders in these schools is the treasure hunt (Reeves, 2002d). During the treasure hunt the question is not "What have we done wrong and how do we fix it?" but rather "What do our results tell us about our most effective professional practices, and how can we identify and replicate those practices?"

In some school systems, data analysis is a source of fear, anger, and retribution. In other systems, however, data analysis is a source of celebration, high fives by teachers and administrators, and joint invitations from union presidents and superintendents to the public to see the data. These leaders and teachers are not sugarcoating the data. Rather, they value the honesty and transparency of public display. "We can't avoid the data," said one teacher, "so now we have to decide how to react to it."

Schools that have improved achievement and closed the equity gap engage in holistic accountability, extensive nonfiction writing, frequent common assessments, decisive and immediate intervention, and constructive use of data. One inescapable conclusion from school reform research, however, is that evidence alone is not enough. We must confront the "knowing-doing gap" (Pfeffer & Sutton, 2000). Leaders and teachers give intellectual assent to the research, and then return to schools and classrooms and . . . *nothing happens*. In the next section, we will consider how leaders must confront the mythology

surrounding educational change; the chapter will conclude with specific strategies to traverse the chasm from knowing to doing, from research to action.

Challenging Educational Mythology

In a profession that prides itself on rationality, education is strangely awash in mythology. Often the mythology has a tinge of truth or a whisper of research, lending sufficient credibility for a sound bite, but not enough evidence to sustain scrutiny. In this section, we will explore educational myths and realities. The most perplexing question to me is this: Why do intelligent and rational people prefer mythology over evidence? These are people who had to pass a research and statistics class in graduate school, and I would have sworn to every reader that if students passed such a class under my tutelage, then they would have brought an appropriate degree of skepticism and critical reasoning to the table. But my sworn testimony would have been in vain. Advanced knowledge of statistics and research does not inoculate anyone from a propensity for mythology, particularly when the myths are seductive and convenient.

Convenient myths abound, but foremost among them is the following: "*It wasn't my responsibility that student achievement was low. It was fate. If demographics, the bell curve, and all forces of the gods are against you, then you can't expect to be successful.*" In more modern terms, the convenient myth is "*I taught it; they just didn't learn it.*" Variations on the theme include every discussion in which adults choose to become victims, shifting responsibility for the success and failure of their students from personal and professional action to the characteristics of the students. Convenient myths provide an abdication of responsibility, and the lives of educational leaders devoid of

responsibility are far less burdensome than the lives of those who take every consequence of their decisions personally.

Just as I insist that teachers and leaders bear significant responsibilities in the lives and successes of students, I am not promoting the idea that students are not without responsibility. Rather, I suggest the reasoned middle ground in which students take responsibility and use their discretion wisely only when teachers and leaders help them use it. Students do not spring full grown from the head of Zeus, but they are the product of years of instruction and nurturing. I have students in a secondary school where I volunteer every week who do not understand that plagiarism is equivalent to stealing. Their older siblings and parents download pirated music from the Internet, and their previous teachers have praised their papers and posters for clever graphics, captions, and paragraphs, all products of downloads. When they use the same technique to produce a research paper in a matter of minutes in secondary school, they think of it as the product of efficiency and positive reinforcement, not the result of nefarious intent and plagiarism. If we want students to take personal responsibility, then we must teach them, directly and clearly, what our expectations are. We play a role in forming their character and decision-making processes; we are not merely their evaluators. Glenn and Nelsen (2000) express this idea well:

> All children are born at risk to problems of dependency. The perceptions and skills that are necessary for self-reliance and effective living require development and maintenance.
>
> Now consider the characteristics of low-risk individuals—people unlikely to fall into the known problem areas and likely to prove themselves successful, productive, capable human beings. They have developed the following:
>
> 1. Strong perceptions of personal capabilities—capable of facing problems and learning through challenges and experiences.

2. Strong perceptions of personal significance—capable of contributing in meaningful ways and believing that life has meaning and purpose.

3. Strong perceptions of personal influence over life—capacity to understand that one's actions and choices influence one's life and hold one accountable.

4. Strong intrapersonal skills—capacity to manage emotions through self-assessment, self-control, and self-discipline.

5. Strong interpersonal skills—capacities necessary to deal effectively with others through communication, cooperation, negotiation, sharing, empathizing, and listening.

6. Strong systemic skills—capacity for responding to the limits, consequences, and interrelatedness of human and natural systems with responsibilities, adaptability, flexibility, and integrity.

7. Strong judgment skills—capacity for making decisions and choices that reflect moral and ethical principles, wisdom, and values.

A primary goal of parent and teaching processes is that of strengthening these areas so that our young people can take on life with an adequate base of these personal resources and assets. (pp. 29–30)

There are factors that are inherent in students that influence their ability to be successful in school and in life, but these factors are malleable and are subject to the influence of teachers, educational leaders, and parents. Schools are not helpless victims. Schools are integral in helping students form their character, make decisions, and acquire lifelong assets. I have asked thousands of seminar participants the following two questions. First, who among you are the first generation in your family to graduate from college? It is not uncommon for 50 percent or more of the hands in the audience to reflect such an achievement. Second, what caused such a stunning achievement on your part? As participants answer the second question, I have never—not once in thousands of inquiries—heard someone testify to the salutary impact of a relative, teacher, or other authority figure who provided

patronizing pats on the head for poor performance. Rather, I see consistent themes in response to the second question:

- I had a teacher who challenged me and made me do far more than I thought I could do.
- I had a parent (or grandparent, godparent, aunt, uncle, clergy member, or other significant authority figure) who told me that I must do great things.
- I felt I had an obligation to succeed—if I didn't, I would be letting a lot of people down.
- I didn't like school at first—not any more than my parents and grandparents did. But after I knew I could do it and could do well, I enjoyed it.

These students clearly do not believe the myth that their destiny lies in their demographics. We do them a serious disservice if we accept the myth of the powerless educator. Through experience, open discussion, and critical thinking in an open and safe environment, we can challenge such myths. Challenging myths is a matter of evidence, not countermythology. The mistake many educational leaders make is attempting to exchange one toxic belief for another— bring in the latest educational expert who will address a hot and crowded gymnasium full of teachers with sufficient zeal, and then produce a miracle. In such a typical model of school reform, we only replace one mythology with another, the second even more short-lived than the first. Challenging mythology entails not an alternative myth but evidence and credible examples from the lives of teachers and leaders. The following examples illustrate this point.

Consider how your own myths were challenged. In a famous Norman Rockwell painting, a young boy's look of astonishment and

perplexity evokes an uncomfortable mix of humor and embarrassment as we notice that the boy has found a Santa Claus outfit in his parents' dresser. Neither an advertisement from a department store Santa nor a warm parental reassurance could ever reestablish the Santa myth for the boy in the picture. As we grow older, our own myths are challenged, including the myths that parents are perfect and invulnerable, that teachers are infallible, and that bad things do not happen to good people. These myths did not die as a result of counter-mythology but as a result of evidence and observation. Let us consider some examples in the world of teaching and learning.

Myth #1: People are happy doing what they are doing now. Teachers in unsuccessful schools would rather continue to be unsuccessful than engage in alternative practices that might lead to improved student success. People are miserable when they are not feeling successful in their personal and professional lives. I have watched the same faculty members change from being angry, defensive, and oppositional to being engaged and enthusiastic. In some cases, faculty members who intended to retire have remained on the job, excited by the prospect of coming to work every day and doing work that is personally and professionally meaningful. What accounted for their change in mood? It was neither psychotropic drugs nor a mood change occasioned by short-term charismatic leadership. Rather, the teachers and leaders made objective observations based on the evidence before their eyes. When student achievement improved, their commitment to their job similarly improved. This phenomenon in which success breeds success is common throughout different types of organizations (Goleman et al., 2002). Employees are not motivated by the promise of less work and reduced challenges. Rather, employees are most motivated by work that is meaningful and by a sense that their personal efforts make a difference.

Myth #2: People resist change because of irrational fear. The previous paragraphs should not leave the impression that resistance to change is inherently irrational and the result of chronic cranks. Rather, many people in schools resist change because they have been burned in prior years on programs that were poorly planned and badly executed. The result is more work with fewer positive results. Resisters can be transformed into allies, however, if they see that the planning and execution of the initiative will be significantly better than in the past. Mere announcements are not enough. Skeptics will want to see clear evidence that the initiative will have the leadership, resources, training, and support necessary for success.

Myth #3: You can't make significant changes until you get buy-in from everybody. Resistance to change is an organizational reality. The prevailing mythology that people are happy performing in ineffective and unhappy circumstances is fed by a corollary to that myth that no meaningful leadership decisions can be made without prior buy-in from all employees. In fact, the wait for buy-in can be interminable because leaders fail to acknowledge the truth that behavior precedes belief. In other words, the cycle of organizational improvement is not "vision, buy-in, and action" but rather "vision, action, buy-in, and more action." The buy-in does not occur until employees first see the results of their actions.

Leaders mistakenly believe that the right speaker, book, or research will create buy-in by reluctant faculty members. I have previously published case studies of successful schools, and these publications have led to numerous visits from teachers and leaders throughout the world (Reeves, 2004a, 2004b). The visits are, above all, testimony to the fact that readers simply do not believe printed case studies or even videotapes. They say that they must see the examples in order to believe them. But a perplexing thing happens.

The reluctant faculty members and administrators who said, "I won't believe that these schools are successful until I see them with my own eyes!" remain skeptical after they are confronted with the evidence. "Those schools are not like us," they complain, or "We could never do data analysis like that" or "They changed their schedule, but our board would never allow us to do that." Distant evidence fails to challenge mythology, as skeptics elevate the importance of environmental characteristics and minimize their own importance in the student achievement equation. Clinging to their long-held mythological beliefs, they prefer myth over reason. Therefore, it is essential that leaders remember this fact: Behavior precedes belief. *If you wait for people to have buy-in, be happy, or change belief systems, then change will never happen.*

Myth #4: You must have perfect research to support a proposed change. The reality is that perfect research does not exist. The United States' No Child Left Behind Act (NCLB) includes more than 200 separate references to "scientifically based research," and the administrative regulations supporting the law emphasize the use of rigorous research techniques, including comparison groups and student achievement as a dependent variable. Astonishingly, the vast majority of research over the past two decades purporting to address the topic of "educational leadership" does not even use student achievement as a dependent variable (Waters et al., 2005). Therefore, while federally supported efforts to improve educational research are welcome, there are also deep flaws in the reasoning that suggest effective policies depend on perfection in research (Reeves, 2002b). There are hardly any true randomly assigned groups in educational research, largely due to ethical constraints. Thankfully, researchers do not assign students to a control group in which students are denied potentially helpful instructional interventions, nor do researchers assign

students to an experimental group with potentially counterproductive
treatment. Imagine the reaction of parents who learned that their
children were assigned to a group of students who were denied adequate literacy instruction, high teacher expectations, or effective
leadership performance. Even after research is completed, the results
can be equivocal, with the term "significant" sometimes related to
research results with practical meaning, but sometimes to research
results that are merely statistically significant (i.e., the results are very
unlikely to be associated with random chance). The quality model
that prevails throughout successful organizations is not waiting for
perfection but rather "Try it, test it, improve it."

   *Myth #5: The risk of change is so great that you must wait until you
have things perfectly organized before implementing change efforts.* The
reality is that there are never risk-free alternatives. The risks of
change—and the human, financial, and organizational risks of any
change effort will be significant—must be compared with the even
more significant risks of maintaining present practices. Is there a risk
to faculty morale and a risk of increasing parent and student complaints if you cancel some classes and increase the number of courses
devoted to intensive intervention for students who need them?
Certainly. Is there a similar risk if you double or triple the time you
devote to math instruction in order to provide necessary catch-up
instruction and grade-level challenges for students who need this
intervention? Without a doubt. But the central question is not about
the risk of change but rather about the forgotten question in most discussions of change: What is the risk if you *fail* to change? It is true
that changes, particularly in schedule or in curriculum, will be incon-
venient for many adults in the system who find the old schedule and
curriculum comfortably familiar. But we must compare the consequences of inconvenience to the alternative risks—the risks and the

lifetime consequences associated with student failure. Too frequently school leaders and advocates for change are put on the defensive, being told that they must prove the effectiveness of their proposals before subjecting their colleagues to the inconvenience of change. I would propose that the burden of proof be shifted to those who defend curricula, schedules, and other policies and practices that are not working.

In interviews with a variety of successful school leaders I asked principals what they knew now that they wish they had known during the first year of their leadership responsibilities (Reeves & Woodson, 2006). The words of one represented the ideas of many:

> I wish I would have known that change never gets easier. At first I thought, I'll take some time to get to know the staff, and then change will be easier. Then I thought, I'll give them some more time to get to know me, and then change will be easier. Then I thought that I'll let the malcontents run out of steam, and then change will be easier. But finally I learned the truth—change never gets easier.

The reality of organizational change is that change never gets easier; it's never convenient, universally popular, without opposition, or risk free. One reason that leadership itself is such a challenging professional and personal responsibility is that effective leadership requires a continuous engagement in moving individuals and organizations from their present state to the leader's vision of an ideal state, and the movement requires change. While great leaders can make change invigorating, exciting, and motivating, and exceptional leaders can provide a continuous stream of feedback that will help communicate the benefits of change, even the best leaders cannot eliminate the inconvenience, opposition, and risks associated with change.

Focusing Change on What Matters Most

Once you have decided to embark on organizational change, it is imperative that change initiatives are focused on those areas that will have the greatest effect on student achievement. The Leadership for Learning Framework allows us to think in systematic ways about the changes that will lead us toward that goal. Briefly, we will focus on what to teach, how to teach, how to meet the needs of individual students, and how to lead.

Let us begin with the forces that have the greatest influence on student achievement. Research from the Wallace Foundation (Leithwood, Louis, Anderson, & Wahlstrom 2004) suggests that effective leadership has a profound and direct impact on student achievement. This work is evocative of the groundbreaking studies of John Goodlad (1984, 1990, 1994) more than a decade earlier in which observations of more than 2,000 schools led researchers to conclude that even when budgets, working conditions, and faculty characteristics were similar, school leadership was profoundly influential. The impact of leadership is most easily observed when a new leader comes into a school, and, while the students, parents, neighborhood, budget, and faculty remain virtually unchanged, the school experiences profound improvements in student achievement. Although the leader surely does not achieve these changes unilaterally, the impact of the leader is unquestionably significant.

Professional teaching practices have an enormous impact on student achievement (Marzano, 2001a, 2001b, 2003; Marzano et al., 2001). Unfortunately, there is an enormous gap between professional development about effective teaching practices and the actual implementation of those practices. Thomas Guskey (2000a) distinguishes

between different levels of professional development influence, ranging from superficial evaluations by seminar participants through actual impact on professional practices and student achievement. This knowing-doing gap (Pfeffer & Sutton, 2000) will resonate with every reader who has witnessed colleagues return to classrooms minutes after an apparently effective professional development presentation and . . . *nothing happens*. The adult learning experience was nothing more than an illusion, a mirage of improved practice in the middle of a desert of indifference. Is this overstating the case? Consider the results of more than 1,500 classroom observations (Learning 24/7, 2005):

- Clear learning objective: 4 percent
- Worksheets: 52 percent
- Lecture: 31 percent
- Monitoring with no feedback: 22 percent
- Students required to speak in complete sentences: 0 percent
- Evidence of assessment for learning: 0 percent
- Evidence of bell-to-bell instruction: 0 percent
- Fewer than one-half of students engaged: 82 percent

These observations are not from randomly selected classrooms and thus cannot be generalized to the entire country. At the very least, however, the findings suggest that every school should conduct similar observations. I recently spoke with the people who originally conducted this research, and while the number of observations of teaching practice now exceeds 10,000, the percentages have hardly varied at all.

   As important as effective professional practice by teachers is, the "how" of teaching is inherently limited by other factors, including the

time allowed for instruction, student work, and teacher feedback, and the quantity of material to be covered. In previous large-scale studies of complex urban systems that have made dramatic progress in student achievement and educational equity (Reeves, 2004a, 2004b), the impact of time is clear. Schools serving students who come to class with reading skills that are years below grade level must be willing to acknowledge that their traditional schedules, designed to provide one year's progress in reading, are insufficient. In some school systems, I have found the variation in reading time to be wildly erratic, with some schools giving three hours every day to literacy instruction and other schools claiming to address the same curriculum in 45 minutes every day. The best curriculum and best pedagogy will have minimal impact if teachers are not given the time they need to address student needs. There is rich literature on the impact of "time on task" (Slavin, 2003), and in some respects the implications are only common sense. If I have 9th grade students who can barely add, subtract, multiply, and divide, I can probably get them to pass an algebra class, but I cannot do so in the one class period per day that is typically provided for such instruction. If I have 7th graders who are reading at the 3rd grade reading level, I can perhaps get them to read on a 7th grade level by the end of the school year, but I cannot do so with a single English Literature class period. Teachers need time. Figure 6.1 shows the experience of one school's faculty when, using the same curriculum, teachers, and final examinations, they provided one group of students with double class periods.

The students who received extra time were those who had been identified as in greatest need. Yet these students experienced significantly lower failure rates. Whenever I share these data, some people react with astonishment and say, "It can't just be time; it's how you

use the time that matters." That is no doubt true, and I am not making the case that when leaders provide extra time for students in need, leaders are relieved of the responsibility for providing effective teaching strategies and intensive professional development. The evidence is clear, however: more time is essential.

Time for teacher collaboration is essential for effective education as well. Effective teacher collaboration that focuses on a collective examination of real student work is a time-consuming and intellectually challenging process. As Figure 6.2 indicates, many sessions are required for a faculty to progress from an anemic level of agreement—19 percent during the first meeting—to an effective level of agreement—92 percent by the end of the fourth session.

Unfortunately, many schools provide professional development about the importance of collaboration but then fail to provide the

6.1 — The Impact of More Time on Student Achievement at Riverview Gardens School System, Missouri

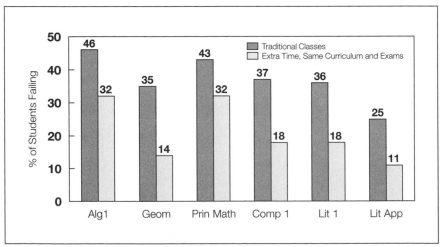

time to implement collaborative practices. This is a prescription for frustration and cynicism. The complaint that "we don't have time to collaborate" should be countered with a consideration of the enormous amounts of time and energy that are consumed when teachers fail to collaborate. The plain fact is that when teachers collaborate as a matter of course—not as an event, but as "the way we do business"—then not only does the quality of collaboration improve, as Figure 6.2 indicates, but also the time required for collaboration will be reduced, as shown in Figure 6.3.

Without effective collaboration, five different teachers can simultaneously hold a dozen different ideas of what the word "proficient" means, with some teachers rewarding effort, attitude, and penmanship, while others focus on time management and cooperation, and still others focus on academic content and written expression. If a professional community does not agree on what student achievement means, then educational leaders cannot allocate scarce resources to

6.2 — The Power of Teacher Collaboration

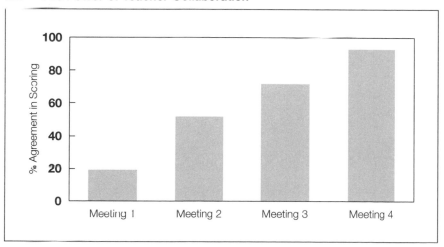

help those students who are most in need and provide enrichment opportunities for students who need advanced work. When an *A* might represent deficient work accomplished on time by a student with a pleasant attitude, and a *D* can reflect high-quality work submitted late by a surly adolescent, then the failure of effective collaboration has terrible consequences for students, future teachers, leaders, and the entire system. In such a system, feedback and grades are meaningless, and students conclude that luck and fate, not their own effort, causes their success or failure in a school.

In addition to providing time for instruction and effective collaboration, leaders must also conserve the time of classroom teachers by helping them focus on those academic content standards that are most important. The term "Power Standards" (Ainsworth, 2003a, 2003b) helps the entire faculty understand what we all know to be true: Not every standard is equally important. However obvious this may be, many faculty members are like a brick wall of resistance

6.3 — Effective Teacher Collaboration Saves Time

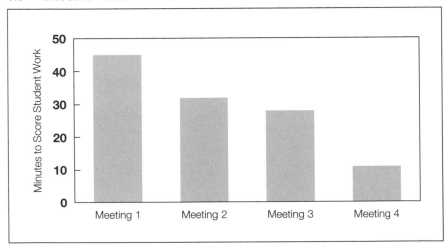

when it comes to giving up elements of their curriculum. "What can I give up?" they ask. "Everything I do is important—and besides, it might be on the state test, so I have to cover it." This deeply held belief in the power of coverage as a substitute for learning can be challenged only with evidence.

The best evidence is an analysis of individual items or clusters of items in formative assessment. In reviewing data from hundreds of classrooms, I have found that there are always students who score well on items and clusters of items that have not been covered and, even more importantly, groups of students who fail to grasp test items on material that has been covered. Documenting teacher work with pacing charts and lesson plans is an exercise in futility if we are unwilling to focus on formative assessment data and then identify the standards that are most important for student success. Interestingly, when I ask the same teachers who claim to be unable to remove anything from their lessons what advice they would have for teachers in the next lower grade, the teachers in the higher grade are remarkably focused, clear, and specific. They have never said, "Doug, I expect the teacher in the next lower grade to cover every single standard." They always provide a list of expectations that focuses on reading, writing, problem solving, critical thinking, time management, individual responsibility, and teamwork. While state and district academic content standards are surely important, they are not alone sufficient to identify the most important elements of teaching and learning. Only a complete commitment to the Power Standards Process will achieve that. Most readers will want to read *Power Standards: Identifying the Standards That Matter the Most* by Larry Ainsworth (2003a).

The Law of Initiative Fatigue

The Law of Initiative Fatigue is my adaptation from the term originally used in the *Harvard Business Review*. The law states

> When resources of time, money, and emotional energy are held constant while the number of old, continuing, and new initiatives rises, organizational implosion is inevitable.

The Law of Initiative Fatigue is graphically portrayed in Figure 6.4. When leaders cling to previous initiatives while attempting to add new ones, they can experience some apparent early success. As the rising line on the left part of the chart indicates, new ideas can be sustained with some early doses of enthusiasm and adrenaline. But,

6.4 — The Law of Initiative Fatigue

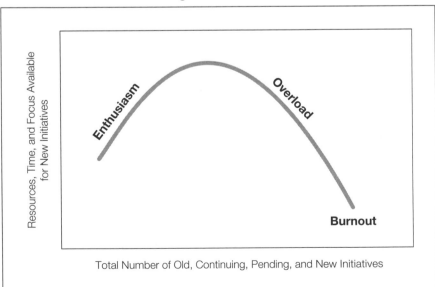

inevitably, the Law of Initiative Fatigue will impose its inexorable will, and enthusiasm gives way to organizational overload, which is precipitously followed by burnout. Not only will the new initiatives fail under such circumstances, but the energy and resources available to old and continuing initiatives are dangerously compromised as well. Thus, the school that attempted to have seven simultaneous reading programs (I am not exaggerating) was able to do none of them well. Similarly, schools that indulge in "flavor of the month" professional development are never able to provide the deep and sustained learning required for the success of any single initiative.

Unless a leader can expand the otherwise finite quantity of time, resources, and energy available in a school, the only response to the Law of Initiative Fatigue is a garden party. The garden party takes its name from a chapter I wrote entitled "Pull the Weeds Before Planting the Flowers" (Reeves, 2002e). There is an important corollary to the Law of Initiative Fatigue: every school has weeds. Just as the most meticulous gardener must continuously remove weeds in order to assure the healthy growth of flowers, leaders must be ever vigilant for persistent weeds with deep roots in the academic garden. The following paragraphs identify only a few of the weeds that abound in schools in every culture.

Announcements—particularly those delivered over loud speakers or provided orally in meetings—can be described best as wastes of time. A growing number of schools have eliminated or dramatically curtailed the frequency and length of morning announcements. To the best of my knowledge, they implemented these changes, and the Earth continued to rotate on its axis, and the rest of the solar system was similarly undisturbed. Students, parents, and teachers still received the information that they needed through posted and written announcements, e-mails, and voice mails. By abandoning the

"microphone fantasy"—the mystical belief that the person in a school holding the microphone also holds the attention of students and teachers—these schools were able to save 20 to 30 minutes every week—as much as 18 instructional hours each year. By eliminating oral announcements in faculty meetings, principals are devoting hours to collaborative scoring of student work and other essential teacher interactions for which time had been previously unavailable. When I asked one remarkable principal how she had so much time available for teachers to collaborate, she replied bluntly, "I stopped talking in faculty meetings about three years ago. We still have meetings, but the teachers take responsibility for our work, and I do all of my announcements in writing. It's a more responsible and respectful way to deal with professionals."

Meetings are the bane of the existence of many administrators. Some superintendents have canceled the vast majority of traditional districtwide principal meetings, preferring to send communications by e-mail and provide personal coaching and support to principals on a differentiated basis. Other superintendents have required all central office meetings to take place on one or two designated "meeting days" per month, so that travel time between the schools and central office is minimized for building principals, and different central office departments are required to coordinate and collaborate on their meeting requirements. Within buildings, meetings that are not relevant to our central concerns—what to teach, how to teach it, and how to meet the needs of individual students—are almost invariably relegated to the dustbin of ineffective management practices. The central question for any meeting is this: Will we engage in activities that require the collective intelligence of the group and therefore make better decisions collaboratively? If there is anything less than emphatic affirmative response to this question, then the rationale for the meeting

must be subject to serious question. When leaders say, "I want my entire staff to get the message at the same time in the same way," the leaders are making the entirely unwarranted assumption that oral communication in a large group is the most effective way for people to "get the message."

Administrators throughout the educational world complain of *paperwork,* but only a few are taking direct aim at one of the primary causes of wasted administrative time: multiple requests for the same information. Some creative central office leaders, such as Deanna Housfeld, retired from the Milwaukee Public Schools, have devised thoughtful ways to reduce duplication. Her creation of the "one-plan" allowed each school leader to provide information in a single document. By identifying the information that schools must provide to a variety of state, federal, district, and grant-providing organizations, the central office was able to ask for information just once, and all additional requests for information must be addressed to the "one-plan" coordinator, who in almost every case already has the information.

Study halls for secondary schools have been described as the last resort of those unable to design a master schedule. In theory, the study hall was designed for, well, study. But rarely has reality departed so far from the label. There are enormous chunks of instructional time that now lie in the wastelands of study halls without study, academic advisories with neither academics nor advice, homerooms without anything resembling the relationship building for which the label was designed, and silent reading periods with not a moment of reading. At the end of the day, we need to ask what students need most. If they are in danger—and reading below grade level presents genuine danger in academic, economic, and even physical terms—then the adult response to danger is not to say, "You're 13—I'll let you decide what is best." When they are in danger, we first remove the danger

and create a safe place—such as a school in which students read on
grade level. In every school in which students are failing, teachers and
leaders complain that there is not sufficient time to meet the needs of
every student. Yet, in virtually every case with such a school, there
are many hours that are unstructured, unfocused, and unrelated to
meeting student needs.

Transitions are another fruitful opportunity for saving teacher
time. Recently I observed two 3rd grade classrooms, right across the
hall from one another. The first teacher was able to make transitions
from one center to another in 17 seconds, while the second teacher
took almost 5 minutes to make a similar transition. Some secondary
school teachers lose 5 to 10 minutes of every class period collecting
homework and getting started, while others collect homework as students walk in the door and students are working on a warm-up exercise before the starting bell has rung.

Assessments are perhaps the most time-consuming activity for
teachers, requiring not only classroom time for administration but
many hours of professional time to create and score assessments. Of
all the time-wasting activities in schools, assessments designed exclusively for the evaluation of student learning and not used to provide
meaningful feedback to students with the expectation of improved
performance must surely be the most pernicious and disrespectful
activities in which we engage. One-shot assessments scream to students
that teacher feedback is irrelevant and that any feedback the students
receive is too late to influence performance. Thus, neither students
nor teachers use one-shot assessments to improve their performance,
and they both marvel at the inability of the other to see the obvious
problem. Teachers bewail the lack of student work ethic and growing
indolence, a complaint of every teacher since Socrates, and students
complain of the obscurity of teacher expectations, an allegation

whined by every student since Plato. The cycle is broken only when teachers decide that the consequence for poor performance on an assessment is not a low grade but the requirement that students perform proficiently.

The one class in which schools rarely experience a gender, ethnic, language, or economic gap is driver's education. Nearly all students pass the test and get their license, though not all on the same day or after the same number of attempts. The stakes are high—the safety of students, family members, and the general public—but the requirements are clear and consistent. If students fail the exam, they receive meaningful feedback and take the exam again. The other area in which student engagement and performance is uniformly high is in playing videogames. Boys and girls, rich and poor, black, brown, and white, English and Cantonese, all play videogames. And all of them—without a single exception—fail at the conclusion of their first game. But in videogames, unlike an algebra final, students use feedback to "get to the next level," and within seconds of receiving negative feedback (their character dies), the students are once again perfecting their skill, equipped with knowledge of how to overcome the next obstacle. In brief, we know what works in assessment as in so many other areas of education. The only question is whether we will transform that knowledge into action. Will we, in brief, take social studies, science, literature, and math at least as seriously as we take driver's education and videogames?

When leaders are willing to confront long-held traditions in schedules and curricula, they at last begin to cross the knowing-doing gap. Research is no longer an abstraction but a guide to the practical realities of daily life in schools. But the changes in pedagogy and institutional structure are only a start. In the next chapter, we will explore some of the most sacred territory of all—classroom grading policies.

– 7 –

Leadership and Effective Feedback
The Dilemmas of Grading*

Deprivatizing Professional Practice

Even when teachers have ample time for instruction and collaboration, our focus on what matters most is incomplete without a discussion of grading practices. Simply put, letter grades do not reflect student achievement in an astonishing number of cases. This situation has long been tolerated because of the pervasive belief that teaching is a private endeavor and grading policies are the exclusive domain of those private practitioners. But a growing chorus of voices is calling for the "deprivatization" of professional practices in teaching and leadership (DuFour et al., 2005). When it comes to providing students with feedback—and grading is one of many powerful sources of feedback—then I will argue that the freedom long enjoyed by private practitioners must take place within boundaries of fairness,

---

*Some paragraphs in this chapter were previously published in an article I wrote entitled "The Case Against the Zero" for *Phi Delta Kappan* in December 2004. These words are used here with the kind permission of Phi Delta Kappan, International.

mathematical accuracy, and effectiveness. When professional practice occurs within those boundaries, then creativity should be encouraged. When practice trespasses across a boundary, however, then it is not simply creative or a matter of personal judgment. It is out of bounds. We have already considered the imperative for teacher collaboration. As Figure 6.2 indicated in the previous chapter, teachers do not easily or automatically agree with each other on what student work is proficient. Such agreement takes intensive work over the course of time. Without it, we are doomed to an unfair system. Imagine if school athletic teams attempted to engage in competitions where neither the coaches nor the officials had a consistent idea of the dimensions of the field or the rules of play. Howls would rise from students, teachers, and parents about the unfairness of it all, just as they do every time an athletic official makes a ruling that differs from the judgment of the fans. But these voices of protest are strangely silent when dramatic evidence of inconsistency is presented in the classroom.

What Do Grades Mean?

Figure 7.1 shows the difference in performance in four areas—language arts, math, science, and social studies—for a large group of students ($n > 35,000$) in one midwestern school system. The assessments included not only multiple-choice items but also short answer and extended response requirements. The low-performing group did not just have a bad day; these students were consistently and significantly lower in their performance than the high-performing group.

If school leaders knew that the lower-performing group needed help, they might be able to provide it. If they had an early warning system, then they might be able to avoid the long-term consequences

of failure that too frequently accompany students whose academic performance lags far behind that of their peers. But in most districts, the only source of information about the needs of these students would be the letter grades in the report card. As Figure 7.2 indicates, leaders would learn very little from these documents, as the grade point averages of the highest-performing and lowest-performing students are barely distinguishable.

The bar on the right—the grades awarded to low-performing students—can best be described as "sucker punch" grading, after the blow delivered to the unsuspecting boxer who does not see the devastating punch until it is too late to offer a defense. These sucker punches are delivered to students every year when they fail classes—particularly in 9th grade—after receiving honor roll grades during the previous year for similar work. The phenomenon is hardly unique to middle schools, as 6th grade teachers regularly make the same complaint about their incoming students who are astonished, after years of

7.1 — Performance Differences for 35,000 Students

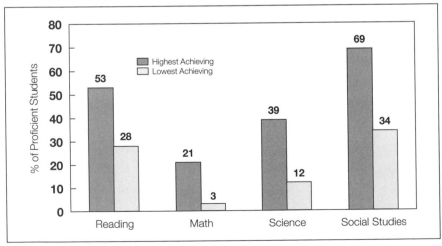

unfiltered affirmation, that their work is not satisfactory. Lest we leave the impression that high schools are bastions of objectivity, consider the evidence in Figures 7.3 and 7.4. The first chart shows the predicted relationship between letter grades and student achievement on a high school graduation exam. It is hardly a high-risk hypothesis, presuming that students who receive grades of D and F are substantially more likely to fail the state graduation exam than students who receive grades of A, B, and C.

But this prediction is sadly mistaken. The real data for several thousand students are presented in Figure 7.4. It shows an astonishing number of students earning grades of A, B, and C who are failing the state graduation exam.

Whenever I ask colleagues around the country to express their hypotheses about why students with high grades are failing basic assessments of reading and math skills, they share some interesting views. Their descriptions of the "A" and "B" students who cannot

7.2 — Minimal Difference in Grade Point Average Between Low-Achieving and High-Achieving Students

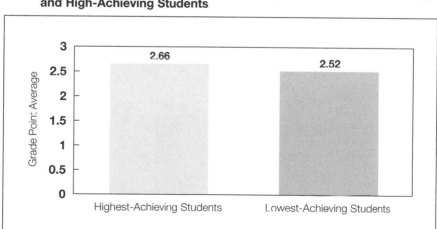

pass a basic English and math exam almost invariably include comments such as the following:

> "A pleasure to have in class"
> "Attends every day"
> "Turns in homework regularly"
> "Willing to do extra credit projects"
> "Never gives me any trouble"
> "Working up to capacity"

None of these statements is particularly objectionable. After all, who
wouldn't want a student who is friendly and cooperative? What is the
matter with offering positive reinforcement to students who do homework and extra credit? Why not give a boost to the quiet students who
are not discipline problems and, all things considered, are doing about
as well as they can? Why? There is only one relevant answer: These

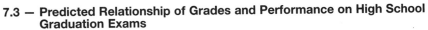

**7.3 — Predicted Relationship of Grades and Performance on High School
Graduation Exams**

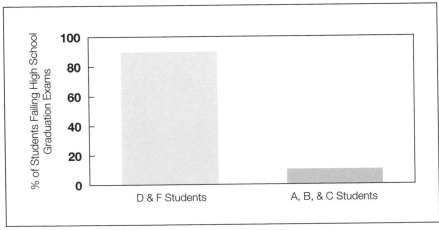

students are not proficient. They cannot read, write, or perform basic problem solving at the standard of their grade level. While there are doubtless virtues in completing homework and behaving in class, we err gravely when we call compliance and politeness "algebra" or "English" or any other label that conflates proficiency with behavior. This is particularly true when good grades for unsatisfactory work and poor grades for satisfactory work are influenced by gender and ethnicity. In Figure 7.4, a disproportionate number of the high grades earned by students failing the state graduate exam belong to minority female students. Similar gender imbalances were observed by Jo Sanders (2002), who found that while girls received higher grades than boys in technology classes, boys outscored girls significantly in external measures of achievement in the same subjects. I recently witnessed the graduation ceremonies at a high school where boys and girls had evenly matched records with regard to college admissions and college entrance exams, but there were six times as many girls as boys in the

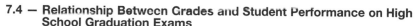

7.4 — Relationship Between Grades and Student Performance on High School Graduation Exams

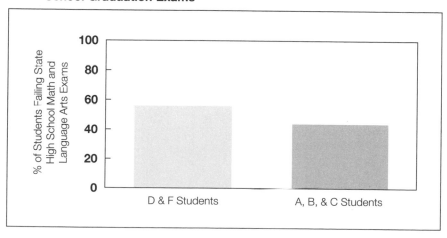

National Honor Society. Let us ask the uncomfortable question: What are we rewarding young women for? Are we rewarding them for being academically proficient in a complex and competitive world, or are we rewarding them for being quiet, compliant, polite, and acquiescent to the authority figures around them? The evidence in this chapter strongly suggests the latter. I can only ask that every reader find a random sample of 30 students who received failing or low grades on your state assessment or any collection of external assessments that you trust. Then examine the letter grades of those 30 randomly selected students. You will find in almost every case grades of C, B, or even A. Then see if you notice a pattern regarding the gender and ethnicity of those students whose grades reflect success but whose externally measured performance shows failure.

The Missing Ingredient in Grading Systems: The Truth

In response to the previous sections, I have heard many teaching colleagues say that while these grading policies may be true of some teachers, they are certainly not part of their own practice. Their grading systems are, they assure me, entirely accurate. Many teachers even use computer systems, so that they are positive that the numbers add up in a precise and methodical way. But neither computerized calculations nor rigorously applied grading systems are enough to save schools from some of the most common and egregious errors in grading. Amazingly, teachers regularly use and leaders frequently tolerate grading systems that may appear to be accurate but are devoid of even the most basic elements of mathematical reasoning and are neither fair nor effective. Let us consider some of the most common errors: zeroes, averages, and misleading labels.

Zeroes

This is not a trick question: If you are using a grading scale in which the numbers 4, 3, 2, 1, and 0 correspond to grades of A, B, C, D, and F, then what number is awarded to a student who fails to turn in an assignment? If you responded with a unanimous chorus of "zero," then you may have a great deal of company. There might be a few people who are familiar with research that asserts that grading as punishment is an ineffective strategy (Guskey & Bailey, 2001). But many of us curmudgeons want to give the miscreants who failed to complete our assignments the punishment that they richly deserve. No work, no credit—that's the end of the story. Groups as diverse as the United Teachers Federation of New York and the Thomas Fordham Foundation rally around this point (Butler, 2004). Let us, for the sake of argument, accept the point: The failure to turn in work should receive a zero. As Figure 7.5 suggests, this 4-point scale is a rational system, as the increments between letter grades are proportional to the increments between numerical grades. The interval from one grade to the next is one point.

7.5 — A 4-Point Grading Scale

- **A = 4**
- **B = 3**
- **C = 2**   **ALL INTERVALS**
- **D = 1**   **ARE THE SAME**
- **F = 0**

But the common use of the zero today is based not on a scale with a range of four points but on a 100-point scale. This practice defies logic and mathematical accuracy. On a 100-point scale, the interval between grades is typically 10 points, with the break points at 90, 80, 70, and so on. The interval between letter grades is 10 points. But when the zero is preserved in a 100-point system, the interval between the D and F is not 10 points but 60 points, as Figure 7.6 indicates. Most state standards in mathematics require that 5th grade students understand the principles of ratios (e.g., A is to B as 4 is to 3; D is to F as 1 is to 0). Yet the persistence of the zero on a 100-point scale indicates that many people with advanced degrees, including more than a few mathematics teachers, have not applied their understanding of the ratio standard to their own professional practices. To insist on using zero on a 100-point scale is to assert that work that is not turned in is worthy of a penalty that is six times greater than work that is done wretchedly and worthy of a grade of D. Earlier I asked what points would be awarded to a student who failed to turn in work if there were a grading scale of 4, 3, 2, 1, 0. No one reading this book

---

7.6 — The Impact of Zero on a 100-Point Scale

- **Notice the interval between scores:**
- **A = 91+**
- **B = 81–90**
- **C = 71–80**
- **D = 61–70**
- **F = Zero?**

ALL INTERVALS ARE THE SAME – 10 POINTS

responded to that question by thinking that the failure to turn in work in such a system would be awarded a grade of "minus 6" (i.e., If $F = 0$, then $0 = -6$ on a 4-point scale)—yet that is precisely the logic employed when the zero is awarded on a 100-point scale.

There are two issues at hand. The first and most important issue is, what is the appropriate consequence when students fail to complete an assignment? The most common answer is punishment. Evidence to the contrary notwithstanding, there is an almost fanatical belief that punishment through grades will motivate students. There are at least a few educators experimenting with the notion that the appropriate consequence for failing to complete an assignment is completing the assignment. That is, students lose privileges, free time, and unstructured class or study hall time, and they are required to complete the assignment. The price of freedom is proficiency, and students are motivated not by threats of failure but by the opportunity for greater freedom and discretion when work is completed accurately and on time. I know my colleagues in the teaching profession well enough to understand that I will not win this point with many of them. Rewards and punishments are part of the psyche of schools, particularly at the secondary level.

But even if I concede the first point, the second issue is much simpler. Even if we want to punish students who fail to complete our assignments—and I admit that on more than one day, my emotions run in that direction with both my students and my own children— then what is the fair, appropriate, and mathematically accurate punishment? However vengeful I may feel at times on my worst days, I'm fairly certain that the appropriate punishment is not the electric chair. Even if I were to engage in the typically fact-free debate in which feelings are elevated over research and thus gave primacy to my personal preference for punishment over efficacy, I would nevertheless be

forced to admit that giving a zero for missing work is a mathematical inaccuracy if I am using a 100-point scale.

If I were using a 4-point grading system, I could give a zero. If I am using a 100-point system, however, then the lowest possible grade is the numerical value of a *D*, minus the same interval that separates one grade from the next. In Figure 7.6 where the interval is 10 points and the value of *D* is 61 points, then the mathematically accurate value of *F* is 51 points. This is not, contrary to popular mythology, "giving" students 50 points but rather awarding punishment that fits the crime. The students failed to turn in an assignment, and they receive a failing grade. They are not sent to a Siberian labor camp. There is, of course, an important difference. Sentences at Siberian labor camps ultimately come to a close, while grades of zero on a 100-point scale last forever. Just two or three zeros are sufficient to cause failure for an entire semester, and just a few course failures lead to high school dropouts, with a lifetime of personal and social consequences.

This issue is as emotional as anything I have encountered since the phonics versus whole language debate. Scholars regress to all-star wrestlers (no offense intended to wrestlers), and research and plain logic are subordinated to vengeance masquerading as high standards. Because the emotional attachment to the zero is so strong, I have given up advocating for 50 as the lowest grade. We can preserve some level of sanity in our grading system and return to a system with a range of four points (4, 3, 2, 1, 0). A's are no longer 100 points but are 4 points. If there is a need for greater specificity, then we can choose an infinite number of digits to the right of the decimal point and thus differentiate between the 3.449 and 3.448 to our heart's content. But at the end of the day, the *F* is a zero, one point below a *D*. It is fair, accurate, and (some people may believe) motivational. But

at least the zero on a 4-point scale is not the mathematical travesty that it is when we apply it to a 100-point system.

Averages

Another common error in grading is the use of the average. Guskey (2000b) and I (Reeves, 2000) have argued that when we make 6th grade students learn about the mean, median, and mode, we do so because at the age of 12, young problem solvers need to learn that the mean—the average—is not always the best way to represent a data set. The same lesson can be well learned by educators and school leaders. Consider three students who earned the following grades on equally weighted assignments and tests:

Sally	Rebecca	James
85	85	85
94	94	94
100	100	100
70	40	0

All three students experienced identical performance until their fourth and, apparently, disastrous assignment. In fact, all three students achieved the same score—a zero —on the fourth assessment, with Sally missing every item, Rebecca failing to put her name on the paper, and James turning in a terrific paper but for the wrong class. How each teacher handled these failures tells an interesting tale about the use of averages and other grading policies.

All three students were earning an average of 93 after three assignments, solid A's for every student by most measures. Sally's teacher wasn't happy with her performance on the fourth assessment,

but the teacher believed in the principle of assessment for learning as discussed in the previous chapter. When Sally failed that assessment, she had the opportunity to retake it, and though it remained exceptionally challenging, her retest allowed her to score a 70. This was still a hard blow, bringing her average grade from an A to B+, with a mathematical average of 87.5. Rebecca's teacher was also upset with her performance, but even though a missing signature was a cause for no credit in this teacher's class, the school had implemented a policy that the lowest grade could be only 20 points lower than the grade for a D, which was 60 points at this school. Thus, the lowest possible grade was 40. This policy represented a compromise between the principal, who wanted the lowest grade to be a 50, and the faculty, who wanted to retain the right to give zeroes. Rebecca received a 40 for her failure to sign her paper, dropping her class average to 79.75, and her grade from an A to a C+. James had a teacher who was confident that the use of averages and zeroes would instill work habits and motivation. These policies led James, who submitted a wonderful paper in the wrong class, to receive a zero, reducing his average to 69.75, or a D+. Rebecca and Sally are fictional characters; James is not.

My youngest son, James, is a diligent, if not always well-organized student. The grades shown are precisely those he received early in his middle school career. I watched as he calculated by hand what had happened to his average grade as the result of one zero. I asked, "What lesson did you learn?" thinking, naively, that he would provide some adult-pleasing bromide about the value of better organization. James sullenly replied, "There goes the honor roll." In an instant, the case study of James established what Guskey's large-scale quantitative research has told us for decades: Grading as punishment does not work and, in fact, can be counterproductive. Rather than motivating students, it demotivates them. Instead of improving performance, it

provides academic game players who know their average but do not apply what they know to improve performance, particularly if the teacher's use of the average renders progress and performance null and void. Strangely, teachers who use the average regularly in their classes find comfort when the average is abandoned by their graduate school professors.

Figure 7.7 displays the progress of three not entirely hypothetical students in my graduate school courses. The student represented by the dotted line is a high school calculus teacher who enters my statistics class on cruise control, mastering every problem, and applying mathematical tools he had used only hours earlier. After immediately establishing his ability, the student slides gently to the end of the semester, neither seeking nor rising to challenges. The dashed diagonal line shows the perfectly linear student whose progress precisely reflects the assumptions of textbooks, syllabi, and professors. Few such students have ever entered a real classroom. The solid line is by far

7.7 — Students' Progress in Statistics and Research Class

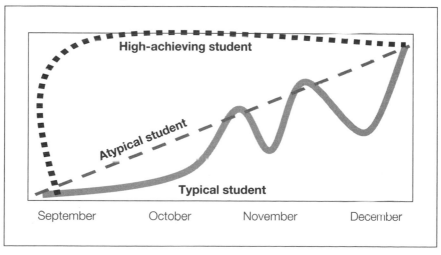

my most common student experience. Future school leaders, required to take a statistics and research class, approach the subject with trepidation as they explain, "I haven't had a math class for 25 years. I'm a social studies teacher [or a school administrator] and am very worried about this. In fact, I don't even know why I should have to take it."

As the semester progresses and their comfort level increases, students eventually realize that I am not requiring them to memorize the formula for the coefficient of variation, but rather I am seeking to give them the research skills that will help them as leaders and educators. As the chart indicates, they reach the "Oh—I get it!" stage toward the end of the semester. Here are the questions that teachers must consider, now that they are students in my class. Should I evaluate their performance based on the average of "I haven't had a math class for 25 years" and "Now I get it," or should I evaluate students based on their proficiency at the end of the semester? Just as there is not a single state algebra standard that requires that students "do algebra quickly," there is no requirement in my class that students who process statistics rapidly in the first class deserve any more credit than those who did so weeks later, after hard work and diligent effort. The progress curves represented in Figure 7.7 can, in a much more complex form, represent the differing student needs in every class, and the blind use of the average recognizes none of these complexities.

What is the alternative? There are two systems I have seen teachers employ that maintain a high degree of rigor and also avoid the errors inherent in using zeroes and averages. In the first system, a secondary school faculty agreed that every student would receive six assessments each quarter. The definition of "assessment" was left to the teacher, as it might be a lab, essay, technology project, or musical presentation, depending on the context of the class. Each assessment would be scored on a 4-point scale as follows:

4 = Exemplary

3 = Proficient

2 = Progressing

1 = Not Meeting Standards

The grading system was uniform and simple:

A = Four assessments scored "exemplary" and two scored at least "proficient"

B = Four assessments scored "proficient" and two scored at least "progressing"

C = Three assessments scored at least "proficient"

Any performance lower than a C was scored as "IP" or "In Progress," a grade that became an F within two weeks after each grading period unless the student submitted work that was sufficient for a grade of C. When students received low scores on assessments, they were encouraged to work harder and resubmit their work. While some faculty members feared that such a system would lead students to delay work until the last moment and cause a diminution in student work ethic, precisely the opposite result occurred. Students knew that they could no longer get a D for little or no work, and they knew that the quality requirements for a C were the same as the quality requirements for a B—with a C representing less quantity but not lower quality. As a result, students had an incentive to do work of higher quality and to do it right the first time. One student confided to me, "It's such a hassle to get a C in this school; you might as well get a B."

Another alternative grading system is the menu approach. This approach appeals to those who are locked into thinking of 90 or some multiple of it as representing an A, 80 representing a B and so on. In this system, students select items from a menu, with a theoretical

total of 1,000 points. There are points for attendance, as there are for participation, papers, research projects, and so on. On the actual menu, however, the possible total exceeds 1,200 points. If a student misses a class and thus the opportunity for some points, the result is not an endless series of excuses and letters from parents but rather the student selects something else from the menu. If a student bombs a test or claims that the dog ate the homework, then excuses are not appropriate, but alternative selections from the menu are the order of the day. The menu system is particularly useful for students who have difficulty mastering long and complex projects. Some students go home to private bedrooms, stereo systems, teddy bears, and parents who check homework and organize projects for them. As time goes along, they play the school game well, manage their own projects, and can probably calculate their current grade more rapidly than the teacher. Other students go home to chaos and have never learned how to break down a complex project into its component parts. The former student can choose a 200-point project and submit it on time. The latter, still learning how to do school, manage projects, and become a successful student, can achieve the same grade by selecting eight 25-point projects, getting feedback and guidance on each of these eight projects. At the end of the semester, both students will have met the same academic standards, but both will have received feedback and support that was appropriate to meet their needs.

Grading systems are only one of many ways in which teachers give feedback to students. With every act of encouragement, every indication of high expectations, and every minute of every class, we provide students with feedback. Thus, grades are certainly not the only focus of consideration in the professional practices surrounding feedback for better student performance. But from the point of view

of students, grades are profoundly important. When grading systems
are mathematically flawed (as in the case of zeroes and averages),
unfair (as in the case of the same performance receiving dramatically
different marks from different teachers), and ineffective (as in the case
when grades are utterly unrelated to student achievement), then
legitimate boundaries established by leaders have been violated.

Student Behavior

The final issue is how, if at all, matters of behavior should figure
into the grading equation. The examples used in this chapter appear
to focus on student achievement. And if we did focus only on achievement, the surly but proficient student would be rewarded for being a
competent jerk. Likewise the earnest and polite student would not
receive high grades based only on behavior that was disconnected
from academic proficiency. The best we can do is to be accurate, with
grades in math reflecting math proficiency rather than the student's
attitude. If it is important to provide feedback on student behavior—
and I agree that it is—then let us follow the model of kindergarten
teachers. Of all the report cards across the educational spectrum, they
combine accuracy, fairness, and clarity that should guide every teacher
throughout the system. In kindergarten, teachers, students, and parents
know that "plays well with others" is not the same as "knows numbers,
shapes, and letters." All participants in the kindergarten enterprise
understand that feedback about following directions and engaging in
appropriate social conduct is not even on the same section of the
report card where we will learn about the student's understanding of
colors, rhythm, and language. In brief, kindergarten teachers understand the differences between behavior and academic performance,
and they are able to account for them with clarity and consistency.

We fail to do that once students enter the double-digit age range, perhaps based on the theory that adolescents are less complex than kindergarteners. But I am hesitant to accept this presupposition. The complexities of adolescence cry out for grading systems that do not reduce education to a single letter. While letter grades remain a necessity in a culture where colleges use transcripts and parents compare grades, surely we can make letter grades more accurate and meaningful than the evidence in this chapter suggests that they are now. Moreover, we can provide feedback on behavior, including making notes on a transcript, if we want to say that a proficient student needs to go to charm school or that a nonproficient student is charming. But let us not confuse one with the other.

This chapter has focused on an essential element of classroom practice, student feedback that is accurate, rational, and effective. In the next chapter we will consider a tool that educational leadership teams can use to monitor their practice and give themselves meaningful feedback.

– 8 –

Using Leadership Maps to Improve Your School

The Leadership for Learning Framework Revisited

This book began with the Leadership for Learning Framework in which the reader was challenged to consider that student achievement is more than a set of test scores (see Figure 8.1). By exclusively focusing on results, leaders and teachers fail to measure and understand the importance of their own actions. High results, the matrix reveals, might be the effect of successful leadership and teaching, or the same results might be luck. Only by evaluating both causes and effects in a comprehensive accountability system can leaders, teachers, and policymakers understand the complexities of student achievement and the efficacy of teaching and leadership practices.

In my travels to schools around the world, I find that many teachers and leaders are already using this framework in a general way. They will come up to me and say, "We're really challenging ourselves, because we don't know if we're as good as we thought we were.

Perhaps we're in the Lucky quadrant." Others will say, "We're not very happy with our scores, but at least we're in the Learning quadrant." A few confess, "We just don't seem to be making any of the necessary changes—we're stuck in the Losing quadrant." Unfortunately, labeling a condition is helpful only if we can follow up that work with interpretation of the data and application of the research in a meaningful way that will lead not only to improved professional practices but to improved student achievement. Leadership mapping is a tool that will allow you to use research data and your own student accountability data in a constructive manner so that you can literally watch your map as it changes over time, create strategies to respond to the inferences from your map, and, most importantly, use those inferences from national research and your own data to implement effective change.

8.1 — The Leadership for Learning Framework

Achievement of Results	**Lucky** High results, low understanding of antecedents Replication of success unlikely	**Leading** High results, high understanding of antecedents Replication of success likely
	Losing Low results, low understanding of antecedents Replication of failure likely	**Learning** Low results, high understanding of antecedents Replication of success likely

Antecedents of Excellence

Creating Your Leadership Map

Building on the Leadership for Learning Framework, the Leadership Map contains a series of nodes that are result plots on a coordinate grid. The vertical axis represents student achievement, with values ranging from 0 to 100 percent of students who are successful. The definition of "success" can be adapted to meet the needs of your school. For example, the vertical axis might represent the percentage of students who score "proficient" or higher on a state exam, the percentage of special education students who complete all the objectives on their Individualized Education Plans, the percentage of technology students who successfully complete certification as a network software engineer, or the percentage of advanced placement students who achieve a score that is sufficiently high to earn college credit. In every case, however, the vertical axis is a measure of student achievement, expressed as a percentage of students who achieve a stated objective. In most schools, there are a variety of sources measuring student achievement, including at the very least annual tests in reading and math, and in most schools a variety of other achievement data. Too frequently, however, teachers and administrators complain of drowning in data as unrelated computer printouts pile up and are never read and never used. Certainly there is no substitute for deep and thoughtful data analysis, and the work of many scholars such as Stephen White is an excellent resource (White, 2005a, 2005b). The Leadership Map, however, provides a single visual display of a great deal of information.

The term "node" to describe the intersecting points on the Leadership Map is deliberate, as the term has multiple layers of meaning. On the surface, a node is nothing more than a "bump, lump, or knob," according to one thesaurus. But Albert-László Barabási (2003)

suggests a much richer meaning for the term. As he studied the science and mathematics of networks, Barabási discovered that nodes, the basic building blocks of networks, have extraordinary and disproportionate power, with some nodes serving as links to a handful of other nodes, and other nodes serving as rich veins of connectivity. This is not the much vaunted 80/20 rule, in which 80 percent of results stem from 20 percent of causes, but closer to a 99/1 rule, in which the vast majority of connections in a network are centered around a few nodes. This turns out to be true whether the networks under study are computer networks, the focus of Barabási's work, or human networks, such as those documented by Malcolm Gladwell in his classic book *The Tipping Point* (2000).

One of the most uncomfortable but necessary discussions in every school is the treasure hunt (Reeves, 2002d). We must ask, "Where are we good, and why did we get that way?" These questions are countercultural, requiring that we overcome institutional resistance to elevating one professional's practices over another. In a recent encounter with a school system that displayed a Leadership Map with an Islands of Excellence pattern (a concept we will explore later in this chapter), I suggested that great good might come from a systematic inquiry into the practices of those schools that combined outstanding student results with systematic documentation of their teaching and leadership practices. The astonishing response by senior leaders in the district who rejected the suggestion was "But that would be *evaluative*," a profane term in a culture that depends on the mythology that every practice is of equal merit and no one leadership or teaching technique should be elevated above any other. The Leadership Map demands introspection, reflection, and, yes, evaluation. The Leadership Map forces us to confront the reality that just as student achievement results are variable, so too are leadership and teaching practices variable in their impact. The

concept of nodes suggests not merely a dot on a map, but leaders and teachers have the opportunity to find patterns of connectivity among nodes so that great teaching and leadership practices can be linked in a systematic manner. Conversely, we can recognize the pathologies of cancerous nodes that link ineffective and destructive practices with poor results in persistent and toxic relationships.

The key to combining results from a variety of different tests is the use of the same measurement—the percentage of students who score "proficient" or higher. Whether the results are initially reported in a raw score, showing the number of test items correct, a percentile rank, showing the relative performance of a student compared to a comparison group, a scale score, or any other measurement, the creator of the Leadership Map must determine how to convert the test data into an indication of proficiency. In a standards-referenced assessment, the language is usually straightforward, as words such as "proficient" or "mastery" are often used to describe student performance at a particular level. Other tests are less clear and some thoughtful judgment must be used. Is merely "passing" the same as "proficient"? Few people who have observed work that earns a D or even C would argue that the quality of that work is remotely close to proficient. In some fields such as mathematical calculation, computer programming, or spelling, proficient performance requires a much higher rate of accuracy than the typical "passing" score of 60 or 70 percent. Norm-referenced tests often fail to provide consumers with raw scores, and they give only a relative indication of student performance. While performance in the "60th percentile" may sound somewhat reassuring (the work in the top half of a theoretical nationally representative group of students), we would be unhappy if we learned that such a score represented accurate answers to fewer than half the test questions. The claim that a student is not as bad as 59 percent of

the students in the comparison group is hardly a compelling case for the use of the term "proficient." While these challenges can be perplexing, they can be overcome. The benefits of representing a wide variety of complex data on a single Leadership Map certainly justify the effort. This may be the first time that faculty members and school leaders can gain a coherent idea of the results of all their work.

A growing number of schools have data walls, with displays of numbers and charts depicting student performance. The Leadership Map, however, not only displays student results but also associates those results with the specific actions of adults that are linked to student results. The horizontal axis of the Leadership Map represents the effectiveness of a strategy that is employed by the school to meet a particular objective. For example, research suggests that student achievement is strongly related to the strategy of nonfiction writing followed by collaborative scoring by teachers, and then rewriting by students. In fact, we can measure this relationship on a continuum from −1.0 (a completely counterproductive strategy that hurts student achievement) to 0 (an ineffective strategy that neither helps nor hurts student achievement) to +1.0 (an effective strategy that has a direct and consistent impact on student achievement.) In the real world, we rarely see relationships at the −1.0 or +1.0 level, but when we find something, such as nonfiction writing, that yields a relationship of +.8 with large numbers of children, then we have a solidly effective strategy.

Consider the case of the Maple Hill School.* When a new principal began several years ago, student achievement was dismal, with only 20 percent of students achieving proficiency on state assessments. Nevertheless, the principal, Ms. Lamb, was determined to start a

---

*Unless otherwise noted, the case studies are authentic syntheses of actual schools and data, but the identities of teachers, administrators, and districts have been changed.

regimen of nonfiction writing, followed by collaborative scoring, editing, and rewriting. The first entry on the Leadership Map is a node that represents an *x* value of +.8, based on the effectiveness of nonfiction writing, and a *y* value of 20 percent, based on the percentage of students who scored proficient or higher on the state assessment. The first mark on the map is shown in Figure 8.2.

The rest of the map is created by entering nodes that correspond to the existing leadership and teaching strategies and actual student achievement results. In the early months of Ms. Lamb's tenure, some of her efforts were implemented and others were not. For example, the school was successful in implementing its nonfiction writing program as well as the expanded literacy block for 180 minutes every day, with two hours devoted to reading and one hour devoted to

8.2 — Leadership Map Charting the Effectiveness of Nonfiction Writing at Maple Hill School

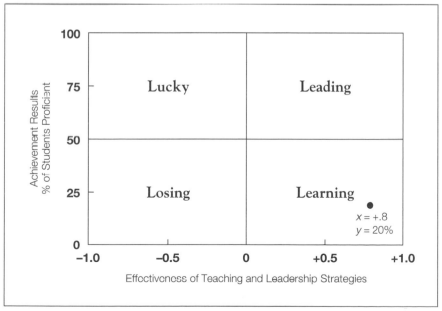

writing every morning. Ms. Lamb's attempts to improve grading systems were less effective, as grading systems in many classrooms continued to be unrelated to actual student achievement. A new reading program that was strongly supported by research was implemented with a high degree of fidelity, as was a program of common grade-level assessments that provided feedback to teachers every month. Equipped with monthly information on student achievement, teachers could better evaluate their teaching practices and determine which were most successful. In addition, Ms. Lamb was successful in transforming music, art, physical education, and technology classes into lessons that had a direct relationship to supporting student literacy and math achievement. A partial summary of these programs, their effectiveness coefficient, along with the real student achievement data, appears in Figure 8.3.

We can translate the data in Figure 8.3 into marks on the Leadership Map for Maple Hill School. Using a sophisticated and systematic process that includes a wide range of leadership and teaching strategies as well as comprehensive student achievement data, a detailed Leadership Map will emerge. In Ms. Lamb's case, a clear

8.3 — Leadership Map Data from Maple Hill School

Leadership Map Mark	Teaching/ Leadership Strategy	Effectiveness Coefficient (X value)	Student Achievement Measurement	Percentage Proficient or Higher (Y value)
A	Nonfiction writing	+.8	State language arts assessment	20
B	Grading practices	0	State assessment, all subjects	18
C	Reading curriculum	+.7	State language arts assessment	20
D	Common assessment program	+.6	State reading, writing, math, science, and social studies assessments	15

profile emerges from only these four strategies and student achievement variables. Figure 8.4 shows the application of the data to Ms. Lamb's Leadership Map.

It is clear from even this preliminary cluster of nodes that Ms. Lamb fits the profile of the "Learning" leader. While she is immensely dissatisfied with student achievement results, she is consistently (but not perfectly) using teaching and leadership strategies that are strongly associated with improved student performance. Put yourself in the position of Ms. Lamb's superintendent. There are other schools in the district where student achievement also languishes in the 15 to 20 percent proficient range. But there is a profound difference between a school

8.4 — Evaluating the Effectiveness of Four Teaching/Leadership Strategies at Maple Hill School

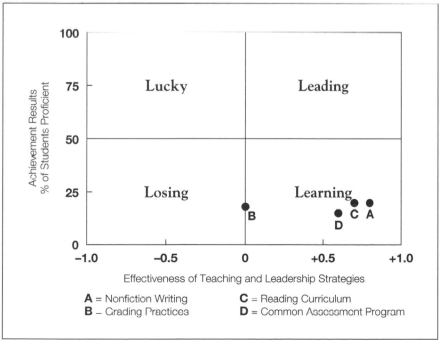

A = Nonfiction Writing   C = Reading Curriculum
B = Grading Practices   D = Common Assessment Program

in which those levels of student proficiency are associated with excuses and the repetition of consistently ineffective practices—the Loser quadrant—and Ms. Lamb's school, which is clearly poised for a turnaround. In fact, this school is a case study in long-term sustained success. For four consecutive years, this school, with a student enrollment of almost 100 percent free or reduced-priced lunch students and almost 100 percent of students from minority ethnic backgrounds, is one of the highest-performing schools in the county, consistently showing more than 80 percent of the students as proficient or higher on state assessments. After a few years of dynamic leadership and consistent application of effective practice, the leadership profile of Maple Hill looks like the one shown in Figure 8.5. The same profile can be

8.5 — The Leadership Map at Maple Hill School After Two Years and Nine Indicators

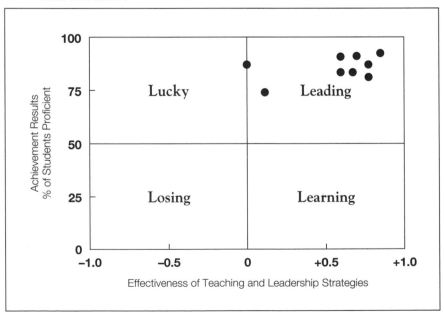

seen in other effective schools across the United States and Canada that also have many poverty-level students, many minority students, and many students classified as English language learners.

Note that the nodes on the Maple Hill map are not perfectly clustered. Some initiatives don't get off the ground, while others are started with enthusiasm but are poorly implemented. Most commonly, there are programs that are diligently implemented, typically based on a requirement from external authorities, but those programs have little or no impact on the intended results. Large numbers of planning, documentation, and training programs fall into this category, leaving even high-performing organizations with nodes scattered on the left side of the map. Despite the lack of artistic perfection in the Leadership Map, the clusters of nodes tell an important story and allow for some important interpretations for leaders and their colleagues.

The horizontal axis of the Leadership Map depends upon the use of research-based strategies and, more importantly, upon research that shows a correlation between particular teaching and leadership actions and student achievement. In Chapter 5, I acknowledged the general limits of correlation analysis, and the same caveats apply here. Correlation is not necessarily causation. In addition, even when correlations do exist, they are not necessarily linear in nature. For example, implementation research on some reading programs shows a distinctly nonlinear relationship between implementation and student achievement, such as depicted in Figure 8.6. The vertical axis represents student achievement in reading, and the horizontal axis represents the degree of program implementation, including the number of hours devoted each week to reading instruction. The hypothetical dashed line represents the linear assumption. Each additional unit of program implementation gains an additional unit of student achievement. But the messy reality is the curve, in which mediocre

implementation is a waste of time, yielding no better results than the absence of implementation. Only with deep implementation—full fidelity to the reading program model, complete staff training, active supervision, frequent collaboration and 10 hours a week of instruction for students—will the curve start to rise, showing the ultimate impact on student achievement.

Another challenge in using simple correlation coefficients, such as Pearson's *r*, is the assumption that only two variables are at work, when we know that life is multivariate. Student achievement has many complex causes inside and outside of school, including attendance, nutrition, teacher expertise, leadership commitment, schoolyard bullying, and a host of other factors. To be sure, multivariate techniques, such as multivariate analysis of variance (MANOVA), discriminate analysis, cluster analysis, multidimensional scaling, path analysis, structural equation, and hierarchical linear modeling, to name just a few, offer more detailed insights into the relative

8.6 — Nonlinear Relations in Leadership and Teaching Initiatives

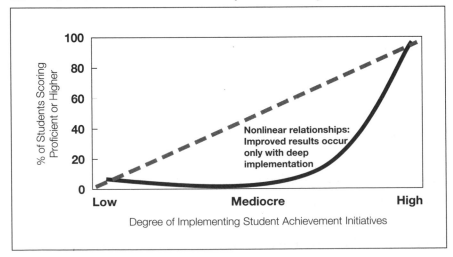

Nonlinear relationships: Improved results occur only with deep implementation

power of different variables. Similarly, there are mathematical ways to express nonlinear correlation coefficients such as the curve in Figure 8.6. As with most such challenges, there are complex and simple ways to deal with them, and for the purposes of the Leadership Map, the virtues of simplicity far outweigh the benefits of complexity.

With multiple variables, we can certainly acknowledge that there are multiple causes for student achievement. But the existence of multiple causes does not allow us to reduce the importance of nonfiction writing on student achievement. Moreover, we also acknowledge other teaching and leadership initiatives that can improve student achievement. To continue the example of nonfiction writing, the evidence does not simply support "more writing" but rather nonfiction writing (description, analysis, or persuasion with evidence), followed by collaborative scoring by teachers, and then followed by editing and rewriting by students. All of these separate causal variables must be in place, not merely a vague commitment to "writing across the curriculum." To return to the challenges of nonlinear relationships, the answer is not to ask readers of this book to calculate nonlinear regression coefficients or multivariate analyses of variance. Rather, the more practical answer to the challenge is to define meaningful thresholds of implementation. The node for "nonfiction writing" with a relationship of +.8 does not appear on the Leadership Map if the principal and teachers merely attend a seminar on the virtues of writing or if they submit to an annual district-required writing prompt. The relationship between nonfiction writing and student achievement holds only for deep implementation, and the author of the Leadership Map can describe in specific terms what that level of implementation means for each program. This includes the number of hours the initiative is applied, monitoring of the initiative by school leaders, and other essential components. As Figure 8.6 suggests,

mediocre implementation is no more deserving of a node on the Leadership Map than the complete absence of implementation.

A Leadership Map can be created automatically using technology-supported services such as those provided by the Center for Performance Assessment or Leadership and Learning International. You can also create your own Leadership Map using the guidelines in Appendix B, and you can receive free Web-based assistance in creating your Leadership Map at www.LeadAndLearn.com. (Select the "Leadership Map" icon.)

Interpreting Your Leadership Map

After creating a Leadership Map, one of three categories of distinctive patterns will emerge:

Cluster Patterns
Lucky
Losing
Learning
Leading

Continuum Patterns
Resilient
Challenge
Victim

Distributed Pattern
Islands of Excellence

The first category of Leadership Map patterns is the cluster. These patterns fall neatly into the labels on the Leadership Map—Lucky,

Losing, Learning, and Leading—and are represented in Figures 8.7 through 8.10.

The Lucky leader enjoys solid student achievement, perhaps because the kindergarteners were reading before they entered school. The leadership practices range from the merely ineffective, represented by the nodes on the "0" line, to the counterproductive and sociopathic, represented by the lines toward the left border of the graph.

The Loser leads a school in the worst of all possible worlds, with poor results and awful leadership and teaching practices. The proto-typical "boss from hell" does not inspire colleagues but alienates them, while the toxic venom of terrible leadership and teaching practices infects the students with malaise, disengagement, and failure.

8.7 — Cluster Pattern: Lucky

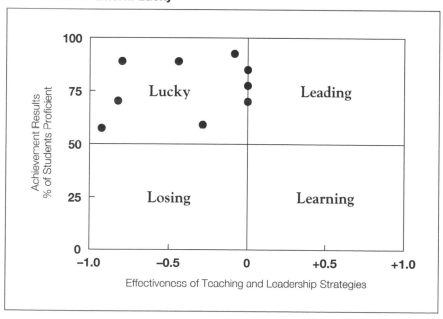

8.8 — Cluster Pattern: Loser

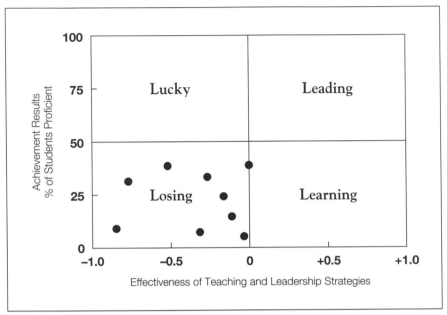

8.9 — Cluster Pattern: Learner

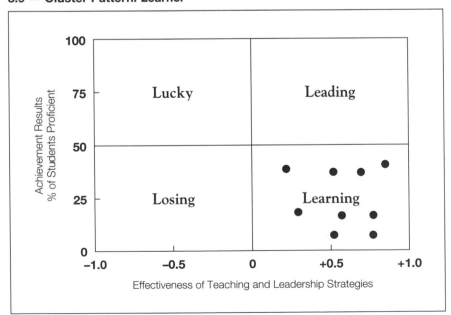

The Learner is a prime candidate for frustration, as the lesson that "behavior precedes belief" is learned the hard way. In the Learning schools, effective leadership and teaching practices are starting but have yet to bear fruit. There is often resistance from the staff and sometimes a lack of will to persist in new initiatives by the teacher. The most frequent question raised in the Learning school is "We're doing all the right things—so when will we see some results?"

The Leading school, like Maple Hill, has learned that morale is highest for students and teachers when there are clear rewards for real success and the long hours and exceptional effort that they have invested as learners.

The second category of Leadership Map patterns is the continuum, in which nodes form a link between two quadrants of the map. These patterns are particularly common in schools that are undergoing

8.10 — Cluster Pattern: Leader

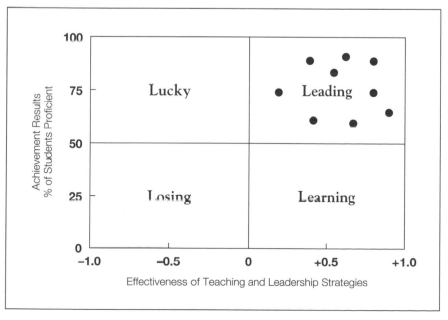

focused improvement efforts while they have many different measurements of student achievement. Thus in Figure 8.11, the Resilient
leader has many effective practices, but only some of the student
results are high on the vertical axis. The label "Resilient" is appropriate for this continuum because the leader, faculty, and students have
clear evidence that their work is starting to pay off. In the journey
from learning to leading, the Resilient continuum is a likely transition.

The Challenge continuum, displayed in Figure 8.12, depicts the
path that almost every turnaround school must travel. On this path,
they learn that there are no silver bullets or any immediate fixes in
school reform. The low-hanging fruit promised by the outside experts
and vendors seems curiously out of reach. Despite the abundance of
evidence to support an initiative, implementation is inconsistent
and incomplete. Straddling the Loser and Learning quadrants, the

8.11 — Continuum Pattern: Resilient

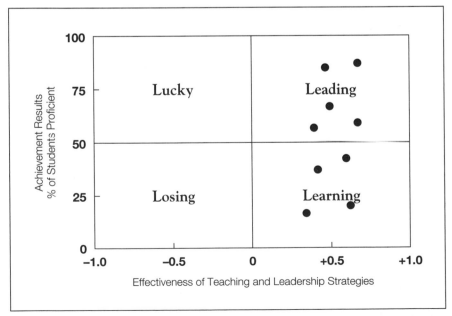

Challenge continuum requires exceptional stamina and extraordinary support from senior leaders.

The Victim continuum represents many schools that are located in suburbs (Petrilli, 2005). Top-performing students gain admission to Ivy League schools and regularly appear in the newspaper as if they represent the entire student body. Tracking is pervasive, allowing a few students to excel, while most students find comfort and anonymity as they sleepwalk through dumbed-down courses. Because they are not performing as badly as their economically deprived neighbors, these schools often escape the worst consequences of external testing requirements. "Sure, 48 percent of our middle schools were not proficient on the state math test," the Victim leaders explain, "but look at the number of National Merit scholars we have!" Teachers and

8.12 — Continuum Pattern: Challenge

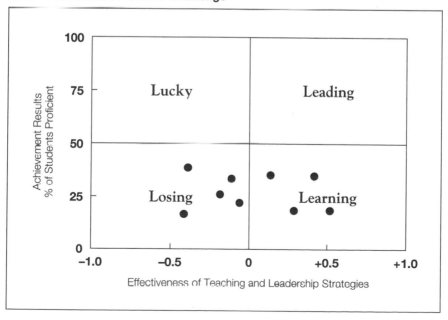

principals in Victim schools have a common refrain: "There's nothing we can do. We can't change tracking because the parents of the high-performing kids demand it. We can't change schedules and provide intervention to students in need because it would interfere with the schedule that parents, teachers, and students find convenient. We can't have high expectations because the way you get along around here is to give good grades for mediocre performance. We can't change our grading system because everybody is emotionally invested in it. We just don't do change—a lot of people have tried it, but they move on once they figure out it won't happen." The Victim culture is heavy on blame and light on personal responsibility.

In the terminology of M. Scott Peck, the late author of *The Road Less Traveled* (1985), the Victim culture could be described as having a character defect. Unlike the neurotic who assumes responsibility for everything, including things far beyond his control, the person with a character defect assumes responsibility for nothing, including factors that are well within his control. The failure to accept personal responsibility, taken to extremes, leads to individual and organizational behavior that is sociopathic (Deutchman, 2005). When one considers the consequences of sociopathic behavior, the parallels to Victim schools are uncomfortably close. In the criminal realm, the sociopath destroys the lives of others without a second thought, as the lives of others are trivial in comparison to the personal needs of the sociopath. In business, the sociopath plunders corporate assets and eradicates jobs, retirements, and futures for employees, while enjoying laudatory coverage from a business press focused myopically on bottom-line results. In education, the sociopath elevates the personal convenience of adults above the critical needs of students. One such leader in a school where more than 80 percent of the students were not reading proficiently said, "We can't offer any more reading instruction—my foreign language teachers

have seniority, and I have to fill those sections before I can offer any more reading classes. We can't offer any more writing instruction, because my faculty says that it takes too much time. But I got a grant for lots of new computers, so my students and teachers are pretty happy, and I intend to keep it that way." None of his colleagues would call him a sociopath. After all, he entered a helping profession, teaching, and has taken on a great challenge in a high-poverty urban school. There are times when he seems to care for adults and students in his charge. But his fervent belief in being a victim of circumstances, utterly impotent in confronting his school's needs, renders this school leader no better than someone who watches an assault take place and turns the corner, indifferent to the peril of another human being. Figure 8.13 shows the victim's continuum pattern.

8.13 — Continuum Pattern: Victim

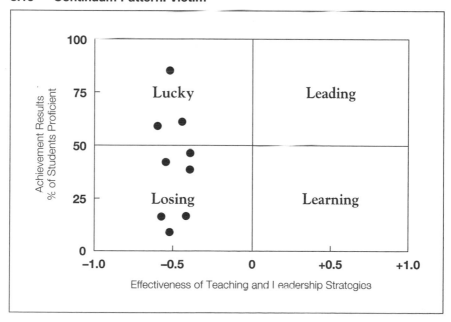

The third category of patterns on the Leadership Map are scattered or distributed patterns. As shown in Figure 8.14, there is a distinct absence of a pattern: nodes are scattered all over the map. Achievement is high and low; leadership and teaching effectiveness are at times outstanding, negligent, and counterproductive. This pattern is called "Islands of Excellence," and the larger an organization is, the more likely that all the patterns discussed earlier in this chapter will converge into this apparent mess of nodes across the Leadership Map. If the inference we draw from apparently random acts of leadership is that cause and effect are randomly distributed, with little systematic inference available, then we will miss the opportunity before our very eyes.

When statisticians study patterns, they are drawn to similarities, thus developing formulas for how apparently disparate nodes are

8.14 — Scattered Pattern: Islands of Excellence

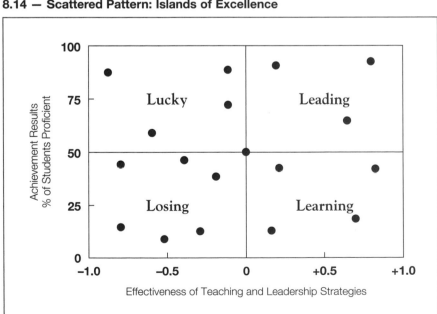

clustered together in a potentially meaningful way. Some of the techniques involved in these thought processes, such as factor analysis, require large conceptual leaps. These processes could include rotating a set of axes in a multidimensional space in different ways so that apparently unrelated nodes will have the opportunity to coalesce around some unifying characteristic—a "factor"—that helps us to understand how apparently disconnected behaviors or characteristics are connected in a meaningful way. This approach is not as abstract as it sounds. Such analysis is at the heart of the consumer profiling that marketers and politicians use on a regular basis. More than a quarter century ago, President Ronald Reagan's advisers discovered the "Reagan Democrats," a group of traditionally Democratic voters who shared some apparently dissimilar characteristics. They were union members, traditionally associated with the Democratic party, but had conservative social values. While traditional demographic analysis labeled these people reliable Democrats, shrewd advisers to Reagan identified these apparently disconnected nodes on the voter map to find a pattern that had gone previously unrecognized—the Reagan Democrat. Twelve years later, Bill Clinton would similarly connect the dots to find the soccer moms, just as George W. Bush would appeal to the NASCAR dads during the 2000 election.

Move the search for nonobvious connections from the political to the educational realm and examples abound. Why did math scores improve in a school? It might not have been the latest pile of curriculum documents stored in an administrative office and enthusiastically displayed to state officials, but rather the unnoticed work of a physical education teacher who, knowing that measurement had been a key skill deficiency of students on recent math assessments, incorporated English and metric measurement into every encounter with students. It might have been the unheralded efforts of the art teacher

who used dramatic visual displays to help students master the concepts of scale, ratio, and mathematical patterns.

Finding patterns in apparently unconnected characteristics is at the heart of the Leadership Map that displays Islands of Excellence. Some real sleuthing is required because the excellence may be deeply buried amid the prevailing mediocre, negligent, ineffective, and counterproductive leadership and teaching practices. In an old joke, a little boy is surprised to find a pile of manure under the Christmas tree. His parents are even more surprised to see him register delight rather than disappointment. When asked why he is so happy, the boy explains, "There must be a pony around here somewhere!" When we are confronted with the complexities of the Islands of Excellence Leadership Map, each element of the map must be inspected to find nodes that offer the opportunity for connections on a larger scale. Similarly, we must find the toxic nodes that are connected to disaffection, disengagement, and impotence, because islands of ineffectiveness battle with islands of excellence for the time, energy, and resources of every leader.

Applying Your Leadership Map for Organizational Change

While the applications of every leadership map should be accompanied by personal reflection, leadership support, and perhaps professional coaching, the remainder of this chapter suggests some applications and action steps that follow logically from typical Leadership Map patterns. The following key questions represent the starting points for leaders as they take their Leadership Map from interpretation to application:

1. What are the sources of our leadership and teaching practices? Which ones were imposed on us from the outside, and which

were chosen by us? If we have some ineffective and counter-productive practices, which are the "self-inflicted wounds" that we can immediately take the initiative to heal, and which are externally imposed damages that must be brought to the attention of a higher level of leadership and policymaking?

2. What are we gaining from our present decision-making framework? What are the personal and organizational rewards that we receive from these practices? Even the most noxious professional practices and personal habits provide some sort of positive reinforcement—that is the only reason we continue them. What do we gain in terms of personal and emotional satisfaction, convenience, or other rewards? How can we align these obviously meaningful rewards with the most productive and successful leadership and professional practices?

3. What is our three- to five-year trend? Are we likely to remain in our current pattern, or are we sliding to a different pattern? If we are Lucky, are we sliding into the Losing quadrant? If we are Leading, are we drifting to Lucky? It might be useful to use different colors to represent the nodes for different years, so that the trends from one year to the next are presented with a clear visual impact.

4. Where are the missing data? What other indicators of student achievement and what other measurements of leadership and professional practices should we include on the Leadership Map?

5. What information about student achievement, teaching practices, and leadership behavior must be expressed in qualitative terms? For example, when the issue is teacher expectations, can we display examples of students who are earning C's and B's and ask ourselves whether these grades reflect our expecta-

tions for proficient work? When the issue is student engagement, can we display anonymous quotations from students that portray in vivid, qualitative terms different levels of engagement ranging from oppositional, defiant, and disengaged to enthusiastic, committed, and completely engaged? When the issue is teacher engagement, can we create a case study that shows all of our most effective strategies being used by an exemplary teacher?

These questions reach deep into the heart of every professional learning community, and the answers are not always comforting. But just as Jim Collins (2001) admonishes us that the journey from "good to great" begins with an acknowledgment of the brutal facts, so also the unending journey toward effective leadership requires a consideration of these essential questions.

You now have a powerful tool for analyzing leadership practices and applying the Leadership for Learning Framework. In the final chapter, we will consider how to put all the pieces together and move from theory and research to action.

– 9 –

Putting It All Together
The Essential Transformations of the Learning Leader

What an exhausting and exhilarating journey! It is exhausting
because the reading is thought-provoking and even daunting, and
exhilarating because the rewards of discovery and challenge make
the effort worth the exertion. I work at a stand-up desk, with a
multivolume dictionary, thesaurus, and references on statistics
and Spanish, Fibonacci and French, idioms and Italian, helixes
and Hebrew all within reach. Authors who force me to use all of
these make me cranky, but those who require none of these are
ear candy, insufficiently engaging my interest. My fondest hope is
that I have fallen into a middle ground between labor and ear
candy, asking you to engage the ideas and stretch intellectually,
without overburdening you with unnecessary detail. In this final
chapter, I will synthesize the ideas and research of this entire
volume into five core ideas. Leadership is about change—how to
justify it, implement it, and maintain it. Your reward for having
persevered to this point is a crystallization of the main points of
this book the essential transformations of leadership for
learning.

From Islands of Excellence to Systemic Impact

"We've got a good start, but we can't seem to take it to scale." This phrase is at the heart of every school reform idea that started with high hopes, enthusiasm, and energy, and was embraced by a small group of early adopters, some of whom, it turned out, had been doing all sorts of effective innovation without benefit of any orders from higher headquarters. During the first year, success stories are diligently reported, as the enthusiastic proponents of the reform speak mainly with one another, reassuring themselves of the effectiveness of their efforts. In even the most troubled schools and systems, I can almost always find Islands of Excellence—classrooms in which 100 percent of special education students are meeting state standards, there is little or no achievement gap related to student demographic characteristics, and second-language learners are reading, writing, and speaking English with joyous enthusiasm. Amid a cesspool of lower expectations, I can find kindergarten students who are writing multiple sentences only months after learning to use a pencil, and 5th grade students who are writing research papers that are rarely required of students four years their senior. These islands of excellence are, however, a double-edged sword. While it is imperative that leaders find, document, and recognize these islands, the leaders must also take the difficult step of organizational leadership by transforming the islands of excellence into systematic impact. This transformation rarely occurs, because we accept assertions that effective change takes five to seven years as a justification for impotence and an argument against initiative. Transformation will happen only when we become dissatisfied with islands of excellence as the start and end of school reform. When, as is so often the case, we compare the enthusiasm of field reports with the reality that, at the end of the

year when it's time to examine systemwide results, there was little or
no change, we respond with a sigh of resignation rather than a commitment to transformation.

When reforms are limited to islands of excellence, there are typically four potential causes:

- The reform itself was ineffective, and the research on which it
  was based was inaccurate or fraudulent—blame the vendor.
- The reform was effective but was not implemented correctly—
  blame the teacher.
- The reform was effective and implemented, but the state test
  didn't reflect what students had really learned—blame the test.
- The reform was effective, implemented correctly in a few
  places, and directly related to improving student performance
  on state tests, but these islands of excellence were so isolated
  that their impact on school or system results was negligible—
  blame the leader.

The last cause is a central leadership failing in which we mistake the
existence of excellent practice with systemic impact of excellent practice. The following scenarios are taken from my personal observations
within the past year.

The curriculum and assessment offices in one district were dis-
patched to see what had become of the literature on which they had
invested so much energy and resources. Once their inquiries extended
beyond the small cadre of enthusiasts, the familiarity of classroom
teachers and building principals with the reform literature ranged
from minimal to nonexistent. Although the district had devoted
three years to the creation of the plan and had distributed thousands
of documents, some teachers claimed never to have heard of it, and

some principals could not find a single document that the district had distributed.

Another district had developed a technology reform that was thoughtfully deployed in some schools, but in others, tens of thousands of dollars of computers sat unopened, in one case stacked in the principal's bathroom. In another district, materials for the new math program had been distributed, teachers had given polite attention to the one-day introductory seminar used to acquaint them with the new curriculum, and the books were even distributed to the students. But even a cursory review of the math folders and assessment files revealed that in some classrooms, the math activities actually used by teachers were focused on the same worksheets that had been illegally copied for more than a decade, and the tests reflected the same agenda of the solo practitioner who explained, "I've been doing this for 22 years—you don't have to tell me how to teach math."

Blaming teachers, forcing teachers to follow a script in the classroom, pleading for "buy-in" from everyone, compromising on essential elements of program implementation, or simply giving up are frequent responses to these dilemmas. As long as there are educational writers who will validate the assertion that change takes just a little longer than the contract term of incumbent administrators, then we have a virtual guarantee that progress will never happen. I did not take you on this journey in order to accept any of these excuses at the end of it. The transformation from islands of excellence to systemic impact requires that we revisit the Leadership for Learning Framework and more narrowly focus on the energy and time of the leader. The complexity of the framework, particularly when covered with nodes that are disjointed islands, can seem overwhelming. How can we make order out of chaos? By

reconceptualizing the Leadership Map from a series of nodes to a small number of hubs.

From Nodes to Hubs

Earlier in this book we used the term "node" to describe the point at which two intersecting lines meet. In the Leadership for Learning Framework, the intersecting lines were the result of ordered pairs in which the vertical axis represented student results and the horizontal axis represented the effectiveness of teaching and leadership strategies. But *Merriam-Webster's Collegiate Dictionary, 10th Edition* (1998) provides surprising clarity with its second definition of "node" as "an entangling complication." While our previous use of the term "node" has conveyed the complexity of networks in a manner far more effective than "dots" or "spots," the very use of the network-related term "node" conveys complexity. And while each node does imply its own system of connections, the science of networks helps us understand that some nodes are much more powerful than others. Figure 9.1 represents the fairly typically disconnected Islands of Excellence phenomenon.

While there are some isolated areas of high achievement, these areas are sometimes associated with good practice, and they are equally likely to be associated with ineffective or deleterious actions of leaders and teachers. Worse yet, some effective actions appear to yield poor results. The term with a double meaning, "chaos," describes such systems well. Colloquially, such a school or system might find affinity with *Webster's* third definition of chaos, "a state of utter confusion." But there is a better definition of chaos, one with implications for leaders. The first meaning of the word, according

to *Webster's* (1998), is "a state of things in which chance is supreme." We are now getting the mathematical foundations for chaos theory, the presumption that a chaotic system is nonlinear and nonpredictable. For leaders who face chaos as part of their daily lives, *The Concise Oxford Dictionary, 10th Edition* (2001), defines the term as "anything where the parts are undistinguished; a conglomeration of parts or elements without order or connexion" (British spelling).

Put the terms together and we find the key to addressing the chaos that is at the heart of islands of excellence in organizations. Leaders who accept that the state of affairs before them is simply "utter confusion" may take the well-traveled and remarkably ineffective paths of either acquiescence or replacing one promising system

9.1 — Scattered Pattern: Islands of Excellence

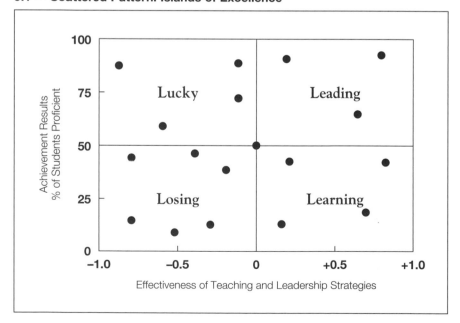

with another. If they make the latter choice, enthusiasm will once again be only a temporary substitute for impact. What is chaos, really? There are three assumptions of chaotic systems: They are random ("chance is supreme"), their composition is indeterminate ("parts are undistinguished"), or the parts are unconnected ("without order or connection"). Let us examine each of these assumptions and apply them to educational systems.

- "Chance is supreme." If success is random, then we really can't replicate it. Successful teachers and leaders just get lucky. By such assumptions (which underlie an astonishing amount of systems and mathematical theories) (Taleb, 2001), we assume victim status and remain safely away from any contemplation of responsibility.
- "Parts are undistinguished." School leaders don't even know who their most successful teachers and leaders are. After all, if they were to analyze data at that detailed a level, it would be bad for morale, and they fear they would have too many complaints. By such logic, these school districts will always be certain to keep success a secret, and while it remains a secret they can reinforce the first presumption of chaos in the system.
- "Without order or connection." Nodes are scattered over all of the Leadership Map, so even if school districts can identify them, they exist as islands, one never connected to another, and thus the chance of replication is so unlikely as to be impossible.

MIT researchers studying apparently random systems found that even if the distribution of nodes appears to be random, the connections among nodes aren't. Connections are, in fact, governed by "power

rules" in which some nodes have dramatically more connectivity than others. If, for example, you looked at a map of the world with dots on it, each dot representing the location of an airport of any size, you would see a mass of dots throughout the world. An airstrip at the Antarctic Research Station or the clearing that passes for an airstrip in Mwingi, East Africa, would be indistinguishable from O'Hare International Airport in Chicago. But if the same map were shown with the dots connected based on actual airline lights, several nodes would soon appear as hubs, as they are the few nodes to which many other nodes are connected. Now Chicago, Atlanta, London, Frankfurt, Paris, Hong Kong, Los Angeles, and only a few other cities would be dominant hubs. If I am planning to travel around the world, the first map of disconnected nodes would give me chaos. When I convert the nodes to hubs, I have the information, prioritization, and the "order"—rather than chaos—that I need to plan my decisions.

Let's reconsider the Islands of Excellence Leadership Map in Figure 9.2 in which the nodes appear to be randomly distributed. One of those nodes, labeled C, represents collaborative scoring of student work. When we connect every other node that is associated with collaborative scoring of student work (e.g., nonfiction writing, common assessments, interdisciplinary curriculum and assessment in music, art, technology, and physical education), then node C is no longer an isolated random dot. Rather, it emerges as one of the most important areas of focus for the leader of this system. If we provide time for collaboration, carefully define what effective collaboration is, and practice, recognize, and support collaboration, then we not only promote node C but indirectly provide support for a host of other effective and promising practices.

Close inspection of Figure 9.2 not only reveals the emergence of node C from a node to an important hub but also allows us to

distinguish between islands and emerging hubs. Not every hub is salutary, as the emerging hub in the lower left corner suggests. Just as C represents a hub of excellence that has extraordinary systemwide potential, the node in the lower left corner, D, might represent the confluence of ill-conceived and poorly executed practices that are equally ineffective in several different areas.

By shifting their attention from nodes to hubs, leaders can sharpen their focus on what matters most. Neither every island of excellence nor every island of mediocrity deserves the leader's attention. Instead, the leader must identify and focus on hubs, both those that hold the key for great improvement in the future and those that are emerging networks of negativity. Effective leaders reject the chaos hypotheses, knowing that effective and ineffective practices

9.2 — From Nodes to Hubs

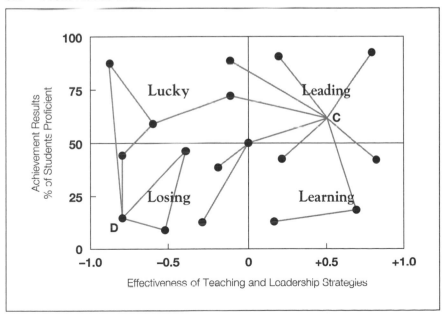

are the result not of random chance but of deliberate choices. Leaders can also gather evidence to reject the chaos hypotheses as they take the time to identify the most effective decisions and professional practices within schools. By employing holistic accountability, leaders know not only what the results are but what the purported causes of student achievement are. Identification and measurement of adult professional practices are essential if we are to move from the secrecy essential for chaos to the openness necessary for order. Finally, leaders make connections, knowing that the absence of connections, even among effective practices and practitioners, will allow chaos to persist and prevent effective practices from being connected throughout the system.

From Frantic to Focused

Leaders are plagued by expectations that are out of line with reality. Their absence at any meeting, sporting event, contest, or performance is viewed by their critics as inattention, indolence, or opposition. Rather than confronting these expectations, some leaders try to be all things to all people, behavior that is exhausting and counterproductive. As we learned in our earlier exploration of chaos theory, the only way to impose order on a random system is to shift our analysis from nodes to hubs. When leaders shift their focus from large numbers of random practices with random effects to a small number of intersections of many nodes—hubs—they nurture, support, and recognize the most effective hubs, and break the toxic connections stemming from the most poisonous hubs.

Focused leaders engage in daily disciplines that maximize their energy, bringing the highest level of concentrated effort on the

challenges that are most important (Reeves, 2002a). These disciplines include some simple tools, such as the Daily Prioritized Task
List and Project Task Analysis (see Appendix D). Focused leaders
allocate their time as if it were a set of precious jewels, each of which
has an expiration date. They cannot store these jewels but can only
allocate them wisely. In addition to the Daily Prioritized Task List,
effective time management disciplines include these practices:

Avoid lines. Be the first or last in a line, but not in the middle
unless you can use that time to read or listen to important information, reflect in a focused and systematic way, or otherwise avoid more
than a few seconds of wasted time. Many military organizations have
a wonderful tradition when it comes to food lines—the officers eat
last. Great school leaders neither cut in line nor wait in line, but use
their minutes wisely, perhaps serving others, gathering important
information, or listening to their constituents. When everyone else
has been served, the leader can have a few bites to eat.

Excuse yourself from pointless meetings. Ask yourself this: Do you
know, within the first 5 or 10 minutes of most meetings, whether
there is a clear objective, whether everyone will make a meaningful
contribution, and whether there is a high probability that the meeting will achieve its objectives? If you answer yes, as most leaders do,
then the difference between the 5th minute of a pointless and
unproductive meeting and the 60th minute at which it was mercifully
adjourned is a personal choice in favor of wasted time. When the
moment of your maximum contribution has arrived and departed,
pose this question to the group: "Is there anything else I can contribute to the meeting?" In an astonishing number of cases, the honest responses are "No," "We don't know," or "We just wanted to share
this information with you." The best response to the latter claim is to
politely but unequivocally say "We have a standard for meetings, and

it's that they are used only to gain the collective wisdom of a group to make better decisions. We never use meetings for announcements or sharing information, and if that is what you have in mind, please give it to me in an e-mail or voice mail. If I can't contribute anything more to a better decision right now, then I need to excuse myself."

However harsh this may seem, taking such a stance will not only save hundreds of precious leadership hours—gems that evaporate at the end of every day—but also set an example for people throughout the organization who now regard a day devoted to attendance at meetings as productive. Unproductive meetings don't contribute to better decisions, but they become antagonistic when colleagues protect turf, represent their vested interests, or otherwise engage in the illusion of productivity. Staying in a meeting and multitasking does not count. This behavior is not only rude, but it sends a signal throughout the organization that this frenzied, unproductive, and ill-mannered behavior is condoned by the leader.

The most important reason to get up and leave meetings is that every hour you are in a pointless meeting is an hour that is not devoted to mentoring and nurturing the "hubs"—those leaders and other members of your organization who have profound systemwide impact. Appreciation, recognition, and personal contact are some of the most extraordinarily strategic uses of leadership time, yet time is rarely allocated in that way because we are too busy with expenditures of time that are distinguished only by tradition and expectation, not by effectiveness.

Be focused. Focused leaders choose their priorities not based on the volume of noise generated by their multiple constituencies but based on the impact that each priority will have. Focused leaders know what their priorities are because they are written down. The format does not matter, as effective leaders of multibillion-dollar

global enterprises have been known to use leather-bound portfolios, personal digital assistants, and plain legal pads. It is the discipline of the content, not the elegance of the cover, that matters. Focused leaders also know their limitations. As the Rule of Six suggests, a focus on more than six high-priority items is too difficult to monitor on a sufficiently frequent basis for thorough data analysis and making midcourse corrections. A network with literally hundreds or even thousands of nodes can have only six hubs over which the leader exercises the greatest leverage.

From Private to Public

One of the most widespread reform efforts in education throughout the world is the use of "professional learning communities," a term that has long been used in leadership literature but has been brought to prominence in recent years by Richard DuFour (DuFour et al., 2005). He makes a compelling case for the transformation of teaching from private to public practice:

> The research in support of the benefits of collaboration is exhaustive, as is the research that links collaborative cultures to improving schools. Yet, despite the abundance of evidence regarding the benefits of collaborative cultures and the virtual absence of evidence to the contrary, it is the norm for public school teachers in North America to work in isolation with individual teachers, like independent subcontractors, teaching discrete groups of students. (pp. 16–17)

Private practice as the status quo in the educational world is hardly an accident. The personal experience of most practitioners is based on a model in which the most vital decisions influencing student learning—curriculum, classroom procedures, assessment, feedback,

rewards, and sanctions—are all matters of personal preference, each classroom disconnected from the next. Although teacher and leadership preparation courses have made the occasional bow to group processes and transparent learning, the essential interaction is a private one between student and professor. Educational systems continue the private interaction model of learning as students themselves become teachers, and "professional development" in many schools devolves into disconnected communication between teachers and administrators. DuFour and colleagues say, "The underlying assumption behind this approach is that if the 3rd grade teacher becomes a better teacher in his or her 'cellular structure' (that is, private kingdom), the school will become more effective in achieving its goals. This premise—the development of individuals ensures enhanced organizational performance—is patently wrong" (DuFour et al., 2005, p. 19).

Even in schools that claim to have professional learning communities, there is a wide range of effectiveness and norms when it comes to the actual implementation of collaboration and transparency. Principals and teachers will swear that they are organized as professional learning communities, but some community members actively resist—to the point of threatening grievances and other protests—analyzing individual classroom data or comparing professional practices among different teachers. Leaders and faculty members in such schools will attend seminars about professional learning communities, engage in staff development, and even arrange for visits to other school districts that have successfully implemented the concept. Then, when I ask for evidence of some of the primary characteristics of professional learning communities, such as common benchmark assessments and monitoring improved student achievement, the astonishing reply is "That wouldn't work for us." When I inquire as

to how it works for so many other school systems, the confident retort is "They aren't like us."

The Norfolk Public Schools in Virginia are one of the finest examples of dramatic progress in student achievement of any urban system in the United States, showing sustained improvements over the past seven years. But I have personally witnessed school leaders from other districts visit Norfolk, enthusiastic about their results and recognition, and walk away from their visit saying, "We could never do what they are doing—our faculty just wouldn't buy in." Norfolk's formula is hardly magic and is based on time-tested strategies. Staff members monitor achievement frequently with formative assessments (the interval ranges from biweekly to quarterly, depending on the school), provide immediate feedback to students and teachers, engage students in nonfiction writing across the curriculum, arrange their schedules to deliver exceptional amounts of time to get every student to grade level, and in general do not tolerate excuses from students or adults. Their comprehensive accountability system provides continuous feedback on the work of students, administrators, and teachers, and many schools monitor parent involvement, student discipline, extracurricular activities, and other factors that are, for them, important indicators of student engagement and achievement. When I hear observers from outside Norfolk claim they just can't do some of these things but nevertheless want to spend grant money and other resources on "doing" the Norfolk system, I wonder how they expect to achieve what Norfolk has achieved without doing what Norfolk has done. This is the strategy that drives people to buy the *South Beach Diet Book*, subscribe to the South Beach e-mail system, and attend lectures by experts promoting the South Beach Diet, all without actually consuming the foods recommended in the regimen. As Twinkies and gin are incompatible with South Beach success, so also

are private and inconsistent curriculum, assessment, and teaching practices incompatible with success in professional learning communities.

Public professional practices are not merely the result of scheduled events, such as collaborative scoring conferences. When public professional practices are fully integrated into a school, colleagues casually exchange ideas, assessments, writing prompts, and student work. Their exciting successes and disappointments are not merely the subject of formal case studies, but of informal discussions. They share their practices and related student achievement results not only in public events, such as the Science Fair for Grownups, but as a matter of daily practice (see Appendix C). Data walls adorn not only the principal's office and faculty meeting room but the hallways, cafeteria, and every classroom. Data walls are never used to humiliate students or teachers but rather are living documents, evidence of the fact that every day the students and adults in this educational system are getting better and better.

Great classroom educators in schools committed to public practice are not pulled away from their students to give lectures to demoralized teachers in a dark auditorium, but rather are the leaders of learning laboratories—their own classrooms—in which a small table with a few adult-sized chairs are placed in a corner. Visitors learn more from watching students and teachers work, learn, struggle, and celebrate together.

From the Bell Curve to the Mountain

The fifth and final transformation for leaders is developing a culminating idea. In complex organizations the goal is not merely to win, because in complex organizations there is no finish line, no ultimate

battle, or no final destination. Instead, there is a continuous series of challenges that call forth the intellect and ingenuity of leaders and every element of the system. At the heart of the difference between those who are committed to long-term sustainable change and those committed to mediocrity is their understanding of the distribution of human potential and achievement. In its best-known description, the bell curve, the prevailing description of human potential and achievement, suggests that a few will wildly succeed, a few will abjectly fail, and most will settle into the comfortable middle. When presented, as it is in most statistics textbooks, the bell curve is relatively benign. It is, after all, known among academics by the benign term "the normal distribution," and surely normal is better than abnormal, isn't it? Indeed, the curve represented in Figure 9.3 seems reasonable.

Biological evidence suggests that the normal distribution has many applications. If you envision the horizontal axis representing

9.3 — The Normal Distribution ("Bell Curve")

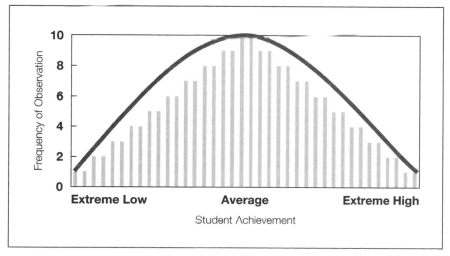

human shoe size, for example, a lot of people wear sizes 7, 8, and 9, but only a few, including several members of my family, are at the extreme ends of that distribution. Herrnstein and Murray (1996) most famously argued in their book *The Bell Curve* that this distribution also applied inexorably to the distribution of human intelligence, but they were hardly the first scholars to make such a connection. Since the early 20th century, researchers in the cognitive, biological, and physical sciences found evidence of the bell curve all around them. One of the great joys of teaching introductory statistics classes to students with diverse academic backgrounds is helping them find symmetry in apparently random phenomena they observe, from the span of antelope antlers to the course of infectious diseases to the parking patterns of faculty members. The bell curve, in other words, has a strong foundation in observed behavior throughout the universe. Indeed, there are many areas of human achievement in which the bell curve appears to have some application. Aficionados of sports statistics can appreciate that the bell curve can describe performance from the normal athlete in the middle of the curve to the extraordinary home run slugger on the far right side or the extraordinary golfer whose scores are on the far left side. Sociologists measuring virtue might find Mother Teresa and Mahatma Gandhi on the right side of the curve, but if they were measuring incidents of psychopathic behavior, they might find virtue on the left side of the curve. As these examples suggest, the application of the bell curve to human performance is not about high or low, good or bad, but about distance from the center or, in statistical terms, deviation from the mean or average of the distribution.

If we stop here, as too many introductory research and statistics courses do, we are left with the impression that the bell curve is simply a law of the universe, and the sooner we accept it and move on

with life, the better off we will be. Herrnstein and Murray (1996) explained that they didn't feel particularly good about their findings but were duty-bound as researchers to report them. People who, however well-meaning, seek to overturn the bell curve might as well rail against nature. A large number of teachers grade "on the curve," assigning the highest grades to students with the most unusual high scores, following what they regard as the inexorable plan of nature, allocating beauty, brains, and test scores to a select few. Long after the publication of *The Bell Curve*, I received the following anonymous note during a large meeting of school administrators: "The bell curve is true!!! After all, if everybody achieved the same standard, who would take out the garbage?" It is not uncharacteristic for someone already in a position of power, authority, and economic success to make such a remark.

Those on the extreme ends of the normal distribution, whether they hit a lot of home runs or have a low golf score, earn a lot of money or pay a low percentage of their income in taxes, have a vested interest in distinguishing themselves from the masses represented in the predominant hump of the bell curve. Lest this elitist tendency be ascribed only to detested royalists, ask yourself how you would respond to the statement, "I've just met the most *average* person! I can't wait for you two to meet!" We value the extraordinary and ascribe exceptional features to those we love and, when we think no one is looking, to ourselves. But when we are on the other end of the analysis, receiving evaluation rather than assigning it, we find "normal" or anything resembling the middle of the bell curve unacceptable. If you are a grandparent, you understand the immediate transmutation that takes place—your child's romantic interest is just barely worthy of marrying your daughter or son. But years later the grandchildren they produce are extraordinary in every measure. How

do we generate the extraordinary from the ordinary? This question is at the heart of the challenge faced by every teacher and educational leader. Although the distribution of ability and background may, indeed, be represented by the bell curve, the best description of our job is to change that distribution. If we receive a bell and deliver a bell, then we have done nothing more than deliver human cargo from one year to the next. But if we receive a bell and deliver a mountain, then we have done something extraordinary indeed. What does the "mountain" curve look like? As Figure 9.4 suggests, the mountain distribution is distorted or, in statistical terms, skewed, to the right of the distribution of human achievement.

The mountain curve is neither a panacea nor, as some critics suggest, a homogenization of students and teachers. It is not a panacea because, despite our best efforts, there are still incidences of low student achievement. It is not a homogenization because there remains a distribution of achievement across many different levels.

9.4 — The Mountain Distribution

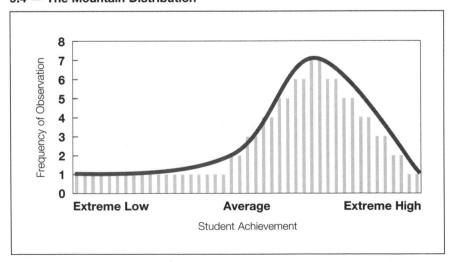

But the characteristics of the mountain curve are quite distinct from the normal distribution or bell curve. First, notice how the mountain curve is skewed to the right. While there remain variations among students, the differences in performance are not the wide distinctions between success and failure that characterize the bell curve, but rather the variations in student performance largely take place within a zone of success on the right side of the curve. Second, note that the shape of the curve appears distorted—it is higher and narrower than the bell curve. This suggests that while there are inevitably distinctions among students, those differences in performance need not be as wide as traditional interpretations suggest. This distribution, for example, is precisely what happens in standards-based reporting systems. When the horizontal axis represents achievement and the vertical axis represents the number of students, then we expect a higher number of students to perform at the right side of the graph, provided that students have the opportunity to succeed in an environment of high expectations and multiple opportunities for success, along with faculty and leaders who are willing to act on the belief that the bell curve is not their destiny. The path from the bell curve to the mountain is not an immediate one but is best illustrated by Figure 9.5.

Each incremental move from the bell curve to the mountain represents a teacher who would not give up, a school leader who did not wait for universal buy-in, a student whose work ethic defied traditional expectations, a parent who sought challenge and encouragement, and a school board member who backed both teachers and administrators who demanded more.

Educators and leaders who read and implement the strategies outlined in The Learning Leader are making a commitment to a journey. Upon reflection, my comparison to a marathon was ill-advised,

because even the longest ultramarathon has a finish line; instead, the strategies in *The Learning Leader* offer a set of mileposts. The journey from islands of excellence to systemic impact will require intellectual engagement and profound commitment. The journey from nodes to hubs is difficult and requires us to acknowledge that all nodes are not equal and that to identify hubs requires analysis that is nuanced, subtle, and politically sensitive. The journey of leaders from frantic to focused requires making choices and, in one of the most important and unusual decisions that leaders can make, standing up and leaving a meeting that is a pointless waste of time. The journey from private to public practice entails profound change, akin to the transformation required in medical practice over the course of centuries. In the span of years from the Greek physician Hippocrates to the present, only recently have doctors acknowledged that they have much to learn from midwives. Countless mothers and babies died while waiting for doctors to admit that, if only their practice and results were more

9.5 — Transition from the Bell Curve to the Mountain Curve

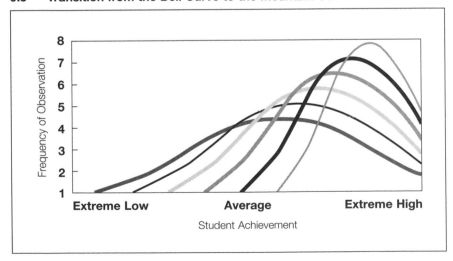

public, their lessons learned could be translated into lives saved. Today, we suffer a similarly agonizing wait while educators and school leaders decide that private practice must yield to the transparency and discovery that public professional practice will provide.

Finally, the journey from the bell curve to the mountain is the longest one of all, but ultimately it is the most rewarding. It is not an idle pursuit. At the dawn of the 21st century, a new generation of scientists is discovering that there are alternatives to chaos, randomness, and the normal distribution (Barabási, 2003). Einstein was right when he asserted that "God does not throw dice." Our lives and those of the children we serve need not be subject only to random chance.

Many people live their lives aspiring to make a difference and to live a life that matters. There need be no such uncertainty in the life of an educator or school leader. Every decision we make, from daily interactions with students to the most consequential policies at every level of government, will influence leadership and learning. After all these words, statistical analyses, and graphs, the preceding pages all come down to this: What we do matters.

Appendixes

– A –

Planning, Implementation, and Monitoring (PIM) School Improvement Audit and Scoring Guide

This appendix was adapted from the PIM study that was described in Chapter 5. The appendix has three primary uses. First, readers can use it to evaluate school planning and implementation practices in their own schools. Some adaptation will be necessary to ensure that local priorities are considered. Second, the rubric format can be used to provide explicit feedback to individual school leadership teams. Third, results of the rubric from many schools can be analyzed to identify systemwide strengths and weaknesses. The author is especially grateful to Donna Davis, Mia Dellanini, Antonia Rudenstein, David Scarbeary, Ray Smith, and Stephen White for their collaboration in the creative and analytical contributions to this appendix.

APPENDIX A — Planning, Implementation, and Monitoring (PIM) School Improvement Audit and Scoring Guide

School: _____

Category	Performance Dimension	Score				Notes
		Exemplary (3 points)	Proficient (2 points)	Needs Improvement (1 point)	Total Score for Category	
A. Comprehensive Needs	1. Strengths					
	2. Assessment results					
	3. Teacher practices					
	4. Acts of leadership					
	5. Engaged stakeholders					
	Subtotals:					
B. Inquiry Process	6. Possible cause-effect correlations					
	7. Strategies driven by specific needs					
	8. Analysis of adults' actions					
	9. Achievements results (effects) linked to causes					
	Subtotals:					
C. S.M.A.R.T. (Specific, Measurable, Accomplishable, Relevant, Timely) Goals	10. Specific goals					
	11. Measurable goals					
	12. Achievable goals					
	13. Relevant goals					
	14. Timely goals					
	Subtotals:					

Category	Performance Dimension	Score			Total Score for Category	Notes
		Exemplary (3 points)	Proficient (2 points)	Needs Improvement (1 point)		
D. Design	15. Purposeful, focused action steps					
	16. Multiple assessments documented					
	17. Demonstrated improvement cycles					
	18. Frequent monitoring of student achievement					
	19. Ability to rapidly implement and sustain reforms					
	20. Results indicators aligned to goals					
	21. Adult learning and change process considered					
	22. Documented coaching and mentoring					
	23. Strategies linked to specific student needs					
	24. Professional development driven by student needs					
	25. Professional development supported and integrated into key processes and operations					
	Subtotals:					
E. Evaluation	26. Summary data provided and compared					
	27. Anticipated knowledge and skills					
	28. Required evidence for evaluation					
	29. Next steps outlined in evaluation					
	30. Results disseminated and transparent					
	Subtotals:					
	Totals:				Total Score:	

SCORING GUIDE FOR SECTION A: Comprehensive Needs

Performance Dimension	Exemplary (3 points) *Meets all criteria for Proficient level and provides specific evidence to meet the criteria below.*	Proficient (2 points) *Provides specific evidence to meet the criteria below.*	Needs Improvement (1 point) *Provides evidence that meets the criteria below.*
1. Strengths	Strengths are described specifically for student achievement, teaching practices, and leadership actions.	Strengths are specified beyond the student achievement area; they include specific strengths of staff and school.	Strengths are limited to student achievement, and mentions of staff strengths are nonspecific or vague.
2. Assessment results	Student achievement is described in terms of state or district assessments, school-based assessments that describe subscale distinctions by subgroups, and classroom or contextual data that describe patterns and trends down to the skill level.	Student achievement data include some evidence of school-level achievement data, narrative, and school/classroom data to support district or state assessment data.	Student achievement data are primarily described in terms of standardized test scores or state-level assessments of student achievement, attendance, and demographics.
3. Teacher practices	Teacher practices are supported by research, describe whether professional development or repeated practice is needed, and describe how monitoring of those practices will be used to improve instruction.	Teacher practices are supported by research, and specific professional development needs are identified.	Teacher practices are generic statements that may identify strategies supported by research but don't link to a specific need for professional development.
4. Acts of leadership	Leadership actions describe the degree to which leaders monitor performance, set direction, provide feedback, or communicate values.	Leadership actions describe the degree to which leaders specifically monitor performance or set direction.	Leadership actions are not specifically distinguished from actions of other staff, or plans lack clear description of leadership actions.
5. Engaged stakeholders	• Evidence of frequent communication with parents regarding standards (beyond traditional grading periods), best practices, and grading (e.g., standards-based report card or nonfiction writing). • Evidence of engaging parents, patrons, and partner businesses or organizations is clearly described. • Web site includes links to various data warehouses for demographic and student achievement assessment.	Evidence of one or more instances of engaging parents in improving student achievement (e.g., online student monitoring, participation in curriculum design, methods to support learning at home).	Evidence of involvement with parents tends to be in areas other than teaching and learning (e.g., percentage of participation in conferences, attendance at school events, newsletters, etc.); complies with minimum state standards for communication with parents.

SCORING GUIDE FOR SECTION B: Inquiry Process

Performance Dimension	Exemplary (3 points) *Meets all criteria for Proficient level and provides specific evidence to meet the criteria below.*	Proficient (2 points) *Provides specific evidence to meet the criteria below.*	Needs Improvement (1 point) *Provides specific evidence that meets the criteria below.*
6. Possible cause-effect corrections	Inquiry routinely examines cause and effect correlations from needs assessment data before selecting ANY strategies or program solutions. Positive correlations at desired levels represent a quantifiable vision of the future.	Inquiry has identified some correlations from needs assessment data to select specific strategies or program solutions planned. Positive correlations at desired levels represent a quantifiable vision of the future.	Effects (results targeted) may or may not align to urgent needs assessed or represent a quantifiable vision of the future. Plan tends to address broad content as improvement needs, without identified correlations between needs and strategies.
7. Strategies driven by specific needs	ALL selected classroom-level research-based programs or instructional strategies are identified for a stated purpose, and ALL standards-based research strategies are designed to address specific needs in student achievement.	Most selected classroom-level research-based programs or instructional strategies are identified for a stated purpose. Most schoolwide programs or strategies (e.g., NCLB research-based programs, collaborative scoring, dual-block algebra, tailored summer school) specify the student needs being addressed.	Few (≤50%) classroom-level research-based instructional strategies or programmatic and structural antecedents are identified based on data that support the need for a specific program or strategy.
8. Analysis of adult actions	Explicit evidence indicates routine data analysis to identify cause and effect correlations. ALL causes are adult actions or the result of adult decisions rather than demographic student or family factors outside of the instructional control of educators.	Most described causes are adult actions or the result of adult decisions rather than demographic student or family factors outside of the instructional control of educators. Plan describes some links between causes (antecedents) and desired results (effects).	Evidence of analysis of cause and effect correlations is not described in the plan. Causes either are absent or tend to be demographic factors outside of the instructional control rather than adult actions and strategies. Plan rarely inquires into cause-effect relationships.
9. Achievement results (effects) linked to causes	ALL effects (desired results or goals) are specifically linked to cause behaviors or antecedent conditions for learning or administrative structures (e.g., time and opportunity, resources, etc.).	Most effects (desired results or goals) are explicitly linked to identified causes, strategies, conditions for learning, or administrative structures.	Few (≤50%) effects are explicitly linked to identified causes, strategies, conditions for learning, or administrative conditions.

SCORING GUIDE FOR SECTION C: S.M.A.R.T. (Specific, Measurable, Accomplishable, Relevant, Timely) Goals

Performance Dimension	Exemplary (3 points) *Meets all criteria for Proficient level and provides specific evidence to meet the criteria below.*	Proficient (2 points) *Provides specific evidence to meet the criteria below.*	Needs Improvement (1 point) *Provides evidence that meets the criteria below.*
10. Specific goals	ALL goals and supporting targets specify • Targeted student groups • Grade level • Standard or content area and subskills delineated within that content area • Assessments specified to address subgroup needs.	More than one goal and supporting target specifies • Targeted student groups • Grade level • Standard or content area and subskills delineated within that content area • Assessments specified to address subgroup needs.	Most goals and supporting targets describe in general rather than specific terms • Targeted student groups • Grade level • Standard or content area and subskills delineated within that content area.
11. Measurable goals	ALL goals and targets describe quantifiable measures of performance. Baseline data are always provided for each goal or objective.	ALL goals and targets describe quantifiable measures of performance with specific assessments.	Few goals or targets describe quantifiable measures of performance. Stated goals seldom reference student needs or growth targets or specific assessment tools.
12. Achievable goals	ALL goals and targets are sufficiently challenging to close learning gaps in three to five years for targeted subgroups.	At least one goal or target is sufficiently challenging to close learning gaps in three to five years for targeted subgroups. Learning gaps are specified.	Goal targets are set so low that achievement will not close learning gaps in foreseeable future, or there are insufficient data to determine whether any learning gaps will be closed by achieving goal targets.
13. Relevant goals	ALL goals and targets align with urgent student needs. ALL goals can be explicitly linked to the mission and beliefs of the school or district.	ALL goals and targets align with urgent student needs identified in comprehensive needs assessment (subgroups specified). Some goals are explicitly linked to the mission or beliefs of the school or district.	Few goals and targets describe urgent student needs identified in comprehensive needs assessment. Links to mission or beliefs are vague or absent.
14. Timely goals	Each goal and target describes a fixed date in time when it will be achieved.	Some goals and targets describe a fixed date in time when they will be achieved, but all goals or objectives specify a specific window of time (within 30 days).	Goals and targets rarely describe a fixed date in time when they will be achieved, and they describe only broad windows of time for any goals.

SCORING GUIDE FOR SECTION D: Design

Performance Dimension	Exemplary (3 points) *Meets all criteria for Proficient level and provides specific evidence to meet the criteria below.*	Proficient (2 points) *Provides specific evidence to meet the criteria below.*	Needs Improvement (1 point) *Provides evidence that meets the criteria below.*
15. Purposeful, focused action steps	Plan describes WHY some action steps are implemented and HOW action steps will be implemented, when, in what settings, and by whom.	Plan describes WHY each focus area or major action step is being implemented.	Plan describes when action steps will be implemented and by whom—but not why or how.
16. Multiple assessments documented	There are multiple forms of student assessment data, including formative, as well as multiple measures of teacher practices and leader actions.	There are multiple forms of student assessment data and some data for teacher practices.	Assessments are more often used to comply with directives than to serve as indicators of change or improved student achievement.
17. Demonstrated improvement cycles	There is explicit evidence of improvement cycles for every school improvement initiative.	There is explicit evidence of improvement cycles for some school improvement initiatives.	Evidence of improvement cycles for school-wide initiatives is unclear.
18. Frequent monitoring of student achievement	Monitoring schedule (≥ monthly) that reviews both student performance and adult teaching practices.	Monitoring schedule (≥ monthly) to review student performance.	Monitoring for student performance or teaching practices is infrequent.
19. Ability to rapidly implement and sustain reform	Capacity for rapid rollout in team responses to data, professional development, and coaching; time allotted for adjustments and opportunities in response to student needs.	Some midcourse corrections are delineated and anticipated in design of improvement plan.	No description of midcourse corrections observed in improvement plan.
20. Results indicators aligned to goals	All results indicators serve as interim progress probes for each S.M.A.R.T. goal.	Some results indicators serve as interim progress probes for S.M.A.R.T. goals.	Results indicators are vague, hard to describe, or difficult to measure.

21. Adult learning and change process considered	Consideration of adult learning issues and the change process is evident in time, programs, and resources.	Some attention to adult learning issues and change process is evident in plan (e.g., limited initiatives, integrated planning, and related support structures).	Evidence provided of adult learning or change process considered in planning. Plan tends to be fragmented with multiple initiatives, little attention to time requirements for implementation.
22. Documented coaching and mentoring	Coaching/mentoring system creates a coaching or mentoring cadre by building capacity and application.	Coaching or mentoring is planned and systemic.	Coaching or mentoring is incidental, viewed as sole responsibility of coach instead of schoolwide effort.
23. Strategies linked to specific student needs	Research-based instructional strategies, programs, and structures selected to impact specified student needs at school. ALL design activities and innovations are strongly correlated to student achievement gains.	Most research-based instructional strategies, programs, and structures are linked to specified student needs at school (school, subgroup, or individual).	Selected strategies, programs, and structures are not clearly linked to student needs as identified in the data. School may lack support in research or best practice.
24. Professional development driven by student needs	Professional development is linked to meeting specific subgroup needs, addresses underlying causes of any substandard performance, is limited to three major initiatives per goal, and prepares educators to improve decision making through planned reflection or analysis.	Professional development is explicitly collaborative, selected to meet identified student needs (school, subgroup, or individual), embedded in functioning school processes, limited to three major initiatives per goal, and scheduled within normal school functions at least monthly.	Professional development is fragmented and may or may not address student needs at school. It is rarely limited to three major initiatives per goal; activities tend to be overly ambitious in number or scope.
25. Professional development supported and integrated into key processes and operations	Support to professional development is provided for all initiatives in multiple ways (e.g., change procedures, cross-curricular applications, integration, subtract obsolete practices, collaboration, and modeling).	Support to professional development is provided in more than one way.	Design has few systems to support professional development efforts.

SCORING GUIDE FOR SECTION E: Evaluation

Performance Dimension	Exemplary (3 points) *Meets all criteria for Proficient level and provides specific evidence to meet the criteria below.*	Proficient (2 points) *Provides specific evidence to meet the criteria below.*	Needs Improvement (1 point) *Provides evidence that meets the criteria below.*
26. Summary data provided and compared	Evaluation compares planned initiatives with actual results from the prior year, examines achievement results based on safety-net power standards by grade, and compares those results to district performance. Student performance is augmented by a specific review of curriculum impact, time/opportunity for students, or the effect of teaching practices on achievement.	Evaluation summarizes data and evidence that examine student performance in multiple content areas; it describes students in need of intervention whose performance puts them at risk of opening learning gaps.	Evaluation tends to limit data summaries to student achievement analyses. Plans tend to examine student performance without specifying students in need of intervention whose performance puts them at risk of opening learning gaps.
27. Anticipated knowledge and skills	Evaluation plan describes explicit new knowledge, specific skills, and attitudes that will result from professional development associated with each goal for students, staff, AND stakeholders.	Evaluation plan describes new knowledge and specific skills or attitudes that will result from professional development associated with most goals for students and staff.	Evaluation plan tends to describe new knowledge, skills, and attitudes in general terms and perceptions rather than specific knowledge or skills.
28. Required evidence for evaluation	Evaluation specifies data and evidence needed to evaluate progress to meet all stated goals, including formative, school-based Tier 2 data explicitly aligned to address those students whose performance puts them at risk of opening rather than closing learning gaps.	Evaluation specifies data and evidence needed to evaluate progress to meet all stated goals, including formative, school-based Tier 2 data and their frequency.	Evaluation tends to use identical generalities for each goal rather than to specify data and evidence needed to evaluate progress toward goals.
29. Next steps outlined in evaluation	Documented next steps outline how changes in teaching and learning will occur, how the leadership team analyzes data, and how evidence was collected and submitted to colleagues and peers for review. The evaluation plan recommends changes from a list of alternatives and delineates a process to secure resources, implement changes, and evaluate them.	Next steps to improve teaching and learning are delineated and supported by a clearly defined improvement cycle in the plan.	Next steps rarely address changes in how teaching and learning will occur. Next steps, if specified, tend to describe future outcome targets (goals) rather than next steps in terms of adult actions.
30. Results disseminated and transparent	Evaluation plan is transparent in describing how results (positive or negative), conclusions, lessons learned, and next steps will be communicated and disseminated to all primary stakeholders (families, educators, staff, patrons, partners, and the public).	Evaluation plan describes how the compared results (positive or negative) are communicated to improve goal setting and ensure that lessons are learned.	Evaluation plan may describe process for communicating results, but seldom specifies next steps or how results will be explained to stakeholders.

Student Achievement Variables

Below are several types of student achievement tests that can be used in conjunction with your PIM analysis to further evaluate school improvement and implementation practices.

Test	Grade Level	Subject Area
Criterion Referenced Test (CRT)		
CRTGr3_MathProf	3	Math
CRTGr3_ReadProf	3	Reading
CRTGr5_MathProf	5	Math
CRTGr5_ReadProf	5	Reading
CRTGr5_ScienceProf	5	Science
CRTGr8_MathProf	8	Math
CRTGr8_ReadProf	8	Reading
CRTGr8_ScienceProf	8	Science
High School Proficiency Examination (HSPE)		
HSPE_MathProf	9–12	Math
HSPE_ReadProf	9–12	Reading
HSPEGr11_WriteProf	11	Writing
Iowa Tests of Basic Skills (ITBS)		
ITBSGr4_LangProf	4	Language
ITBSGr4_MathProf	4	Math
ITBSGr4_ReadProf	4	Reading
ITBSGr4_ScienceProf	4	Science
ITBSGr7_LangProf	7	Language
ITBSGr7_MathProf	7	Math
ITBSGr7_ReadProf	7	Reading
ITBSGr7_ScienceProf	7	Science
Iowa Tests of Educational Development (ITED)		
ITEDGr10_LangProf	10	Language
ITEDGr10_MathProf	10	Math
ITEDGr10_ReadProf	10	Reading
ITEDGr10_ScienceProf	10	Science
Nevada Analytic Writing Examination (NAWE)		
NAWEGr4_WriteProf	4	Writing
NAWEGr8_WriteProf	8	Writing

Creating Your Leadership Map

Step 1: Gather Student Achievement Data

Identify the percentage of students who score proficient or higher on state assessments. You can also use other indicators of student achievement, such as the percentage of special education students who have met their Individualized Education Plan objectives, the percentage of Advanced Placement students who achieved a score on the AP exam sufficient to earn college credit, the percentage of technology students who earned external credentials, such as certified network engineer, or any other meaningful student achievement variable that can be expressed as a percentage from 0 to 100 percent. For free Web-based assistance, go to www.LeadAndLearn.com and click on Leadership Maps.

Table B.1

Student Achievement Indicator	Percentage of Students Scoring Proficient or Higher Ranging from 0 to 100%

Step 2: Identify Teaching and Leadership Strategies Associated with Student Achievement

For each strategy, estimate an effectiveness coefficient. You can use the table of estimated effectiveness coefficients from research in the references as a guideline, but you should also use local school, district, state, or national research that is more appropriate for the specific needs of your school. For more information, please visit www.LeadAndLearn.com for an updated list of effectiveness coefficients.

Table B.2

Teaching or Leadership Strategy	Estimated Effectiveness Coefficient (ranging from −1.0 to +1.0)

Step 3: Create Leadership Map Ordered Pairs

Using the data from Tables B.1 and B.2 create a series of ordered pairs that you will plot on your Leadership Map. The x-axis (horizontal axis) is taken from the estimates of effectiveness for leadership and teaching strategies. The y-axis (vertical axis) is taken from the percentage of students who score proficient or higher on the assessments used to measure student achievement.

Table B.3

X Value—Estimated Effectiveness of Leadership and Teaching Strategy (Table B.2)	Y Value—Percentage of Students Scoring Proficient or Higher (Table B.1)

Step 4: Plot the Ordered Pairs on Your Leadership Map

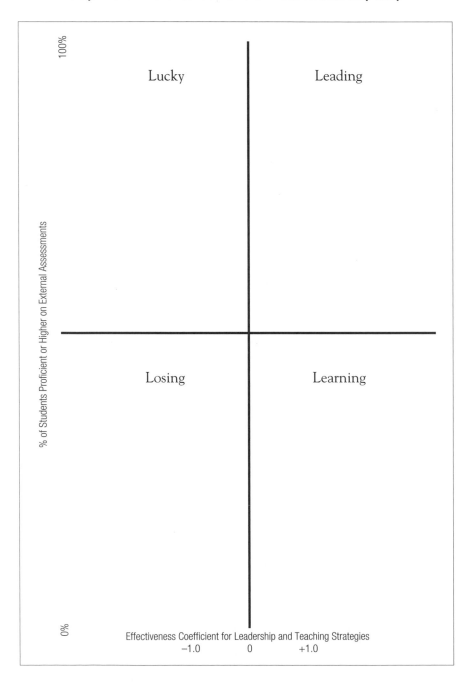

– C –

Guidelines for Data Walls or the Science Fair for Grownups

One of the most powerful techniques that educators and school leaders can use to improve decision making in the classroom, school, and district is the data wall. Ideally, the data wall is a portable display, using the cardboard three-panel displays frequently used for student science fairs. When administrators gather to discuss their ideas for improving student achievement, the data walls provide a rich source of information about the strategies employed in each school. Within each school, the data walls can be the focal point for faculty discussions on improving student achievement. For principals and teachers who are already using data to guide their instructional decision making, the use of a data wall will not create any additional work. For leaders who are not using data to guide their decisions, the data walls provide a valuable technique to jump-start their work. Most importantly, this technique will ensure that the analysis of student data is not isolated to a single seminar or a staff development program on data, but rather it becomes a continuous part of faculty and administrative decision making throughout the school year.

Three Essential Parts of the Data Wall

1. External data, such as state test scores.
2. Internal data (classroom assessments or other school measurements involving teaching practices chosen by the school that reflect its unique needs).
3. Inferences and conclusions (drawn from the data).

Information for the Panels

Left Panel

Includes tables, charts, and graphs that illustrate state test scores for the school and district. There may also be narrative comments, such as *"84 percent of our students are proficient or higher in mathematics according to the state test scores, and 78 percent are proficient according to a district test. A review of the last three years of data shows consistent progress on both state and district measurements, with particular gains in the problem-solving portion of the math assessments."*

Middle Panel

Includes data on teaching strategies associated with the tested subjects followed by another brief narrative, such as "The charts above show that the number of mathematics assessments including student writing has increased significantly in the past three years. Those assessments have emphasized the problem-solving portions of the state test. The charts also show a strong increase in interdisciplinary mathematics instruction, with the frequency of math instruction in music, art, physical education, technology, science, and social studies much greater for the most recent school year than was the case in earlier years."

Right Panel

Includes inferences and conclusions, such as "Our analysis of the data suggests that multidisciplinary instruction in math and writing in math have both been effective strategies to improve student performance. Therefore, we have planned to expand these strategies in the following ways [provide examples of the strategies specifically applicable to the individual school]. We remain very concerned about the 16 percent of students who are not proficient on the math portion of the state tests and have developed individualized learning plans for each of these students. In addition, we have added the following intervention strategies for all nonproficient students [include specific strategies applicable to your school]."

Other Notes to Prepare for the Science Fair for Grownups

1. Principals will not make formal presentations—the data walls speak for themselves. Principals should be prepared to respond to questions from colleagues about their data walls.
2. The primary function of the data wall and science fair is to allow principals to ask one another questions and share with each other informally how they achieved their successes. (*If the science fair takes place during a multiple-day leadership conference, then the displays should be set up during the breakfast of the first day and left up throughout the conference.*)
3. The process of continuous collaboration must continue all year, not just at the retreat. The data walls can be the focus of internal staff development, joint faculty meetings with other schools, and planning for instructional interventions and professional development activities.

4. **Critically Important:** The data walls are not for the purpose of impressing outside observers, the superintendent, or any other external audience. The primary purpose of the data walls is for the principals to share information with their fellow principals and, most importantly, with their faculties.

5. Principals will have to make choices regarding which data to use. They will want to show the information that is most important, drawing clear conclusions, and making the point to the faculty members that they are not merely displaying data but *using* data to inform their leadership decision making.

– D –

Daily Priorities Lists

Daily Prioritized Task List

Create a new daily prioritized task list every day. Throughout the day add new requests for your time. If you have more than six A priorities for today, then you must either defer some of the A-level tasks or change some of those tasks to B-level priority.

Name: _____   Date: _____

Page _____ of _____ pages

Task	Priority (A,B,C)	Date of Origination

Project Task Analysis

Projects must be broken down into manageable tasks. Any task that takes more than the time allowed for a single uninterrupted work session must be broken down into several different tasks. In general, if a task takes more than three hours to complete, it is not a task but a project.

Project Name: _____ Start Date: _____

Task	Person Responsible	Start Date	Deadline

Acknowledgments

Every book is a collegial effort, but this book in particular depended upon the efforts of many of my colleagues at the Center for Performance Assessment and our partnership school systems. The research in Chapter 5 was conducted with the kind permission of the Clark County School District in Nevada. I extend my particular appreciation to former Superintendent Carlos Garcia and current Superintendents Augustin Orci and Walt Rulffes and the Clark County School District Research, Accountability, and Innovation Division. Much of the research work on the Planning Implementation and Monitoring (PIM™) study was the work of my colleagues Stephen White and Ray Smith at the Center for Performance Assessment and Dr. Antonia Rudenstein. David Scarbeary provided exceptional technical and analytical insights, and Mia Dellanini managed the entire project.

My thinking on leadership has been informed by a number of scholars, friends, and colleagues. Footnotes are inadequate expressions for the following scholars whose thinking so profoundly influences my work: Albert-László Barabási, Richard Elmore, Michael Fullan,

Howard Gardner, John Goodlad, Tom Guskey, Jeff Howard, Robert Kaplan, Mary Grassa O'Neill, Bob Marzano, David Perkins, Mike Schmoker, Robert Slavin, and Noel Tichy. Practicing school leaders who have had a profound impact on my work particularly with regard to the role of leaders in accountability include: Bill Andrikopolous, Joyce Bales, Jim Dueck, Karen Gould, Bill Habermehl, Bob Jasna, Thomas Lockamy, Ray Simon, Betty Sternberg, and Terry Thompson. I thank the following school systems for their partnership: Savannah–Chatham County Public Schools, Georgia; Hazelwood School District, Missouri; Rockford Public Schools, Illinois; Metropolitan School District of Wayne Township, Indiana; Elkhart Community Schools, Indiana; Norfolk Public Schools, Virginia; Montgomery County Educational Service Center, Ohio; Connecticut State Department of Education, Connecticut; District of Columbia Public Schools, Washington, D.C.; Bering Strait School District, Alaska; North Thurston Public Schools, Washington; Beaverton Public Schools, Oregon; West Contra Costa Unified School District, California; Twin Falls School District, Idaho; Jurupa Unified School District, California; New Haven Public Schools, Connecticut; The Stupski Foundation; and Clark County School District, Nevada. At the Center for Performance Assessment, I am indebted to Larry Ainsworth, Lisa Almeida, Greg Atkins, Bonnie Bishop, Cheryl Bonnell, Nan Caldwell, Damon Carr, Donna Davis, Anne Fenske, Tony Flach, Todd Gilmore, Kendra Hockenberry, Robin Hoey, Mary Kate Karr-Petras. Matt Minney, Liz Monsma, Peggy Morales, Jason Mueller, Angela Peery, Peg Portscheller, Kelly Valentine, Cindy Wasinger, and Nan Woodson.

My collaborations with ASCD are always a pleasure. The professionalism of the staff and the commitment of the entire organization to international education helped lighten the author's burdens. I am

particularly indebted to the following from ASCD: Leah Lakins, Associate Editor, Scott Willis, Director, Book Acquisitions and Development, and Nancy Modrak, Director of Publishing. Cathy Shulkin once again reviewed every word of the manuscript, asking challenging questions, improving clarity, moderating my affinity for polysyllabic expression, and helping me avoid embarrassing errors. The errors that remain, of course, are my own.

My grandmother was a school superintendent in the early years of the 20th century, when women in senior leadership roles were even more rare than they are today. It is therefore not surprising that her progeny included a daughter, Julie Reeves, who continues to teach and lead in her ninth decade. Her life is both a compelling example and gentle rebuke to anyone who would claim that either busy lives or physical limitations are reasons to resist the callings of teaching and leadership. Though she never received a penny for teaching, she has taught generations of students, ranging from the smallest children, to teens with whom few others had any patience, to her peers who share her passion for lifelong learning. While I was working on this project, she was researching a paper on the legal career of Abraham Lincoln and serving on the board of a national arts organization. When my father could not read the papers written by his law school students, it was my mother who patiently read them so that he could continue his teaching career even after his eyesight failed. Dedicating this book to her is only a particle of the acknowledgment she deserves for a lifetime of service to students she knew and loved and to students who never knew of her contributions to their education.

Douglas Reeves
Swampscott, Massachusetts
October 2005

References

Ainsworth, L. (2003a). *Power standards: Identifying the standards that matter the most.* Englewood, CO: Advanced Learning Press.

Ainsworth, L. (2003b). *Unwrapping the standards: A simple process to make standards manageable.* Englewood, CO: Advanced Learning Press.

Armstrong, T. (2000). *Multiple intelligences in the classroom* (2nd ed.). Alexandria, VA: Association for Supervision and Curriculum Development.

Barabási, A. L. (2003). *Linked: How everything is connected to everything else and what it means.* New York: Plume.

Barzun, J. (2001). *From dawn to decadence: 500 years of Western cultural life: 1500 to the present.* London: HarperCollins.

Baumeister, R. F., Campbell, J. D., Krueger, J. I., & Vohs, C. D. (2004, December 20). Exploding the self-esteem myth. *Scientific American.* Retrieved July 12, 2005, from http://www.sciam.com/print_version.cfm?articleID=000CB565-F330-11BE-AD0683414B7F0000.

Bennett, L., Jr. (1992). *What manner of man: A biography of Martin Luther King, Jr.* (8th ed.). Chicago: Johnson Publishing Co.

Brand, C. (1996). *The g factor: General intelligence and its implications.* New York: Wiley.

Buckingham, M. (2005a). *The one thing you need to know: . . . About great managing, great leading, and sustained individual success.* New York: Free Press.

Buckingham, M. (2005b, March 1). What great managers do. *Harvard Business Review,* 70–78.

Buckingham, M., & Clifton, D. O. (2001). *Now, discover your strengths.* New York: Free Press.

Buckingham, M., & Coffman, C. (1999). *First, break all the rules: What the world's greatest managers do differently.* New York: Simon & Schuster.

Butler, C. (2004, June 3). Minimum grades, minimum motivation. *The Education Gadfly*. Retrieved July 13, 2005, from http://www.edexcellence.net/foundation/gadfly/issue.cfm?id=151#1850.

Calkins, L. M. (1994). *The art of teaching writing* (2nd ed.). Portsmouth, NH: Heinemann.

Cameron, K. S., & Caza, A. (2004). Contributions to positive organizational scholarship. *American Behavioral Scientist, 47*(6), 731–739.

Casciaro, T., & Lobo, M. S. (2005, June 1). Competent jerks, lovable fools, and the formation of social networks. *Harvard Business Review*, 92–99.

Churchill, W. (1974). *The world crisis*. London: Library of Imperial History, in association with the Hamlyn Publishing Group.

Coleman, J. (1966). *Equality of educational opportunity*. Washington, DC: U.S. Government Printing Office.

Collins, J. C. (2001). *Good to great: Why some companies make the leap . . . and others don't*. New York: HarperBusiness.

Concise Oxford Dictionary (10th ed.). (2001). Oxford: Oxford University Press.

Covey, S. R. (2004). *The 8th habit: From effectiveness to greatness*. New York: Free Press.

Darling-Hammond, L. (1995). *A license to teach: Building a profession for 21st-century schools*. Boulder, CO: Westview Press.

Darling-Hammond, L. (1997a). *Doing what matters most: Investing in quality teaching*. New York: National Commission on Teaching & America's Future.

Darling-Hammond, L. (1997b). *The right to learn: A blueprint for creating schools that work*. San Francisco: Jossey-Bass.

Darwin, C. (1859/2005). *The origin of species*. Chestnut Hill, MA: Elibron Classics. (Original work published 1859)

Deutchman, A. (2005, July). Is your boss a psychopath? *Fast Company, 96*, 44–51.

DuFour, R., Eaker, R., & DuFour R. (2005). *On common ground: The power of professional learning communities*. Bloomington, IN: National Educational Service.

Durant, W. J. (1933). *The story of philosophy*. New York: Simon & Schuster.

Durant, W. J. (1935). *The story of civilization*. New York: Simon & Schuster.

Durant, W. J. (1950). *The age of faith: A history of medieval civilization—Christian, Islamic, and Judaic—from Constantine to Dante: A.D. 325–1300. The story of civilization pt. 4*. New York: Simon & Schuster.

Ellis, J. (2004). *His excellency: George Washington*. New York: Knopf.

Elmore, R. (2000). *Building a new structure for school leadership*. Washington, DC: Albert Shanker Institute.

Evans, P., & Wolf, B. (2005, July–August). Collaboration rules. *Harvard Business Review*, 96–104.

Fennell, T. (1997). Bernard Ebbers, a Canadian-born telecommunications mogul who prefers cowboy hats and blue jeans to pinstripes and silk ties. *The Canadian Encyclopedia*. Retrieved July 17, 2005, from http://thecanadianencyclopedia.com/index.cfm?PgNm=TCE&Params=M1ARTM0011444.

Friedman, T. L. (2005). *The world is flat*. New York: Farrar, Straus, and Giroux.

Fuhrman, S. H., & Elmore, R. F. (Eds.). (2004). *Redesigning accountability systems for education*. New York: Teachers College Press.

Fullan, M. (2005). *Leadership & sustainability: System thinkers in action*. Thousand Oaks, CA: Corwin Press.

Gardner, H. (1993). *Frames of mind: The theory of multiple intelligences* (2nd ed.). New York: BasicBooks.

Gardner, H. (1999). *Intelligence reframed: Multiple intelligences for the 21st century*. New York: BasicBooks.

Gerstner, L. V. (2002). *Who says elephants can't dance? Inside IBM's historic turnaround*. New York: HarperCollins.

Gladwell, M. (2000). *The tipping point: How little things can make a big difference*. Boston: Little, Brown.

Glenn, H. S., & Nelsen, J. (2000). *Raising self-reliant children in a self-indulgent world: Seven building blocks for developing capable young people* (Rev. ed.). Roseville, CA: Prima Publishing.

Goleman, D. (1995). *Emotional intelligence: Why it can matter more than IQ*. New York: Bantam Books.

Goleman, D. (2000). *Working with emotional intelligence*. New York: Bantam Books.

Goleman, D., Boyatzis, R., & McKee, A. (2002). *Primal leadership: Realizing the power of emotional intelligence*. Boston: Harvard Business School Press.

Goodlad, J. I. (1984). *A place called school*. New York: McGraw-Hill.

Goodlad, J. I. (1990). *Teachers for our nation's schools*. San Francisco: Jossey-Bass.

Goodlad, J. I. (1994). *Educational renewal: Better teachers, better schools*. San Francisco: Jossey-Bass.

Gray, J. (1992). *Men are from Mars, women are from Venus: A practical guide for improving communication and getting what you want in your relationships*. New York: HarperCollins.

Guskey, T. R. (2000a). *Evaluating professional development*. Thousand Oaks, CA: Corwin Press.

Guskey, T. R. (2000b, December). Grading policies that work against standards . . . and How to fix them. *NASSP Bulletin, 84*(620), 20–29.

Guskey, T. R. (2005). Five key concepts kick off the process. *Journal of Staff Development, 26*(1), 36–40.

Guskey, T. R., & Bailey, J. M. (2001). *Developing grading and reporting systems for student learning*. Thousand Oaks, CA: Corwin Press.

Haycock, K. (1998, Summer). Good teaching matters . . . a lot. *The Education Trust, 3*(2), 3–14.

Herrnstein, R. J., & Murray, C. (1996). *The bell curve: Intelligence and class structure in American life*. New York: Simon & Schuster.

Hersey, P. (1985). *The situational leader*. New York: Warner Books.

Hersey, P., & Blanchard, K. H. (1977). *The management of organizational behavior* (3rd ed). Upper Saddle River, N. J.: Prentice Hall.

Ingersoll, R. M. (2003, January 7). To close the gap, quality counts. *Education Week*, 7–18.

Jenkins, R. (2001). *Churchill*. London: Macmillan.

Johnson, J., & Duffett, A. (2003, August 25). *An assessment of survey data on attitudes about teaching, including the views of parents, administrators, teachers and the general public*. Retrieved July 15, 2005, from http://www.publicagenda.com/research/pdfs/attitudes_about_teaching.pdf.

Kachigan, S. K. (1986). *Statistical analysis: An interdisciplinary introduction to univariate & multivariate methods*. New York: Radius Press.

Kagan, S., Gardner, H., & Sylwester, R. (2002, Fall). Trialogue: Brain localization of intelligences. *Kagan Online Magazine*. Retrieved July 18, 2005, from http://www.kaganonline.com/KaganClub/FreeArticles/Trialogue.html.

Kagan, S., & Kagan, M. (1998). *The complete MI book*. San Clemente, CA: Kagan
    Cooperative Learning.
King, S. (2002). *On writing: A memoir of the craft*. New York: Pocket Books.
Kouzes, J. M., & Posner, B. Z. (2000). *The five practices of exemplary leadership: When lead-
    ers are at their best*. San Francisco: Jossey-Bass.
Kouzes, J. M., & Posner, B. Z. (2003a). *Credibility: How leaders gain it and lose it, why
    people demand it*. Jossey-Bass Business & Management Series. San Francisco:
    Jossey-Bass.
Kouzes, J. M., & Posner, B. Z. (2003b). *The leadership challenge* (Rev. ed.). San Francisco:
    Jossey-Bass.
Learning 24/7. (2005, April 7). *Classroom observation study*. Study presented at the meet-
    ing of the National Conference on Standards and Assessment in Las Vegas, NV.
Leithwood, K., Louis, K. S., Anderson, S., & Wahlstrom, K. (2004, September). *How lead-
    ership influences students learning*. The Wallace Foundation. Retrieved July 13, 2005,
    from http://www.wallacefoundation.org/WF/KnowledgeCenter/KnowledgeTopics/
    EducationLeadership/HowLeadershipInfluencesStudentLearning.htm.
Levine, M. (2002). *The myth of laziness*. New York: Simon & Schuster.
Levine, A. (2005, March). *Educating school leaders*. The Education Schools Project.
    Retrieved July 11, 2005, from http://www.edschools.org/pdf/Final313.pdf.
Marzano, R. J. (2000). *Transforming classroom grading*. Alexandria, VA: Association for
    Supervision and Curriculum Development.
Marzano, R. J. (2001a). *Designing a new taxonomy of educational objectives*. Thousand
    Oaks, CA: Corwin Press.
Marzano, R. J. (2001b). *A handbook for classroom instruction that works*. Alexandria, VA:
    Association for Supervision and Curriculum Development.
Marzano, R. J. (2003). *What works in schools: Translating research into action*. Alexandria,
    VA: Association for Supervision and Curriculum Development.
Marzano, R. J., Pickering, D., & Pollock, J. E. (2001). *Classroom instruction that works:
    Research-based strategies for increasing student achievement*. Alexandria, VA:
    Association for Supervision and Curriculum Development.
McBrien, J. L., Brandt, L., & Brandt, R. S. (1997). *The language of learning: A guide to
    education terms*. Alexandria, VA: Association for Supervision and Curriculum
    Development.
McCullough, D. G. (2002). *John Adams*. New York: Simon & Schuster.
McCullough, D. G. (2005). *1776*. New York: Simon & Schuster.
McLean, B., & Elkind, P. (2003). *The smartest guys in the room: The amazing rise and scan-
    dalous fall of Enron*. New York: Portfolio.
Merriam-Webster's Collegiate Dictionary (10th ed.). (1998). Springfield, MA: Merriam-
    Webster.
Morse, G. (2005, June). Hidden harassment. *Harvard Business Review, 28–30.*
Neff, T. J., & Citrin, J. M. (1999). *Lessons from the top: The search for America's best busi-
    ness leaders*. New York: Doubleday.
Oberman, I., & Symonds, K. W. (2005, January–February). What matters most in closing
    the gaps. *Leadership, 8–11.*
Peck, M. S. (1985). *The road less traveled*. New York: Simon & Schuster.
Perini, M. J., Silver, H. F., & Strong, R. W. (2000). *So each may learn: Integrating learning
    styles and multiple intelligences*. Alexandria, VA: Association for Supervision and
    Curriculum Development.
Perkins, D. N. (1995). *Outsmarting IQ: The emerging science of learnable intelligence*. New
    York: Free Press.

Perkins, D. N. (2003). *King Arthur's round table: How collaborative conversations create smart organizations.* Hoboken, NJ: Wiley.

Petrilli, M. J. (2005, July 11). School reform moves to the suburbs. *New York Times.*

Pfeffer, J., & Sutton, R. I. (2000). *The knowing-doing gap: How smart companies turn knowledge into action.* Boston: Harvard Business School Press.

Prichard Committee for Academic Excellence. (2005). *High achieving high schools report.* Retrieved July 13, 2005, from http://www.prichardcommittee.org/ HS%20Report.pdf. Author.

Prince, C. (2002). *The challenge of attracting good teachers and principals to struggling schools.* American Association of School Administrators. Retrieved July 13, 2005, from http://www.aasa.org/issues_and_insights/issues_dept/challenges_teachers_ principals.pdf.

Reeves, D. B. (2000, December). Standards are not enough: Essential transformations for school success. *NASSP Bulletin, 84*(10), 5–19.

Reeves, D. B. (2001a). *Crusade in the classroom: How George W. Bush's education reforms will affect your children, our schools.* New York: Simon & Schuster.

Reeves, D. B. (2001b). *101 questions & answers about standards, assessment, and accountability.* Denver, CO: Advanced Learning Press.

Reeves, D. B. (2002a). *The daily disciplines of leadership: How to improve student achievement, staff motivation, and personal organization.* San Francisco: Jossey-Bass.

Reeves, D. B. (2002b). Galileo's dilemma: The illusion of scientific certainty in educational research. *Education Week, 21*(34).

Reeves, D. B. (2002c). *Holistic accountability: Serving students, schools, and community.* Thousand Oaks, CA: Corwin Press.

Reeves, D. B. (2002d). *The leader's guide to standards: A blueprint for educational equity and excellence.* San Francisco: Jossey-Bass.

Reeves, D. B. (2002e). *Making standards work: How to implement standards-based assessments in the classroom, school, and district* (3rd ed). Denver, CO: Advanced Learning Press.

Reeves, D. B. (2004a). *Accountability for learning: How teachers and school leaders can take charge.* Alexandria, VA: Association for Supervision and Curriculum Development.

Reeves, D. B. (2004b). *Accountability in action: A blueprint for learning organizations* (2nd ed.). Englewood, CO: Advanced Learning Press.

Reeves, D. B. (2004c). *Assessing educational leaders: Evaluating performance for improved individual and organizational results.* Thousand Oaks, CA: Corwin Press.

Reeves, D. B. (2004d). The case against the zero. *Phi Delta Kappan, 86*(4), 324–325.

Reeves, D. B. (2004e). *101 more questions & answers about standards, assessment, and accountability.* Englewood, CO: Advanced Learning Press.

Reeves, D. B. (2005). *It's all about the client: Consulting for results.* Englewood, CO: Advanced Learning Press.

Reeves, D. B., & Woodson, N. (2006). *Real leaders, real schools.* Phoenix, AZ: All Star Publishing.

Roberts, W. (1990). *Leadership secrets of Attila the Hun.* London: Bantam.

Rosenthal, R., & Jacobson, L. (1968). *Pygmalion in the classroom: Teacher expectation and pupils' intellectual development.* New York: Holt, Rinehart and Winston.

Rothstein, E., Rothstein, A., & Lauber, G. (2003). *Write for mathematics.* Thousand Oaks, CA: Corwin Press.

Rothstein, R. (2004a). Class and the classroom: Even the best schools can't close the race achievement gap. *American School Board Journal, 191*(10), 16.

Rothstein, R. (2004b). *Class and schools: Using social, economic, and educational reform to close the Black-White achievement gap.* Washington, DC: Economic Policy Institute.

Sanders, J. (2002). Something is missing from teacher education: Attention to two genders. *Phi Delta Kappan, 84(3),* 241–244.

Schmoker, M. J. (2001). *The results fieldbook: Practical strategies from dramatically improved schools.* Alexandria, VA: Association for Supervision and Curriculum Development.

Schmoker, M. J. (2004). Tipping point: From feckless reform to substantive instructional improvement. *Phi Delta Kappan, 85(6),* 424–432.

Searcey, D., Young, S., & Scannell, K. (2005, July 14). Ebbers is sentenced to 25 years for $11 billion WorldCom fraud. *Wall Street Journal,* p. A1.

Simpson, J. O. (2003). Beating the odds. *American School Board Journal, 190(1),* 43–47.

Slavin, R. E. (2003). *Educational psychology: Theory and practice* (7th ed). Boston: Allyn & Bacon.

Smith, C. (2004). *Mandela: In celebration of a great life.* Cape Town, South Africa: Struik.

Spearman, C. (1927). *The abilities of man.* New York: Macmillan.

Sternberg, R. J., Forsythe, G. B., Hedlund, J., Horvath, J. A., Wagner, R. K., Williams, W. M., et al. (2000). *Practical intelligence in everyday life.* Cambridge, U.K.: Cambridge University Press.

Surowiecki, J. (2004). *The wisdom of crowds: Why the many are smarter than the few and how collective wisdom shapes business, economies, societies, and nations.* New York: Doubleday.

Taleb, N. N. (2001). *Fooled by randomness: The hidden role of chance in the markets and in life.* New York: Texere.

Tichy, N. M., & Cohen, E. B. (1997). *The leadership engine: How winning companies build leaders at every level.* New York: HarperBusiness.

Van Velsor, E., & McCauley, C. D. (Eds). (2004). *The center for creative leadership handbook of leadership development* (2nd ed.). San Francisco: Jossey-Bass.

Waters, J. T., Marzano, R. J., & McNulty, B. A. (2003). *Balanced leadership: What 30 years of research tells us about the effect of leadership on student achievement.* Aurora, CO: Mid-Continent Research for Education and Learning.

Waters, J. T., Marzano, R. J., & McNulty, B. A. (2005, April 2). McREL's school leadership that works framework: Applications and implications. Paper presented at the meeting of the Association for Supervision and Curriculum Development, Orlando, FL.

White, S. (2005a). *Beyond the numbers: Making data work for teachers & school leaders.* Englewood, CO: Advanced Learning Press.

White, S. (2005b). *Show me the proof: Tools and strategies to make data work for you.* Englewood, CO: Advanced Learning Press.

Whitmire, K. (2005, Summer). Leading through shared values. *Leader to Leader, 37,* 48–54.

Willingham, D. T. (2004, Summer). Reframing the mind: Howard Gardner became a hero among educators simply by redefining talents as "intelligences." *Education Next, 4(3),* 19–24.

Index

In this index *f* behind a page number indicates there is a figure in the text.

About the Author

Douglas B. Reeves is chairman and founder of the Center for Performance Assessment, an international organization dedicated to improving student achievement and educational equity. Through its long-term relationships with school systems, the center helps educators and school leaders to improve student achievement through practical and constructive approaches to standards, assessment, and accountability.

Dr. Reeves is a frequent keynote speaker in the United States and abroad for education, government, and business organizations and is a faculty member of leadership programs sponsored by the Harvard Graduate School of Education. Dr. Reeves is the author of more than 20 books and many articles including the best-selling *Making Standards Work: How to Implement Standards-Based Assessments in the Classroom, School and District* (Advanced Learning Press, 2001), now in its third edition, *Assessing Educational Leaders: Evaluating Performance for Improved Individual and Organizational Results* (Corwin Press, 2004), *Accountability for Learning: How Teachers and School Leaders Can Take Charge* (ASCD, 2004), *Accountability in Action: A*

Blueprint for Learning Organizations (Advanced Learning Press, 2005), *he Daily Disciplines of Leadership: How to Improve Student Achievement, Staff Motivation, and Personal Organization* (Jossey-Bass, 2002), *The Leader's Guide to Standards: A Blueprint for Educational Equity and Excellence* (Jossey-Bass, 2002), and *Reason to Write: Help Your Child Succeed in School and in Life Through Better Reasoning and Clear Communication* (Simon & Schuster, 2002). His work has appeared in numerous national journals, magazines, and newspapers. Dr. Reeves has been selected twice for the Harvard Distinguished Authors Series. He won the Parent's Choice Award for his writing for children and parents and was recently named the 2006 Brock International Laureate, one of the most significant education awards in the world.

Beyond his work in large-scale assessment and research, Dr. Reeves has devoted many years to classroom teaching with students ranging from elementary school to doctoral candidates. His family includes four children, all of whom have attended public schools, and his wife, Shelley Sackett, is an attorney, mediator, and school board member. Dr. Reeves lives near Boston.

Related Resources: School Leadership

At the time of publication, the following resources were available; for the most up-to-date information about ASCD resources, go to www.ascd.org. ASCD stock numbers are noted in parentheses.

Audio
Accountability for Learning: How Teachers and School Leaders Can Take Charge by Douglas B. Reeves (Audiotape #205061; CD #505085)

Balanced Leadership: What Research Shows About Leadership and Student Achievement by Tim Waters, Robert J. Marzano, and Brian McNulty (Audiotapes #204169; CDs #504303)

Leadership for Learning by Carl Glickman (Audiocassette #203063; CD #503059)

Networks
Visit the ASCD Web site (www.ascd.org) and click on About ASCD. Go to the section on Networks for information about professional educators who have formed groups around topics such as "Restructuring Schools" and "Learning and Assessment." Look in the Network Directory for current facilitators' addresses and phone numbers.

Online Courses
Visit the ASCD Web site (www.ascd.org) for the following professional development opportunities:

Effective Leadership by Frank Betts (#P8OC0)

What Works in Schools: An Introduction by John Brown (#PD04OC36)

Print Products
Accountability for Learning: How Teachers and School Leaders Can Take Charge by Douglas B. Reeves (#104004)

The Art of School Leadership by Thomas R. Hoerr (#105037)

Creating Dynamic Schools Through Mentoring, Coaching, and Collaboration by Judy F. Carr, Douglas E. Harris, and Nancy Herman (#103021)

Educational Leadership, April 2004: Leading in Tough Times (Entire Issue #104029)

Educational Leadership, February 2005: How Schools Improve (Entire Issue #105032)

From Standards to Success: A Guide for School Leaders by Mark R. O'Shea (#105017)

How to Thrive as a Teacher Leader by John G. Gabriel (#104150)

Leadership Capacity for Lasting School Improvement by Linda Lambert (#102283)

Resilient School Leaders: Strategies for Turning Adversity into Achievement by Jerry L. Patterson and Paul Kelleher (#104003)

School Leadership That Works: From Research to Results by Robert J. Marzano, Timothy Waters, and Brian A. McNulty (#105125)

Transforming Schools: Creating a Culture of Continuous Improvement by Allison Zmuda, Robert Kuklis, and Everett Kline (#103112)

What Works in Schools: Translating Research into Action by Robert J. Marzano (#102271)

Video and DVD
What Works in Schools (Three programs on DVD with a 140-page Facilitator's Guide #603047)

Improving Instruction Through Observation and Feedback (Three Videos with a Facilitator's Guide #402058)

For more information, visit us on the World Wide Web (http://www.ascd.org), send an e-mail message to member@ascd.org, call the ASCD Service Center (1-800-933-ASCD or 703-578-9600, then press 2), send a fax to 703-575-5400, or write to Information Services, ASCD, 1703 N. Beauregard St., Alexandria, VA 22311-1714 USA.